AF334805

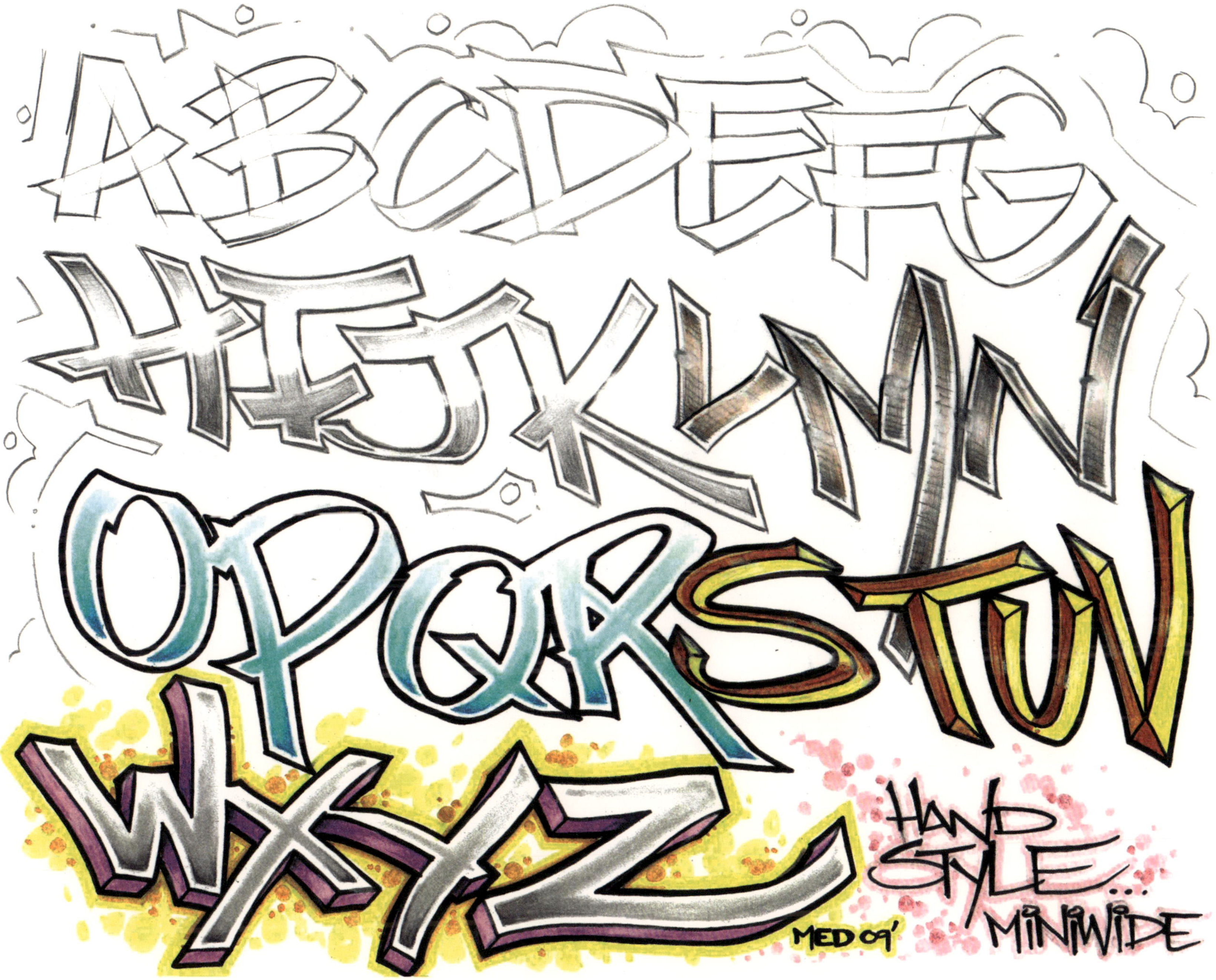

A B C D E F G
H I J K L M N
O P Q R S T U V
W X Y Z
MED 09'
HAND STYLE...
MINIWIDE

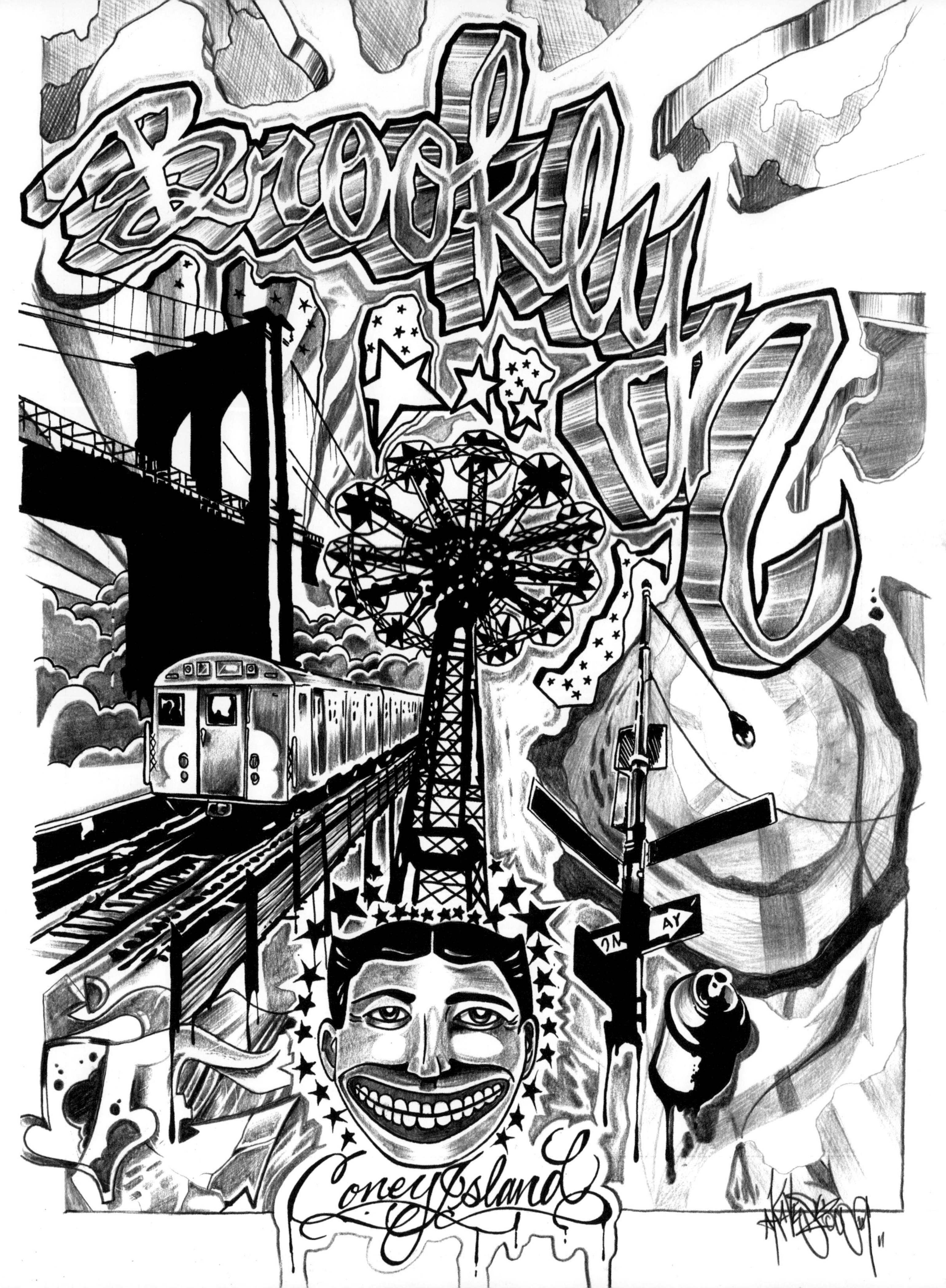

Brooklyn
NYC
Coney Island
ONE WAY

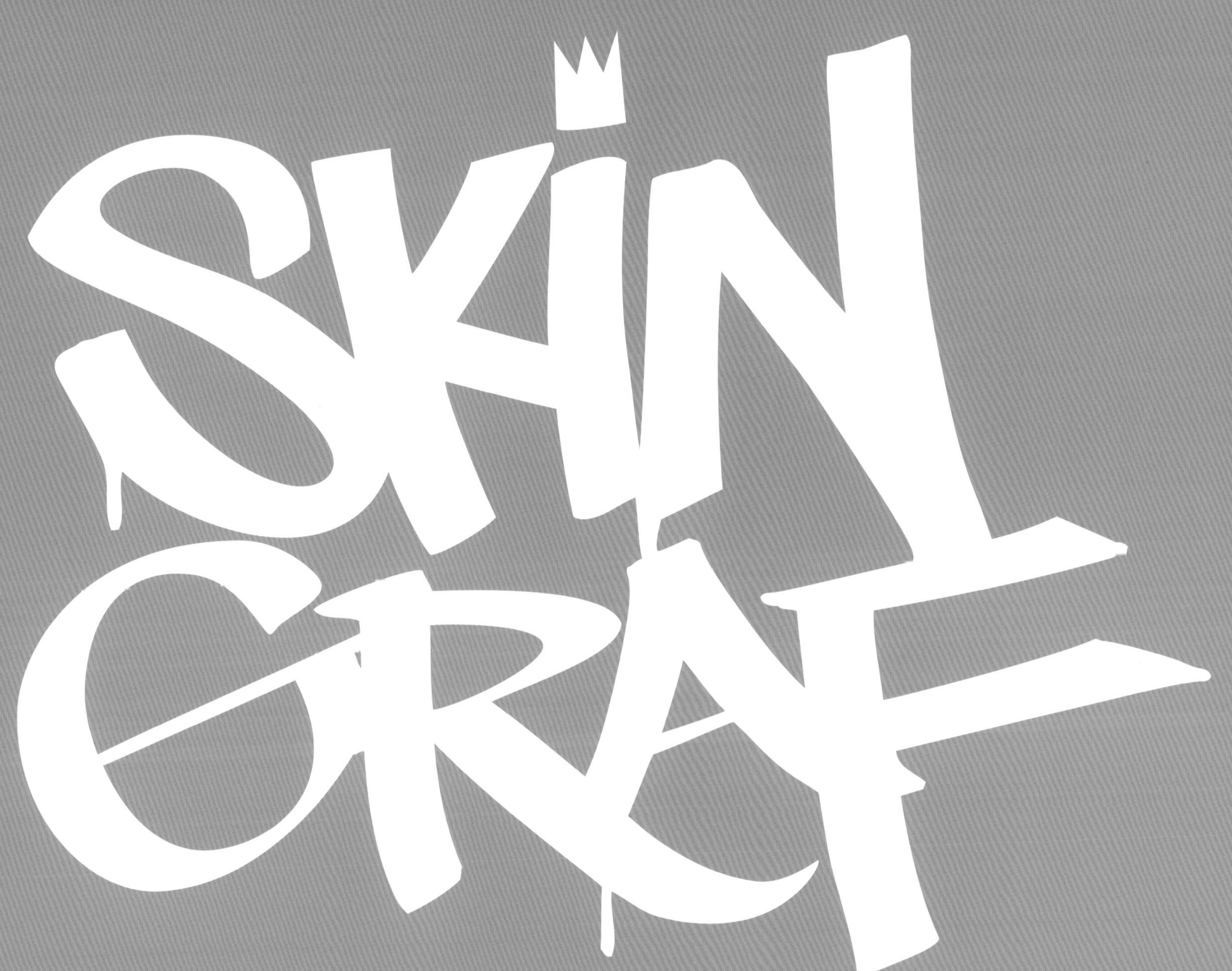
SKIN
GRAF

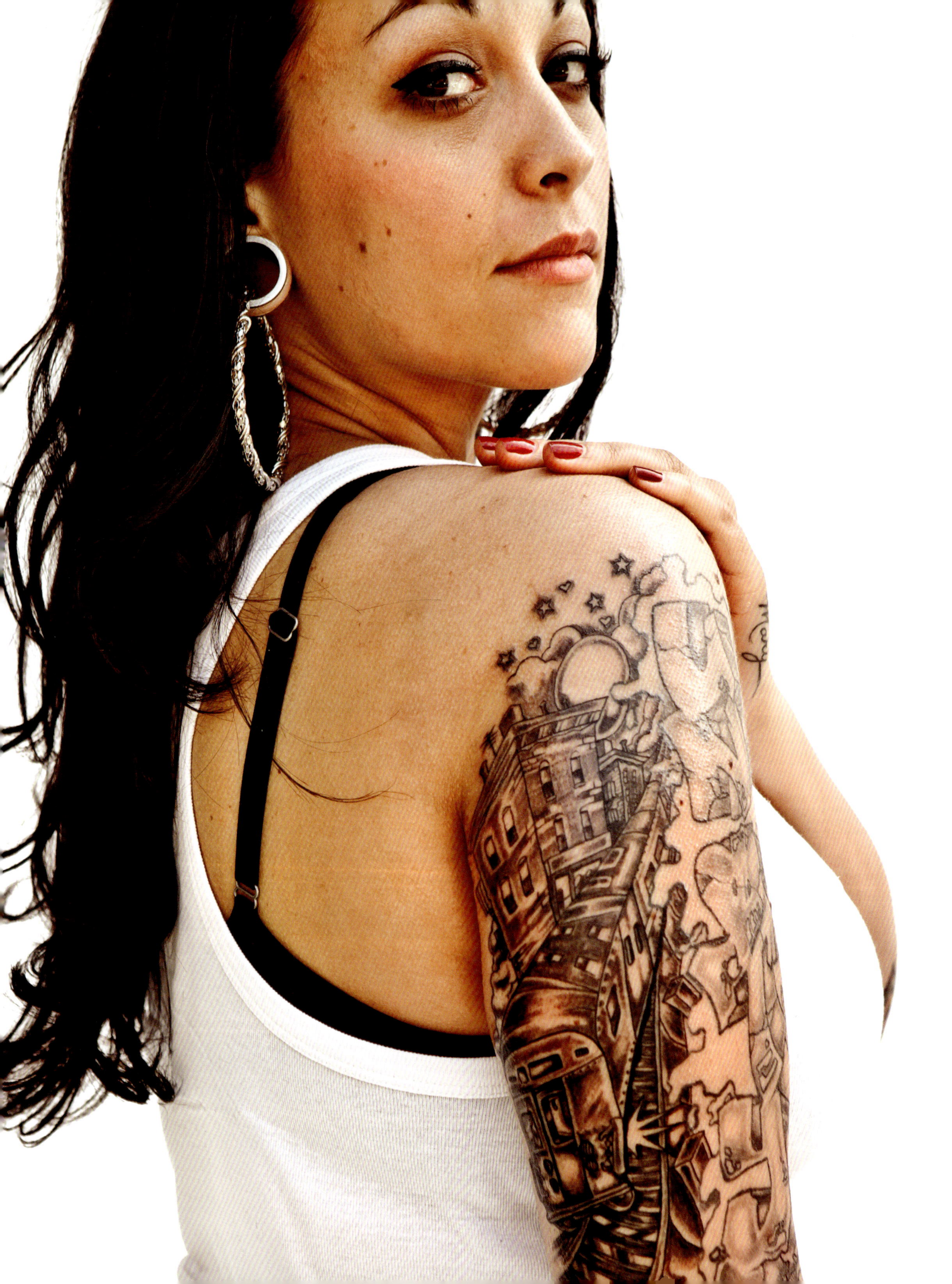

MICHAEL "KAVES" McLEER & BILLY BURKE

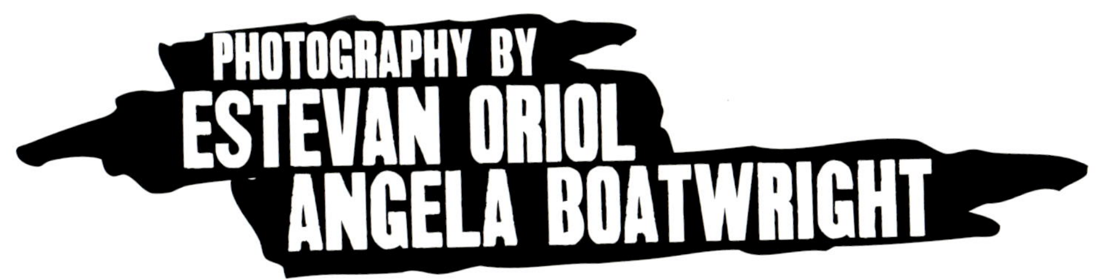

SKIN GRAF

· MASTERS OF GRAFFITI TATTOO ·

PHOTOGRAPHY BY
ESTEVAN ORIOL
ANGELA BOATWRIGHT

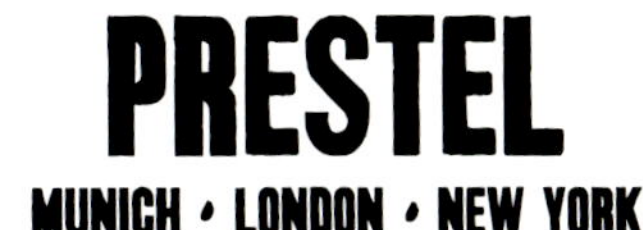

PRESTEL
MUNICH · LONDON · NEW YORK

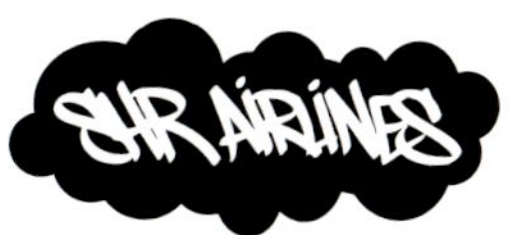

Published by Prestel, a member of Verlagsgruppe Random House GmbH

Prestel Verlag
Neumarkter Strasse 28
81673 Munich
Germany
Tel.: +49 89 41 36 0
Fax: +49 89 41 36 23 35

Prestel Publishing Ltd.
4 Bloomsbury Place
London WC1A 2QA
United Kingdom
Tel.: +44 20 7323 5004
Fax: +44 20 7636 8004

Prestel Publishing
900 Broadway, Suite 603
New York, NY 10003
Tel.: +1 212 995 2720
Fax: +1 212 995 2733
E-mail: sales@prestel-usa.com

www.prestel.com

Library of Congress Cataloging-in-Publication Data

McLeer, Michael.
 Skin graf : masters of graffiti tattoo / Michael "Kaves" McLeer, Billy Burke ; Photographs by Estevan Oriol and Angela Boatright.
    p. cm.
 "An SHR Airlines Book."
 ISBN 978-3-7913-4663-2
 1. Tattooing. 2. Graffiti. I. Burke, Billy. II. Title.
 GT2345.M45 2013
 391.6'5–dc23
                        2012037435

Editorial direction: Karen A. Levine
Editorial assistance: Ryan Newbanks
Proofreading: Dianne Woo
Design: Donna McLeer / Tunnel Vizion Media
"Skin Graf" lettering: Kaves
Production: The Production Department
Separations: Fine Arts Repro House, Hong Kong
Printing: Midas Printing International, Dongguan, China

Verlagsgruppe Random House FSC-DEU-0100
The FSC-certified paper 157gsm NEO matte art has been supplied by Moorim Paper Co. Ltd., Korea

Front cover: Seen, Melrose Avenue, Los Angeles, 2012
Frontispiece: Kaves tattoo, 2012

Contents

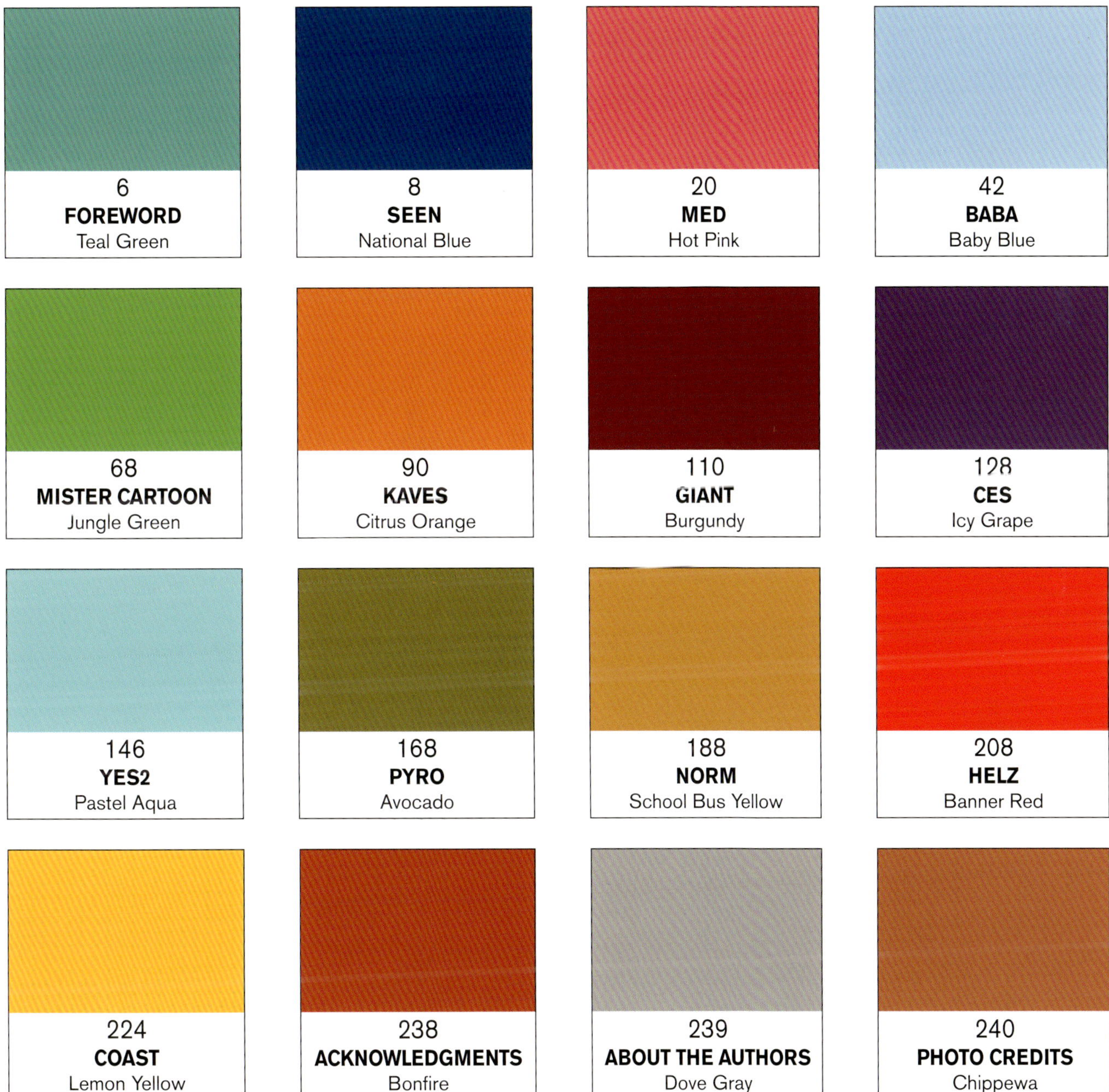

HARD AND FRESH NEEDLE IN THE FLESH
Why Graffiti and Tattoo Came Together

Michael "Kaves" McLeer and Billy Burke

The Egyptians told their stories on walls with hieroglyphs. Graffiti writers today spray walls, trains, and just about anything else with a flat, agreeable surface.

Even that form of expression has a long history. Early humans were blowing pigment against their hands, leaving a negative outline of their palms and fingers on the walls of caves in Europe as early as 35,000 years ago. The 5,000-year-old remains of tattooed Ötzi the Iceman—found frozen in the Ötztal Alps on the Austrian-Italian border—tell us that art on skin was happening long before it was stigmatized by modern society.

One might argue that the timelessness of these artistic expressions is proof positive that there was street culture—as it would later be known—before there were even streets! In any place on earth that humans have inhabited, during any time period, documentation of life through art lives. It is human nature to express oneself by either marking surroundings or marking bodies. It is only natural to imagine that one day these two rebel forms—graffiti and tattoo—would converge.

The pioneering graffiti artists of the early 1970s didn't paint caves, but they would often paint in cave like environments beneath New York City. If graffiti started on the streets and in subway tunnels, Western tattooing started in seedy, cobblestoned back alleys. Tattooing has existed on the fringes of society for centuries. In much the same way as writers were put in jail for bombing trains in Technicolor, tattooing was banned in many places all over the world, and it still remains illegal in some countries today. The outlaw essence of these two raw forms makes them blood brothers, so to speak, and a lot of blood has literally been spilled in order to bring these mediums to the prominence and respect they currently enjoy.

The way a train carries a writer's name—emblazoned bright and bold for all to see—is similar to the manner in which a person living with an artist's tattoo carries that mark; he or she is a vessel that hosts this fine art for the extent of their mortal existence. As they say in the world of graffiti, it's just another "up," only there is no need to battle cops or the acid baths that trains get doused in after they've been sprayed by so-called vandals. Tattoos are the new burners, and they "run" for a long time.

Pirates, poets, artists, street preachers, street teachers—both graffiti artists and tattoo artists can be seen as cultural curators. Their work depicts the times and conditions in which they live, and it exists as commentary on social status, telling stories of these otherwise undocumented outlaws through visual mediums. Many law-abiding citizens get tattoos, and the art they choose to scar into their bodies helps to tell their stories too. Stories of hope and pain and triumph and fantasy. Tales tall and tales true.

Graffiti and tattooing have always been the art of the outlaw and the outsider. Graffiti artists aren't a perfect fit for their anarchist neighbors, and they aren't a perfect fit for their fine art/street art brothers and sisters either. Until recently, they were an orphaned group, banished both literally and figuratively to live and eat on the avenues. And tattoo artists have lived in a world dominated by outlaw motorcycle culture for many decades. The artists in this book have managed to carve out their own place in the hardcore tattoo world—a major accomplishment, since for a time they have existed as outsiders twice removed, dancing on the fringe of the fringe.

But the writing on the wall and on the skin says the times they are a-changin'. The traditionalists—the bikers and the sailors and the tribalists—have learned to embrace the ways of the graffiti artist largely because the graffiti world, much like the tattoo world, lives and dies on the strength of loyalty, respect, and apprenticeship. Respect your master and you too can become one—that is the great lesson that graffiti and tattoo share with us.

The writers in this book have found a way to immortalize themselves through their work, and that's what makes them stand a head above their peers. Today their art is also thriving by way of skin—an organism that lives and breathes each and every day. This collective of legendary writers-turned-tattooists have left their mark on the people—and their history, as you will soon read, is the by-product of a brotherhood bound by tradition and language. A wall can be buffed, but a tattoo is all up *in* you.

The artists here represent two worlds colliding and merging to create something greater than the sum of their parts. The outlaw has become the visionary, the vandal has become the pioneer. These artists are nouveau historians, cultural anthropologists documenting the dreams and crucial cries of the otherwise unheard, disenfranchised people of this planet.

Oh, and some people get tattoos because they look cool.

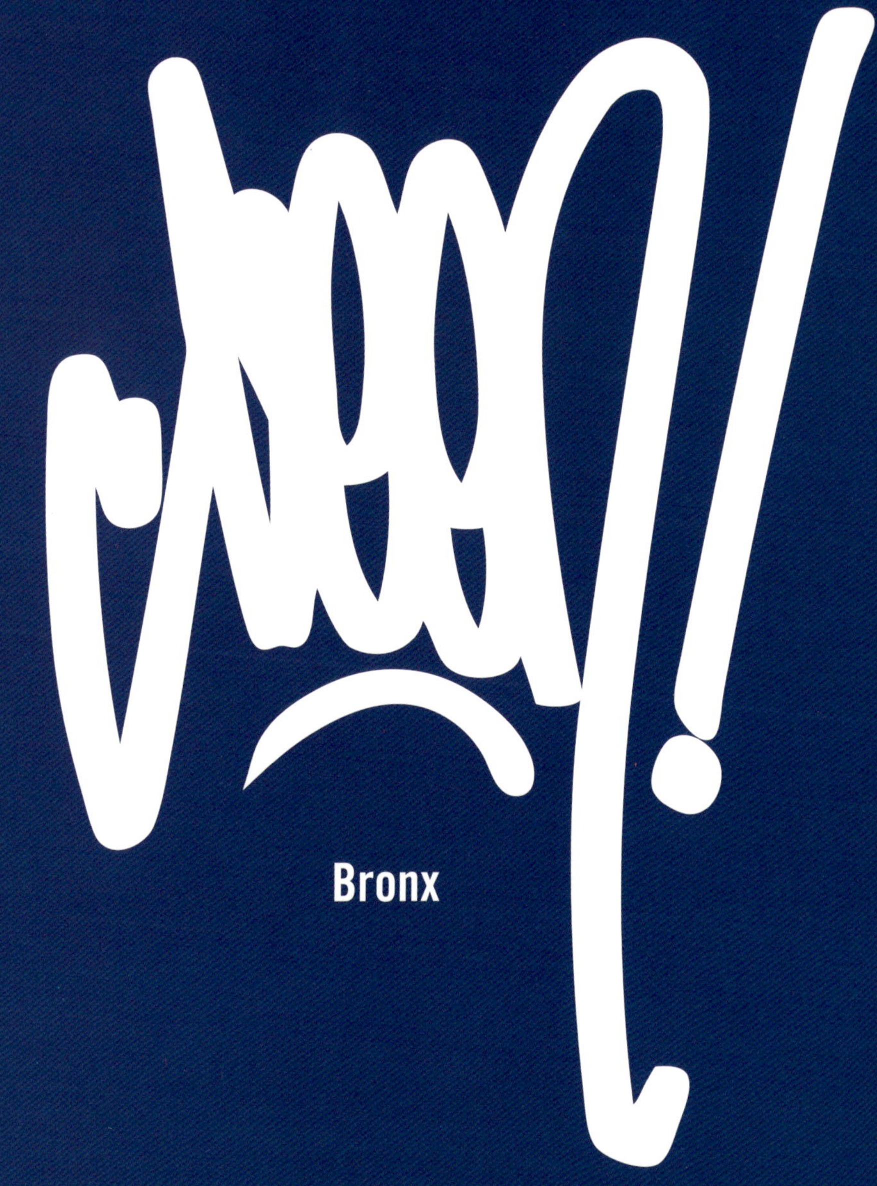

Bronx

> *"My shop became like the shop because we were willing to think and draw outside the box. It wasn't about pulling the flash off the wall."*

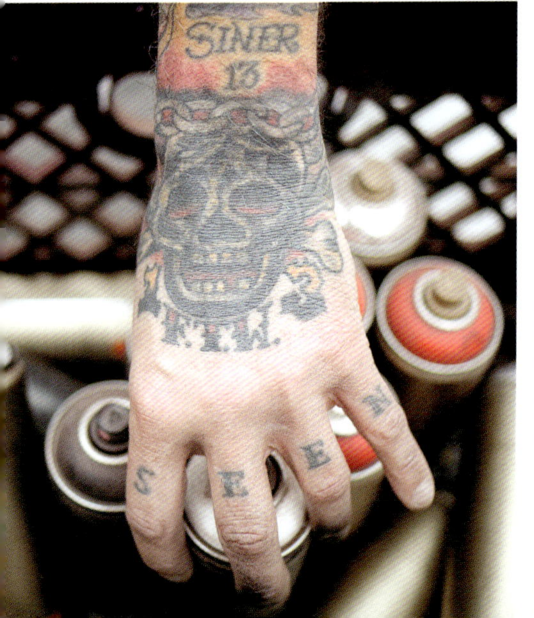

SEEN

Seen is the undisputed godfather of graffiti-inspired art on skin. His graffiti career started in the early 1970s, and his subway paintings are some of the most iconic and recognizable works in the history of a now worldwide movement. By the time he'd picked up a tattoo machine, there was nothing left for him to achieve as a writer. Seen is that Italian dude from the Bronx who had nuts big enough to hop on a plane to Los Angeles and paint his name real big and bold on the Hollywood sign, creating an image visible from miles and miles away. The fact that Seen doesn't understand the word *boundaries* is the reason why he's had such an influence across so many cultural platforms.

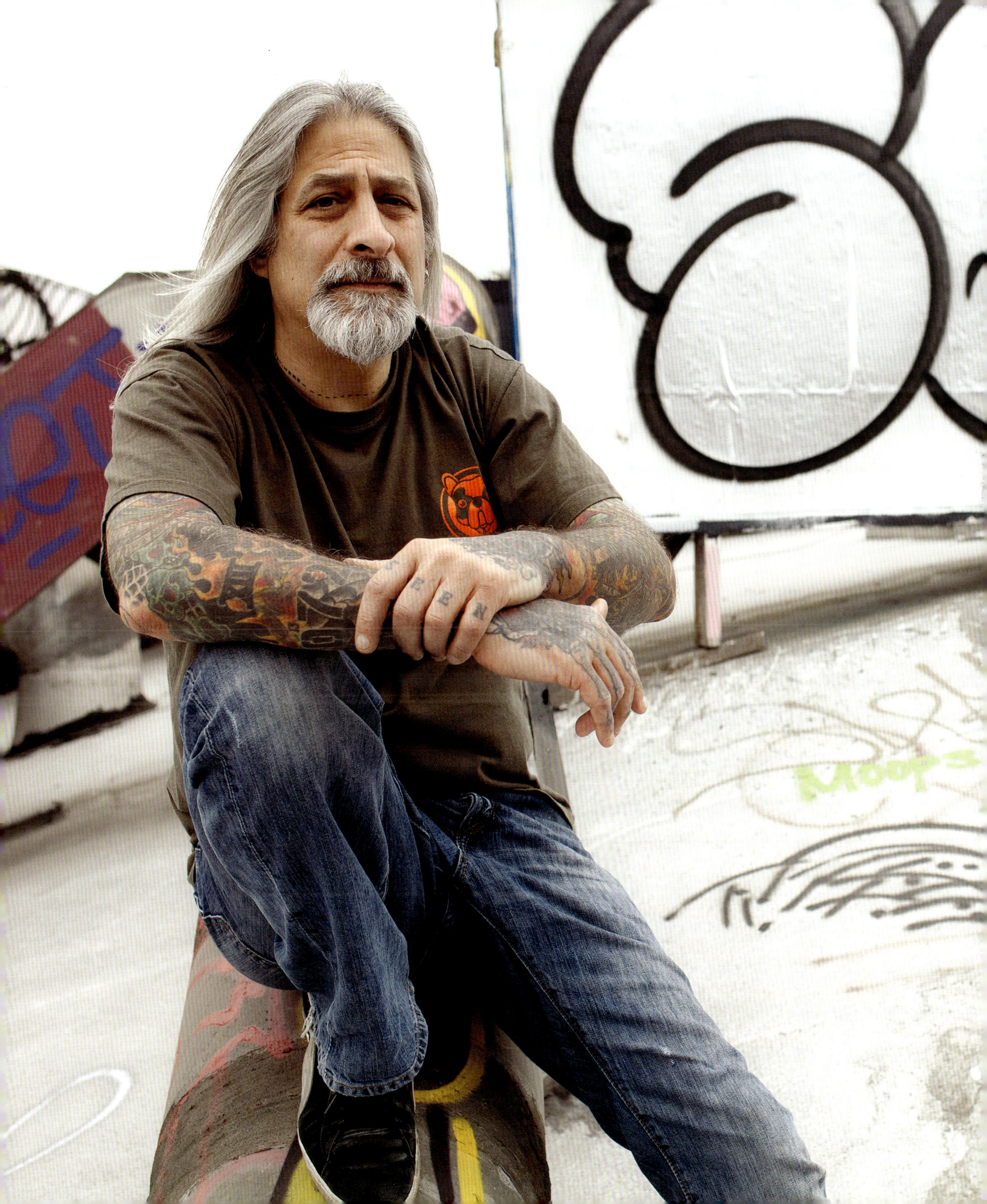

MOOP

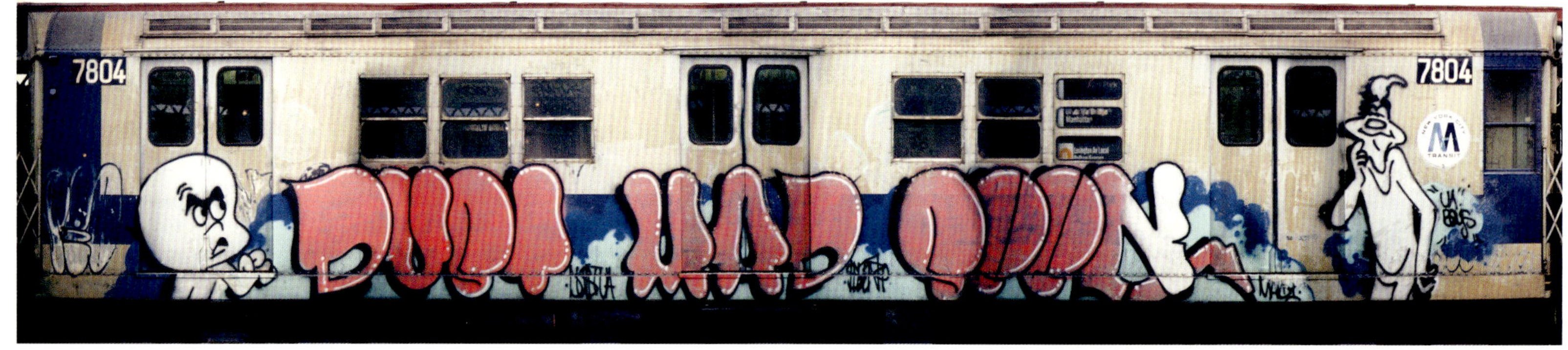

Dust, Mad, Seen train car, New York City, 1980

I was around eleven years old when I got started. I didn't know what graffiti was about. It was a fairly new thing that was happening at that time. But for me, it was like '73 and I just used to walk the avenue with my mom, it was a shopping area. And I looked up and saw the elevated trains roll by on the tracks with graffiti written on them. What it said, what it was about, I had no clue. I don't know what possessed me to think that I have to try to do this. You know, at eleven, I made an attempt on my own one day. Basically I went to the avenue on my own the day that I knew how to get there, and I went up on the elevated tracks and waited for a train to come by and I did like, motion tagging. I would get on the train, take a tag, get off at the next stop, and wait for another train coming back in the same direction because at that point, I was so young, I didn't know where it was taking me. So I would go one stop out and one stop in, one stop out and one stop in, and that's how I started taking the tags.

But you know, that's not what I think I really wanted to do. For some reason, I wanted to be outside. I realized that the train yard for the number 6 line was my home line, and that's the line that I became known for. It was only one stop past my home station. That's where I first attempted to paint on the outside of a train. That was somewhere around '73, and from that point on it was like a marriage made in heaven. I mean, I used the 6 yard as my playground as a youth.

Eventually, I dragged my brother … I dragged my cousins and friends in there with me. And as time went on, I started to learn the way the groups worked. The truth of the matter is, I probably didn't get any recognition until the late seventies. Let me explain something: in '78, during that major "buff" campaign when the city knocked out a lot of the kings from the old days, there were kings of writing that never returned after '79 or '80. I think it was a good thing I wasn't in the game hardcore back in the early days, because I probably would have shot

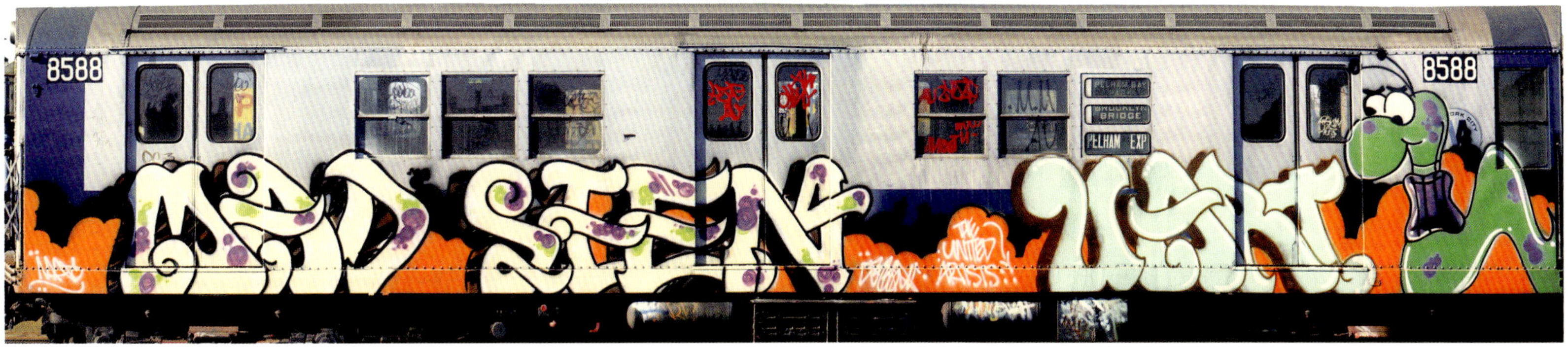

Mad, Seen, Uart train car, New York City, 1980

my load and been gone with the rest of them. I was still learning the game, how to go about it, racking paint, how to paint, where the layups are, this and that. So for me, this was a new thing, and I was learning by myself aside from my cousins and my brothers. None of us really knew what we were doing. By 1980 the game started to fall into place.

To me, what was done in the seventies was just being redone in the eighties, but it was perfected and it was multicolored. It was a time where the media was grabbing it—television, newspapers, magazines, they were all interested in it. It's really crazy how something you did as a kid for fun, for yourself more than anything else, became such a phenomenon back then. After I painted the Hollywood sign—and shortly afterward it came out in print in *Spraycan Art*—it escalated me to another level. I'm not tootin' my own horn here, but people started treating me like I was some sort of a god at that point. But I'm not a superstar. I bleed like everyone else.

I've been lucky and blessed that everything that I've done in my lifetime to survive out there has related to some sort of art. Back in the old days, I used to airbrush T-shirts. I used to customize cars and bikes. I did everything that you could imagine. Somewhere down the line, I always seemed to be a little bit of a hater of whatever was happening during my time. When my airbrushing days were coming to an end, I was ready to move on, and I thought, what is the next step? Let me see this tattooing stuff. I fell into it. Maybe more by accident, I would have to say, but it was the next step for me.

What happened with me was, I ended up playing with a machine that belonged to a friend of mine who worked in a tattoo shop on Long Island. One time he brought his machine home. I picked it up in my hand and wondered if I could do a tattoo. It was just a fluke. But the truth is, I felt comfortable having it in my hand. Because I had been

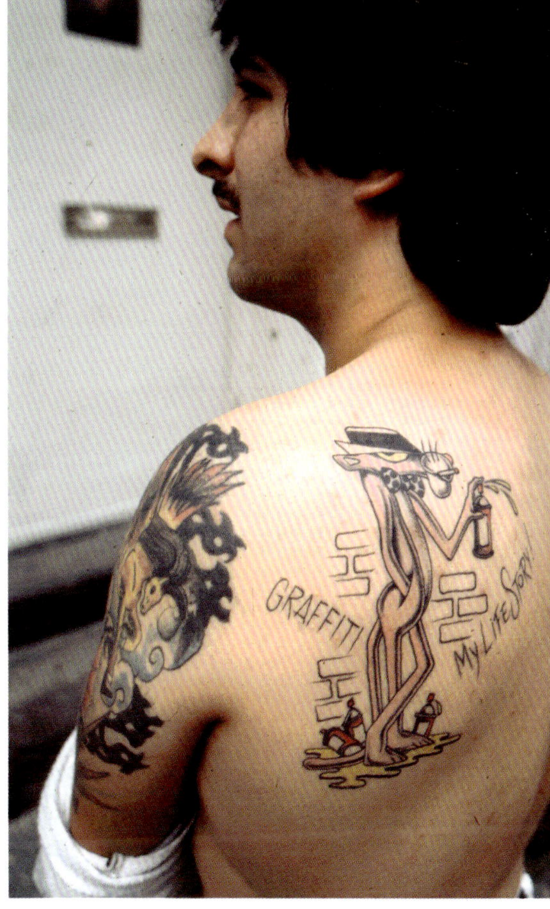

Seen, 1985

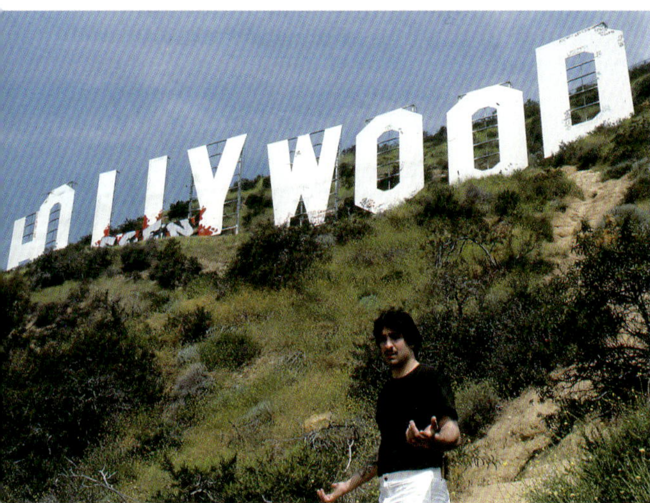

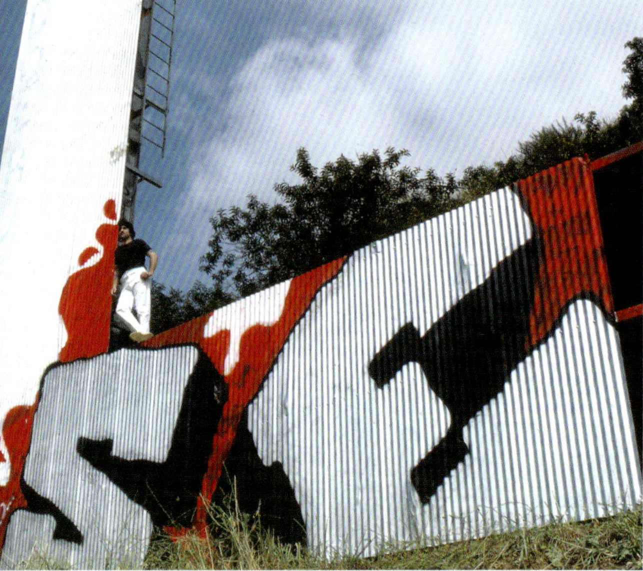

Seen piece on Hollywood sign, Los Angeles, 1985

getting tattooed since I was fifteen years old and hanging around tattoo shops—and there weren't many of them back then—I must have been watching and understanding what was happening. I felt at ease. I gave the first person a very good experience…it wasn't like I was gouging or whipping skin like some people. We all know what people who don't know what they're doing can do to your skin. But it was a smooth tattoo and I was impressed with myself. At that point I was like, "Wow—I might like the idea of doing this."

Back then it was still hard to get equipment. There were a couple of companies out there, but you needed to prove that you were in business. So it wasn't that easy to buy from any supply company that existed back then. I had to figure out how I was going to get some machines if I was going to play. Finally I got my hands on two machines, believe it or not. It was a pair of machines from Big Joe Kaplan out in Mount Vernon. It was a little tricky back then, but I think I kind of walked into the picture at the right time.

After I started tattooing, others in my area who were known for graffiti followed in my footsteps. I'm not saying everyone followed in my footsteps, but a good amount had gone my way after seeing what I did. Just like when I did airbrushing back in the day. There was a following of people from graffiti moving into airbrushing. And it was a good thing.

The only shop that existed in the Bronx at the time was Angelo's Tattoo. It's still out there. Angelo had closed down for a while. He came back later after it was legalized. He opened Champion Tattoos, but he was the only one in the Bronx at that time other than me. I was on the other side of the Bronx doing my thing while it was illegal. And me, I knew what I was up against and the law wasn't my main worry, you know. It was other people who had established businesses for many years and it was a controlled business…you know? I knew that's what I would have to deal with if I was going to put up huge billboards out on the street, advertising in unheard-of places. I went as far as advertising in movie theaters, I went as far as advertising in weekly papers and daily papers, and I started making paper flyers and putting them on bus stops when I first started. At that time I was just bombing, like with graffiti. I was having fun with it. And the thing was, I was doing something that nobody was doing, something people were afraid to do in New York City because it was still illegal. When you had to go make an appointment, some people, especially in Manhattan, would say, "OK, you call me when you get to this phone booth and then meet me over here." It was like a James Bond movie. But you know what? Nobody at the time realized that in New York City it was just a $50 health code violation.

When I came up from painting the trains, I was airbrushing clothing for people who saw me on the trains. They were able to get a T-shirt or a sweatshirt or something painted by me. And then all of a sudden I'm tattooing. So now they could get a tattoo from me. At first, when I started tattooing, it wasn't about me making a lot of money. It was about me trying to survive, and believe me, I swear, I calculated. I said to myself, "What else do I need to do to make $40 a day to live? If I can make $40 a day at the end of the month, I can pay all my bills, I can live, I can eat."

It went from me tattooing friends to their friends and then their friends, and I was working out of my house. The truth of the matter is, I don't give a fuck who you are. I don't want strangers using my fucking pisser. Do you know what I'm saying? I don't want strangers walking through my house where I don't know if you're going to come up behind me with a pistol to my head.

Things were starting to escalate with the amount of people coming up to my place. Now I have strangers coming on their own, not even brought by friends, people I don't know at all. And I'm like, this has got to stop. So my father owned some property on the main strip of Tremont Avenue where he kept his office; he was in the construction business. I was like, "Pop, maybe you got a little space that's available or something?" There was his office and then he had another glass room in there that was originally his private office. It had the venetian blinds and everything. It was cool.

Now I had people coming up, but he's got secretaries there. Eventually I had to have folding chairs outside my workroom so the people could all line up. It was becoming an inconvenience for his secretary because I had people coming in whenever. And then I found that I even needed help running things. I had a telephone in there. And now I needed help helping people. So I took a friend of mine through there, and I was like, "You know what, Marty, I'm going to give you a job. You can make some money hanging around here all day long and help me out." So I put him on the payroll to handle people and to handle the phones for me.

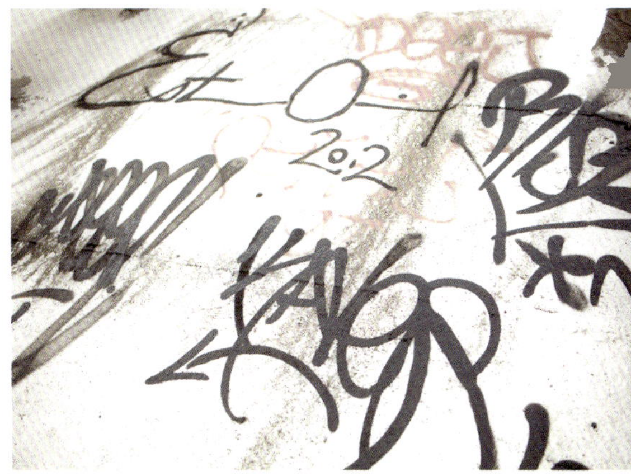

Seen, Kaves, Risk, Estevan tags on Melrose Avenue rooftop, Los Angeles, 2012

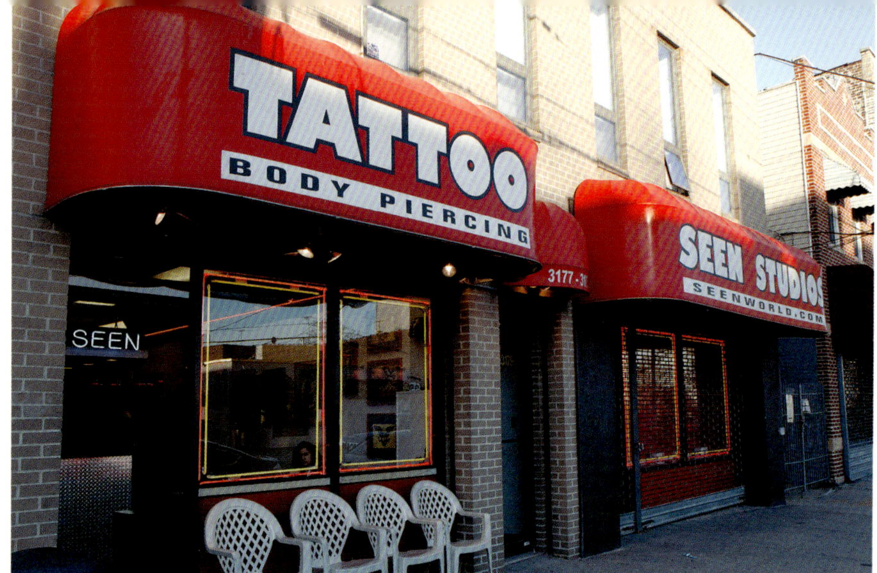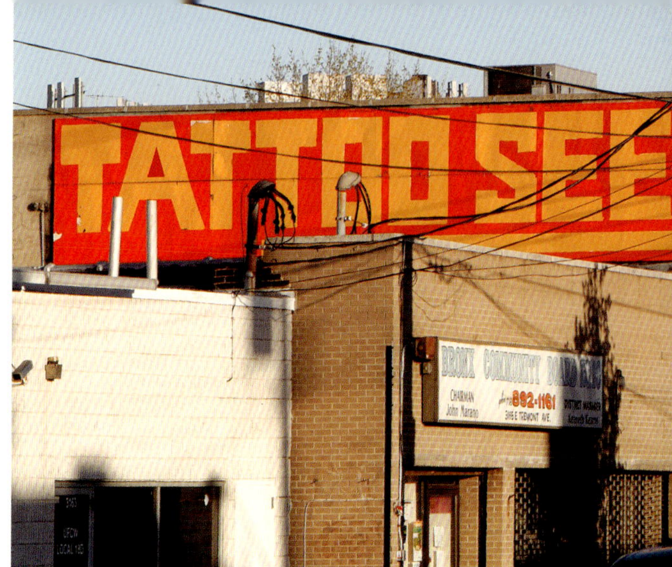

Exteriors and interior of Tattoo Seen Studios, Bronx

I was on the second floor in a little space. There was a line all the way down the steps, I shit you not. There were people sitting on the steps waiting to get tattooed. In the room, we had so many chairs. I was thinking to myself, "I can't do this many people in a day," so it got to the point where I was like, "Pop, I need a bigger space." He says, "You know what I can do for you? I could cut my office in half." He cut his office in half and put up a dividing wall. He created a workspace, a waiting area, and everything. It still wasn't big enough, but it housed what I needed to do so I could deal with it for a while.

People were coming up, and it was getting crazy. I was still saying, "I can't do all these people in one day. Maybe I could get another person up here to help me out with tattooing." I got somebody up there, actually one of my guys who used to airbrush. I taught him how to tattoo—well, actually, I taught him to an extent. He ended up going cowboy on me and made a mess out of everything. He worked out fine doing what was needed for the time, but people still wanted a tattoo from me. It took years for me to get customers used to somebody else.

My shop became like *the* shop because we were willing to think and draw outside the box. It wasn't about pulling the flash off the wall. But when I was growing up, if you even had the balls to walk into a shop back then, you had to stay in line, otherwise you might go through the plate-glass window. The tattoo back in those days was on the wall and what the colors were there is what you got. And if the plastic showed it facing this way on your arm, that's what you got. You couldn't even ask to flip it to face how you wanted. And God forbid you said you wanted periwinkle blue. They would beat you down. It was insane.

And there's heavy politics when it comes to other shops. When the shit hit the fan, it wasn't always about the open and close thing. You know, it wasn't always about just dealing with the authorities. I got on

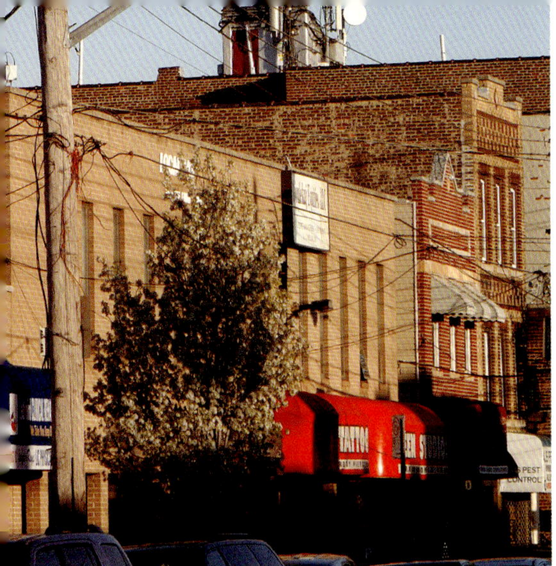

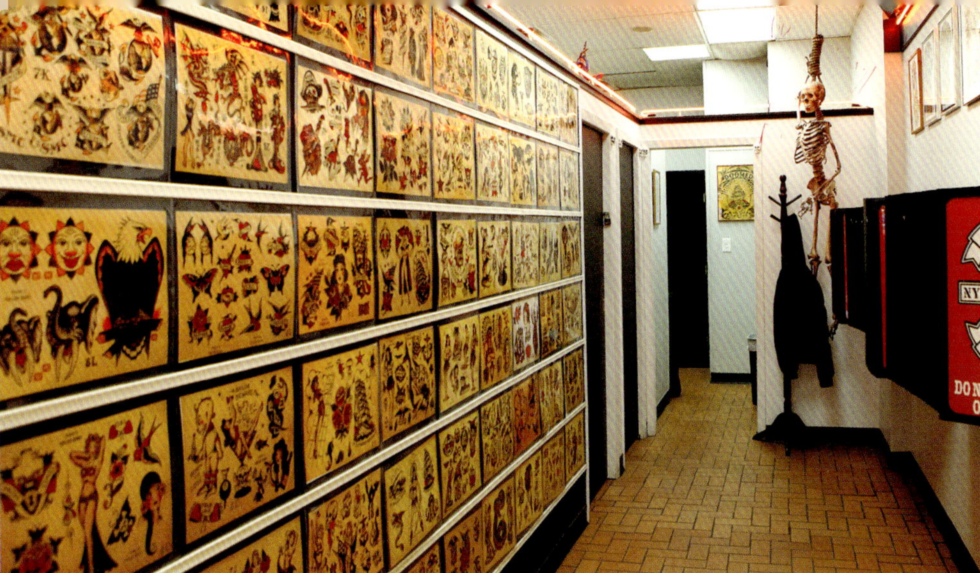

the phone and said I could come to their shop and we could talk about this or whatever. They'd say, "Well, you can do that, but I don't know if you're going to make it out of here alive." They would threaten me. I said, "You know what? When you're ready to talk to me like a man, I'll talk with you. Until then, goodbye." And I hung up.

I had to ask family for help because I wasn't sure what to do at this point. I know what happens to guys in this situation. I've seen it happen. I mentioned something to a family member, and believe it or not, two weeks later I got another phone call. Now one of the sons of the owner I knew really well. The owner called and was like, "You know, you and my son got along well. I don't know why we have some stupid shit like this." The tables had turned.

Anyway, a storefront had become available. I asked my dad if I could take that. I said, "Look, I don't want it for nothing. I don't want to pay less than anybody. I want to pay what you would rent it to somebody." He said OK. My brother is in construction, so we gutted the whole place, turned it into a tattoo shop. Business multiplied overnight. I still got shit—I still had to worry about what's happening, you know? Even though someone says, "OK, you're my friend now," I still had to look over my shoulder no matter what.

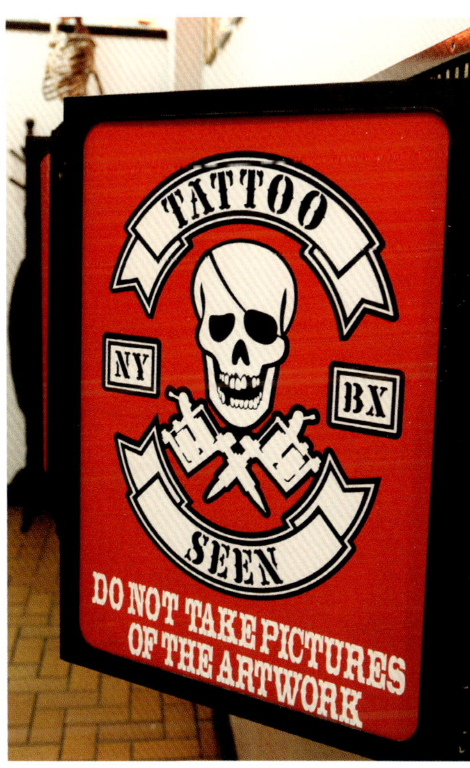

Interior of Tattoo Seen Studios, Bronx

I offered custom work at a time when custom work was very limited. That's what made me so busy. I custom draw. At that time I had no flash on the walls. What you wanted, I drew it for you and then I tattooed it on you. It wasn't until later on that I started using flash as a secondary thing. You know, you got to keep up with the Joneses, as they say.

I felt natural with the tattoo machine. The spray can probably gave me the most challenge because the cans are always changing—the pressures, the brands, the caps. There are so many different elements

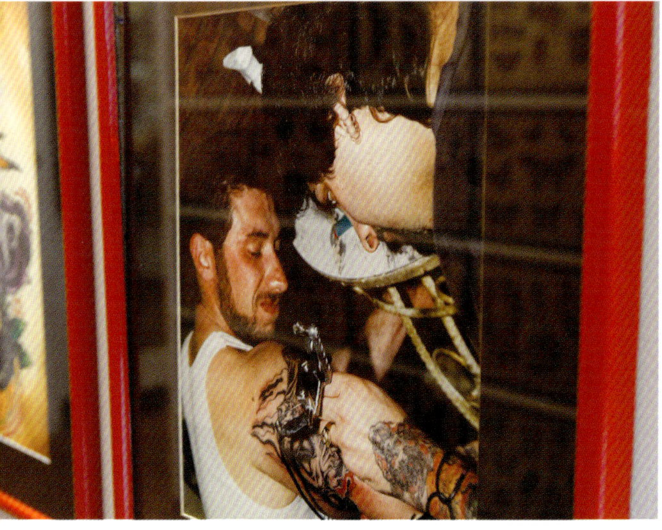

Seen tattooing a client, early 1990s

that are constantly changing in the spray can. So I'm always being challenged by that. I'll always be behind the eight ball when it comes to the spray can. Tattooing, however…I came to a point before I retired from the tattoo business where I was starting to find myself and develop my own style. The sad part is I walked away at that point, you know, I didn't explore that any further.

I'm going to be honest with you: if a person could unscrew their arm and leave it with me and come back and pick it up later, maybe I would have tattooed a little bit longer than I did. But I was getting tired of sitting with people, having to talk with people. I felt like I was talking about the same old stories, to the first customer and then the next customer, the next customer, the next customer. I've repeated myself over and over. Other than the artwork being a little different, it was the same thing day in and day out, and I was kind of getting bored by that. It came to a point where I started becoming more of a boss. I say "boss" because I had to oversee and run the business. I didn't want to be a boss. I didn't want to run it. I want to create art. When I was tattooing or drawing custom work for people, I was creating art. I started to lose that, and I started to burn out because it became so big. And I didn't want to become that big. Like I said, I was happy making $40 a day to pay my bills.

Would I ever tattoo again? I would be happy to tattoo people I know who have always wanted tattoos from me—close friends—but not a stranger. I could not work for a stranger and I could not work for money. I would have to do it for the joy of tattooing somebody.

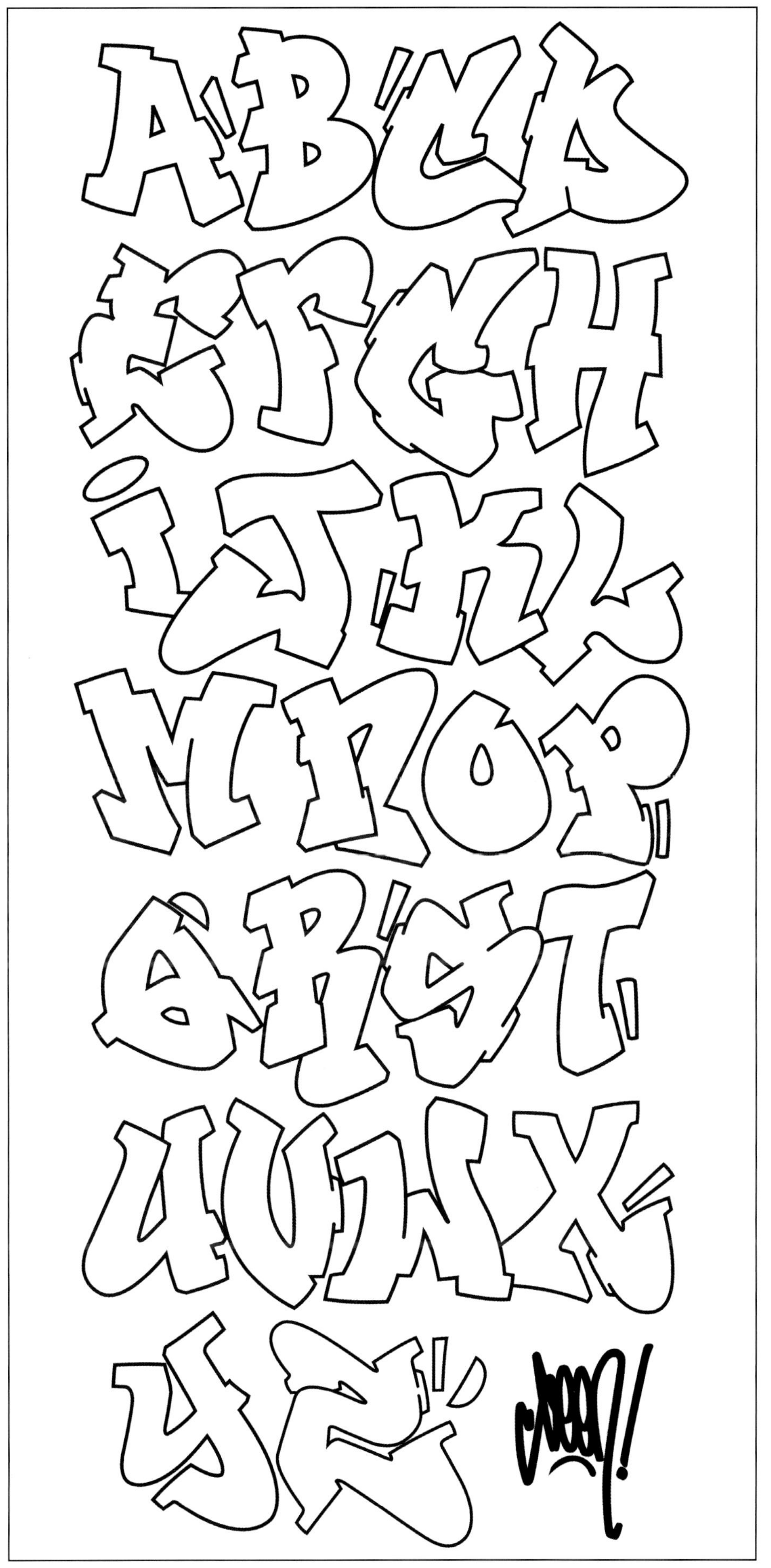

Seen, tattoo flash alphabet

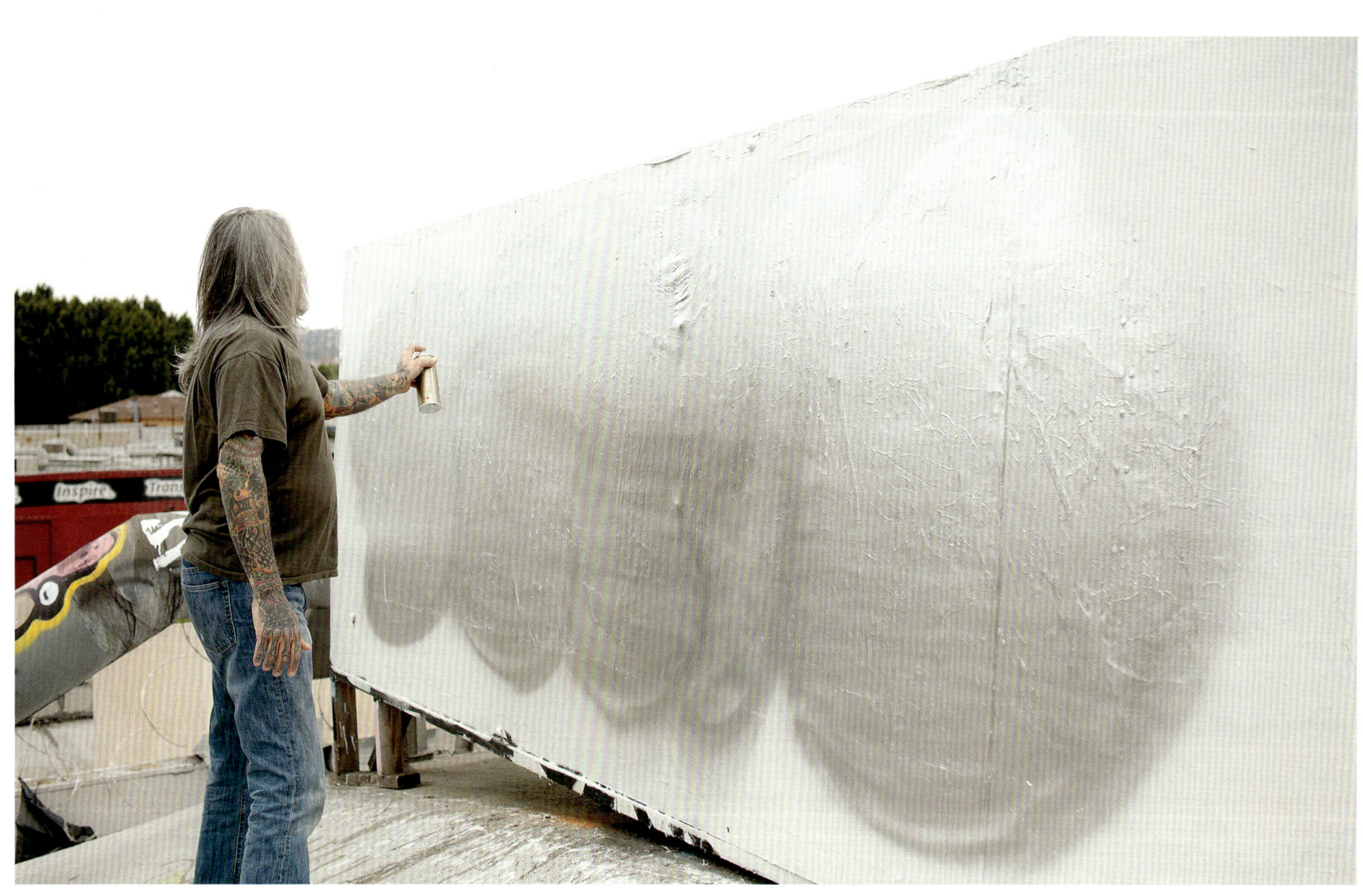

Seen on Melrose Avenue rooftop, Los Angeles, 2012

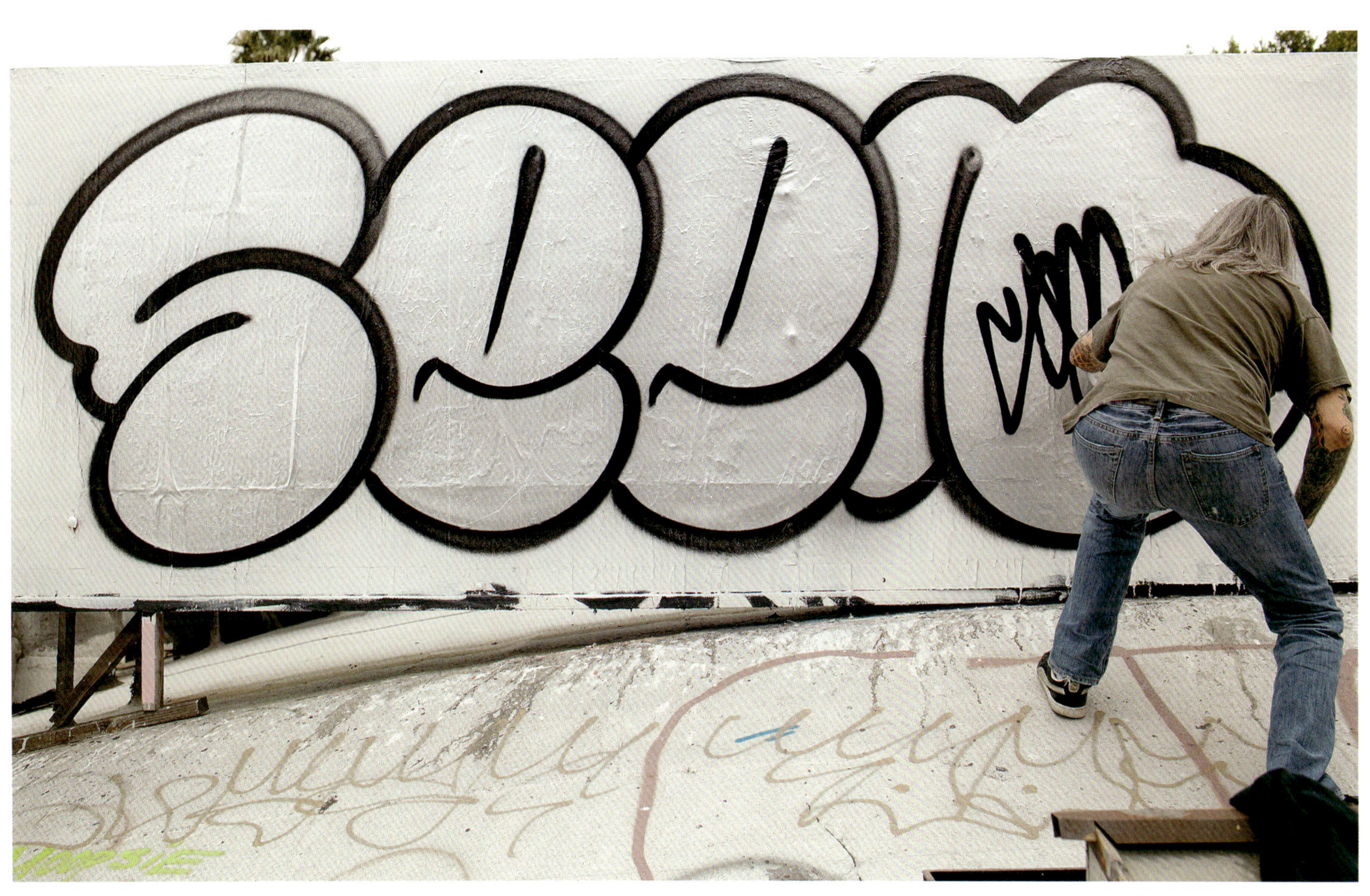

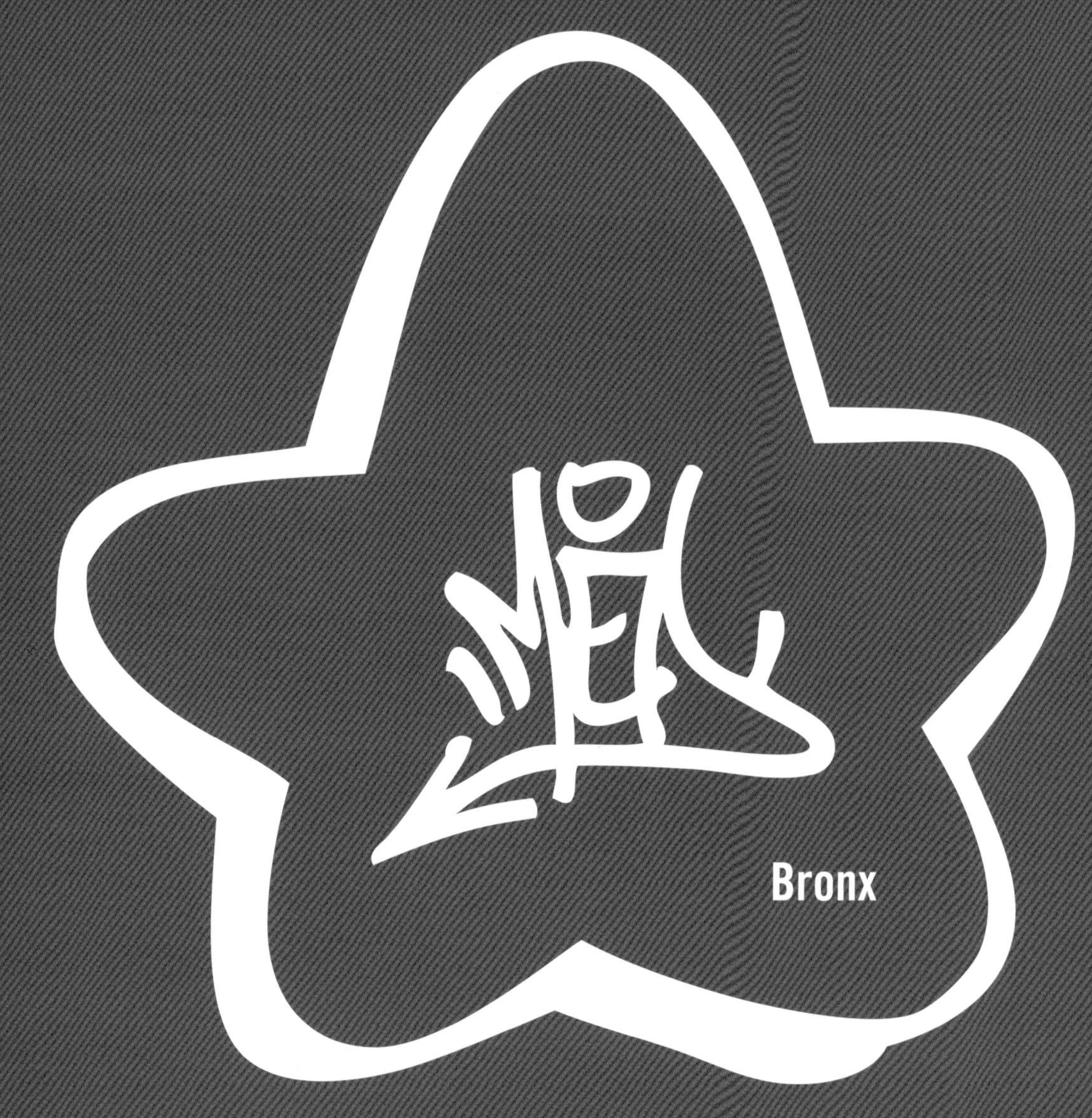

"I got released and came home from jail still a graffiti writer but now also a tattooist. And the rest is history."

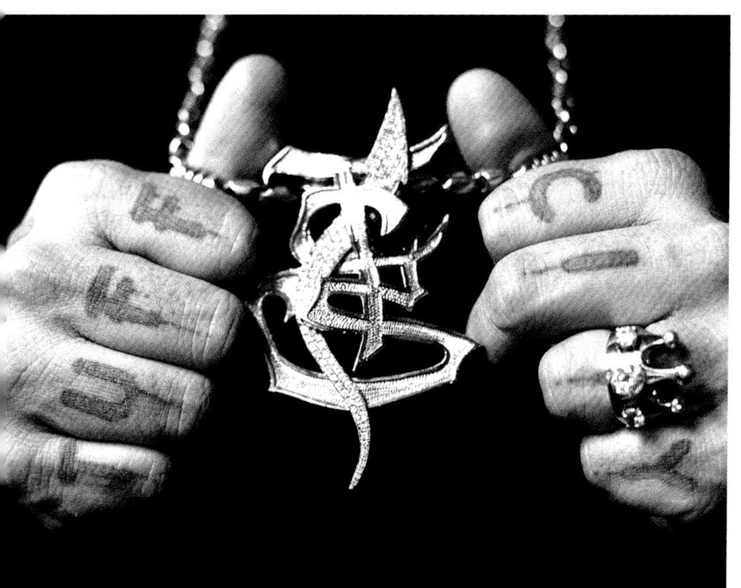

MED

Bronx native Med is a writer who made a name for himself on subway cars and highway walls back in the 1980s. He was a wild child at a time in New York history when delinquent teens could run amok with minimal interference. He would later channel his kinetic energy into tattoo. Med's talent and charisma led him to open his own parlor, Tuff City Styles, after working tattoo with the legendary Seen. Today, Med's shop—the interior of which mirrors a train yard—is a mecca for graffiti writers.

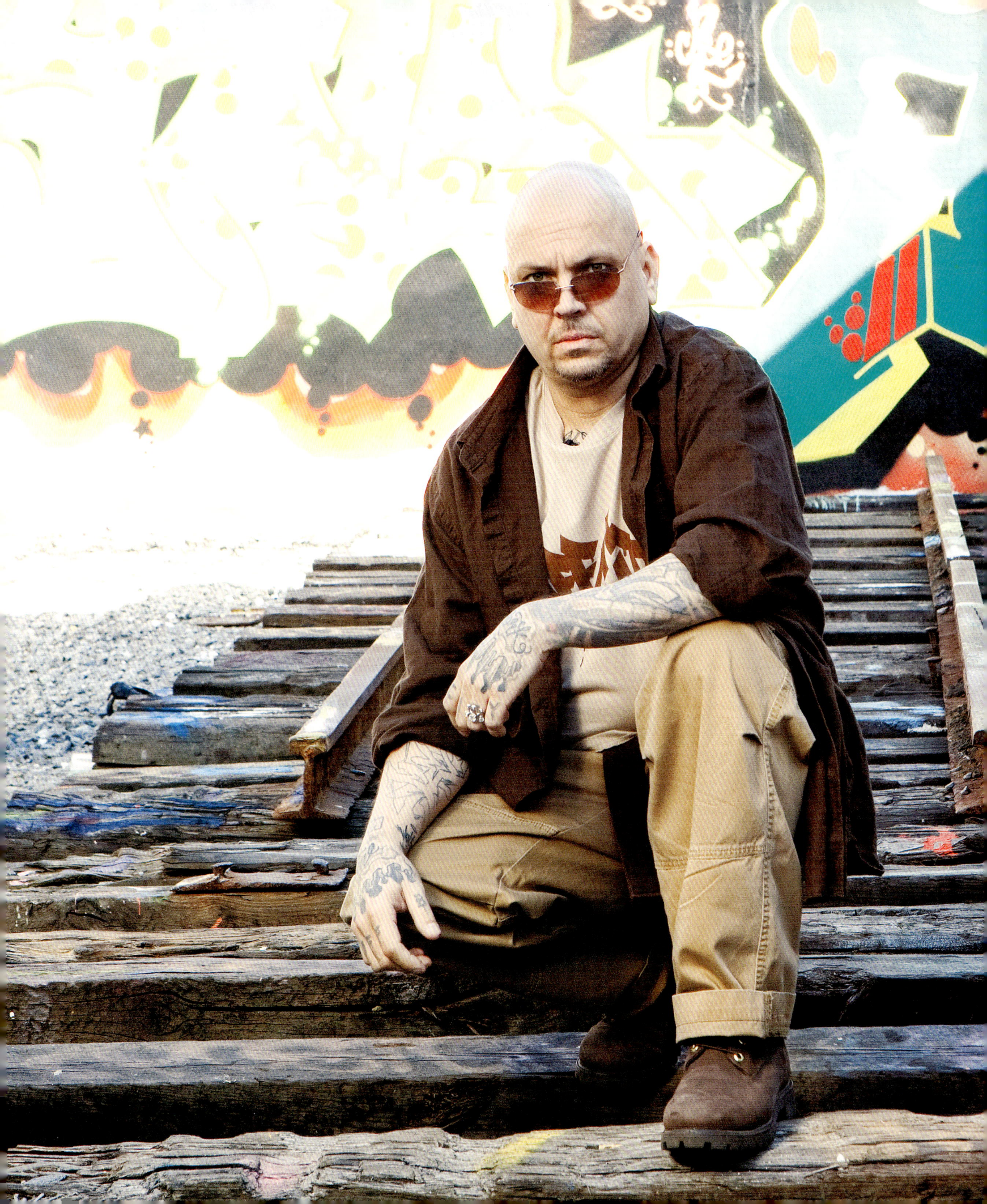

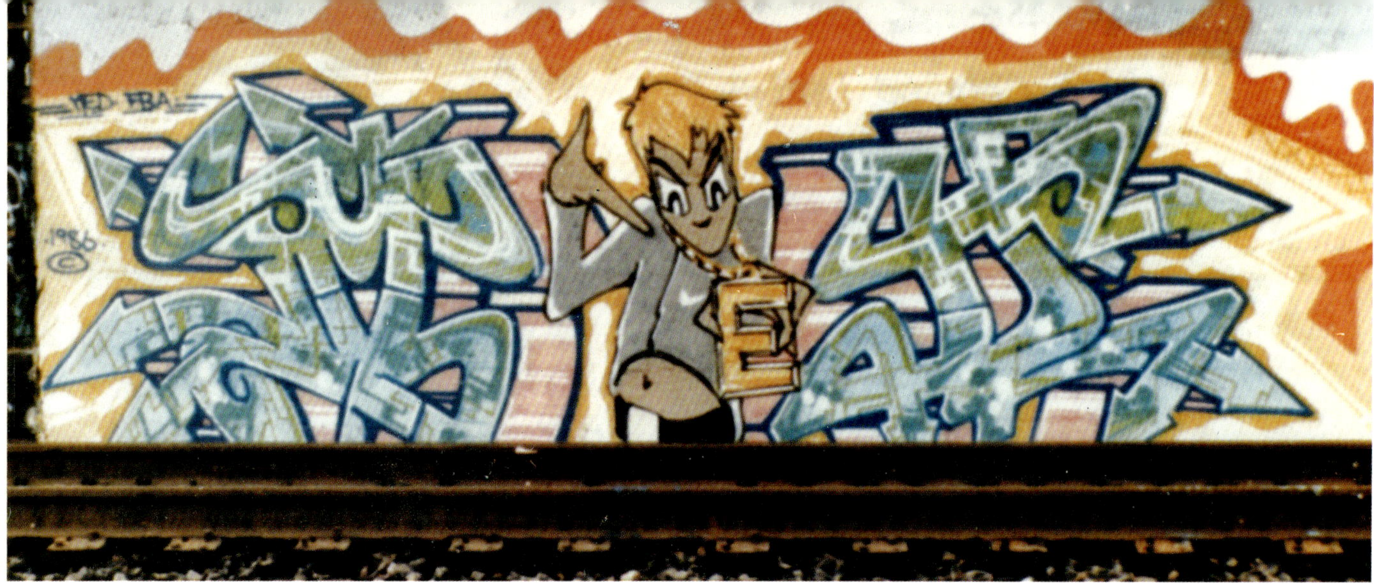

Med piece, Bronx, 1986

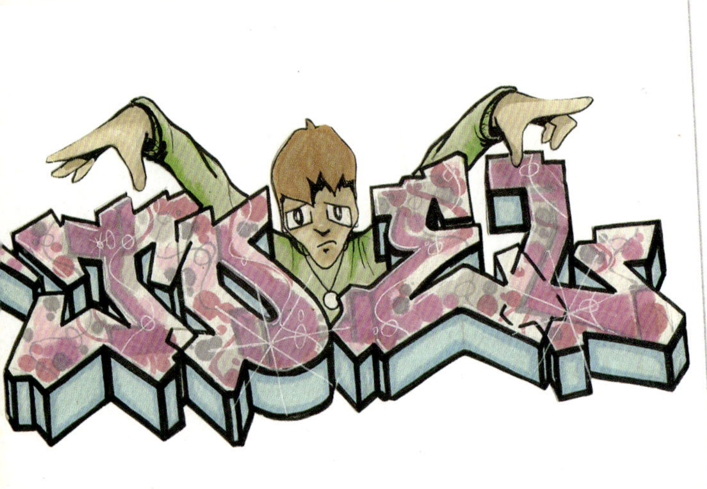

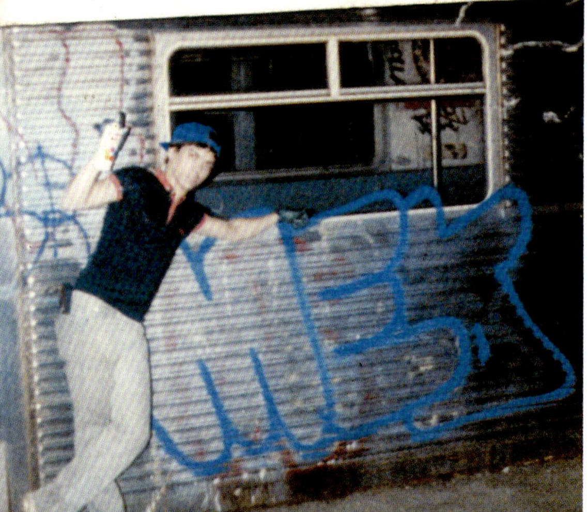

TOP: Med piecebook drawing, 1985
BOTTOM: Med, City Hall, 1986

I started writing graffiti at ten years old. Started doing it in my closet and in the stairwell of my building. At that time in the Bronx, it was all over the trains.

Then at twelve years old I was put into a group home by the state because I was such a wild kid and they felt my parents couldn't control me. At the group home they would send you home for the weekend, give you a subway token and send you home to your parents, telling you to come back on Monday. All my neighborhood friends stopped hanging out with me because they thought I was such a wild kid.

I had no one to hang out with when I was home on those weekends, so I would sit in my room and practice what I saw on the trains. I would take my drawings with me back to the group home, and all the kids would bug out, and I think it was that enthusiasm that gave me the fire under my ass to keep going, because the work I was doing was being appreciated. But it wasn't until 1982, when I was around fifteen, that I did my first train.

Mitch 77 was definitely someone I was really inspired by, also Iz the Wiz and Seen. Those were the big guys for me in the early eighties. It was their work I was seeing on the trains. Around '82 I started going to the layups. At that point I started getting influenced more by the people who were around me.

People in my peer group—like West, and the IBM [Incredible Bombing Masters] and FC [First Class] crews—were doing nice colorful stuff on the 1 line. Poem in the Bronx also had a strong influence on me. Of course there was Cap too—it was a respect thing for him, not an art

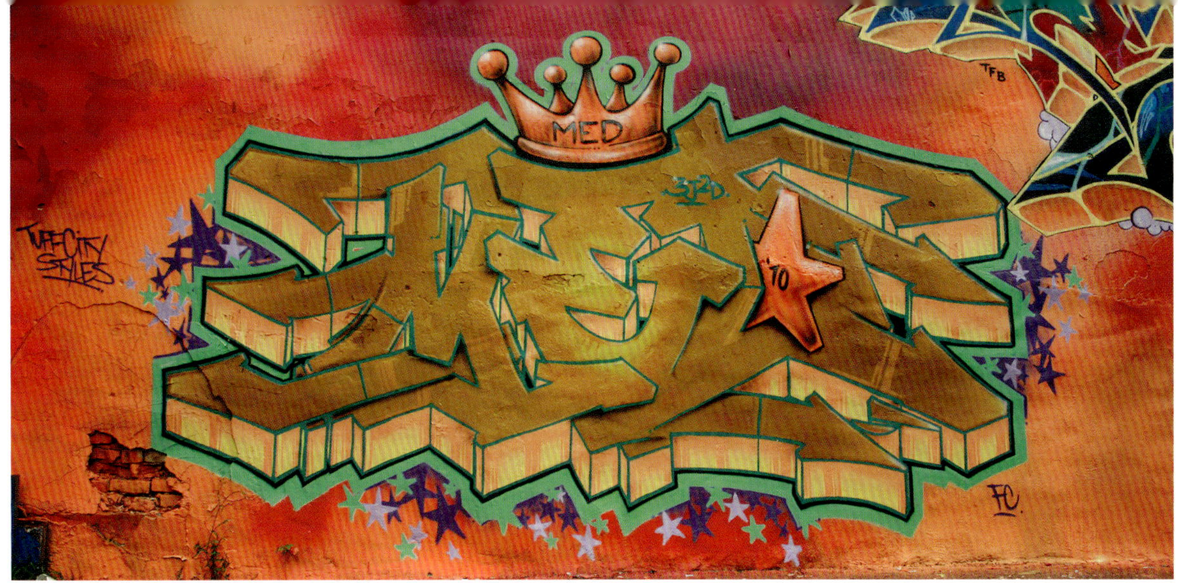

Med piece, Montreal, 2010

thing. He was a white guy who was just blasting over everybody and still walking around, and that was a really cool thing.

I got down with MPC [Morris Park Crew], FC, and UA [United Artists] through Duster. Those were big moments in my career, because with those crews, you couldn't just get down with them. FC took it serious— it was like a fraternity, highly organized and all that. You had to get nominated by someone, then someone had to second the nomination, and then you had to get voted in. Then, like I said, having Cap put me down with MPC was an honor; I was like "Oh my God, this nigga just put me down with MPC!" He recognized that I had been destroying the city and the trains and that was a milestone for me. And then to get put down with United Artists by Duster was big, since those guys were really artistic. To be part of that, I knew they respected what I was doing artistically.

I guess I have been blessed to experience both sides of graffiti. I have been on the destructive side of taking tags, hitting the highways and destroying everything, and then also the artistic side, where it is like, OK, do a nice colorful window down or a whole car. I have been blessed to get respect on both sides. That makes me feel like I have accomplished something.

The eighties were definitely volatile. The majority of my time was spent in wars. I met Cope through us warring with each other. They came to my building and wrote on my front door in Co-Op City, and then we chased Quik from his house one night with baseball bats and knives. Then we went looking for Cope on his block. It was a violent time— fights, crossing each other out. I couldn't concentrate on doing nice

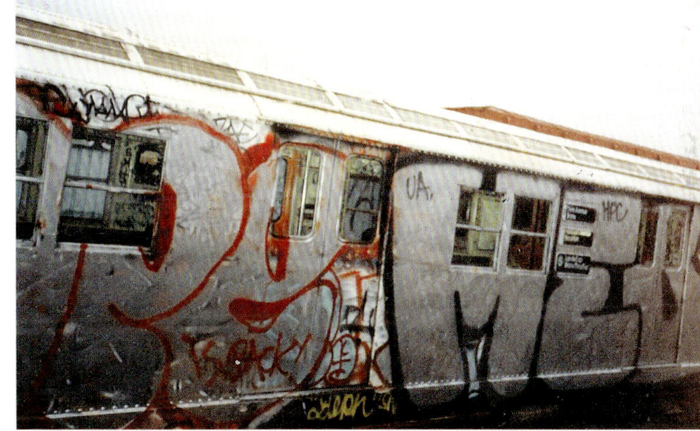

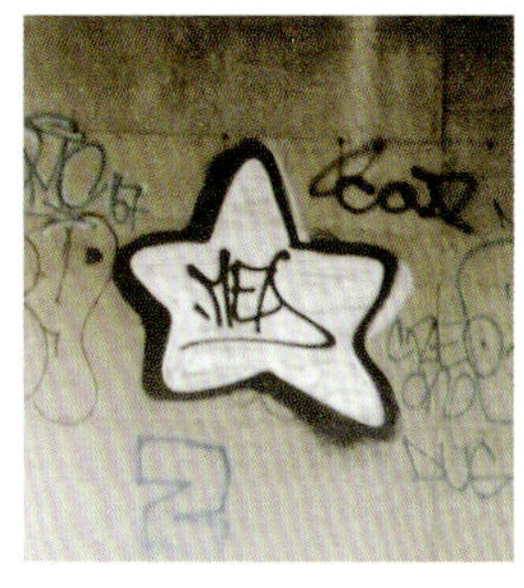

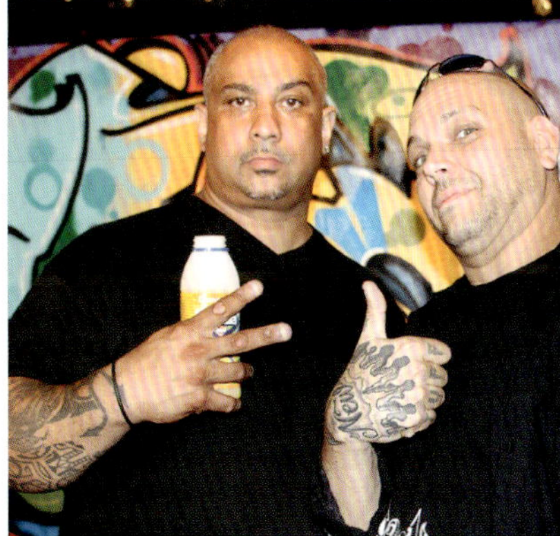

TOP: Cope, Med train car, 1988
BOTTOM: Med tag, Pitkin Yard, Brooklyn, 1987 RIGHT: Cope (left) and Med, 2012

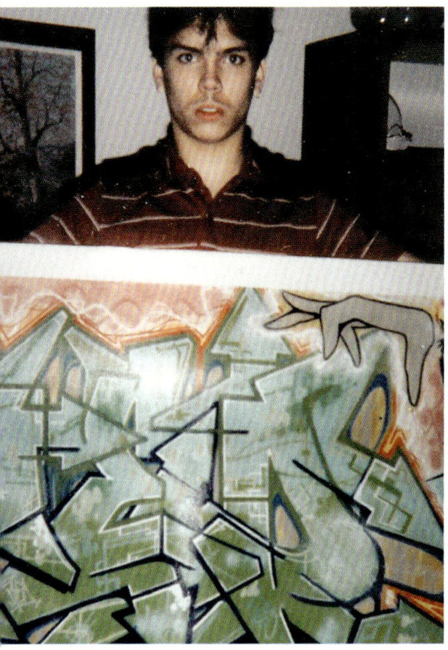

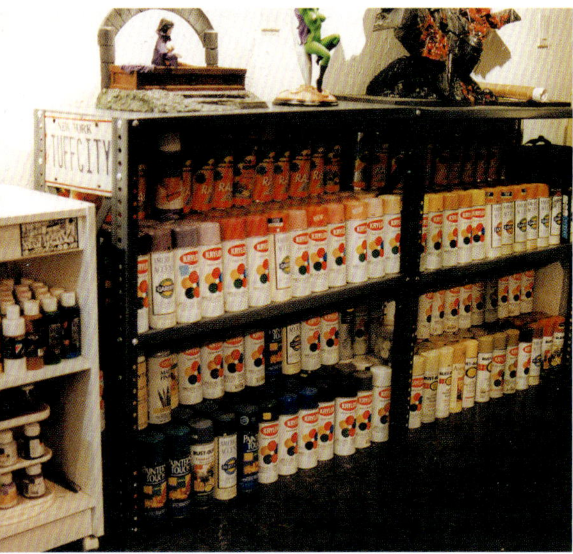

TOP: Med with canvas, 1985
BOTTOM: Med's paint collection at his apartment, 1996

pieces at the time, because if someone we were beefing with found out about it, they would just come and cross it out. Out of that Cope and I came to be friends and have been for twenty years, but at a point in time we were ready to really kill each other.

I got tattooed by one of the Moskowitz brothers. I don't remember which one—either Stanley or Walter. It was nothing, just my graffiti name, a *Med* in script. It was like a stupid little fuckin' $30 tattoo, and it wasn't that I even knew who anybody was at the time. I just looked in the Yellow Pages and saw "Tattoo Sun Rise Highway Long Island," and I was like, "Oh, I know how to get there because we used to steal paint from out there." That was a notorious street to steal paint from. But the whole experience was just in passing.

At that time tattooing didn't really have any presence in graffiti, you know. Maybe one or two of us might have had a Big Joe tattoo of a spider or a dragon or something stupid, but that was it. There really were no graffiti cats getting down hard with tattooing.

I mean, I remember being fourteen; I had just come home from the group home and started high school and was hanging out with friends. The OG in my neighborhood was like, "You don't know how to do tattoo? You just get a needle and thread and dip it in india ink, then you poke it in your skin." And we were like, what?!

So my whole crew got a bottle of Higgins india ink and went in the staircase. I did my name on my hand, and my other boy did his hand. It really had nothing to do with graffiti or anything, it was just that one night, and again, it was just a passing thing.

The lifestyle I was living and the graffiti crowd I was running with were wild. I was stealing, I was robbing people, I was getting high, and that eventually got me locked up. Over time I had accrued a number of different charges. Then I jumped bail and moved out to California with Duster. I was living in Los Angeles—this is around 1988. After a short time, I moved back to New York and those charges were waiting for me when I got home. I had to go do time, I got a two to six.

I got locked up and I was on Rikers Island. On like the first day, I was in the dayroom drawing. Some inmates were watching me and one of 'em was like, "Oh shit, look what he is drawing. Yo, that looks good. You tattoo?" I was like, "Not really, but I have done it before," and they were like, "Oh word? If I can get you some stuff, will you tattoo me?" So I was like, "Yeah." That is how it started.

I was on Rikers doing hand-poked tattoos with, like, the crudest shit. Like plastic from a shaving razor or an ID card burned onto the ceiling and scraped and mixed with water to make ink. You would be amazed what motherfuckers will make ink with in the penal system. Anyway, I started doing this heavy, and shit was dope. I was tattooing and getting respected, I didn't have beef, my shit wasn't getting stolen or robbed, they were loving me. They were like, "Yo, my man can fuckin' draw." And so that just sparked it more in me.

Eventually I got shipped to state prison, and this white biker—who actually was also, as crazy as it sounds, a graffiti writer named Zane from Roosevelt Island—was like, "Yo, I can make you a tattoo machine if you tattoo me." The dude was a graffiti writer who built me my first tattoo machine in jail. And from that point on, boom, I was running a tattoo shop in jail. Like literally, I had ink getting sent in from the street. I ran the commercial art department, so I was drawing flash all day, every day.

All the officers were cool with me. They would call me from cell block to cell block to tattoo guys. I would go in the yard with the book of flash and motherfuckers would be like, "Yo, I want a tattoo." I would be like, "OK, show me what you want. OK, boom, that's going to cost this, have your people send me $150." The money would come through, I would go tell the officer, and he would call me out of my cell and take me to the dude's cell. I would get my gloves on and tattoo the guy.

If the sergeant was coming around, they would come by and be like, "Stop," so I would wait for him to pass and then start tattooing again. I did this for four years in prison. I had money in the commissary, I had respect from everyone, every race—black dudes, white dudes,

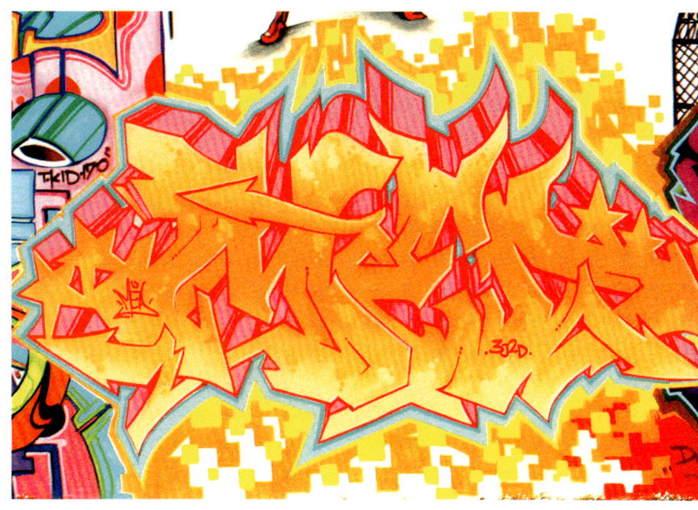

Med piece, Rikers Island, 2011

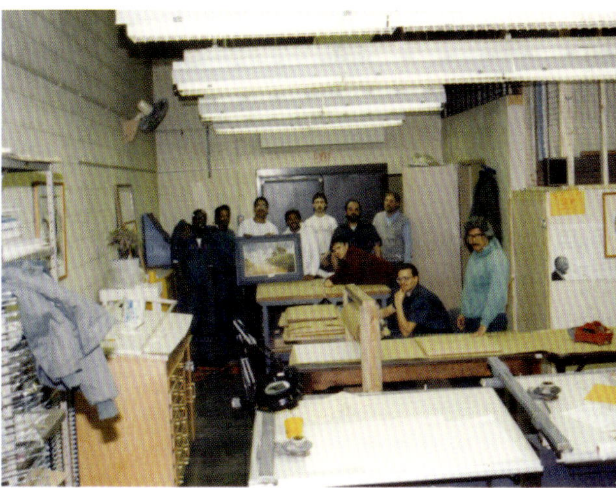

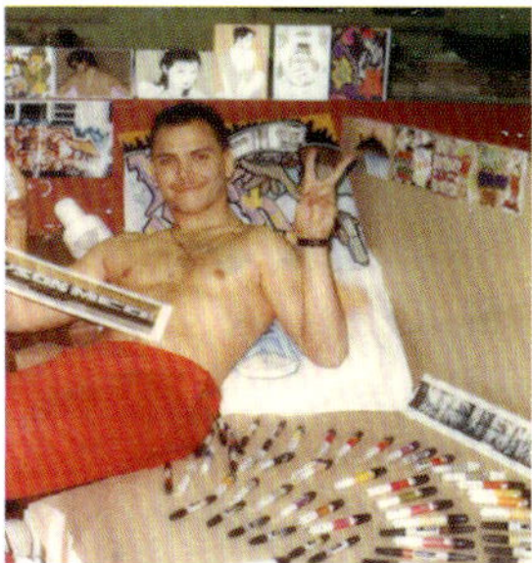
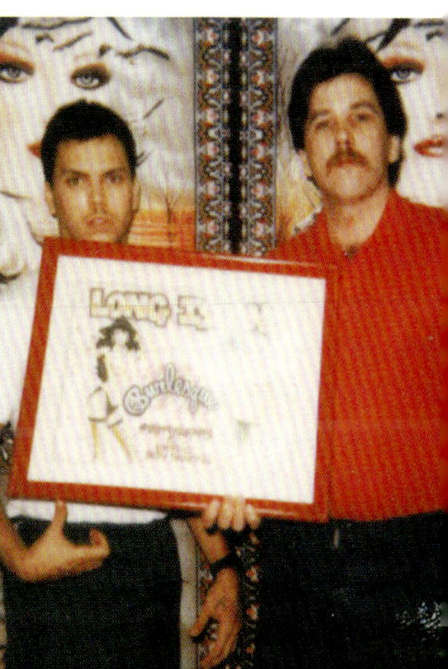

TOP: Commercial art class, Greene Correctional Facility
BOTTOM: Med RIGHT: Med, Greene Correctional Facility

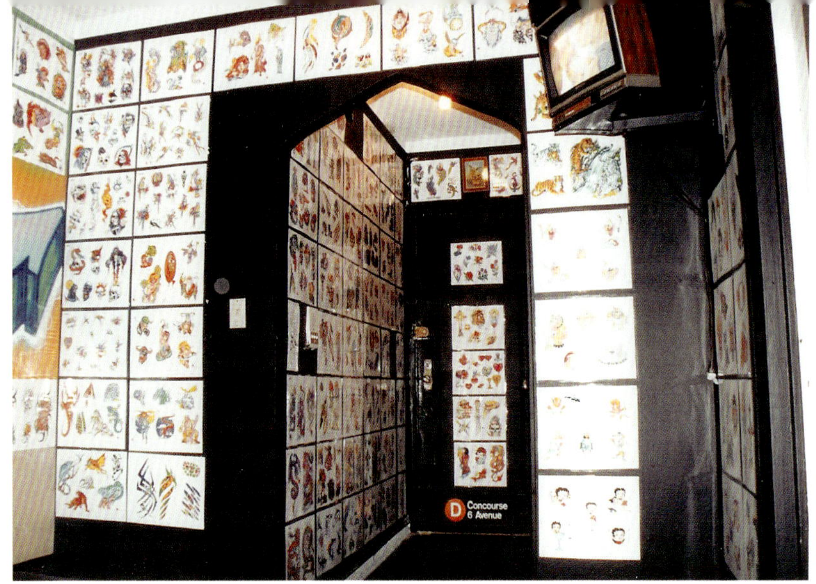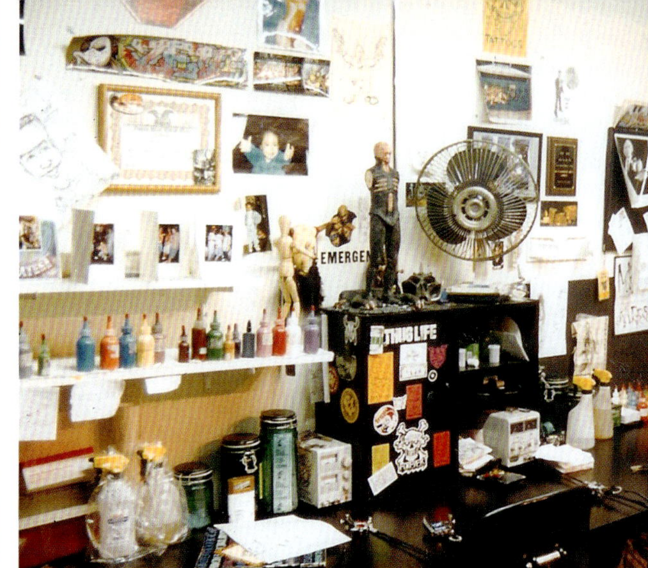

FROM LEFT: Interiors of Tuff City Tatts, Bronx, 1993

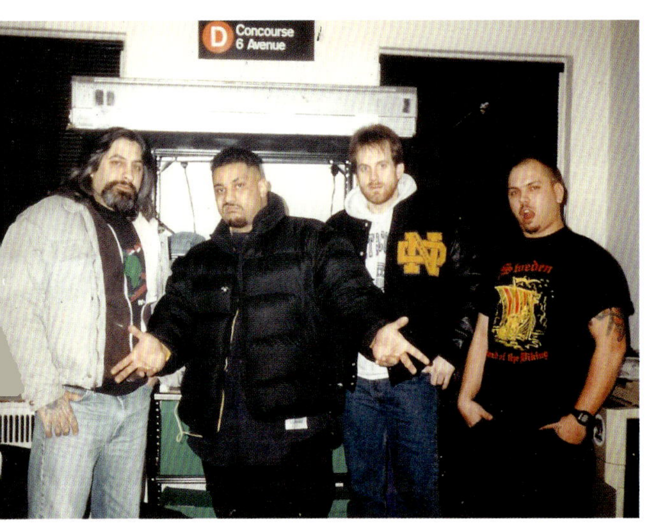

Seen, Cope, PJ, and Med at Tuff City, 1993

Spanish dudes. They were all like, "This nigga's nice and I want to get a tattoo from him." Technically I had a full-blown running shop in prison. Nobody before me had taken it to that level. People come home today and they are like, "Yo, niggas still talk about you upstate."

Then I got released and came home from jail still a graffiti writer but now also a tattooist. And the rest is history. I came home from jail in '91 and was tattooing the family members of people I was upstate with, other friends, going house to house. I did this for about a year, and Seen had just started recently as well. He had been learning at, I think, Big Joe's and around this time had just gotten his own spot.

It was an office above his father's building, and after seeing me go house to house, he was like, "Why don't you come and tattoo out of my spot? I will give you some space and a chair to just do it here." It wasn't a money thing; he never asked me for money. It was just like, "Here's a table, why don't you do it here?" This is like 1992. At the time the tattoo shop didn't have a name. I remembered that Seen had a silk-screening business before called Tuff City Tees that had closed down. I always liked that name. I was like, "Why don't we call it Tuff City Tatts?" He was like, "That's a great name."

So I'm tattooing there for a few months, and then Seen brought someone in to work there, and this guy was paying Seen money to be there. I sensed that he started to feel weird about getting paid from this guy. Meanwhile, I'm there and not paying him anything. I went away for a week, and when I came back, the name of the shop was changed to Tattoo Seen. There were new business cards, and Tuff City Tatts was no more.

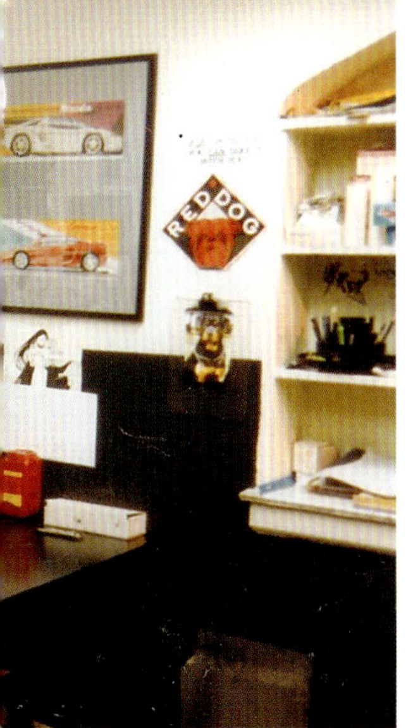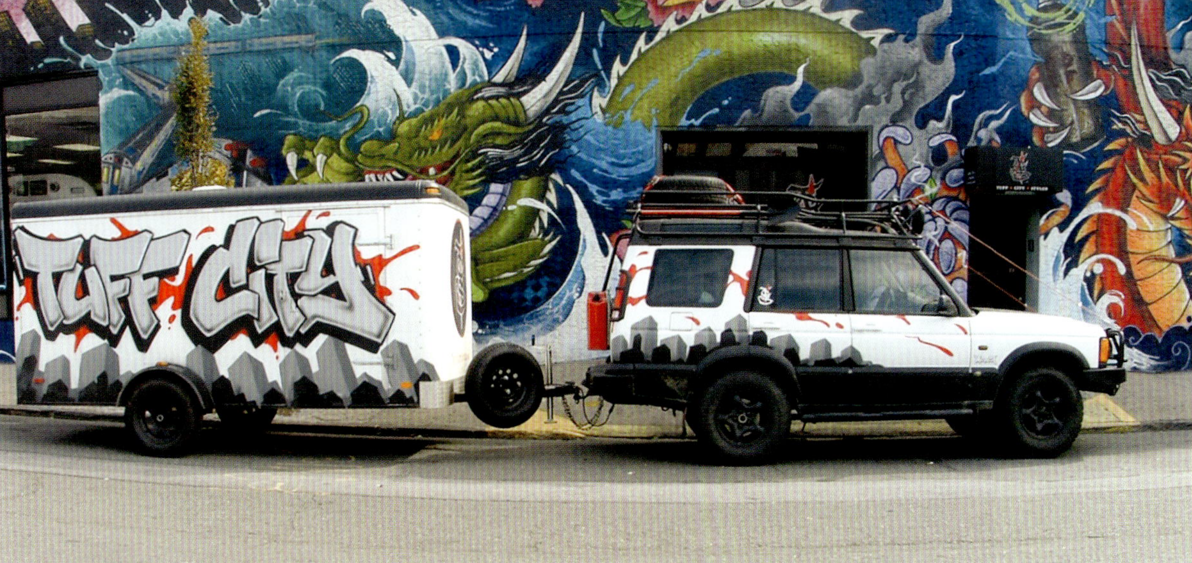

Tuff City Styles, Bronx, 2012

I worked there for another month, but I started to feel kind of weird about the whole thing. I went to Seen to talk about it. I was like, "Listen, man, I'm going to open my own thing. I'm going to move to the other side of the Bronx—to the ghetto—and I'm going to keep the name Tuff City Tatts, and I hope that's OK."

He was like, "Yo, no problem. You're going to move to the other side of the Bronx? Cool. Thank you. Respect. You want the name? Cool." I had his blessing. That felt like the real beginning of my life. In 1993 I got a studio apartment on the Grand Concourse. I blew it up so much that with all the traffic, my neighbors and landlord thought I was a drug dealer. The landlord wrote me an eviction notice claiming illegal activity. I was like, "Listen, I'm just tattooing in there," and he was like, "Either way, it's a business, and this is not a commercial space." The year on the lease was about up, and I had to go.

That forced me to get my first storefront. This was sometime in late '94 or '95. At the time tattooing was still illegal. The ban was still in effect, but I was in the Yellow Pages and had a big fuckin' neon sign in the window that said *Tattoo*. We just defied it for years, and no cops ever came.

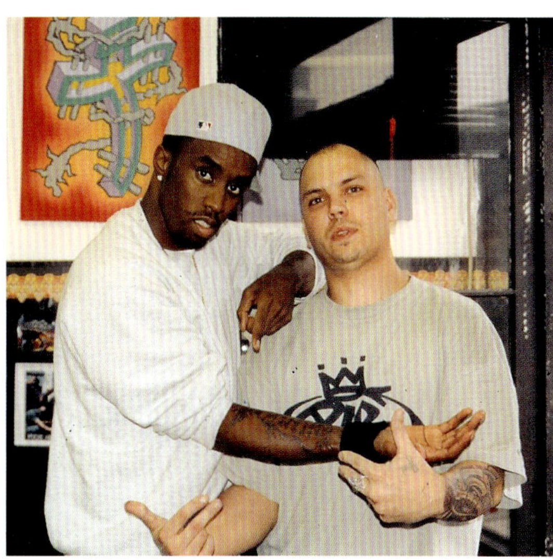

Sean Combs (left) and Med, Tuff City, 1996

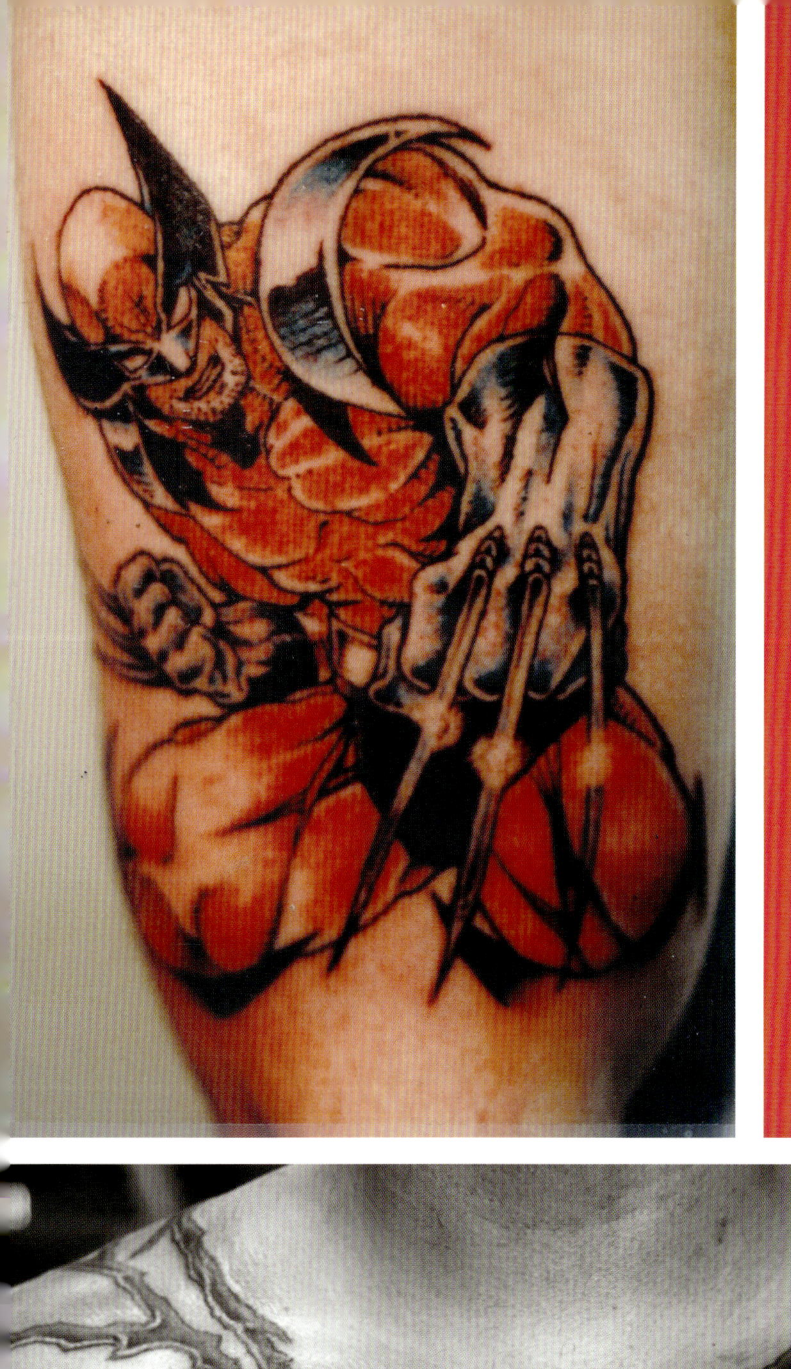
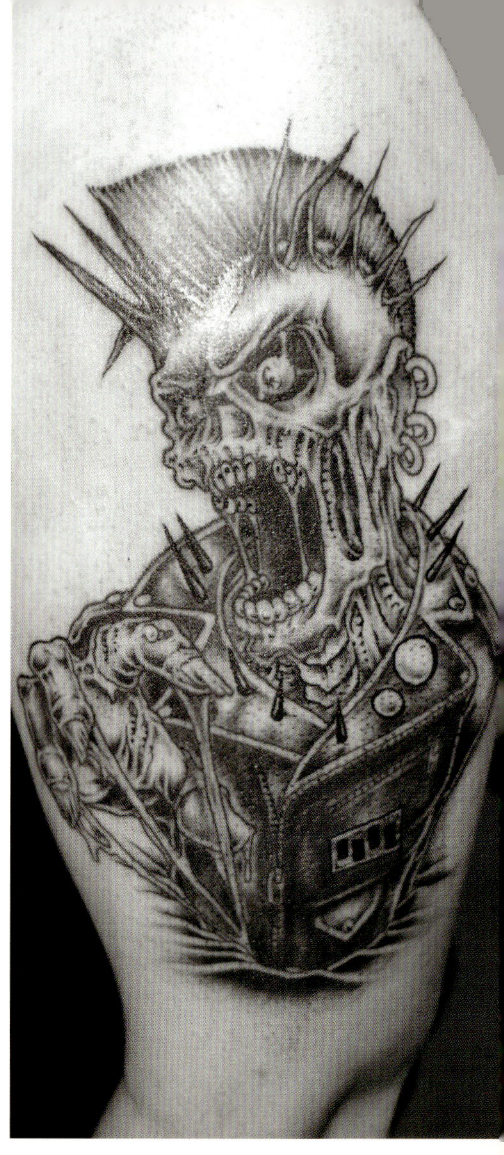
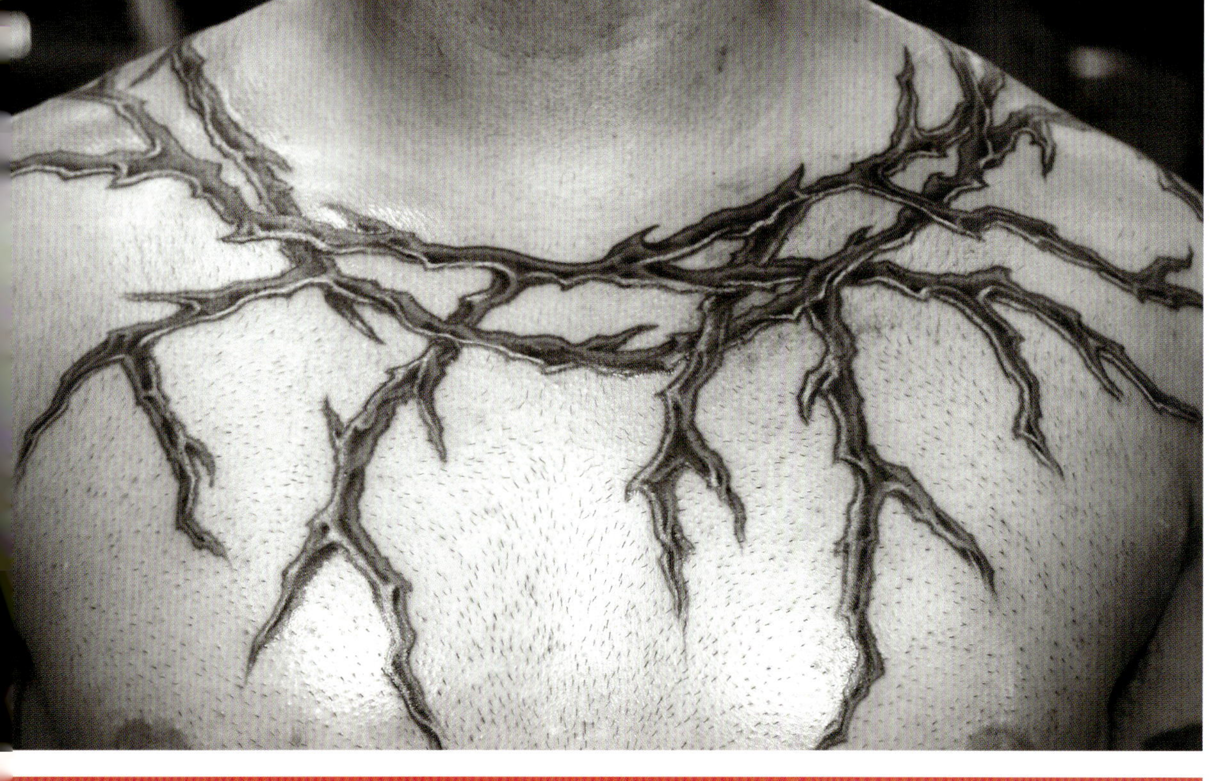

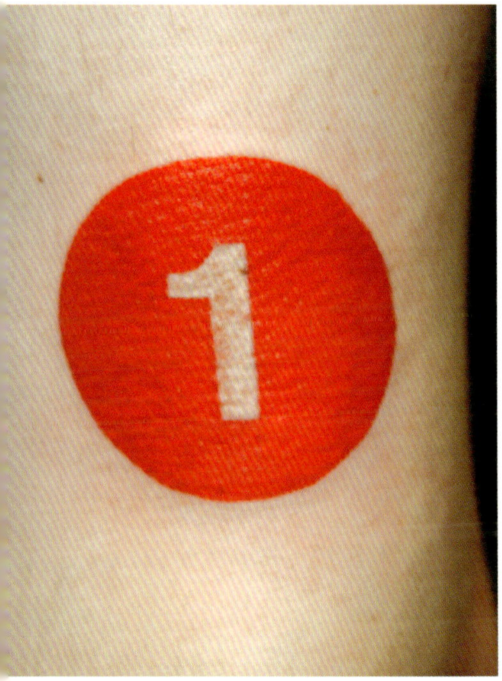

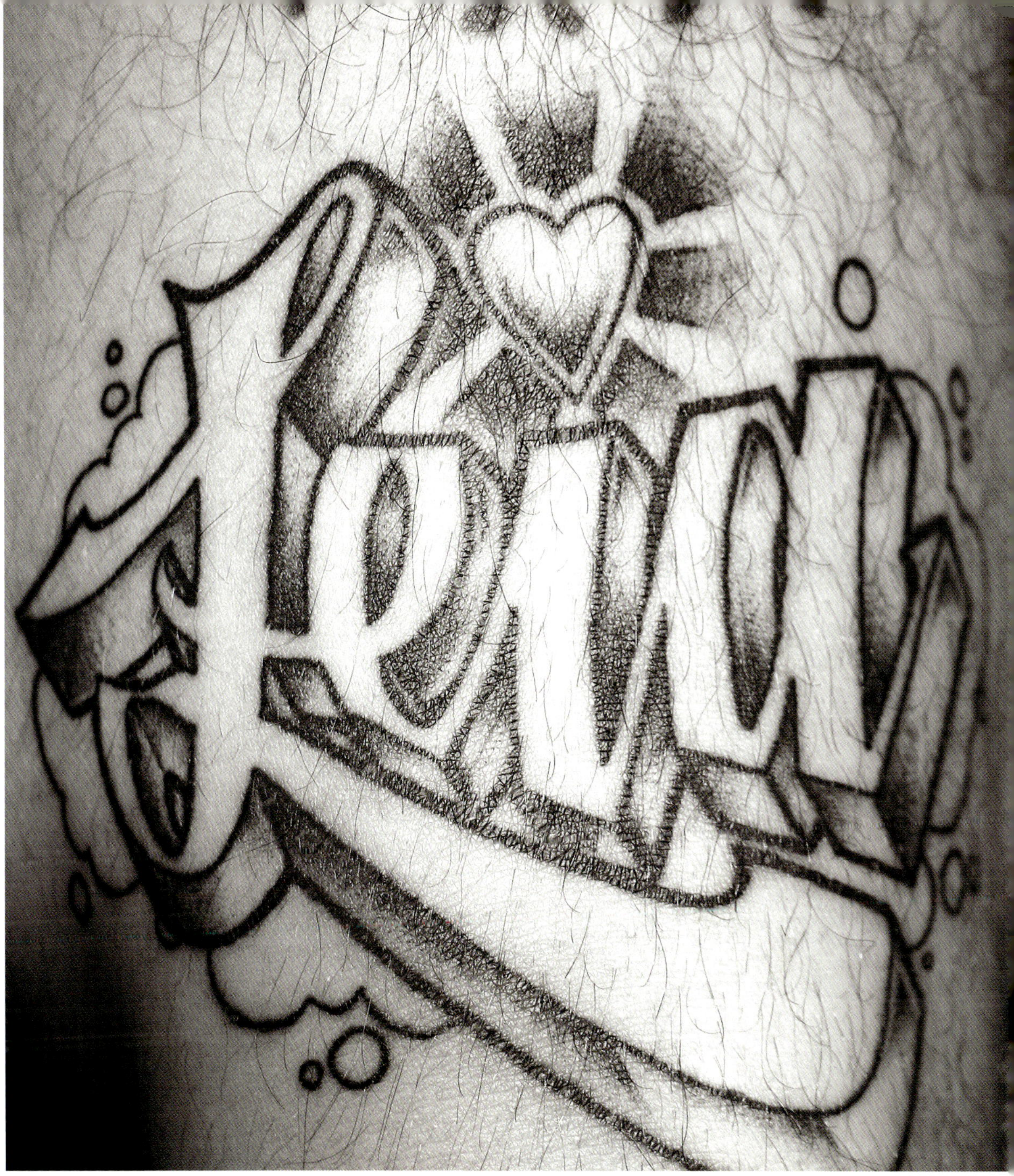

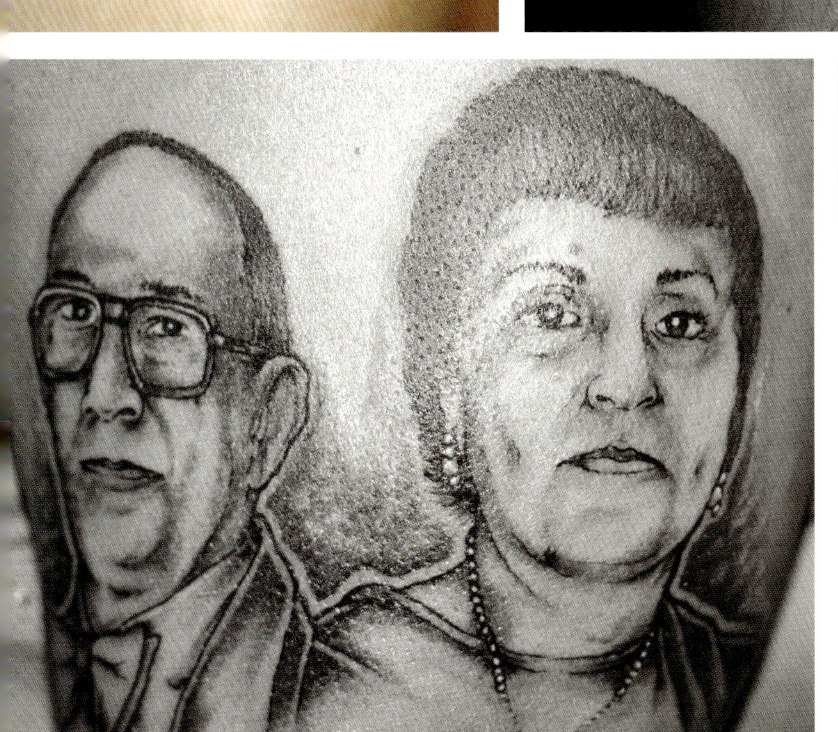

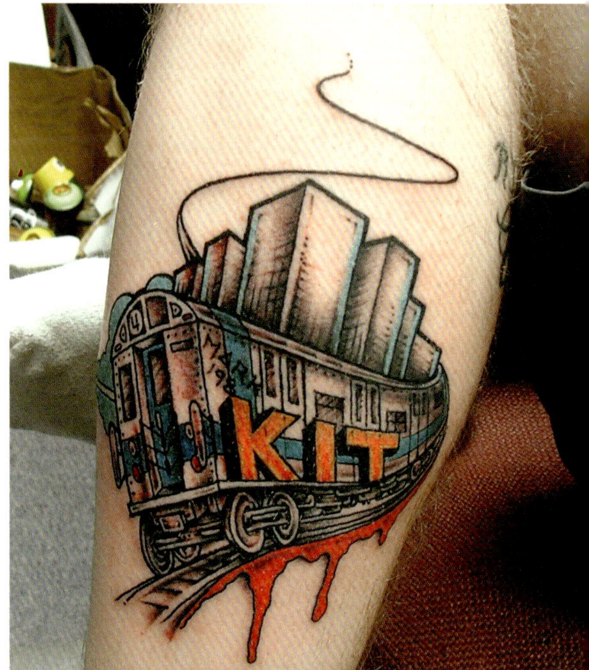
KIT

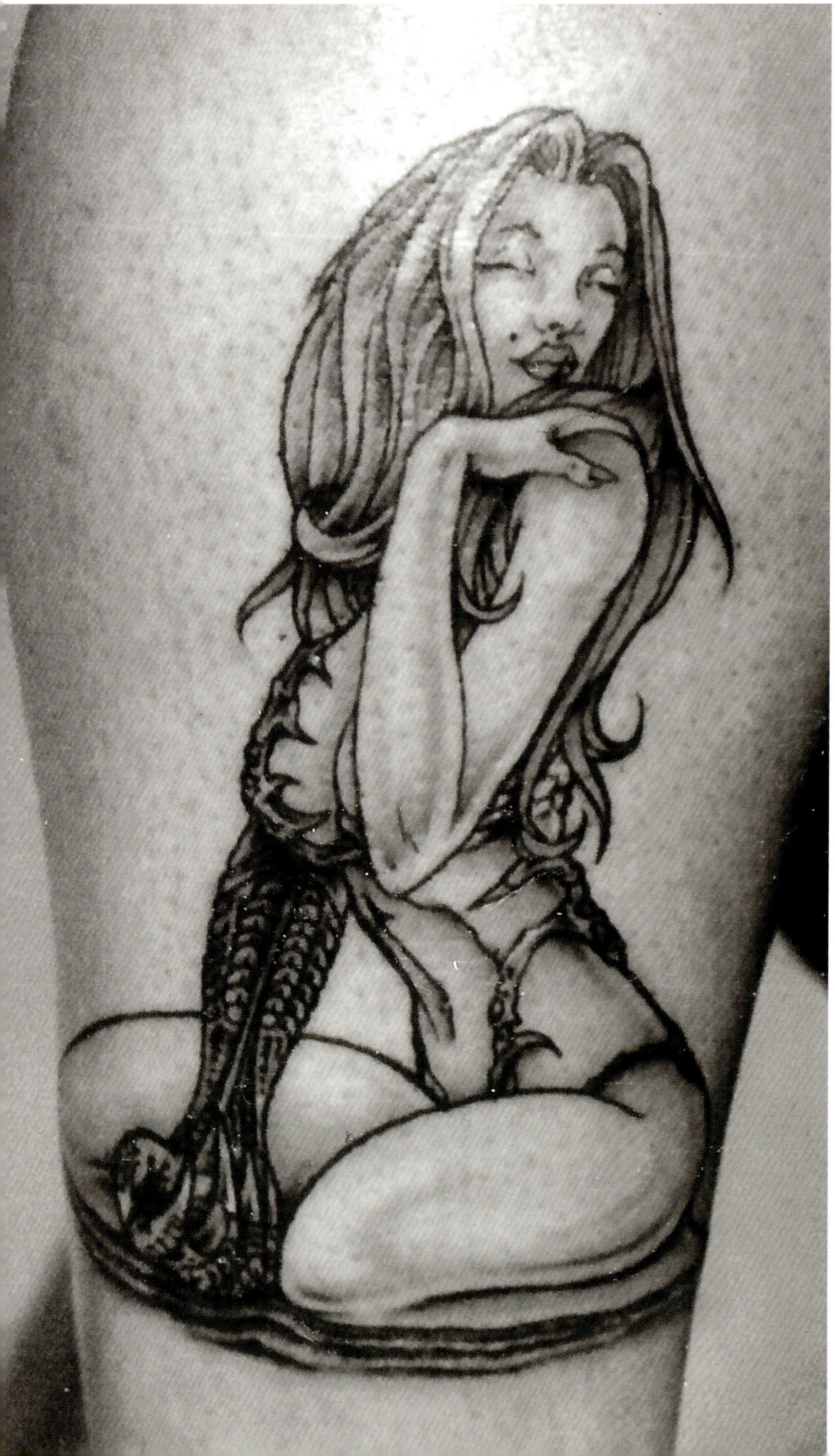

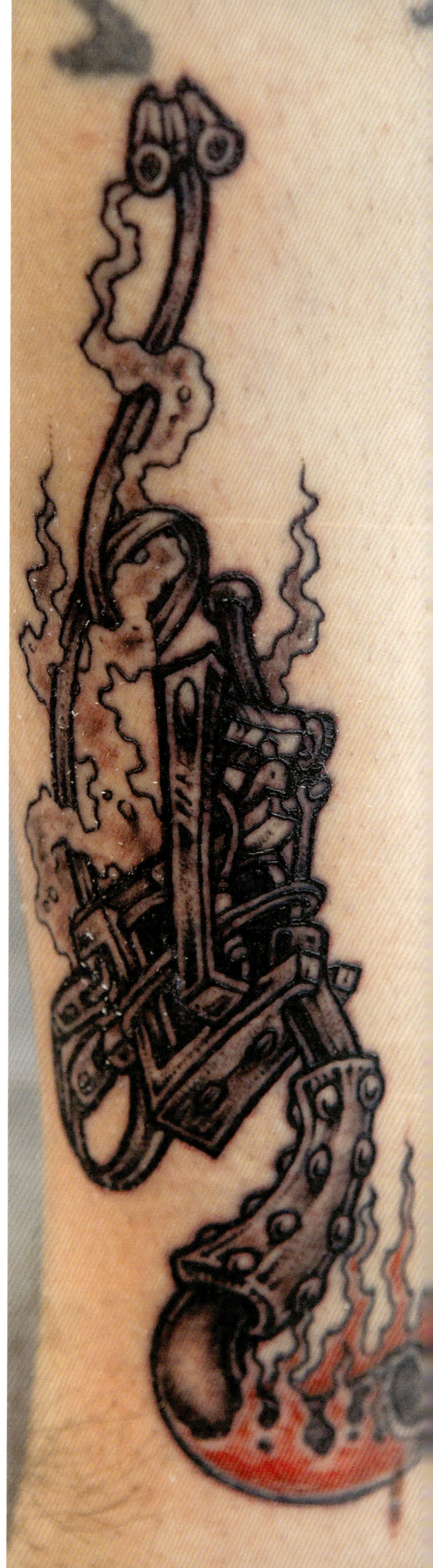

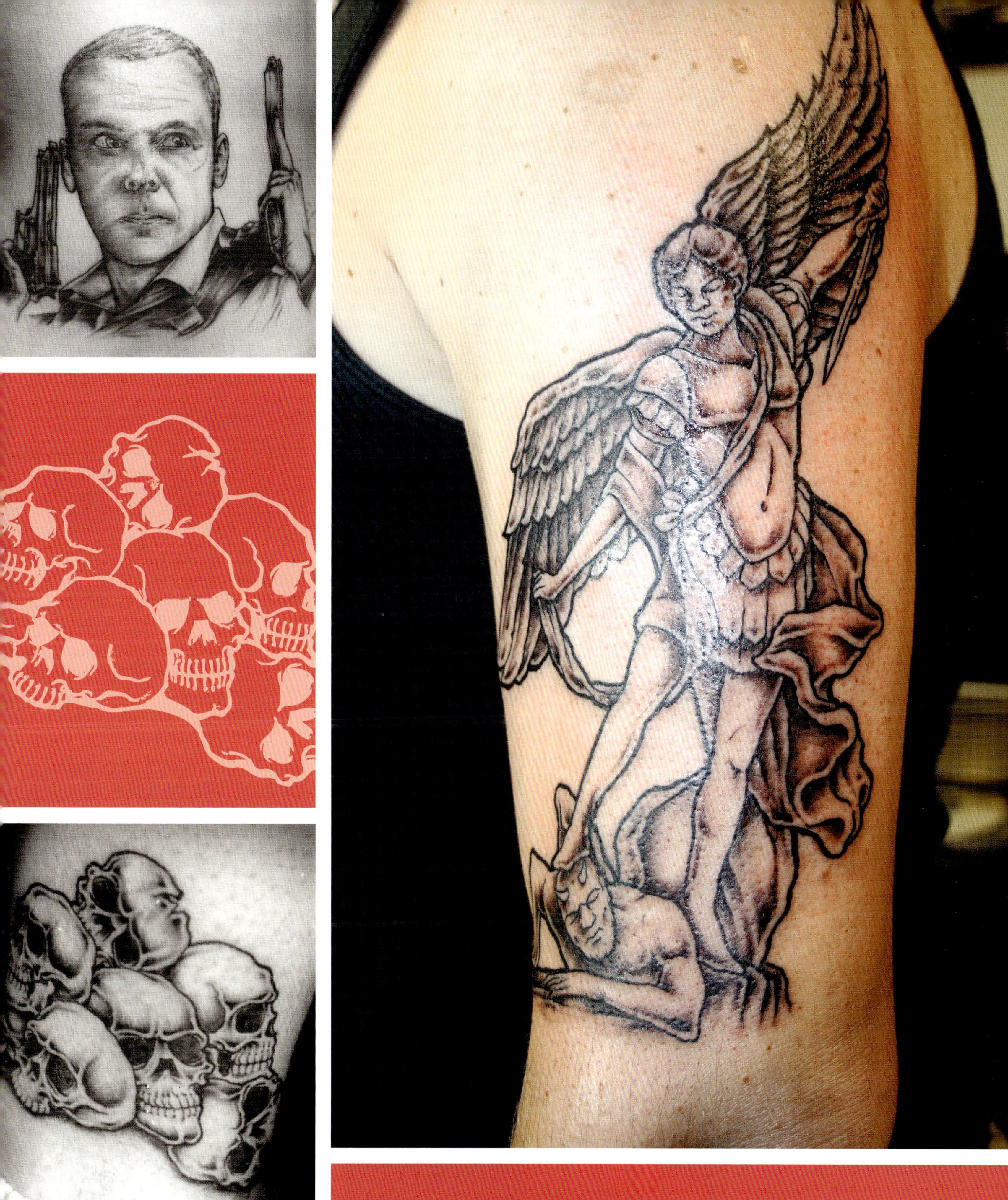

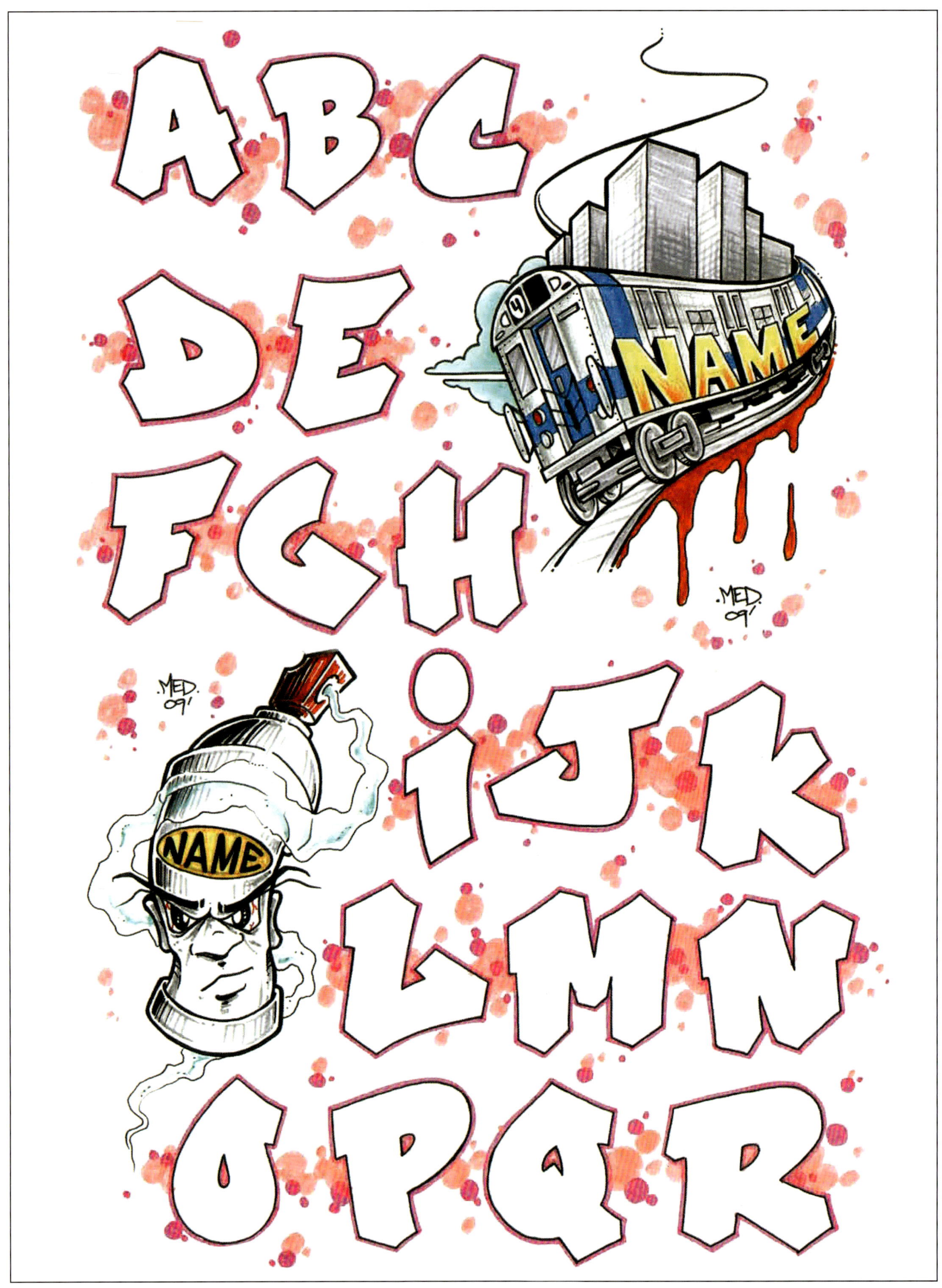
NAME
NAME
.MED. 09'
.MED. 09'

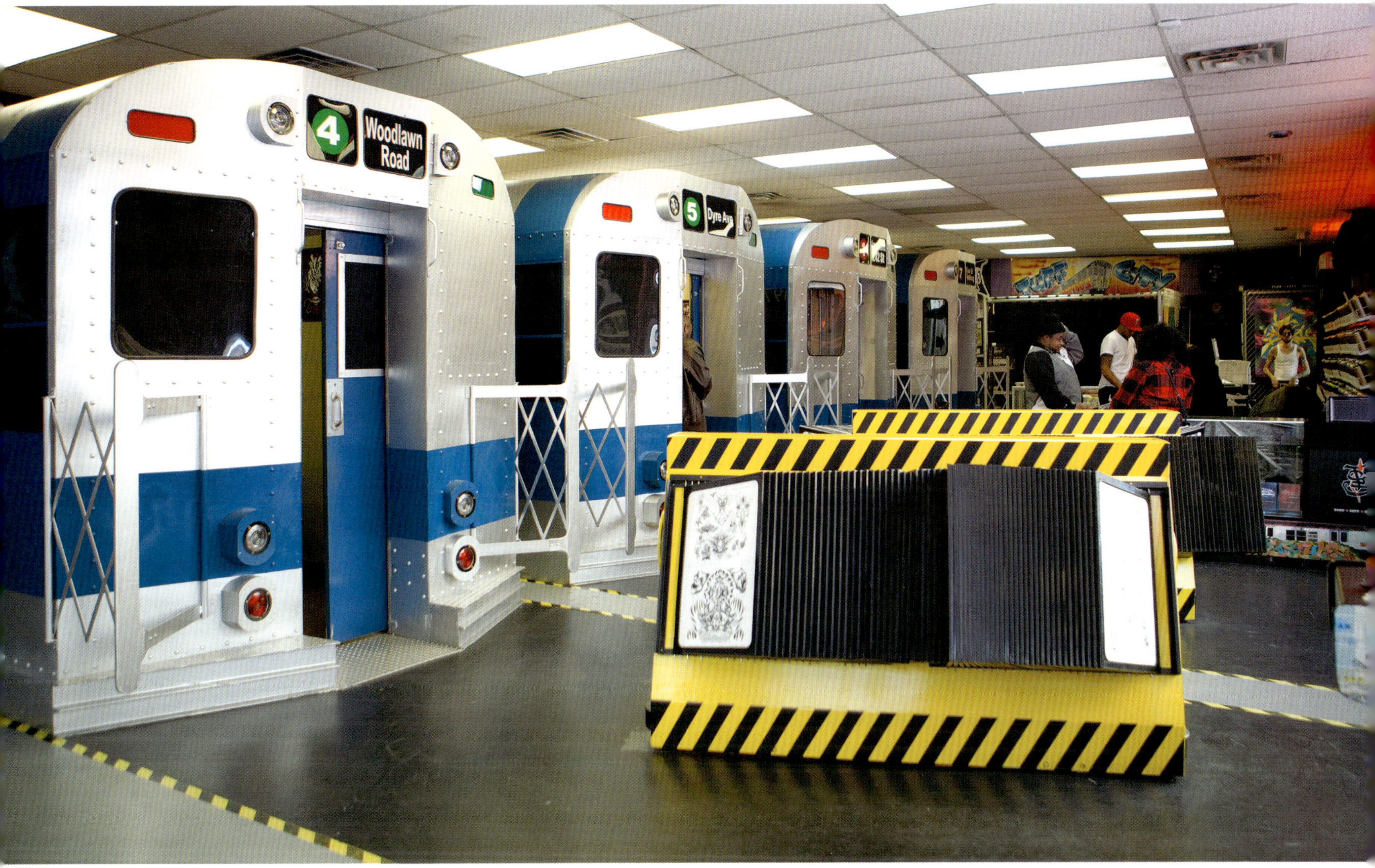

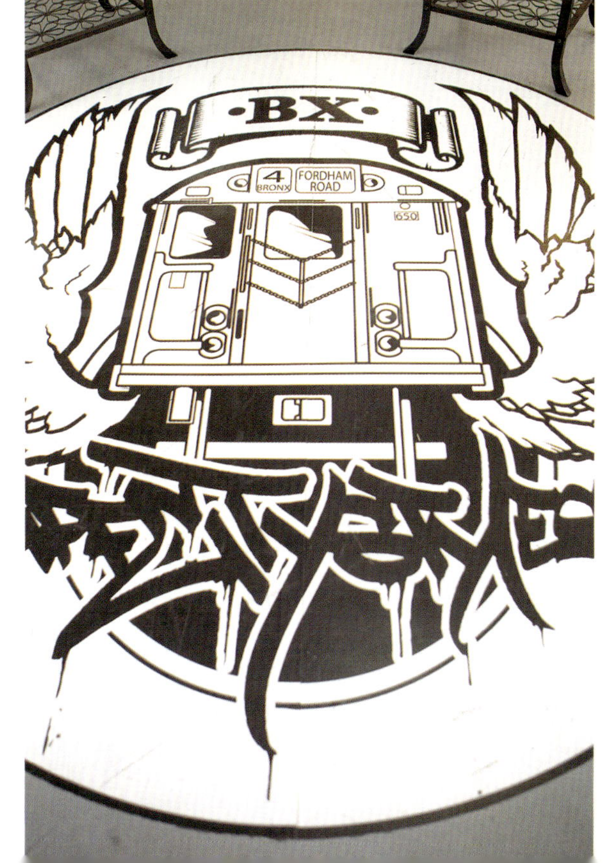

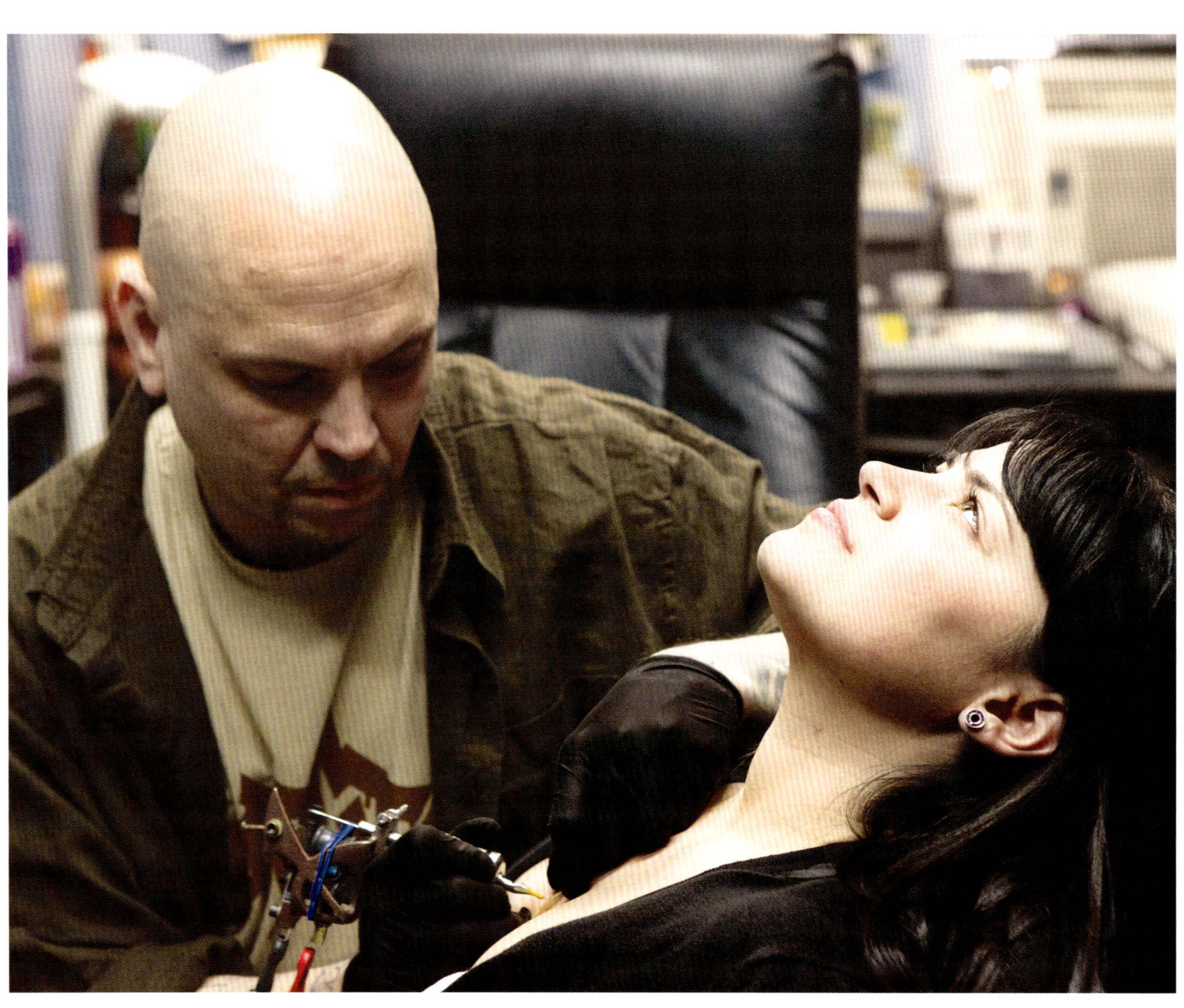

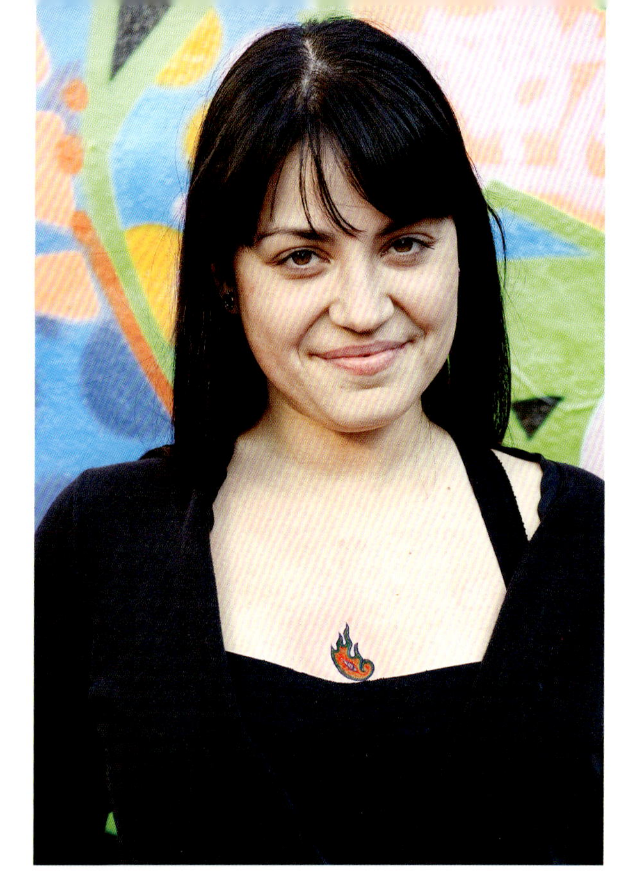

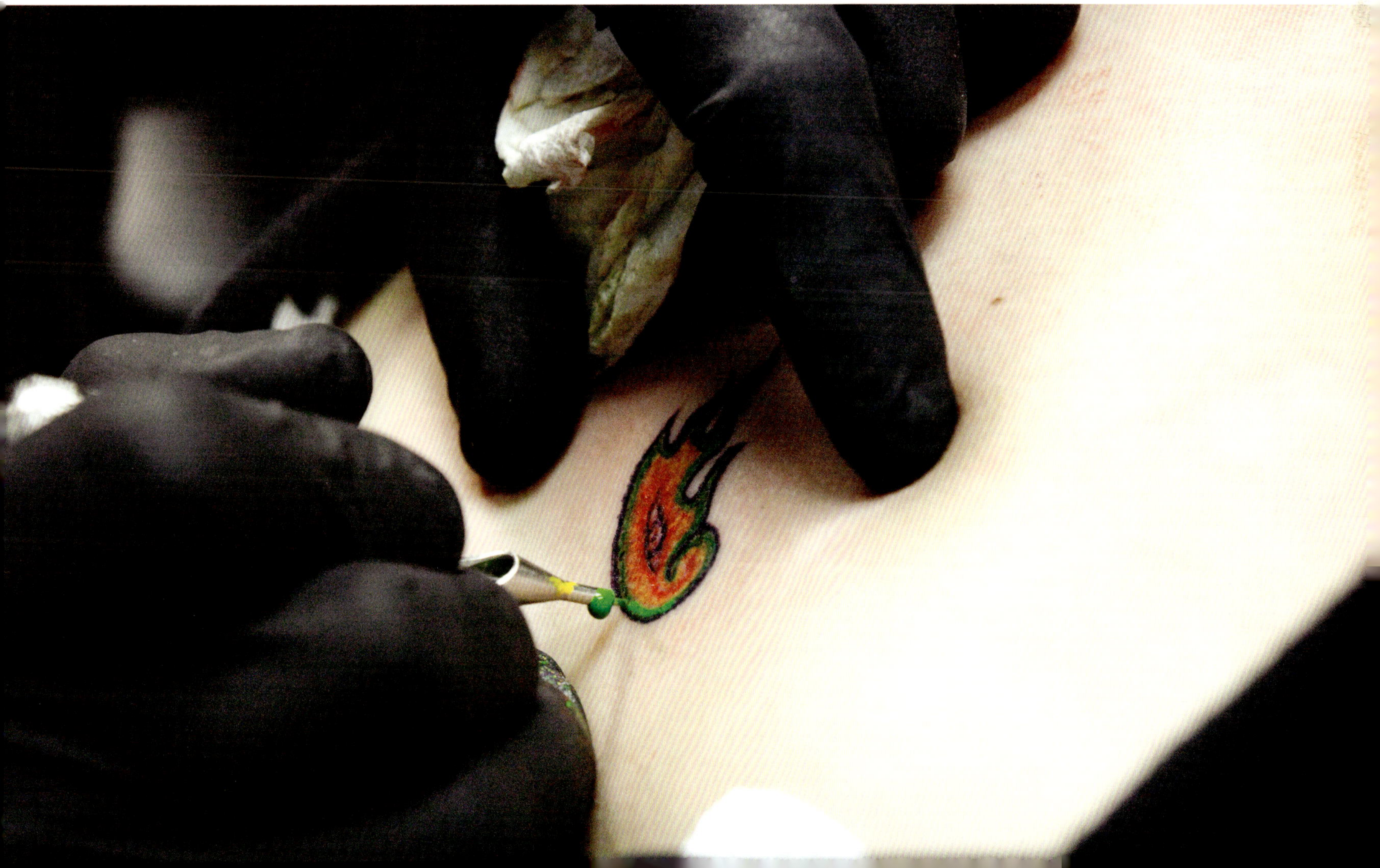

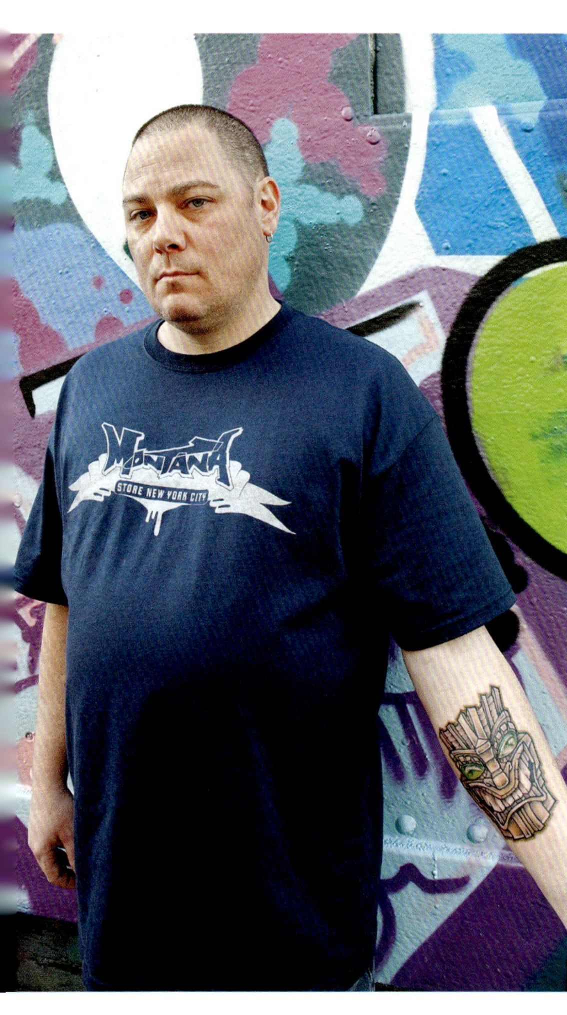

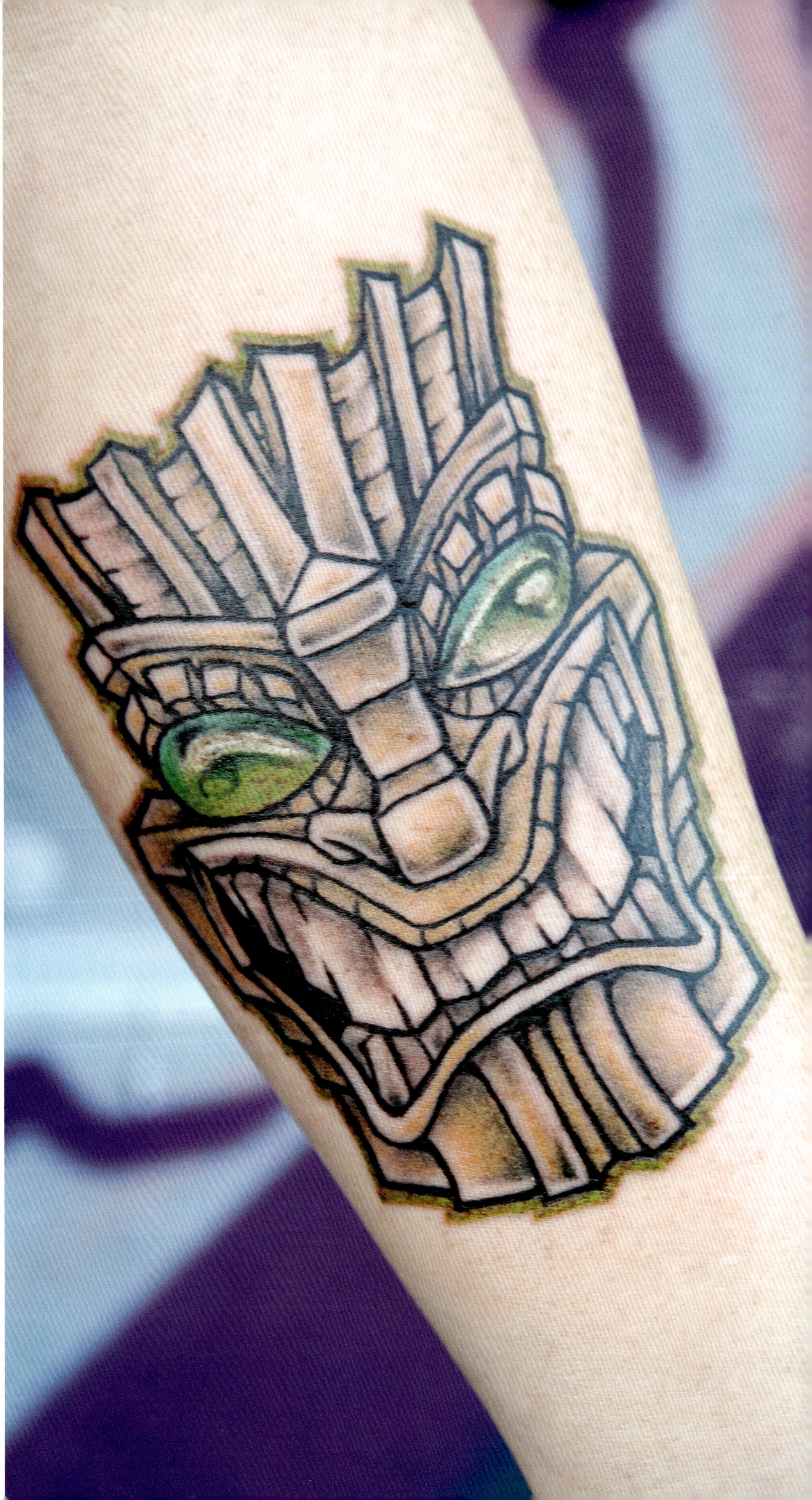

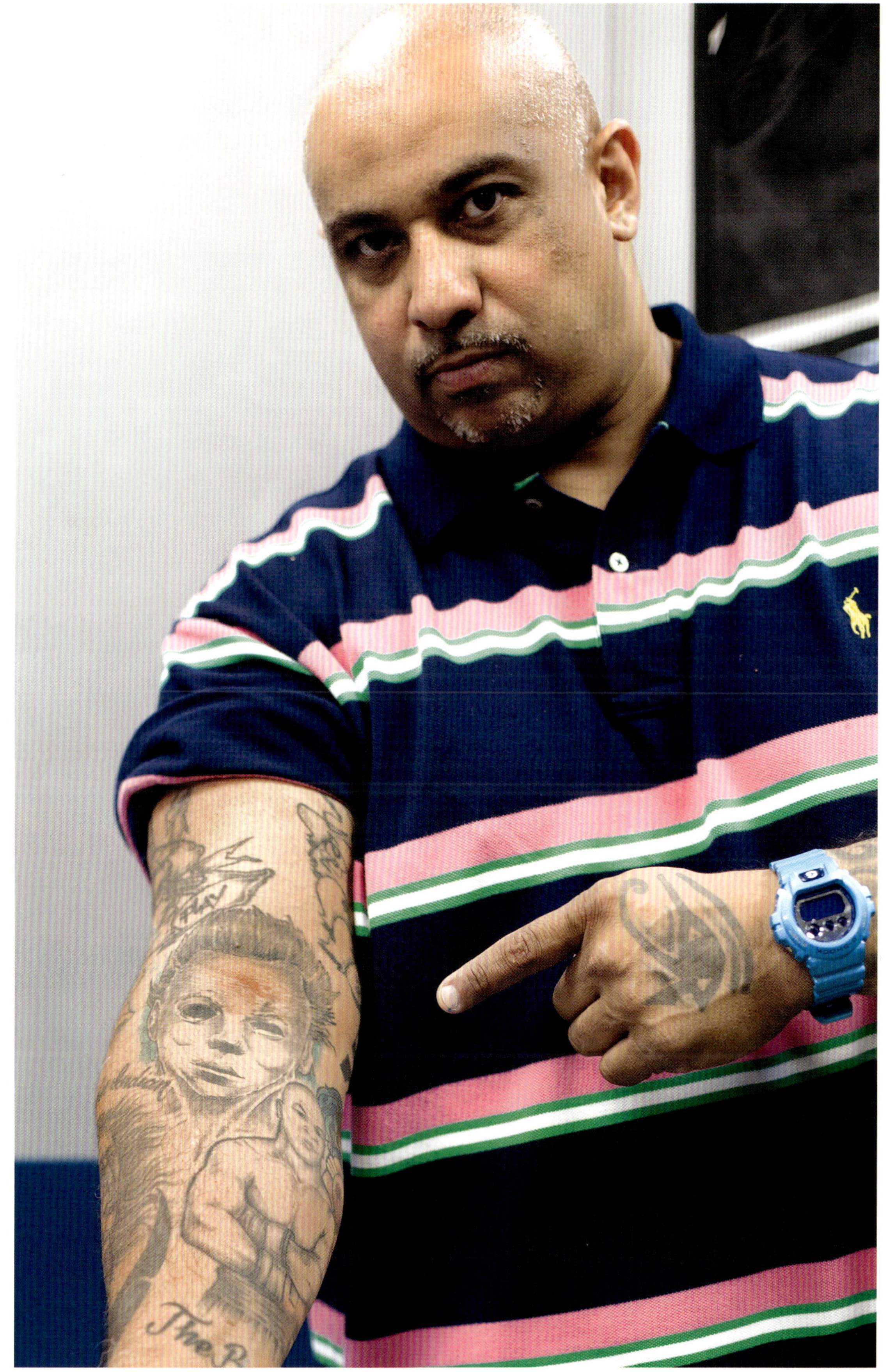

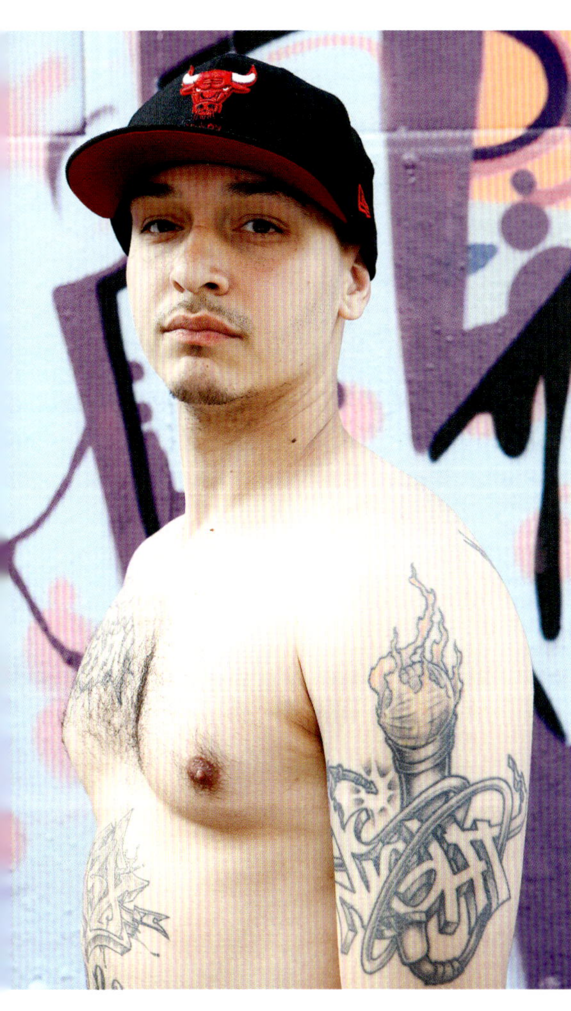

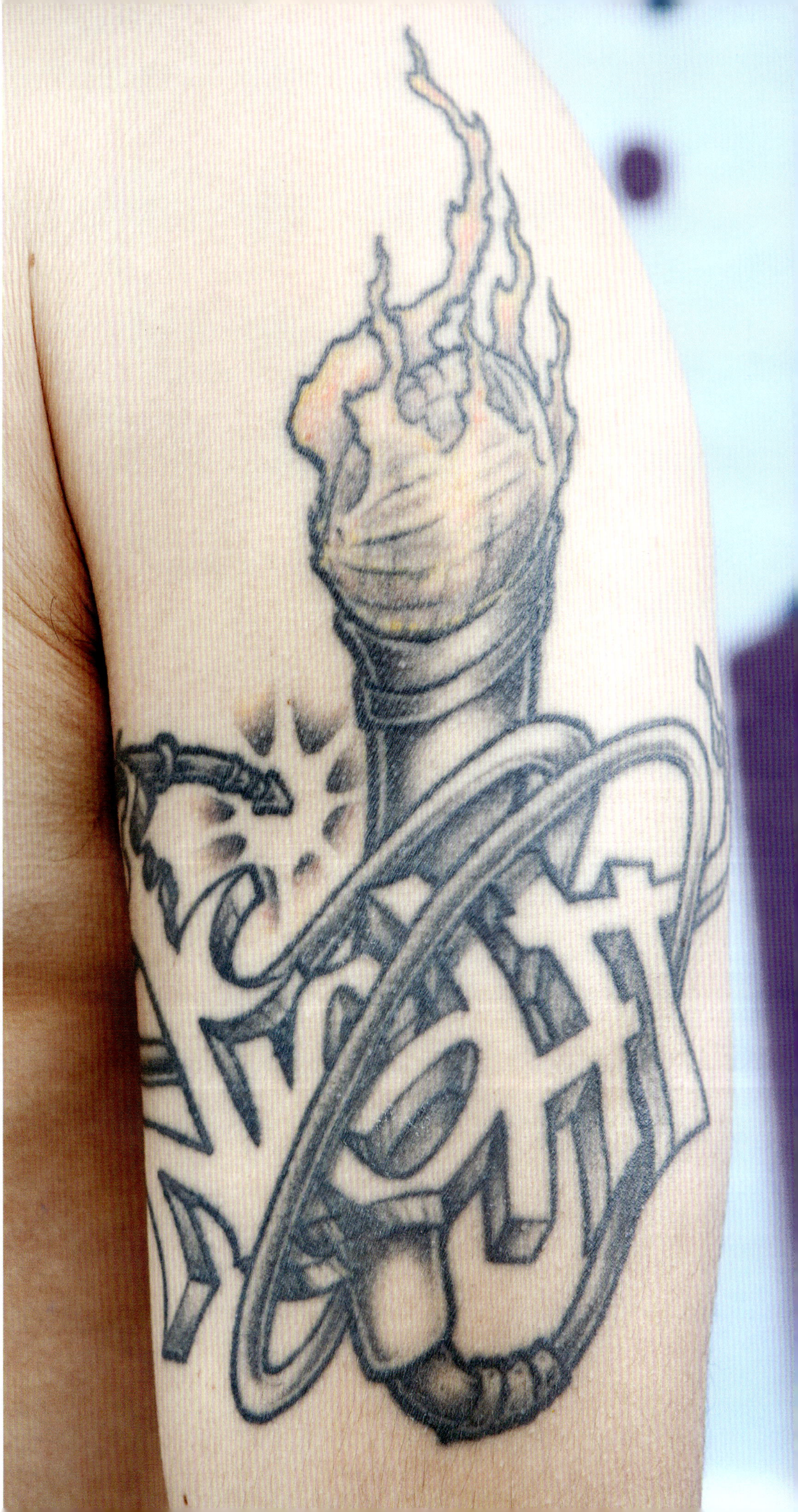

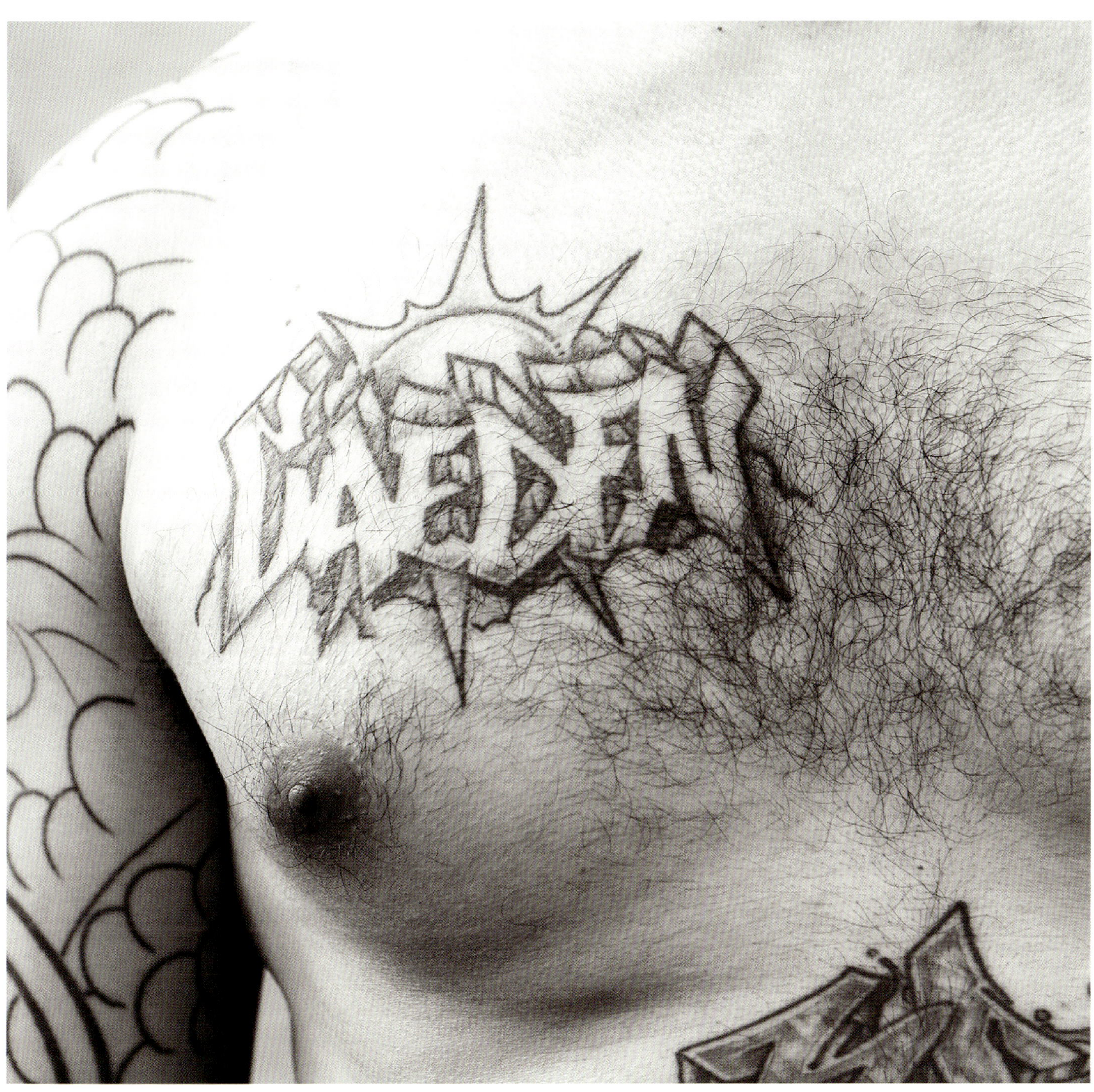

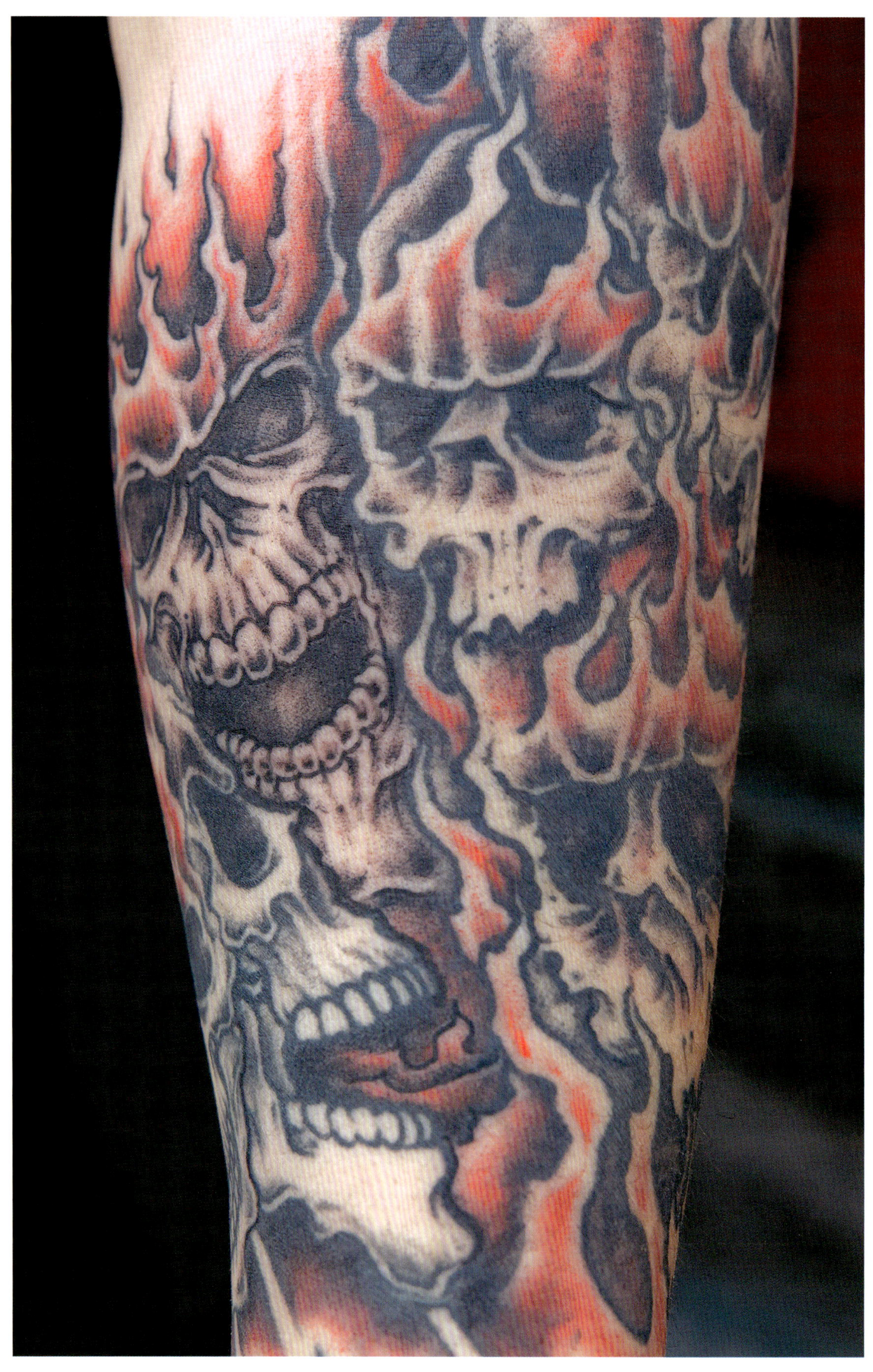

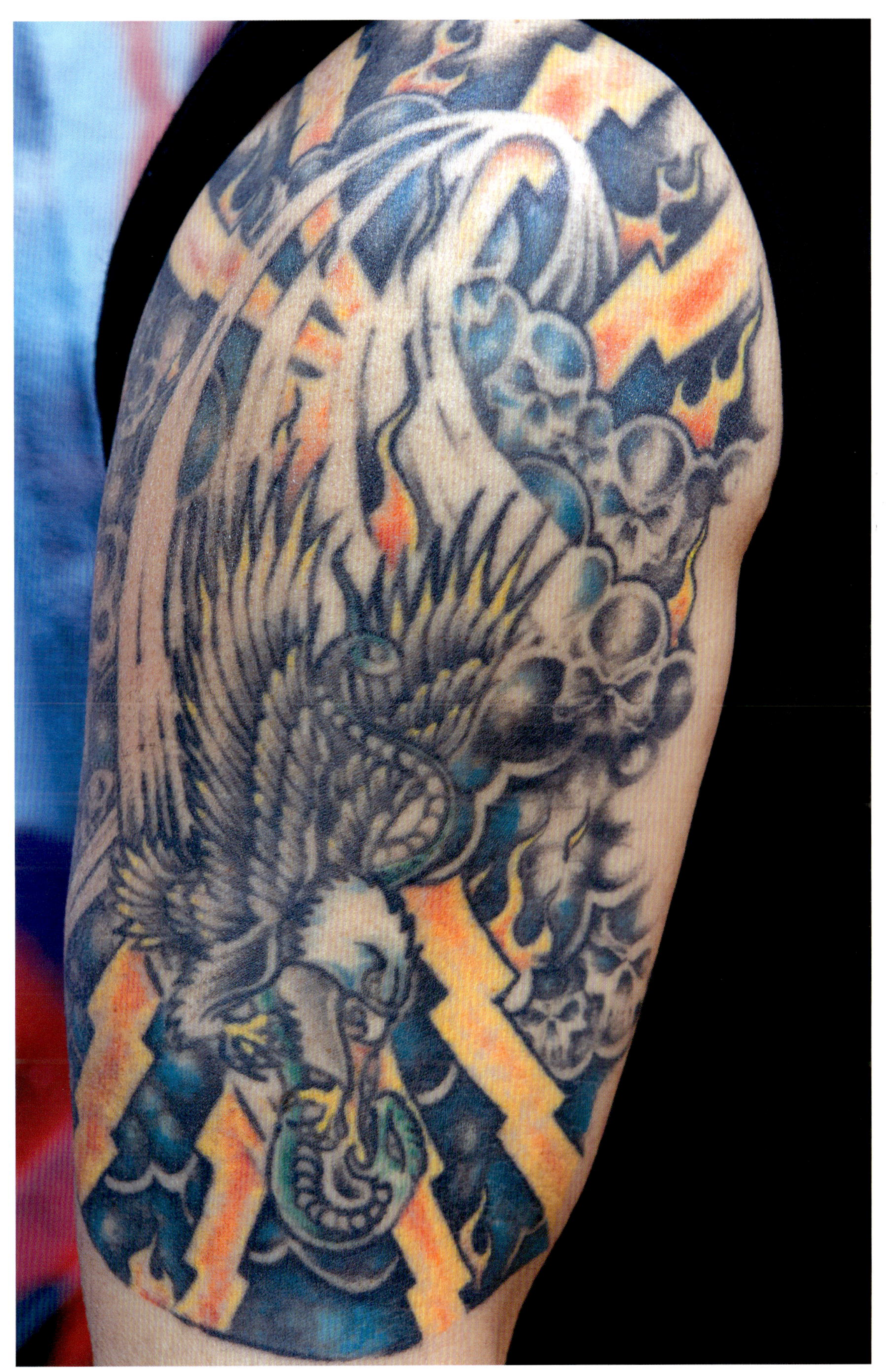

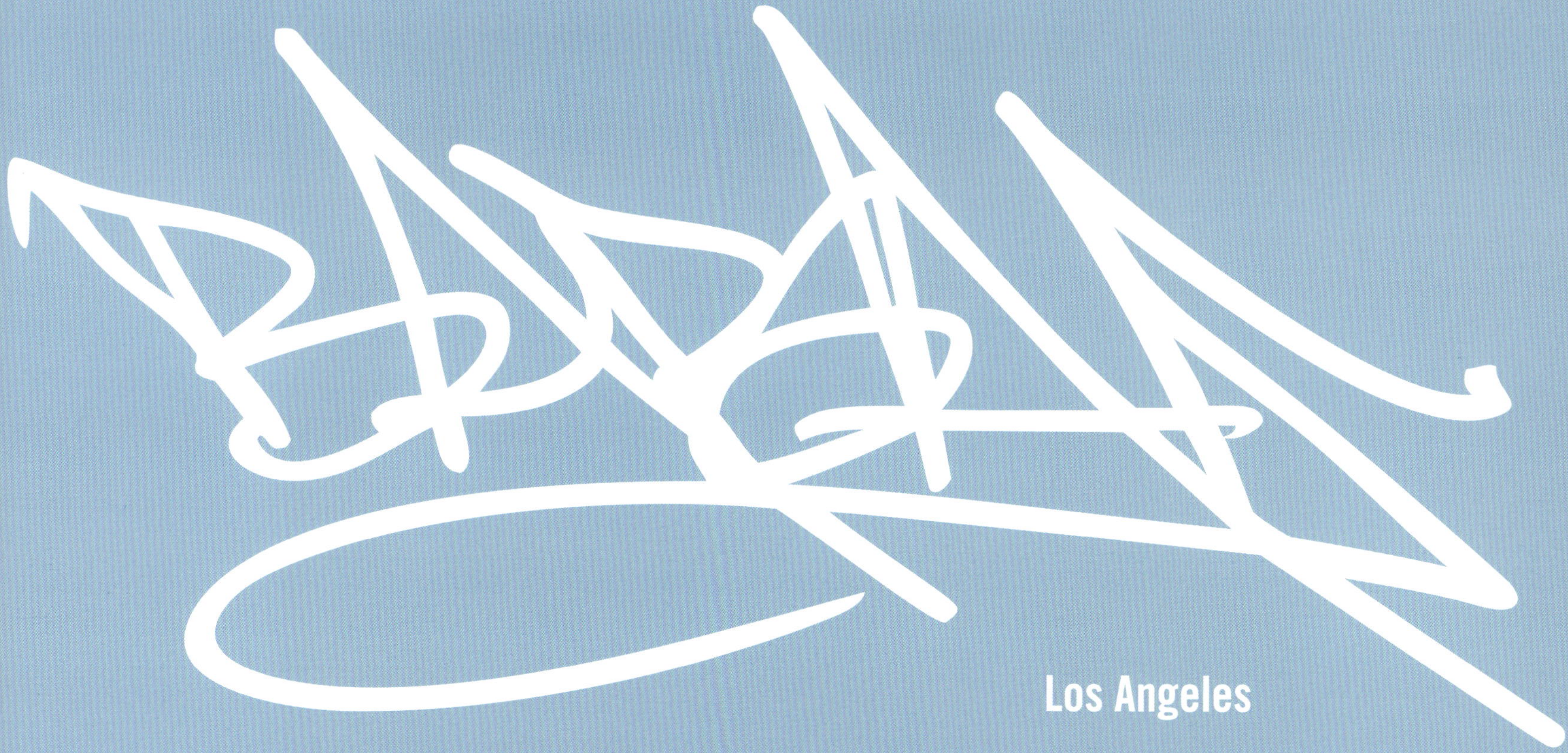

"When I asked Jonathan Shaw to teach me tattooing, he asked, 'What can you do that we don't have already?' But I could do graf. I can rock you some letters."

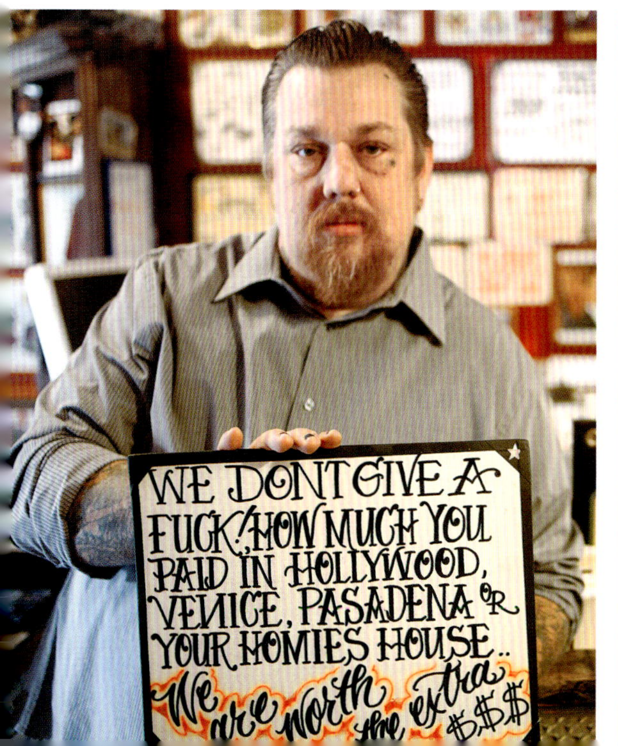

BABA

Baba's passion for graffiti culture has fueled his passion for tattoo culture. He is a traditionalist who believes in putting in work. The diversity of this California native's DNA is in sync with the varied DNA of his writing trajectory: he studied the aesthetics of classic New York City graffiti and processed it through his Mexican American/ punk American prism, creating along the way his own unique tattoo vocabulary and laying the foundation for some of the globe's most respected graffiti crews.

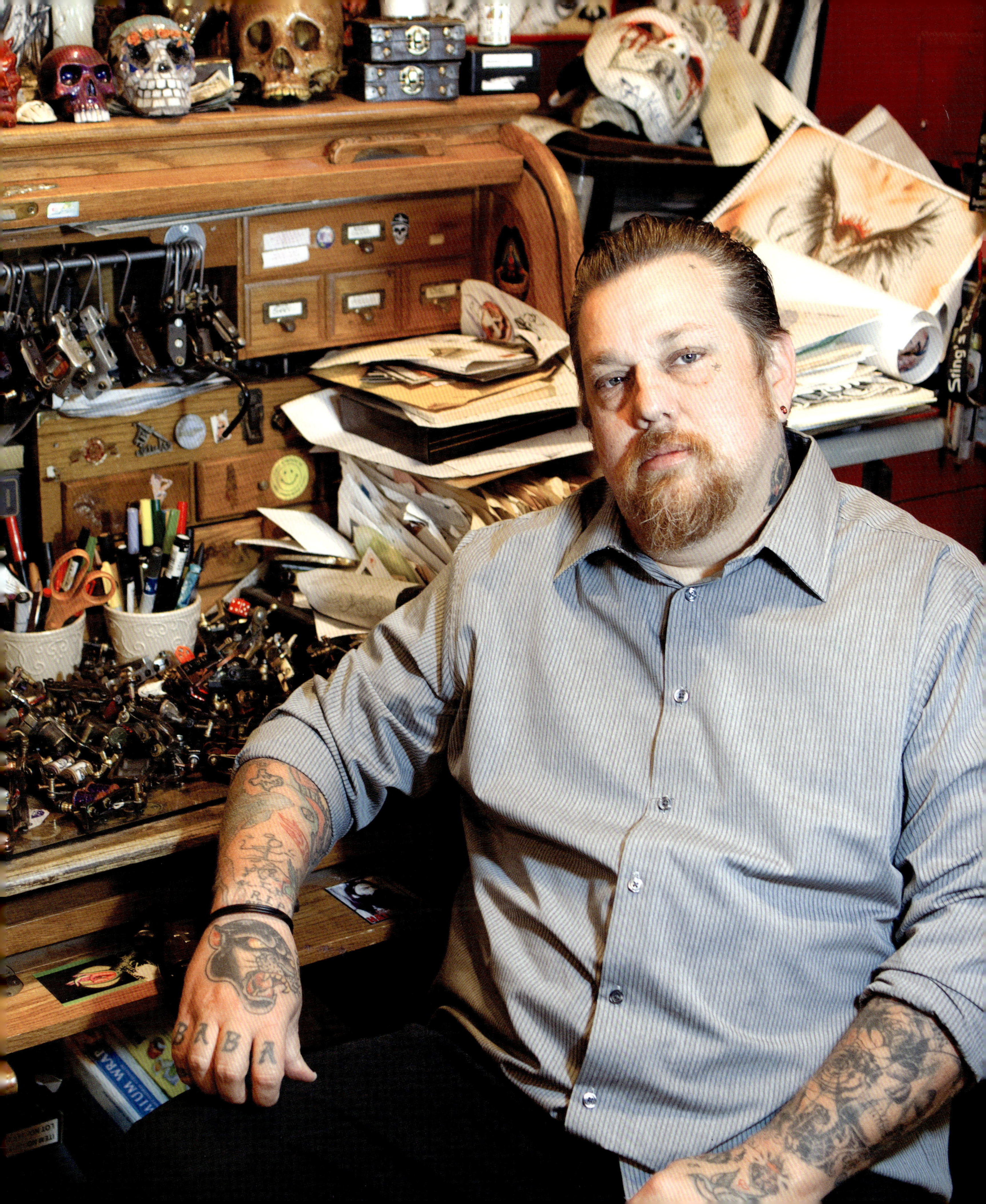

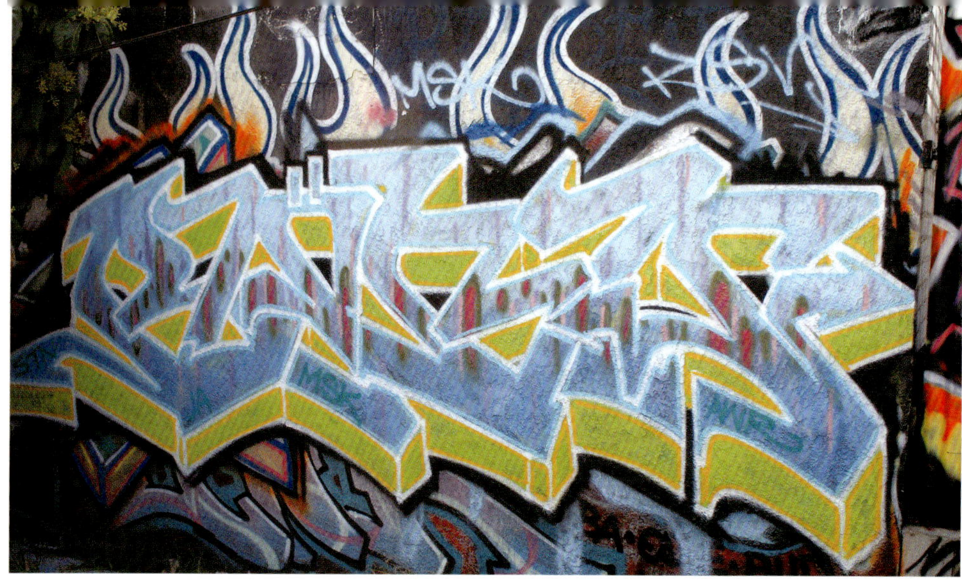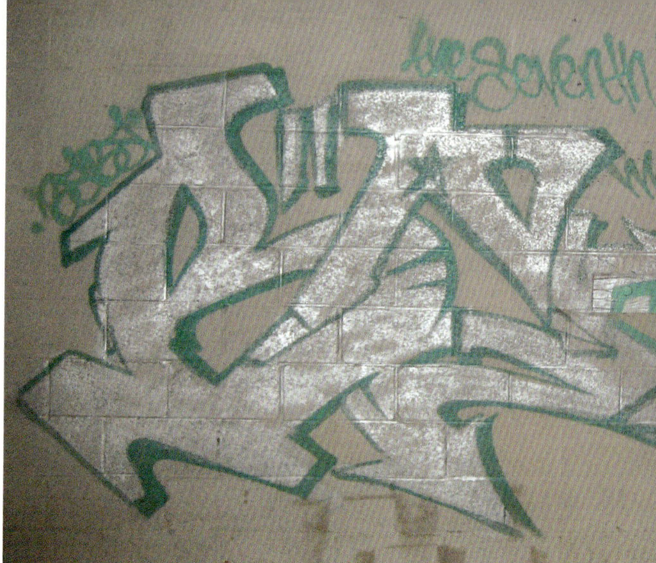

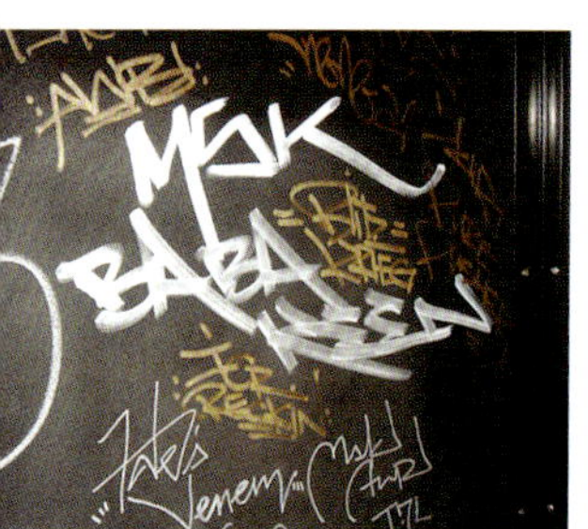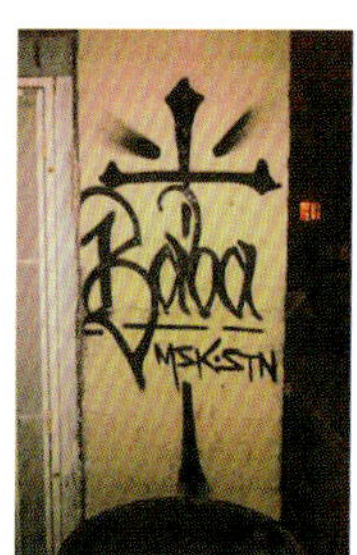

I'm the owner of Vintage Tattoo, a member of the Second to None crew and United Artists in New York City, and founder of Mad Society Kings [MSK]. I'm half Mexican and I grew up in Van Nuys. The BVN gang, which is Barrio Van Nuys, and the Cruisers are the two local gangs out there, so growing up around that culture, I was always fascinated with graffiti. The letters that they used were amazing and it probably got instilled at an early age, but I didn't really tap into it until the eighties. In 1979 I got jumped into BPO, which is Burbank Punk Organization. It was a punk-rock gang where you basically fought Nazis. Instead of doing graffiti the way that they were doing graffiti, I started emulating the Chicano style. We would go all around the city and just tag *BPO* everywhere. We were at war with Suicidals. We'd go down to Venice and trip.

I met this girl named Joni Binder. Now she's the president of the San Francisco Museum of Modern Art's Modern Art Council. Joni was dating Andy "Zephyr" Witten, so I met Andy at an early age and saw his shit and I was just like, "Wow, what the fuck is this?" To go from blocks and tags and early gang tags to seeing Zephyr's shit was unbelievable. At that time nobody had anything like that. We're talking like, '81, '82, and Zephyr came out here for a show, I believe, in Santa Barbara. He was out doing his stuff everywhere and I was hooked. I tried my best to find everything I could on graffiti, and Zeph was my first influence.

Because of that gang stuff, I got locked up in a boys' home and I met Danny Boy [Danny O'Connor], who would join Everlast to form the band House of Pain. We've known each other since like ninth grade. We found this really hardcore bootleg tape of *Style Wars* and all that shit. We were doing this stuff with another writer named Candy Man.

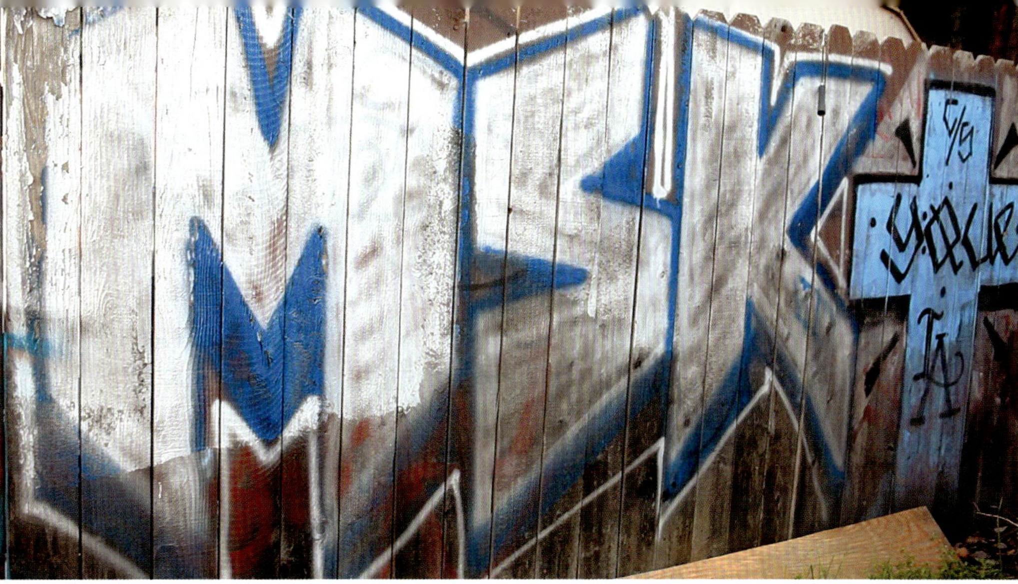

He was a gang member from CPA [Canoga Park Alabama]. Those were my early influences. I started dating this girl named Paula whose older brother was Mario Davila, who's now director of the After School Arts Program [ASAP], the arts education department of LA's BEST, an after-school enrichment program. His best friend was this guy named Jack, who wrote *Jokcr* or *Dante*, and he brought K2S [Kill to Succeed] into my life. He was showing me all the shit by Belmont Tunnel. It was like, '83, '84 when I first saw Belmont and the stuff that the K2S crew was doing. I've been hooked ever since.

Me and Relic, we were the first people to get up on the Levitz building—an LA landmark that is gone now. In 1986 we were doing burners and Duster UA [from New York] was doing his thing. Then we go over to see [what he painted], and literally our jaws dropped. We were so disappointed because all he did was a big *Dusty* but in script. We were just like, "Wow, we finally get to paint with Duster and he does this lame little shit." Then we go on the freeway to see what we just did and all you see is scribble, scribble, then *Dusty*. We knew right there that everything we knew about graffiti was wrong. We didn't know this shit because we didn't know about trains or anything. That's when me and Relic and Repo started getting heavily into freeway bombing. We took it to another level, and then 1987, I got in KSN [Kings Stop at Nothing].

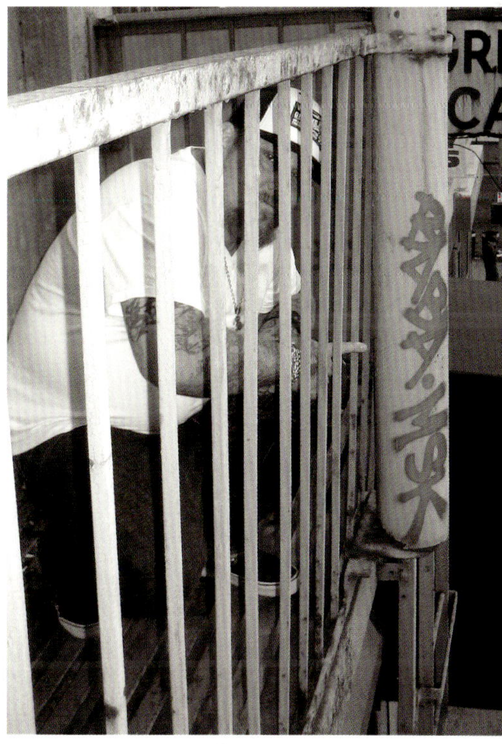

Baba, New York City, 2010

KSN was like the all-star team for LA. They took a bunch of members from different crews, so when I got in KSN, I was happy. But I soon discovered that graffiti was so rock star. It was so far away from what it was supposed to be about: getting up. I was really, really disillusioned with the whole graffiti scene. I got pissed off and started a crew called AWR [Angels Will Rise].

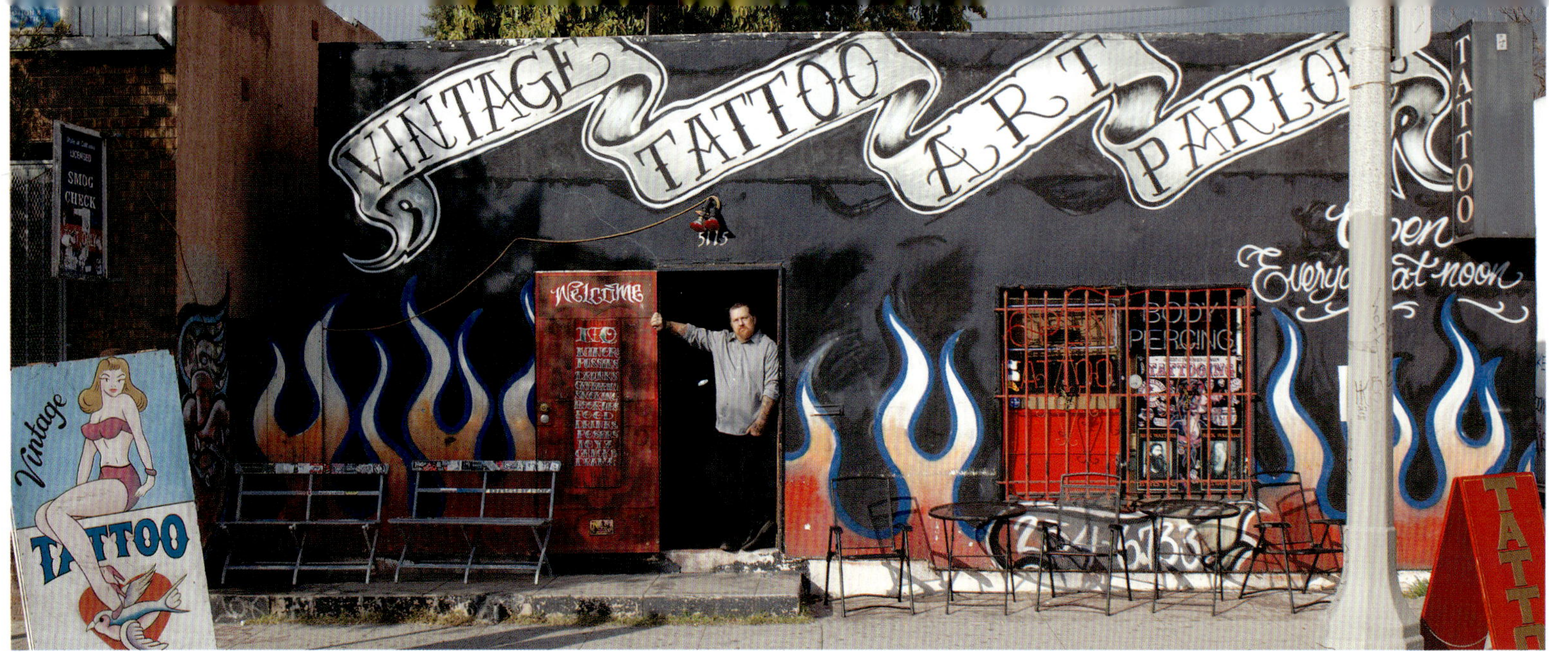

Baba at Vintage Tattoo, Los Angeles, 2012

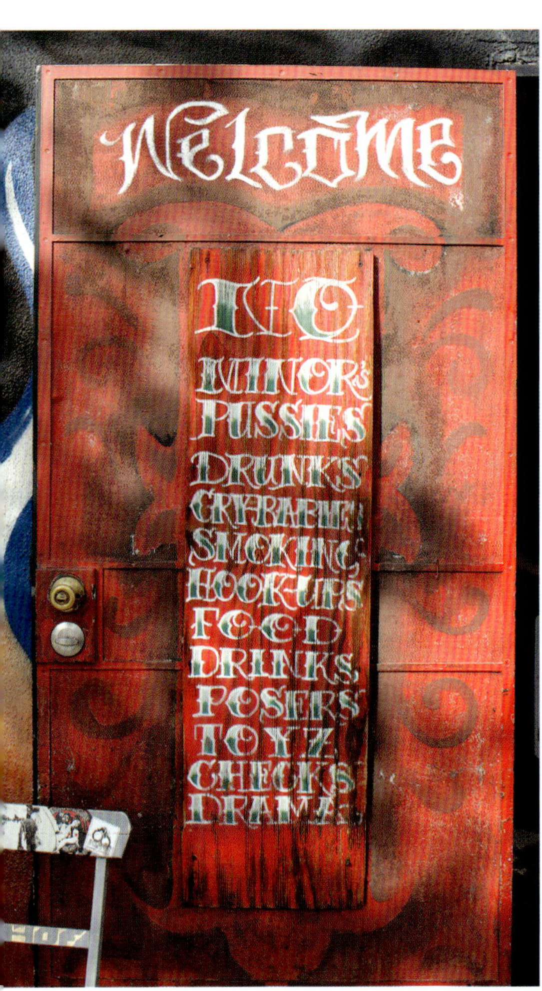

Vintage Tattoo door, Los Angeles, 2012

The AWR crew looked up to the KSN crew, but KSN didn't care about them. So I was talking about everything I learned and all this other stuff about how graffiti's about just getting up—even if you have only a crayon, just get up. You don't have to sit here and be paid or whatever to do your best. You just get up. I thought right then and there that I was going to start a crew that took everything that was right about graffiti and make it right again, and that was the beginning of MSK. I started it at the motor yard. Mad Society Kings was born right there. I don't want to say disgust, but it was born out of heartbreak over the way KSN was. Officially, I'm not taking any credit for what MSK is now. I just founded it. I gave them their recipe and they went on and became fucking badass chefs.

When I moved in New York in '89 and I was doing my own graffiti thing, trying to get in galleries and shit like that, I started airbrushing for musicians—New Kids, Vanilla Ice. I thought, I am in New York, am I an LA writer? I'm making money, how much higher can I get off this shit? Martin Wong had a bunch of paintings—he was a major artist and collector of graffiti art. Getting into a New York gallery? I did it. That was the dream. But I was lost after that. I thought I wanted to change careers. I made a bunch of money and got tattooed. I walked into Jonathan Shaw's shop and magic happened.

When I was a kid in Van Nuys, we used to hang out at the local tattoo shop. The guy would squirt alcohol at us and chase us out, like, "Get out of here, fucking little kids!" One day we went in and there was this beautiful blond girl getting tattooed on her thigh. She had the mad, strawberry blond bush. I'm seven years old and I saw pussy for the first time at a tattoo shop. I fell in love with pussy and tattooing right then and there. I've loved tattooing ever since, but then with punk rock and skateboarding happening, I forgot about it. And then when I went to New York and walked into Jonathan's shop, that magic was there. I asked him to apprentice me and he told me, "Fuck off, get out of here, fuck you, I don't want nothing to do with you." You know, like we all say when people ask to get apprenticed. I just kept coming back. I was very persistent.

I moved back to LA in '92 and got hired at LA Tattoo before it even opened. I was the first employee. I started doing some real stuff there, and later on some other guy showed up. It was Mike Brown, and he was my second mentor. He taught me everything I know about lettering, black and gray, shading, gradients, light sources, all of that. He and Jonathan Shaw were my two biggest mentors. When I asked Jonathan Shaw to teach me tattooing, he asked, "What can you do that we don't have already?" But I could do graf. I can rock you some letters. So I did alphabets for Jonathan. In the early nineties, like, '89 to '91, he was doing graffiti. Those were all my drawings, all my color schemes and shit. I would have to sit there and color them and give them to him. I had that to offer, and at that time Richie Mirando [Seen] was doing stuff. I think Richie was the first writer to make the transition from graffiti to tattoo. We all looked up to him, and Richie was doing stuff like throwing highlights in pieces. He was doing biker stuff with highlights and different shading, graf style.

All I wanted to do was graffiti tattooing at first. That's all I did. When I first started tattooing, I would just rock burners on people. It was fun. It lasted for a while, and then one day this Japanese tourist comes in, points to the wall, and says, "I want that." I had to do a piece of flash. I was lost. It was just a heart with a dagger. I still have the piece. It's up on the wall. When I left LA Tattoo, I took that one piece of flash because it was my first nongraffiti tattoo and I still have it up. I fucked that tattoo all up. That's when I realized I needed to buckle down and take this shit serious. That was like, '92.

I eventually founded Vintage Tattoo because Hollywood at that time had no real appreciation for the history and traditions of the American art of tattooing. American tattoos are basically stamps. The East Coast had a style of heavy black shading up against color. The West Coast had a style of more shades of color. I wanted to keep the traditions alive.

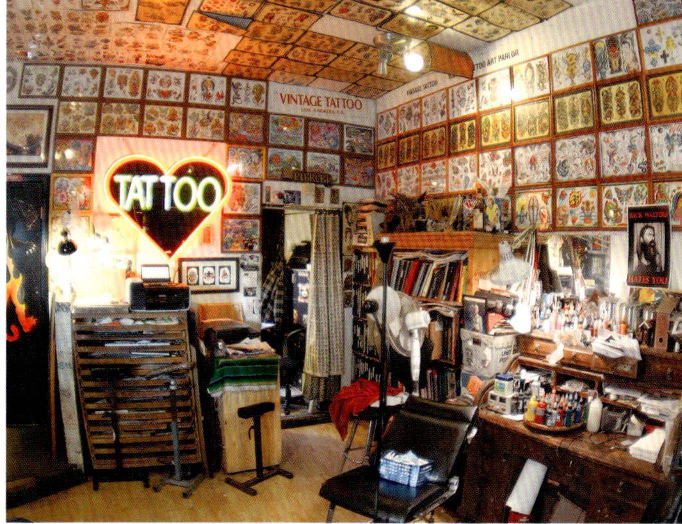

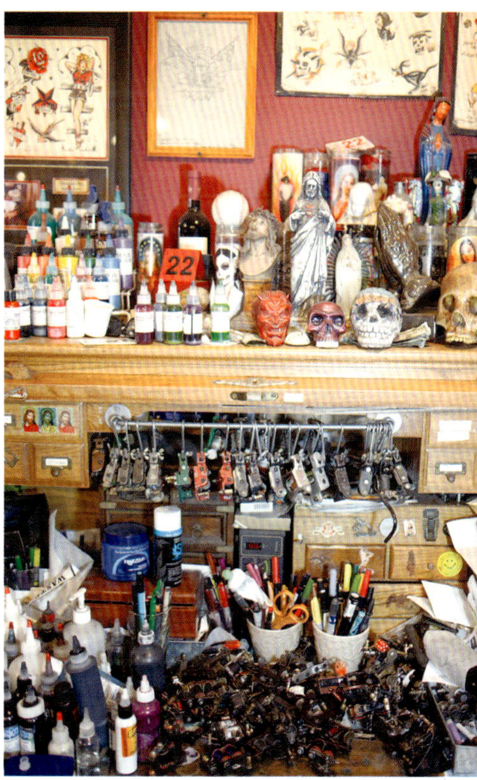

Interiors of Vintage Tattoo, Los Angeles, 2012

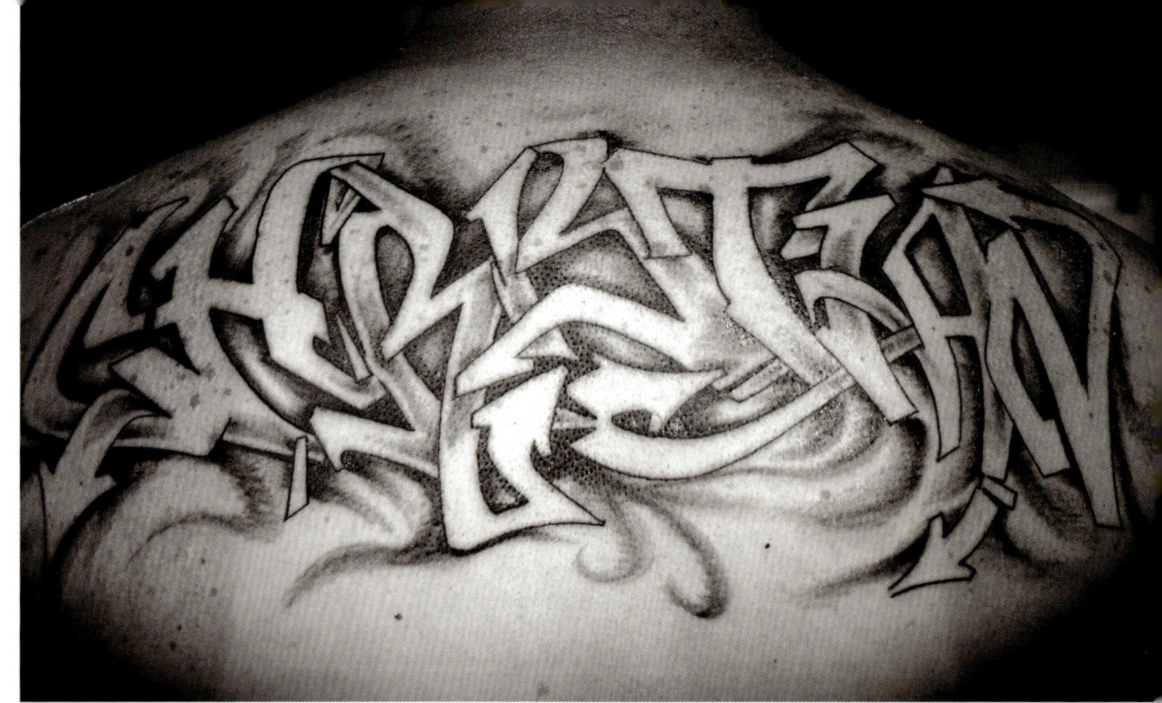
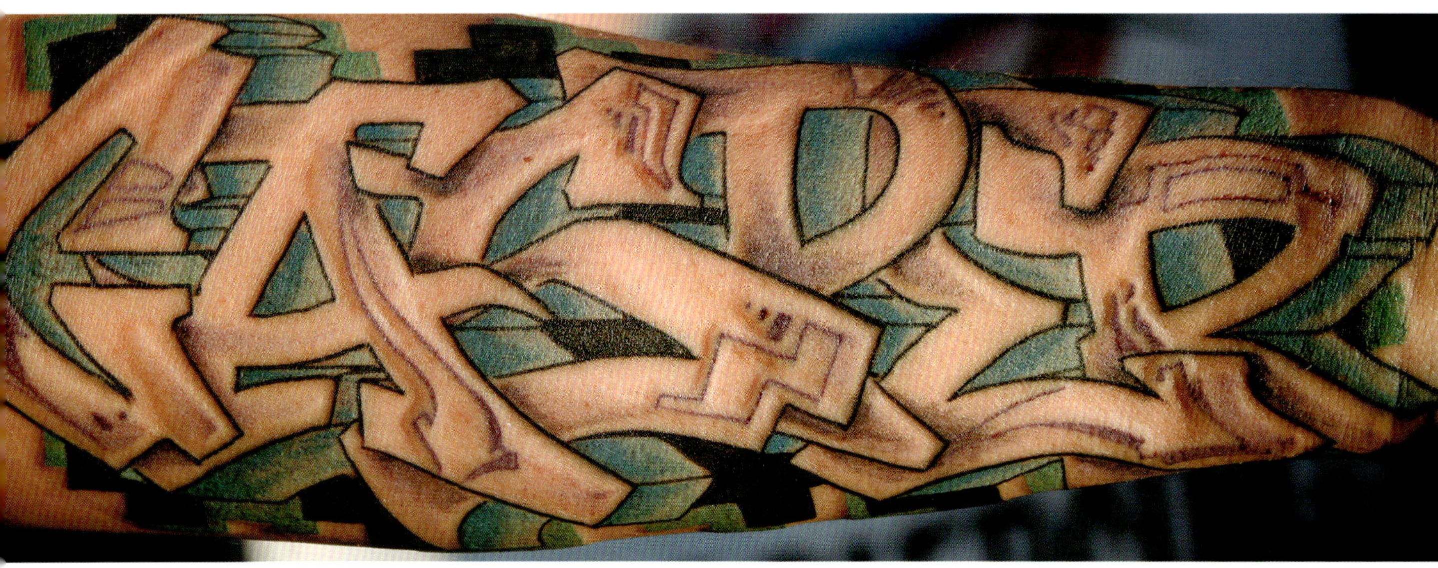
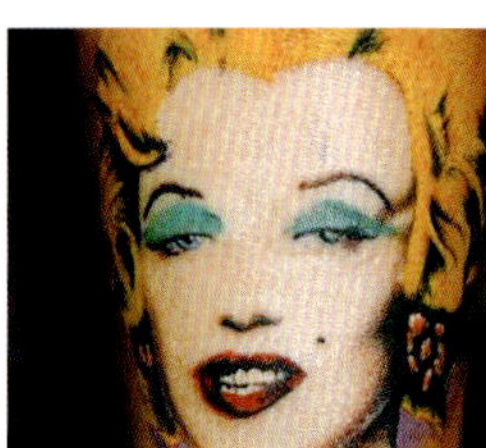

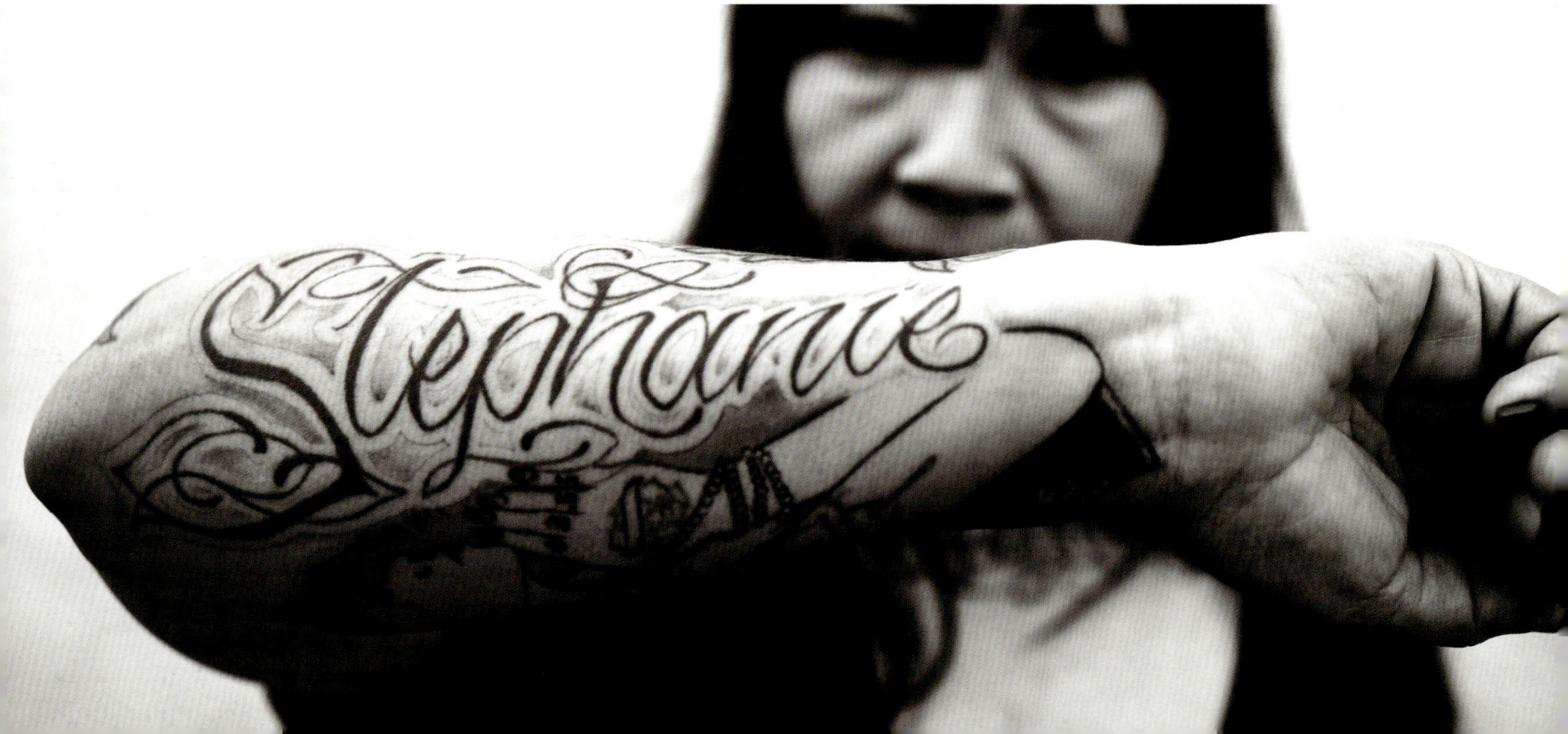

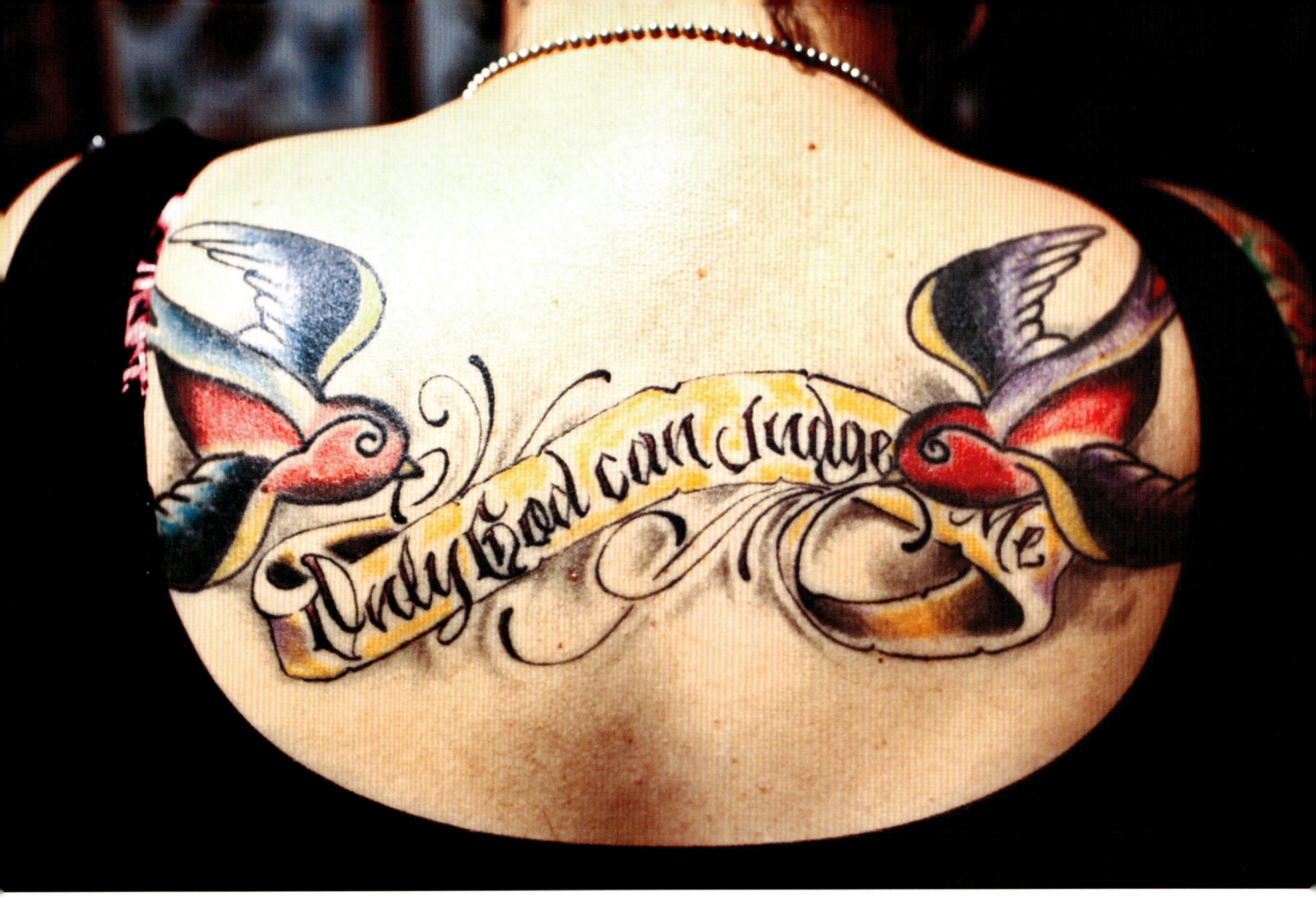

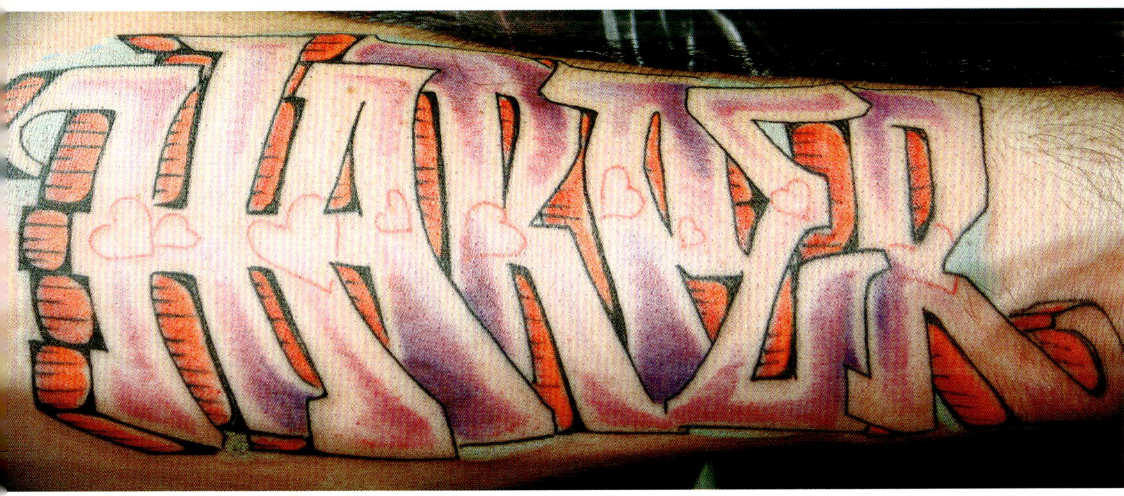
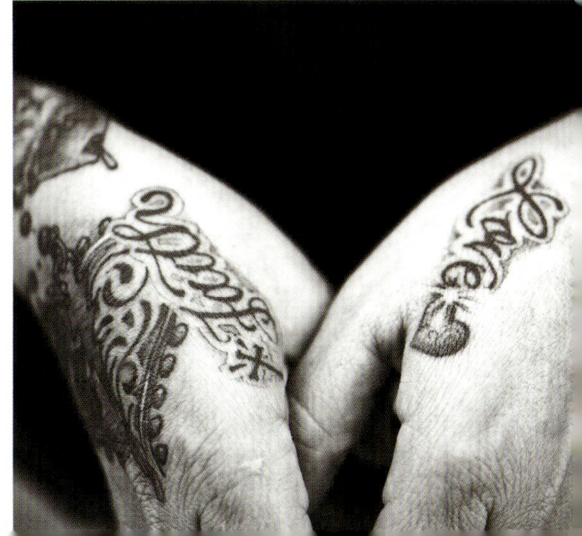

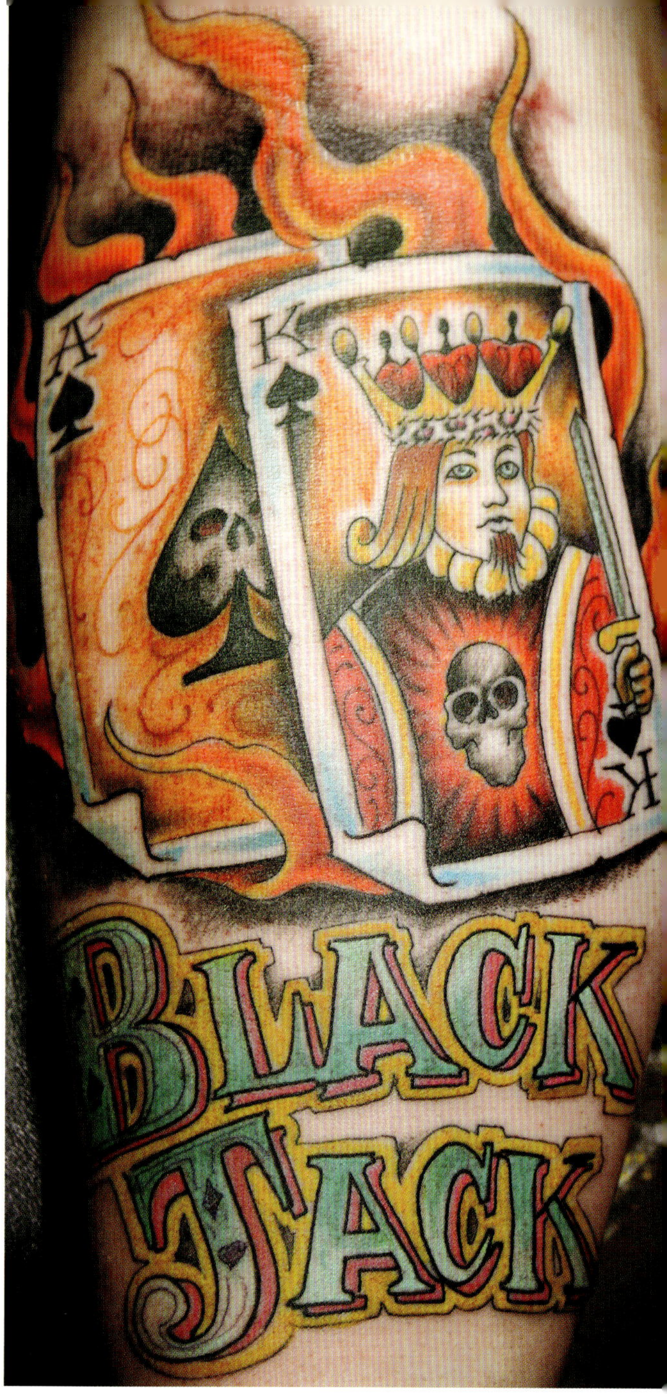

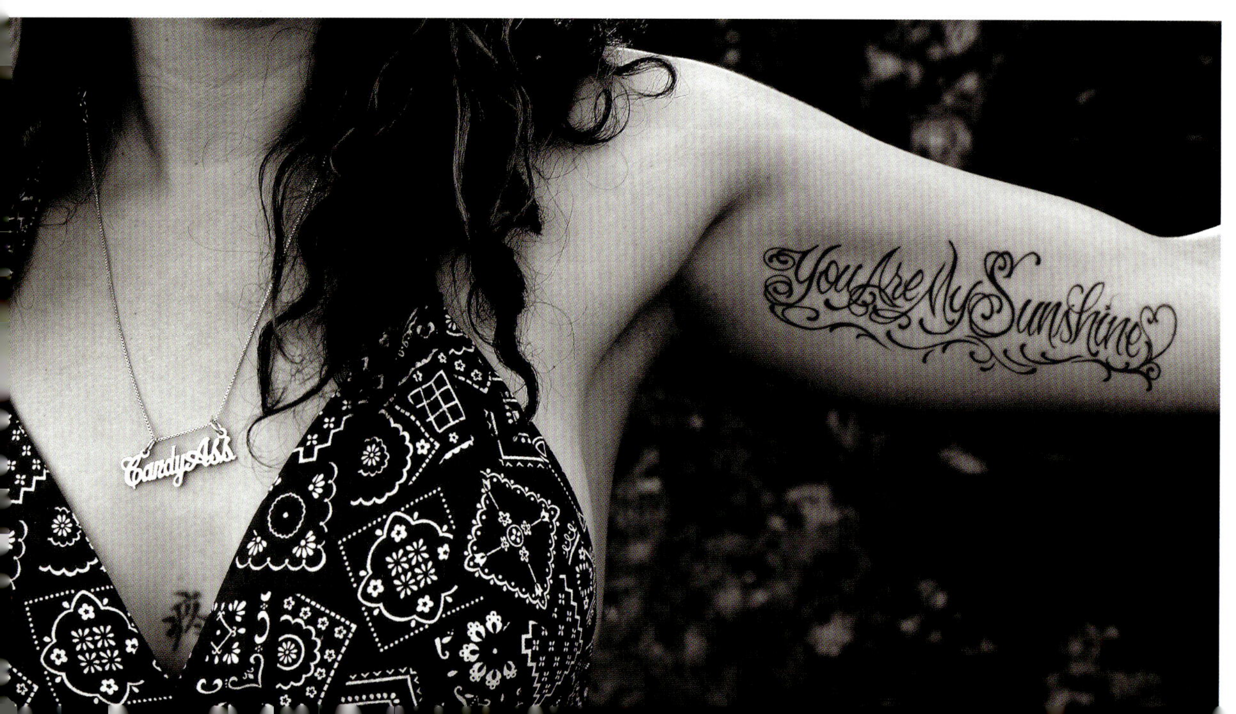
Immortal Beloved
BLACK JACK
You Are My Sunshine
CandyAss

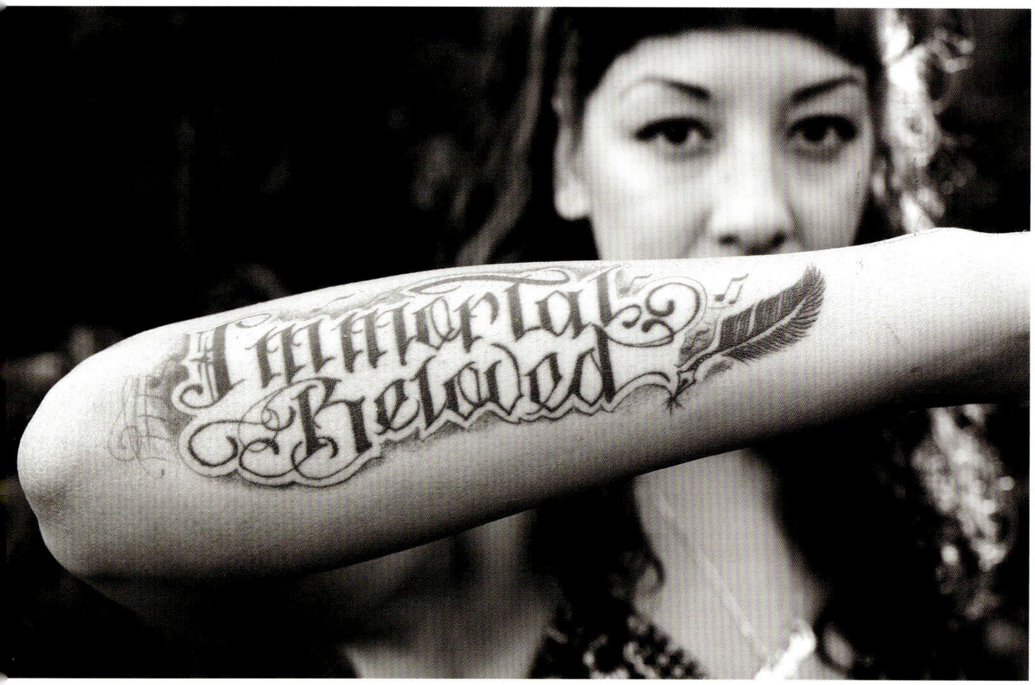

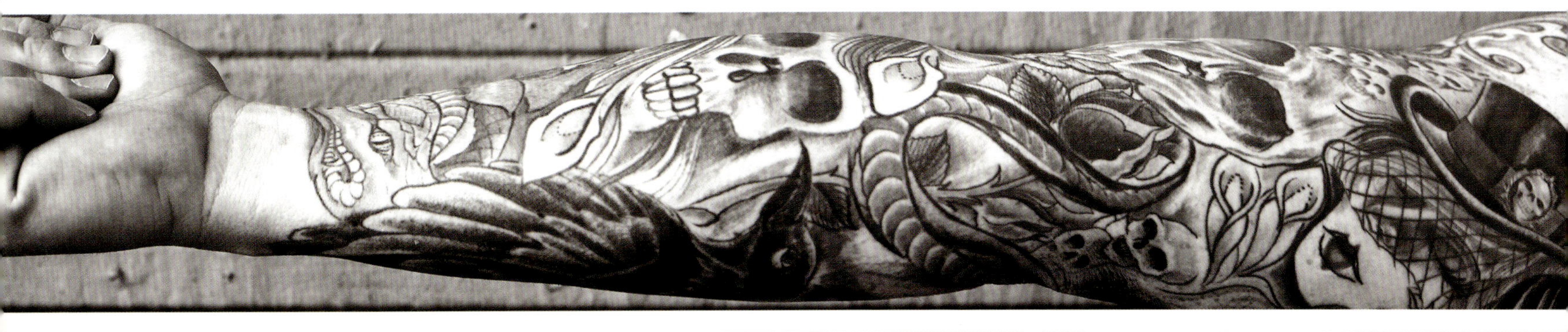

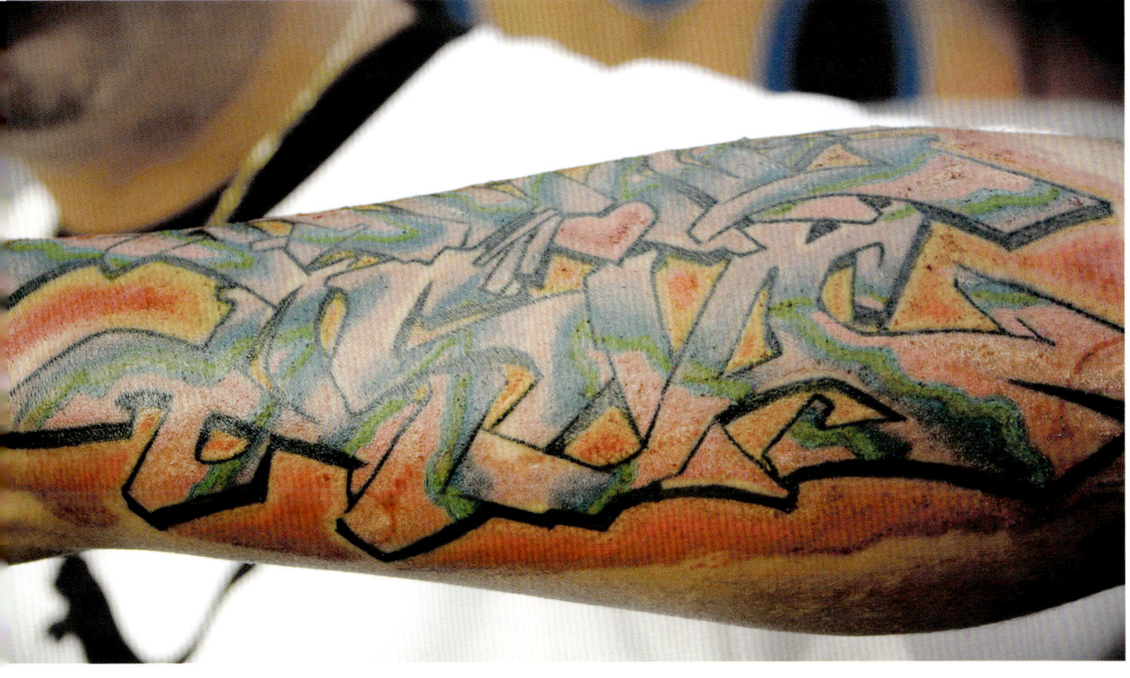

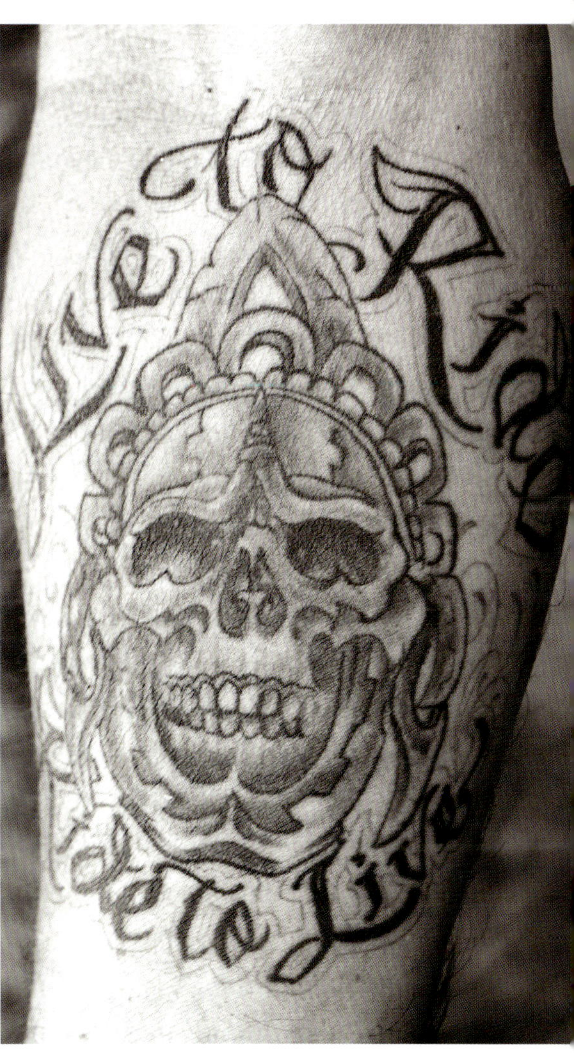

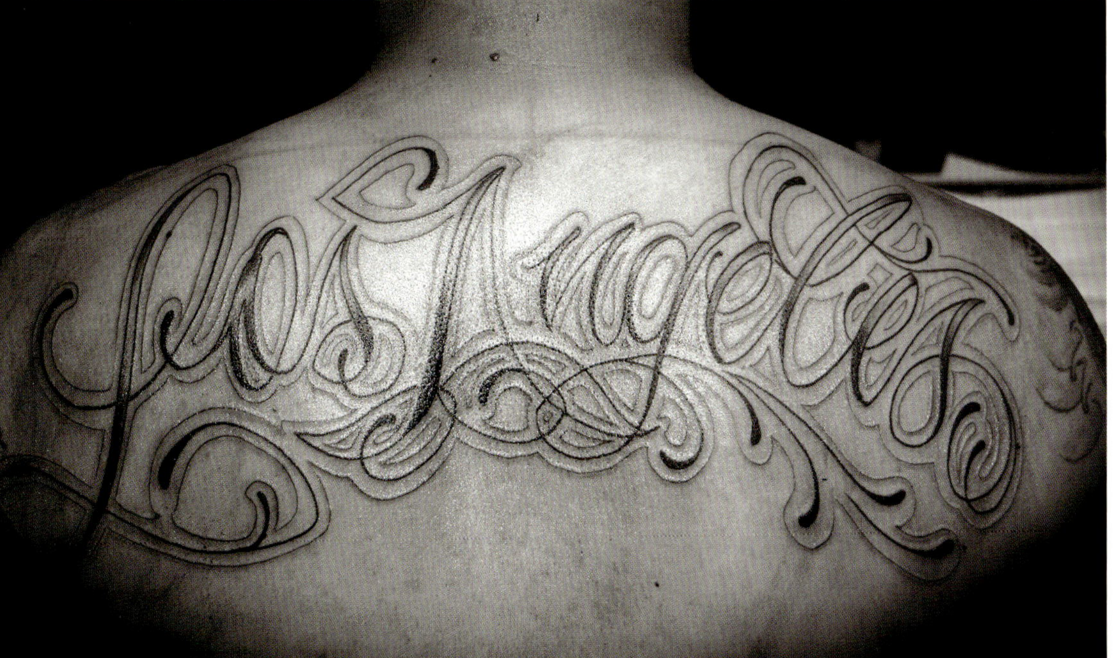

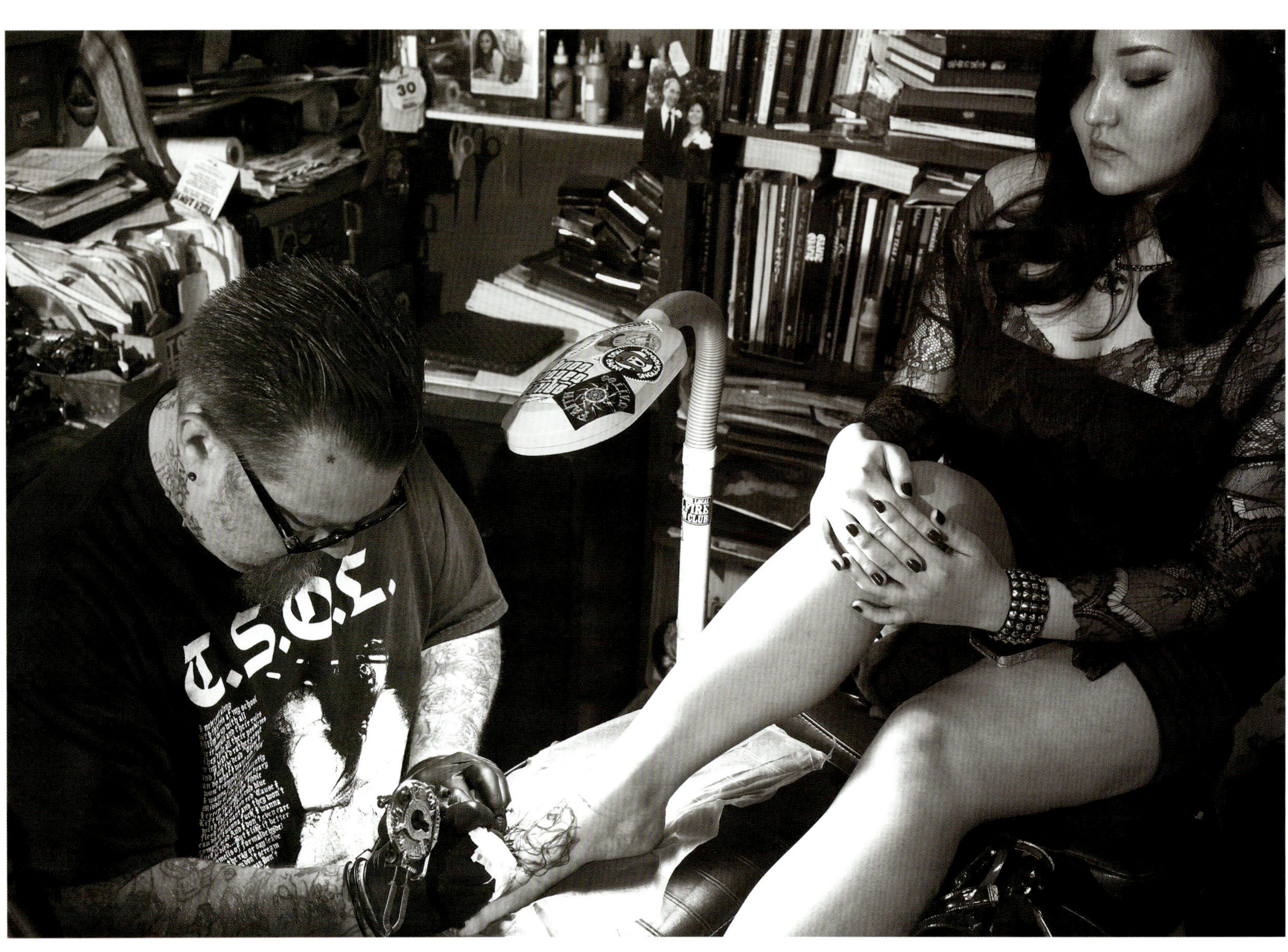

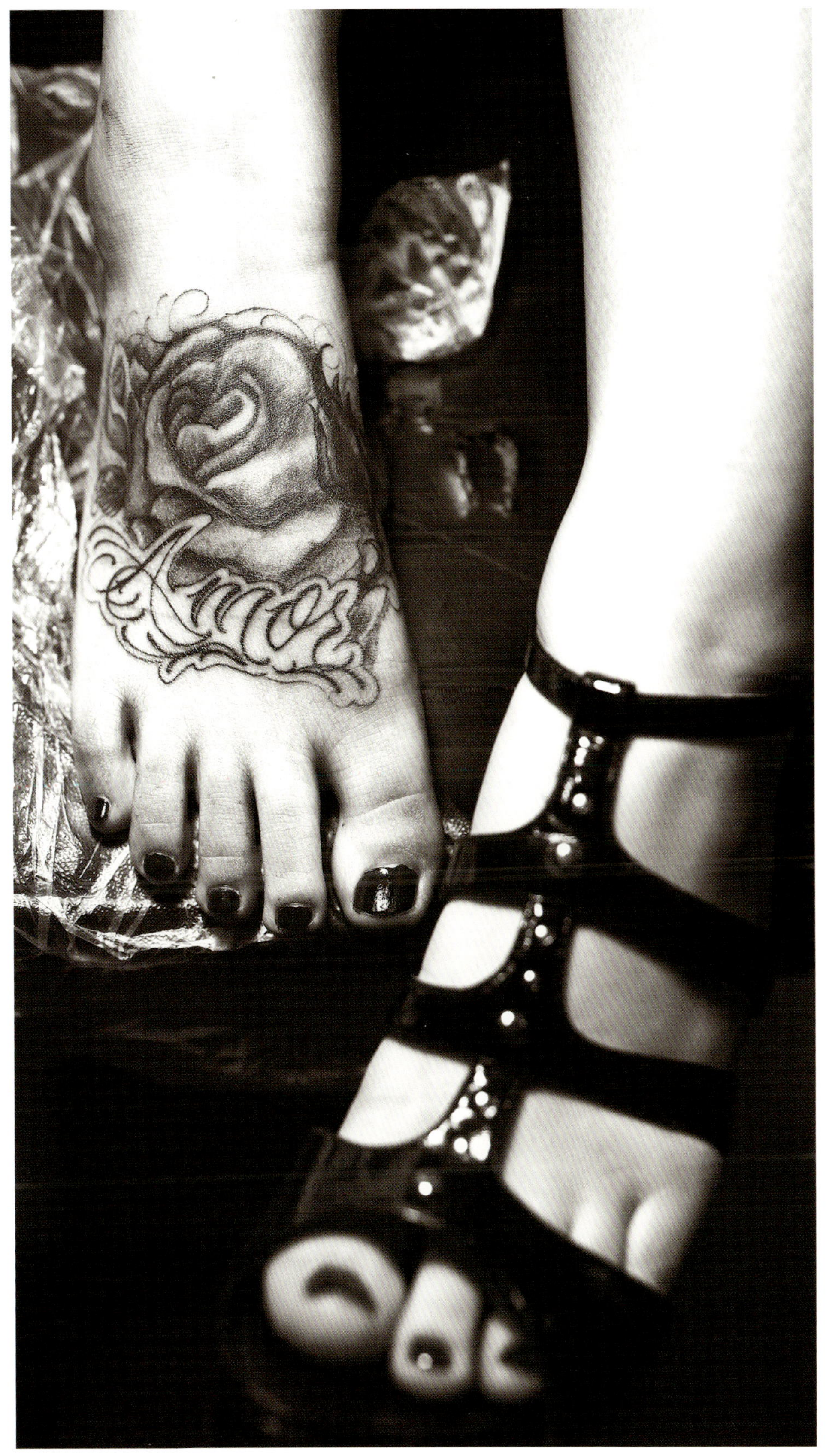

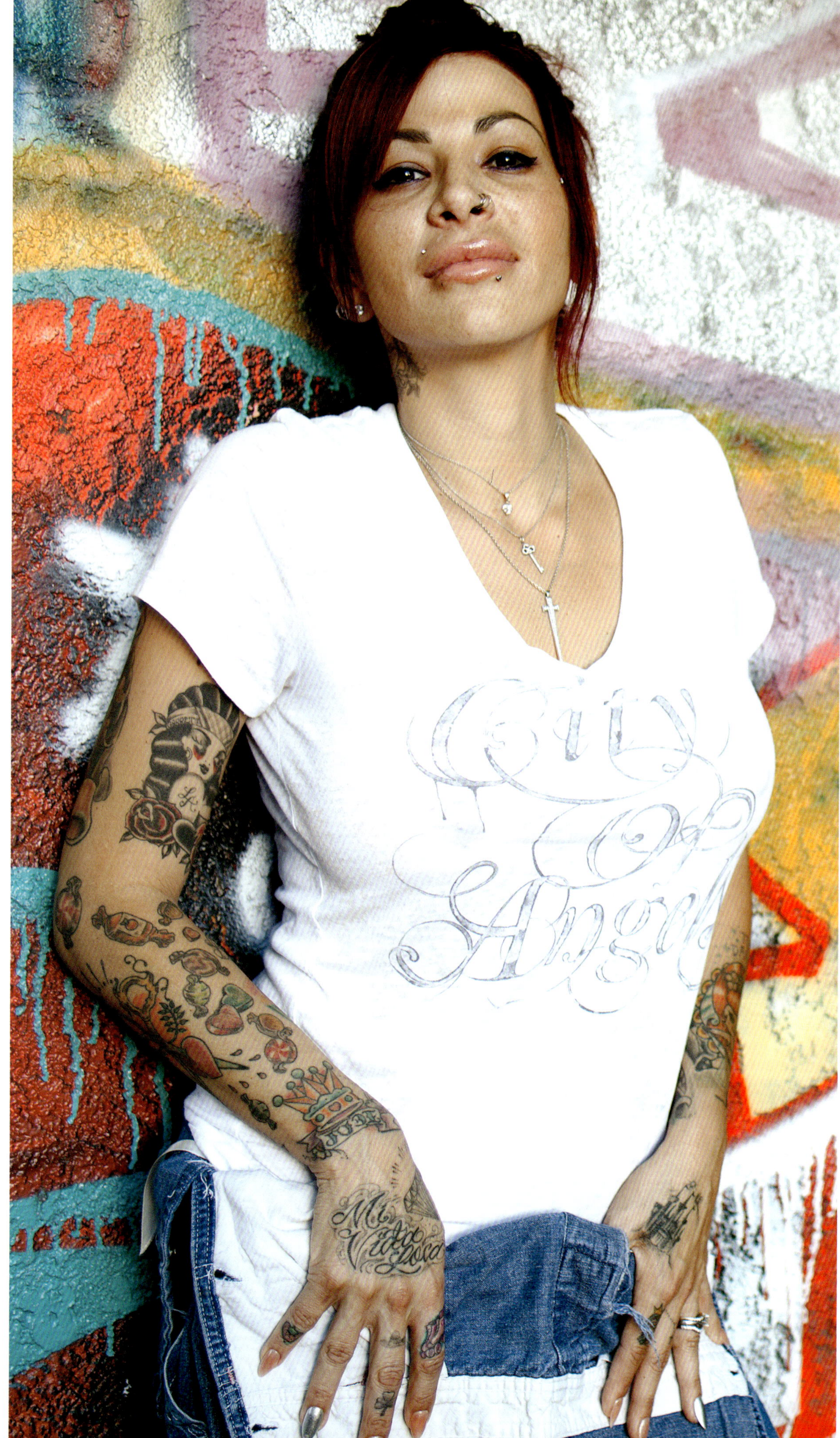

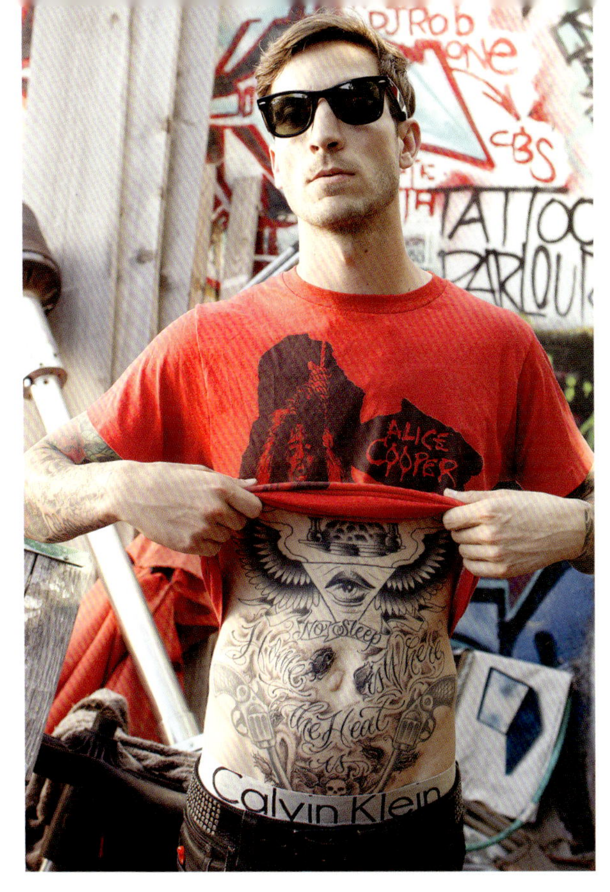

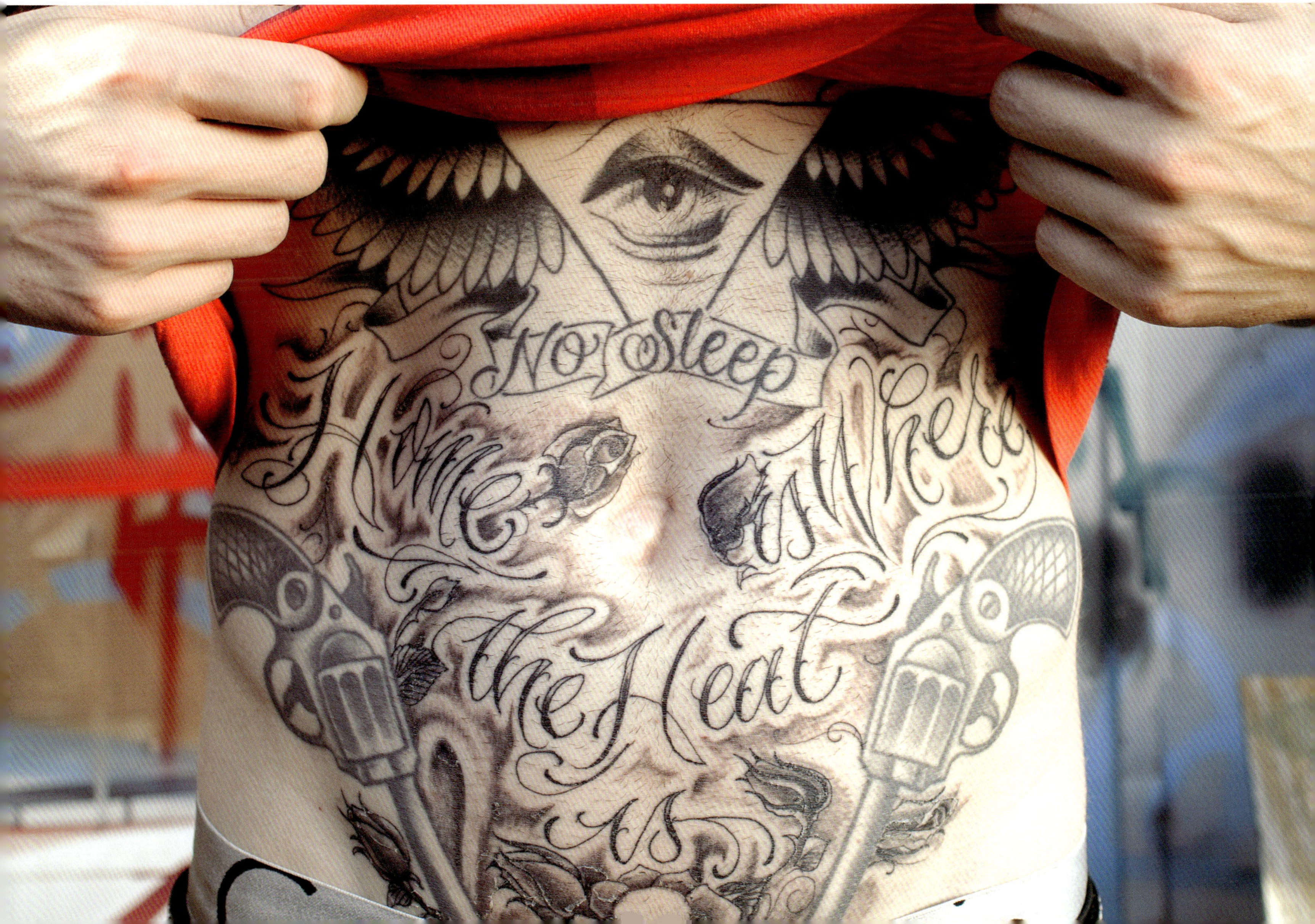

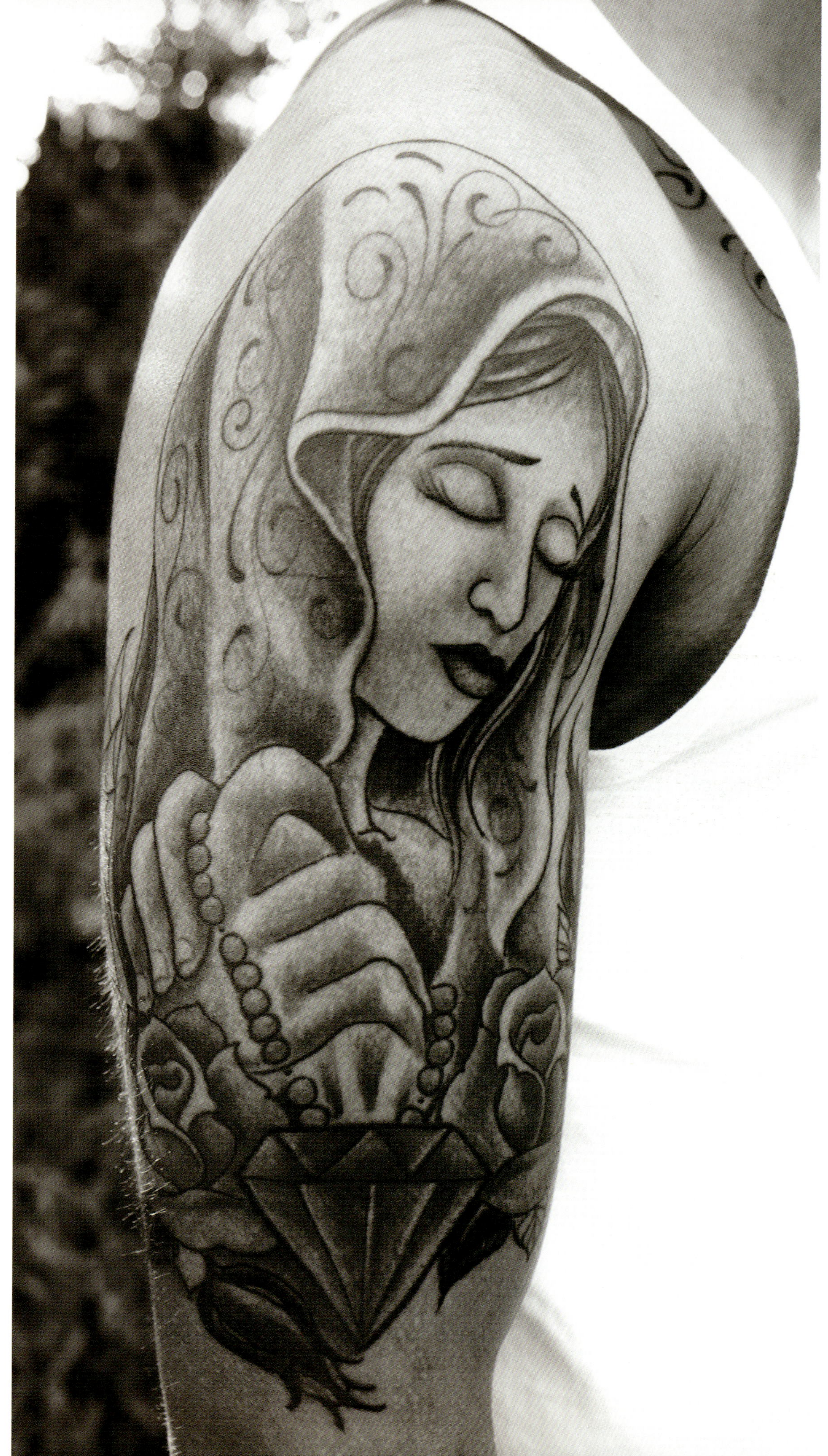

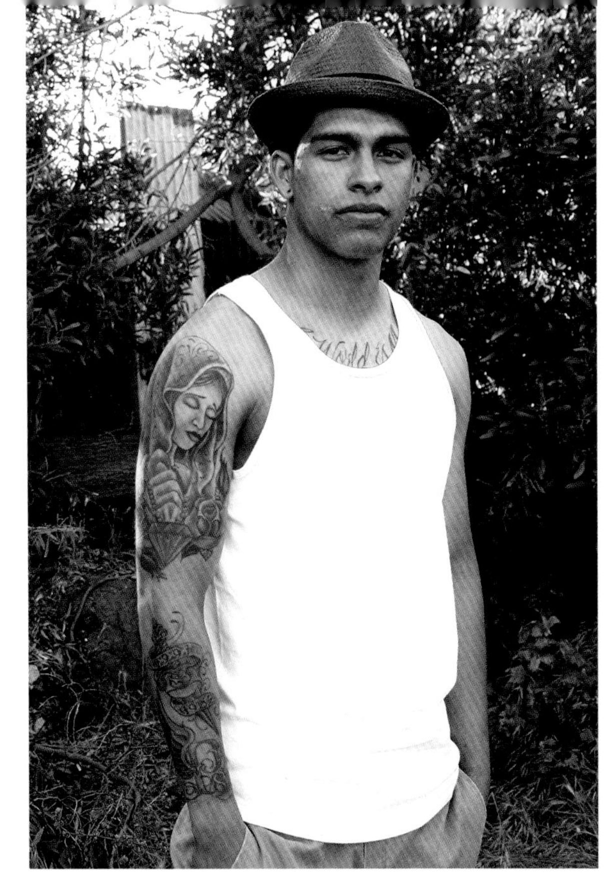

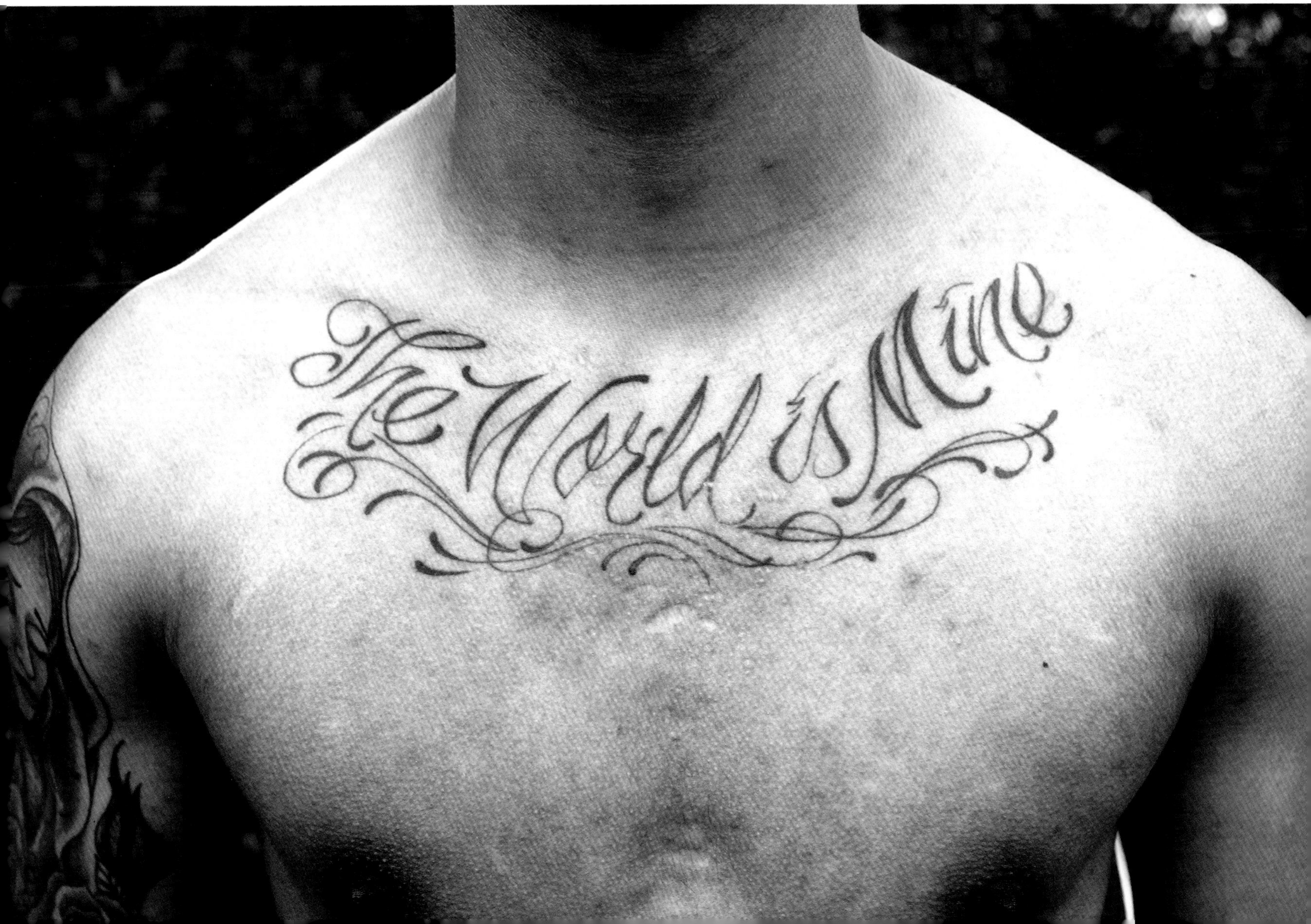

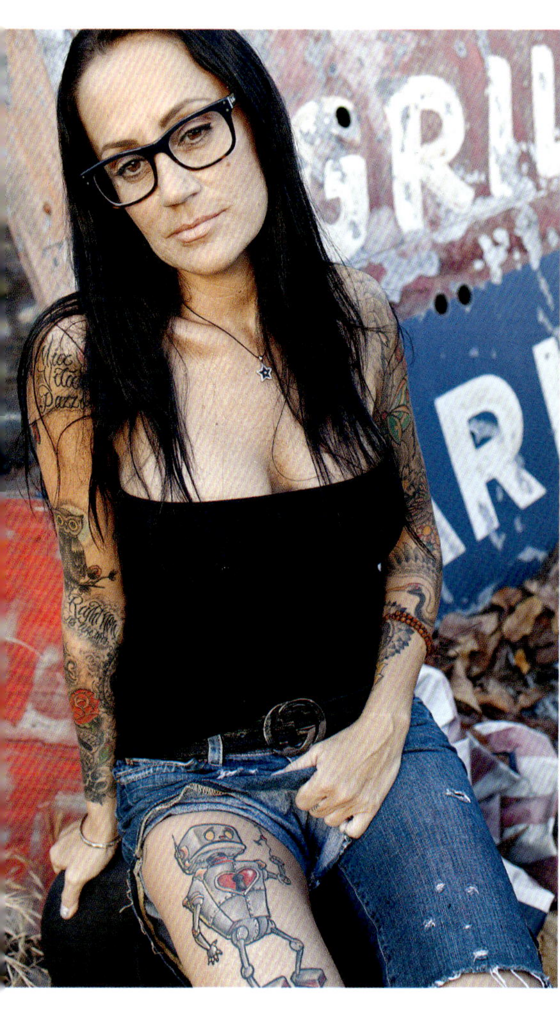

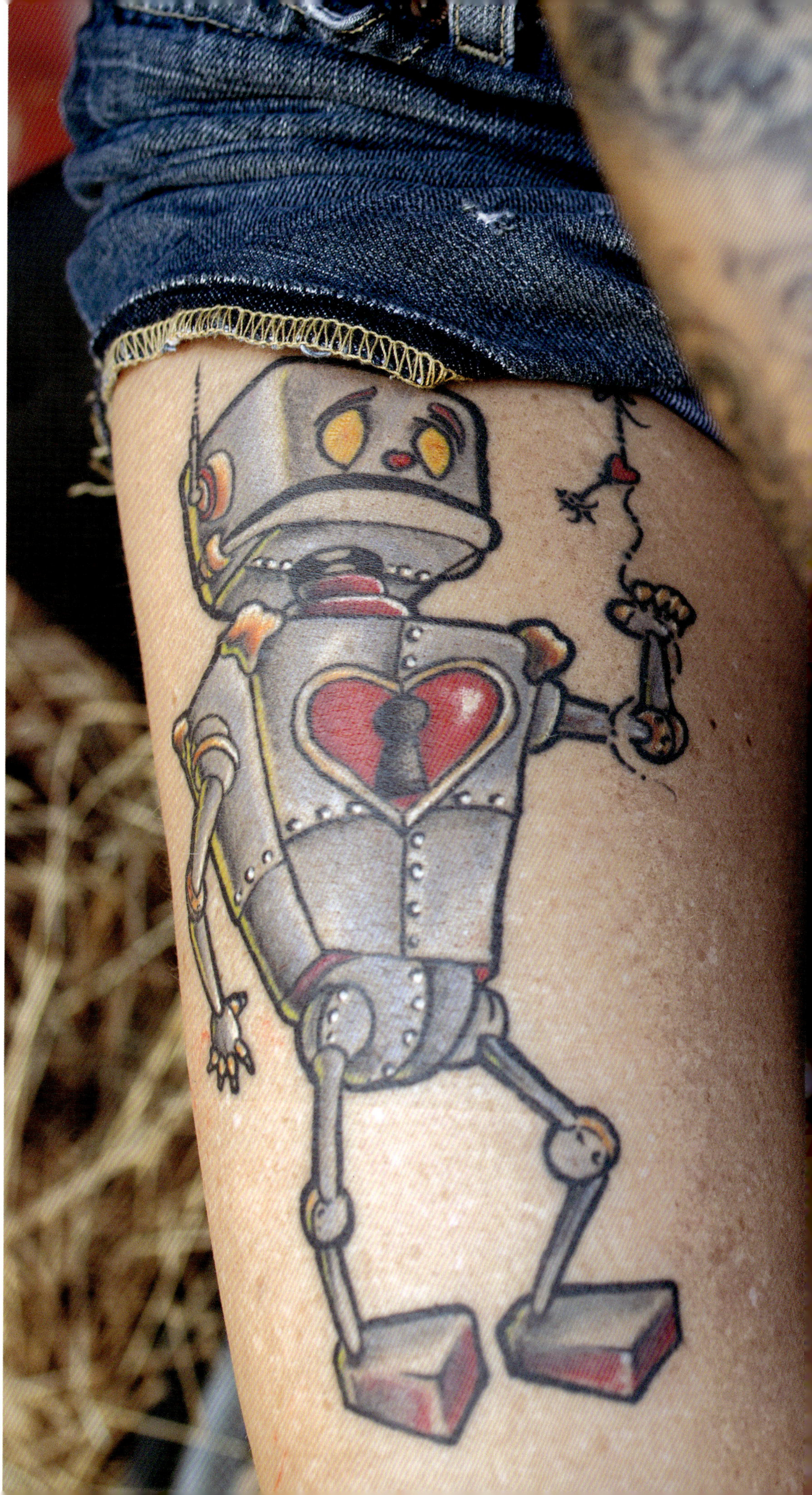

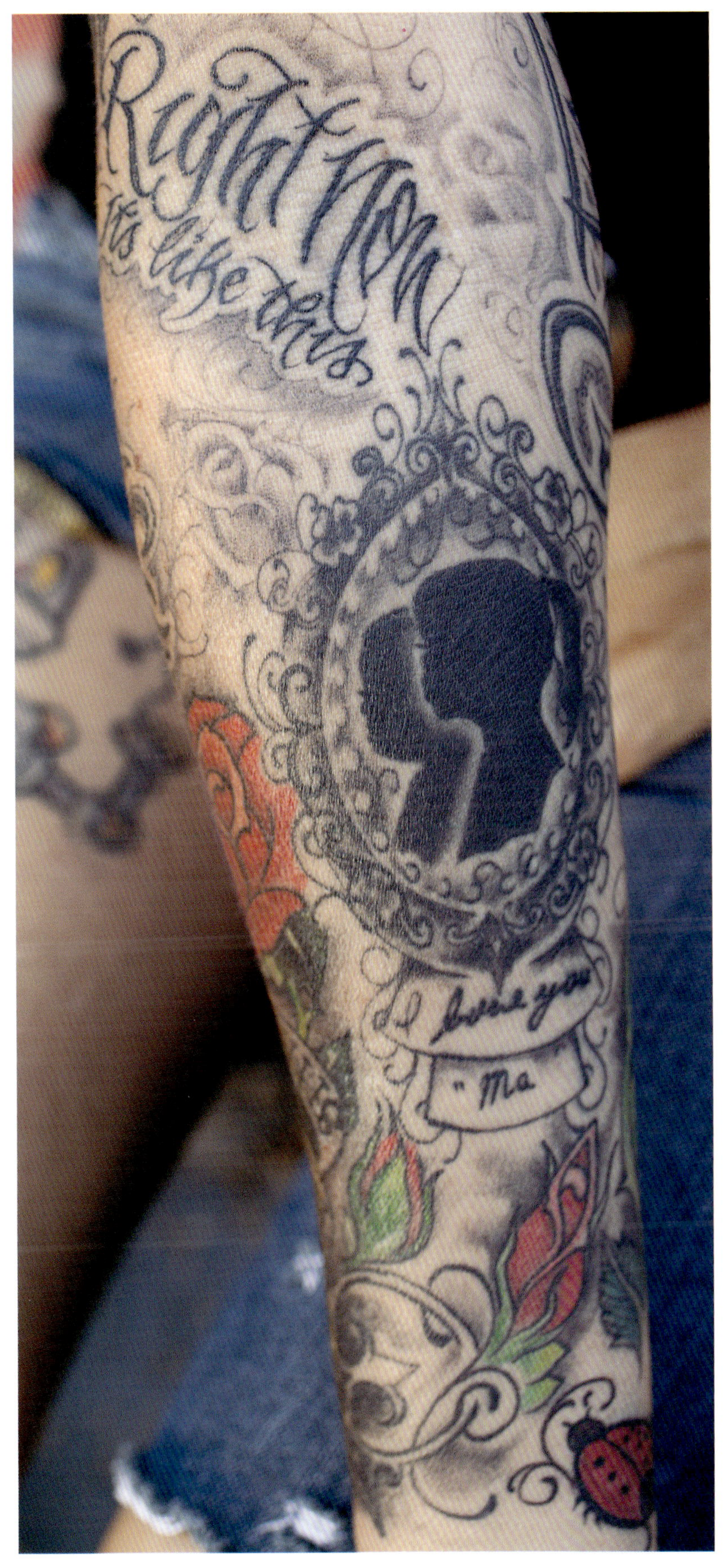

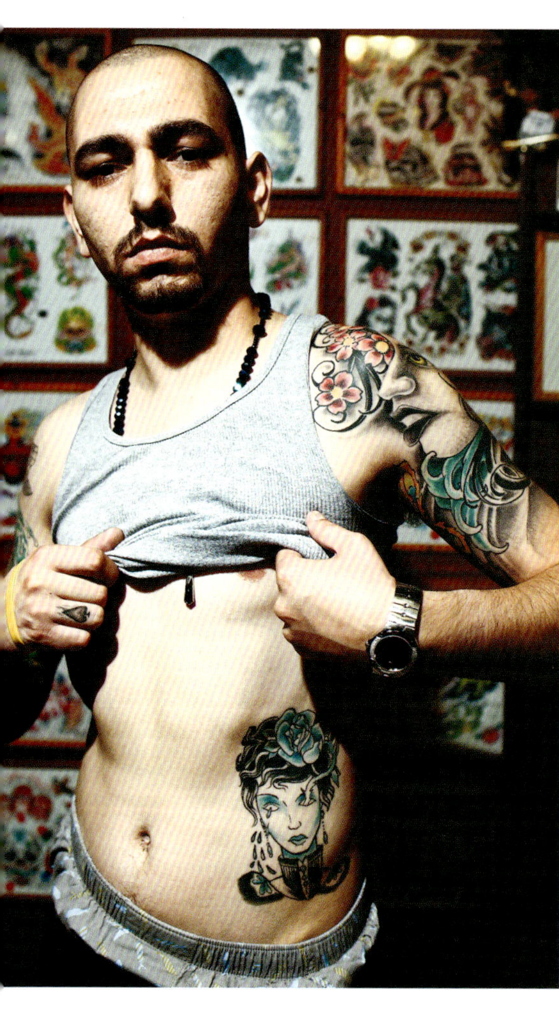

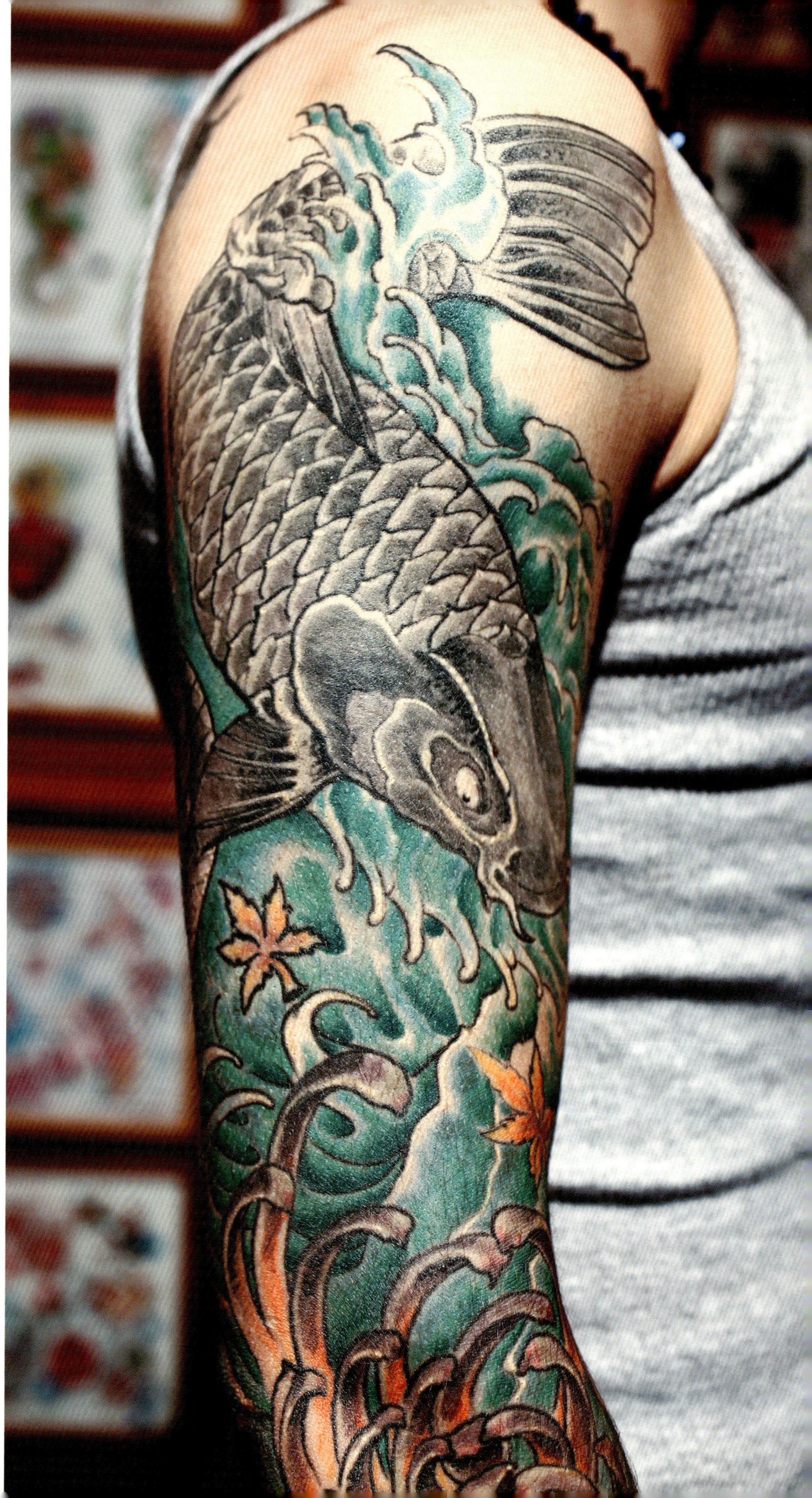

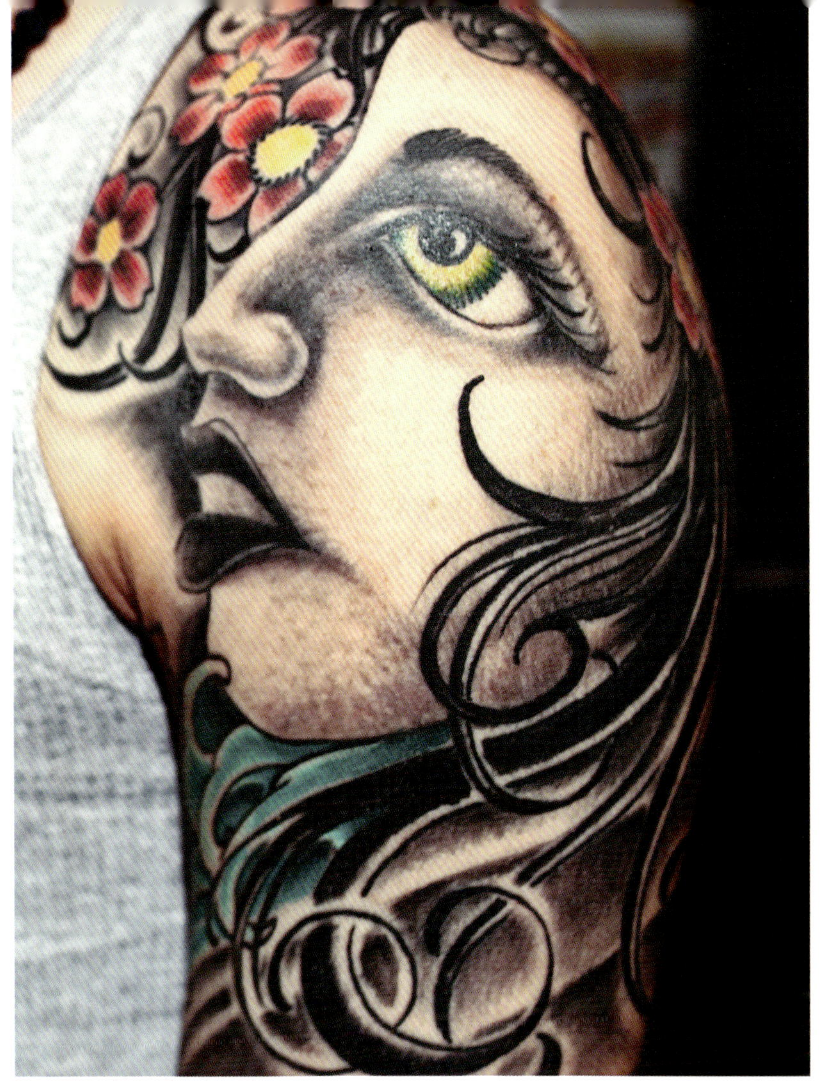

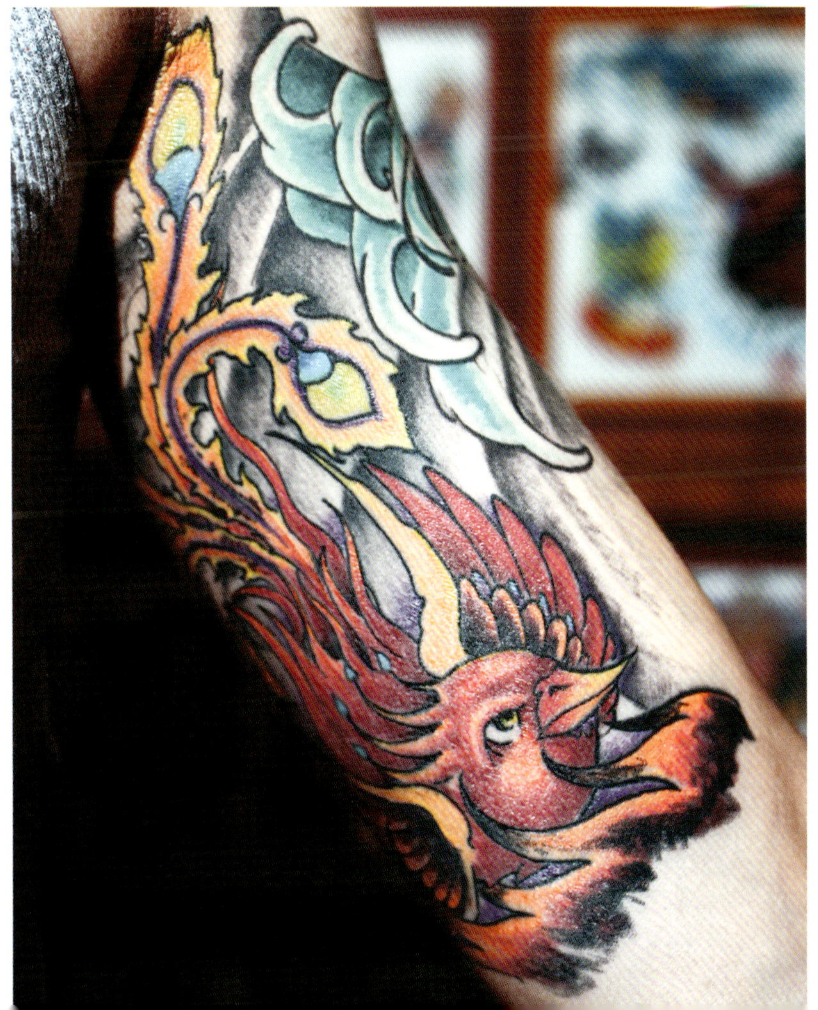

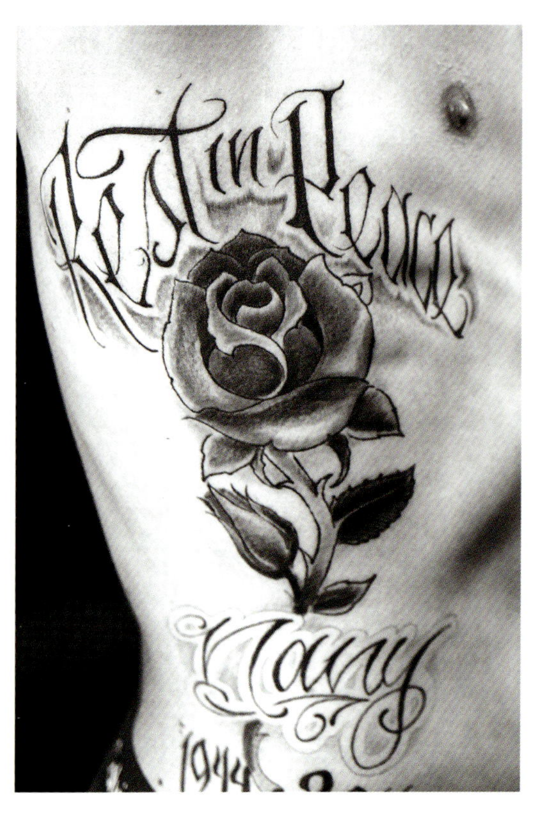
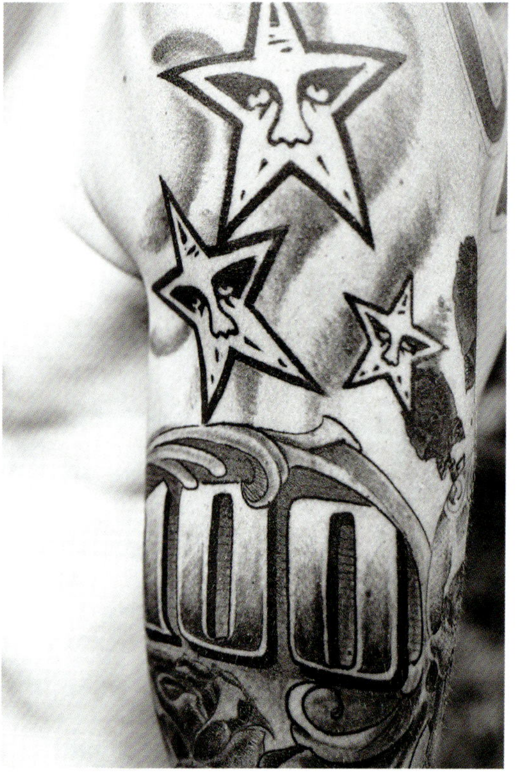
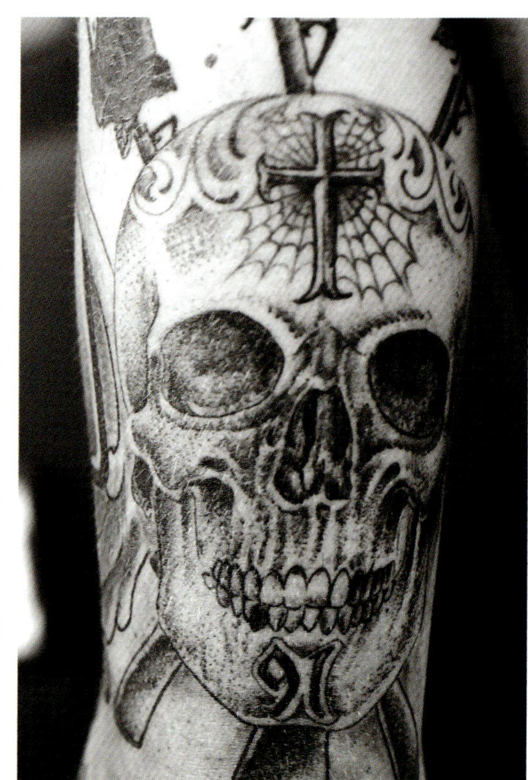

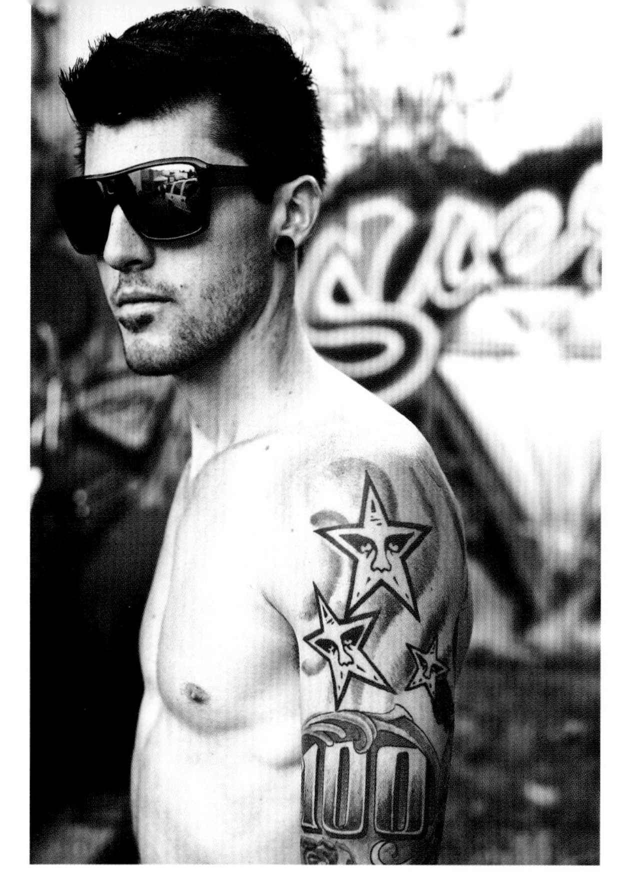

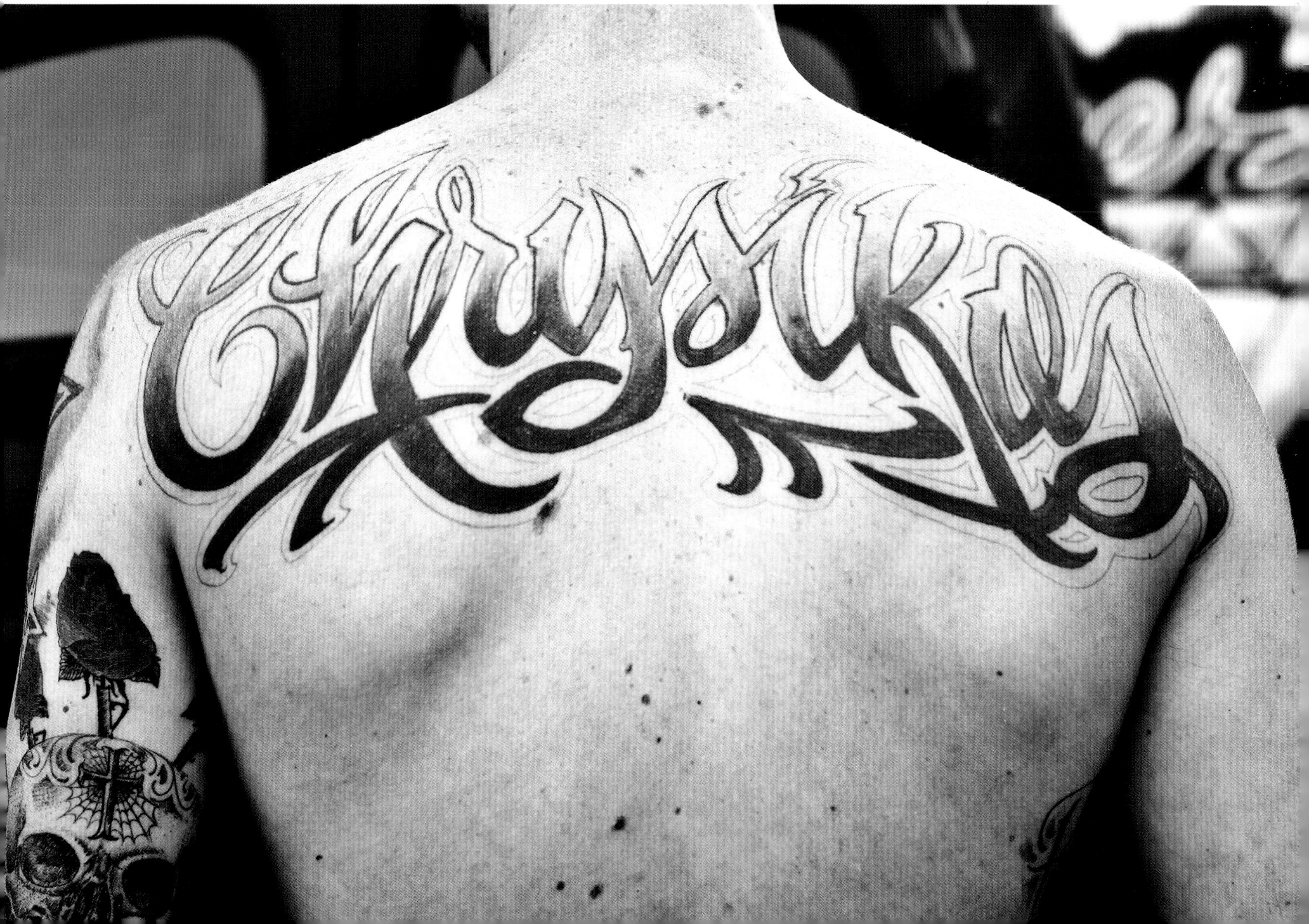

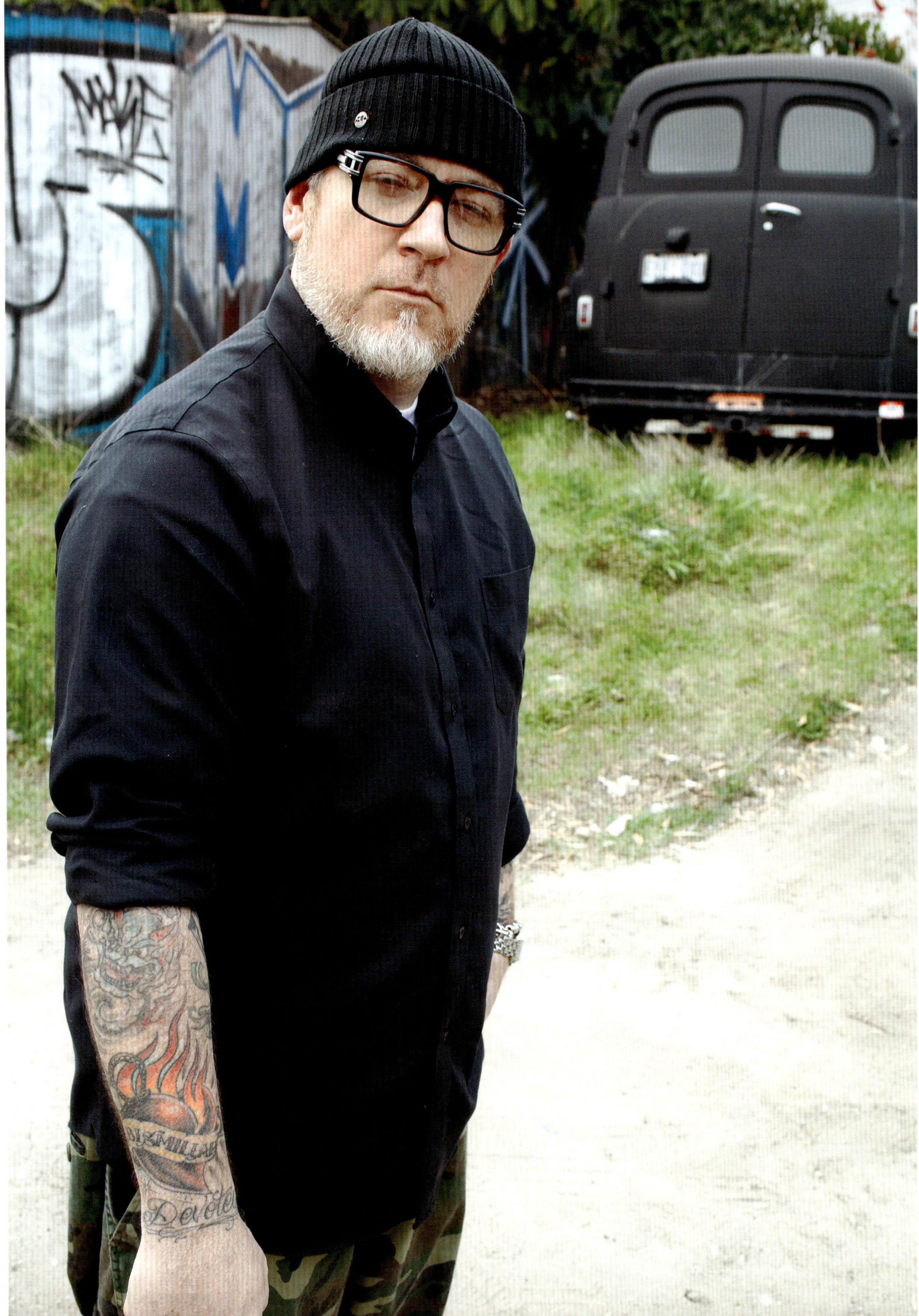

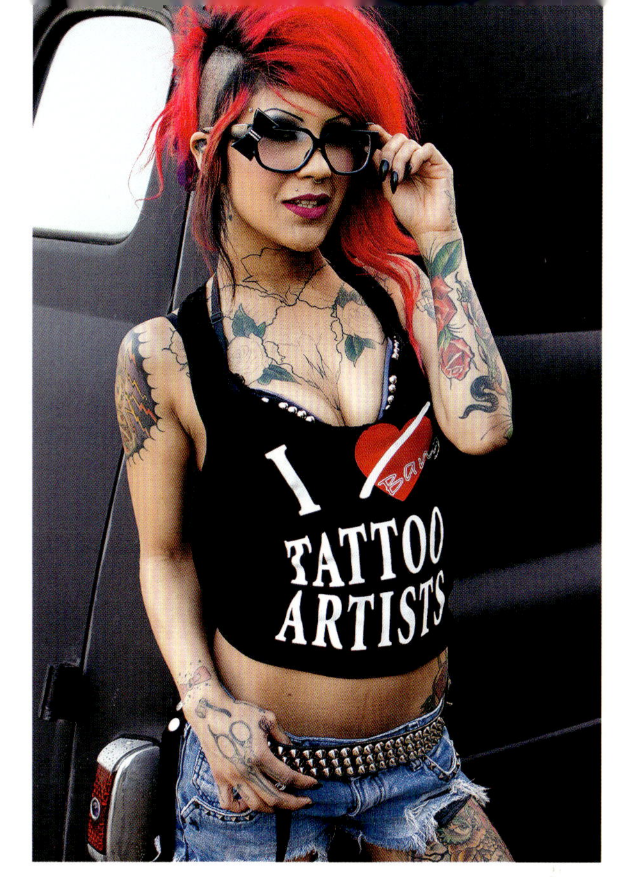
I ♥ TATTOO ARTISTS

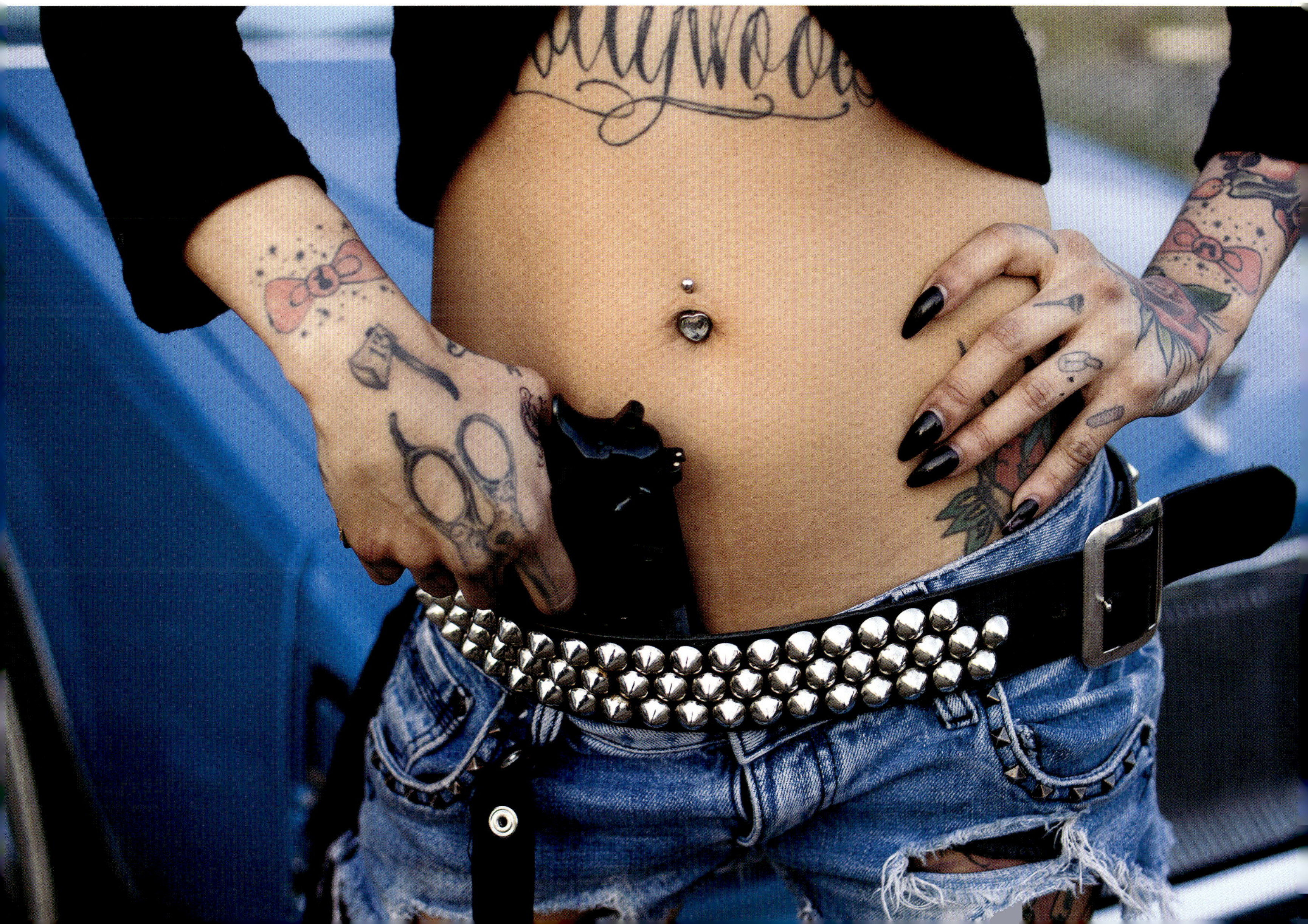

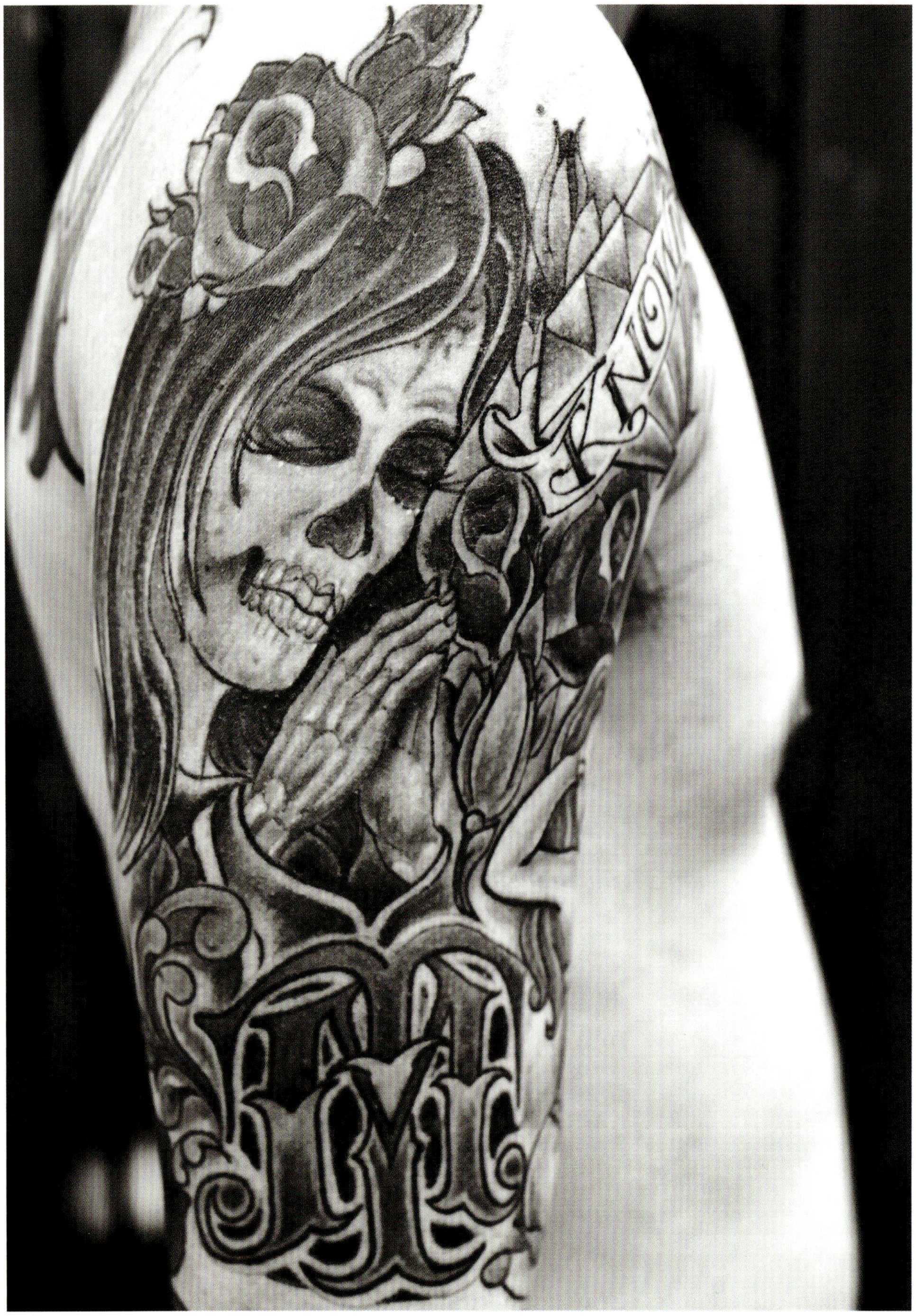

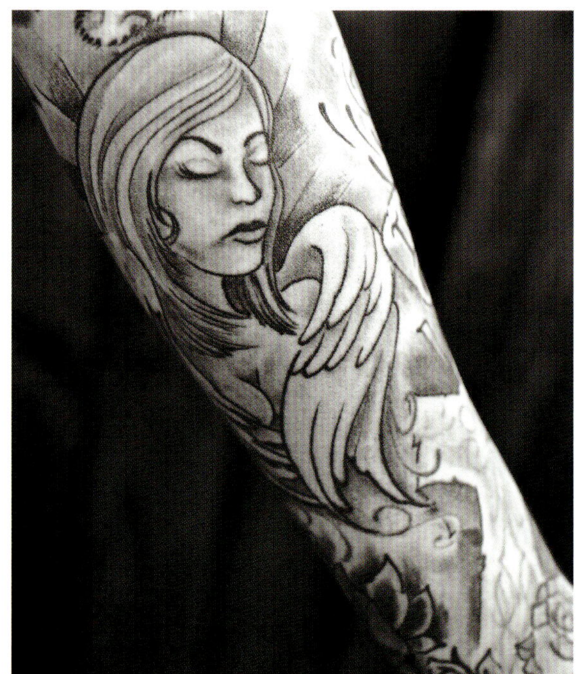

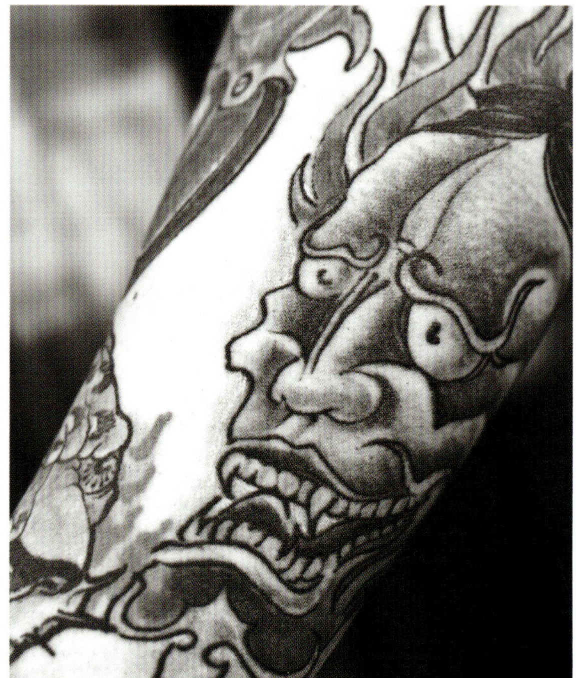

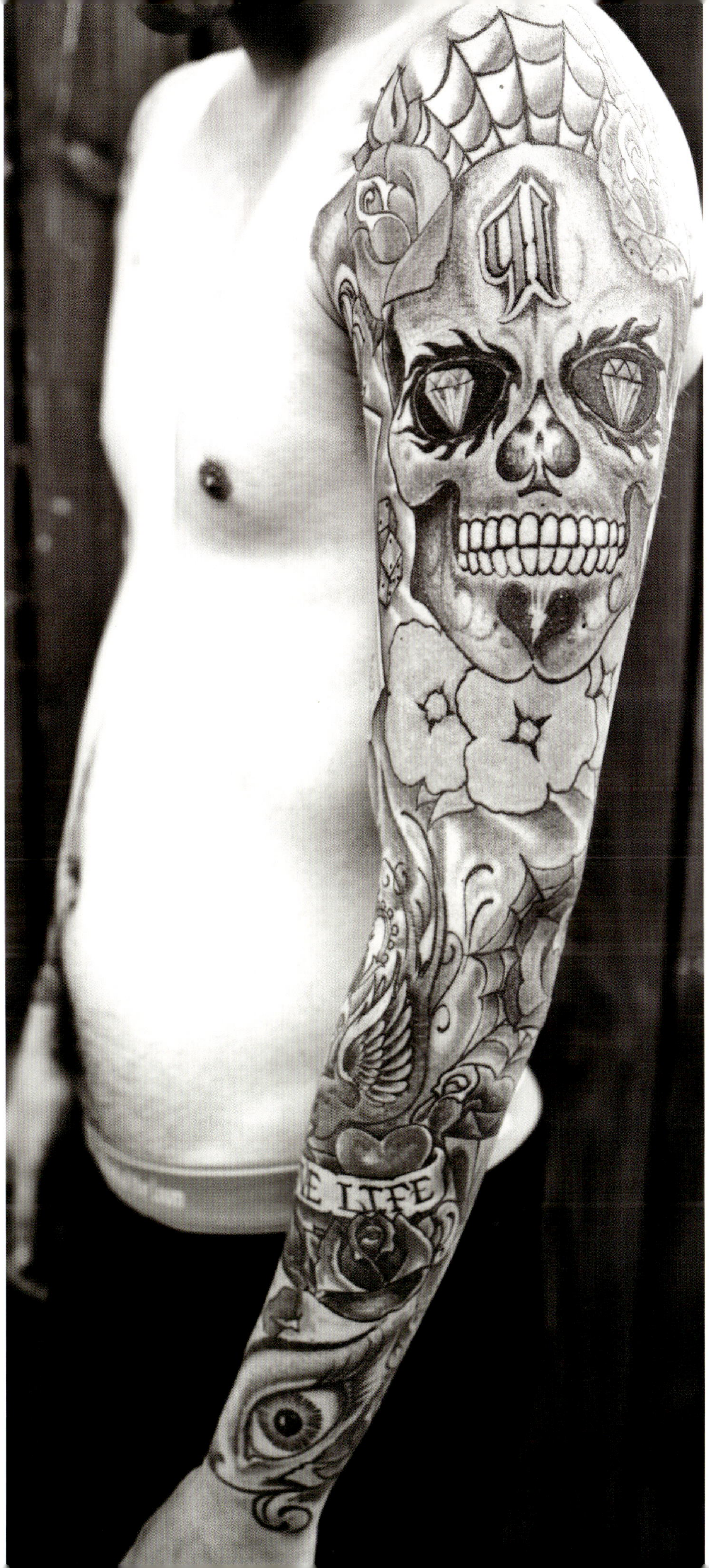

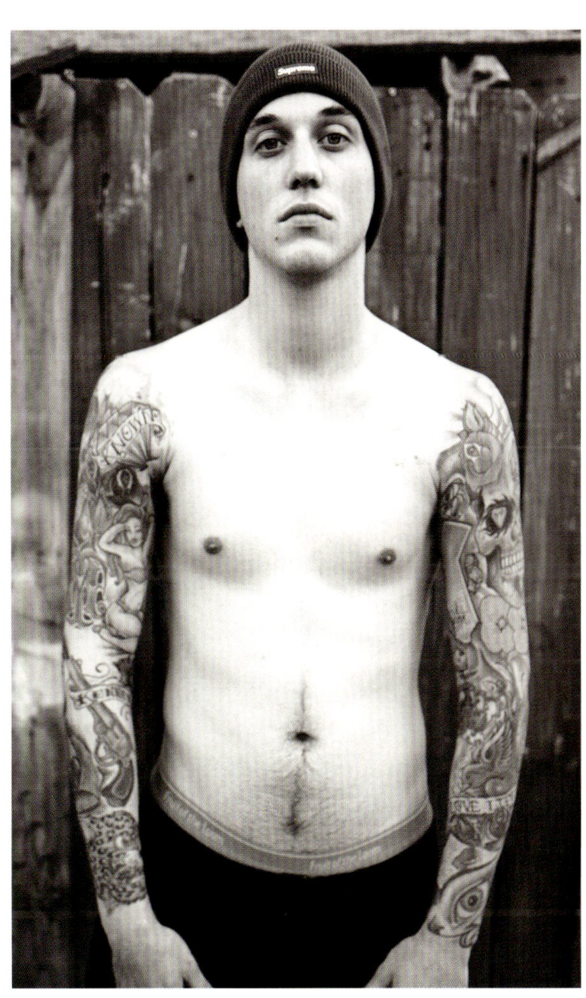

MISTER CARTOON

Los Angeles

"It was difficult for me to get into the industry with a bunch of old guys not wanting young kids to come in the game with skill. Now I think it's completely different. A lot of these tattoo artists are ex-graffiti writers now. So they welcome hand styles and unique style and someone being dope so they can make money at their shop. That's more of the way it should be looked at."

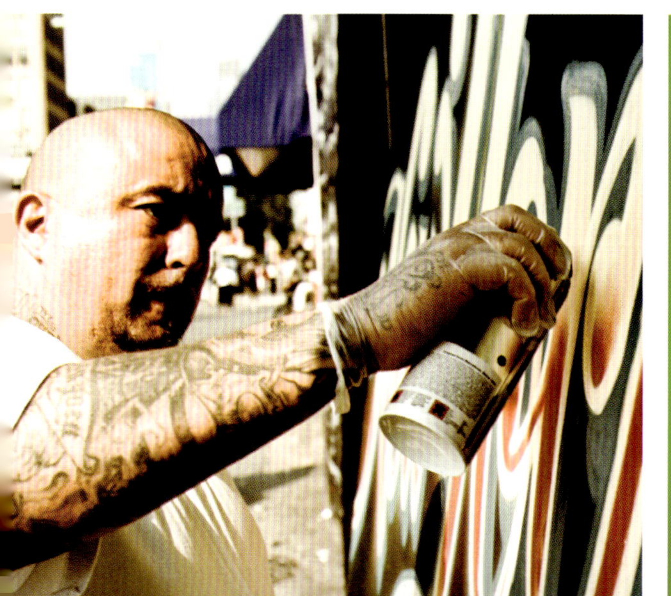

MISTER CARTOON

Here are some words that one might associate with Mister Cartoon: *Los Angeles*, *Mexico*, *American*, *Chicano*, *hip-hop*, *lowrider*, *pride*, *respect*, *heart*. His work is an amalgamation of all of these powerful words, and his fans the world over recognize this truth. He took his youthful passion for the culture of writing and applied that energy to the detailed work he slings with his tattoo machine. The list of celebrities he's decorated is too long to list, but the culture he's come to personify eclipses any list of famous faces.

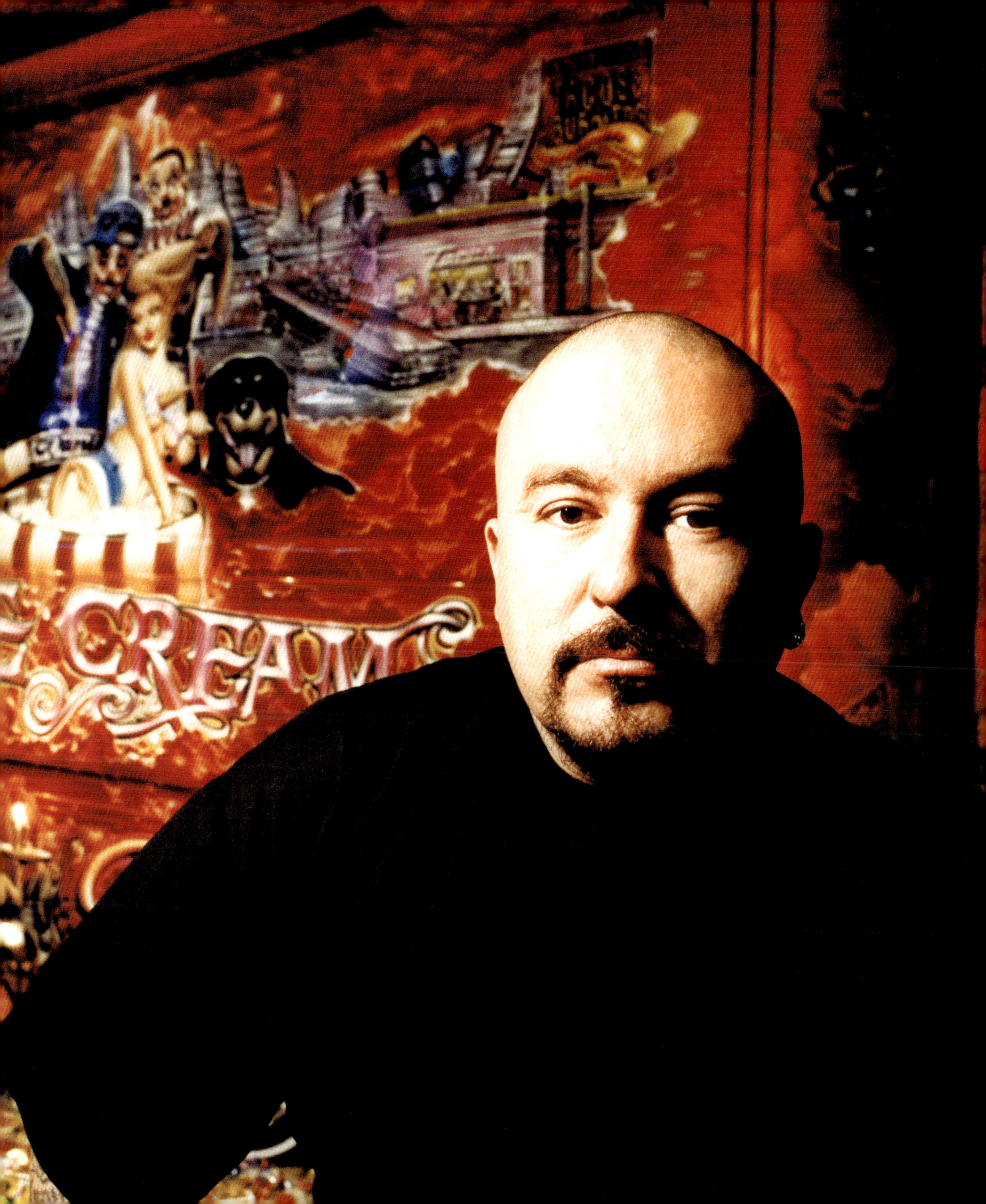
CREAM

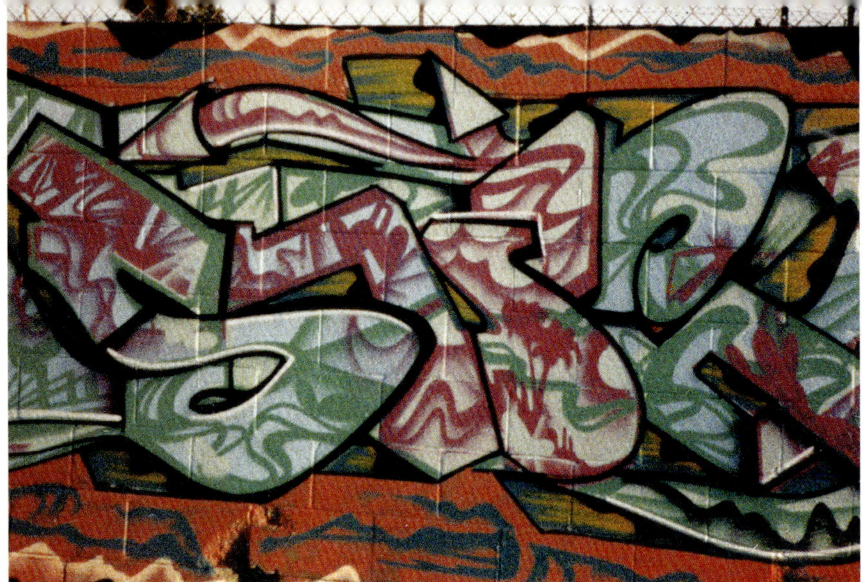
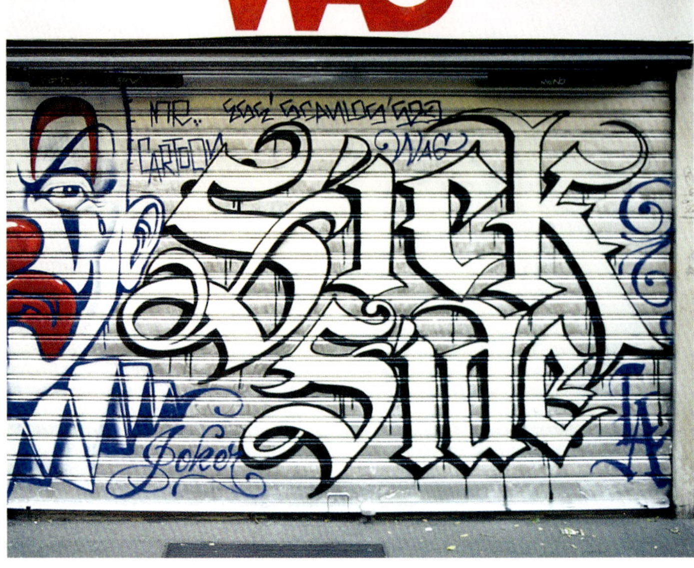

FROM LEFT: Mister Cartoon piece, Los Angeles, late 1980s; Mister Cartoon, *Sick Side*, Milan, Italy, 1997; Mister Cartoon, *Only the Brave* piece for Diesel Cologne, Los Angeles, 2010

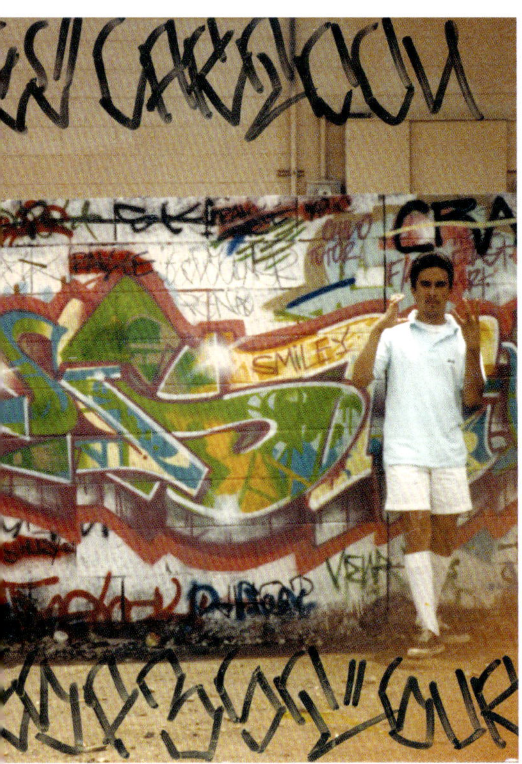

Mister Cartoon, Los Angeles, late 1980s

I first experimented with graffiti around fourteen, but I didn't understand it until I was fifteen. I can remember KD and White playing on the radio and it was Doug E. Fresh and Slick Rick. I can just remember my heart pounding, you know, hearing the show and hearing the songs. I wanted to find my place in hip-hop in the eighties. Everyone wanted to break-dance, but unless you are real athletic and have some shit about you, that wasn't for you—and it wasn't for me.

Seeing graffiti for the first time sends a rush through you. Then you just always kind of chase that, and you keep experiencing it on certain days, maybe seeing a new style of graffiti or just seeing something that's not supposed to be there.

I remember seeing graffiti in Blondie's video "Rapture" and it blew me away because you could read it easily. It was a Lee piece, *L-E-E*, and I couldn't believe that there was popping in front of it—full pop-lock style of dance. I wanted to emulate that. Then there was a movie called *Beat Street* that came out and that was about a breaker, a DJ, and a graffiti writer. Remember that movie? Worst movie in America. If you watch that right now, you can't get through four minutes of it. It's so terrible. They didn't even use a real graffiti writer. They used a guy from the art department. When I saw it, the work still looked fresh, though, because it had these arrows on it, and we never saw anything like that on TV. MTV just started it, so there wasn't a bunch of graffiti, couldn't google "graffiti writer," you know? And we tried to emulate New York graffiti bombing style because the gangster *cholo* letters have been around since zoot suit time in the forties. New York's style kind of connected with that music and the message—guys like Grandmaster Flash, Kurtis Blow—those are the grooves that were busting in the eighties. Even in LA, we were hearing that. So graffiti was for me. That's where I fit in. I could draw.

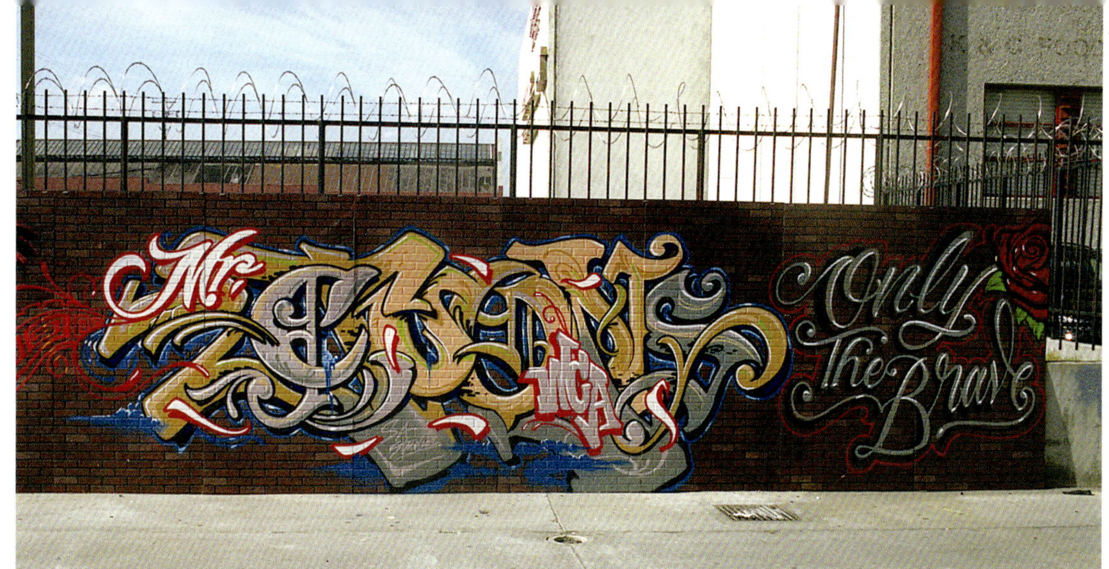

It all changed for me when I met a kid named Clever. Clever grew up in Gardena, in South Central. I met him at the Hawthorne mall one time, and he had this young Mexican kid with him. The kid's name was Abel. We called him Sphere at the time, and I was Flame 1. We both had long hair in the back—had our hair combed back, little pompadours. Turtlenecks, Raiders caps. And we loved graffiti and we didn't know what we were doing, so we just kept doing it until we figured it out. And at the time silver paint had just come out. We would use a True Blue outline or a Cherry Red, and you were the man if you were doing a silver piece. It was crazy. Someone figured out that silver went over everything. I started doing that.

My early influences were Rival, Pyro, Whisk, Minor, Risky, Dream, Green—you know, half of them were from West Coast Artists, other guys were from other crews like K2S [Kill to Succeed]. I was influenced by their style, which is more of a Chicago style of graffiti. And then later on CBS [Can't Be Stopped] was another crew coming out, and BC [Beyond Control].

The graffiti scene when I was coming up was all about getting fired up and just figuring out how to do it. All the guys that I looked up to, my crew, were over it. They were burned out on it. They were starting to get tattoos, and Rival already had sleeves back in '90. He was heavily tattooed and working on motors and shit like that, so I started to see that guys were going toward that and hanging in tattoo shops. Being that Rival knew Charlie Roberts and all those different characters, I started to meet a whole different young crowd at Spotlight Tattoo, and most of them could do graffiti as well. So it was a natural transition for me to go from graffiti into tattooing: two lowbrow, underground styles of art.

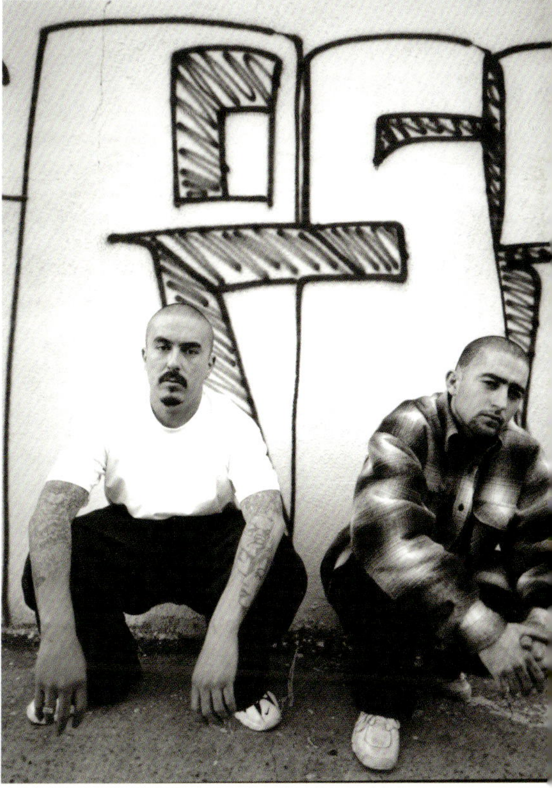

Mister Cartoon (left) and Lil Lucky, Los Angeles, 1998

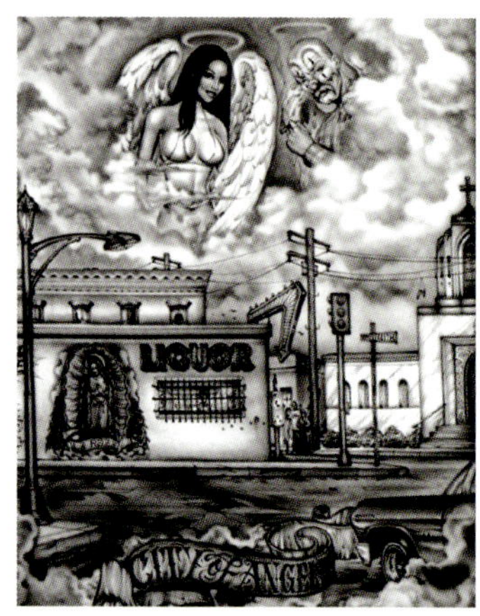

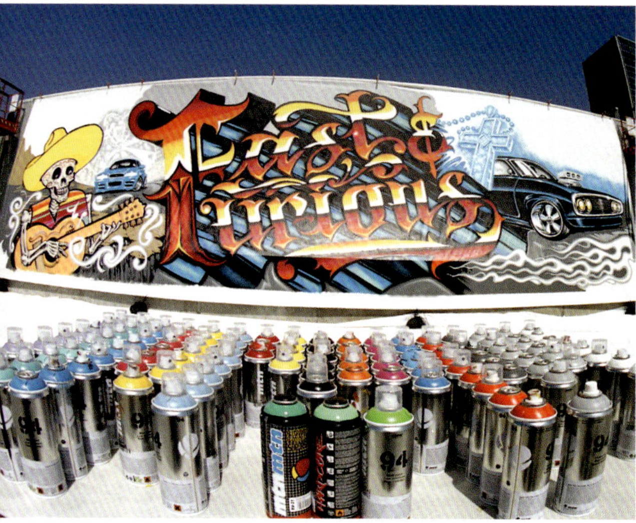

TOP: Mister Cartoon, *City of Angels*, 2005
BOTTOM: Mister Cartoon, Revok, Tloks, *Fast and Furious*, Los Angeles, 2009

The Jefferson yard was a K2S yard, and that's where we learned how to basically put up our pieces. And there was a young kid named Sinner and his older brother, Sane. Sinner is not one of the most famous graffiti writers from LA, and Sane was more my age. Sinner was only a couple years younger but still hanging out with us. And we would do giant murals, man. It was crazy that we would pull this stuff off. We didn't know what we were doing, you know. We would be in South Central painting the side of a Jamaican rasta place. Those types of guys would let us do murals on their place. They understood the art and they were open.

In places like South Central, we could do murals. Everywhere else they would get nervous, but there they encouraged it. I used to work on every shop on Western and Florence. The whole time we were listening to the Beastie Boys' first album and writing graffiti. It was the best time of my life. I loved it all. You always hear what old-time graffiti writers were talking about back in the day. But things have changed. We've seen the change with computer technology coming into graffiti. Now it's going to be ten times harder for these kids to do original stuff because they're so influenced by what the world is doing. But they'll be there. Graffiti art will spawn the next wave of tattoo artists. The next wave of designers for movies or next wave of fashion designers is going to come from graffiti art, from that form where you can get arrested, where people are telling you that you're doing something you're not supposed to do.

In the streets, there are different levels of graffiti writers. If they're gangsters, they ride that fine line of whether they are gang members or graffiti writers. Back then, it was mainly graffiti writers with their own subculture. It was mixed, with Latinos, white kids, Asians, black kids, all of us hanging out together, you know what I mean? And there was no tripping with all that. We all got along, we all did our thing. With gangsters, it was very segregated. As years went on, it seemed like a whole new generation of tag bangers came out and started to mesh graffiti and gangs together.

I think the first time I heard about a graffiti writer being a tattoo artist was Seen. That was crazy when we heard that Seen stopped doing graffiti and was tattooing, because we thought he would never stop doing graffiti. He made a retirement statement saying, "I stopped." So I guess it had to be him, the first one to own a tattoo shop and be a graffiti writer. And actually it was the first time I'd seen any tattoo artist do a piece that looked like a piece that was done by a writer.

I started getting tattooed long before I ever thought about myself as a tattoo artist. I was already working on my sleeves before I got the nerve or the courage to think that I could tattoo. I was already a professional artist, so for me to start fresh and new in front of everybody seemed crazy, and I didn't want to look like I had no balls doing it. Being a professional artist made it a big handicap for me to come into the tattoo world. No one wants to see a professional painter or artist do tattoos because they think they're kind of cheating in a way. The thing is, I never went to art school so I don't qualify as an artist, but I was a professional.

I think walking into Spotlight Tattoo sparked the fire inside of me. It made me fall in love with tattoos. The atmosphere of the shop, everyone who hung out there—it was unlike any other tattoo shop. There wasn't a lot of foot traffic, it was just people who wanted good tattoos, and you could go there to get a piercing, and it was the best shop I've ever seen.

I learned how to tattoo, and it was basically me and Estevan [Oriol]. I learned how to tattoo pretty much practicing on Estevan in the beginning, with homemade machines. We hung out in tattoo shops all the time. I started tattooing a lot with Tattoo Tony, and he was one of the first professional tattooers to just tell me anything I wanted to know. I didn't have any information other than this. So I learned a lot from him. He thought he was learning from me, like learning how to draw and all that stuff, but I was learning the techniques of how to tattoo from him, and he helped me get to a certain level.

The change happened for me when I saw Tony hanging out with Baby Ray. I called Baby Ray for some supplies to borrow, and he rigged me a new machine and told me I should be learning how to tattoo properly. He really showed me the art of the tattoo. Baby Ray showed me how to price tattoos, what I should be getting, and how I should approach people and deal with people. He showed me real tattoo life and terminology and life skills in general. He showed me the ropes on everything that I know about a tattoo shop.

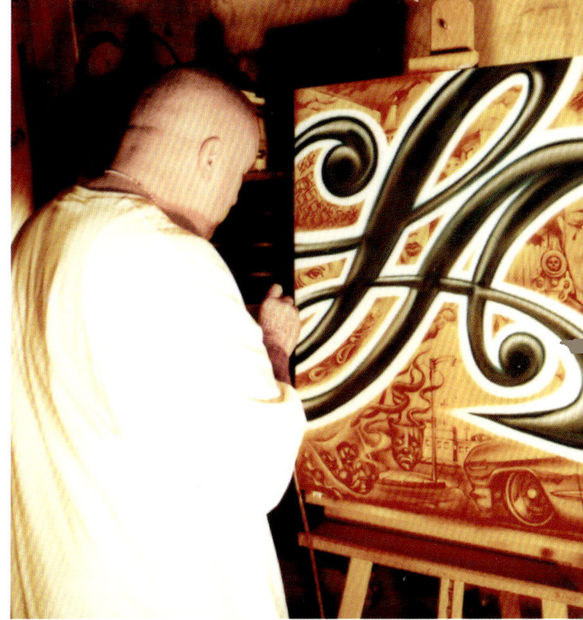

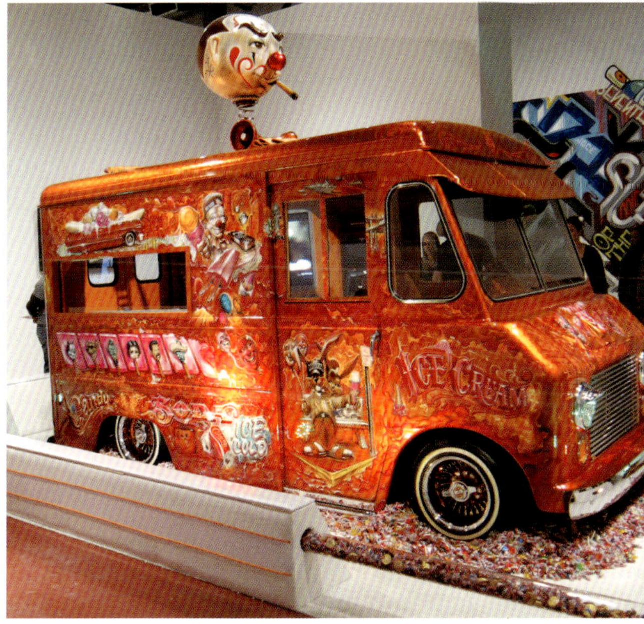

TOP: Mister Cartoon painting a canvas, 2012
BOTTOM: Mister Cartoon ice cream truck on view in *Art in the Streets* exhibition, Museum of Contemporary Art, Los Angeles, 2011

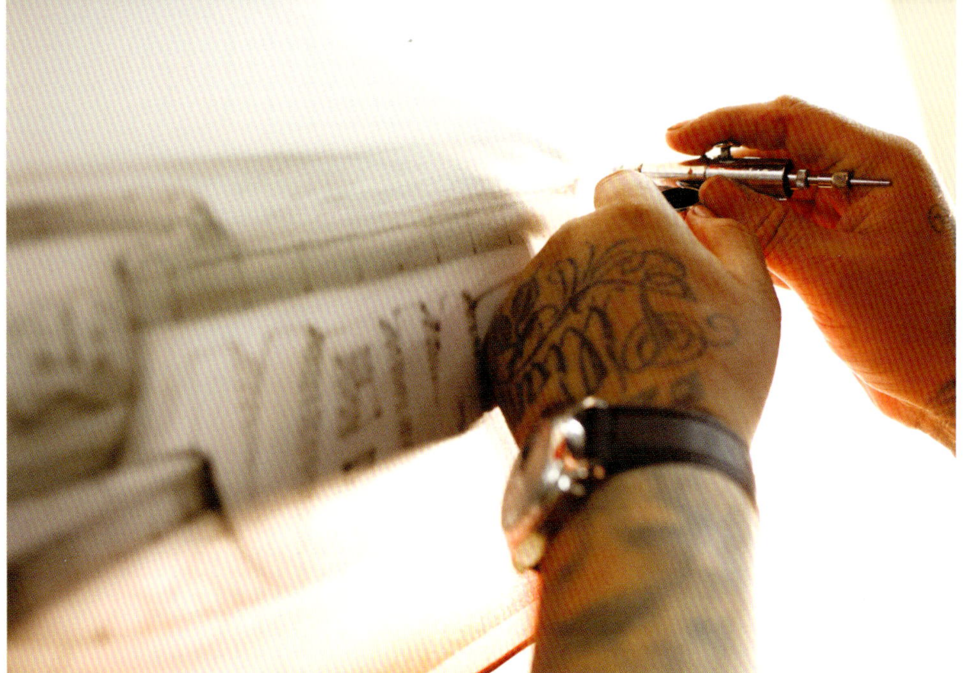

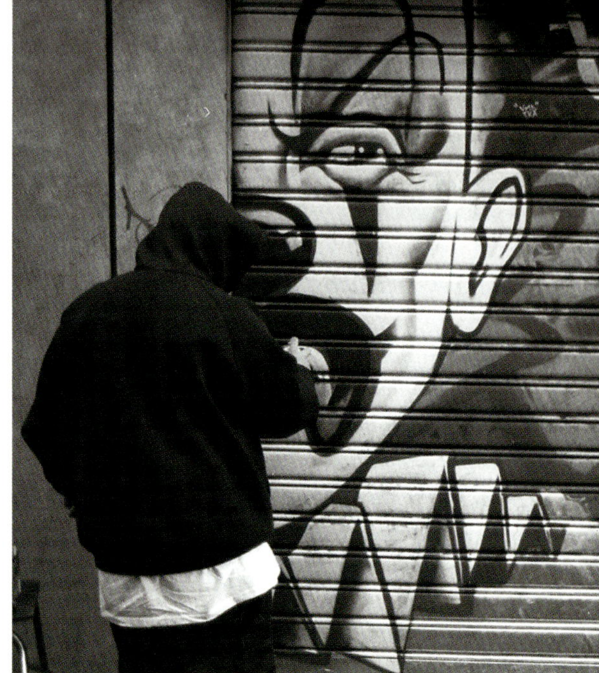

FROM LEFT: Mister Cartoon airbrushing a van for Vans, 2012; Mister Cartoon painting *Sick Side* piece, Milan, Italy, 1997; Mister Cartoon tattooing B-Real at the Inkslingers Ball, Hollywood, CA, 1995

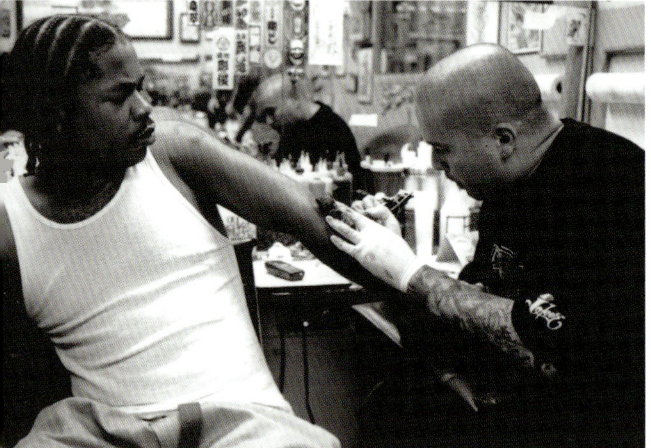

Mister Cartoon tattooing Xzibit at Spotlight Tattoo Shop, Los Angeles, 1998

My early influence was seeing tattoos done by a boy from Long Beach. He was the first one I have seen doing prison envelopes and style for Christian church posters and invites, and stuff they'd hand out on the streets and at car shows. And it was the first time I had really seen masterful black and gray. The girls looked pretty; they weren't from too far in the seventies, they were the way girls look now. He was the first one I've seen laying lettering. It was the highest level of gangster tattoos that I've seen. And then I saw Jack Rudy, which was almost airbrush-looking, portrait style. You can tell he was using professional machines because they looked so washed. Seeing those guys at an early point really tripped me out.

I always considered myself a graffiti writer. It's funny. I guess your first form of art is forever, you know? I approach things the way I approach graffiti. I look at people, and I think they're biting my style. I think about crossing people out, and I forget I'm forty-two years old and a father of four, that I own a home.

Times have changed now. It was difficult for me to get into the industry with a bunch of old guys not wanting young kids to come in the game with skill. Now I think it's completely different. A lot of these tattoo artists are ex-graffiti writers now. So they welcome hand styles and unique style and someone being dope so they can make money at their shop. That's more of the way it should be looked at. I think there's no better time for graffiti writers to start tattooing.

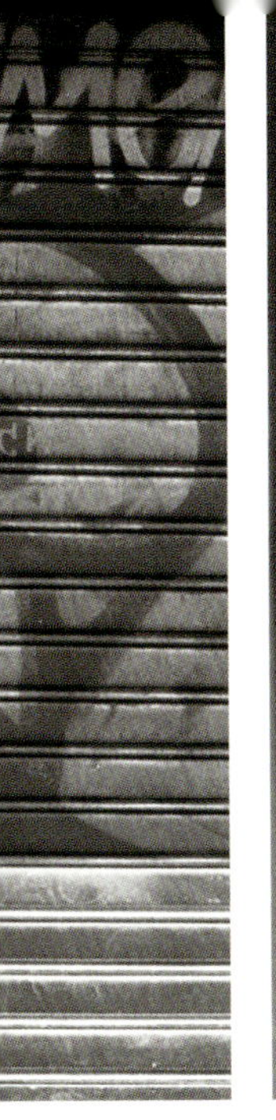
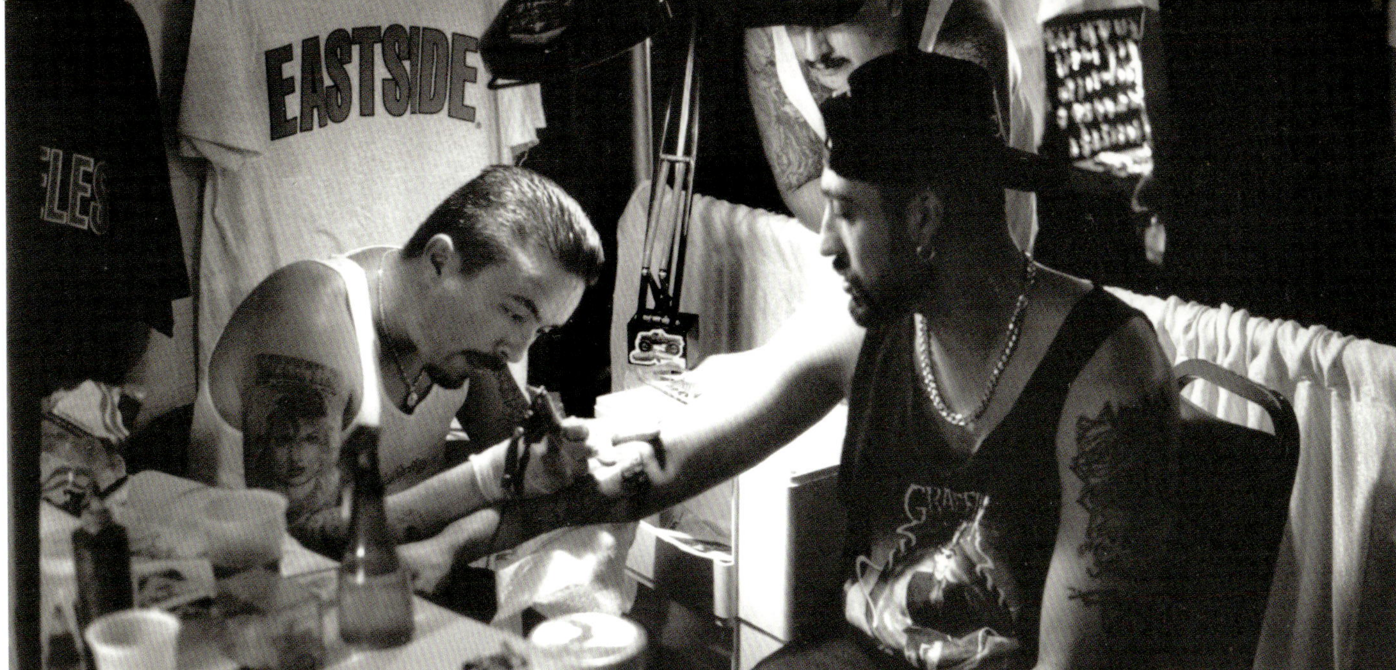

There's a big difference between tattooing and graffiti. In graffiti, if I do a character in a certain way and people identify that character as mine, if you go paint someone's wall in another neighborhood with the same character, you're going to be considered a biter. Now, if I designed a tattoo and someone else gets a picture of that tattoo and makes a pattern out of it and puts that tattoo on somebody else, it's not frowned upon. You don't sign the tattoo, but everyone knows that you did it. Tattooing is a form of borrowing. It always has and it always will be. In graffiti, you're not borrowing, you're biting. That's the big difference. So I had to become relaxed with people doing my patterns. They became public patterns.

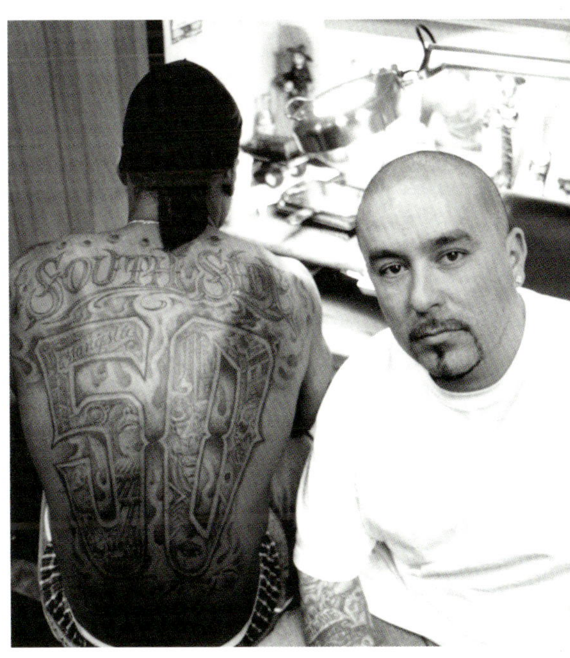

50 Cent (left) and Mister Cartoon, Los Angeles, 2003

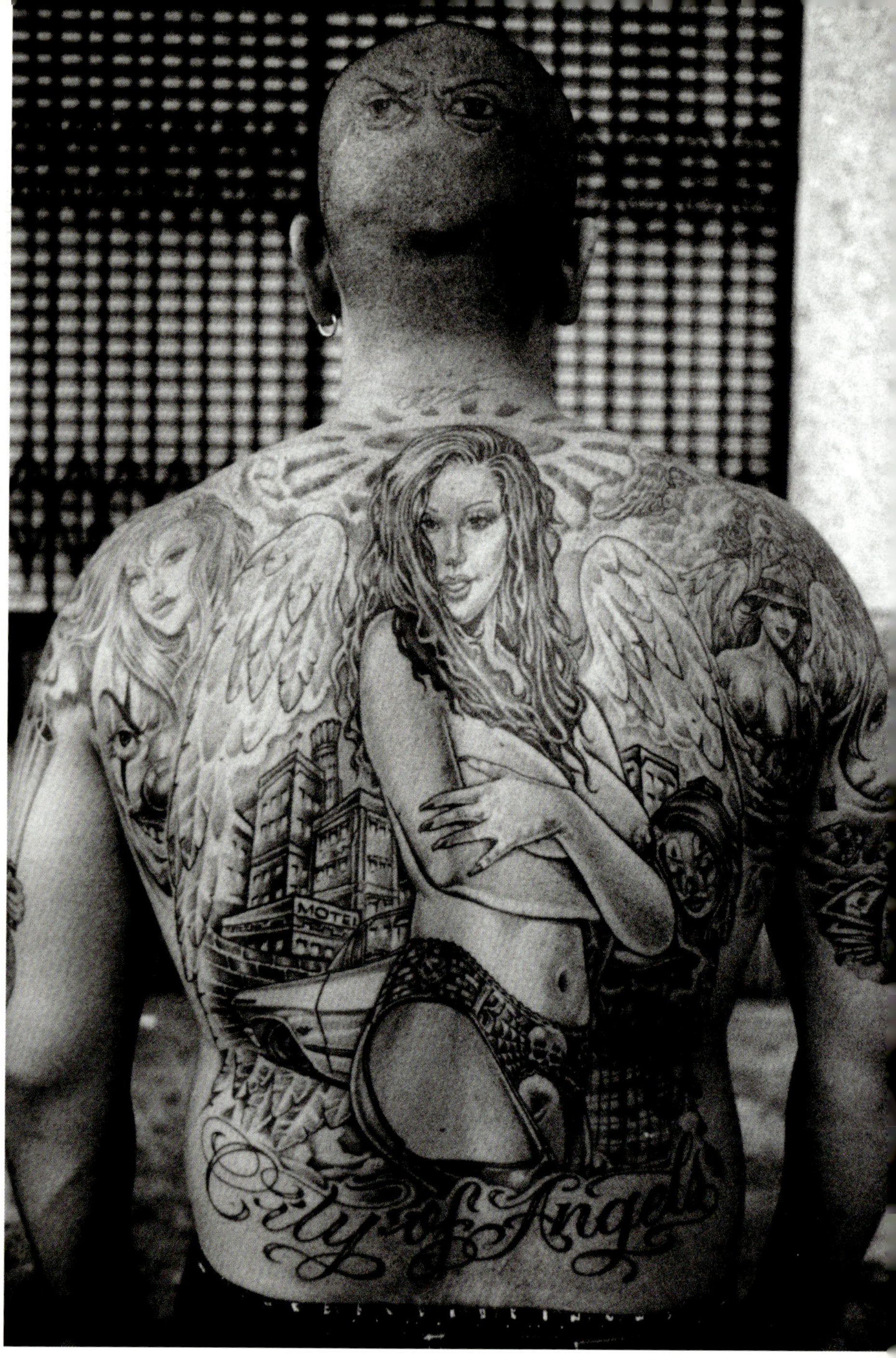

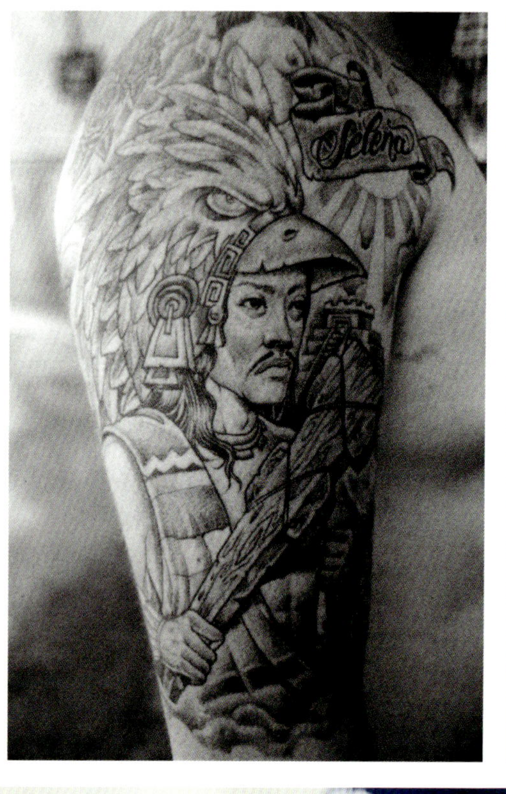
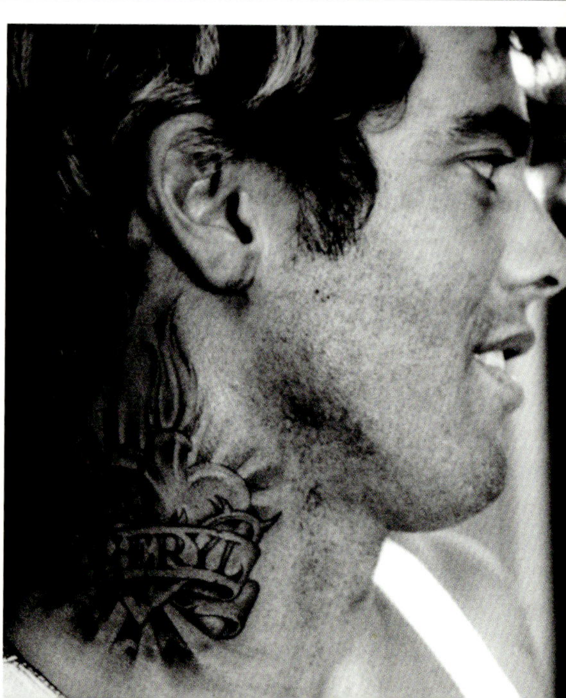
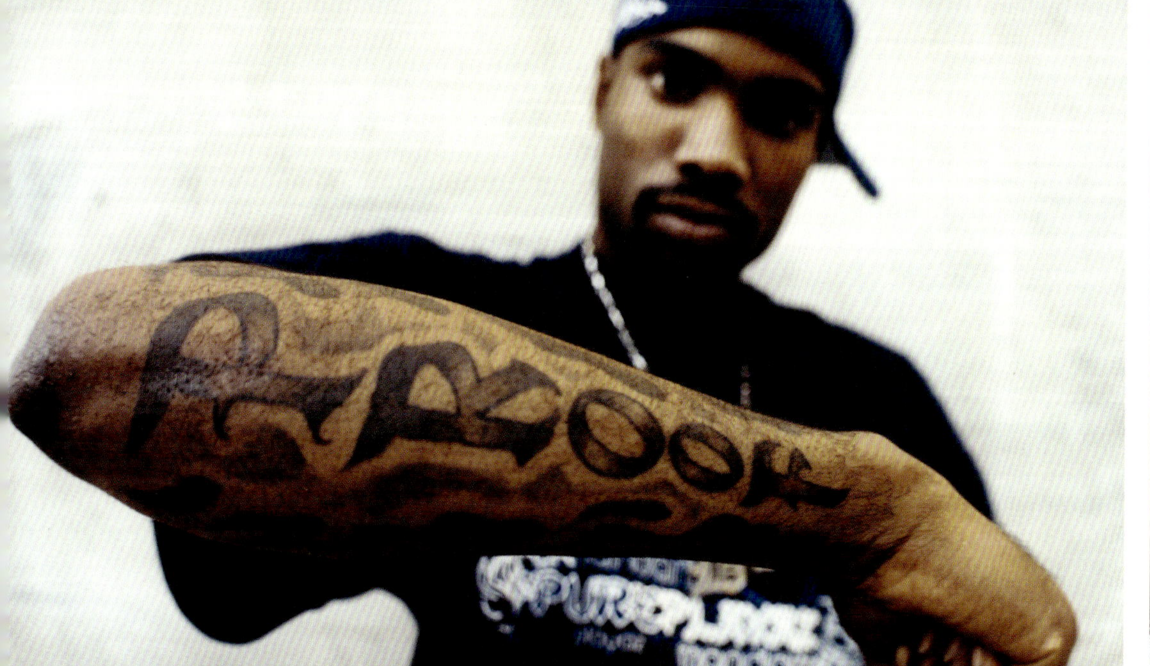

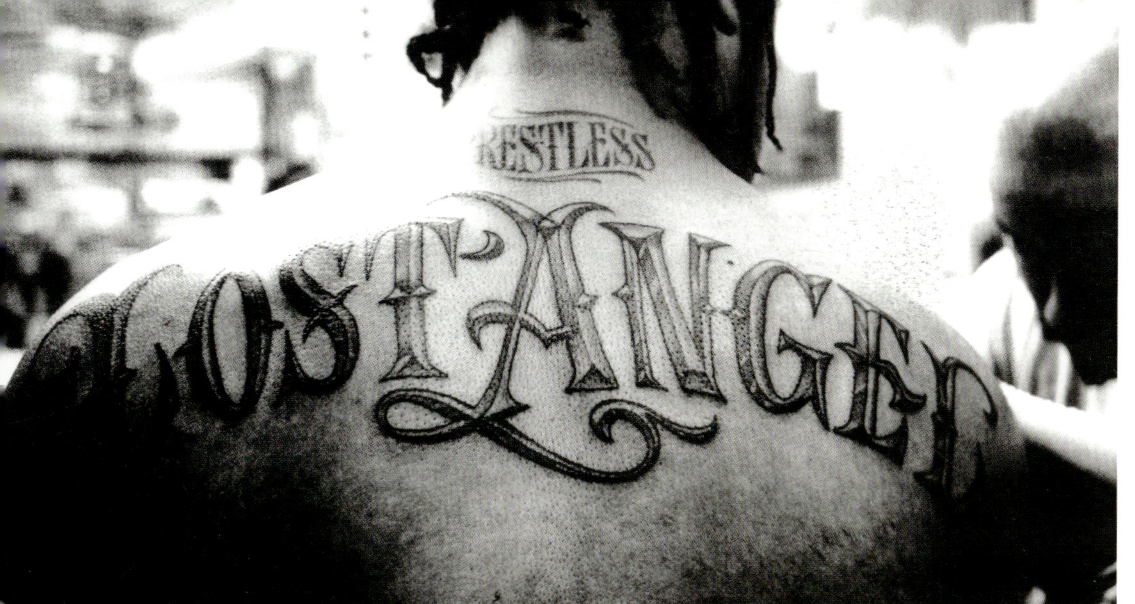
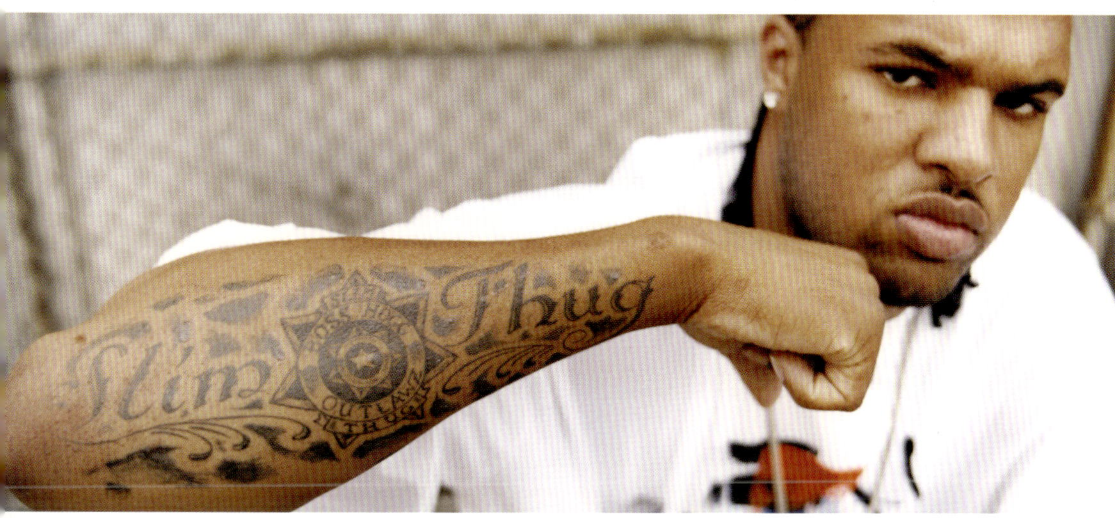
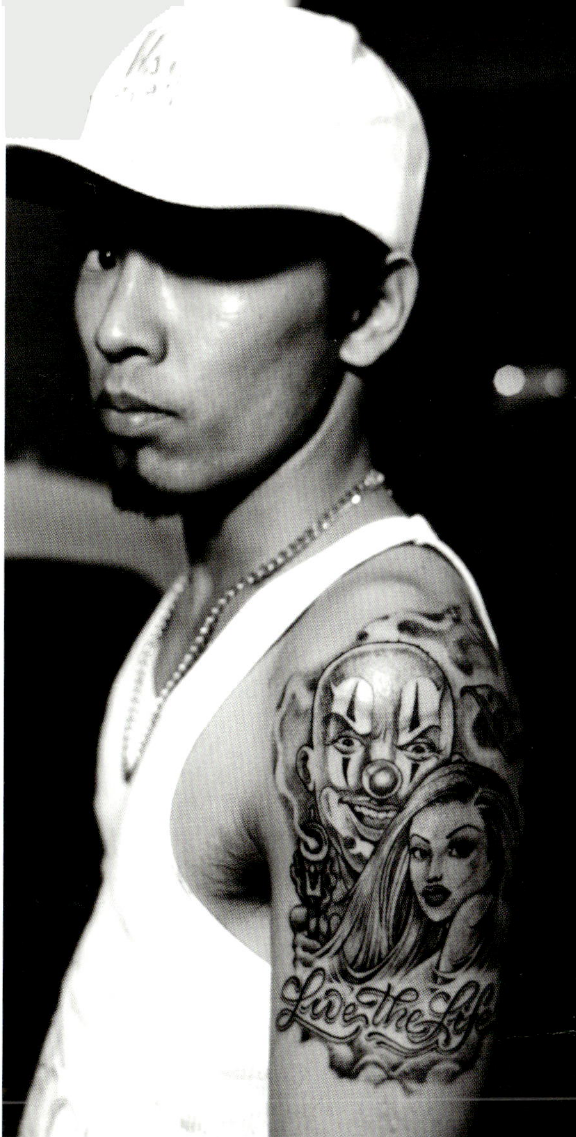
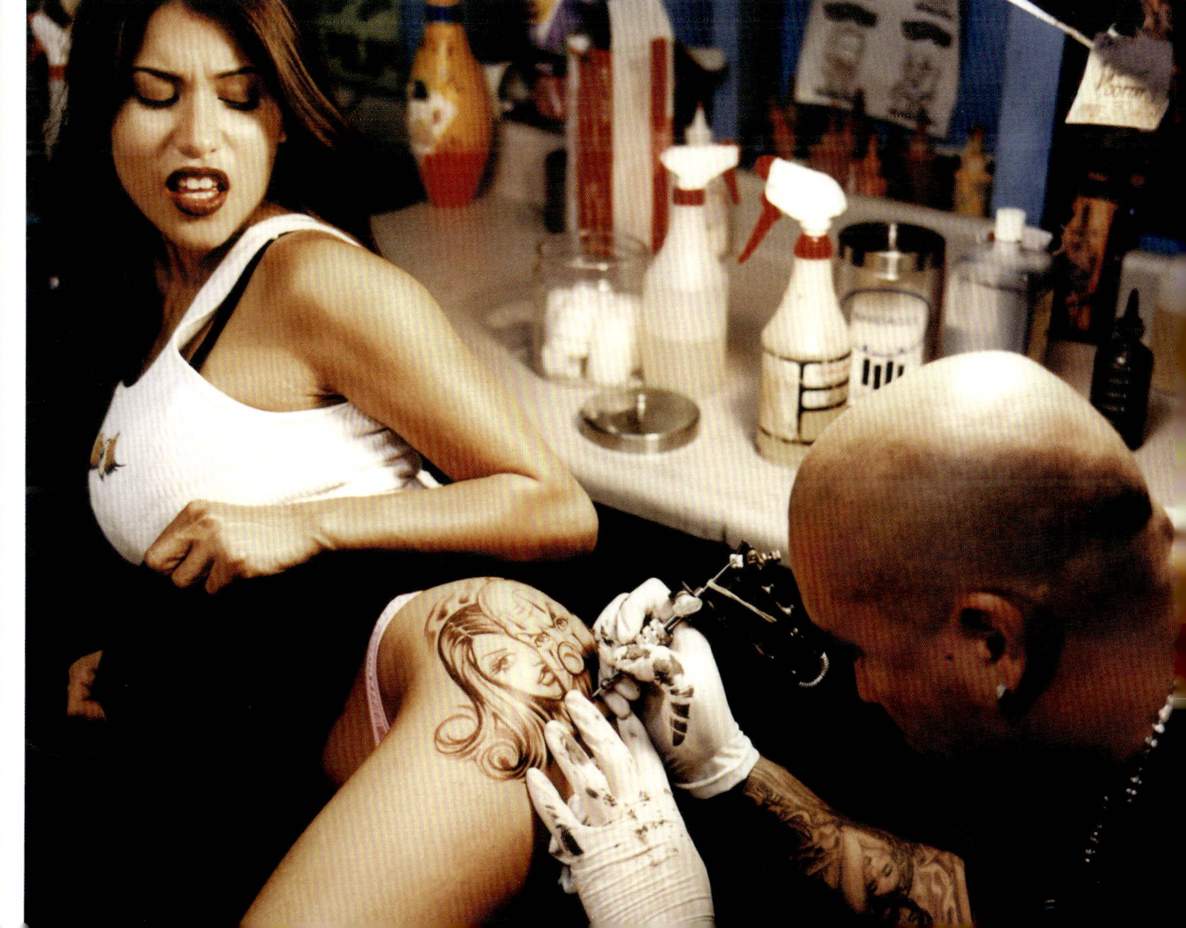

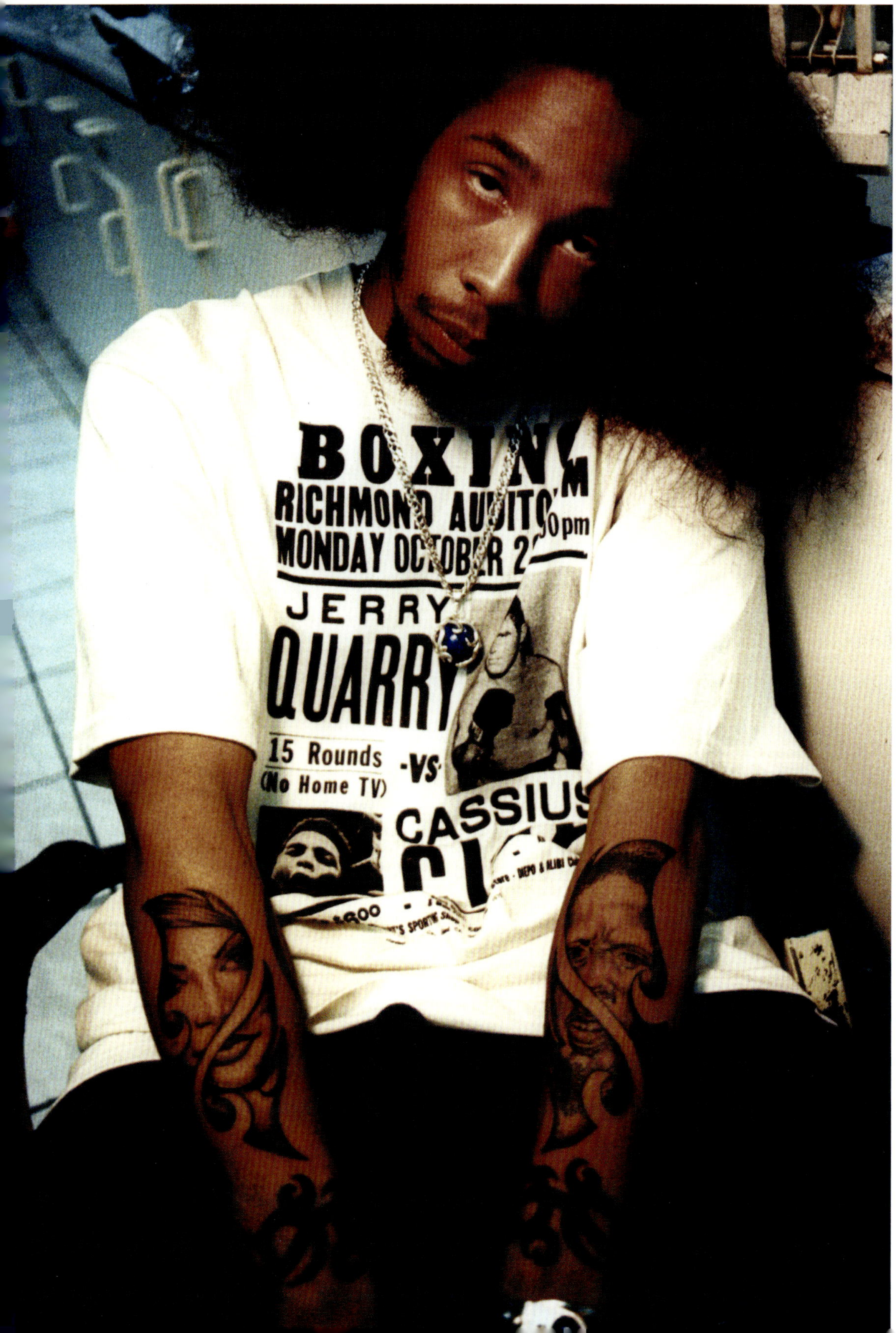

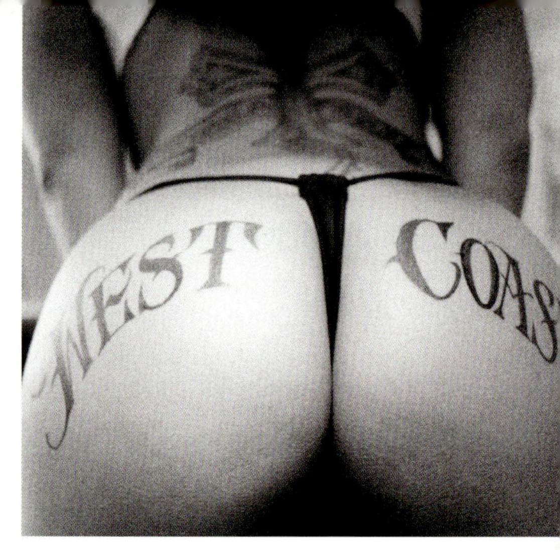

WEST COAS
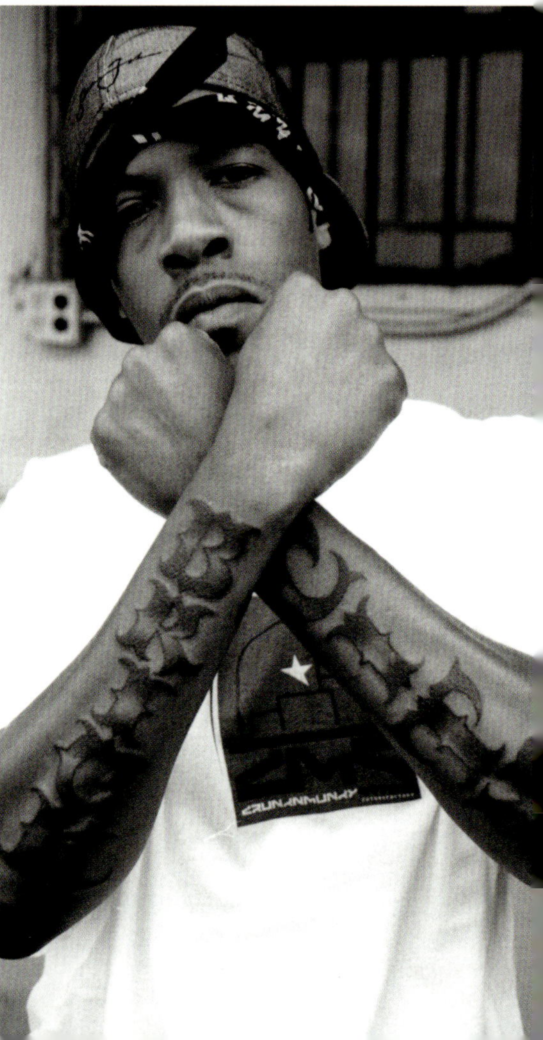

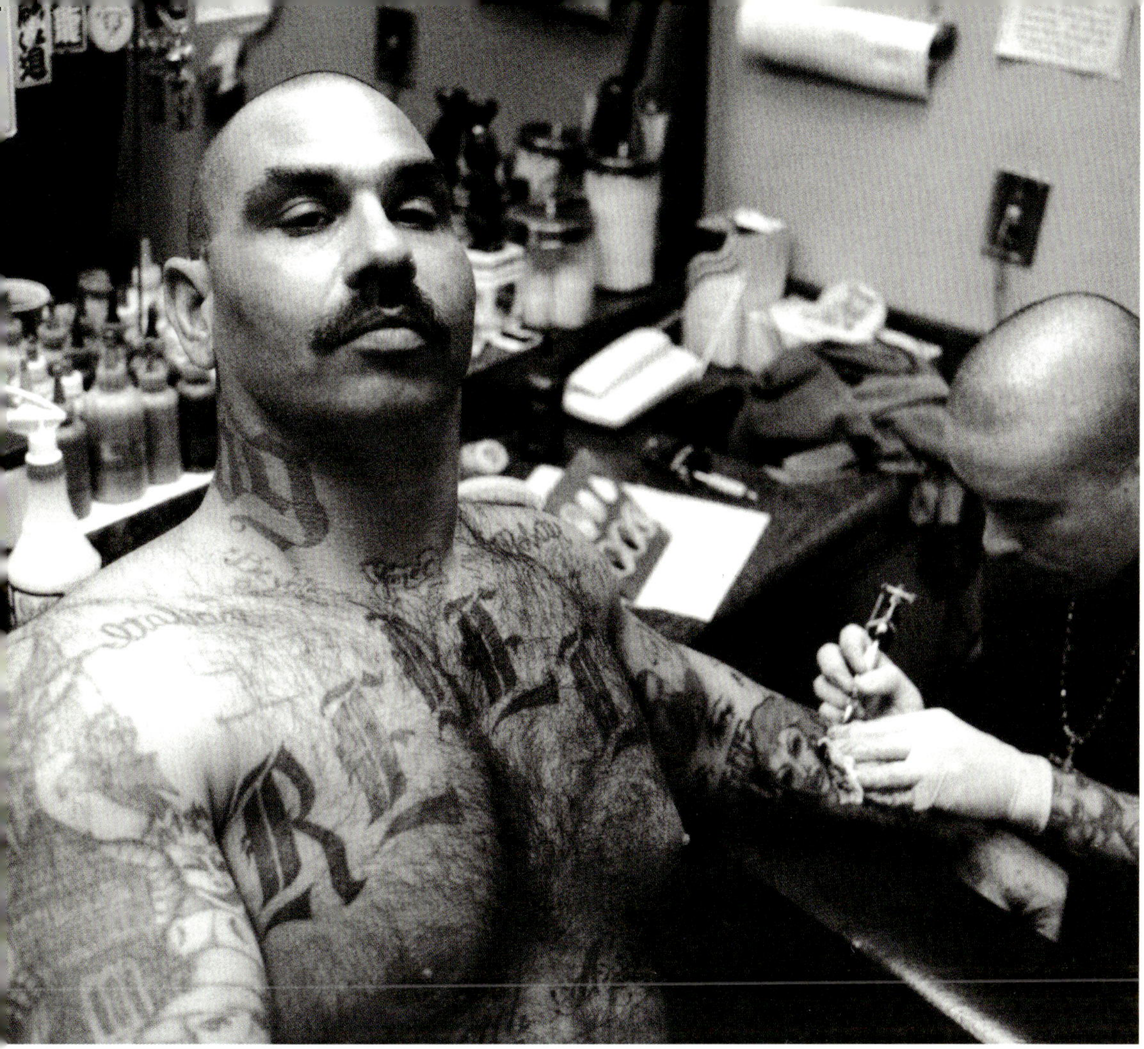

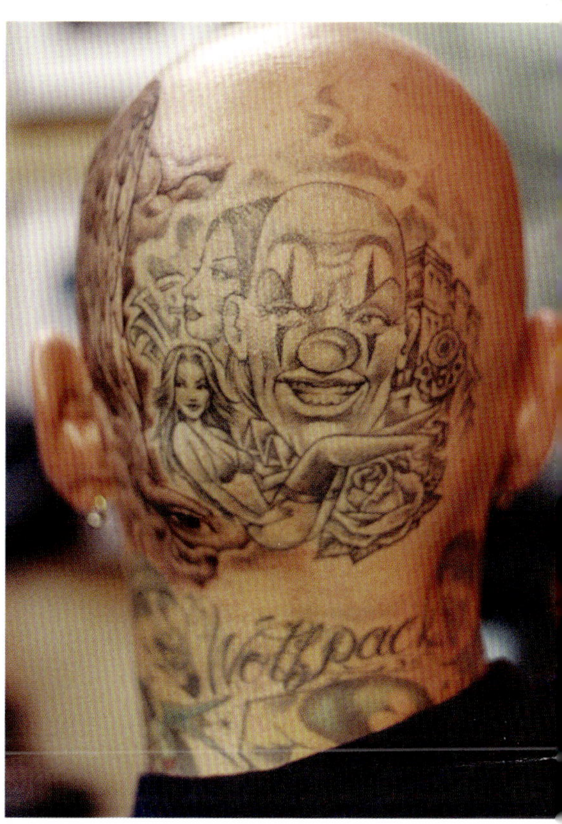

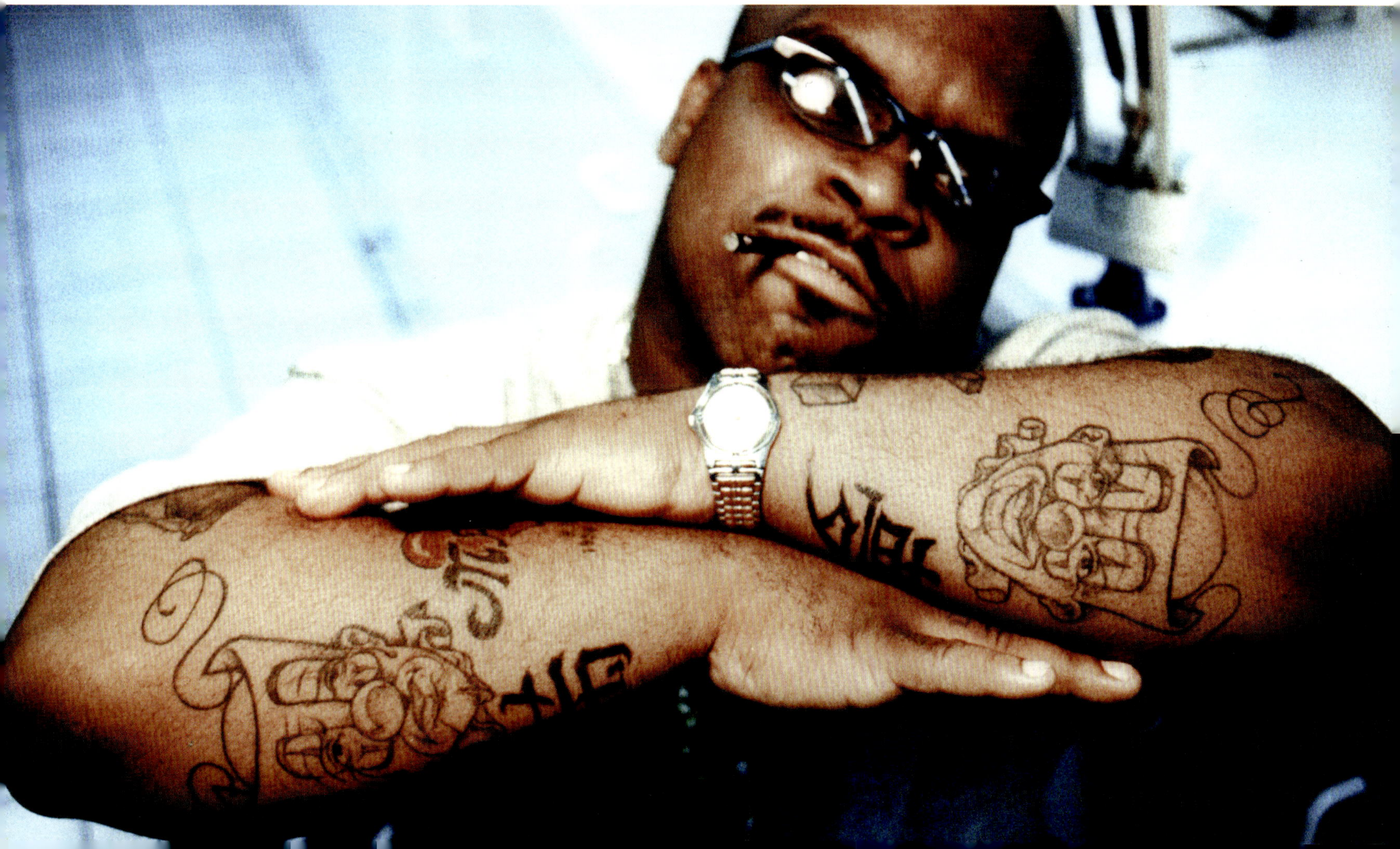

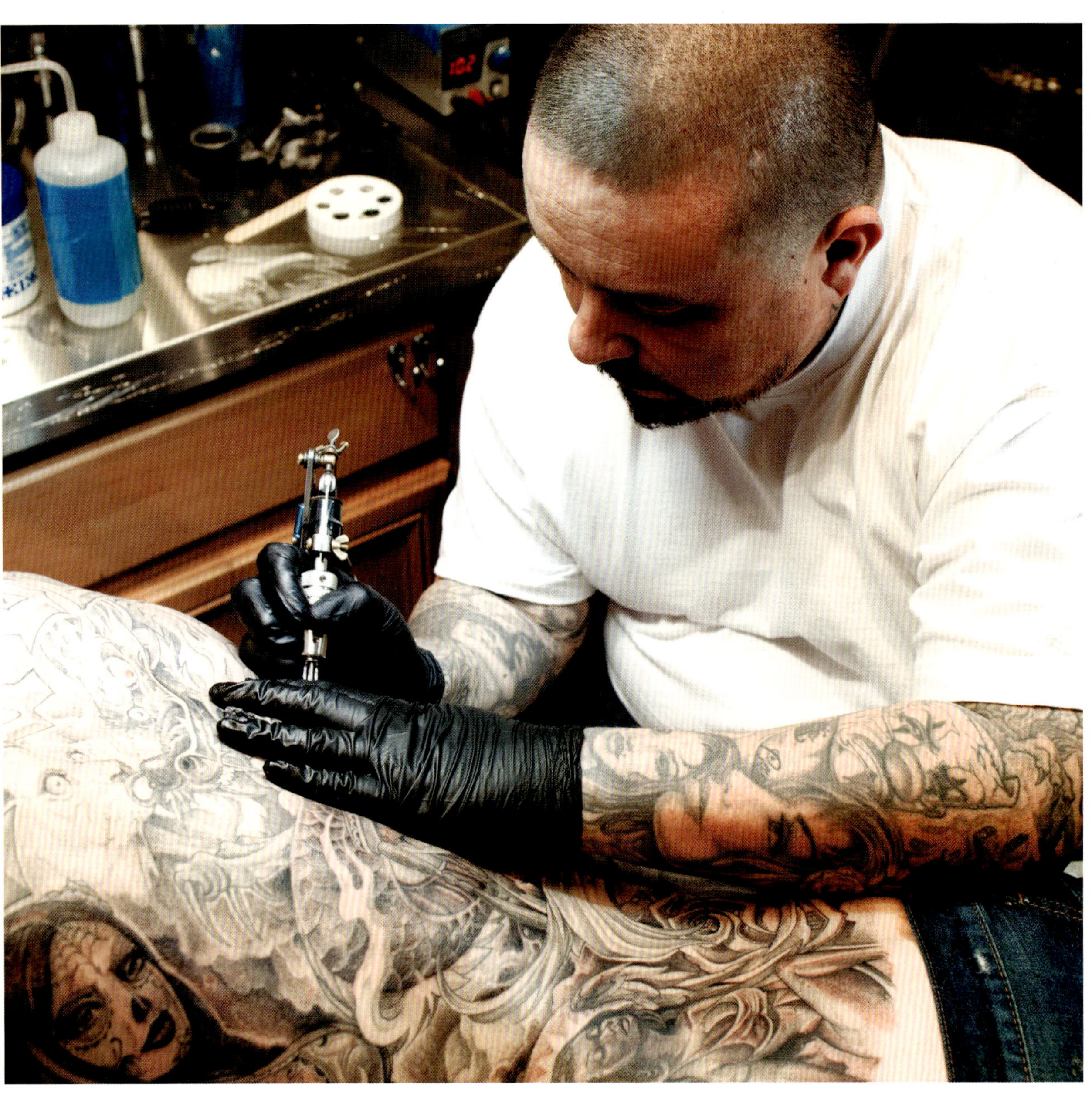

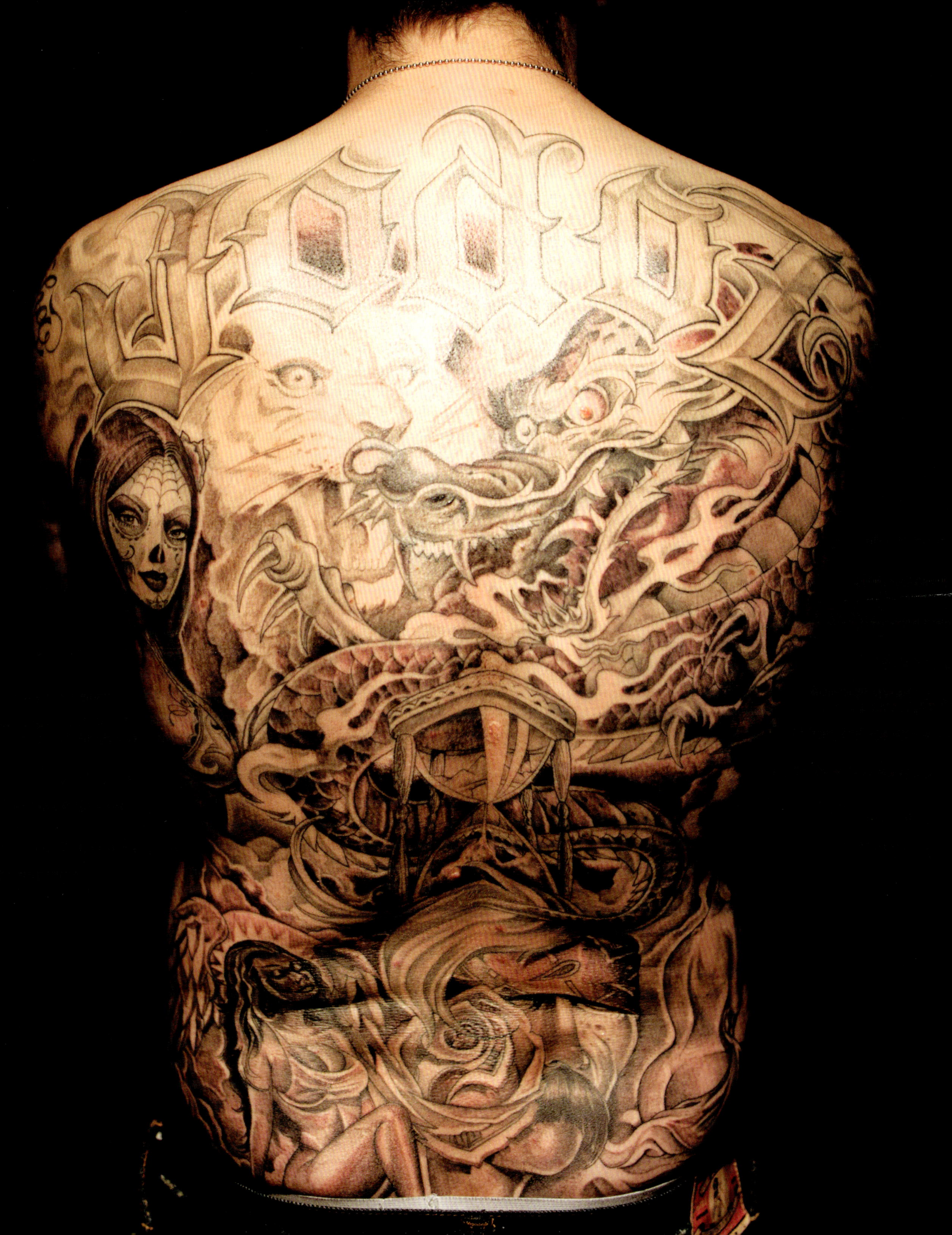

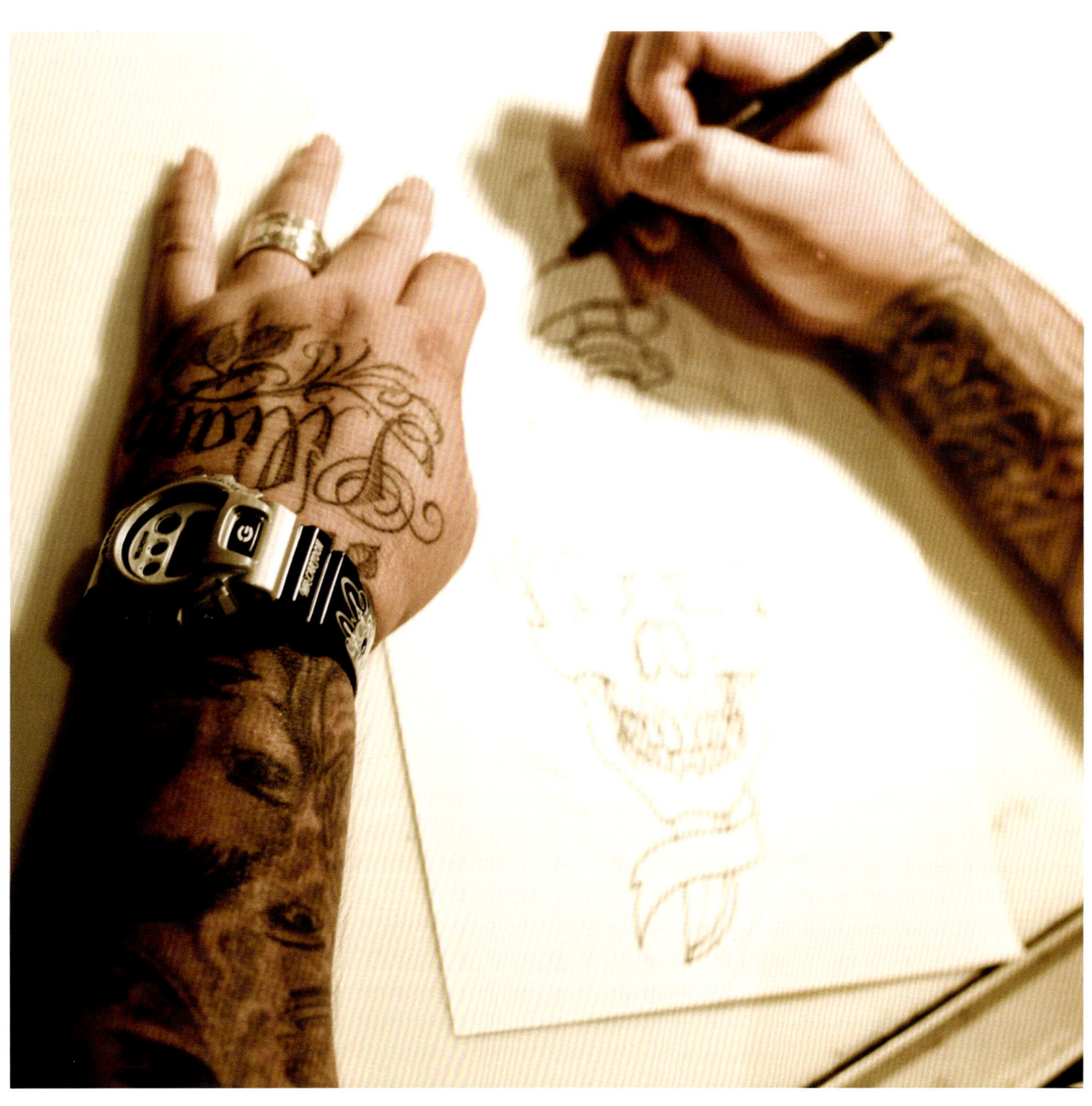

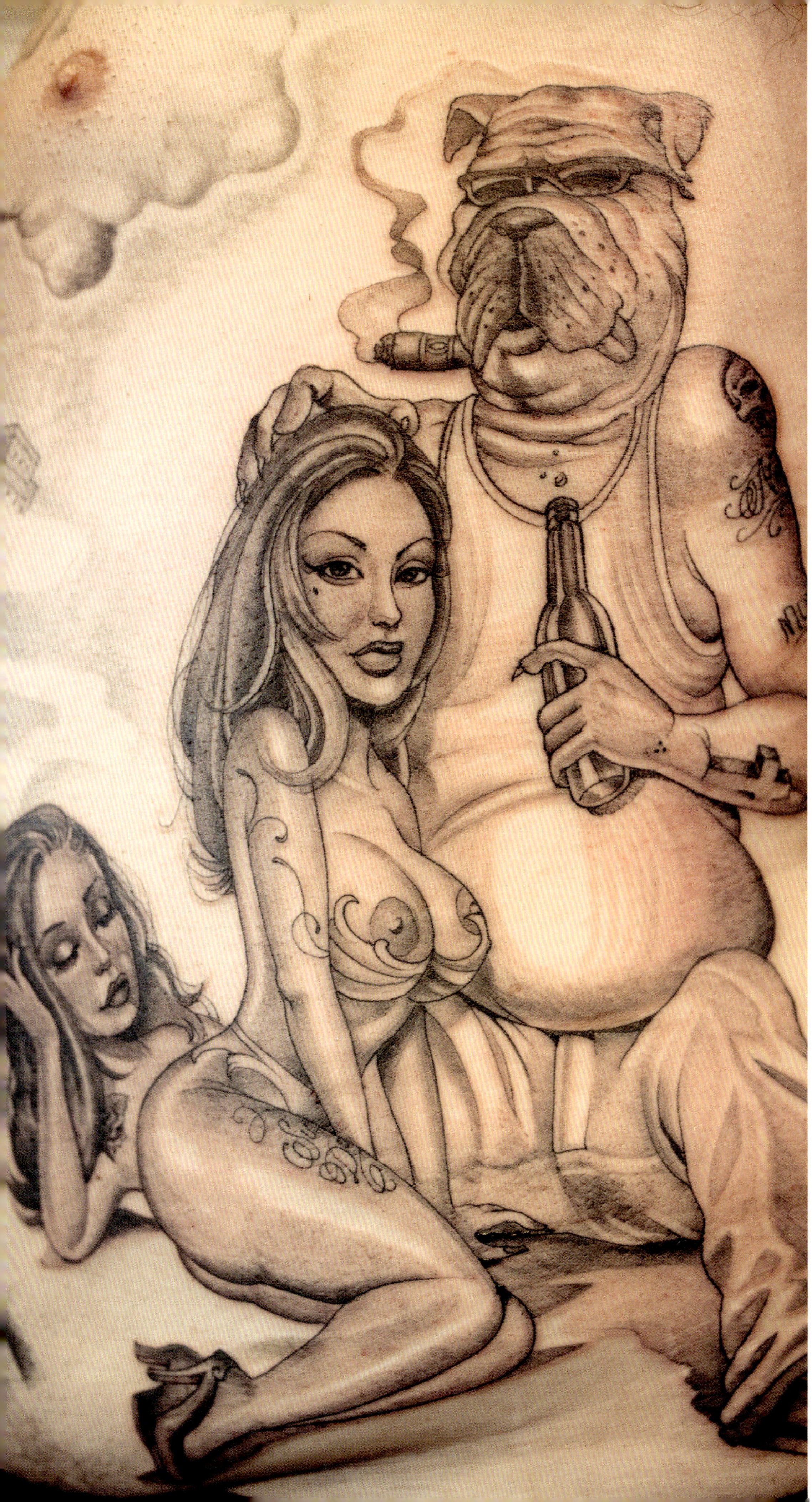

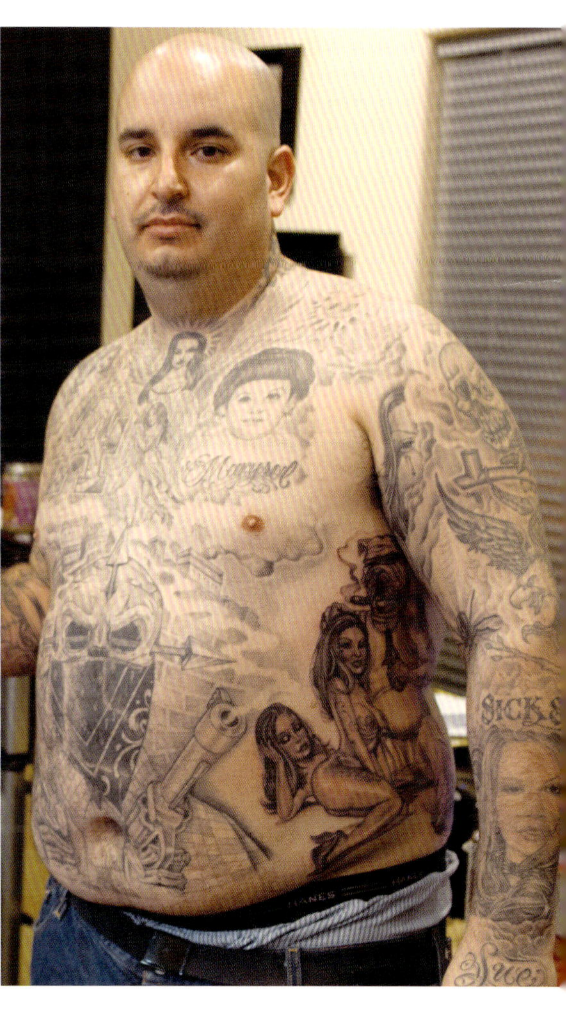

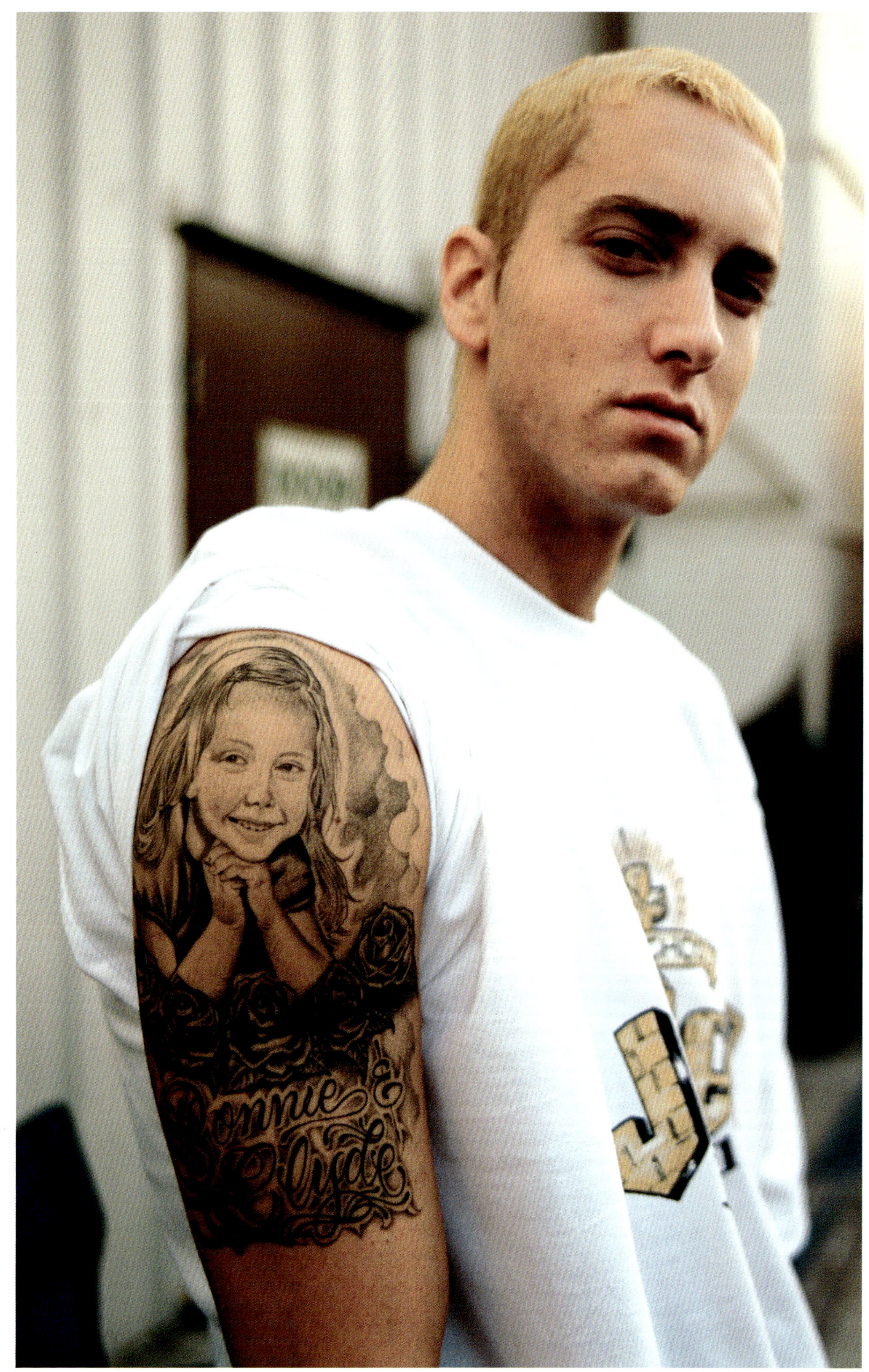

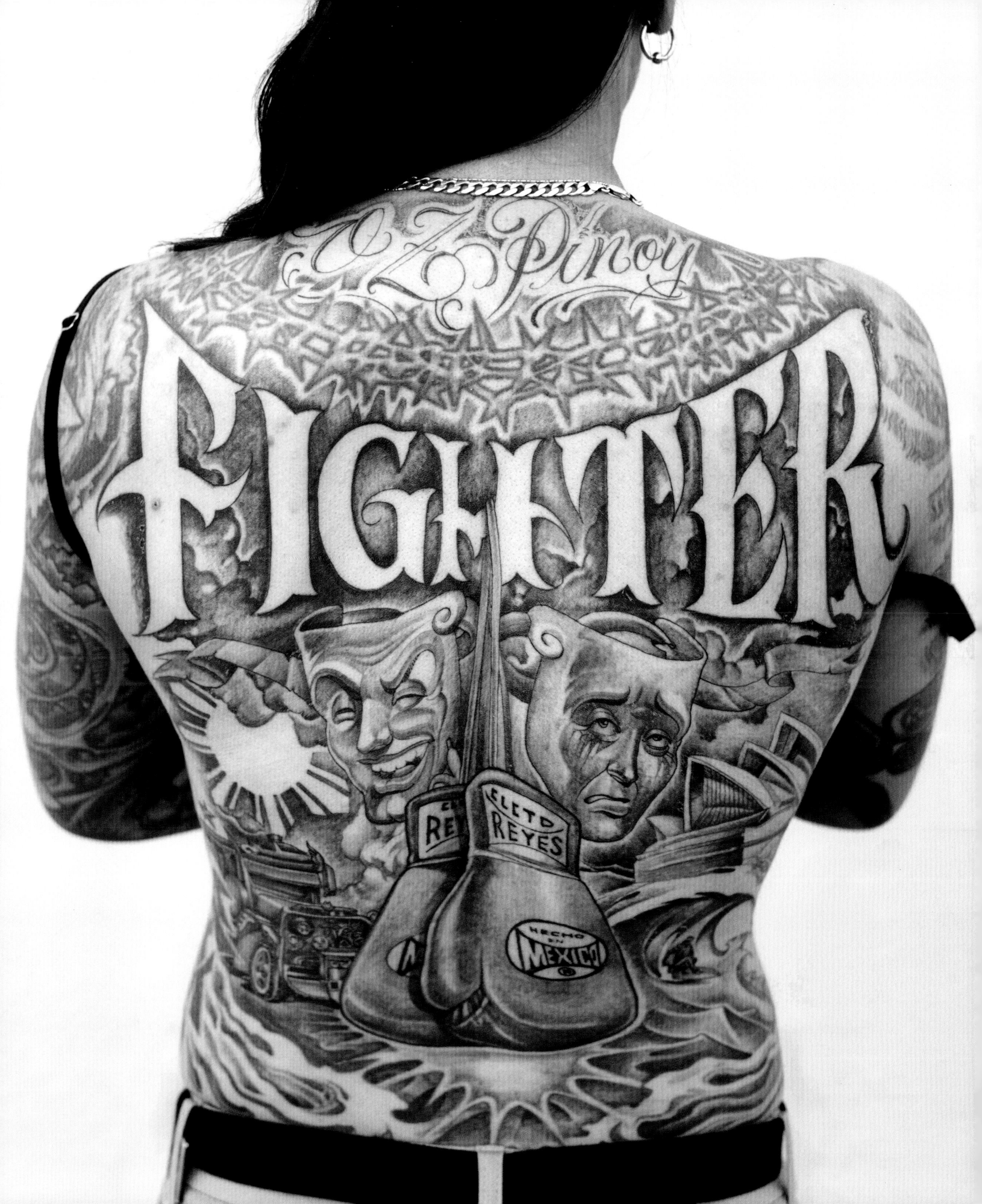
Pinoy
FIGHTER
CLETO
REYES
CLETO
REYES
HECHO
EN
MEXICO

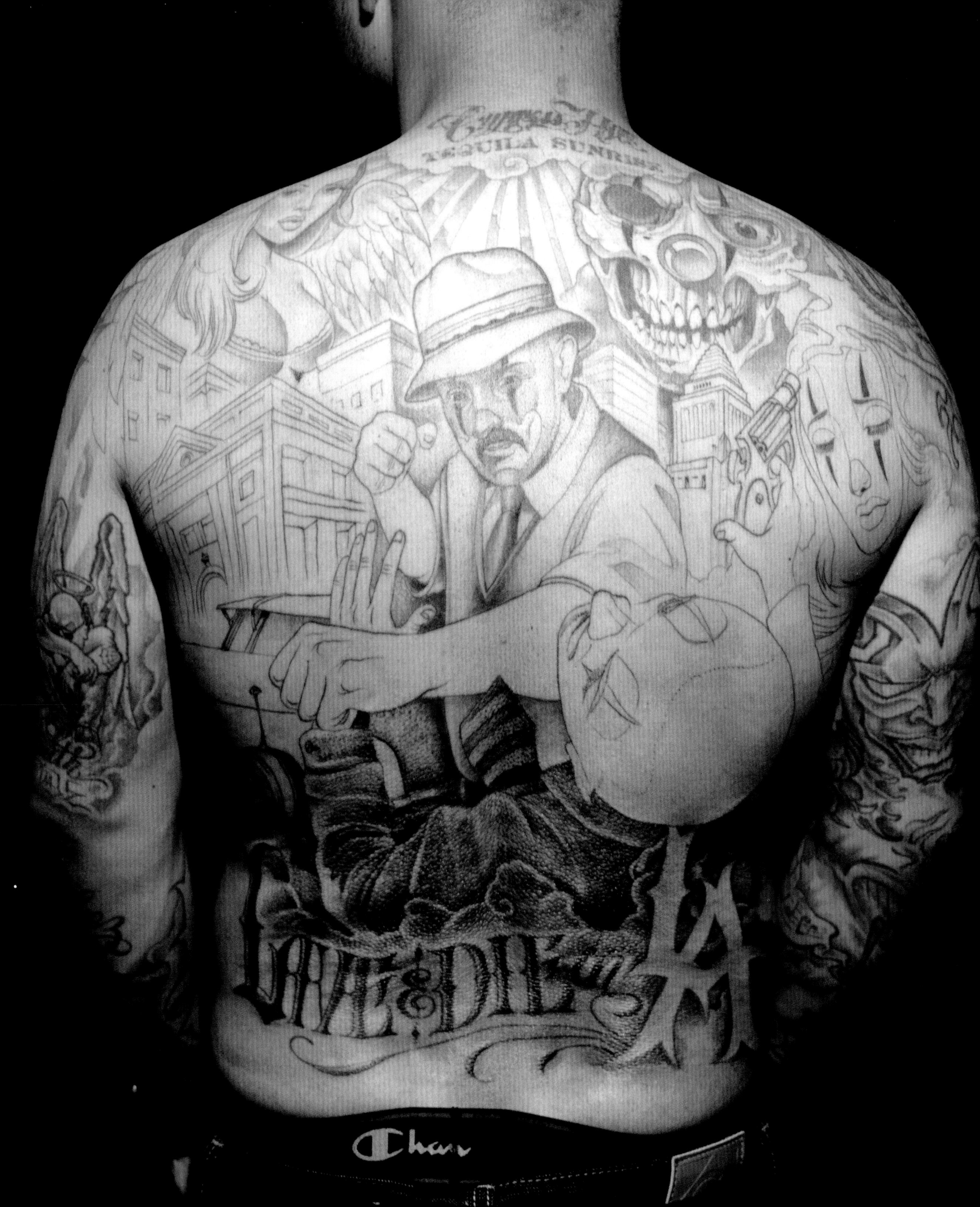

TEQUILA SUNRISE
LIVE & DIE IN LA

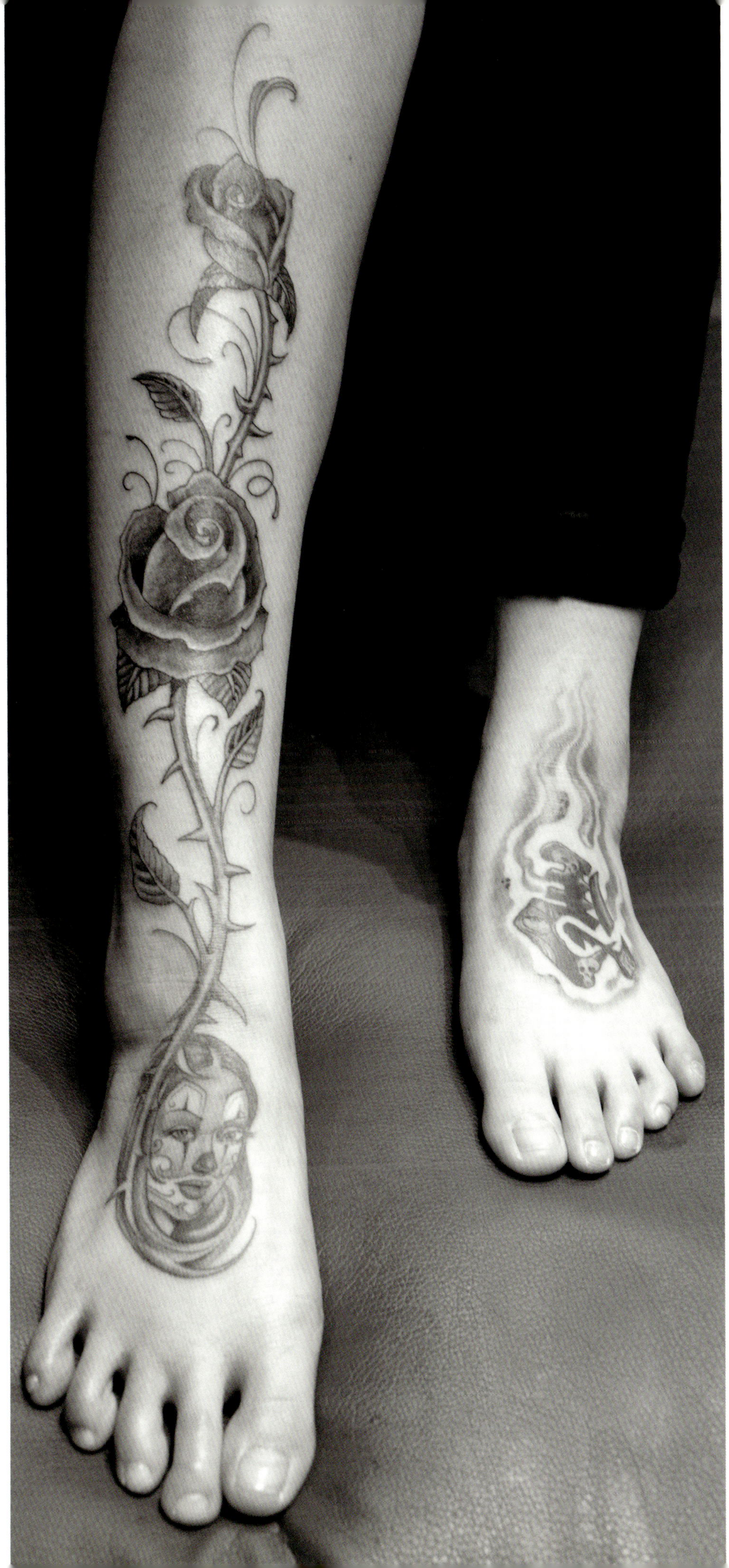

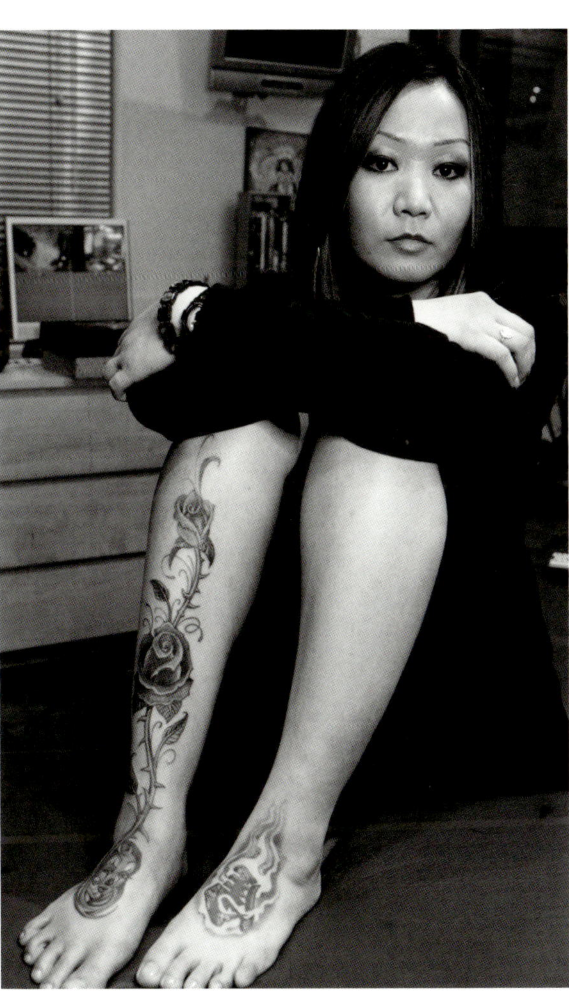

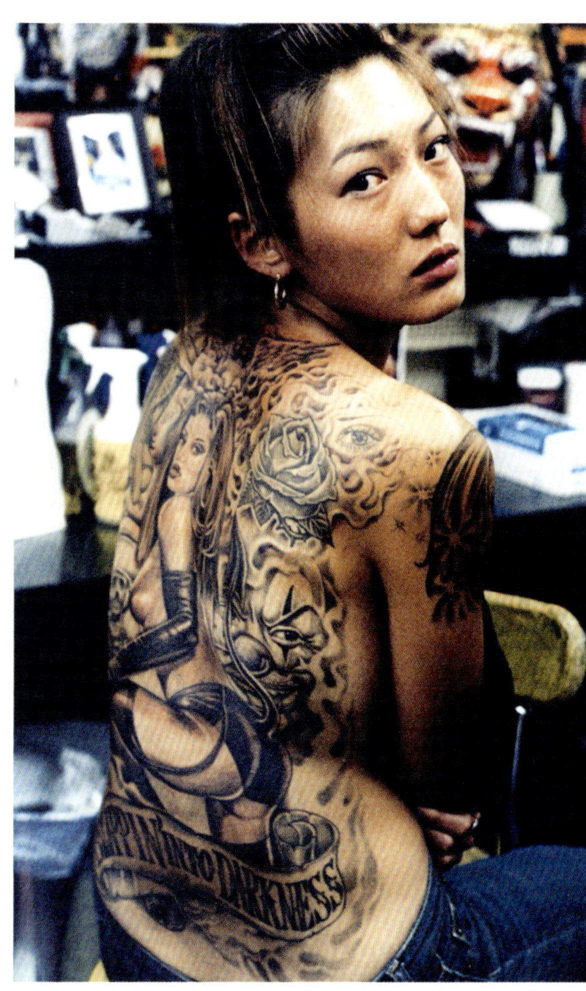

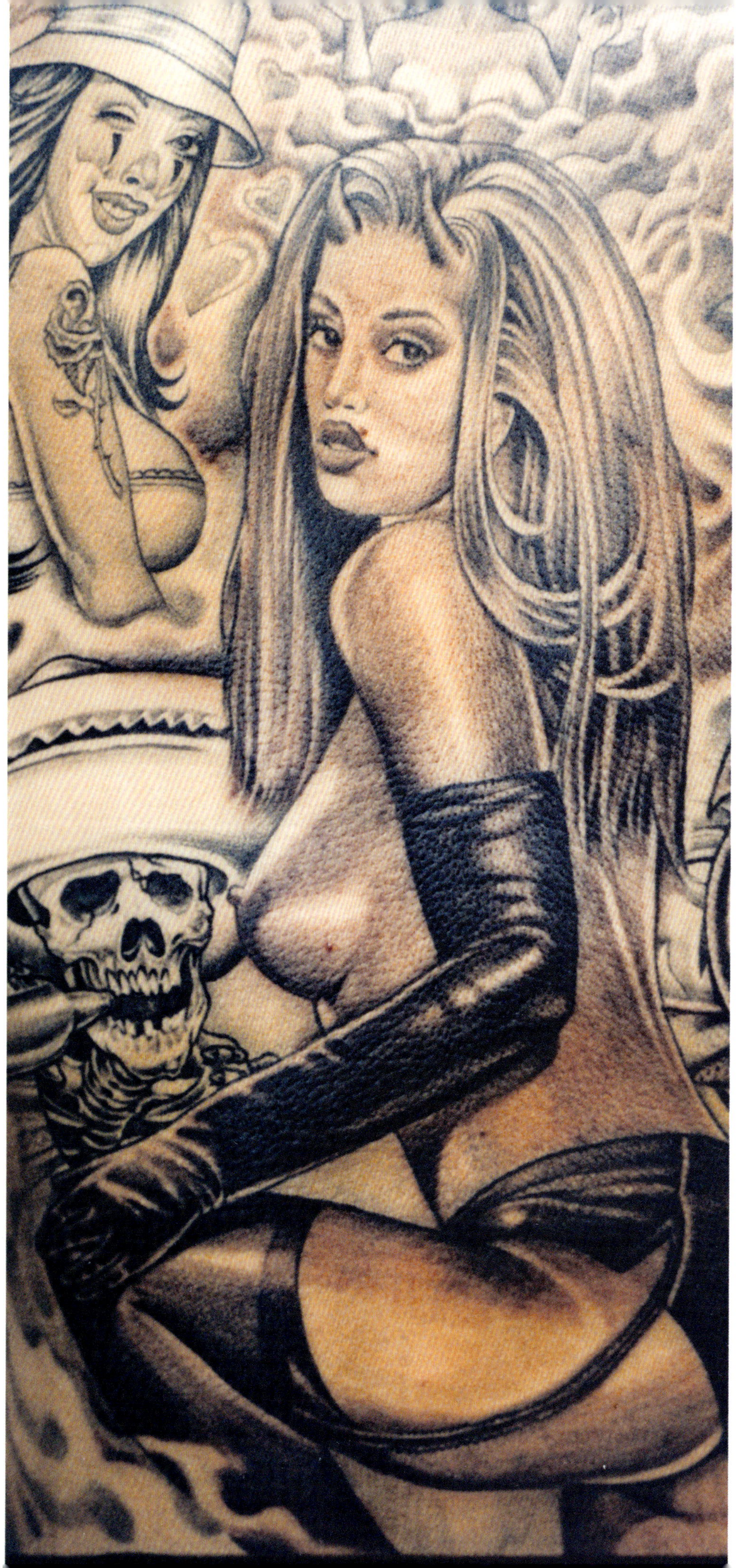

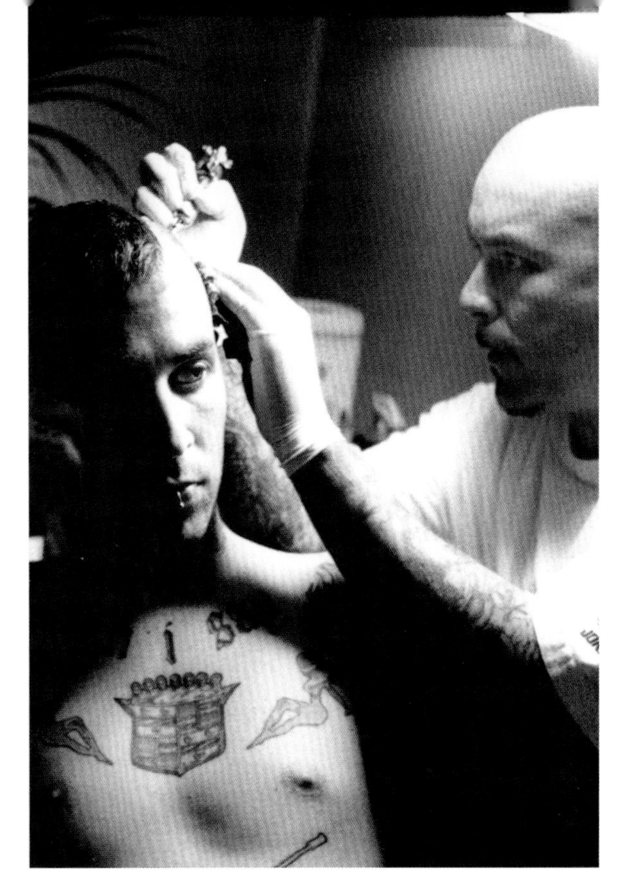

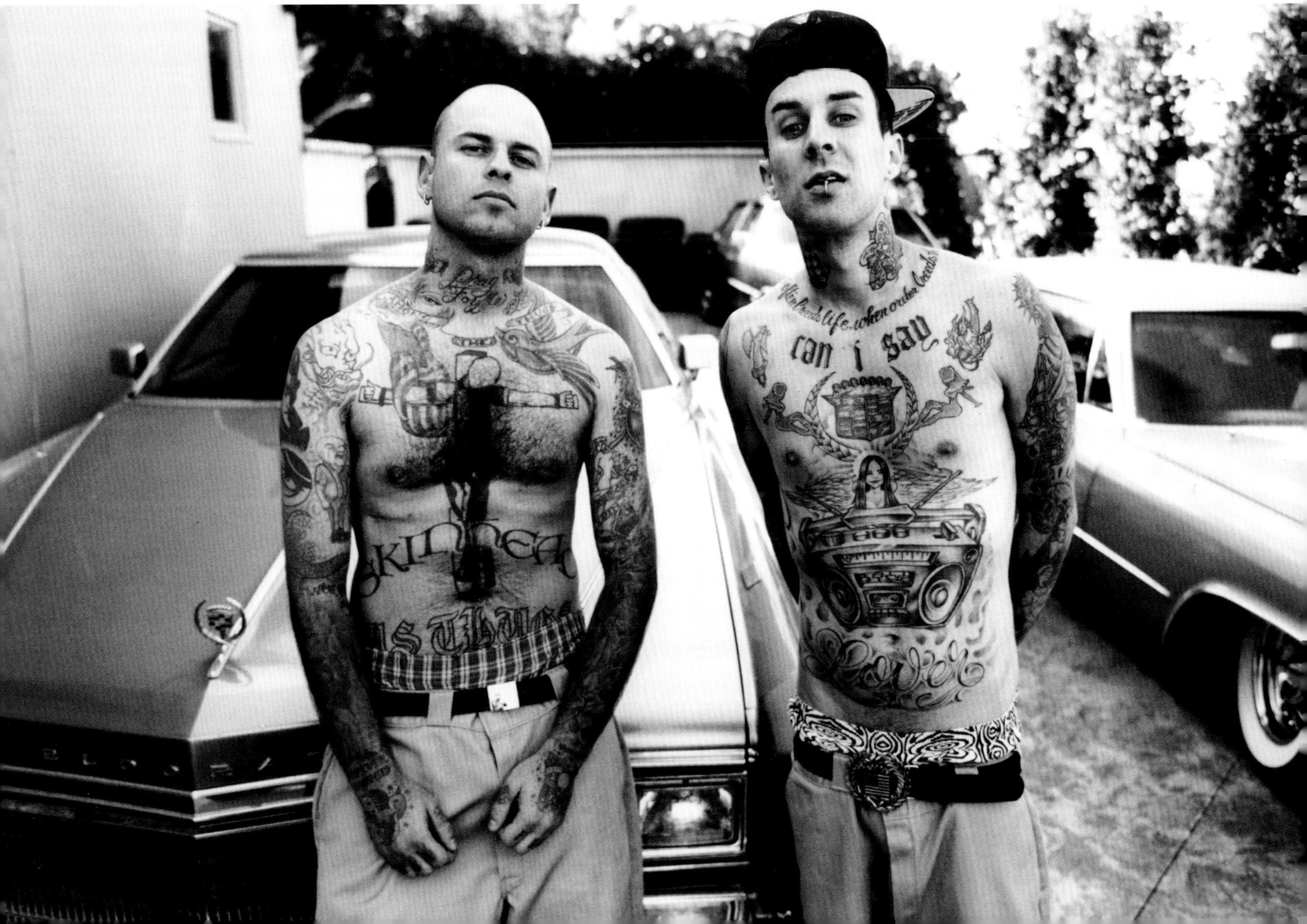

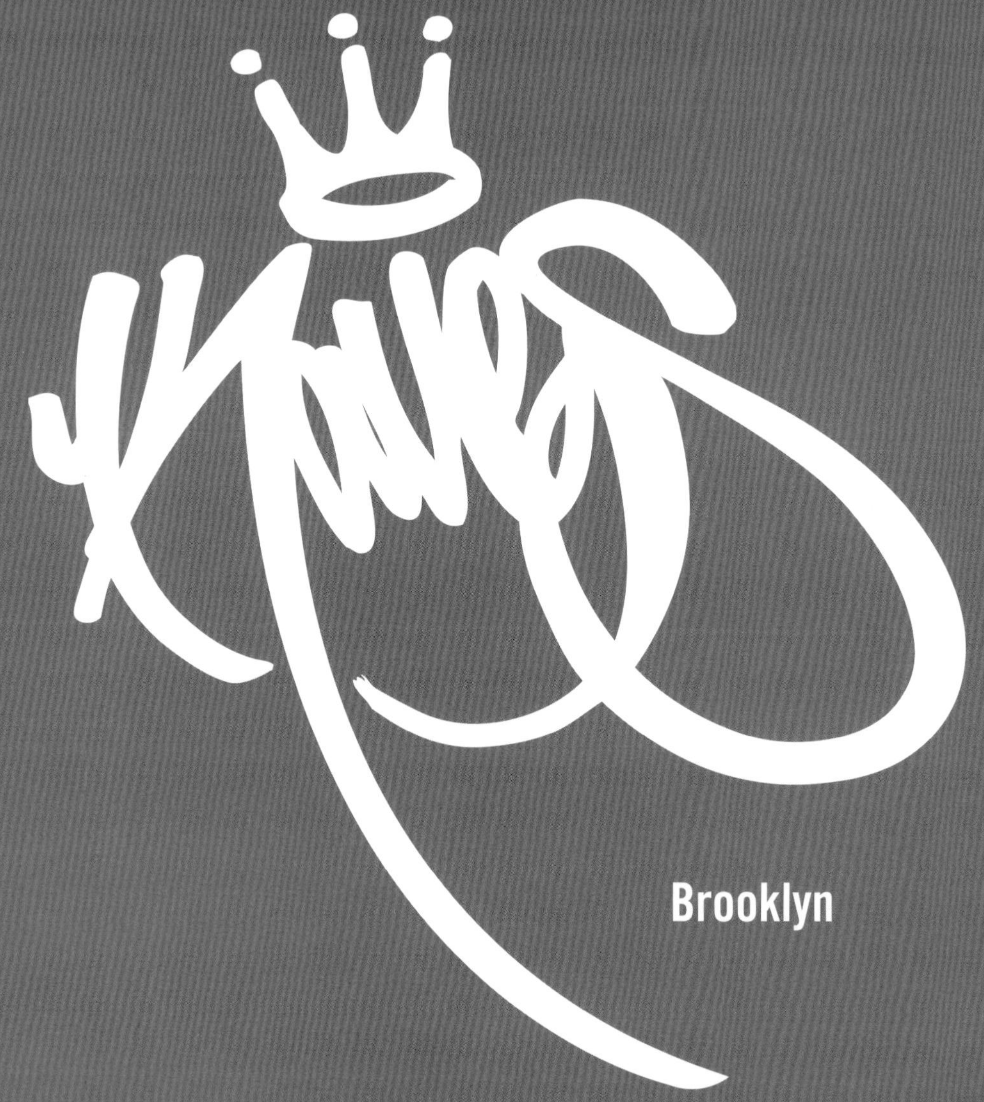

"It was one of those rare moments in my life where everything made sense. Just like when I first got a spray can in my hand. I saw it as a mark that I could make on the world, and make a name for myself doing it."

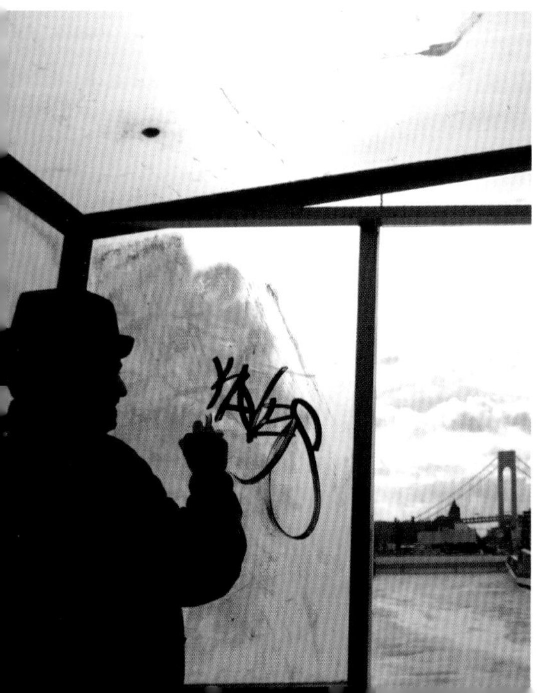

KAVES

Kaves is a Brooklyn original. A pioneer in his largely working-class Irish and Italian Bay Ridge neighborhood, he was break dancing and rapping and writing on trains before such an elaborate cultural cocktail was deemed acceptable in those parts. His rap/rock band, Lordz of Brooklyn, has toured the globe, and his experiences on the road opened up for him a world of tattoos that went beyond the traditional sailor-style work he'd known from the old neighborhood. His writer's hand would add something new to a classic formula. He currently owns, operates, and is the main tattooist at Brooklyn Made Tattoo, in the very same neighborhood where he made his bones. The shop is a vivid reflection of Kaves's old soul and is dripping with authentic Brooklyn nostalgia for his international, as well as 'round the way, clientele.

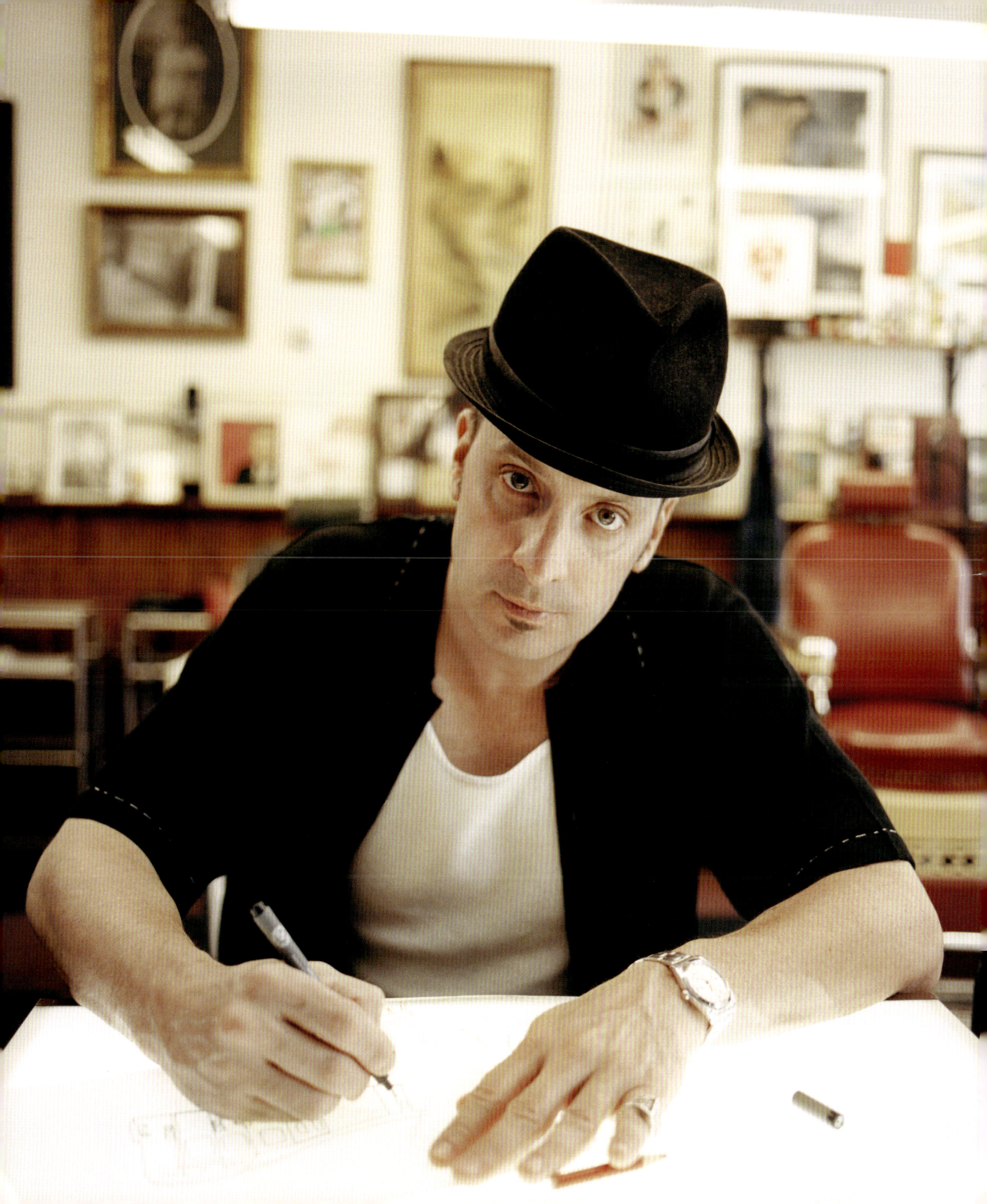

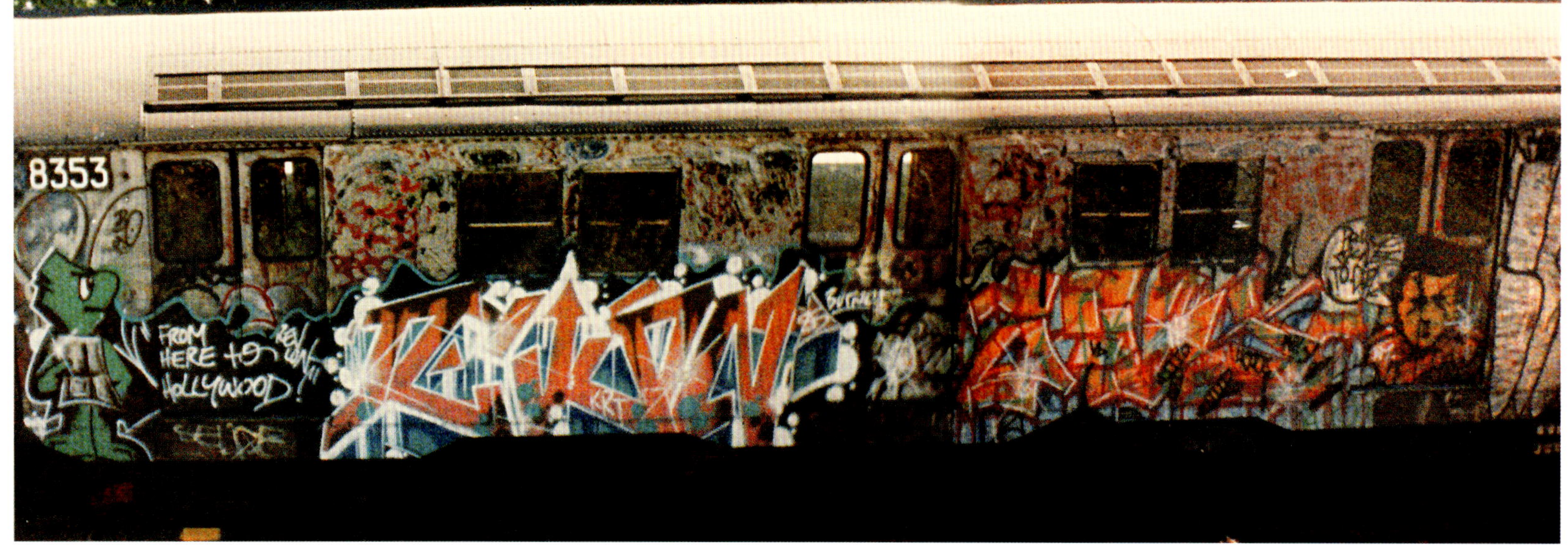

Kaves, Revs train car, New York City, 1985

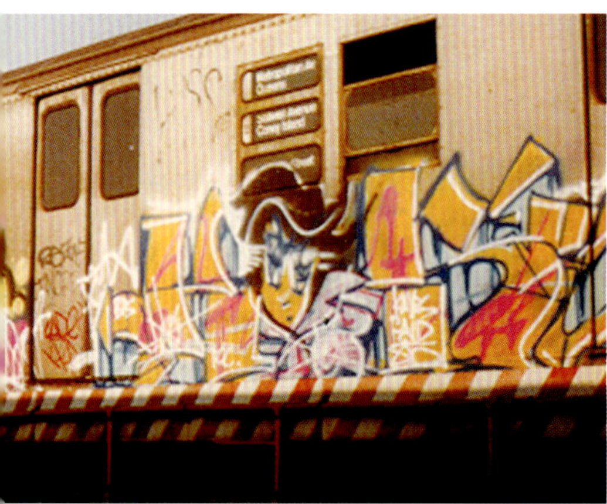

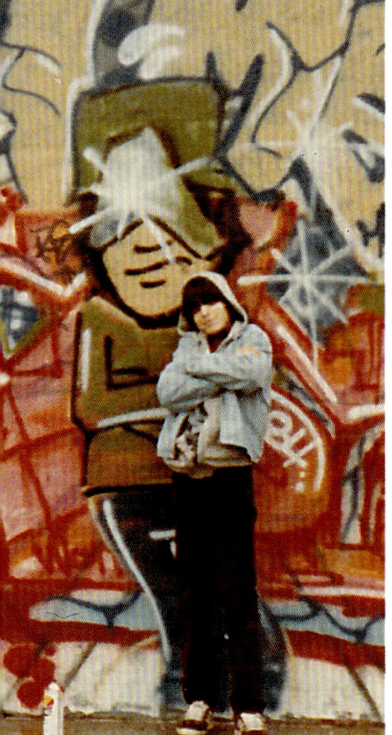

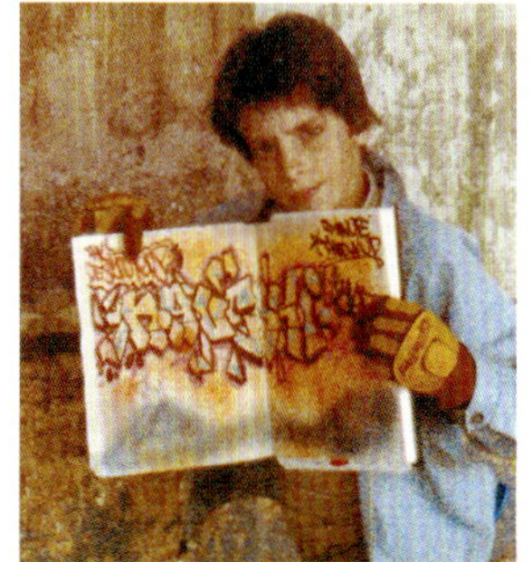

TOP: Kaves train car, New York City, 1985 **BOTTOM:** Kaves with his piecebook, 1983 **LEFT:** Kaves in front of his paddleball-court piece, Brooklyn, 1984

I started writing graffiti in late 1979. I was ten years old and I was going through a turbulent time in life. My parents had recently divorced, and my mother moved us to a block in Brooklyn where life was sort of a blank slate. I had to figure out how to fit in all over again.

The normal stuff a ten-year-old would be interested in, like baseball and sports or whatever, just wasn't cutting it for me. I was angry and I was looking for something to give me a voice and to call my own. Also, I was very talented artistically, but there was no after-school program for a young artist in my neighborhood. As luck would have it, there were a handful of writers who also lived on my block. Kids in school talked about markers and tagging, but on my block I found the secret society, and I knew I could be good.

An older writer in the neighborhood named RR saw me writing on the block and took an interest in me. He was that guy in the neighborhood, a rough dude, the Rocky Balboa type, and he took me under his wing. He handed me down the name of his brother, as his brother had just retired from writing. He showed me the rules and introduced me to the game. That's where it all started. You have to remember, this is when the city was a different place than it is today. It was a very dangerous playground, but it was ours and no one could take that away from us.

The graffiti scene had been in motion since the seventies, but it was a bit more peaceful then, as guys were coming off the hippie movement and fucking with LSD and marijuana. By the time the eighties came around, New York was in a toilet bowl; the city got dirtier and people got meaner, real grimy and slimy. Drugs were plaguing the city, and it started becoming even more of a jungle than it already was.

There was also a big crackdown on the heavier gangs of the seventies, and many graffiti crews picked up where they left off. Kids cliqued up

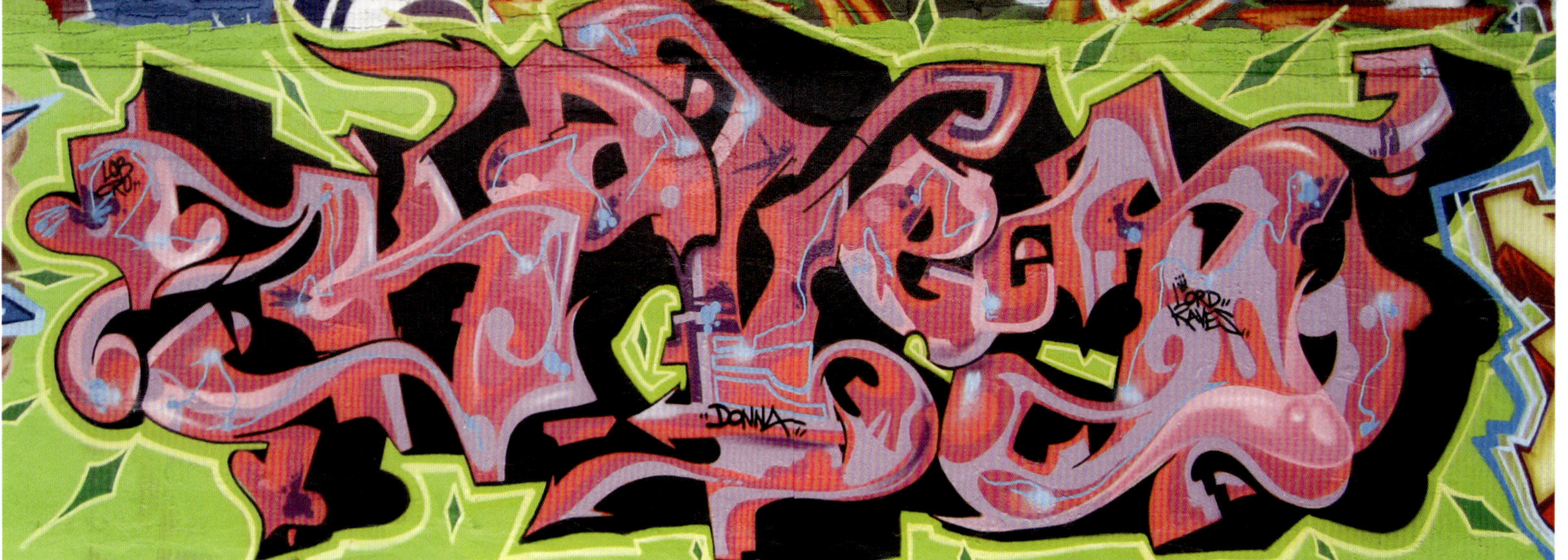

Kaves piece, Hunts Point, Bronx, 2011

and it became a very violent time. Some kids were out there to bomb and get up, some kids wanted to do pieces and be creative, and other kids wanted to just fuck shit up or fuck you up. It was survival of the fittest. You needed to roll with a deep crew and be ready to hold your own or you weren't gonna last very long.

I noticed tattoos at a young age because of the older kids in my neighborhood. These kids were very colorful and charismatic; you looked up to them. And as soon as you were thirteen years old or whatever, you wanted in. Also, the local street celebrity in the neighborhood was the tattooist; there were no rock stars around. Michelangelo was that guy in my neighborhood.

My father would pick up my brother and me on the weekends and he would ask us what we wanted to do. I would say I wanted to go to the Bronx or Harlem to check out graffiti. Even though he thought I was crazy, he would take us up there, and along the way he would tell us his war stories. He was part of the Pig Town crew in Flatbush, and he had a tattoo done by Tony Polito when he was a kid. I remember that I would always ask him about this dot on his hand, and he would tell me it was where they tested out the ink before he got the tattoo. I never questioned it, but years later, hearing him and his friends talk, I learned that when you got inducted into the Pig Town gang, you went to Tony Polito and got your tattoo and a mark on the hand, which showed you were down.

As a kid, I always romanticized gang culture, and the graffiti crew I started in my neighborhood was modeled after my father's gang. For him it was hair grease and hot rods, and for the Verrazano Boyz and, later, the Lordz of Brooklyn [LOB], it was spray cans and subway cars. But our whole vibe and the way we carried ourselves, well, that was all from those stories of my father.

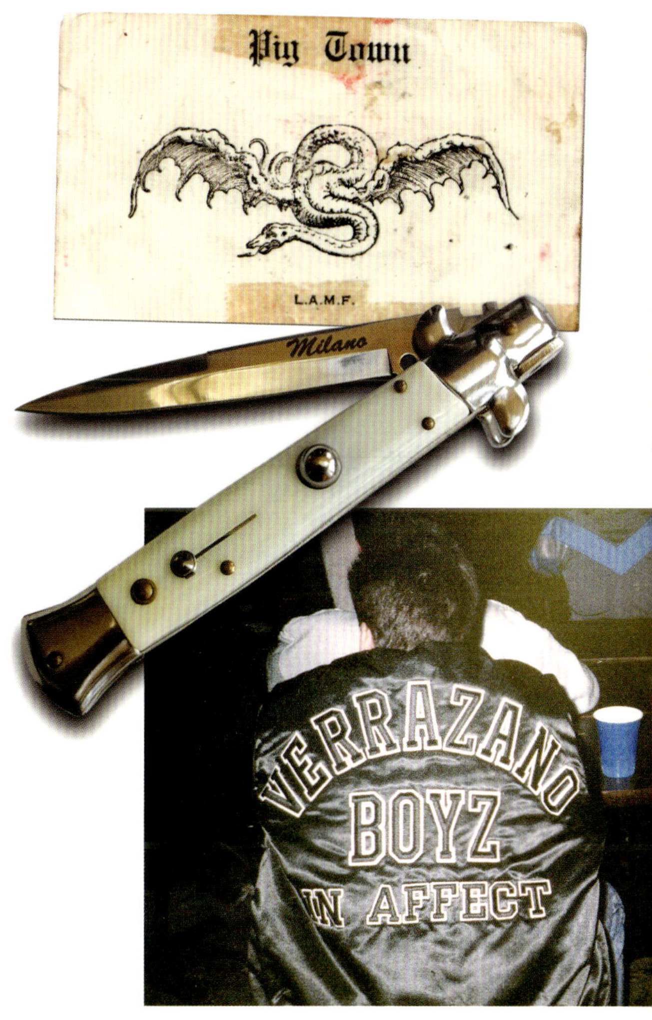

TOP: Kaves's father's Pig Town gang card and switchblade
BOTTOM: Verrazano Boyz jacket, 1987

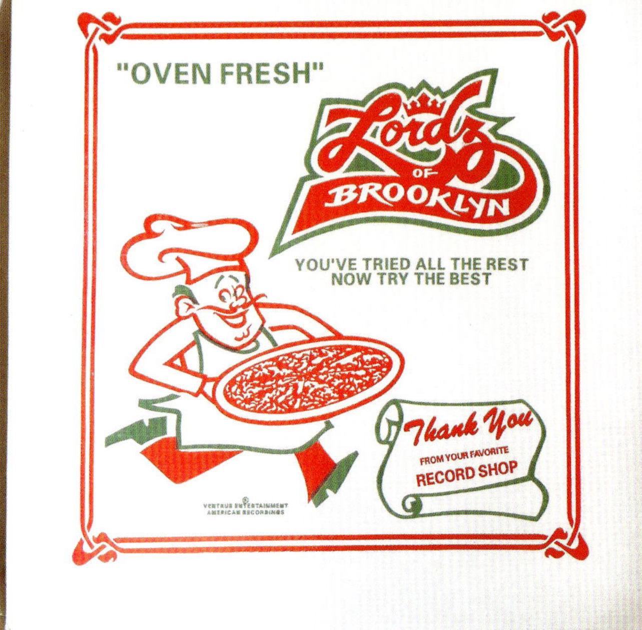

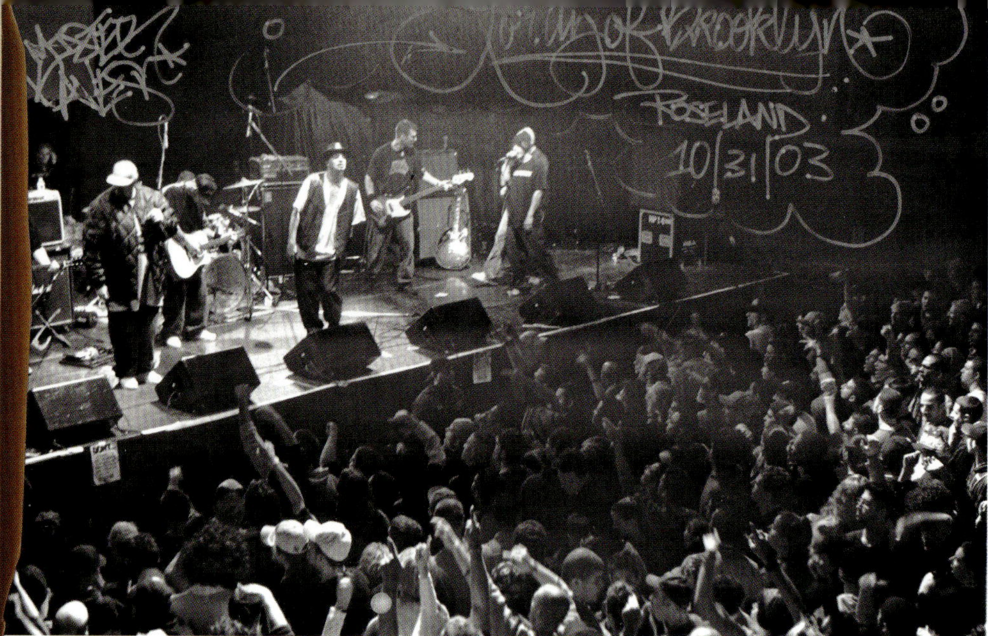

FROM LEFT: Promotional pizza box for Lordz of Brooklyn's 1995 album *All in the Family* (American Recordings); Lordz of Brooklyn performing at the Roseland Ballroom, New York City, 2003

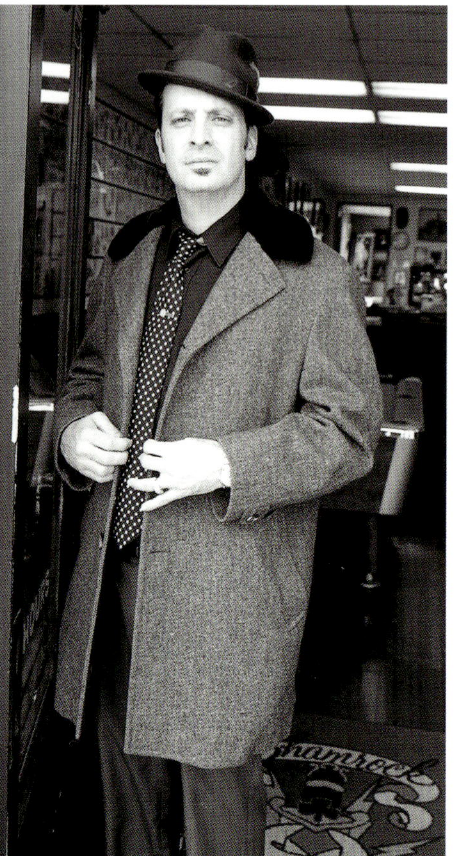

Kaves at Mark Mahoney's Shamrock Social Club, Sunset Boulevard, Los Angeles, 2012

I got my first tattoo a bit later in life than most. My mother and sister died, and it was the way I felt I could best express the heartache and pain that I was going through. It was a time for me to shed the old skin and reinvent the new; it was part of the therapy that I needed. I went to Chris Garver. The next tattoo I got, I committed to my band and my crew. I got *Lordz of Brooklyn* on my back, since that's what I broke my back for my whole life.

After making a name in the graffiti world and then having some success in the music business, I was in the neighborhood and looking for what I was going to do next. Then one day Danny Boy, from the band House of Pain, was at my house and he had a tattoo machine someone gave him, and I'll never forget what he said. He said, "Take this. If anyone can build a house with it, it is you." Again, it was one of those rare moments in my life where everything made sense. Just like when I first got a spray can in my hand. I saw it as a mark that I could make on the world, and make a name for myself doing it.

At that time Seen and Med were two graffiti writers in the Bronx who were making big names for themselves in tattoo. Seen was a bit hard to get to, but when I told my friend Jest from ALife what I was looking to do, he connected me with Med, as I did not know Med personally at the time.

Med and I met and immediately connected, so we decided to open a tattoo shop in Brooklyn called Tuff City Brooklyn Ink. He already had a Tuff City in the Bronx. The first tattoo I did, I stuck with what I knew. I didn't do a Japanese dragon, I did a graffiti piece. It reminded me a lot of the trains: they were moving, and the materials were crude, and you had to take those elements and turn them into something beautiful.

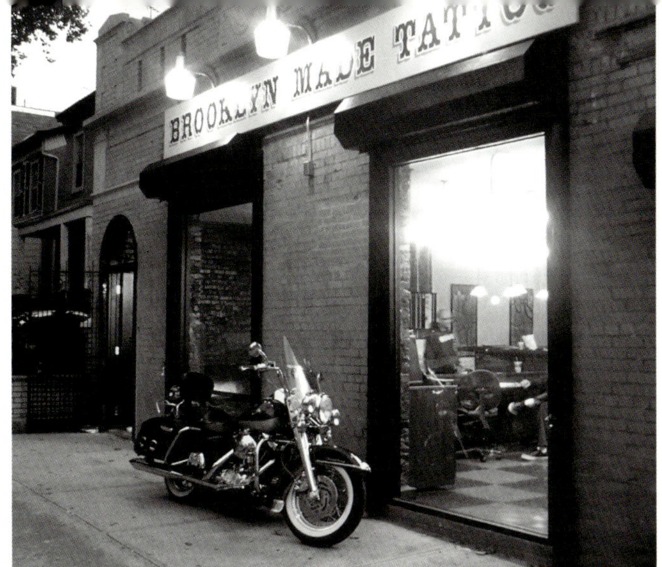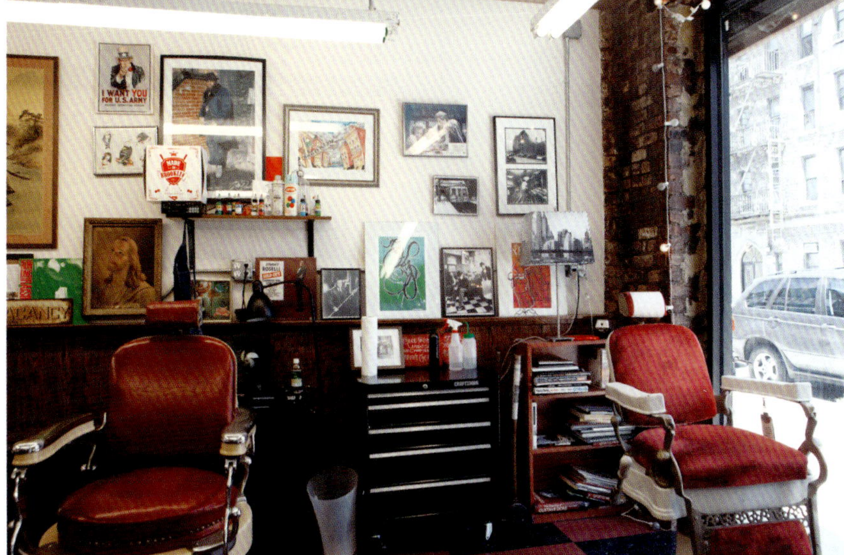

I knew it was something that I wouldn't master overnight and, like graffiti, it took me thirty years to get to where I am. I've been tattooing for twelve years, and I'm still learning every day.

As an artist, that learning never stops. I have been blessed to have Baba help me out early on, and in the last few years I have been blessed to have the noted tattoo artists Mark Mahoney and Freddy Negrete take me to the side and drop some wisdom on me.

The other person was Mister Cartoon. I got close with Estevan during the Soul Assassins and Lordz of Brooklyn tour. We built a strong friendship, and Cartoon was down with the Soul Assassins and I was around him a lot. I was very influenced by the way he captured the neighborhood and told these street stories in his work. This was around the beginning of when he first started tattooing, and some of the guys from LOB were the first people he tattooed. Watching him do those LA landscapes, I was like, I've been doing those of Brooklyn in my piecebook for years. I saw a way to make it my own. Cartoon was a big inspiration early on.

In my opinion, skin is the hardest canvas to work on. It's a living, breathing thing, and you never know who is going to sit in the chair and where they are going to tell you they want you to tattoo them. Down the neck, the armpit, you never know what to expect. The palm of the hand, the inside of a lip, or whatever—it is always changing. At least with the walls and trains, you always knew what to expect. Tattooing is very physical graffiti because you're stretching and pulling and working the skin. It definitely can be challenging, and it is a unique experience every single time.

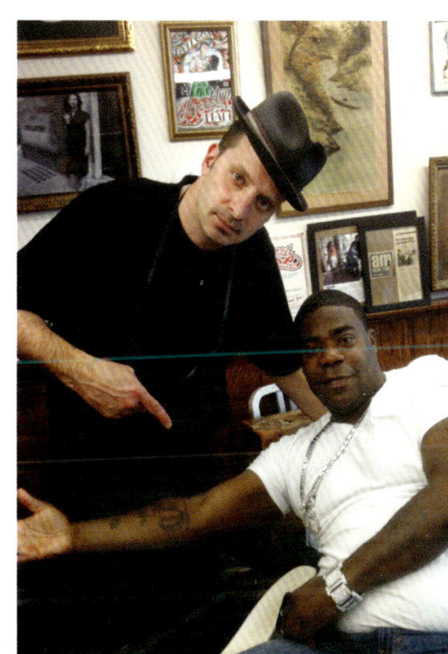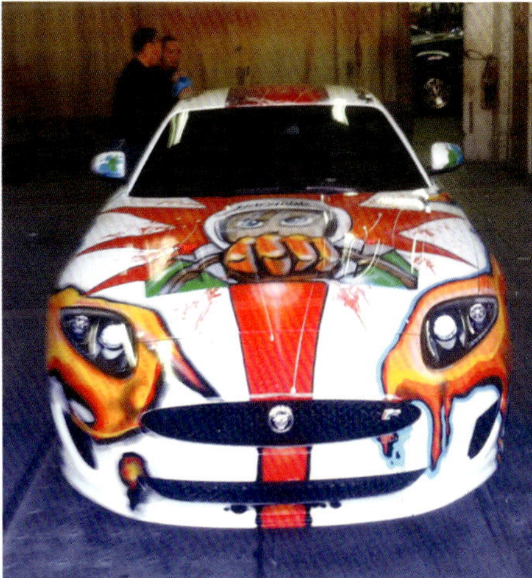

TOP: Kaves (left) and Tracy Morgan at Brooklyn Made Tattoo, 2012 BOTTOM: Jaguar painted by Kaves, 2012

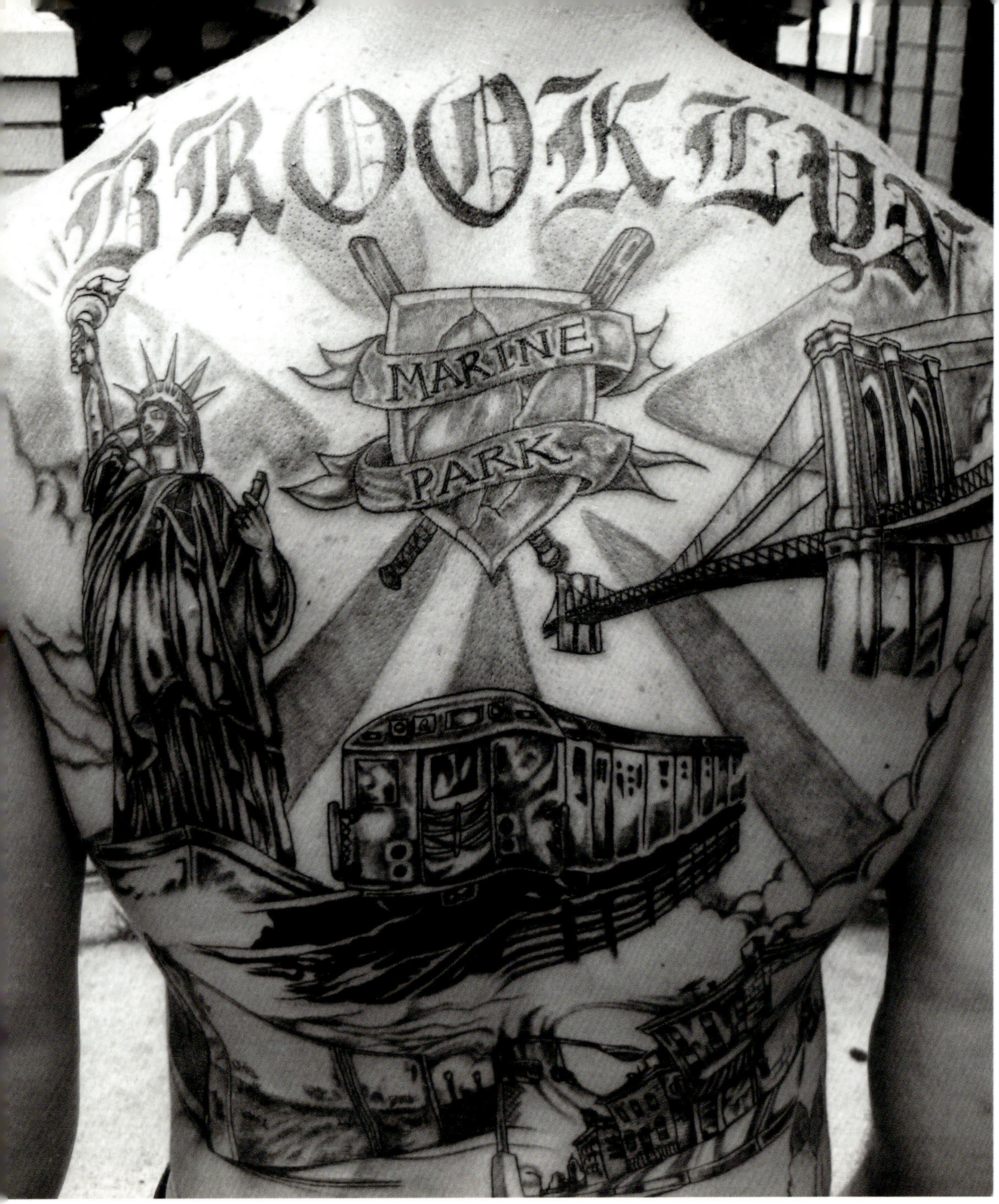

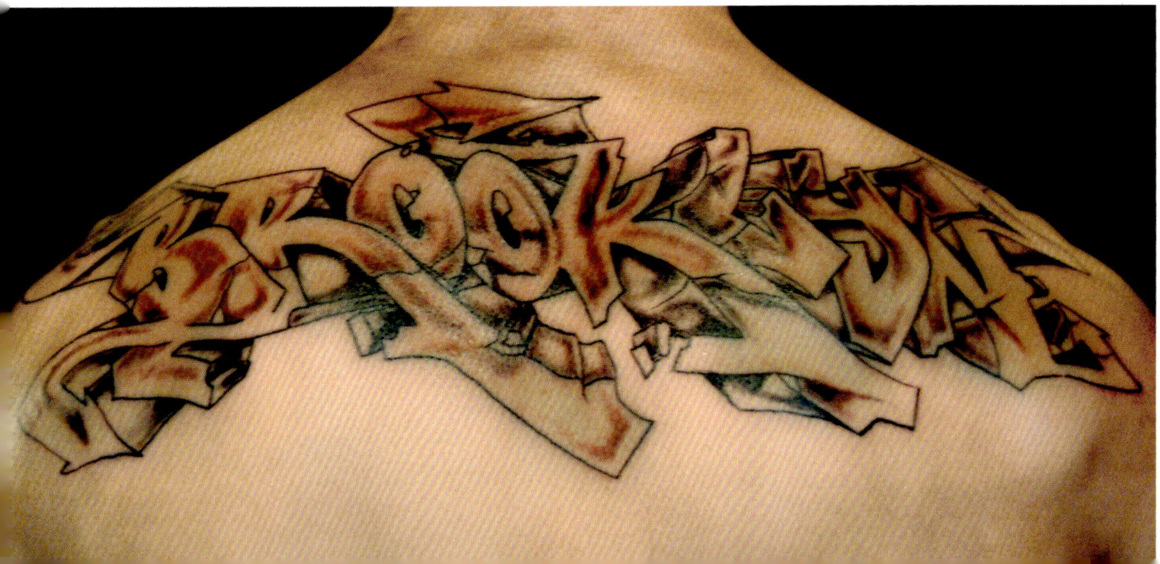

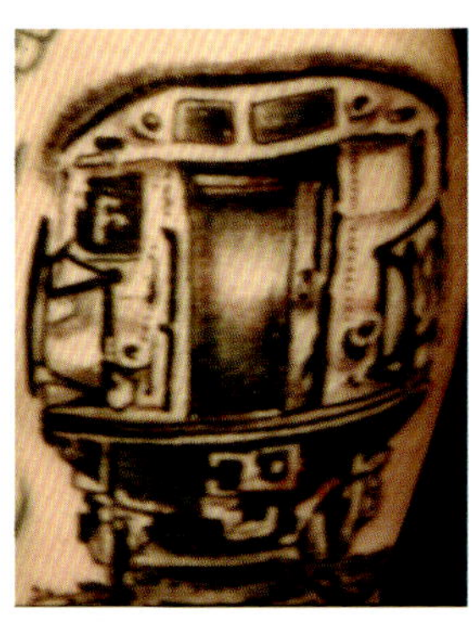

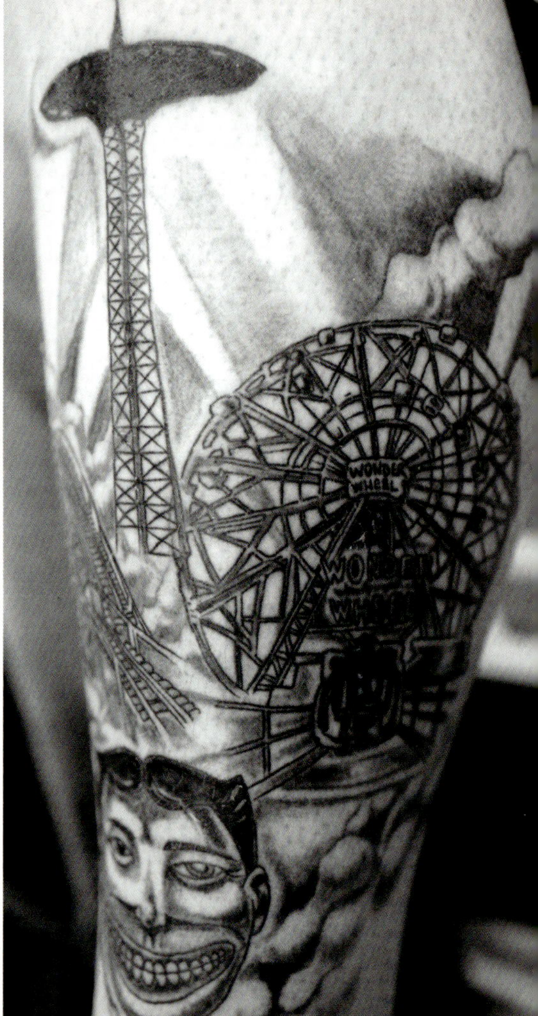

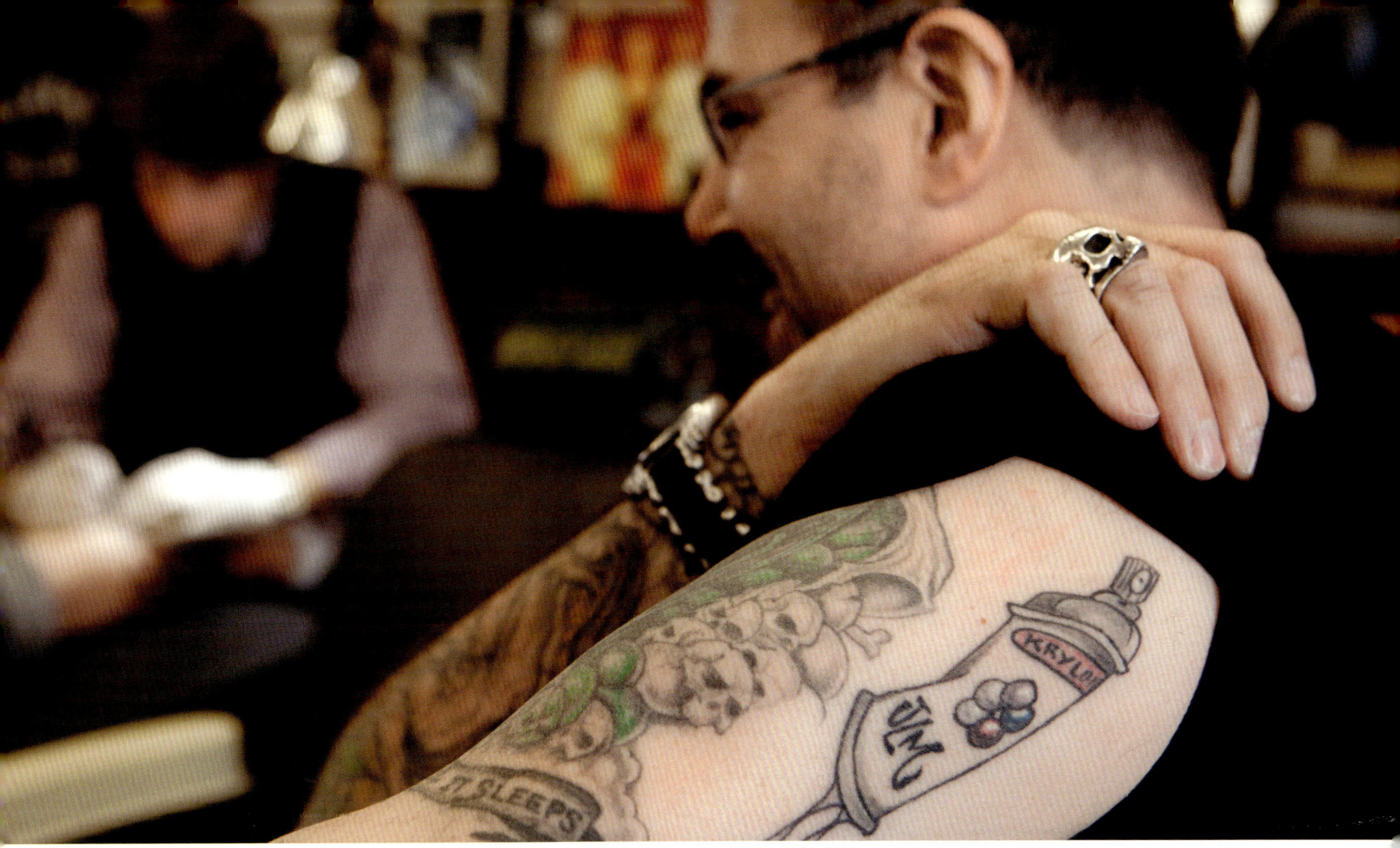

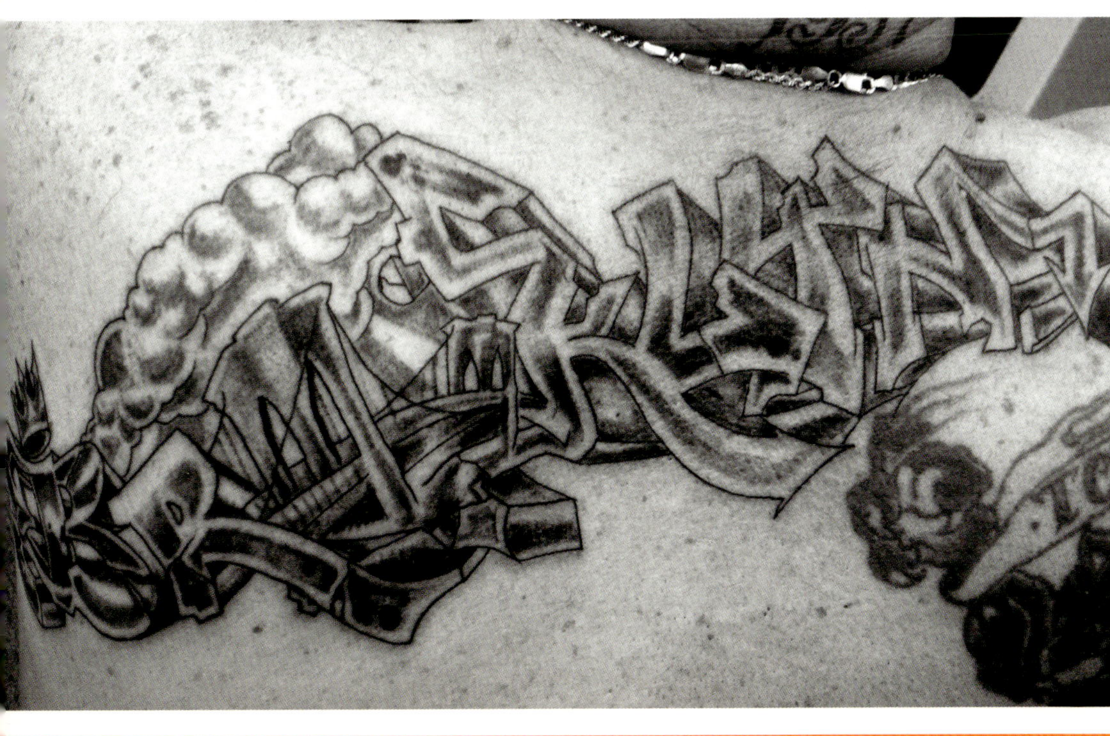
KRYLON
JMC
T SLEEPS

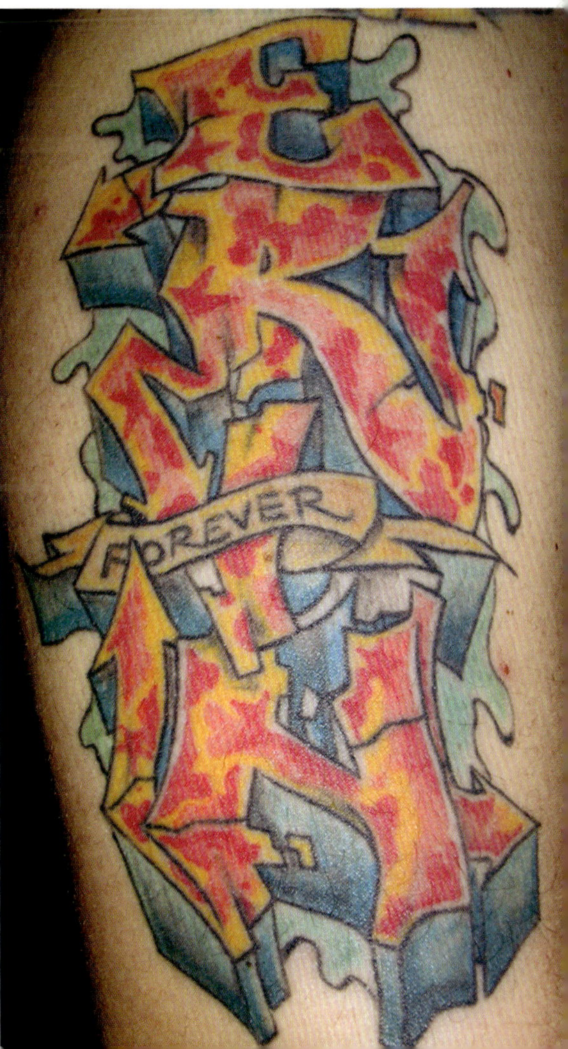
FOREVER

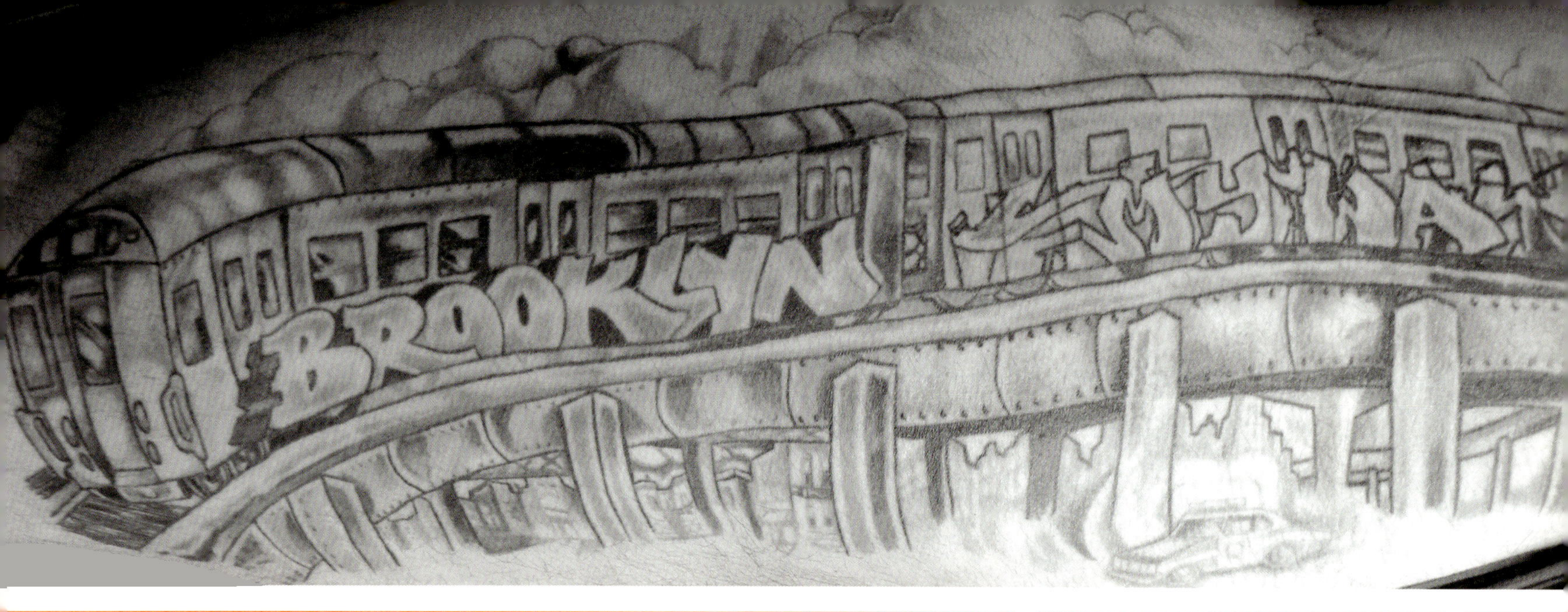
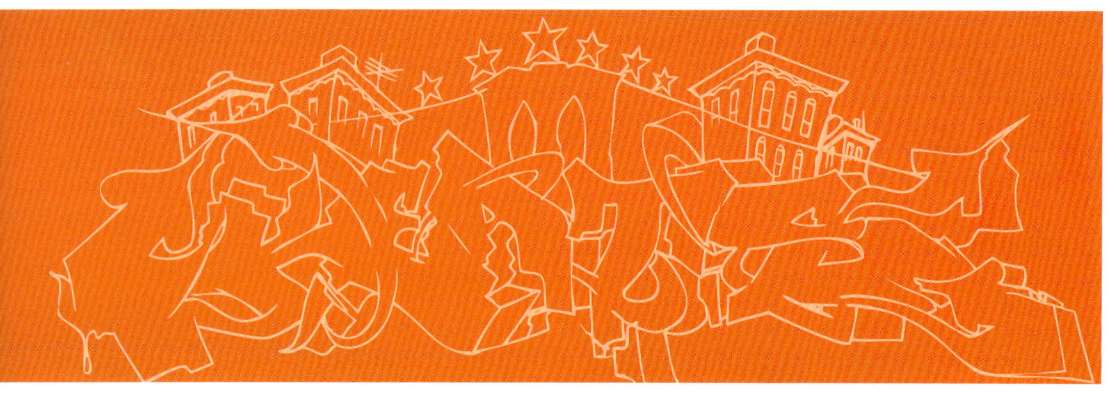
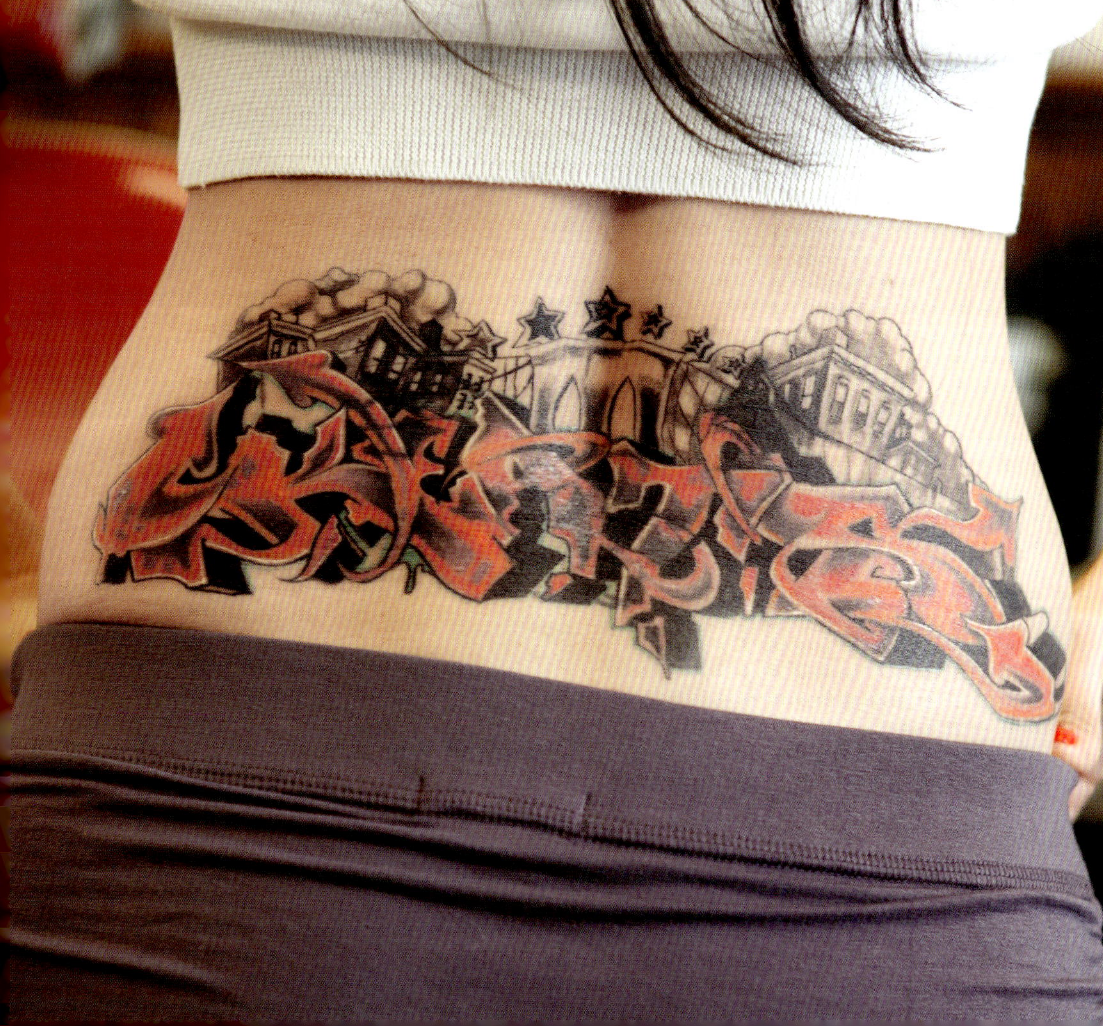
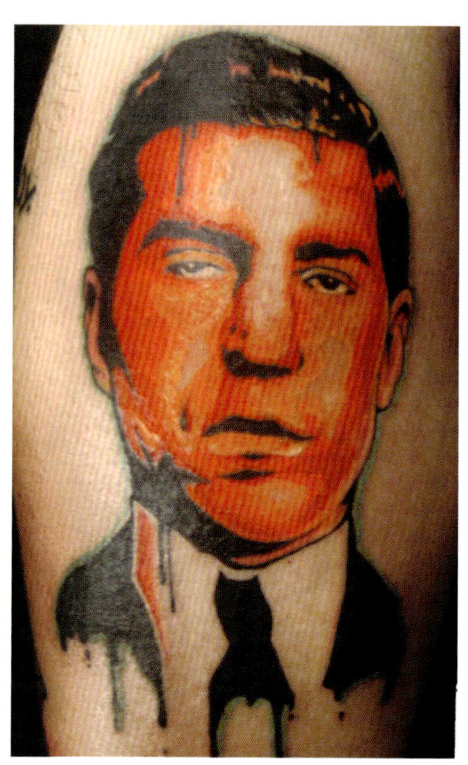
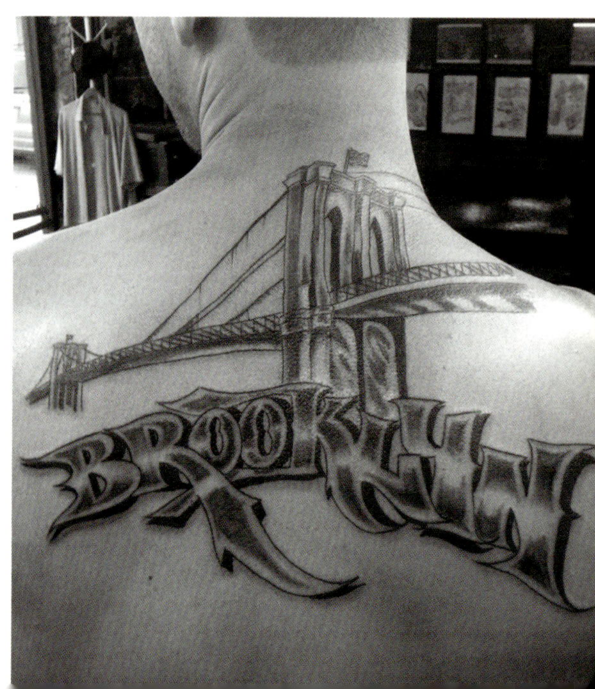

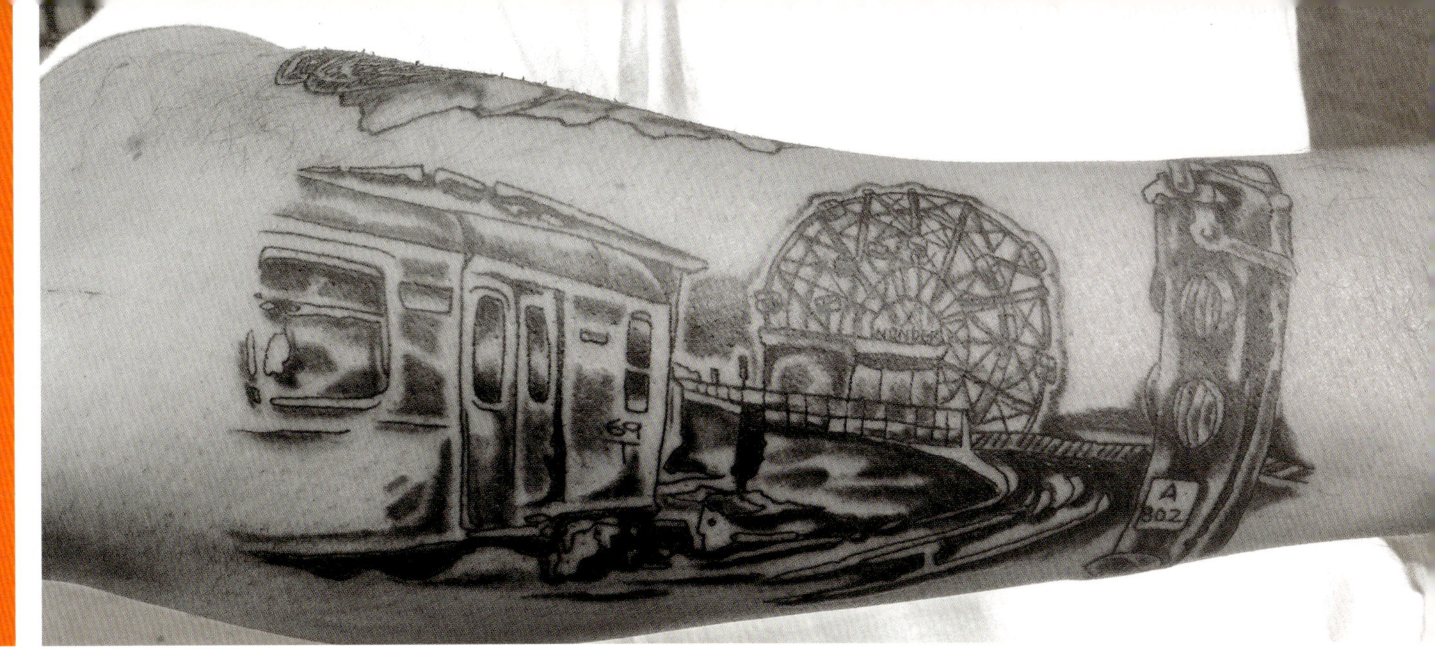

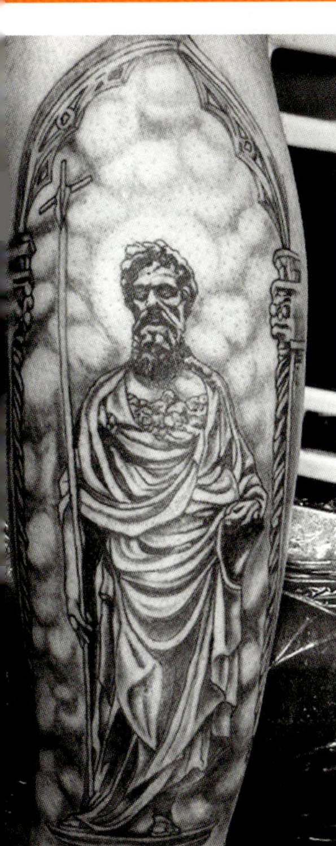

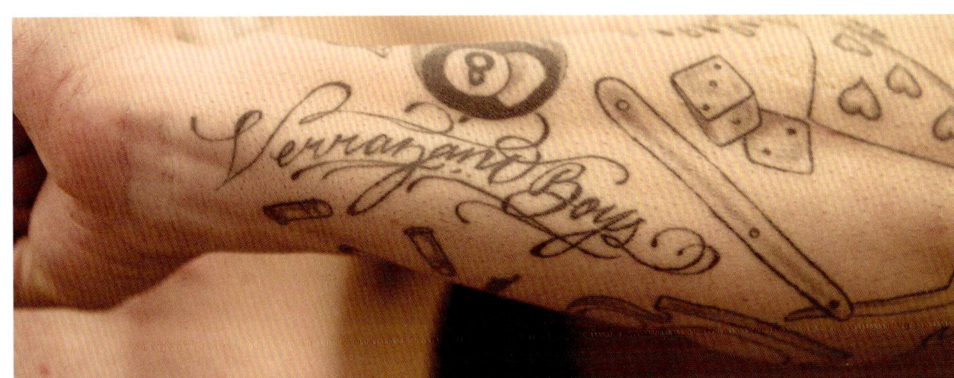
Verrazano Boys

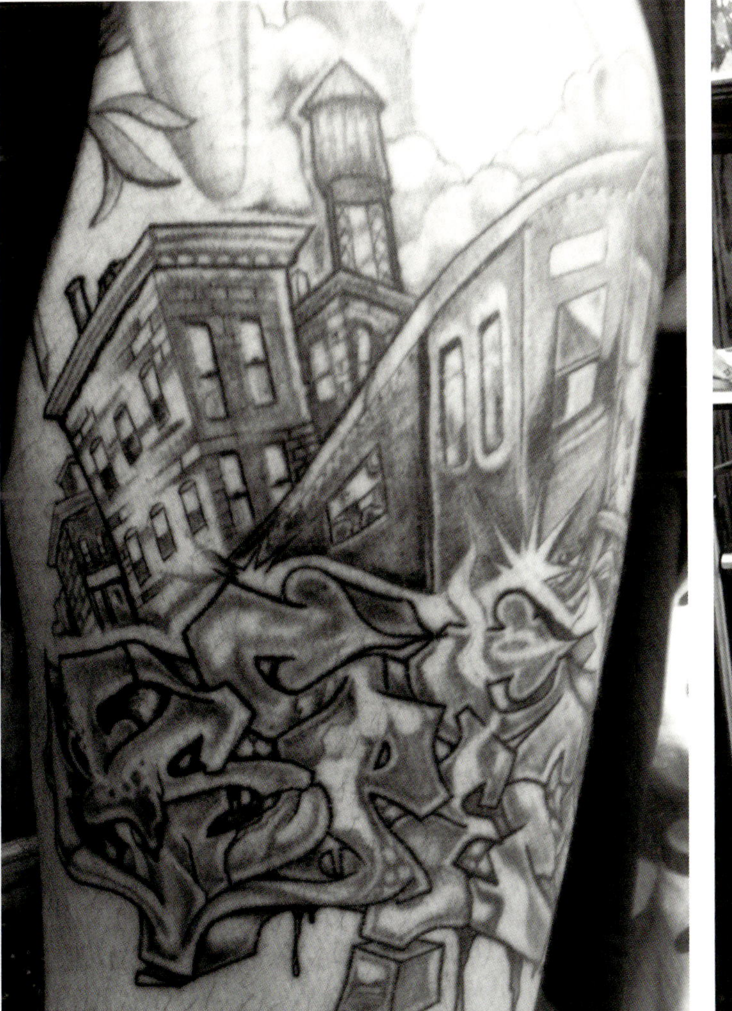

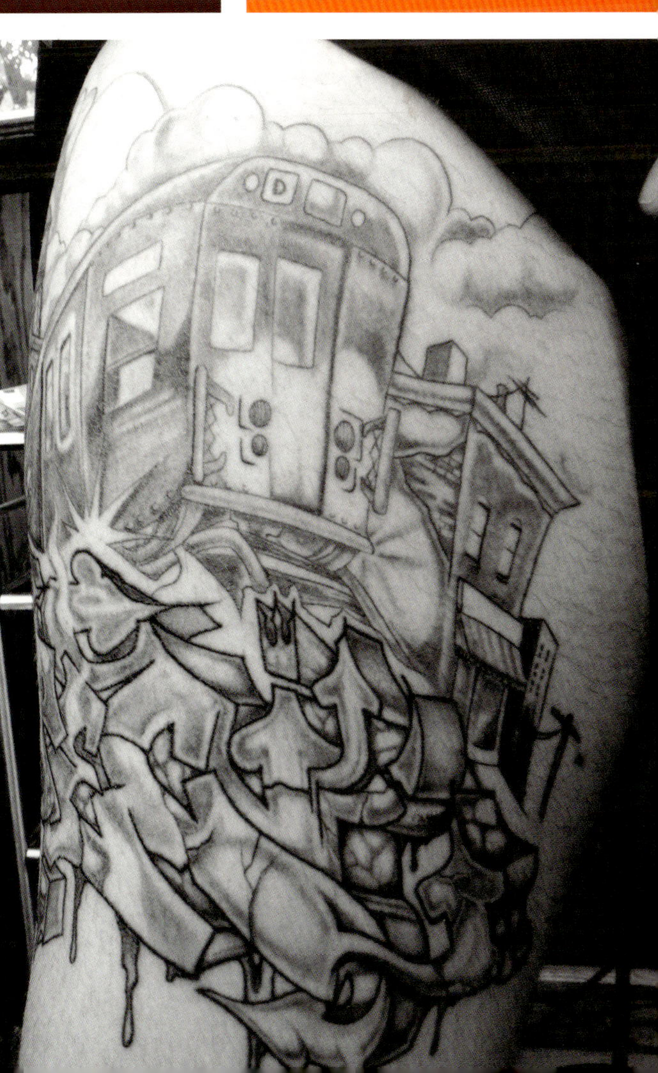

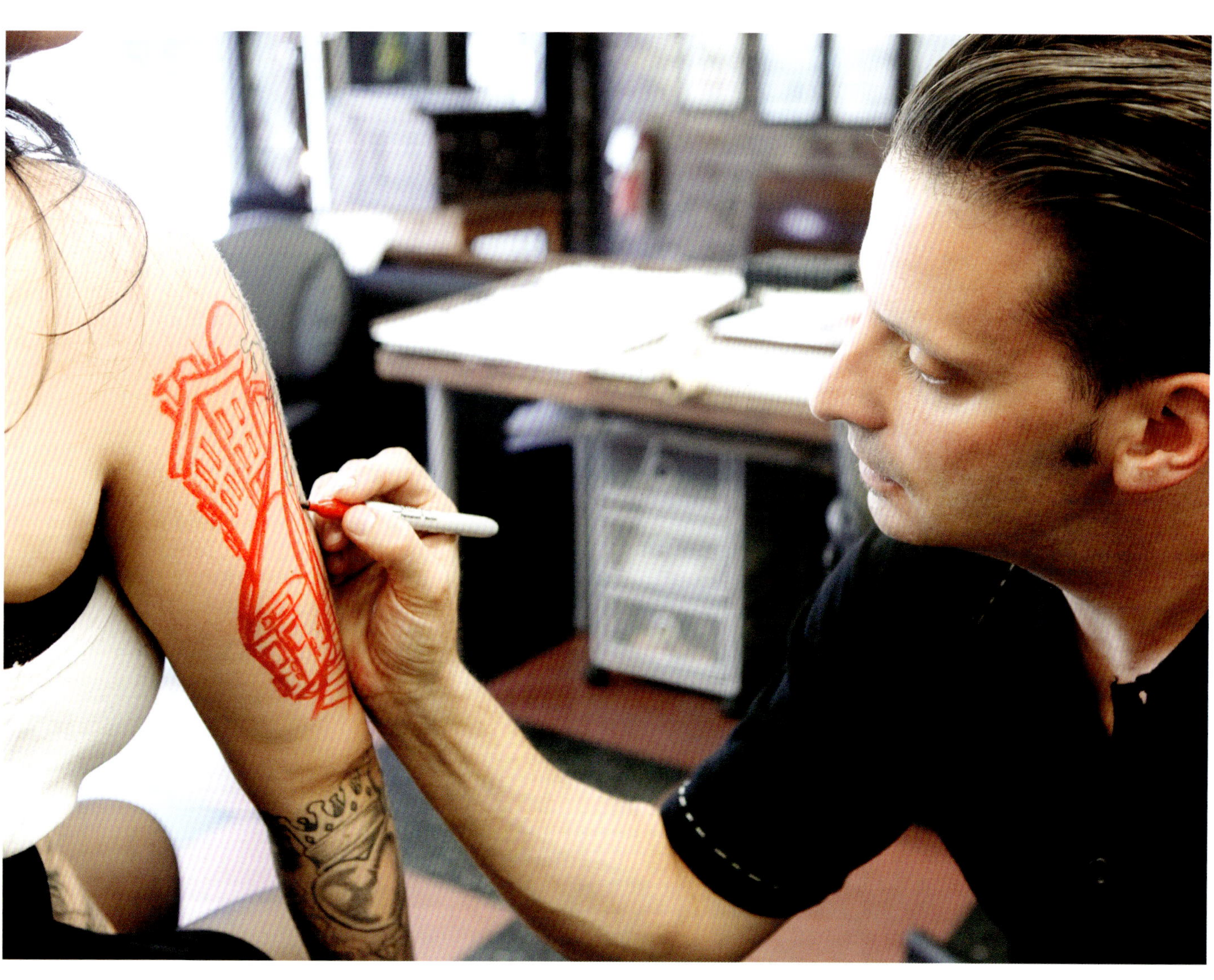

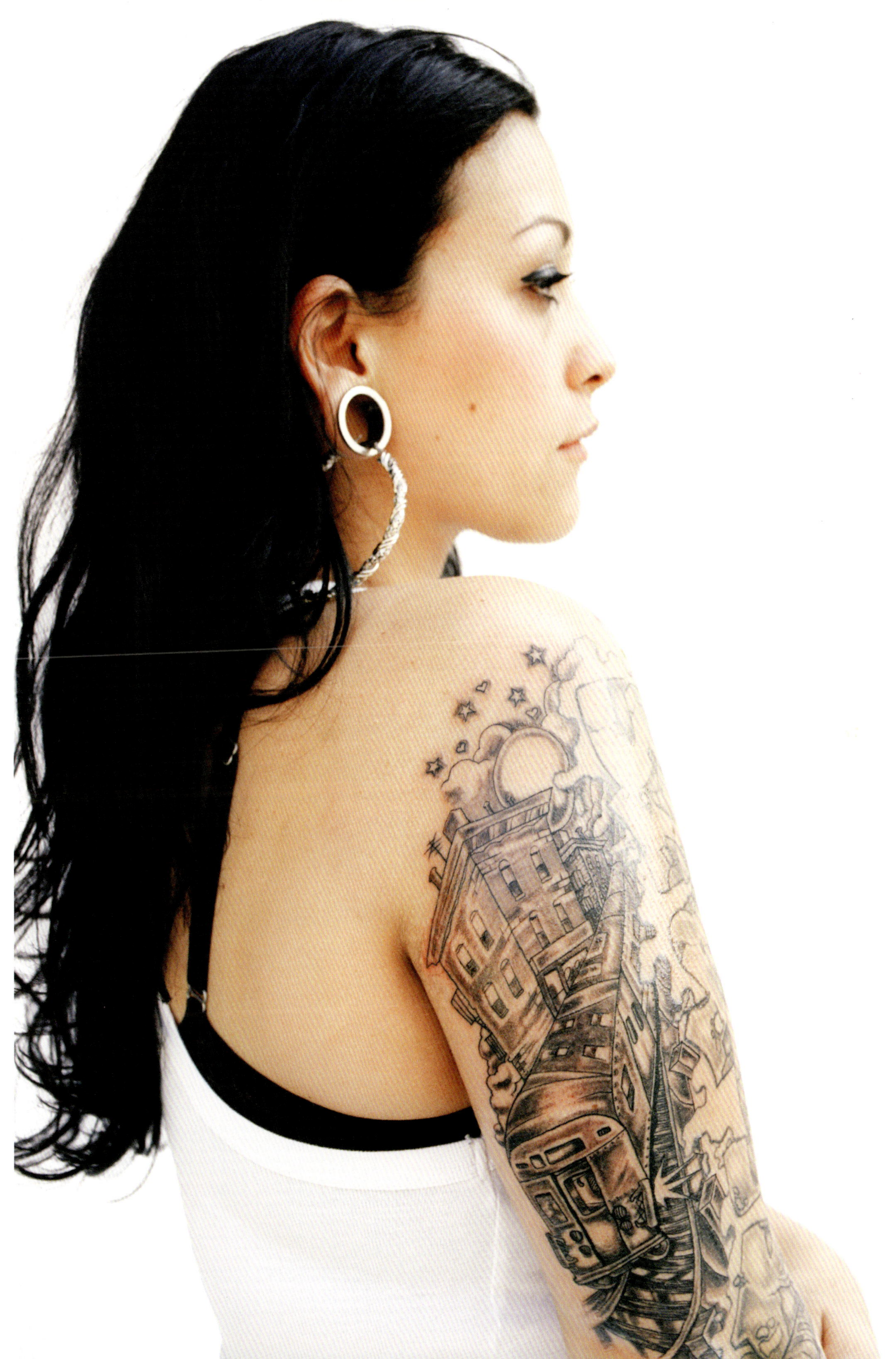

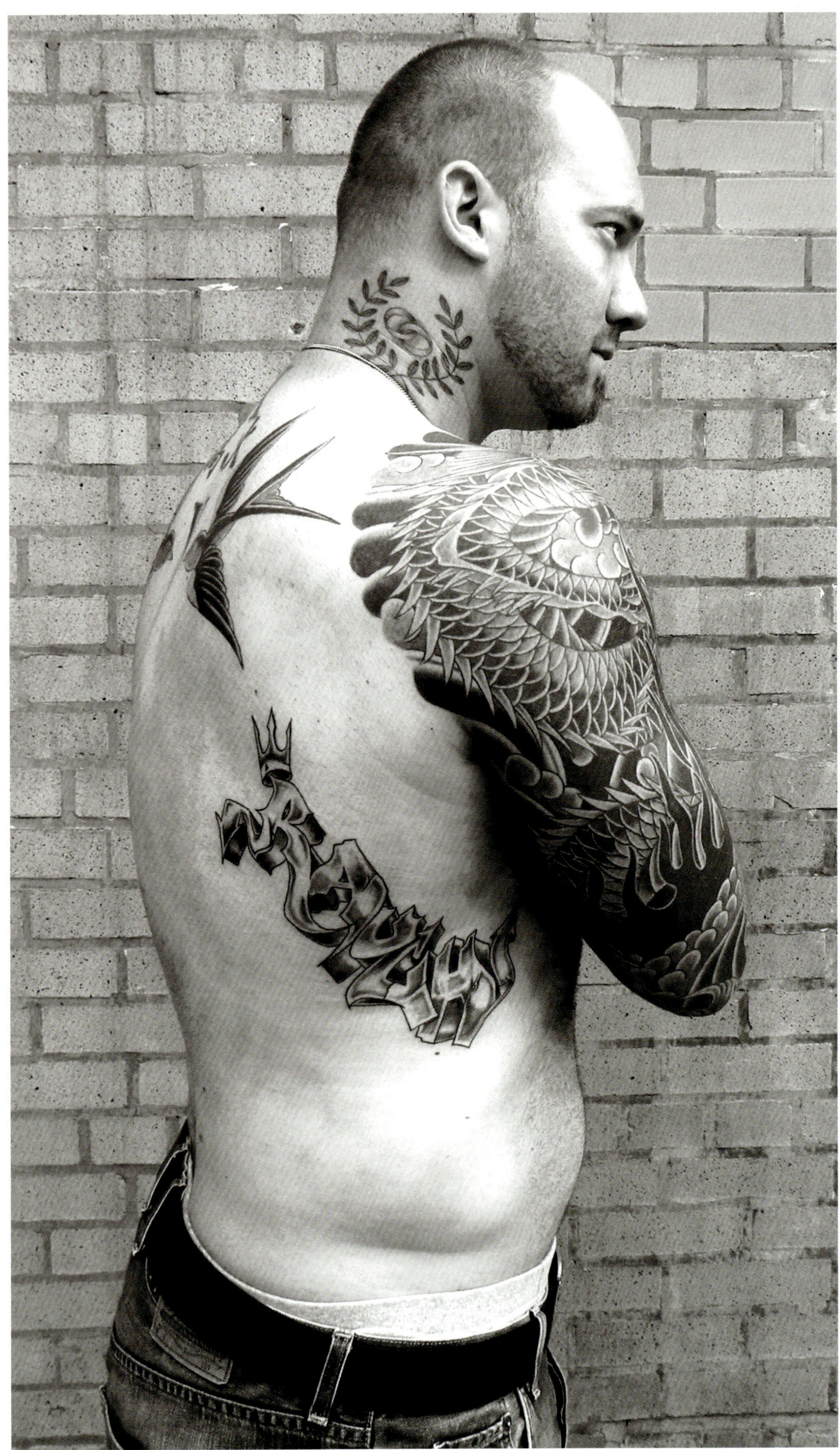

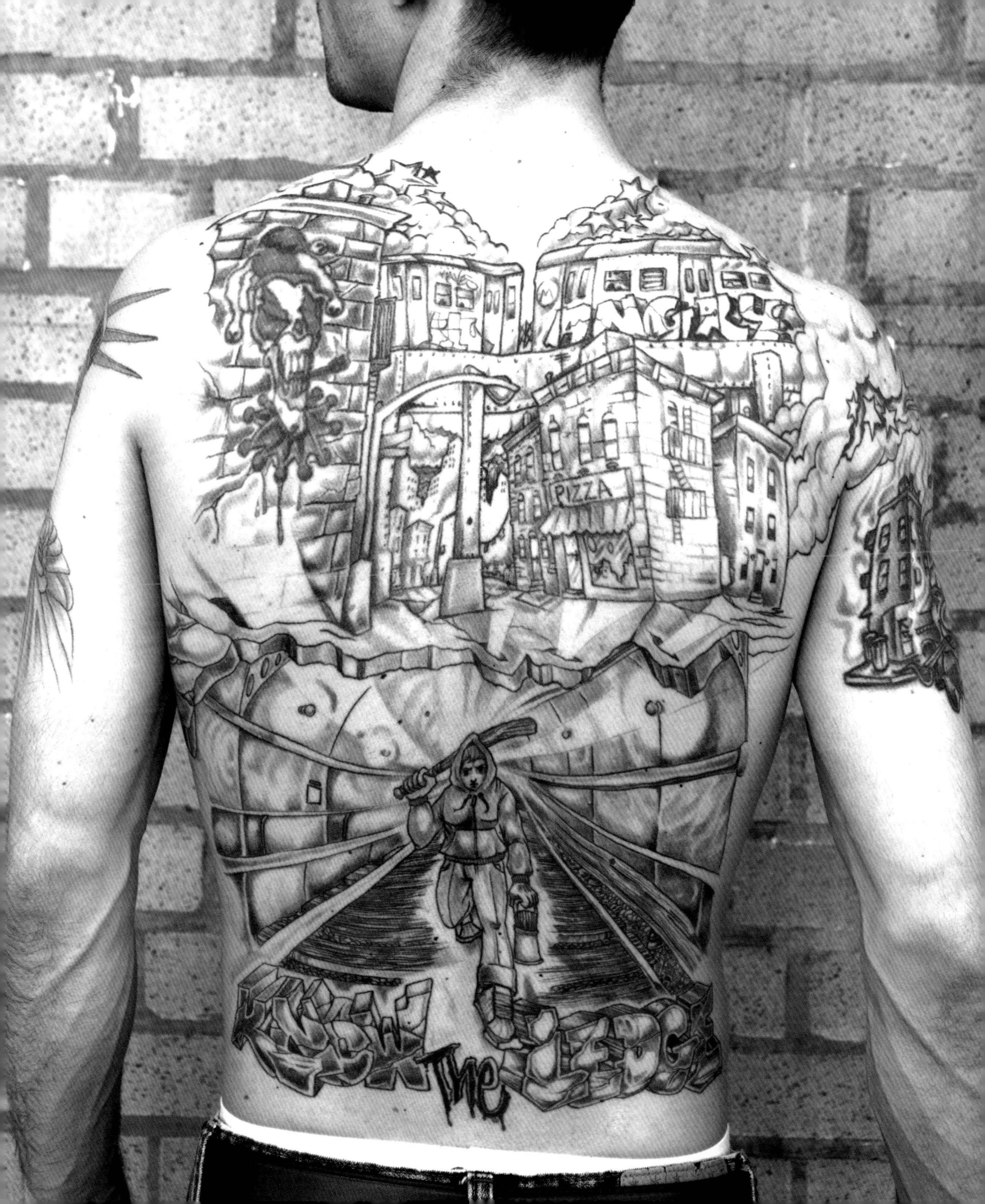
ANGLES
PIZZA
THE

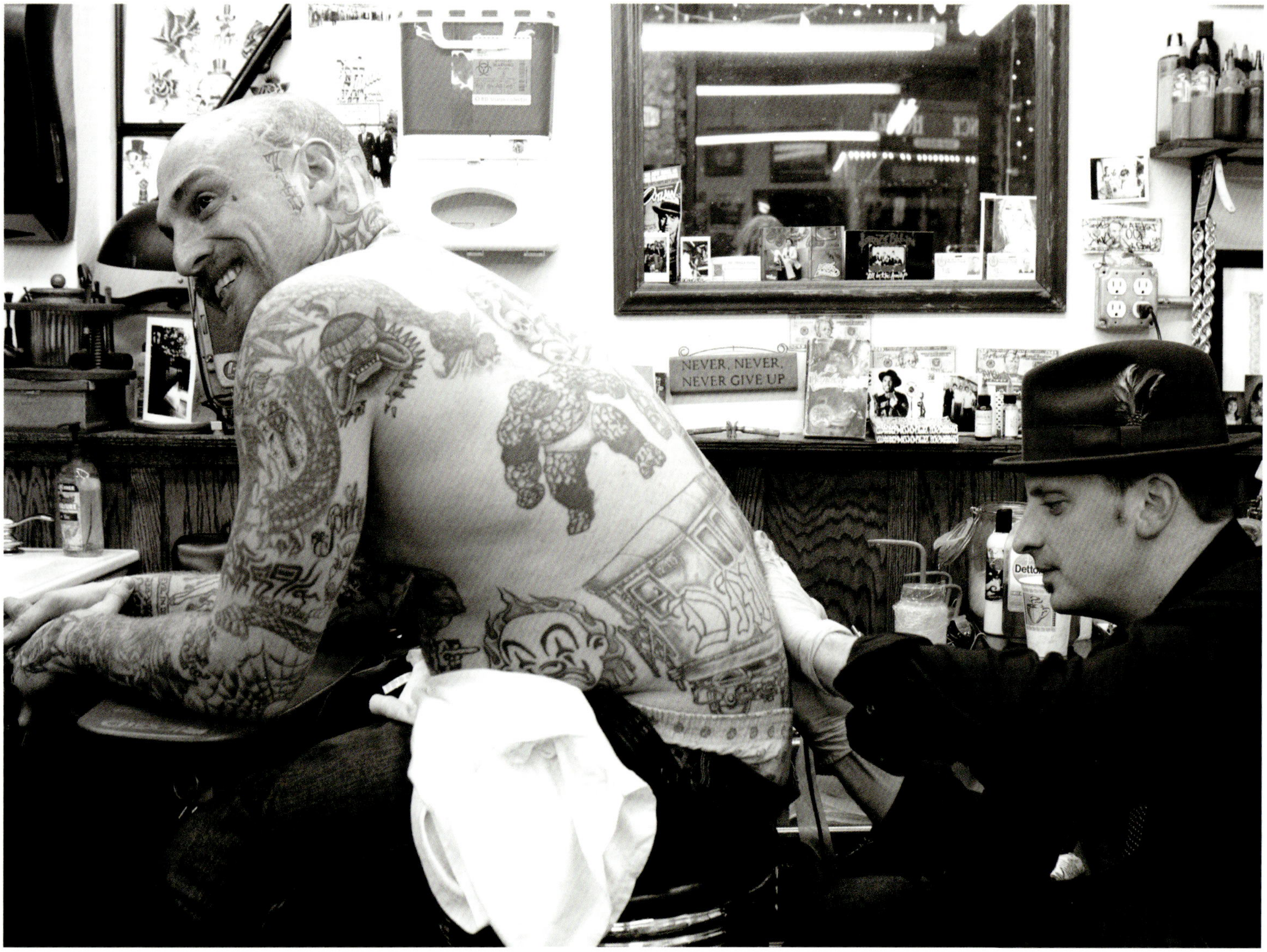

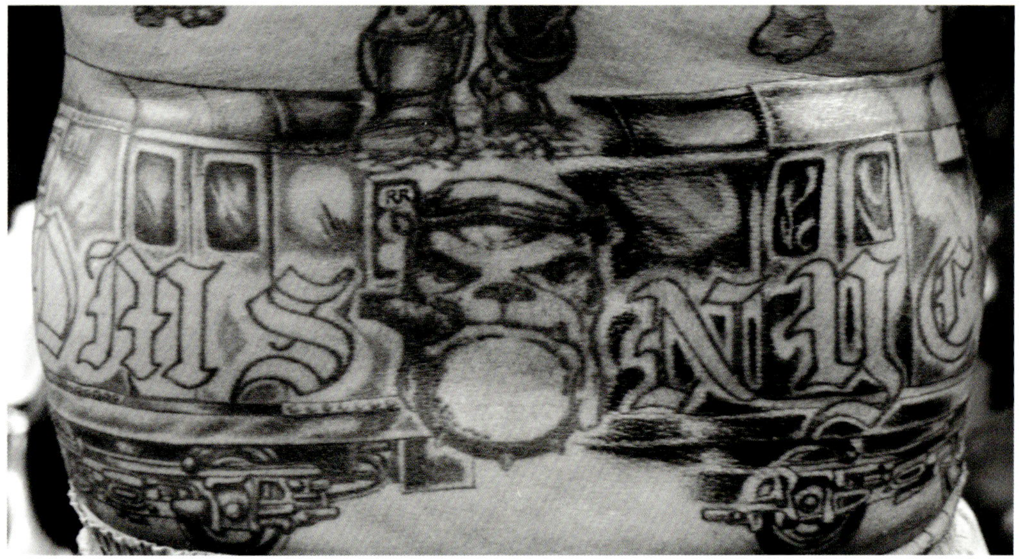

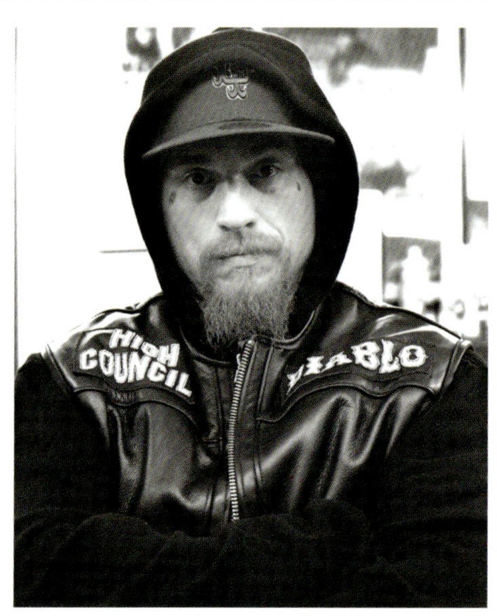

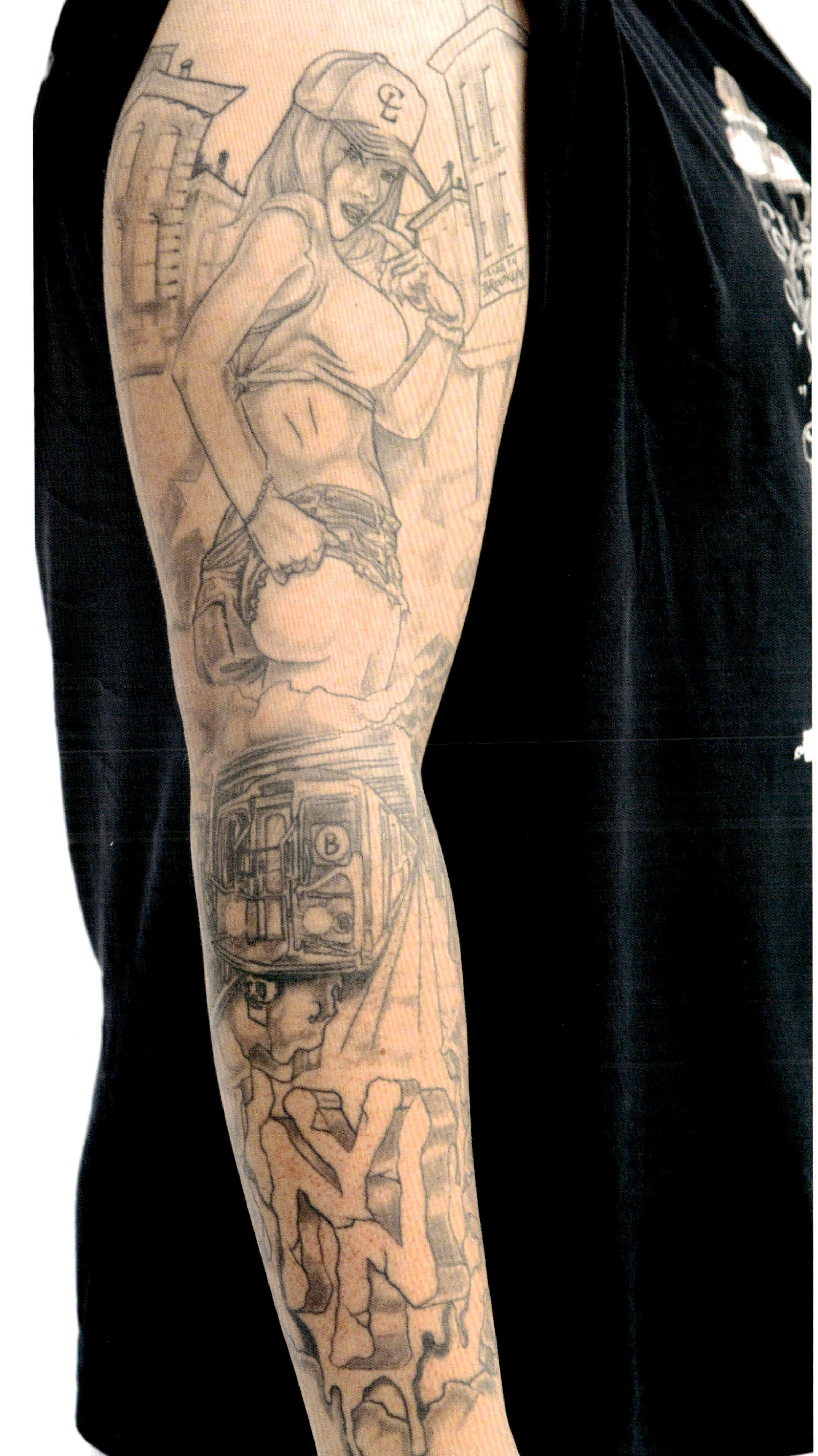

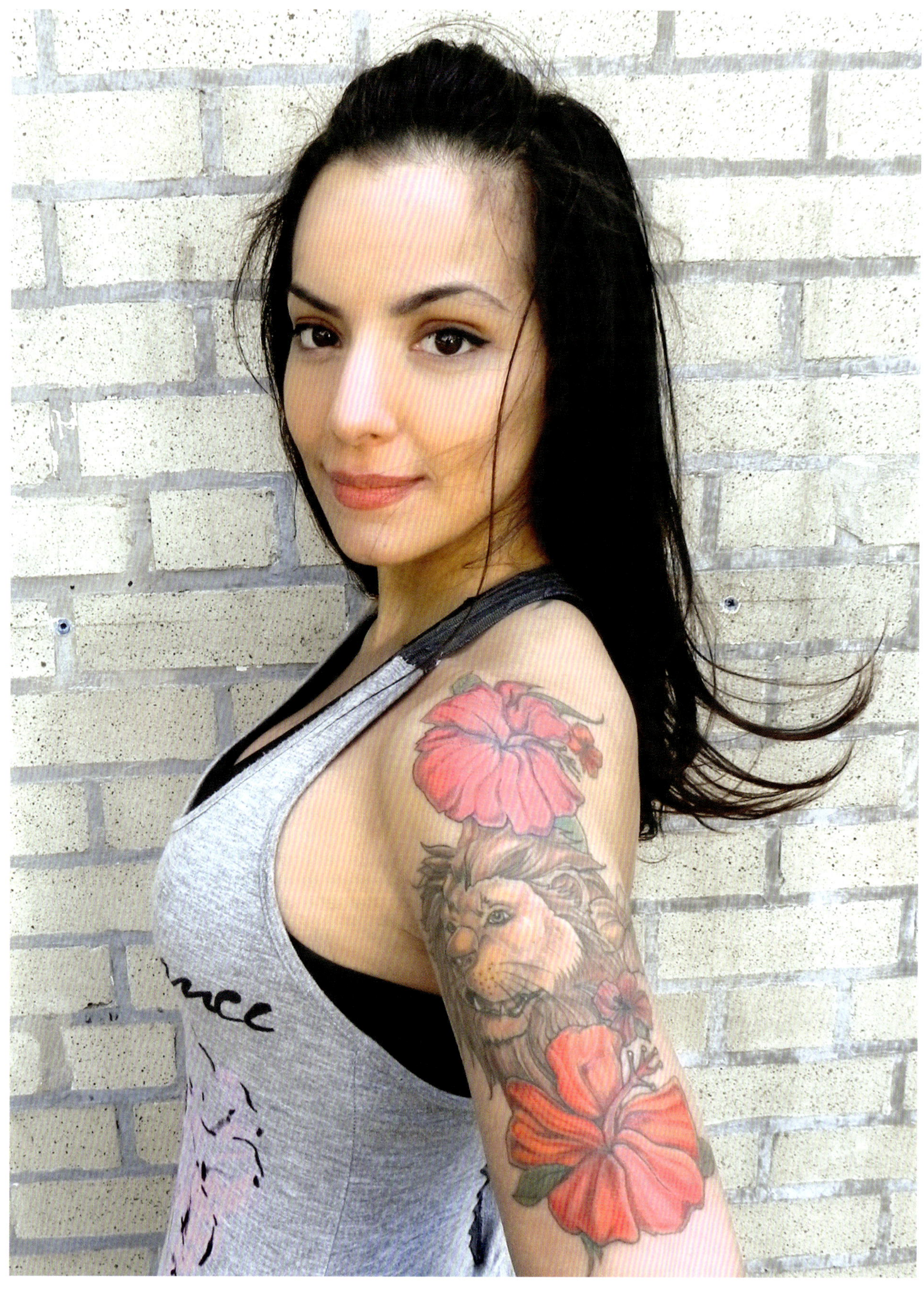

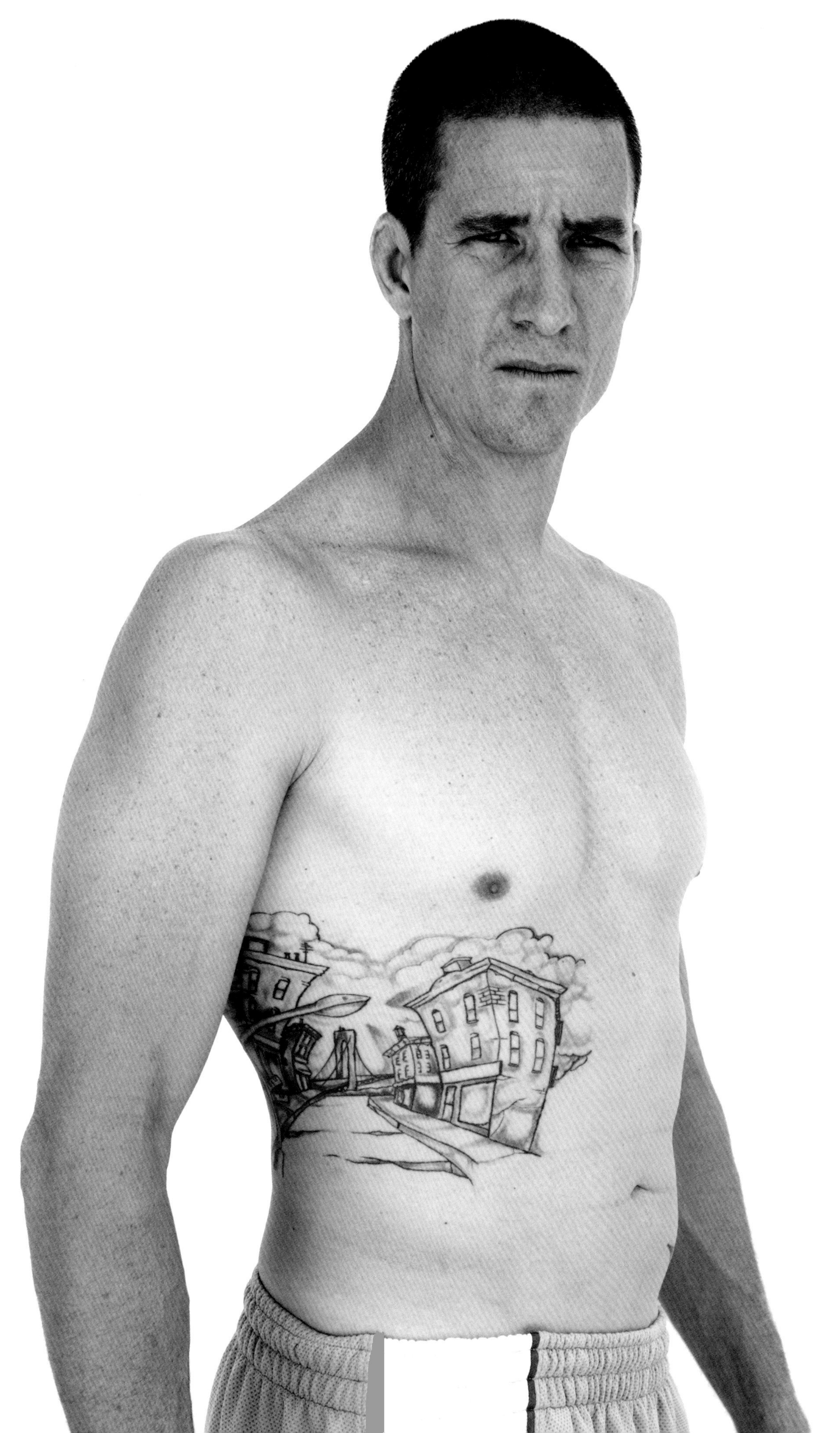

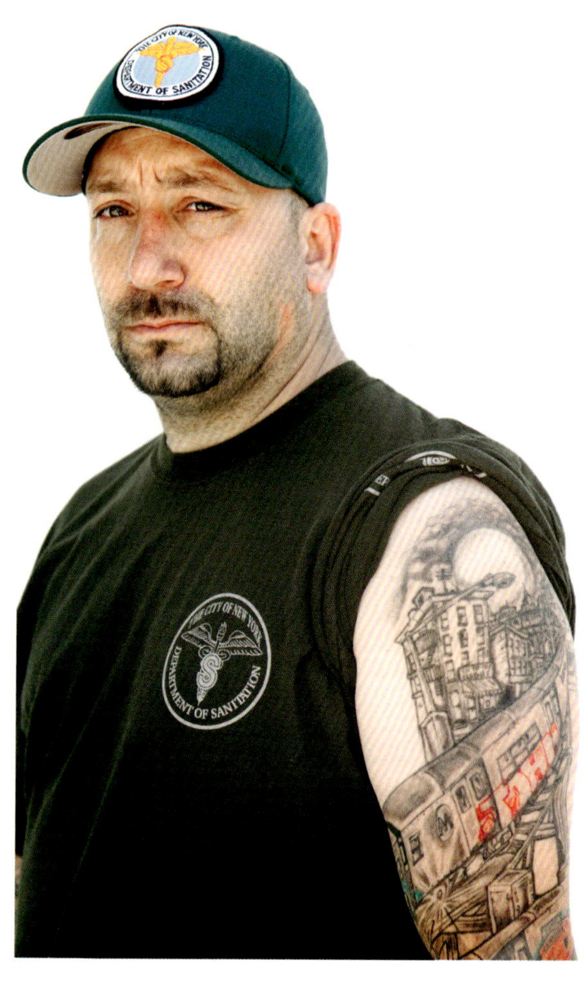

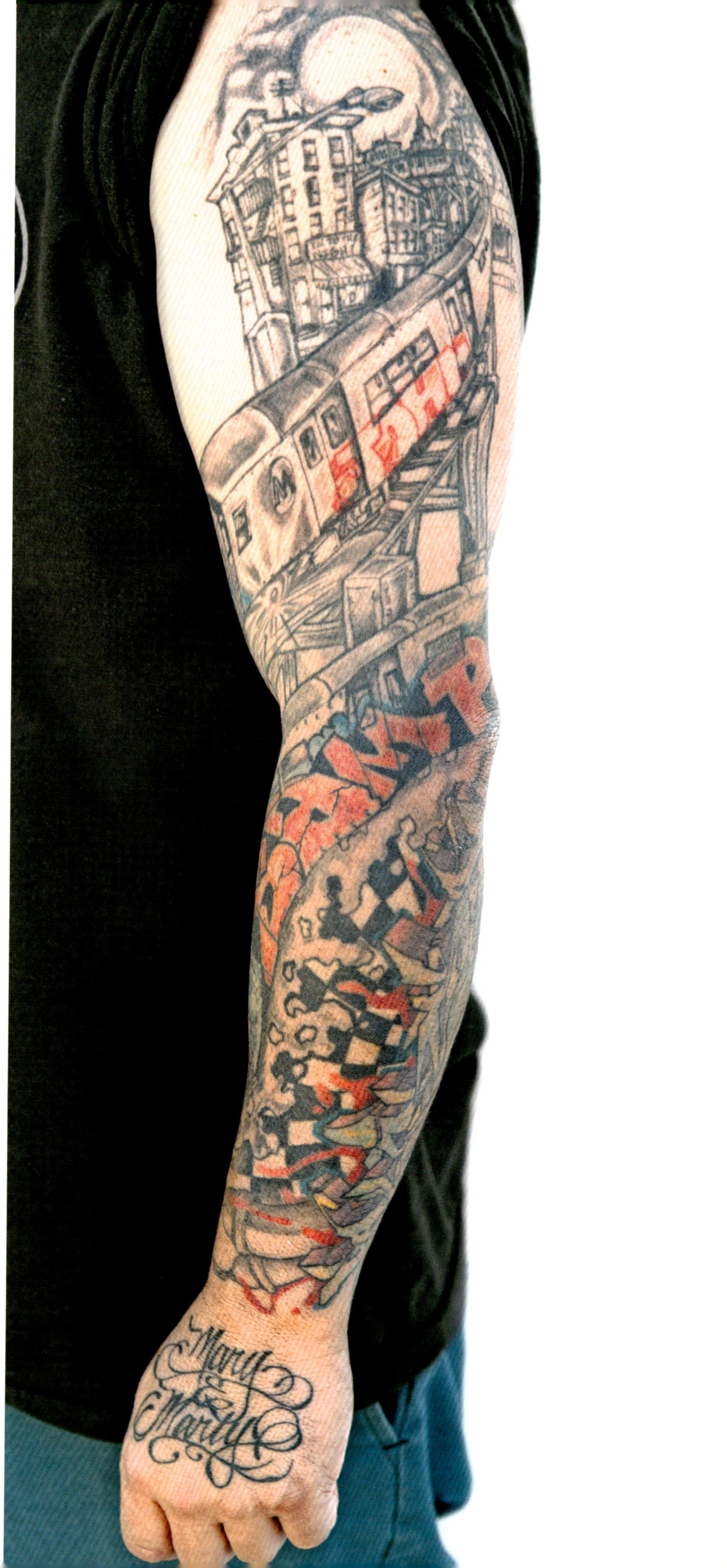

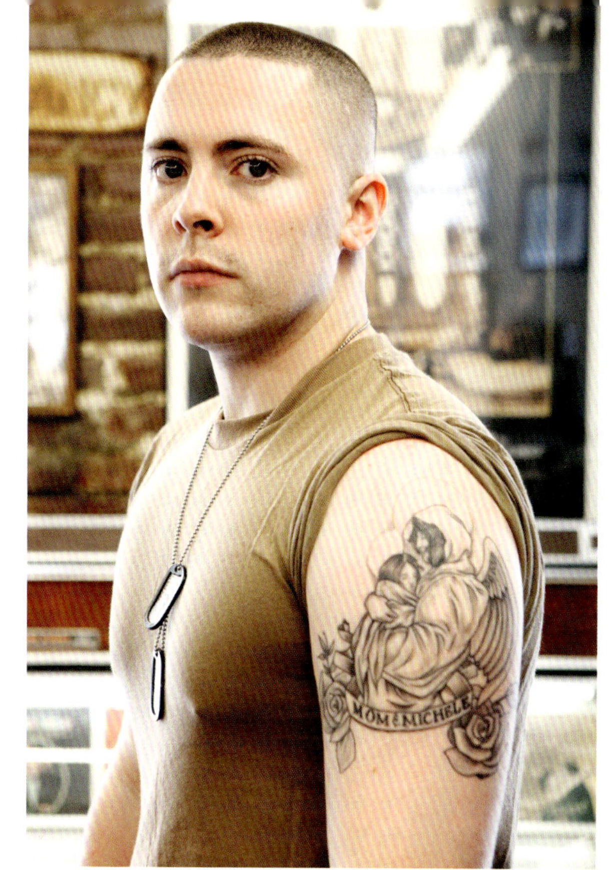

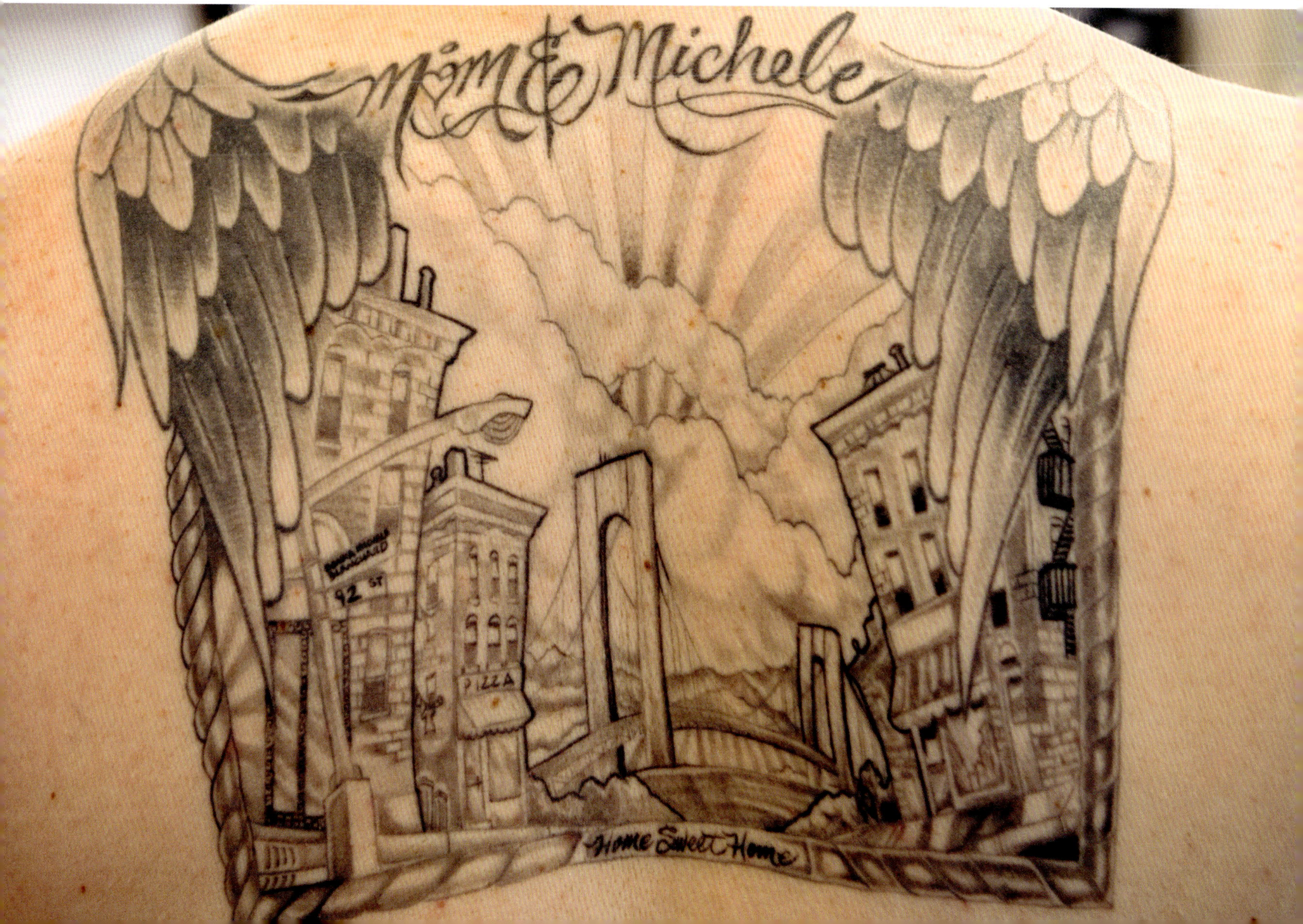

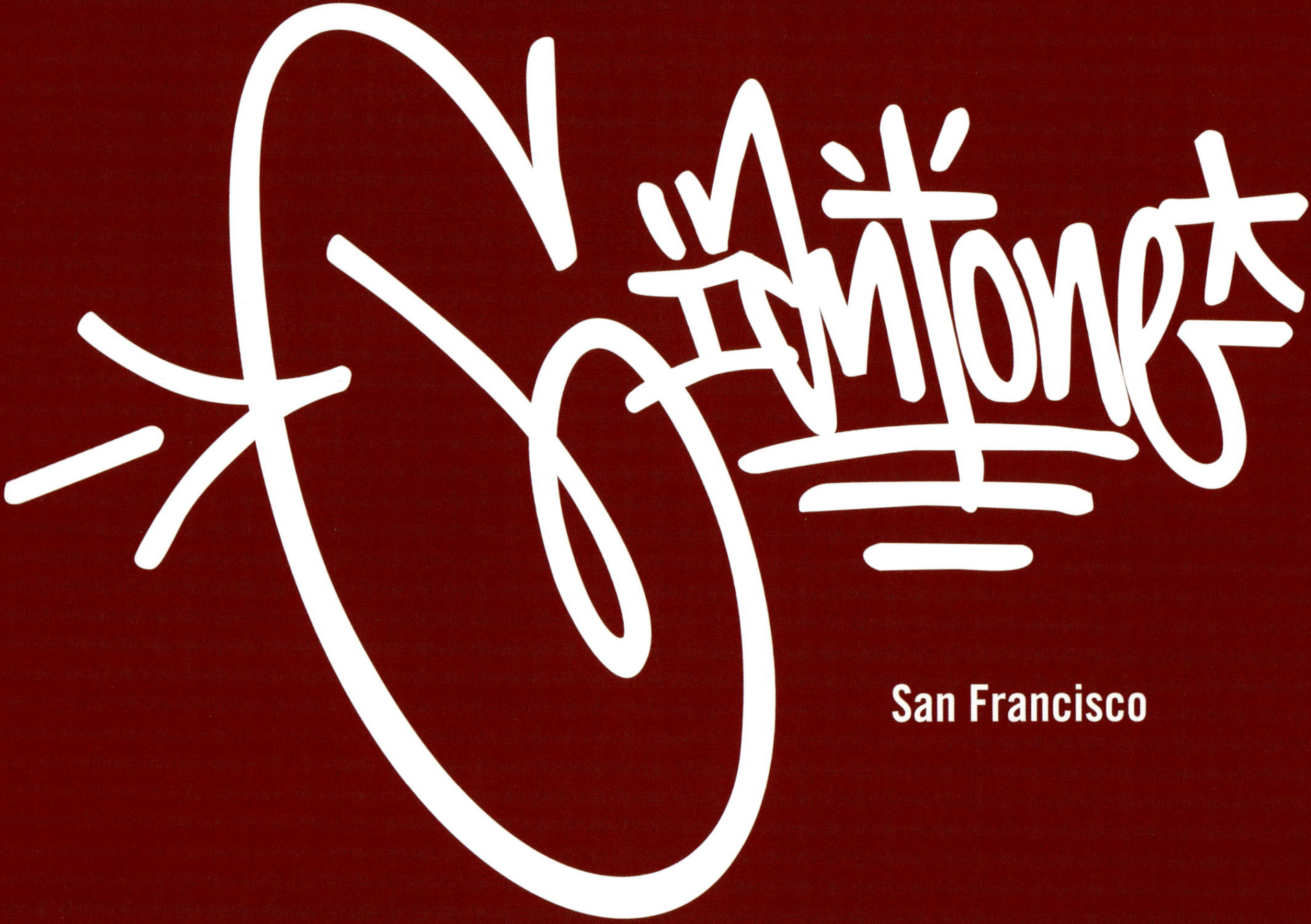

San Francisco

*"In tattooing and graffiti, every day is an opportunity to get up....
I think with the graffiti thing, you can't really slack. It's
better just to quit than go out as a toy or go out with some
wack style. Every time I paint, I still want it to be better than
the one I did before."*

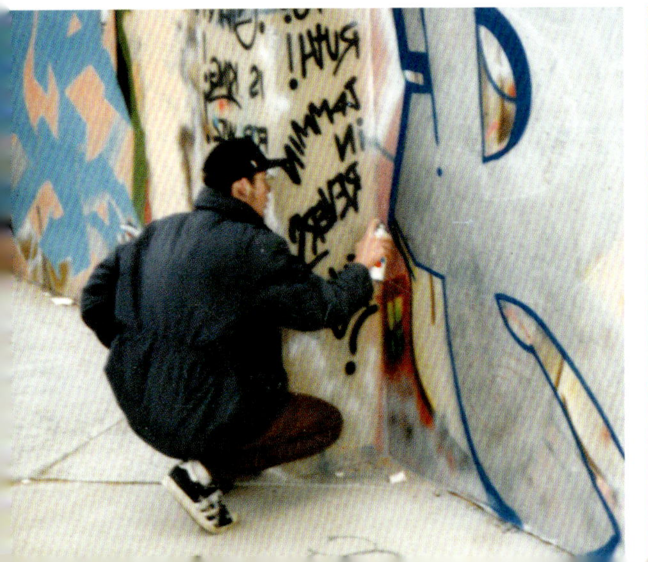

GIANT

Giant came up in Albuquerque, New Mexico. Graffiti whispered to him at a young age, and the voice would get louder after meeting a young New York transplant and graffiti ambassador named Agree (RIP), who was himself influenced by Kaves. Giant's name inside the writing culture is strong, and his style is a reflection of all of the places and spaces he's inhabited. His tattoo work is a true representation of what America looks like when stripped to its core: black and white and gray, with Mexicans and punks and bicyclists leading the way.

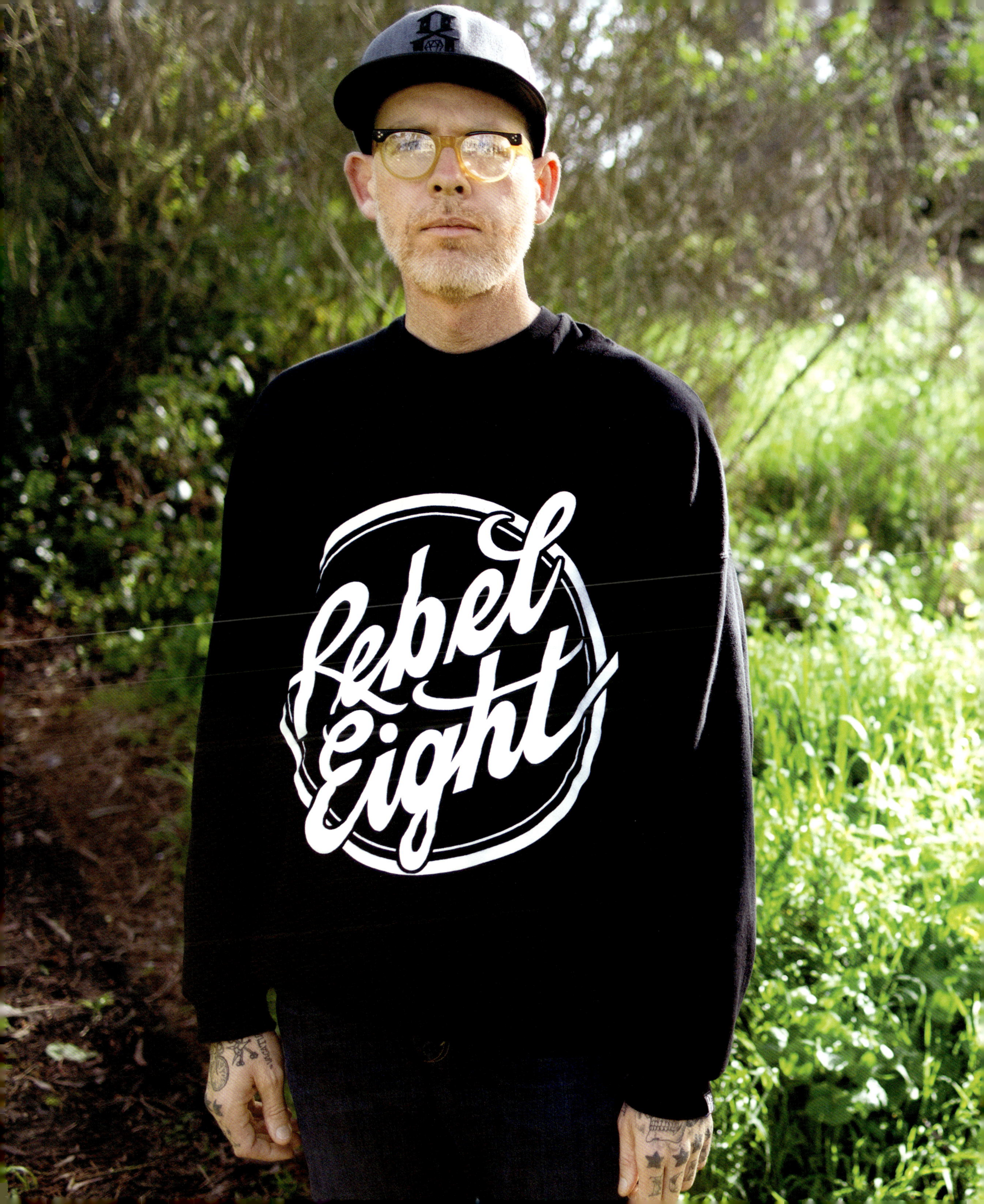

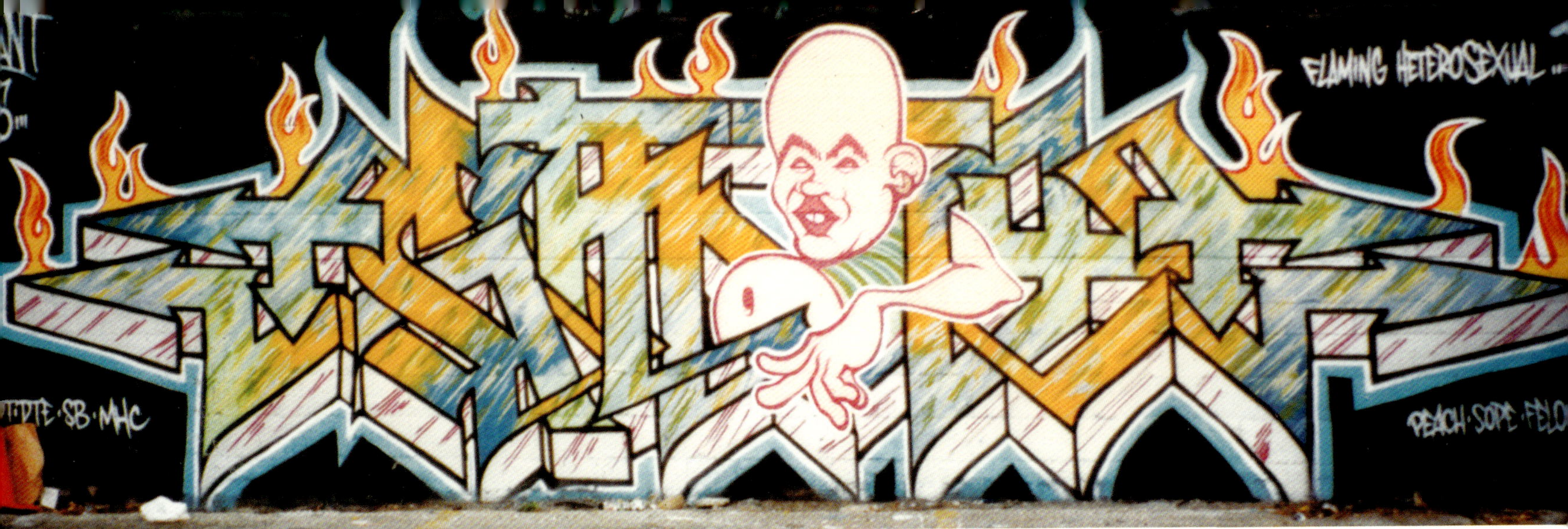

Giant piece, San Francisco, 1995

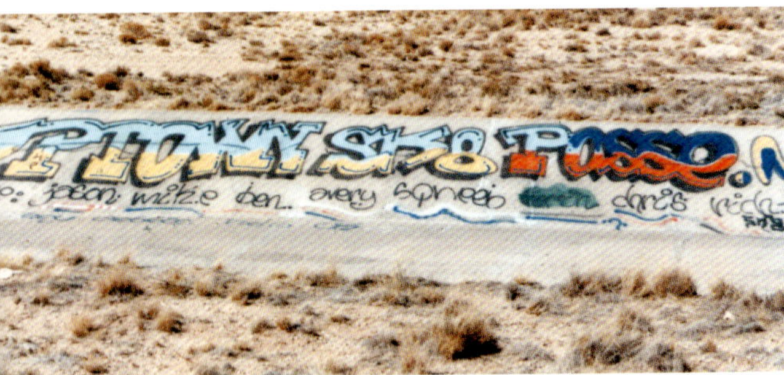

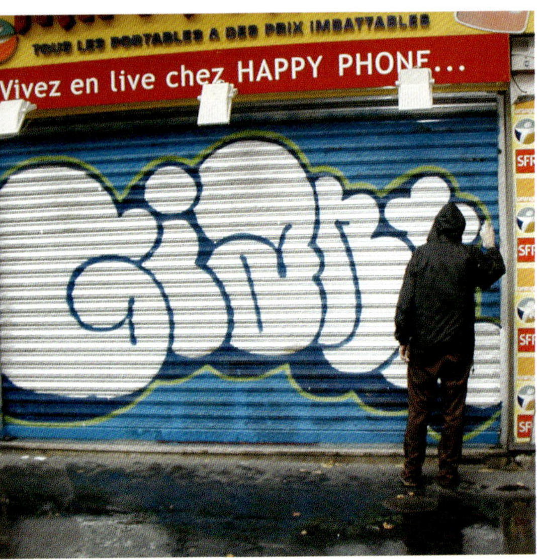

TOP: Giant piece, Albuquerque, NM, 1989
BOTTOM: Giant piece, Paris, 2005

My name is Mike Giant, and I've been a graffiti writer since 1989. I started writing in Albuquerque, New Mexico, where I was living at the time. I was going to school at the University of New Mexico. I was studying architecture. The first piece I did was at a spot that I skated at a lot, and I painted just using the paint that I could find in my dad's garage. After that, I started doing a lot more graffiti in that area, mostly at night.

After four or five pieces, I started writing *Giant*. Before that I was writing my initials. From there I just started painting walls. They were mostly on the freeway, all over the place. I put an ad in my college newspaper saying that I was a spray-can artist, and that I was looking for legal walls to paint. This random dude got back to me and took me to a place on the other side of town. It was the foundation of a factory that went bankrupt during construction, so it was left unfinished. The whole thing was just below the surface of the ground. If you looked from the road, you could just see an open field. You wouldn't even know that there was this big complex of walls and stuff. It was perfect. I was able to paint there for many years, and that's where I really started to learn everything.

The walls of that factory were actually the first place I met other writers. Other writers from around Albuquerque would congregate there, and we started to connect. Around the same time, I was a guest on the weekly hip-hop radio show that my college radio station put on. A guy named Agree, who had just moved to Albuquerque from New York City, called the show and asked to talk to me, so we connected that way. At the time his graffiti was the best that I had ever seen—him and this other guy, Doc.

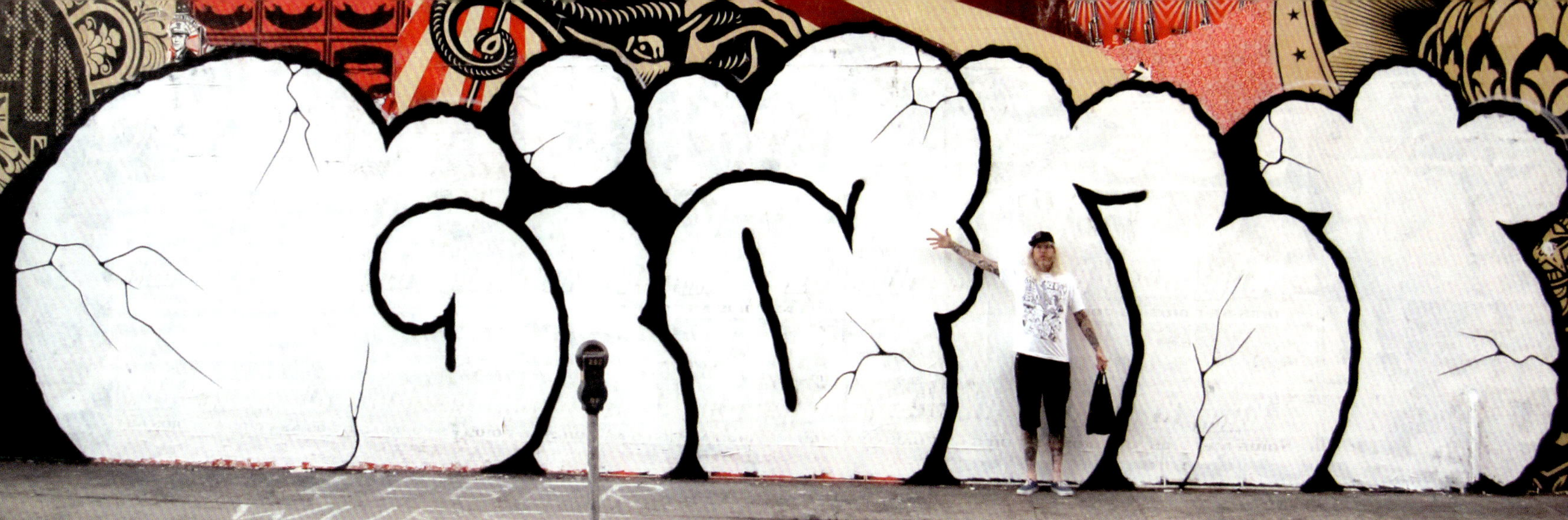

Giant piece, Los Angeles, 2010

I met both of them and they took me in. They took me painting and put me down with their crew, which was really important. I know how good that feels when you get put down by the people you're just in awe of. I wouldn't even paint with them the first day I went out with them. I felt like, I'm not worthy, you know? They did a piece for me and they were super tight. Those guys, they taught me everything.

Doc was from Venice, California, and that's where he was schooled. He got to see a lot of the WCA [West Coast Artists] crew graffiti and also the beginnings of the AWR [Angels Will Rise] crew as well, which I got to witness firsthand when I went to Los Angeles the first time with Doc, which was crazy. He taught me how to use paint and how to use caps and color theory because I'm color-blind, so basically all the color sense that I have even today is based on what I learned from Doc. He was really, really awesome at that.

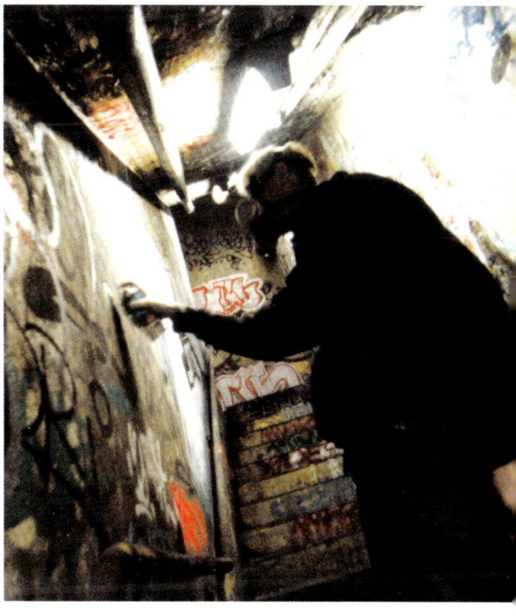

Giant at work in San Francisco tunnels, 1996

I painted in Albuquerque for a few years, then I got offered a job in '93 working for Think Skateboards in San Francisco, and I jumped at the opportunity. Before I left Albuquerque, I was writing with ATK crew, which was All Time Kings. That was the crew Agree brought from New York with him. When I moved to San Francisco, I immediately hooked up with guys that were in IHU [I Hate U] crew, who were mostly East Coast: Sope, Felon, and Jase. Pretty soon after that they put me down with BA [Burning America] crew, which was Jase's crew that he brought from Baltimore.

I guess my first exposure to tattoos was in Albuquerque. When I first got to New Mexico, it was mostly black and gray stuff that I saw on older Mexican and Latino guys. I guess I did see some at the car shows that my dad would take me to, and there was kind of a mix

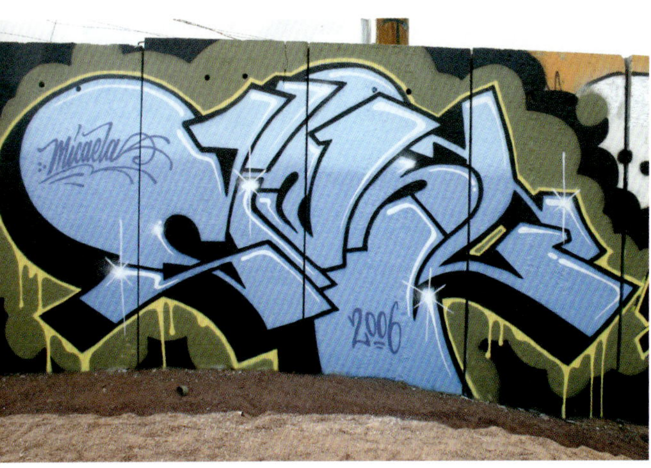

Giant piece, Albuquerque, NM, 2006

of biker stuff and *cholo* stuff. My family went to the flea market and sometimes we would see stuff there. Man, that was the late seventies even, because we got to New Mexico in '78. It was like, '78, '79, we would walk the whole market, and I was just at the right height to see everybody's arms as they walked by. I was into art in general, but I knew that that was something special.

Also, I got picked on a lot when I first got to New Mexico. I was this super-tall white kid. I totally stuck out. They used to flip me off and I'd be like, "Fuck you," and they would just laugh. They would laugh at the way I flipped them off. They thought it was so funny that I did it different. Stuff like that would get me punched, you know? It was ridiculous. The kids who picked on me, their older brothers and their dads were covered in black and gray tattoos and they were visible. That was a power thing to me. Those kids acted like I was fair game, but at the same time they had absolute respect for these guys that were covered in tattoos. It's one of those things. I felt I needed to look like those guys for them to stop picking on me.

It wasn't until I was, I think, nineteen that I got my first tattoo. I got a graffiti banner on my arm. It just says *Giant*. My buddy Joker designed it for me. And my buddy Carlos, he writes *Went.* He still lives in New Mexico. He did the tattoo for me. I paid a bottle of Jack Daniel's for it because Carlos wanted to give me the tattoo for free. We were super tight with the owners of the shop, and these biker dudes are like, "Fuck that! What do *we* get out of that?" and Carlos was like, "What do you want?" They're like, "Tell him to bring Jack Daniel's." I brought a big bottle and I gave it to them as I went in and I got my tattoo. It was a good first experience. It was ghetto. It was fucking sketchy. Bikers and booze.

Pretty soon after I got my first tattoo, I moved to San Francisco. It was October of '93. I was working at Think Skateboards. A lot of the guys I worked with had tattoos, and I asked them who did their tattoos. Through that I ended up meeting a guy named Nalla Smith. He was working at Ed Hardy's Tattoo City, which was an amazing shop back then—still is, I think. It was extra incredible as far as I was concerned back then. I got a few tattoos from Nalla and I traded art for those tattoos, which was really cool. He just liked what I was doing, and I was super flattered by that.

Then I started getting tattooed by Chris Conn while he was still at Tattoo City as well. I started to see Scott Sylvia. He was working at a place called 222. God, how did that escalate? I guess I just kind of kept getting tattooed by mostly those guys. My buddy Jason Candell did an early piece on my leg, a big graffiti piece. I had asked Nalla a few times if he had any interest in teaching me how to tattoo, and he kept telling me he didn't really have the means to do that. I just kind of put it out of my mind that it wasn't going to happen, even though other people had offered me the same kind of foot in the door, so to speak. But then a few years later, around '98, Nalla asked if I still had interest in learning how to tattoo, and I did. So he put the equipment in my hands.

I did my first tattoo on my leg. It's still there. It's just like a big graffiti piece. I just outlined it. I did it all with a number 4 needle. I think it was a shader machine—it was the only machine I had. I just dug away at my leg for like, four hours. I showed my roommates and they were like, "Oh my God. That's what you've been doing in there all day?"

I would say there are quite a few similarities between getting into the graffiti game and getting into the tattoo game. I think a lot of it is access to information. When I started writing graffiti, I only had the *Subway Art* book, maybe *Spraycan Art*. I don't think I'd seen anything else in print about graffiti at that point. I'd seen *Style Wars*, the movie, at some point too. But I didn't know much at all.

When I started painting, I pretty much just had the walls in my neighborhood as inspiration. But then once I met Agree and Doc, they had magazines and books and all this incredible information. They had access to styles from all over the world. All of a sudden, it was just this incredible underground library, and I just consumed the shit out of it. It was the same in tattooing—it's funny, because my transition into the world of tattoos was made a lot easier because I knew lots of graffiti artists who had already been tattooing for many years. It was kind of a no-brainer to them that I was going to start to tattoo. I think I got the right information and the right tools quite a bit faster than other people would've gotten. I had an incredible teacher right off the bat. I think that's what helped me excel in tattooing and build a name for myself as a tattoo artist the way I feel I have in the graffiti game.

In tattooing and graffiti, every day is an opportunity to get up. Every T-shirt that we print is me getting up on someone's chest. My work has paid my way, but I need to sit and draw. When life catches up with me and I can't draw for a month or two for some reason, the bills start backing up. It's one of those things. Like, I can't slack. I think with the graffiti thing, you can't really slack. It's better just to quit than go out as a toy or go out with some wack style. Every time I paint, I still want it to be better than the one I did before.

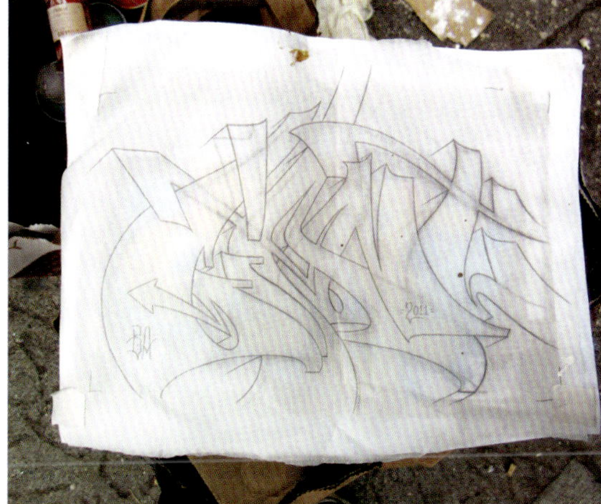

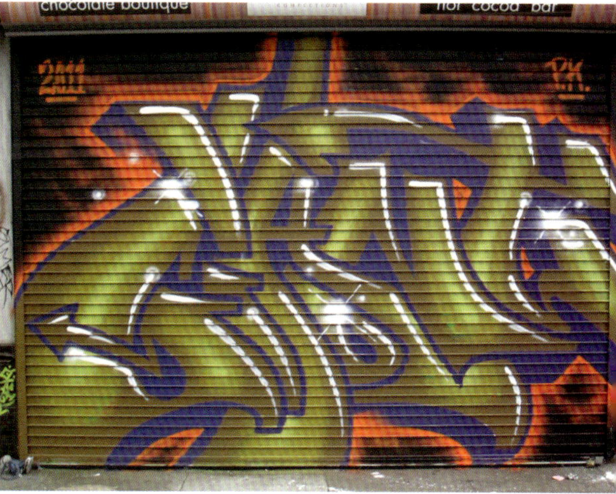

TOP: Giant sketch for piece on Haight Street, San Francisco, 2011
BOTTOM: Giant piece on Haight Street, San Francisco, 2011

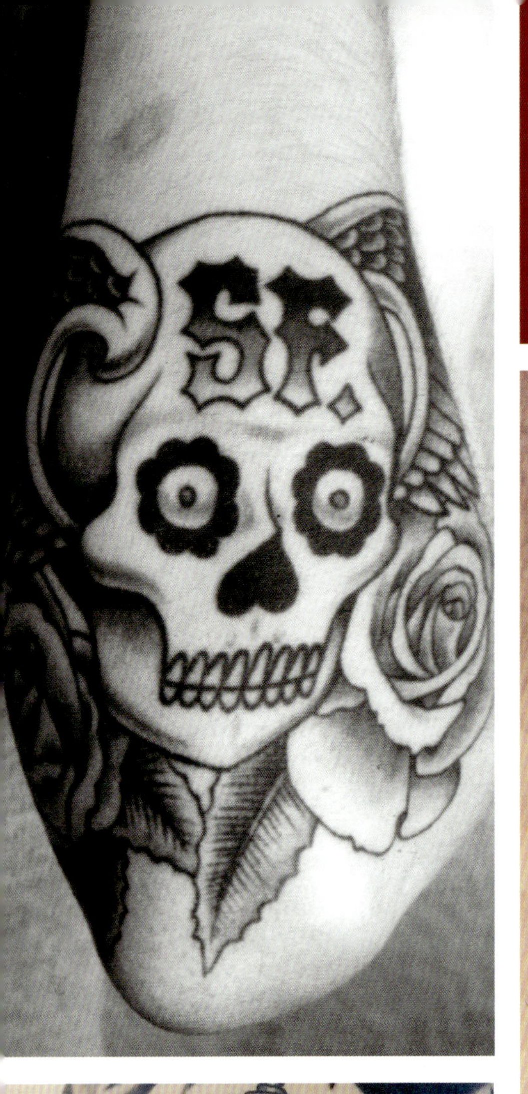

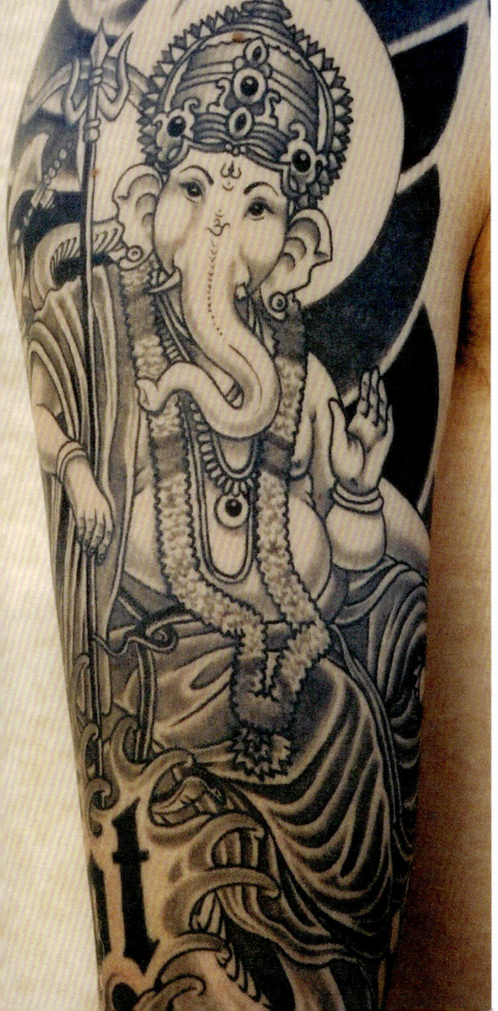

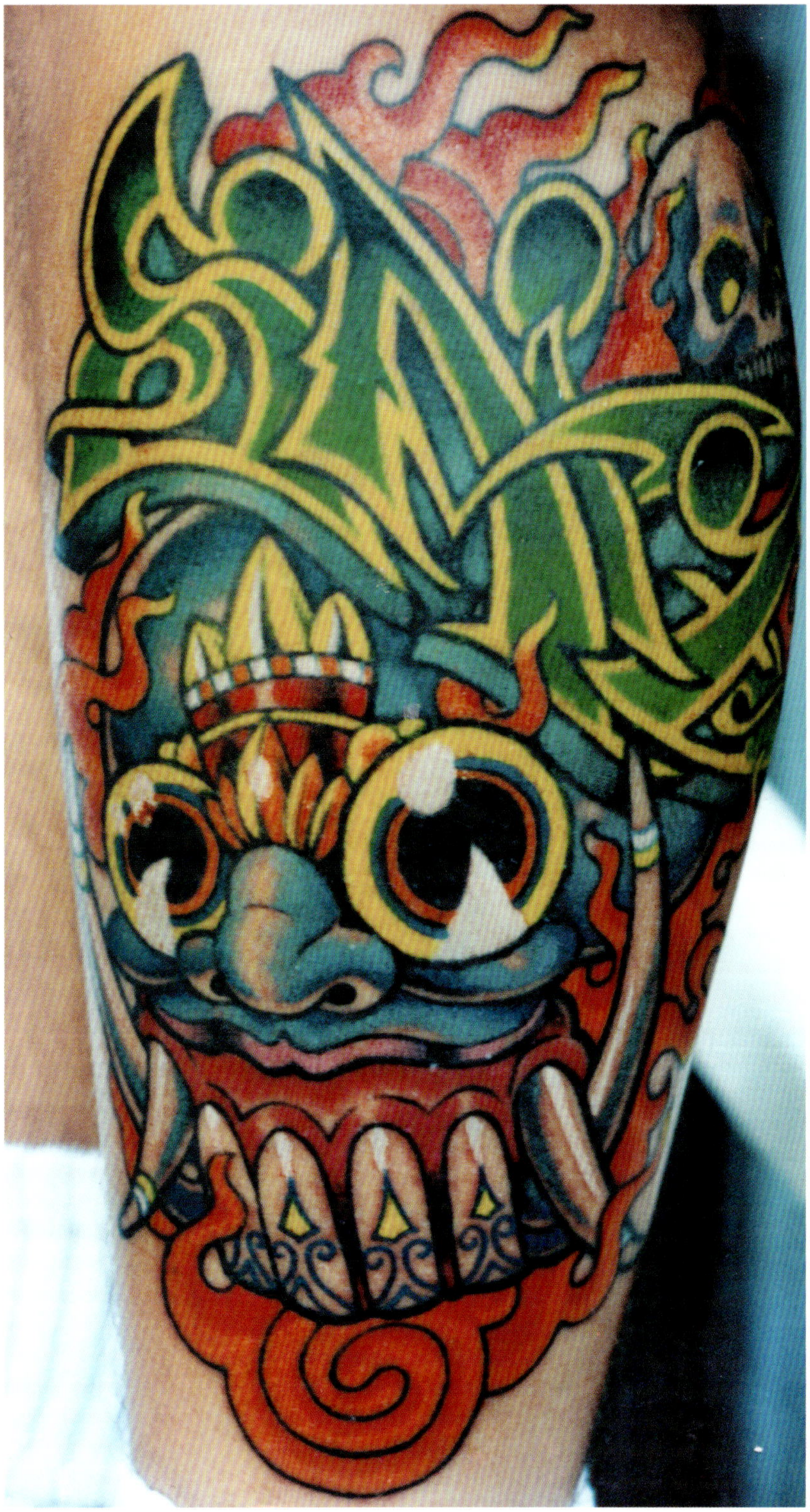

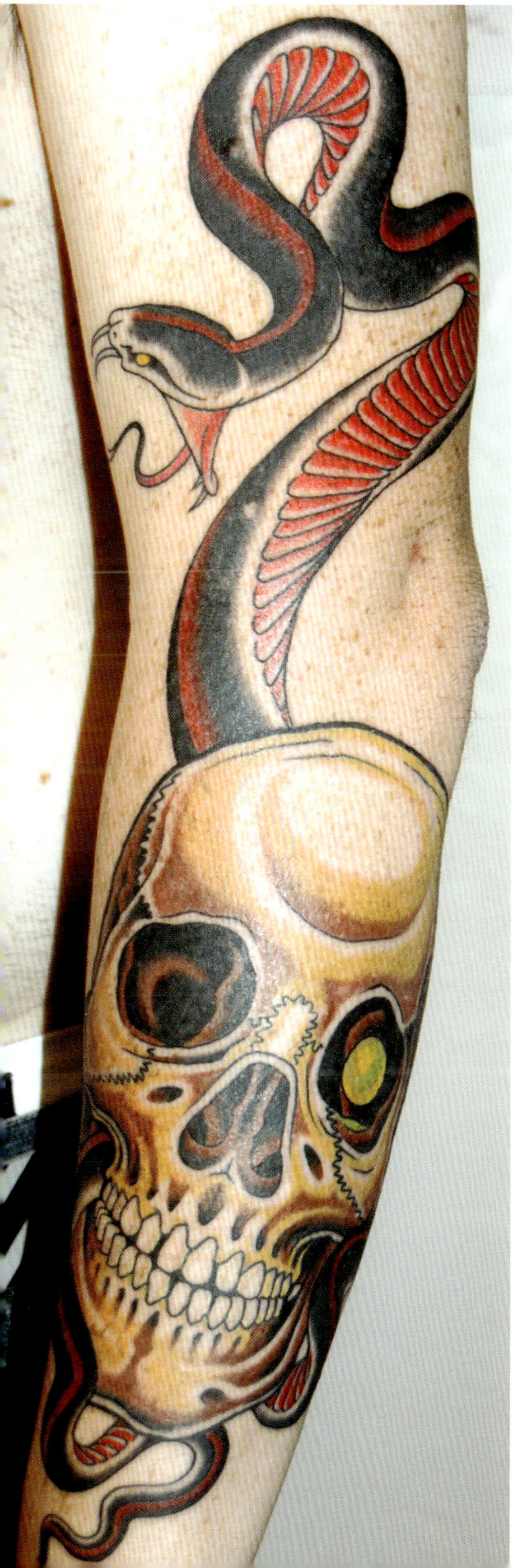

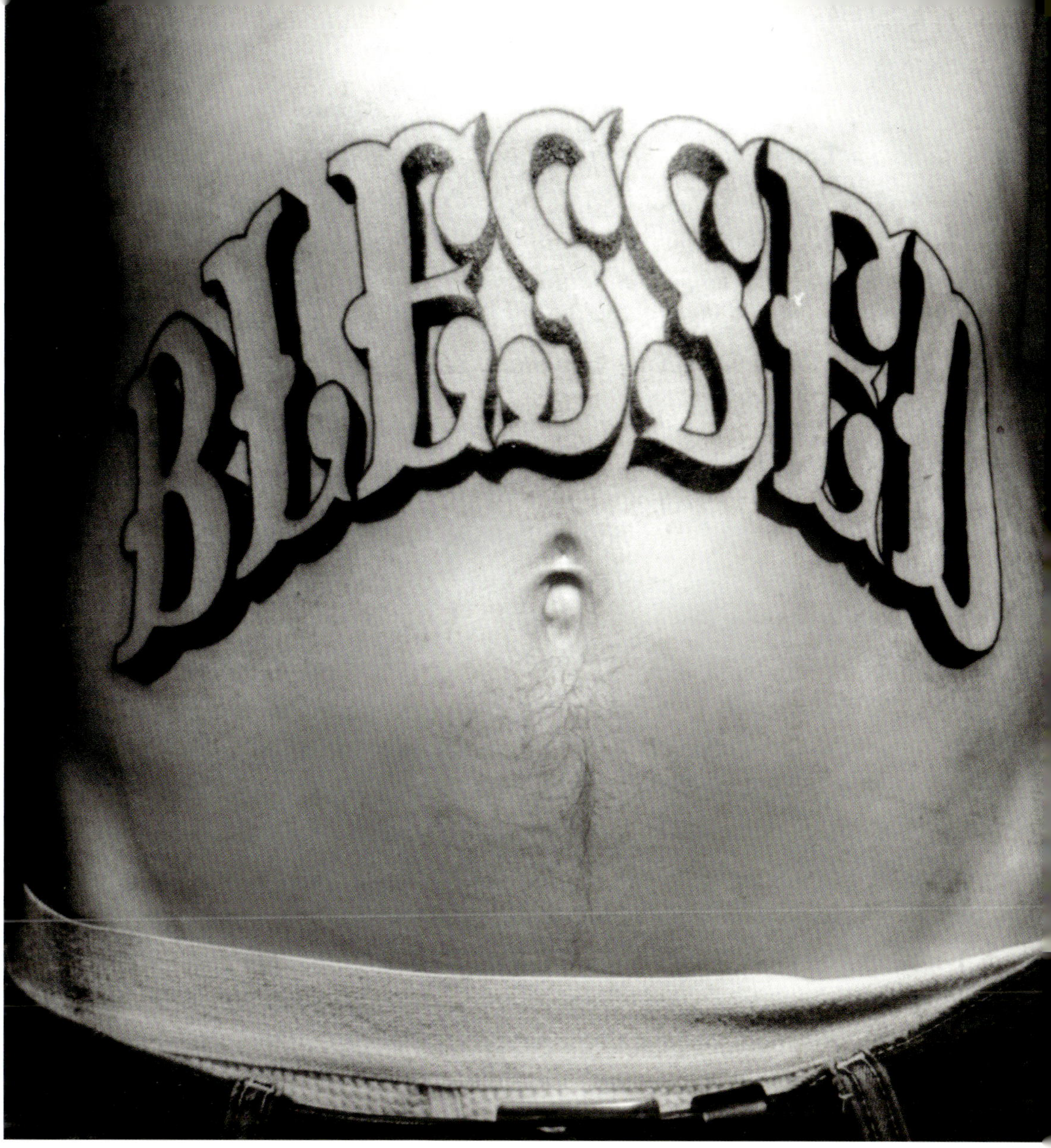

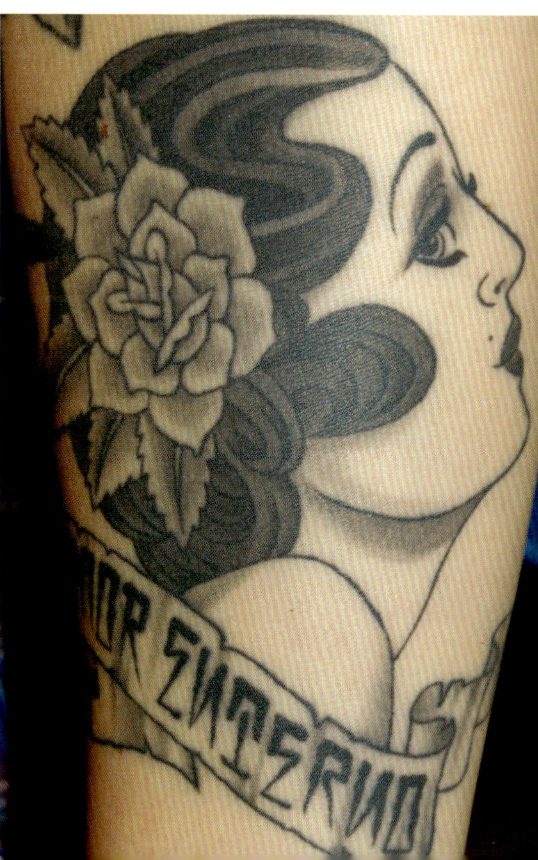
OR ENTERIN

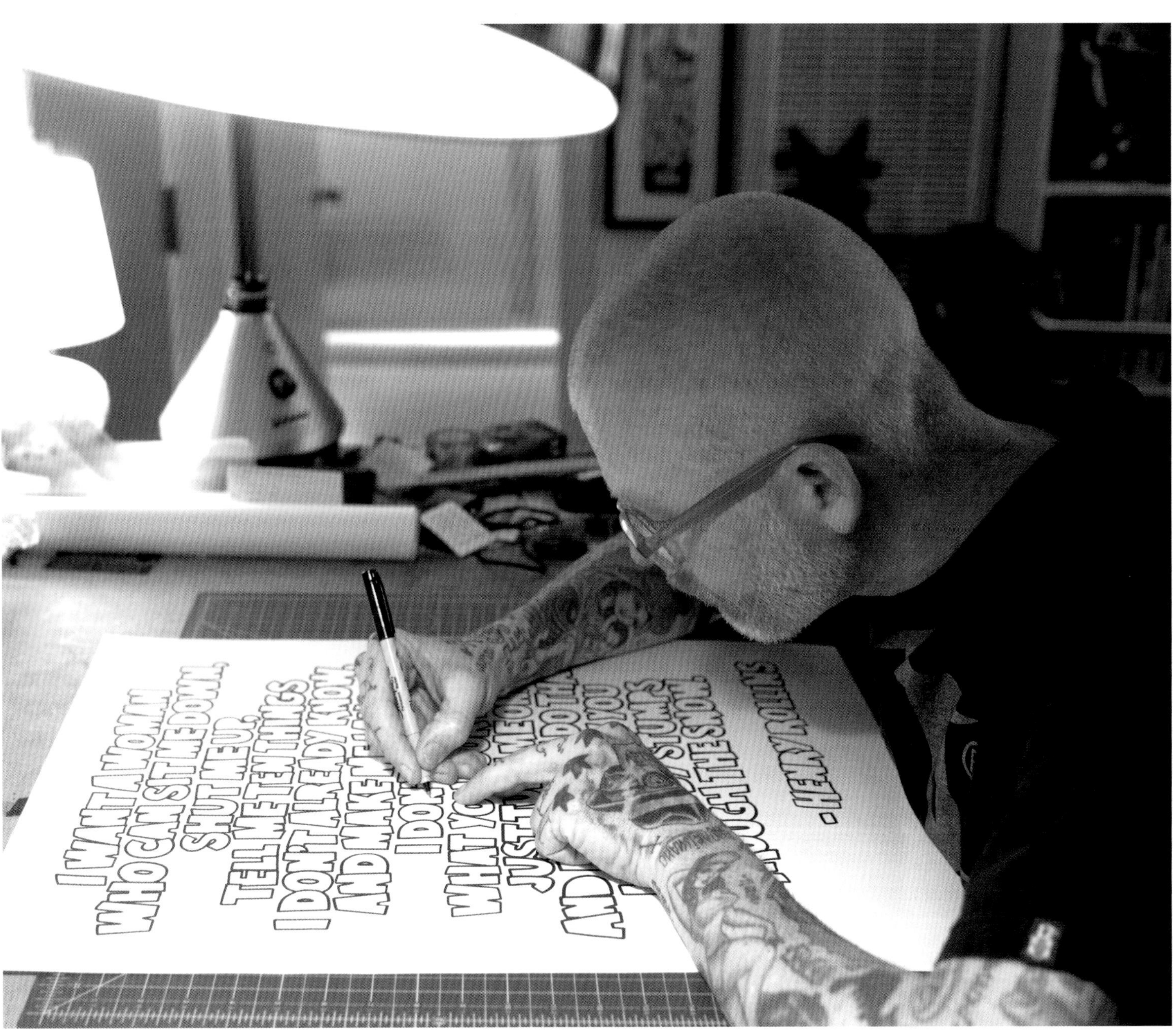

I WANT A WOMAN
WHO CAN STARE ME DOWN
SHUT ME UP.
TELL ME TEN THINGS
I DON'T ALREADY KNOW.
AND MAKE ME
THROUGH THE SOUL.
- HENRY ROLLINS

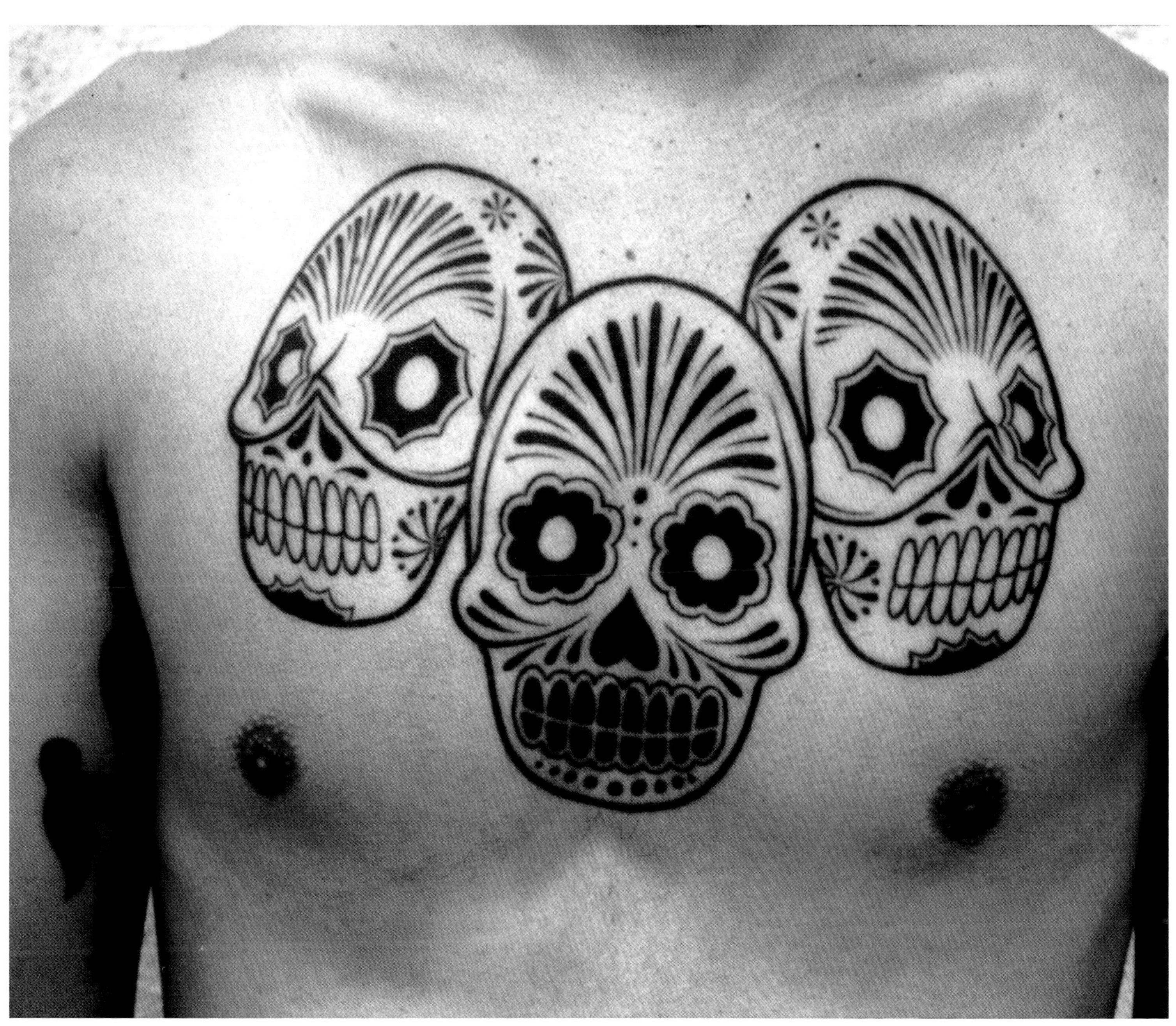

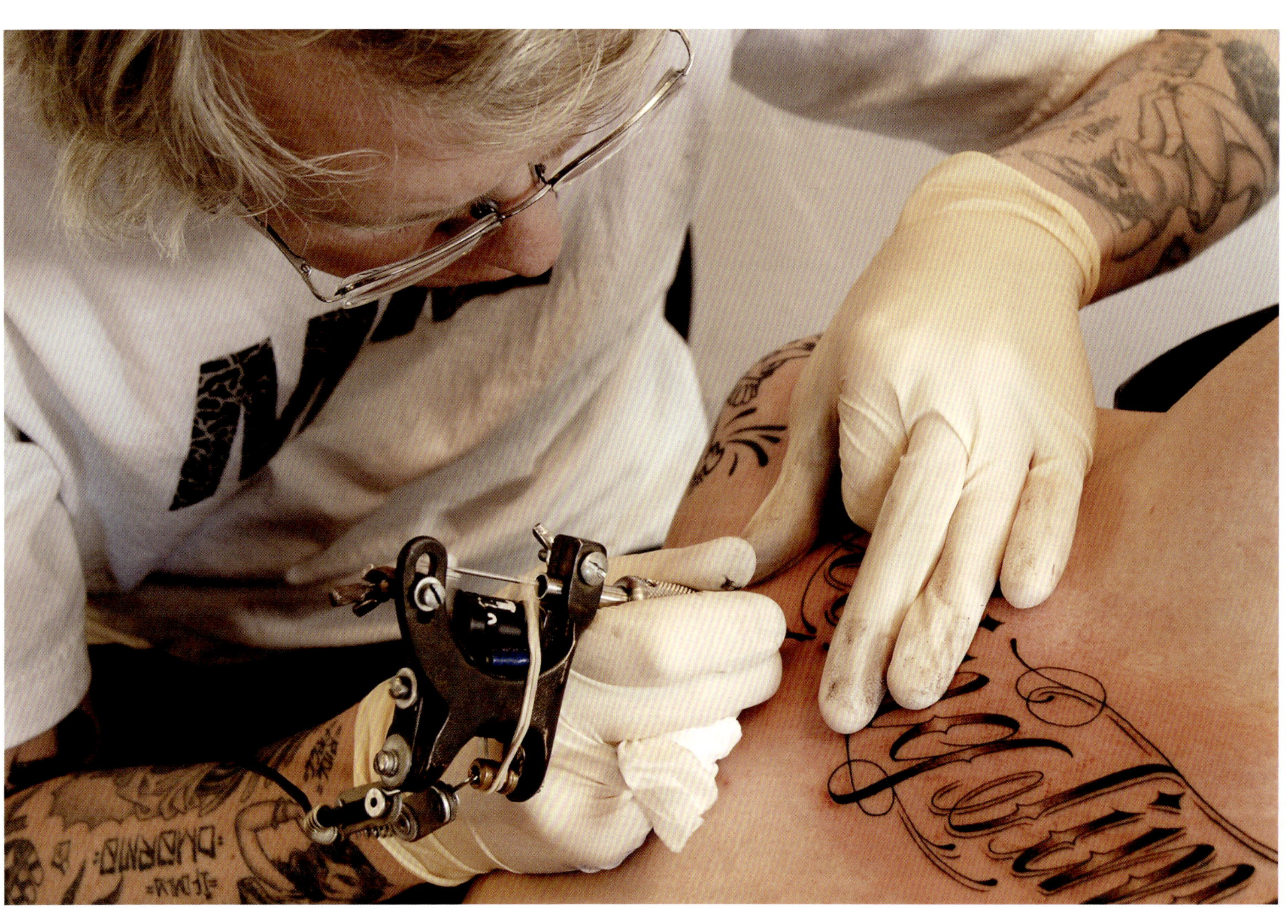

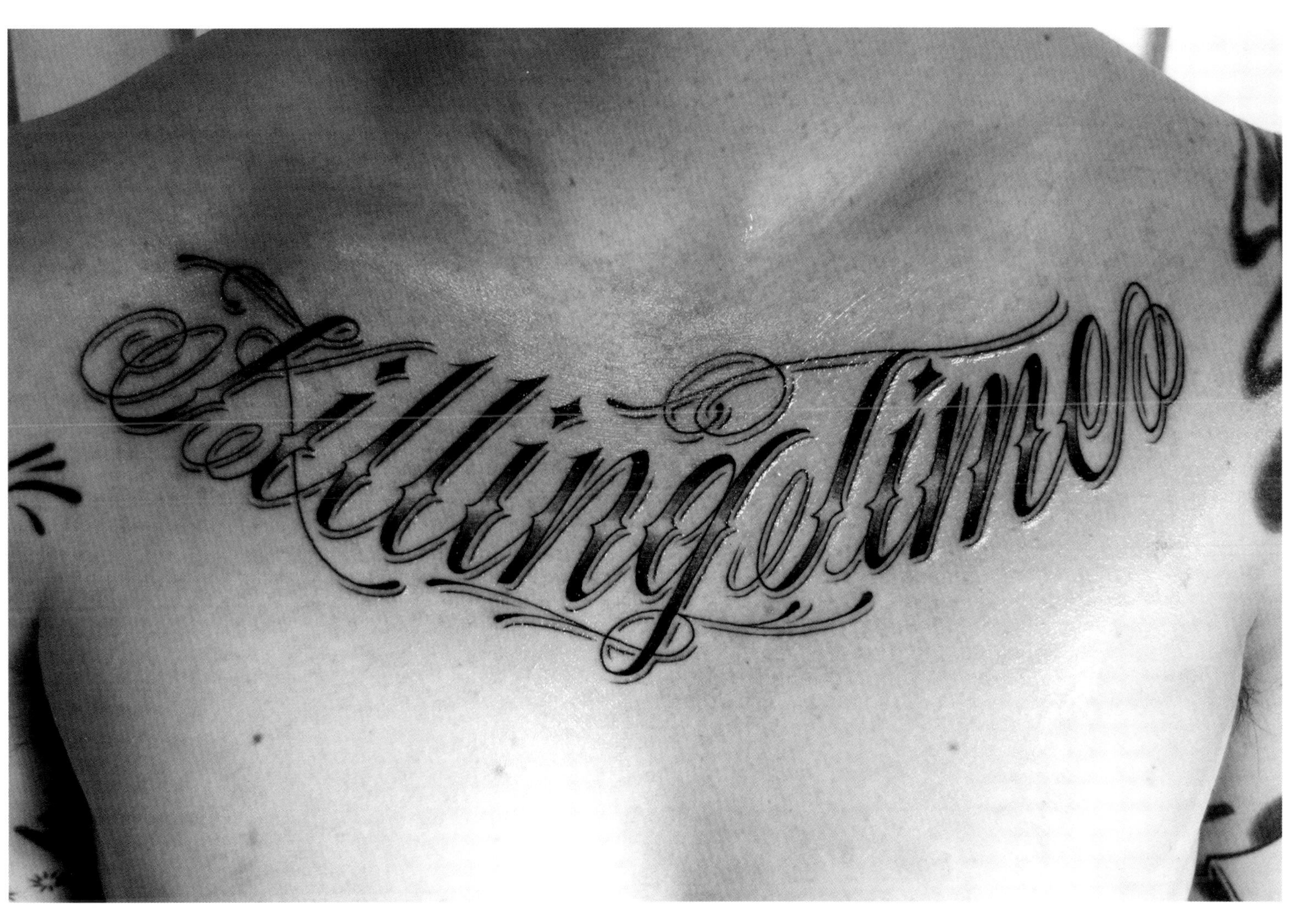
Killing time

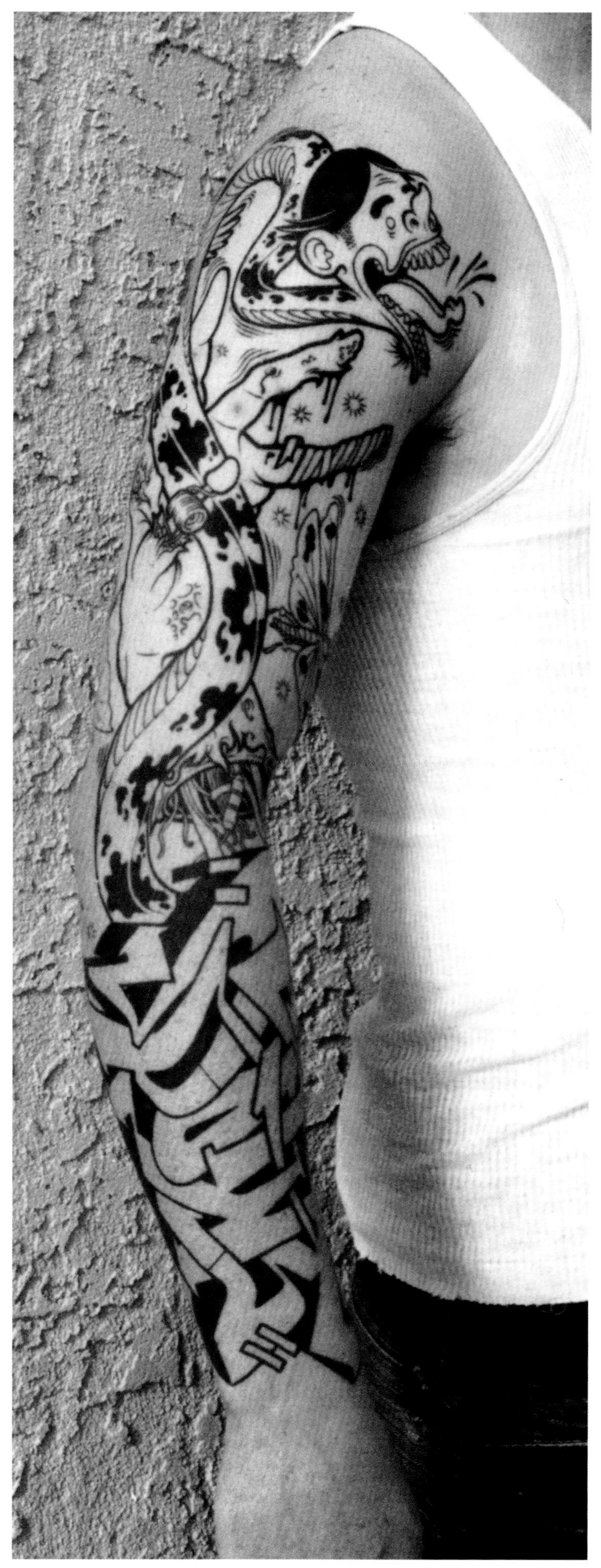

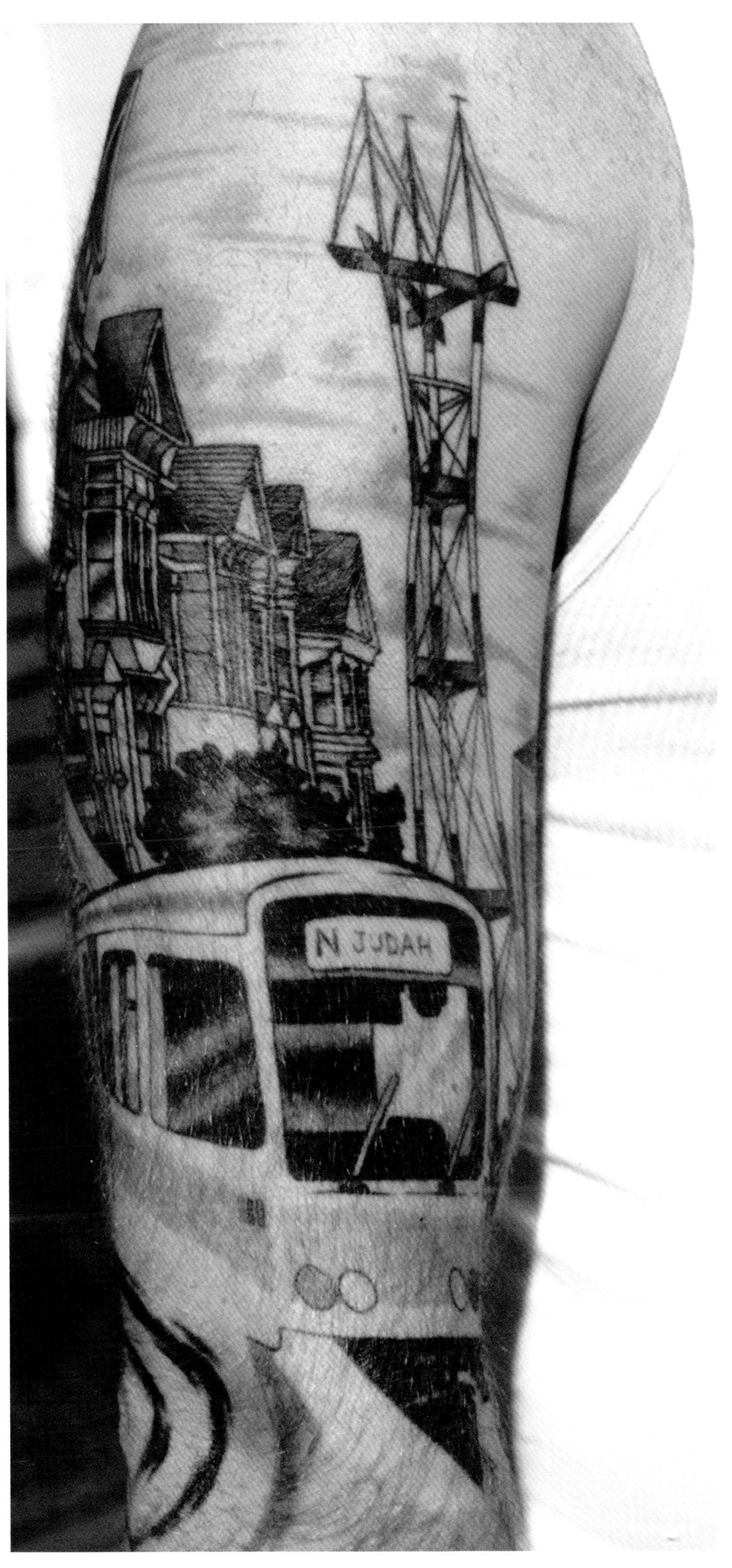
N JUDAH

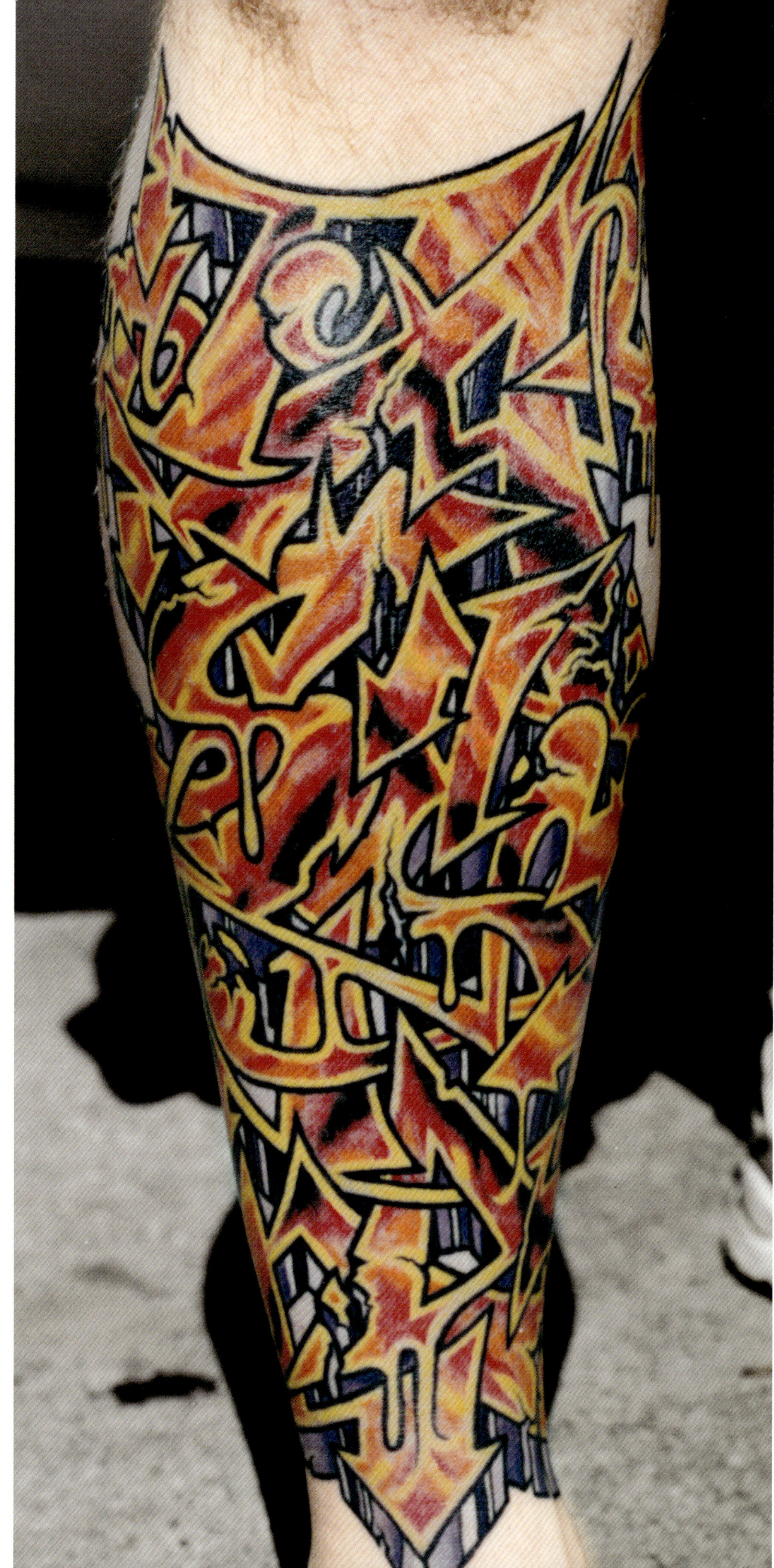

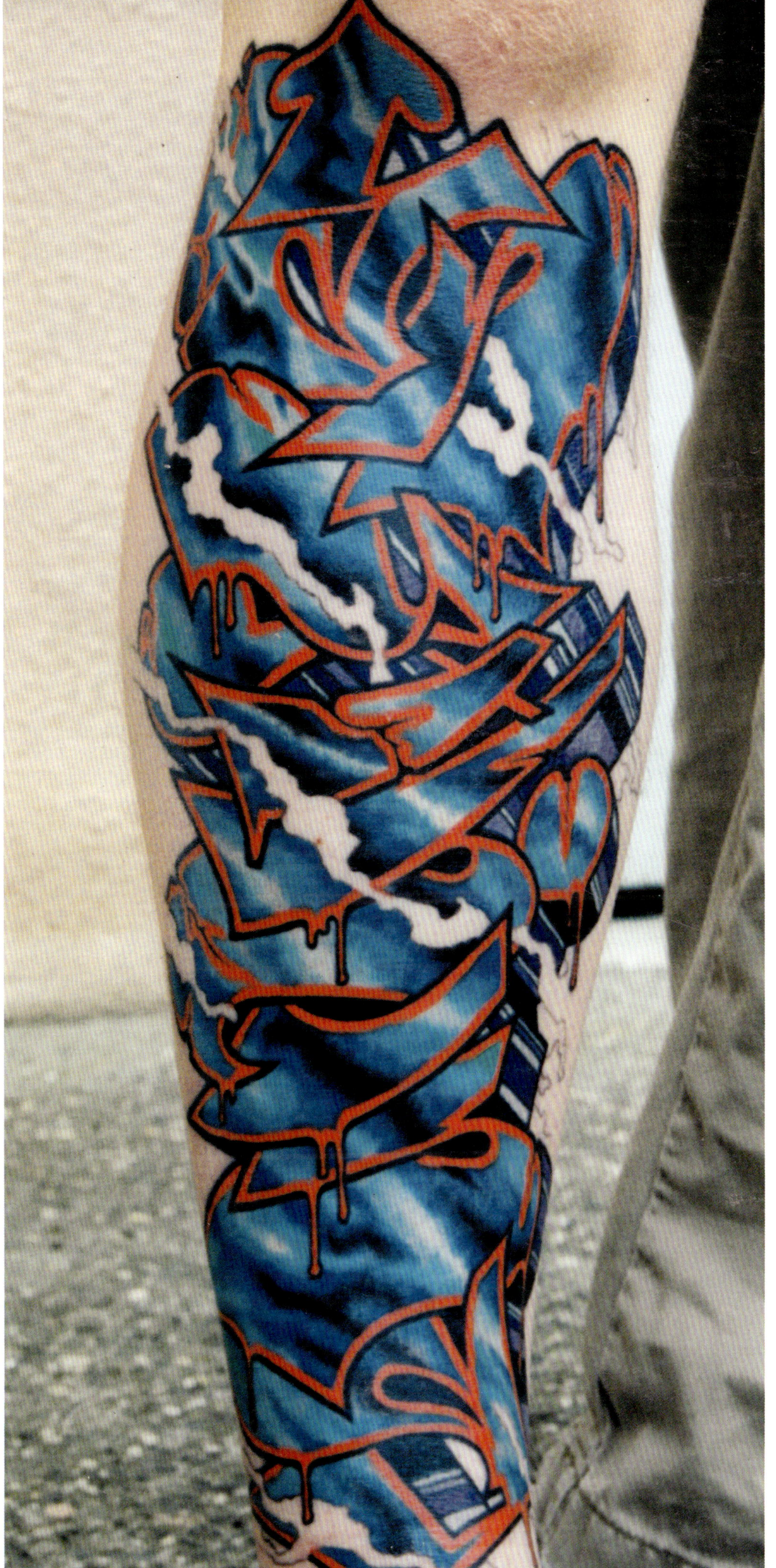

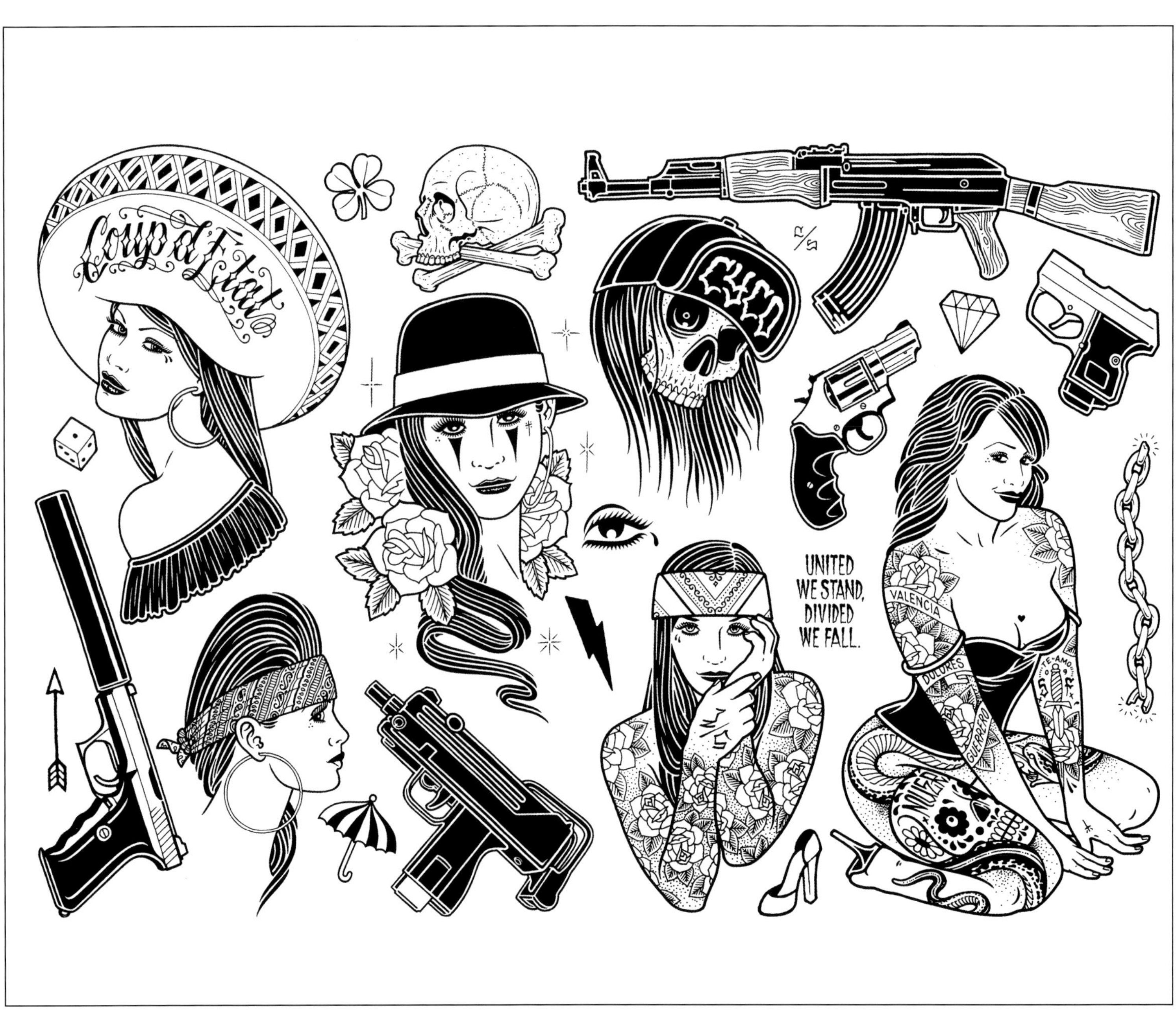

Coup d'État
UNITED
WE STAND.
DIVIDED
WE FALL.
VALENCIA

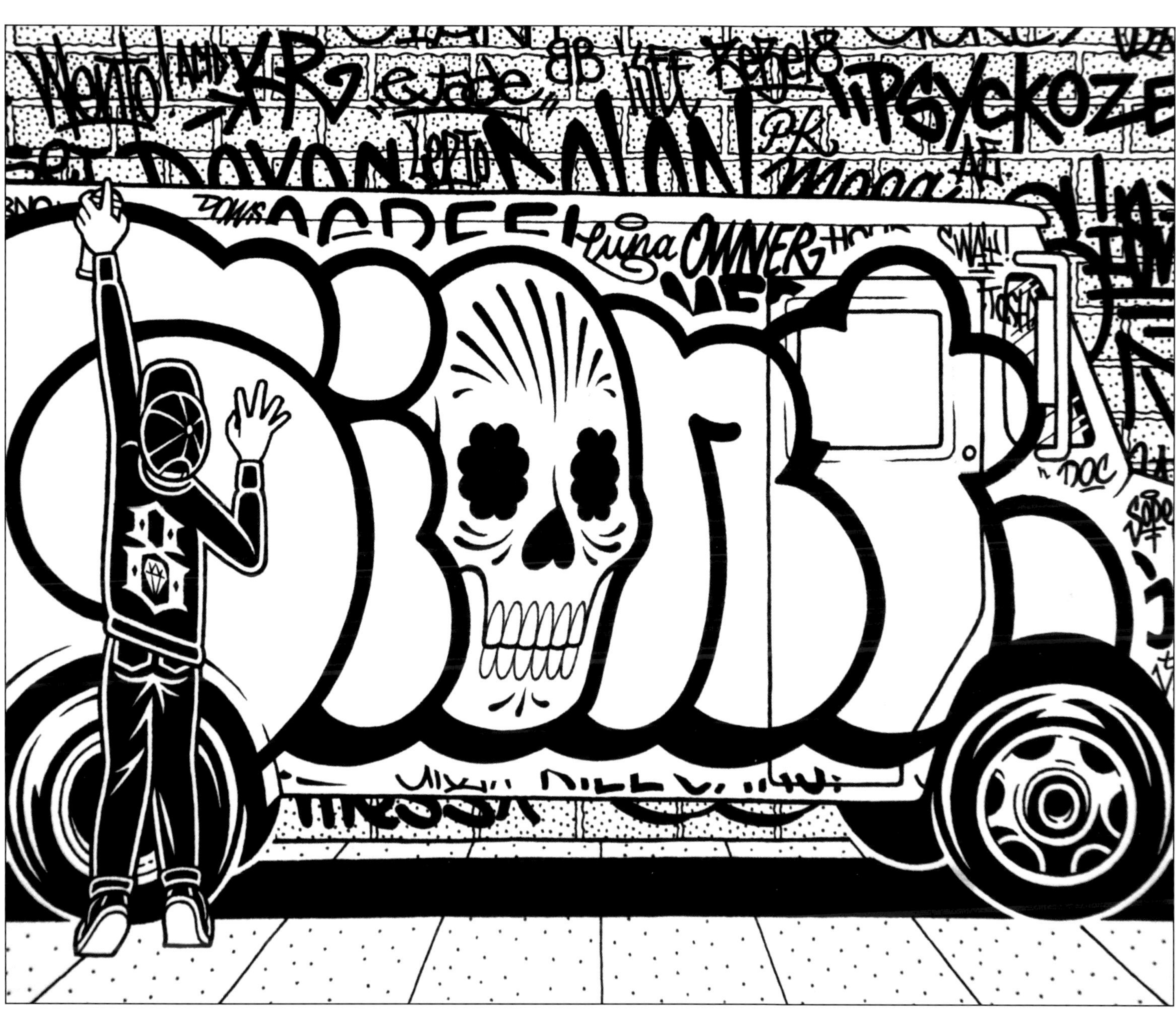

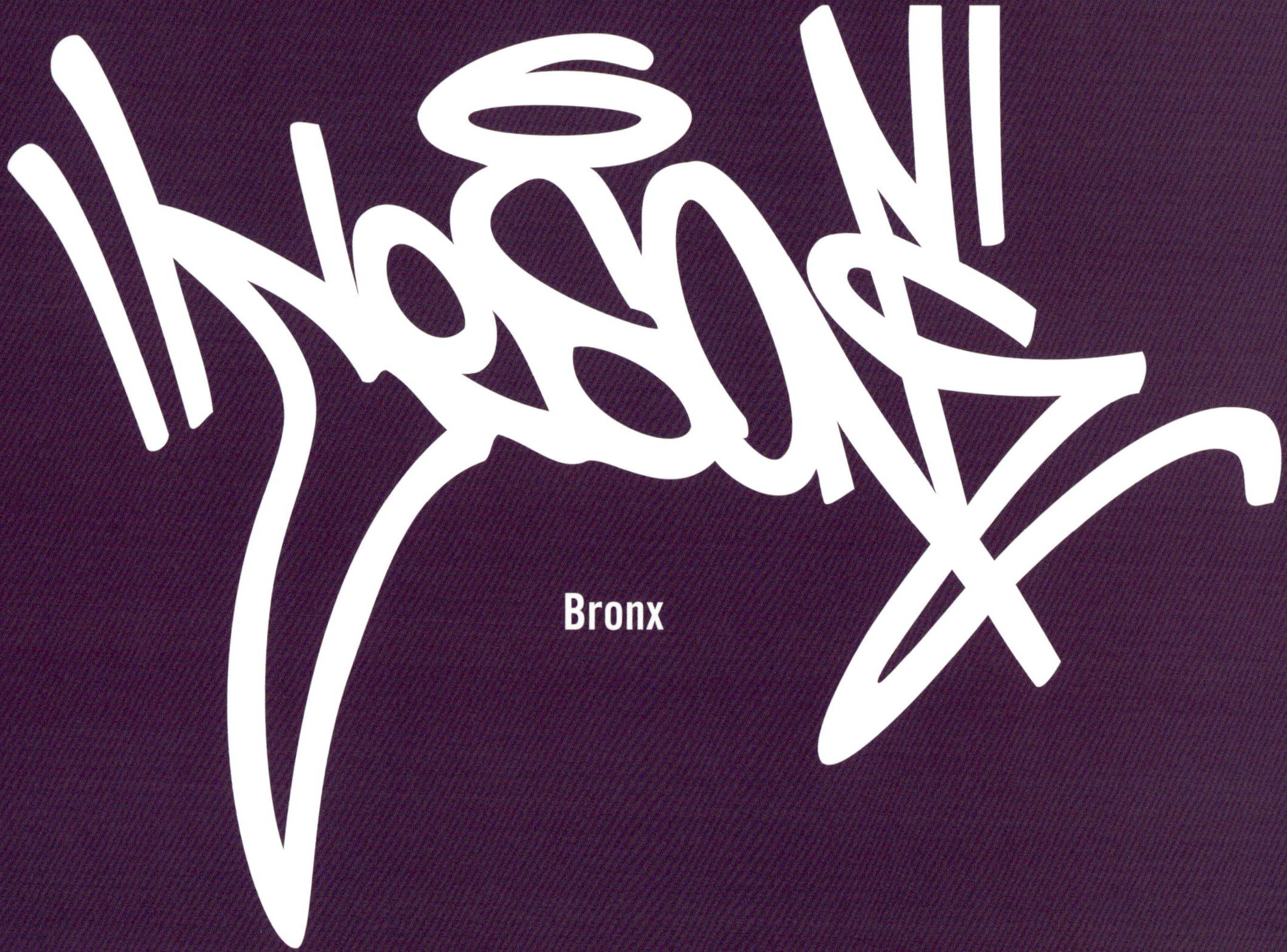

"I was in the right place at the right time. Eventually, being that I built a name for myself, people would come in and say, 'Oh, you're a tattooer now and you do graffiti? I want to get a graffiti tattoo from you.' It kind of just gave me a place and a purpose."

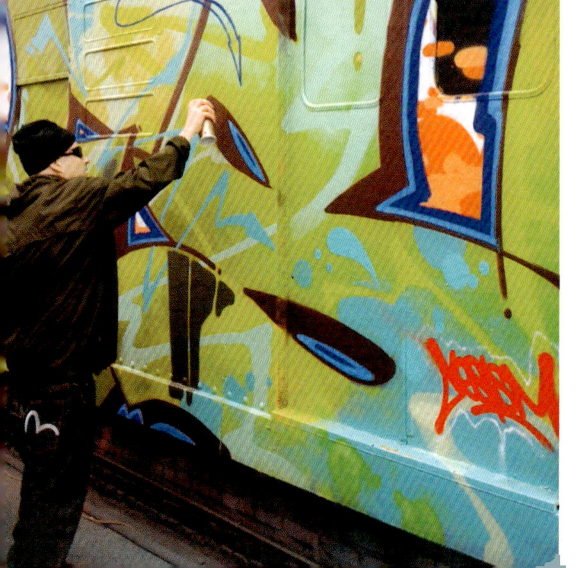

CES

New York native Ces became a tattoo artist as an afterthought. He came of age as hip-hop culture was rising up like the Holy Roman Empire. Once Ces decided that graffiti was his mode of expression, he campaigned hard, painting numerous trains, planes, and automobiles along the way. Today, Ces's distinctive style has inspired legions of graffiti writers around the world, and tattoo fans travel far and wide to get the heat of his burners etched into their flesh.

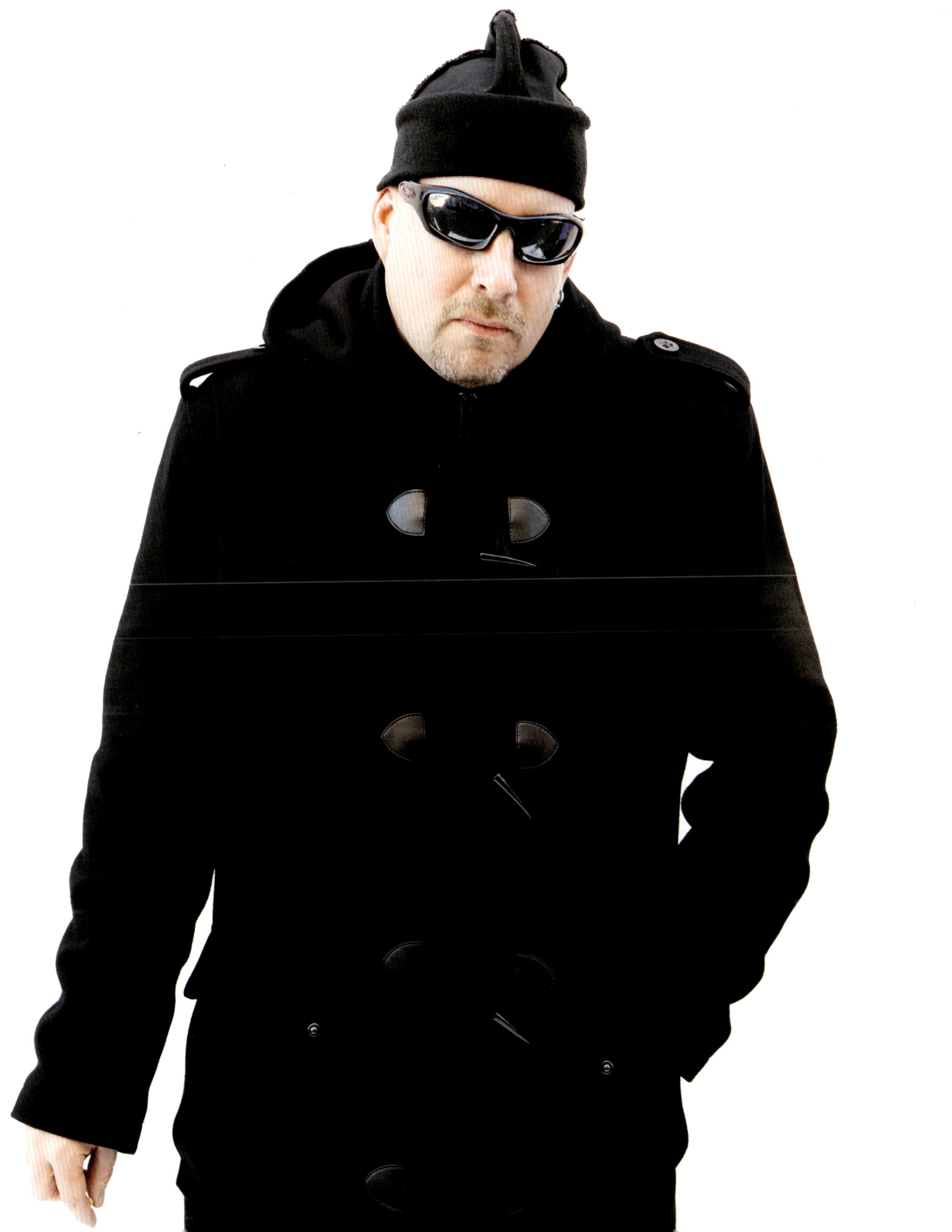

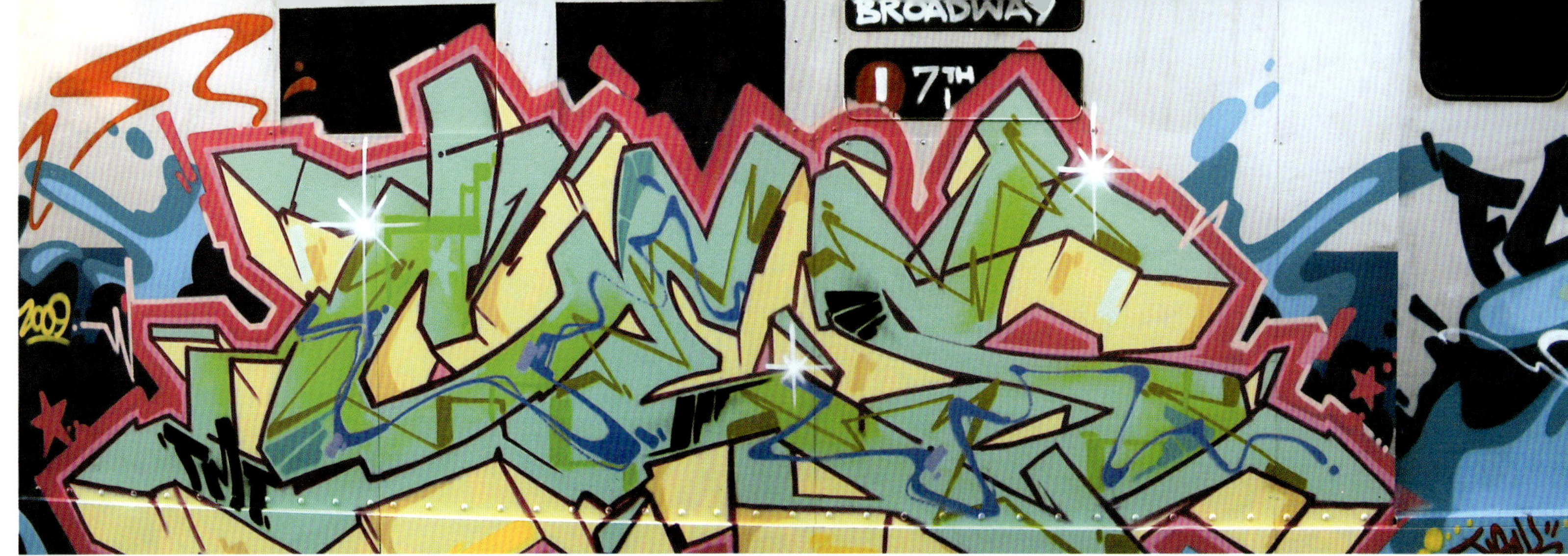

Ces piece, Tuff City, Bronx, 2009

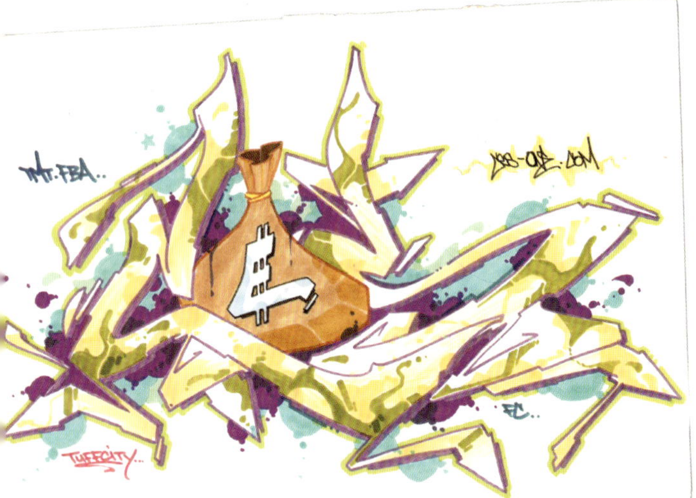

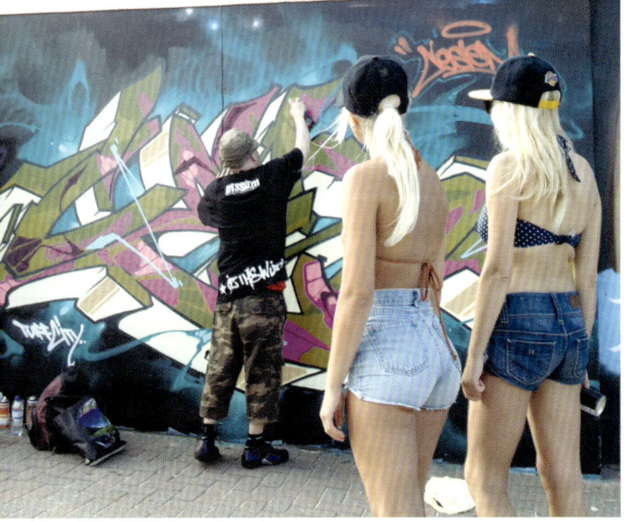

TOP: Ces piecebook drawing, 2010
BOTTOM: Ces working in Melbourne, Australia, 2012

I first started writing *Ces* in 1983, here in New York. At that time I spelled it *S-E-S*, but that lasted maybe one summer because doing two S's—the same, like bookends—became difficult. I switched it to *C-E-S* to give it a different look, and it was a bit easier. So I was writing that from '84 until about '86. I stopped from '87 to '91. I lived a crazy life without graffiti, but I always watched it even then. I came back to it in '92 and never stopped.

I was born able to draw well. I knew from the first day of kindergarten that I was different from the other kids when we had drawing time. Later on I was seeing a lot of kids in my neighborhood writing. I think the things I was exposed to or how I grew up all played a part. It seemed, in the summer of 1984, everyone who was a part of my life wrote graffiti. Even my father wanted to try. I mean, like, it was that big. It was that important.

It's funny, because years later I run into people from back then and they say, "Is that you? You still do that? Remember when we used to do that?" And I'd be like, "Yeah, I kind of still do," like, kind of embarrassed about it. I was really into it while they were out making money or doing other things. They all get married and have kids, and I'm saying, "No, I still do graffiti like we did back when we were twelve."

One of the first important crews when I was young was TCV—The Crazy Vandals. It was this dude Vet from Westchester County, and he kind of mentored me. He took me out to these really beat-up places where I wouldn't have gone on my own, and I met other writers through him. It grew like that. The crews that I got down with in the years to come, I never thought I'd be part of them as a kid. People I was a fan

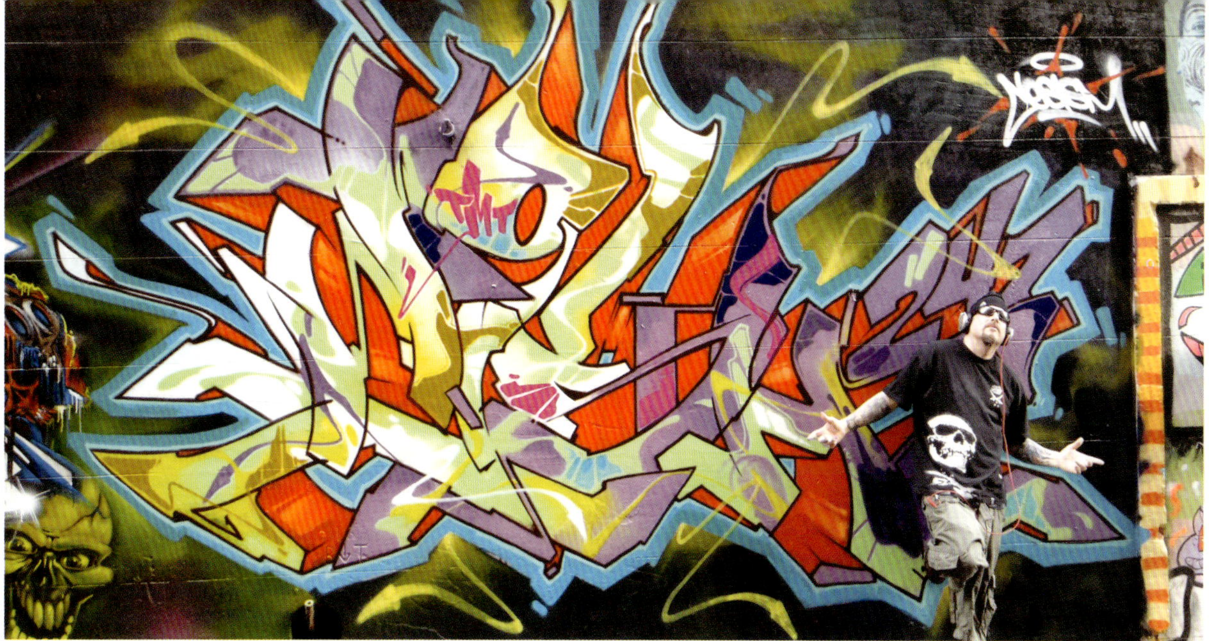

Ces piece, Melbourne, Australia, 2009

of were larger than life to me, and so it's just the perseverance and passion of what I wanted.

There are still moments to this day, when I'm around around certain writers I really admired as a kid, where I check myself for like ten seconds and think, "Am I really doing this with this guy right now?" You've got to hold on to that. You always have to remain a fan of it. You can't put yourself in front of it. The smells and the stealing of paint—now I'm sponsored by a paint company and I get flown to different countries. It's not the same as when I was a kid. But I do remember it, and I'm glad I was there for it, and that's where I really keep true a lot of the time.

I was just in Australia at a big event, and these guys out there paint like razor sharp and I'm not as clean as them. So the first few times painting, I'm thinking these guys are going to judge me, like I don't have the skill they do, and I can try, but that's not really where it's at for me. I'm standing back from the wall and they're like, "Yours is the natural, you know, we could never do that." It just reminds me how I say that to the older guys I know, so it's full circle again.

I started noticing tattoos obviously as an artist and having an eye open to everything around me. I noticed tattoos pretty early, but it was more like bikers and sailors, that kind of thing. I didn't really see myself having anything to do with it. Someone took me to a tattoo shop when I was maybe seventeen, eighteen. I wasn't going to get a tattoo. We just went because he came home from the Marines and he was getting a tattoo, if I recall. It was like the scariest place ever. The guy had his eyelids tattooed and I was like, no, I'll never, never deal with this.

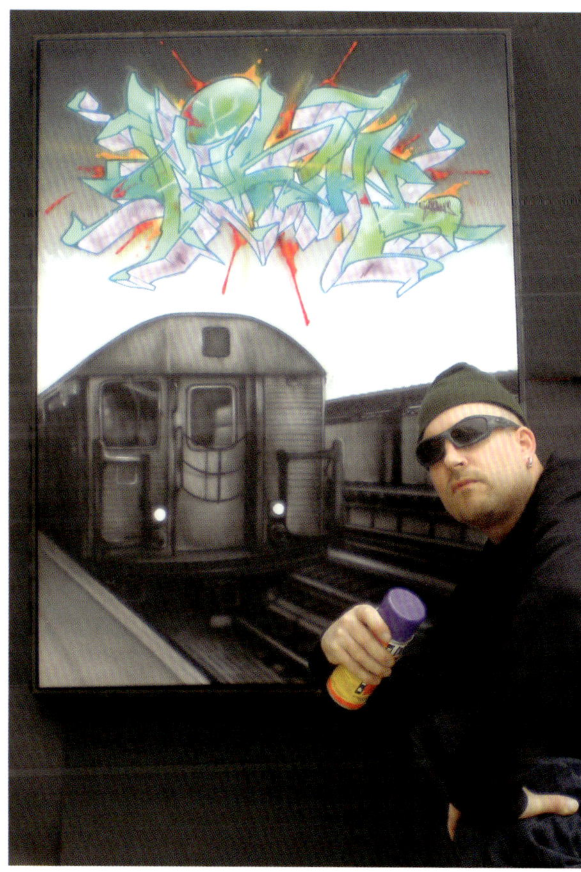

Ces painting, 2007

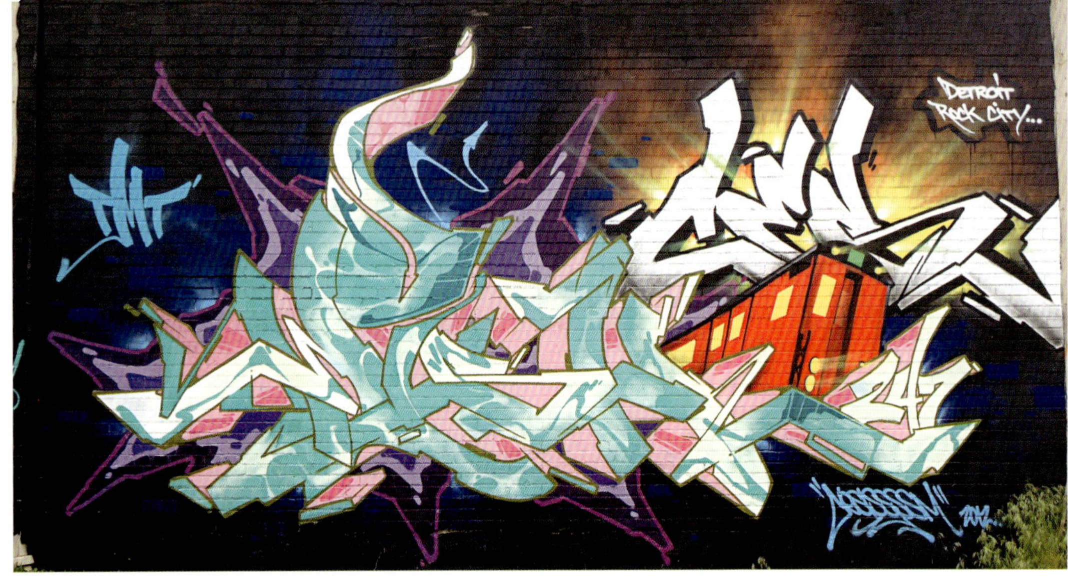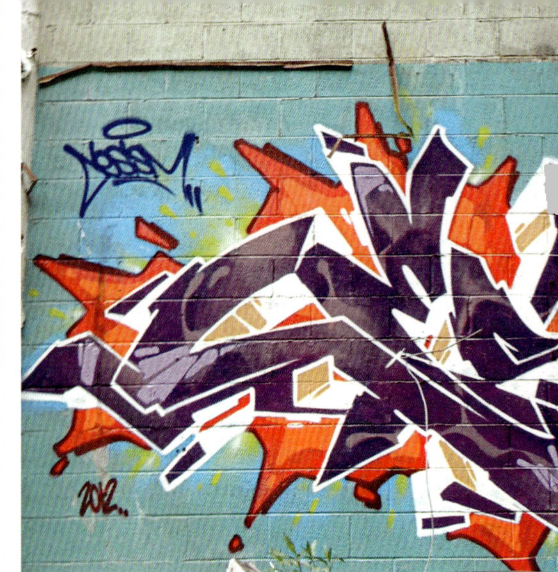

FROM LEFT: Ces, *Wish*, Detroit, 2012; Ces piece, Montreal, 2012; Ces piece, Detroit, 2012

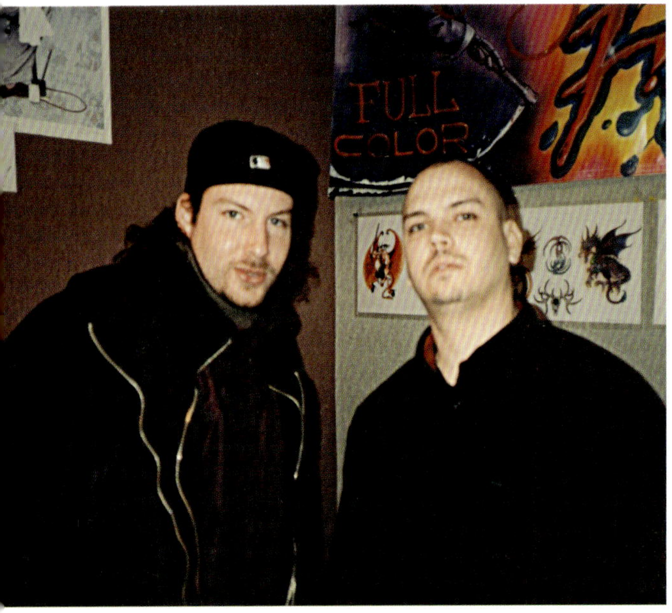

Ces (left) and Med, 1996

As years went on, I was meeting artists like Med and other people. They were like, hey, you should really try this, and my only memory of it was that scary place as a kid where there were all these guys who looked at me like I was crazy. I didn't want nothing to do with it. Then I came and hung around with Med in the shop. It wasn't part of my lifestyle, but the more I hung around and the more I saw, I was like, you know what, I'll try it. I got some machines and tried it on some kids in my neighborhood, fixing tattoos for them, and then I picked it up.

I like walls and trains and canvases and paper, because they don't bleed or talk back. But then again, there's the work that you can do, the money that you can make, and being around your friends. I mean, prior to coming here to Tuff City and working with Med, I actually was a sanitation worker in Brooklyn. I dropped that. I had benefits and I had my freedom, but I wasn't an artist. Tattooing helped take me in that direction. It was kind of a means to an end. Like I'm supposed to be here.

When I first started working with Med, I just watched a lot. It was just me being there and picking it up and pushing myself into it. I do graffiti, I could do that—I was doing drawings for people. And then I watched my drawings get done by Med on people—mostly graffiti stuff, because I didn't know that much about tattooing. I saw panthers and scorpions and roses and I have no relation to that stuff.

When I first started tattooing, I was emulating or copying, because that's what people come in for a lot. They'll come in and they'll say, I want this rose. So you add your own flair to it and try to give them

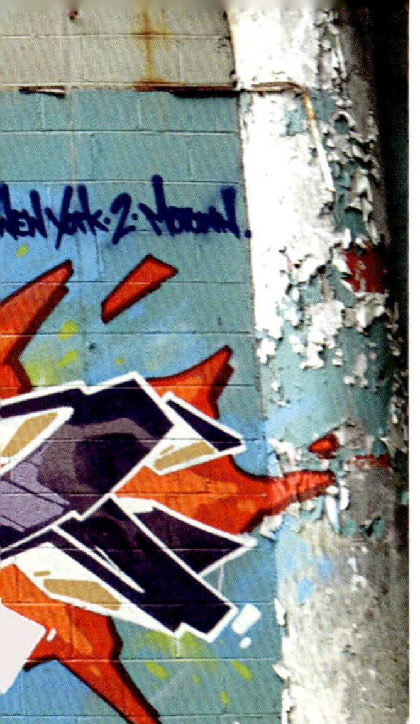

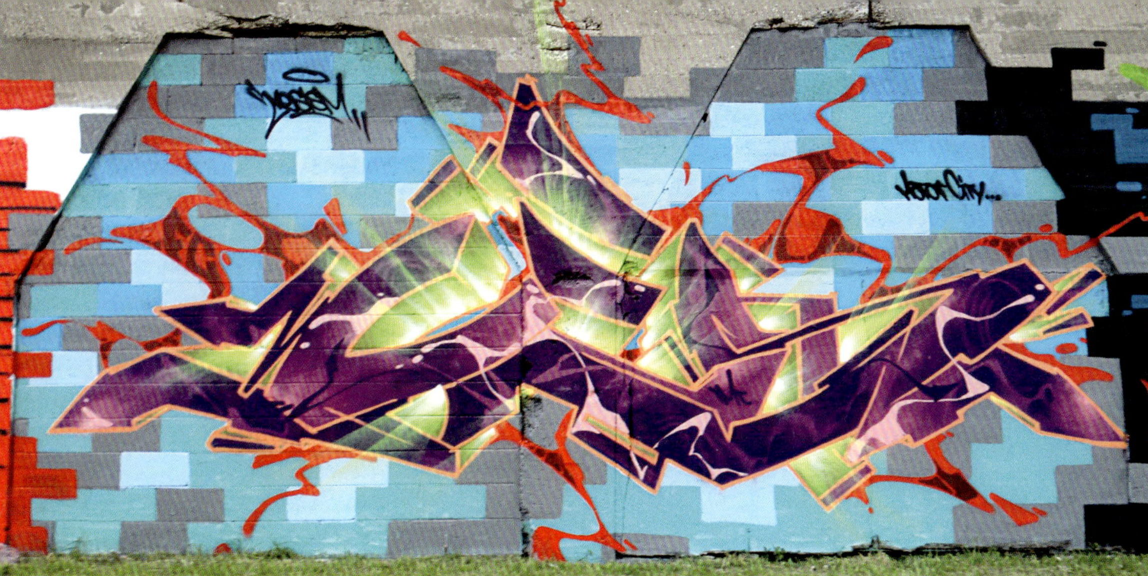

something more custom. I was in the right place at the right time. Eventually, being that I built a name for myself, people would come in and say, "Oh, you're a tattooer now and you do graffiti? I want to get a graffiti tattoo from you." It kind of just gave me a place and a purpose.

I didn't experience any kind of adversity from the traditional tattoo community. Nobody said, "You guys aren't living the life of a tattoo artist," or anything like that. We were welcomed. I remember meeting a bunch of guys that had something in Maine called the Mad Hatter's Ball or something like that. I went with Med, and Zephyr was there as well. Little Vinnie and Aaron Cain and all these famous guys were there, Guy Aitchison. We met a lot of people, and I watched them work. Just like you would have kings in graffiti, it was the same kind of situation. Seeing that and then meeting some of these guys— and they were like, "Oh, we love graffiti." It became clear that this tattooing world is just like the graffiti world: sketching, developing the composition, deciding where it's going to go, picking colors, just like you would in a painting.

I know too many people who just lie in bed and go nowhere. Me? I like to do as much as I can. I like to enjoy life. I change constantly. I'm a creative person, so I'm crazy. Sometimes nothing will make sense. Which is good.

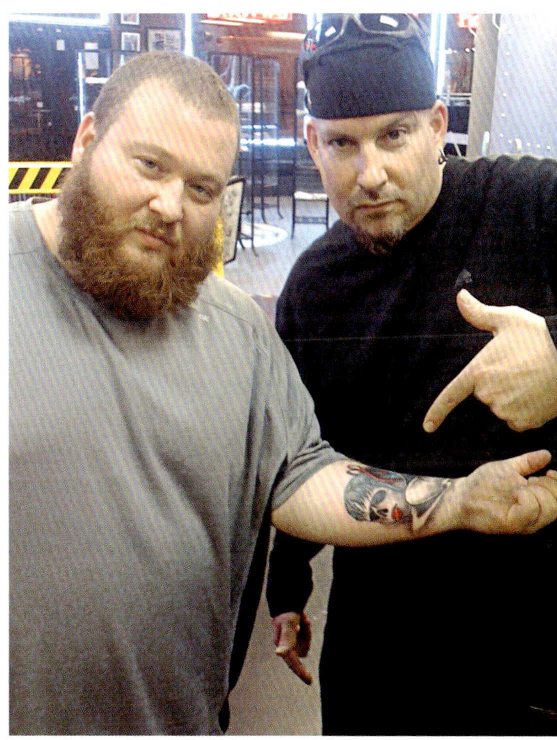

Action Bronson (left) and Ces at Tuff City, 2012

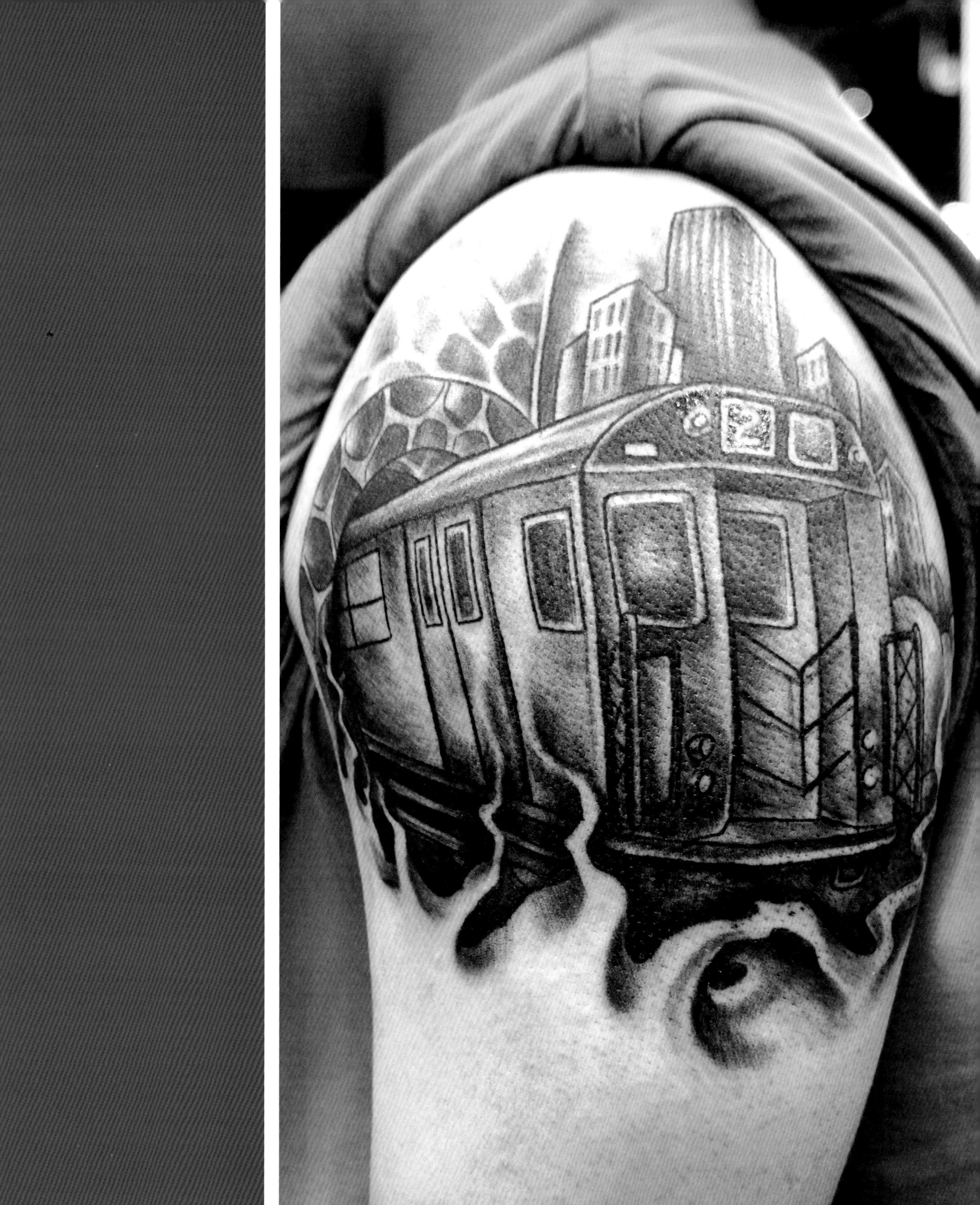

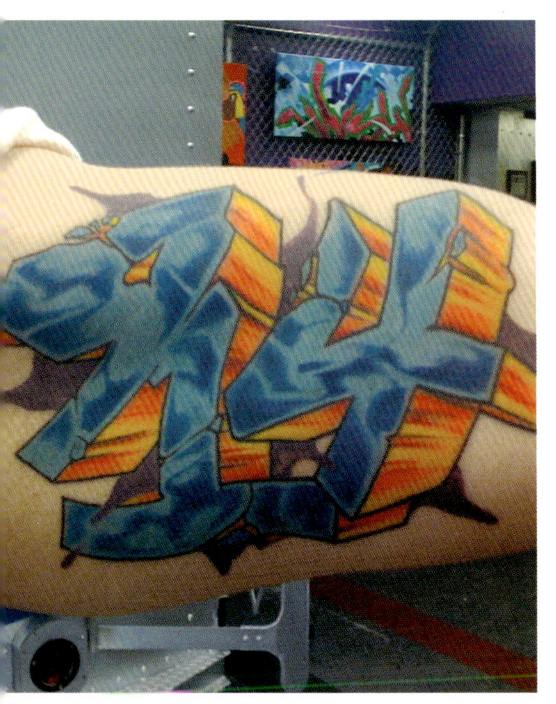
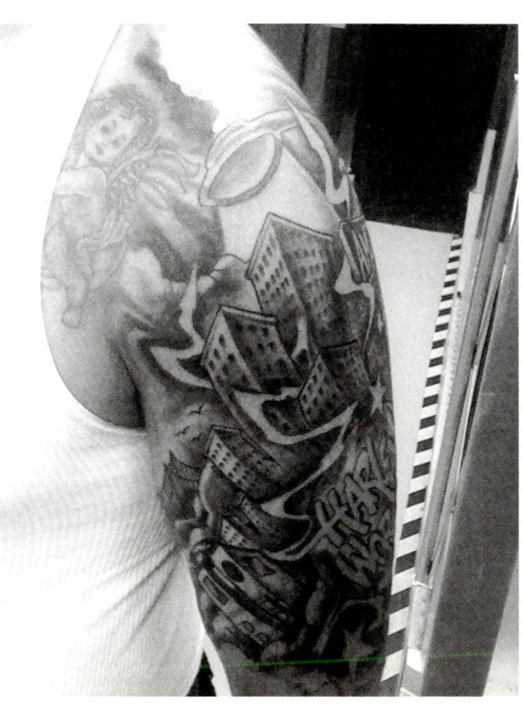
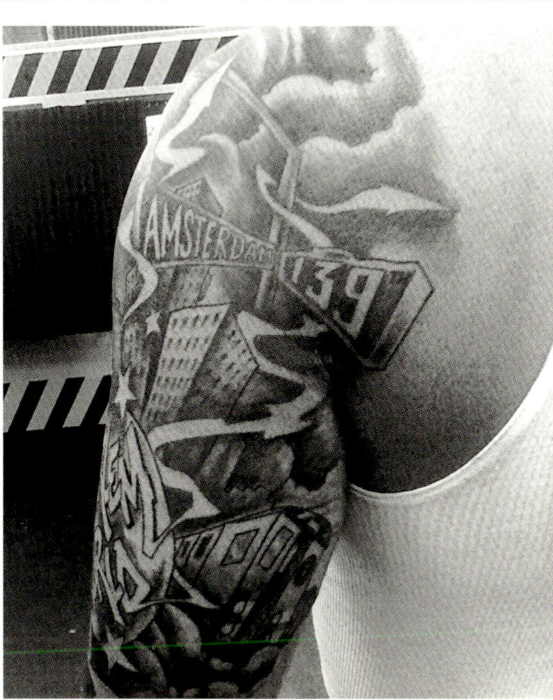
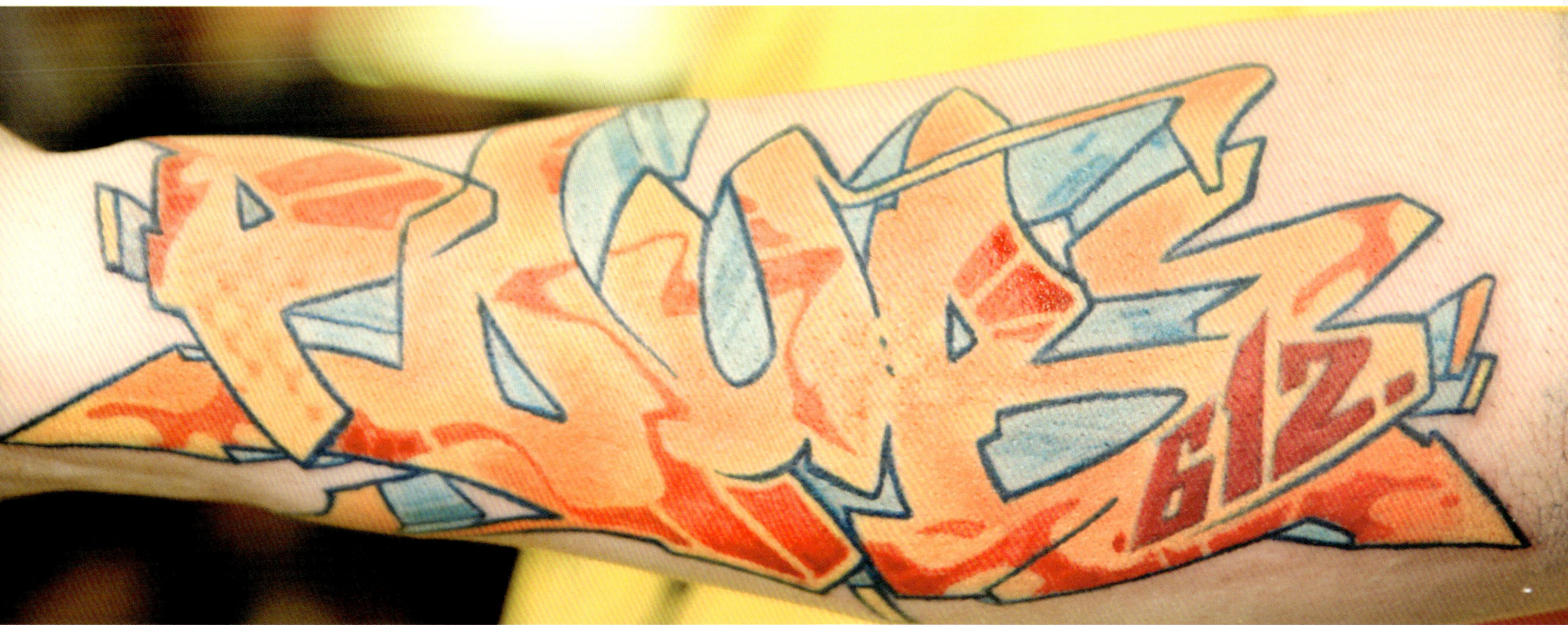

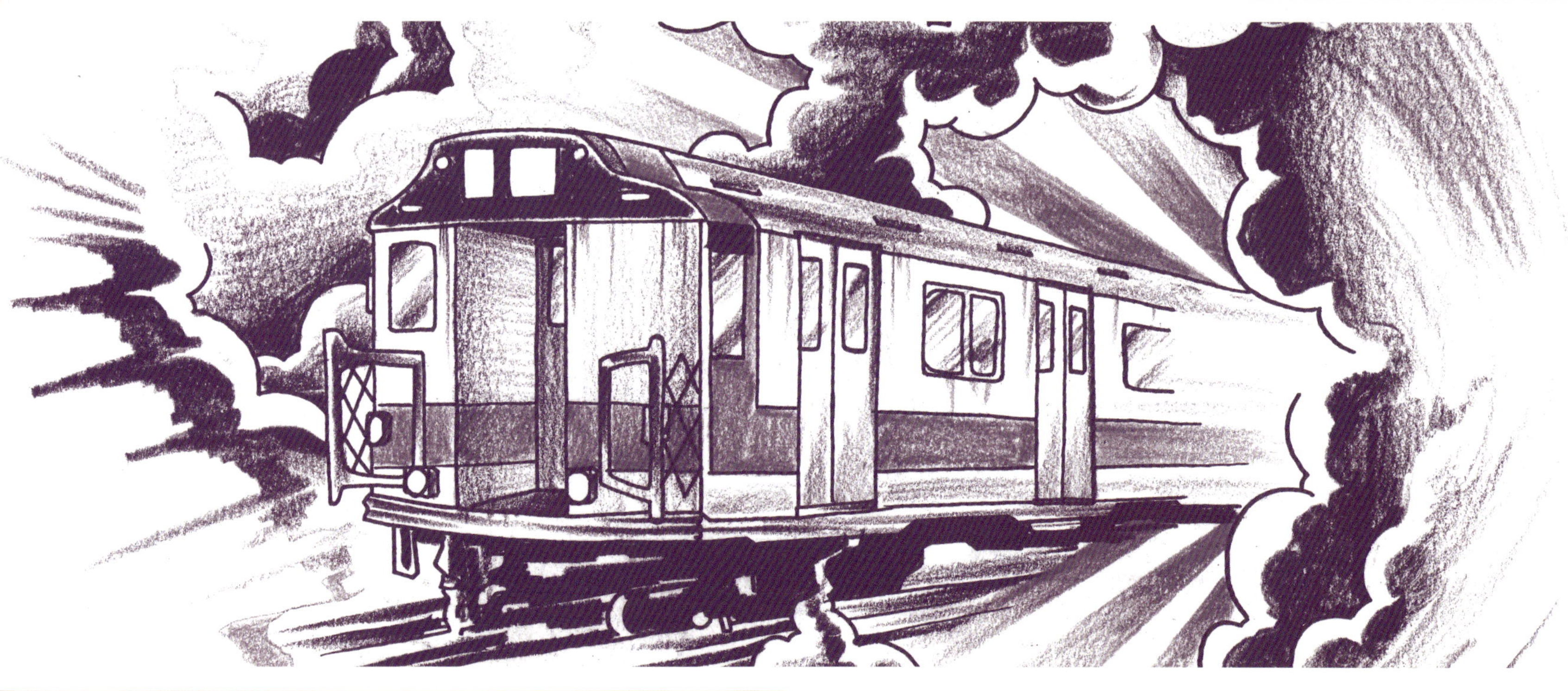

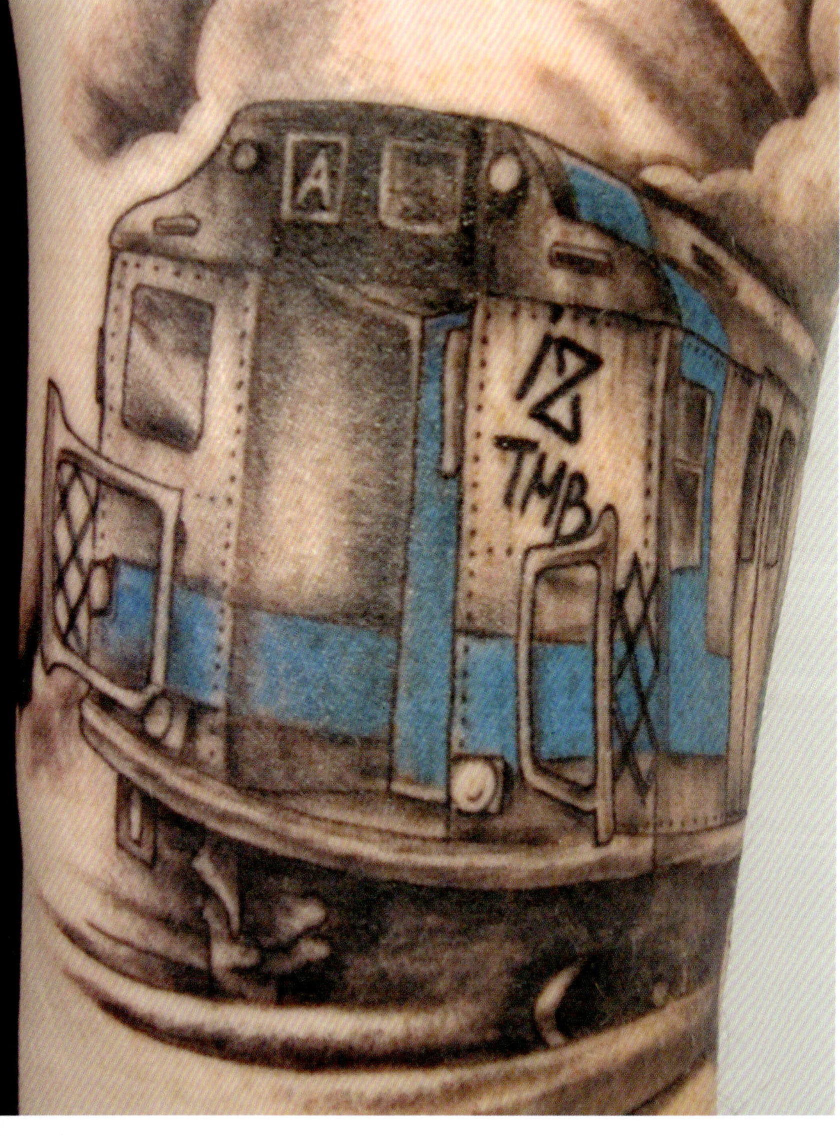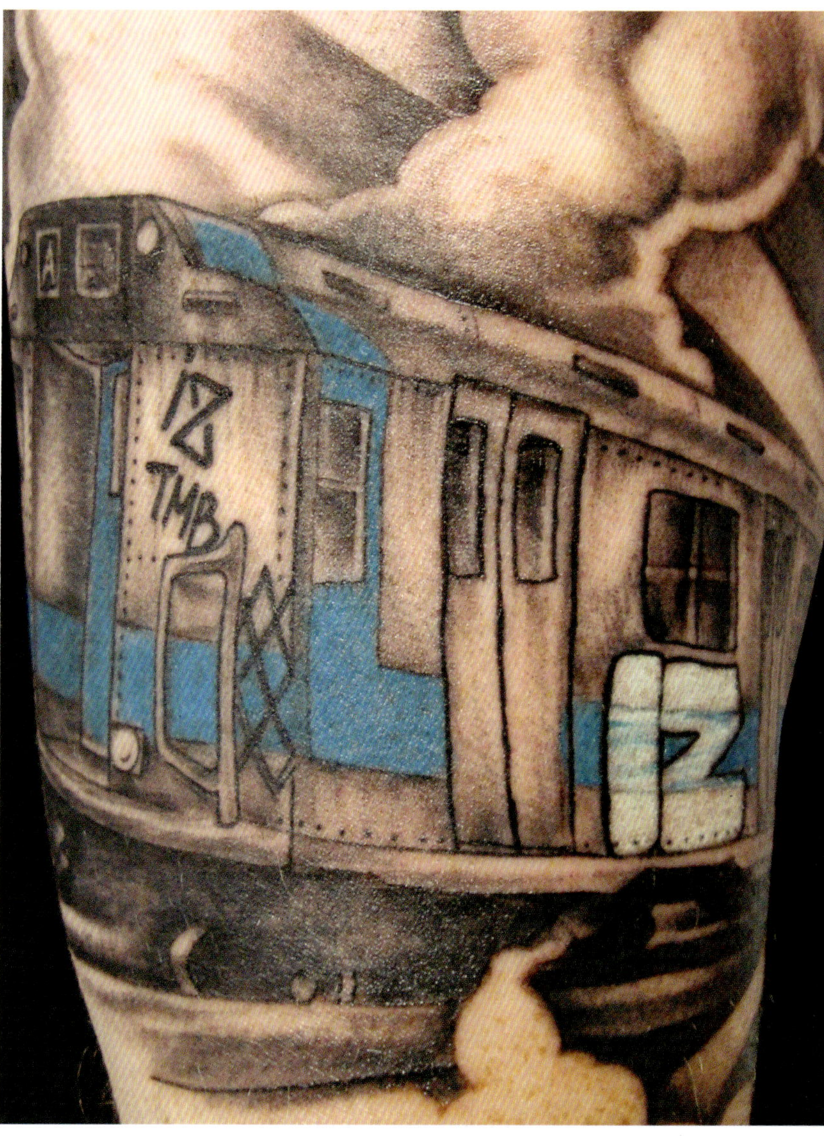

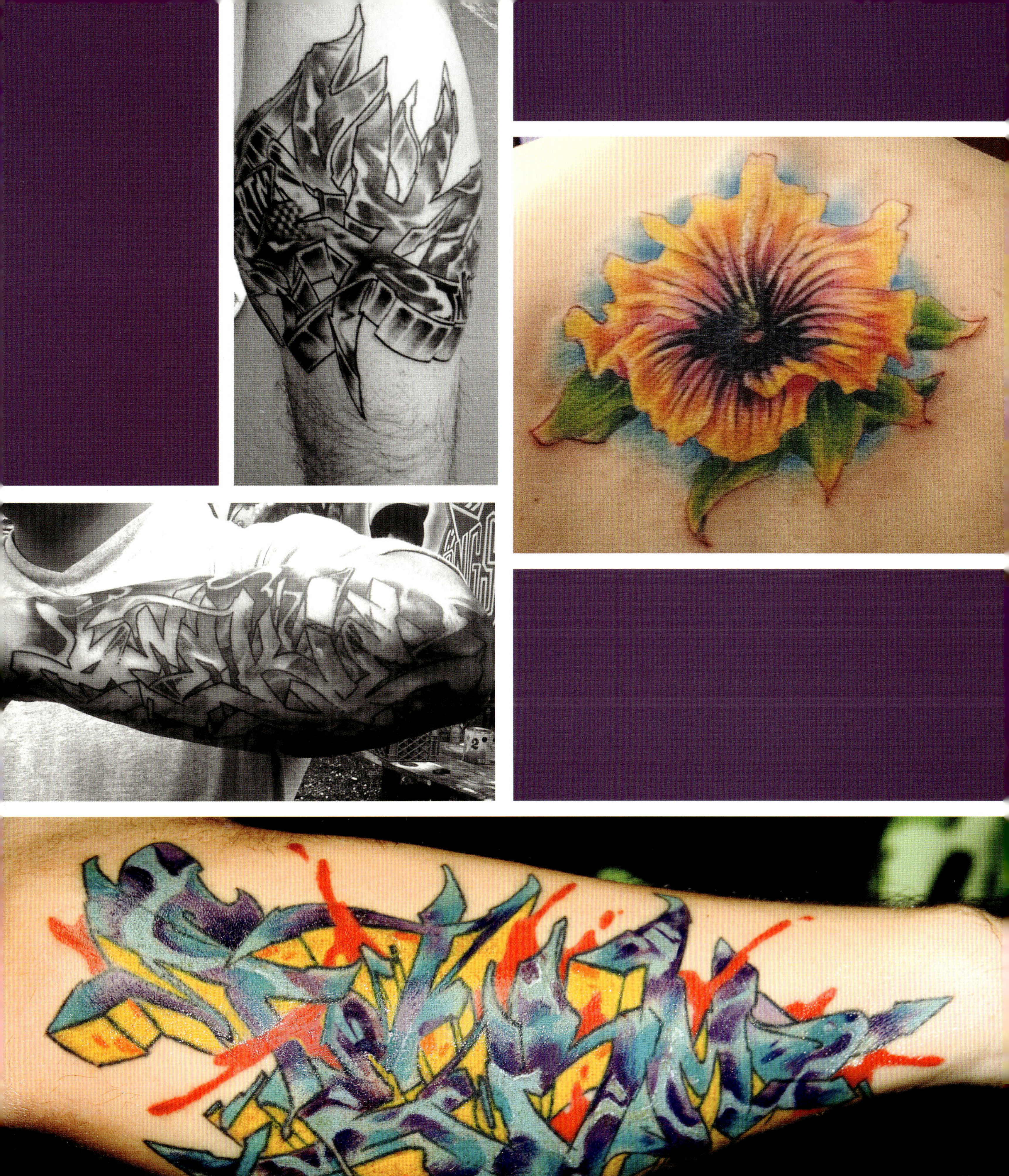

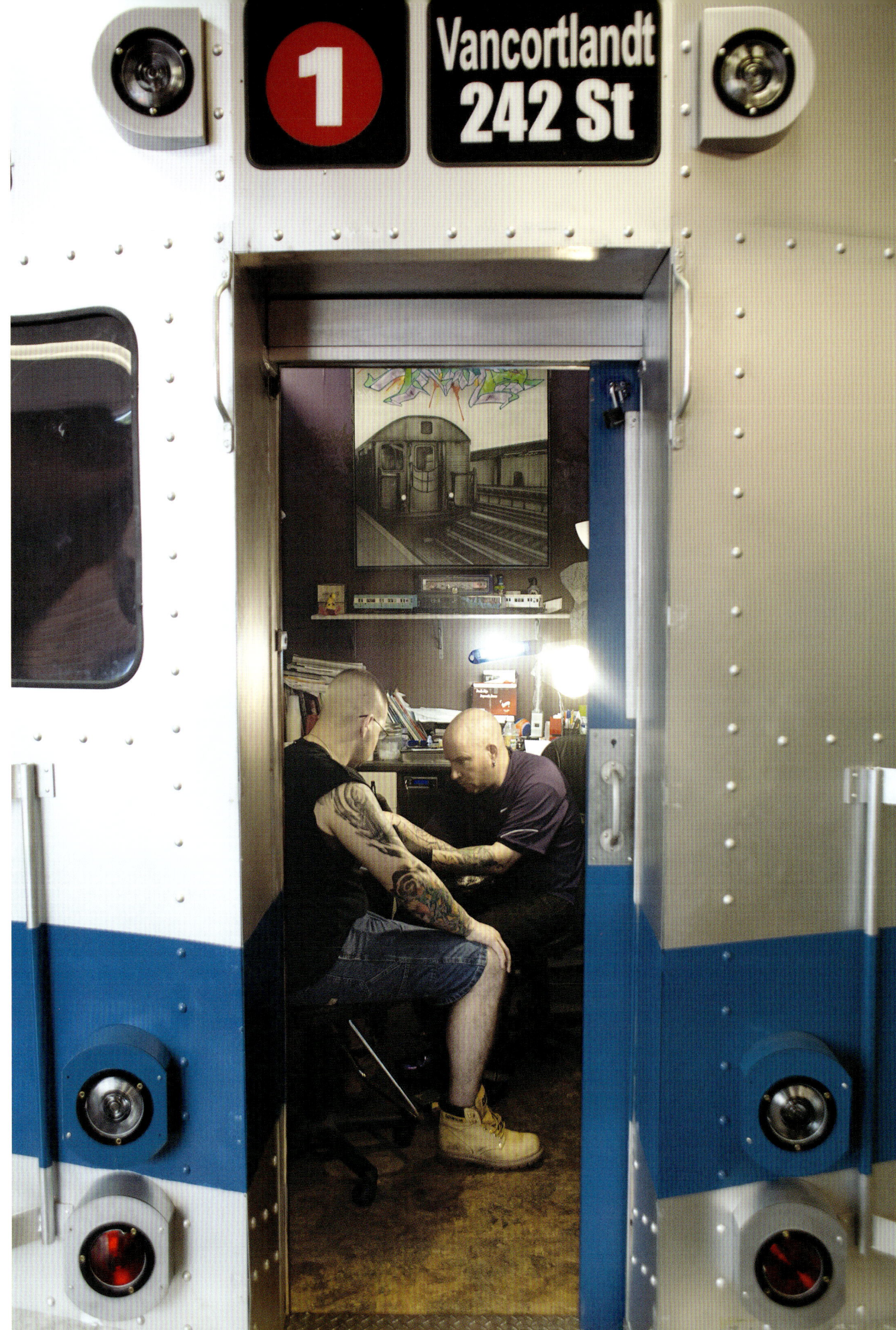
1
Vancortlandt
242 St

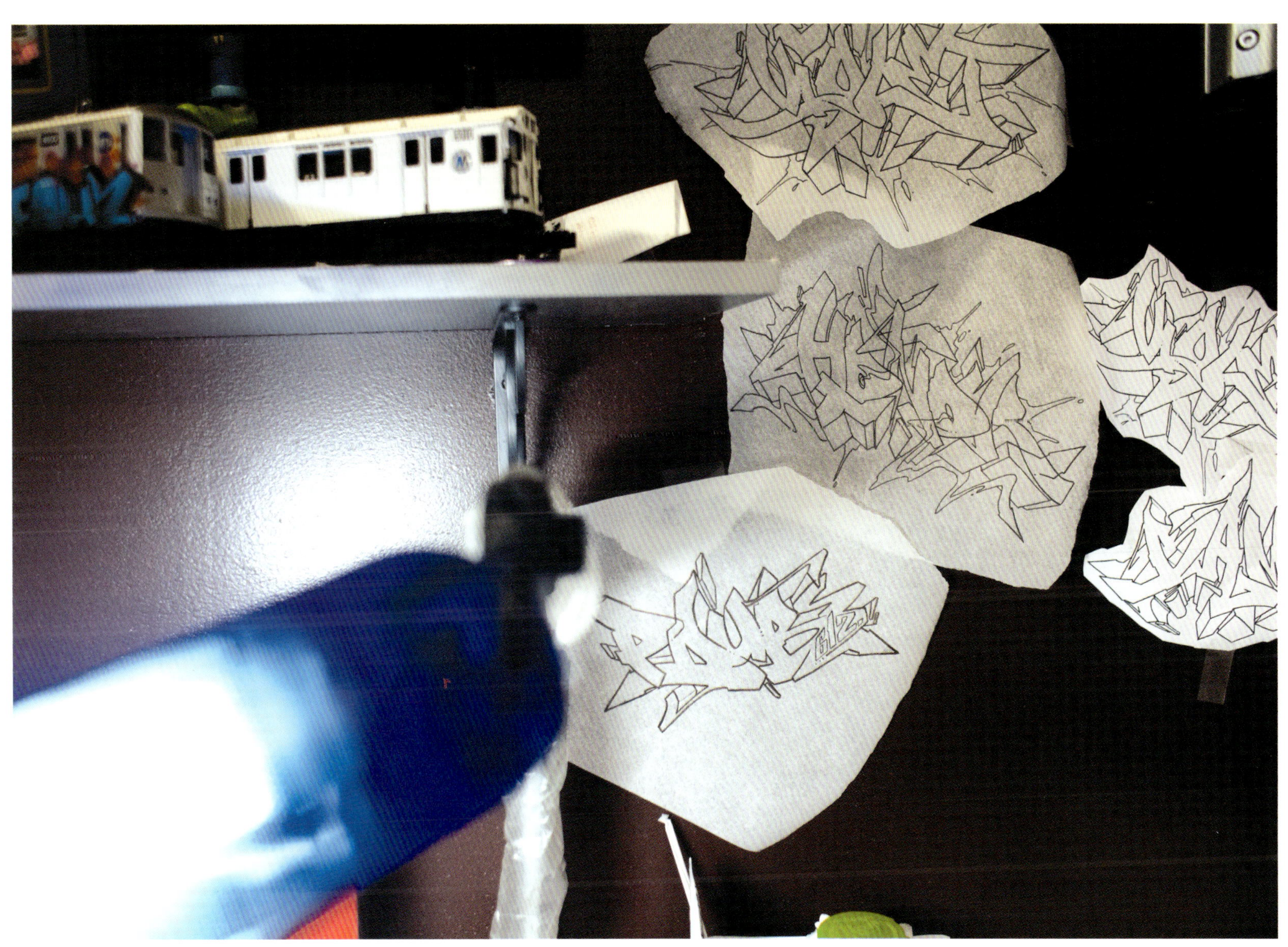

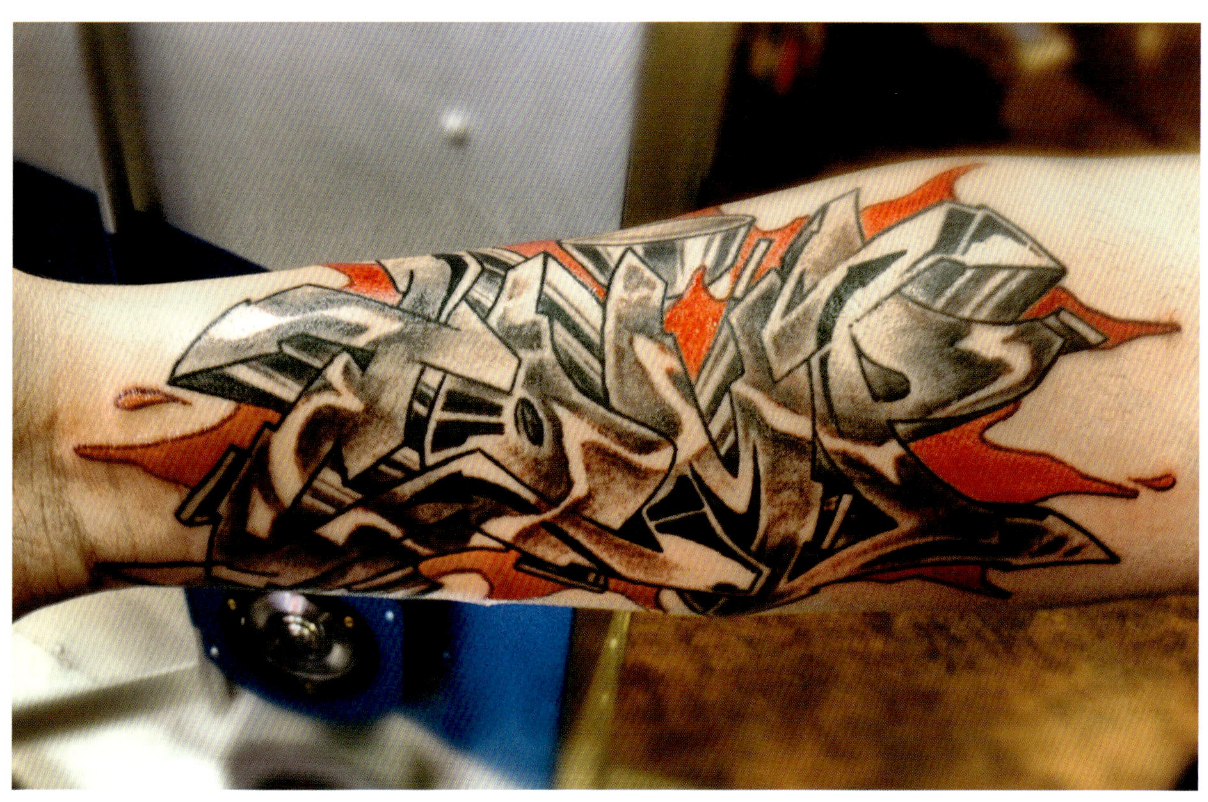

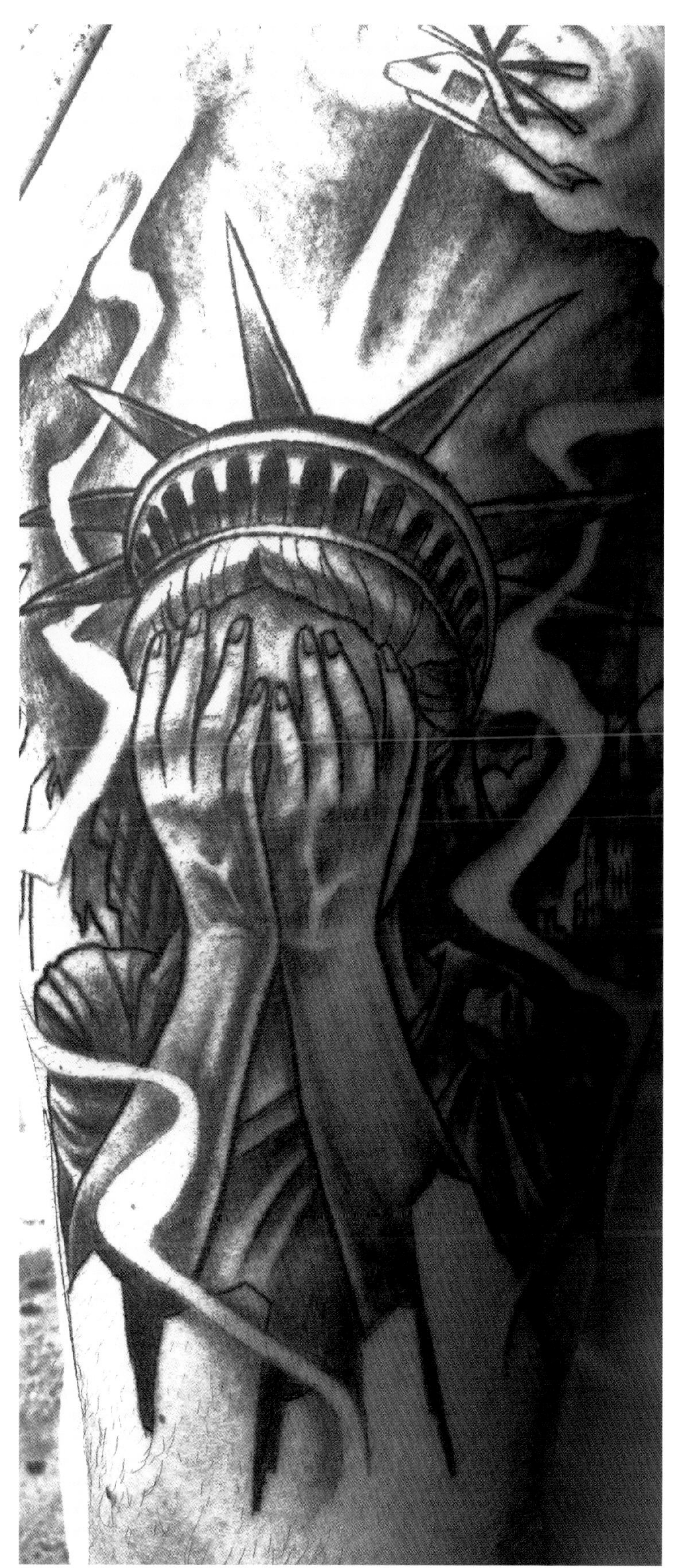

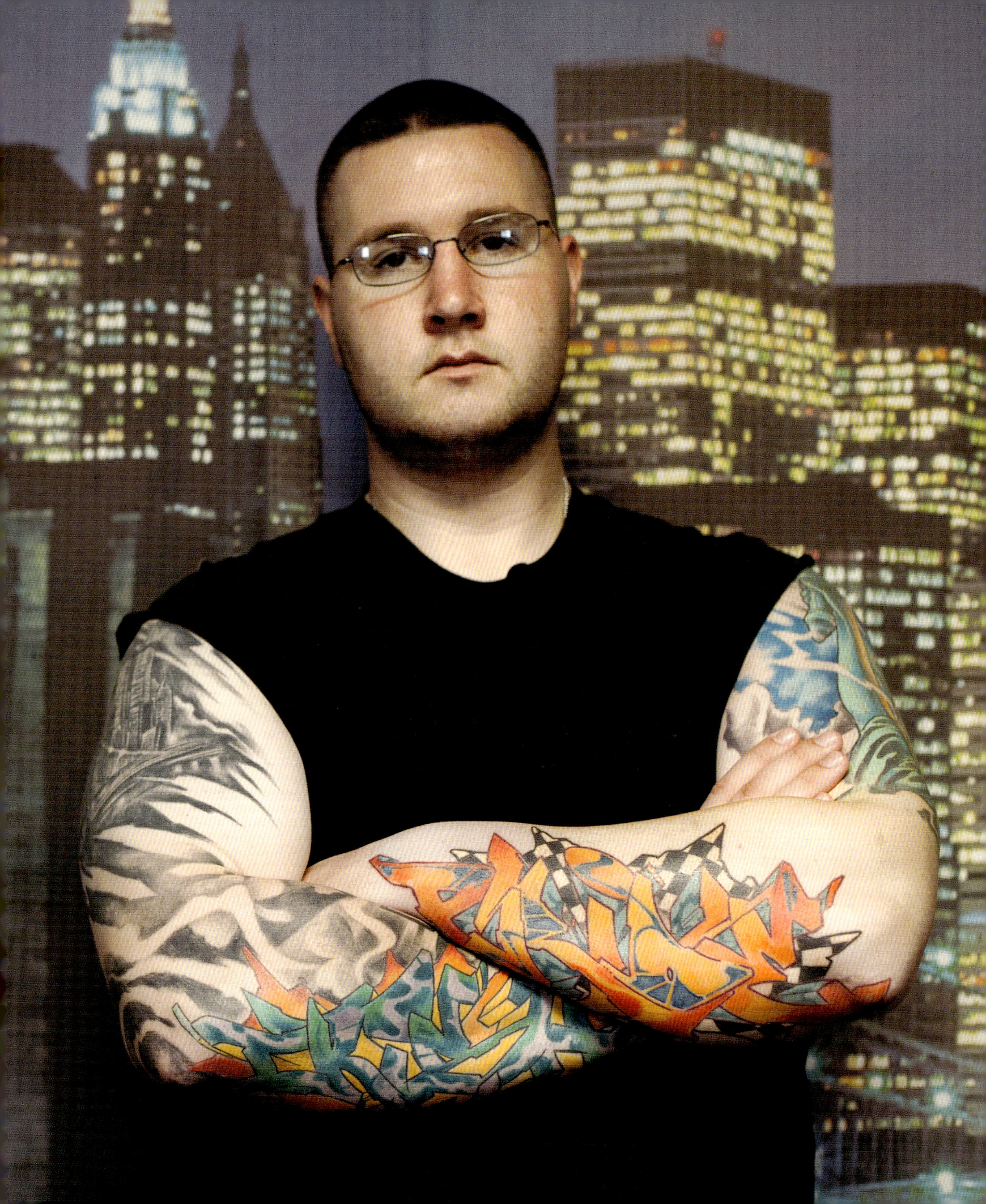

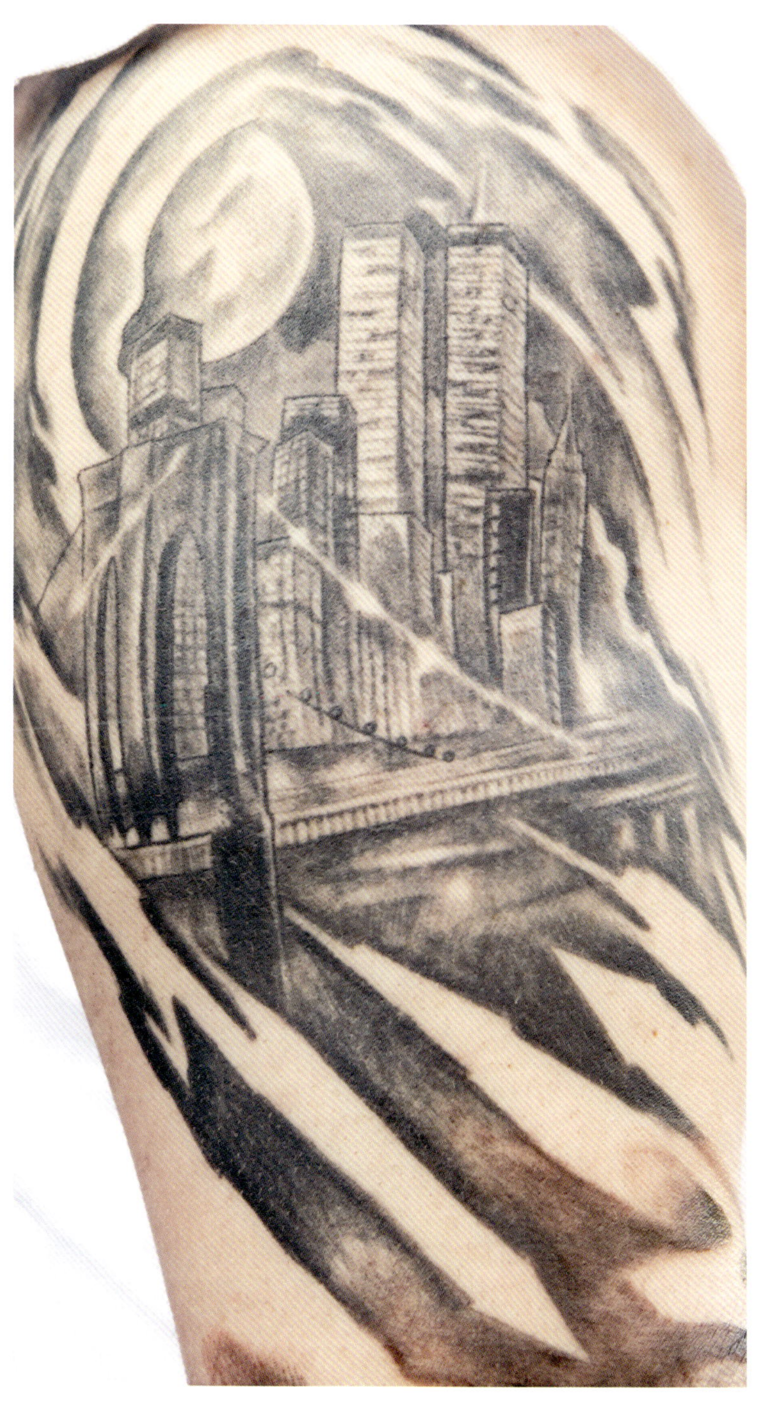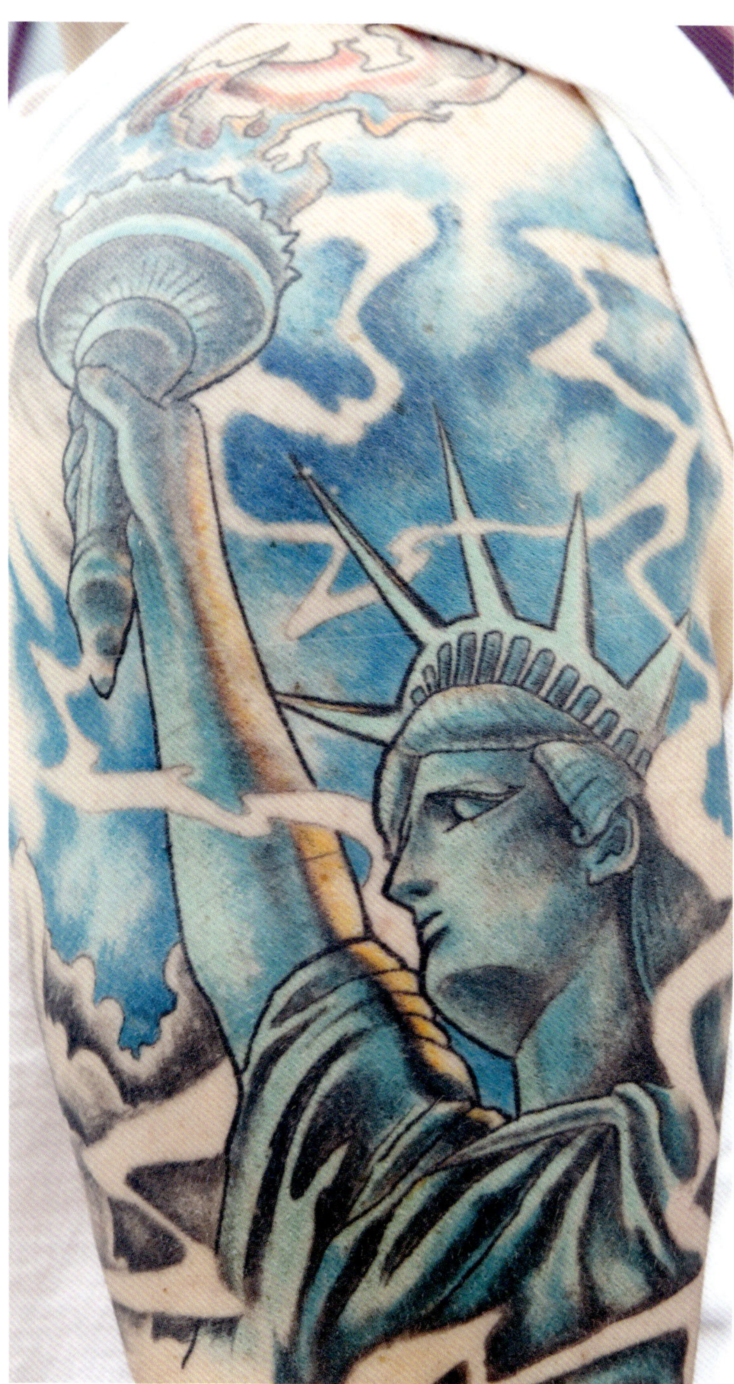

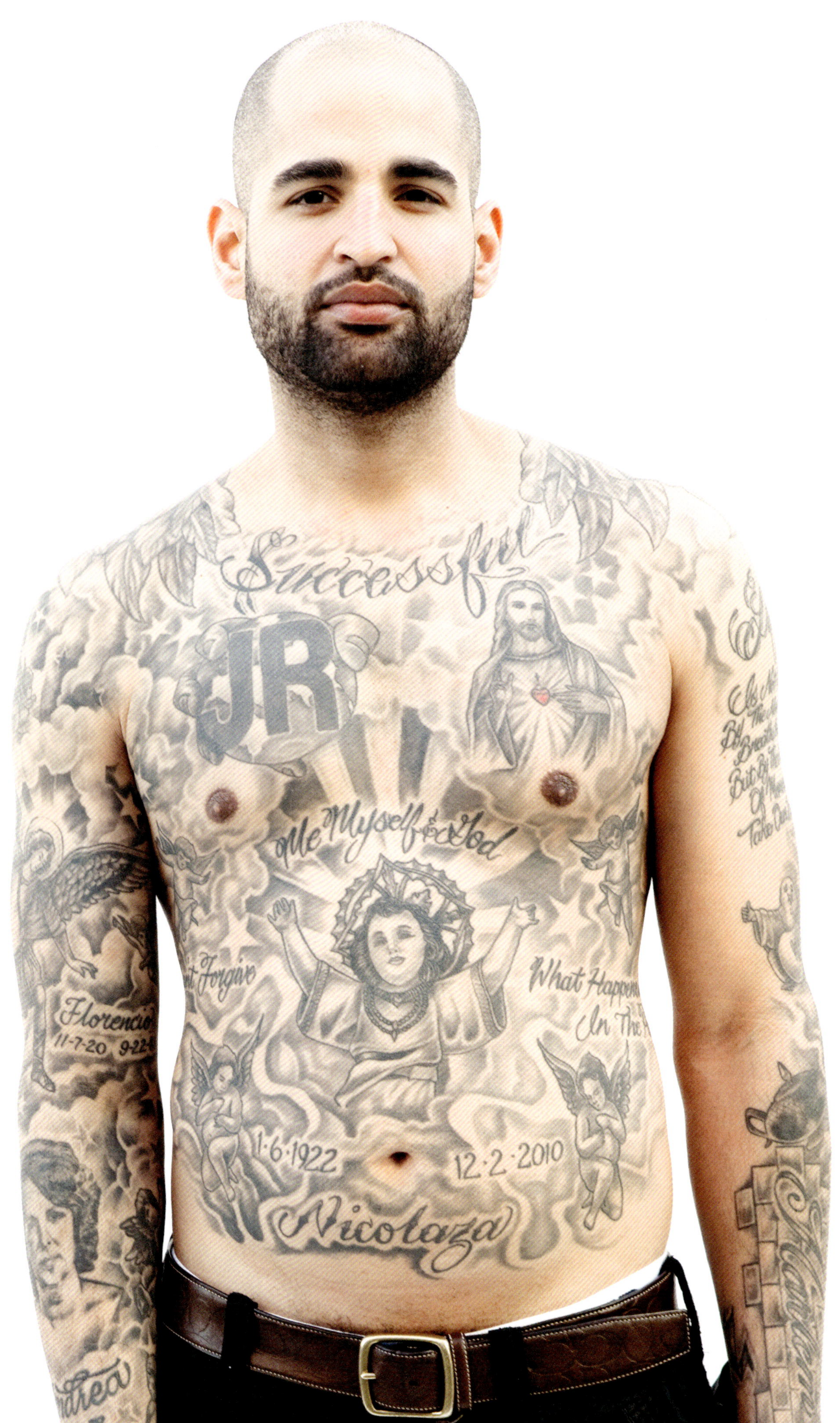

Successful
JR
Me Myself & God
nt Forgive
Florencio
11-7-20 9-22
1·6·1922
12·2·2010
Nicolaza
What Happen
In The

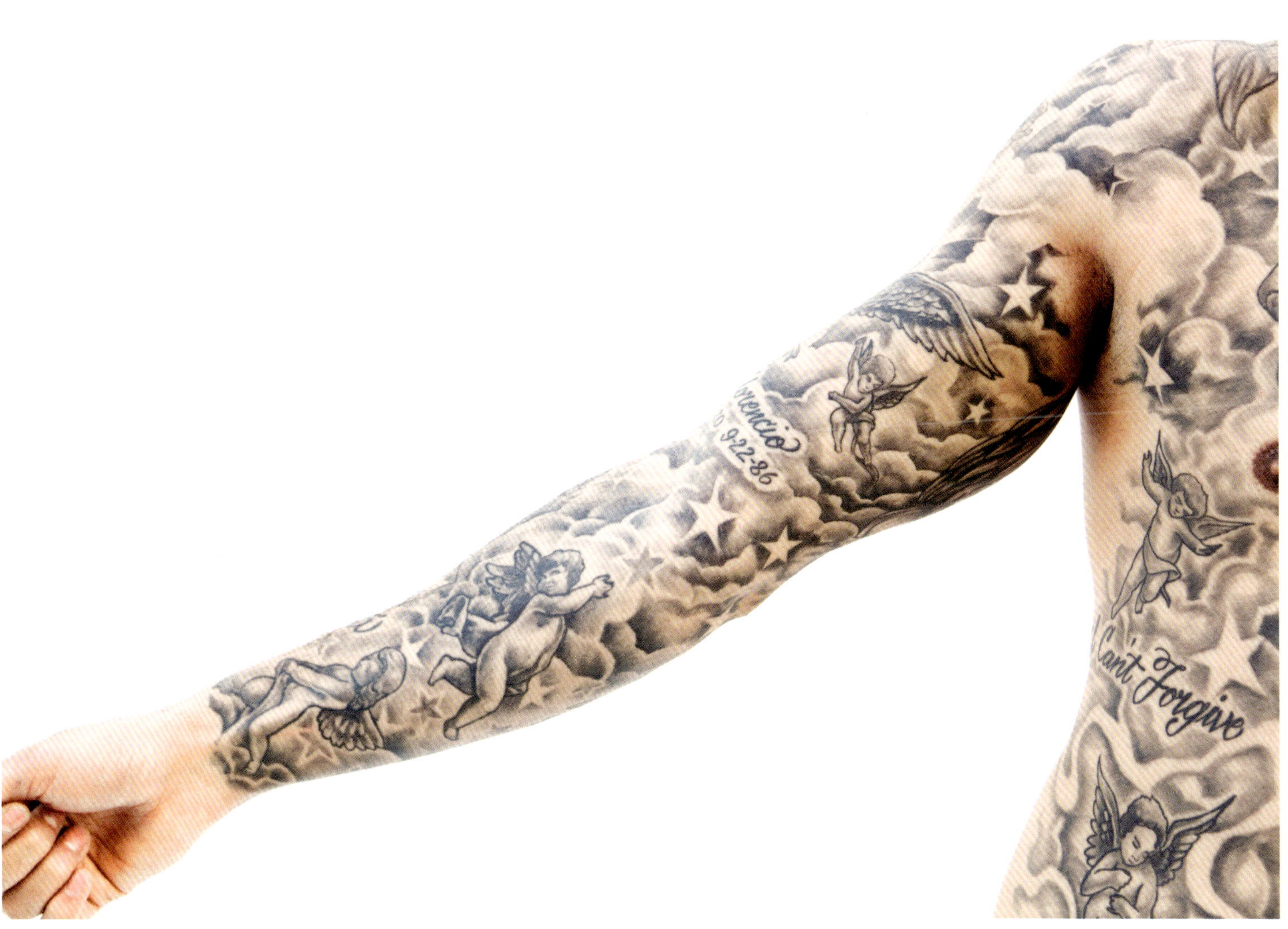

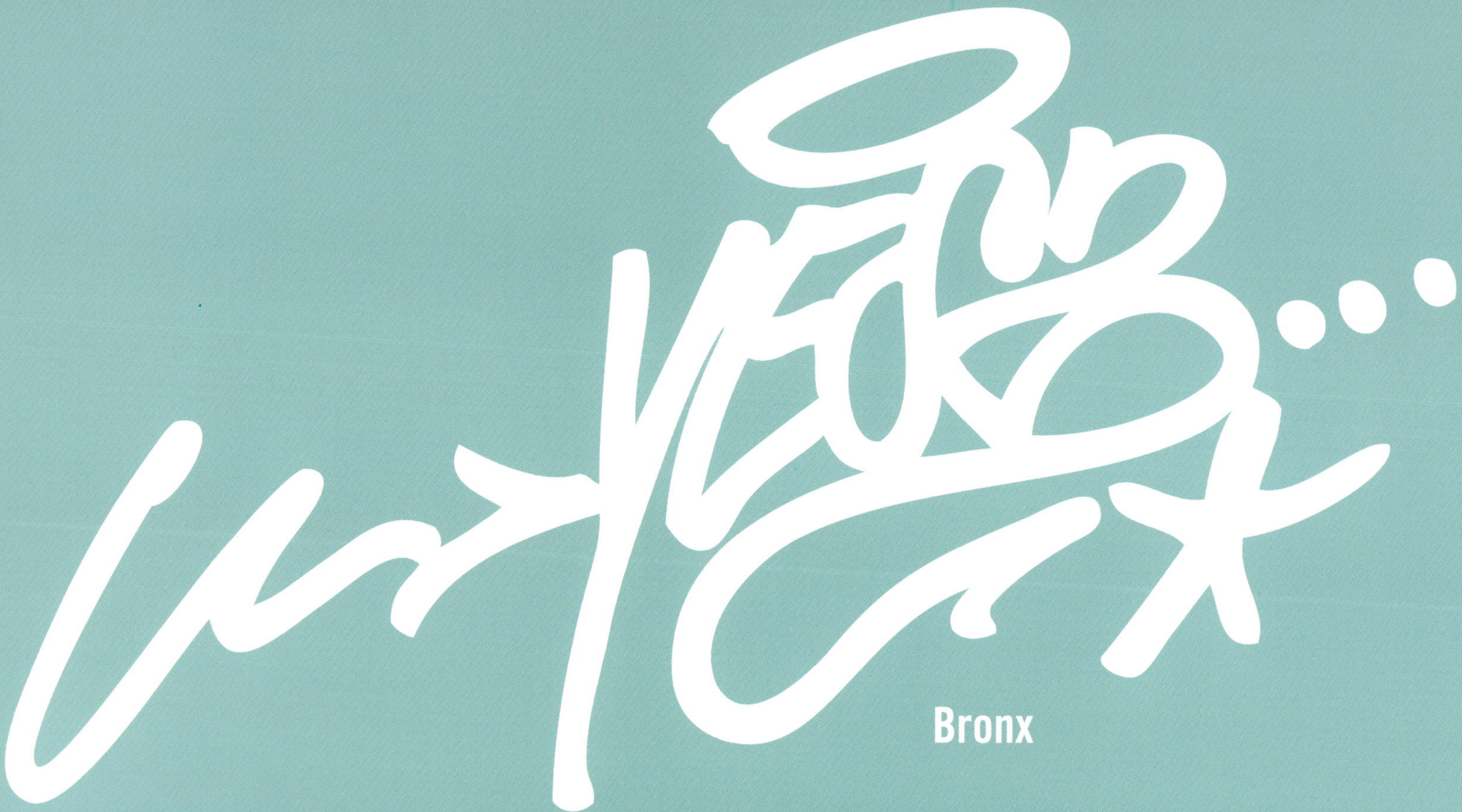

"The graffiti stuff comes natural to me and I like to do it, but over the years I have come to totally appreciate old-school work. Designs that were drawn to be tattoos first and foremost. Early on you're dazzled by the bright colors and stuff, and then eventually you get back to the basic stuff. It's like sugar, man—still the best. NutraSweet? I don't trust it."

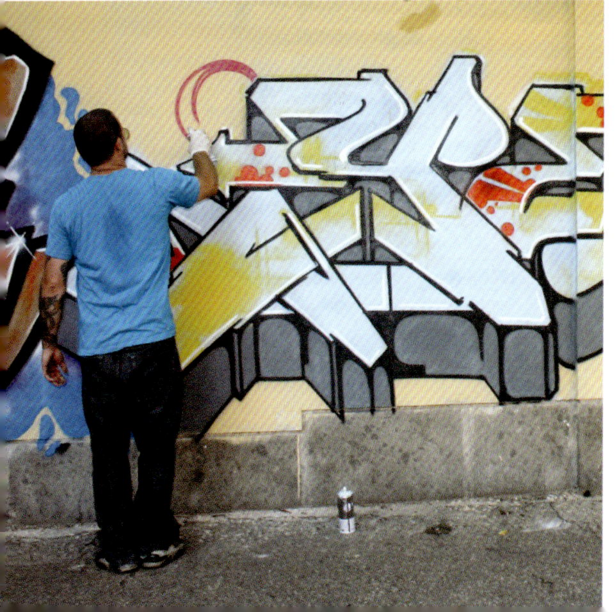

YES2

Yes2's dad worked for the Metropolitan Transit Authority, so as a young writer he had a more intimate understanding than most of how the system worked. But Yes2 wanted to bomb the system—graffiti vernacular for painting trains (don't get any crazy ideas, Homeland Security). The trains were fading away by the time he was ready to blow up some spots, so he applied his efforts to the streets and highways of New York. When he realized that he could stay true to the art of writing while getting paid to do so, he became a tattooist in demand.

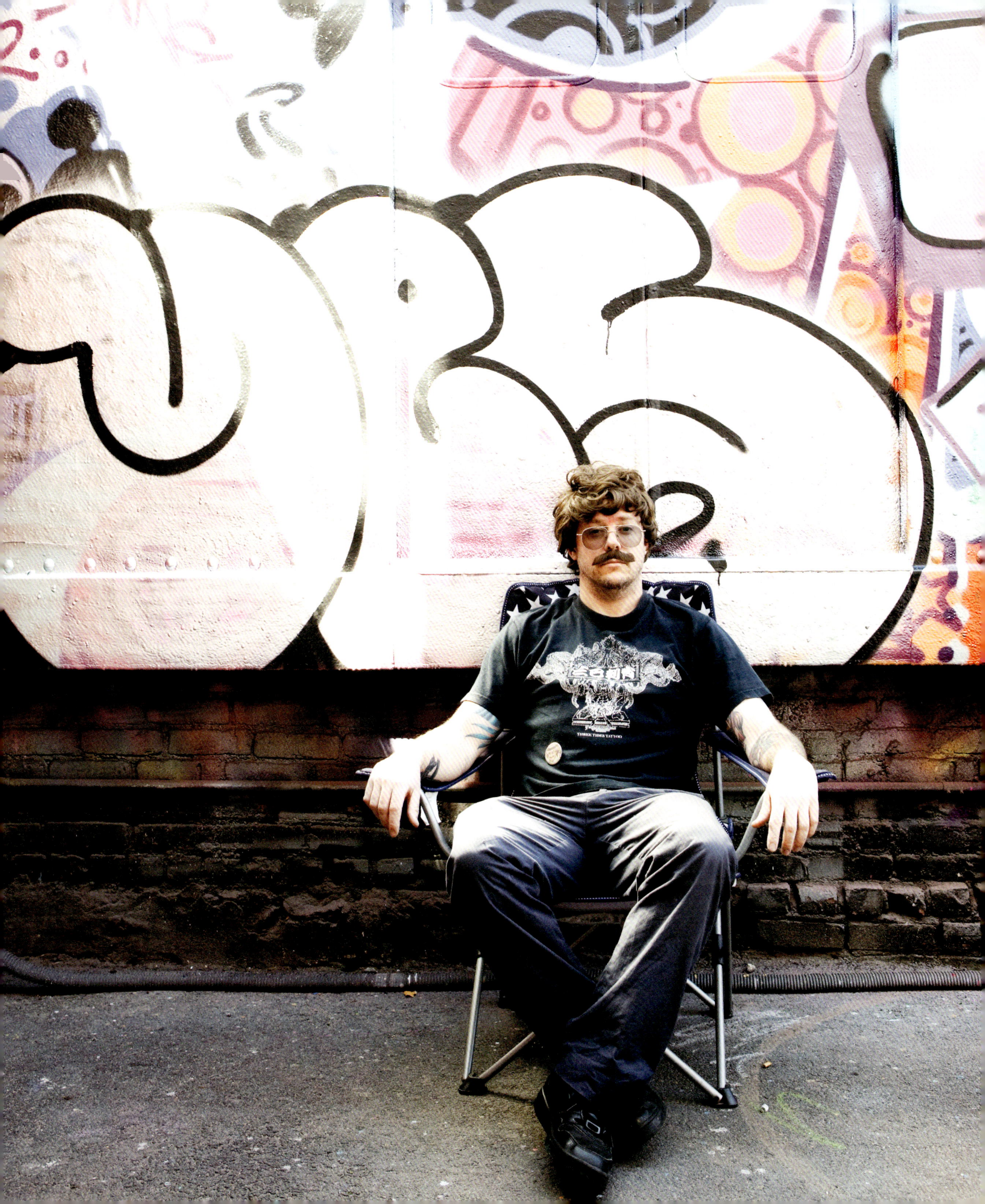

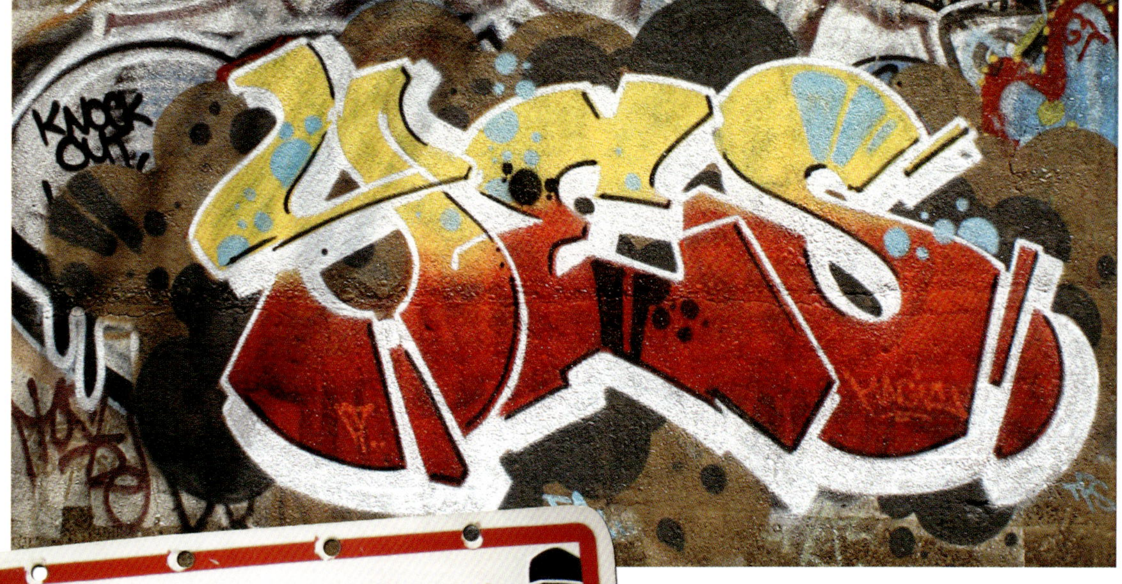

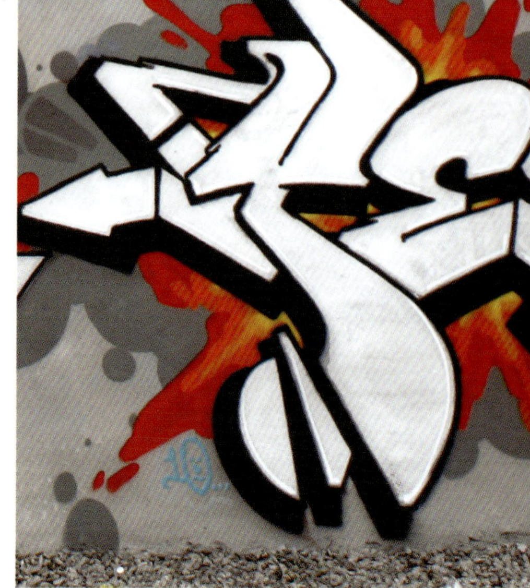

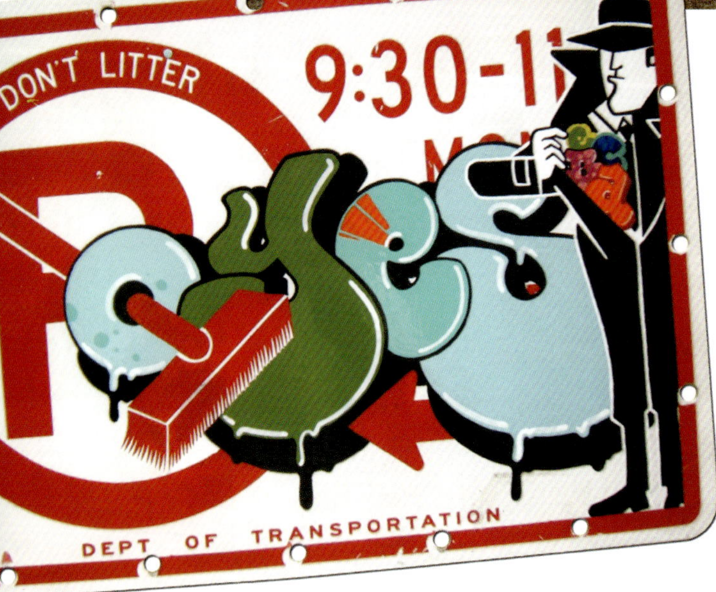

Yes parking sign, 2006

The first thing I actually put on a wall I think was in 1988. I grew up in the Bronx, and that shit was just everywhere. My father worked for the MTA, so we always rode the trains because he had the free employee train pass back then. They would let the whole family go on for free, and [the trains] were obviously destroyed, but I really didn't know what I was looking at when I was young. Then one day my friend met an older writer from our neighborhood. I think that guy drew my friend's name or something, and I was like, "This shit is cool." My friend and I started making up names, drawing random names and stuff. Then I started to notice the other graffiti that was around me.

My dad was oblivious to it, like, "Ah, that bullshit you scribble." He obviously didn't want me doing anything illegal, but back then he wasn't so disdainful, and it was kind of like background noise you didn't even notice. My parents' main thing was more, "Don't go near the tracks, don't get electrocuted, don't get hit by a train." They were more angry after my room accumulated a ton of graffiti—I destroyed my bedroom.

At first I wrote *ES* or *ES1*, and that was a little limited because it had only two letters. There was another writer with a similar name, and he had a lot of problems with people going over his stuff a lot, and then they would end up going over mine, thinking I was the same guy. I was still pretty young at this point—this was around '89—and I hadn't done much with the name, so I was like, "I kind of don't like it too much anyway. Why don't I just change it?"

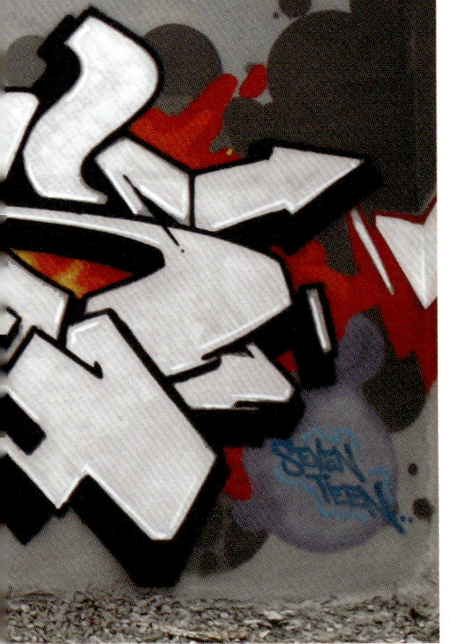

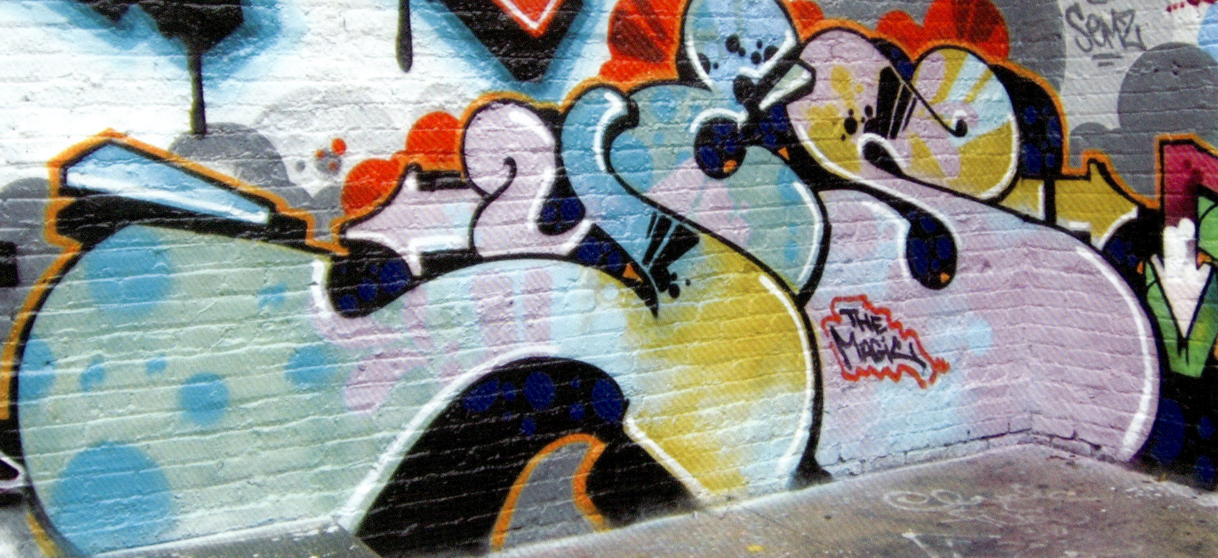

I looked at the alphabet and thought what would be the best letter to add before it, to be a good addition to the name as well as being a name that no one else had. There was another guy from my neighborhood who really didn't write too much who wrote *Yes*, and he was like, "Yeah, go ahead and use it, you should keep that going. I really don't write anymore." I decided to put the 2 on it just out of respect for him.

In the late eighties the city had pretty much cleaned up the trains, but the highways were still totally destroyed. I wanted to get my name out there, so naturally I hit the highways. There were a ton of people hitting them at that time. Just like the older guys will tell you that they never thought the trains would end, I never thought they would clean the highways. Like, who the fuck cares, you're whizzing by and you're not even supposed to be looking at the wall.

Anyway, around '94 or '95 I got with a crew that called themselves IMOK [If Mother Only Knew] and they were doing a lot of stuff. It was a pretty interesting crew for that time because there were guys from the Bronx, a lot of guys from Boston, Westchester, and Connecticut. At that time most crews were from a particular neighborhood. This was pretty cool because it was guys from the tri-state area and we were mainly hitting the highways, and since people from all over were traveling, I guess it made sense.

Actually, Med was one of the dudes that I saw a lot on the highway. He was really going crazy and having what was known as war in graffiti with other people. Like the real hardcore writers, if someone goes over them, they're going to go fucking crazy and not be able to rest until

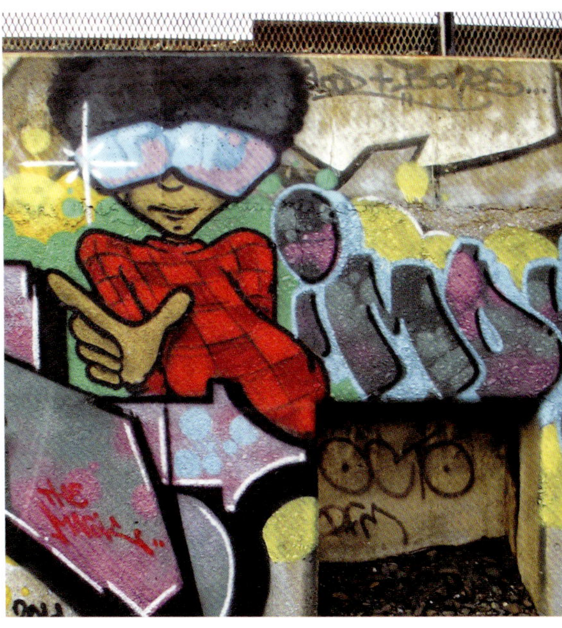

Yes character, 2011

they go back over [the other one's spot]. And if the other guy has the same zeal, he is going to be doing the same shit. I remember seeing these things last for years sometimes. Guys would be going back over each other in multiple spots, like reclaiming the spots.

When I was young, I went to tattoo parlors a bunch of times with older guys from my neighborhood, and it's crazy to me because I do tattoos now. But they would bring me along because they knew I was into drawing and graffiti and they would be like, "You want to take a ride? You could help me pick out my tattoo."

I remember a lot of people were getting killer clowns tattooed on them, clowns with fuckin' knives, or the swirl in the eye, like that crazy hypnotized look. These guys were getting multiple killer clowns, like every time. And when they brought me they would be like, "Which killer clown should I get?" And I would be like, "Uh, this one looks cool." At the time I thought that I would never even get a tattoo, I was like, "Fuck that, I don't want one of these clowns." But obviously…

I don't know how or why I ended up deciding to get one. I think it actually kind of happened because I started to hang out at Med's shop, Tuff City. The shop was a little more underground back then. I wanted to meet Med on the graffiti tip, so that is probably what put it in my head to get one. I still had this whole plan that I was only going to get one and not be like everyone else, but that only lasted a couple of months before I was back for more, like everyone else.

Med gave me my first tattoo. I got it on my upper back, real simple lettering I had drawn up, and he hit me with the old fuckin' paper towel full of rubbing alcohol. Then he smacked my shit like, *wham!* and it was welcome to fucking whatever old tattoo saying he said for people who got their first tattoo.

I was hanging out at Tuff City a lot and was sketching out shit for people. I remember Med one day asking me if I wanted to get down, and at the time I had no idea what a blessing that was. And to be honest, it was kind of intimidating. I was good at drawing, but putting something permanent on people's skin? No thanks. Then again, I was working at an art store making no money, and he asked me again one day. This was right before the tattoo boom, like a year before they made it legal. I don't know if he liked me, saw potential, or just needed a hand, but I took him up on it. I said, "Fuck it, I'll try it out and see what happens."

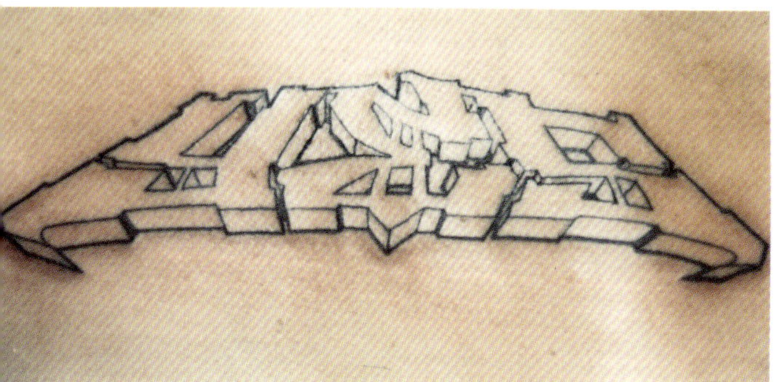

Yes tattoo by Med

My apprenticeship was less formal than for other people I saw coming through. But I definitely cleaned a million tubes and swept and shit. I definitely got blessed, though. It was formal in the sense of how Med taught me. I wasn't allowed to tattoo in the shop for a long time; eventually I had to bring people to the shop myself to get tattoos on the barter system, them getting a good—or possibly bad—tattoo for free and me getting their skin to practice on with Med observing.

When I first started tattooing, Med met Adrian Lee from San Jose, and it was some shit you never saw before. It looked airbrushed or something, and in the beginning I was really influenced by him. Also, there's an old-school shop around here called Big Joe's, which had a basic, solid, traditional style that I really liked.

Seen is another one who was tattooing a lot of people. His stuff had a graffiti look and also reminded me of some of the Big Joe's stuff that I liked. I think he learned from them and started tattooing there. It was clean, bold outlines, solid color and solid work.

The graffiti stuff comes natural to me and I like to do it, but over the years I have come to totally appreciate old-school work. Designs that were drawn to be tattoos first and foremost. Early on you're dazzled by the bright colors and stuff, and then eventually you get back to the basic stuff. It's like sugar, man—still the best. NutraSweet? I don't trust it.

With graffiti, you have total freedom to do whatever the fuck you want, and you're normally doing it where you are not supposed to be doing it. And don't forget, you've got to get it done fast. With tattoos, you have to give the person what they want and take a bit more of your time to get it right, and you can't fuck up. With spray paint and graffiti you can paint over a mistake, but you can't do that with tattoos.

And of course, tattooing pays. If I could get paid to do graffiti, I would possibly opt to do that. But I like tattooing, otherwise I wouldn't still be doing it all of these years later. Tattooing is work, and graffiti is more recreational, something I do when I'm not tattooing.

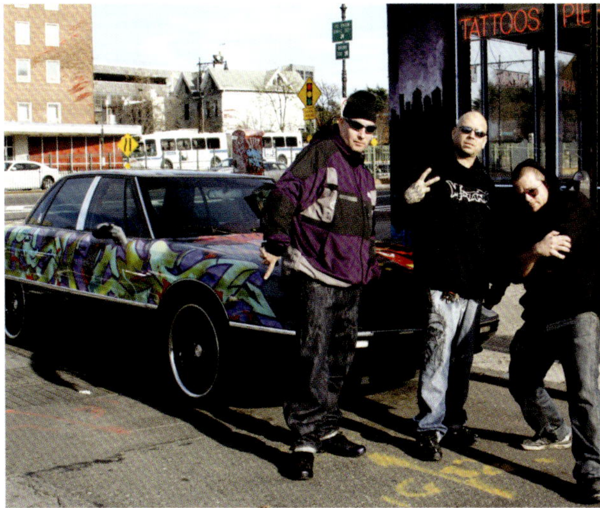

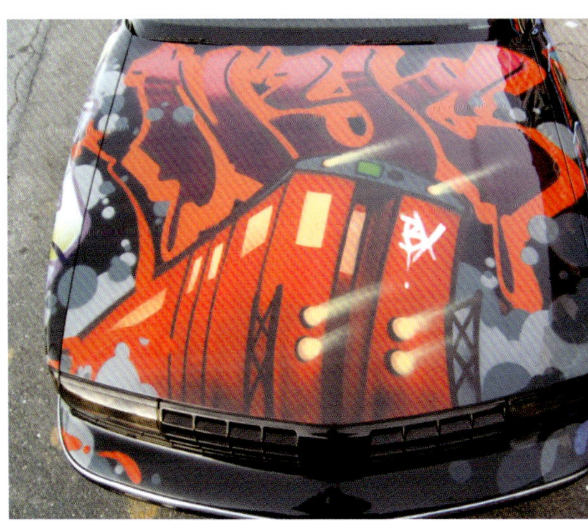

TOP: Ces, Med, and Yes2
BOTTOM: GFX graffiti car painted by Yes2

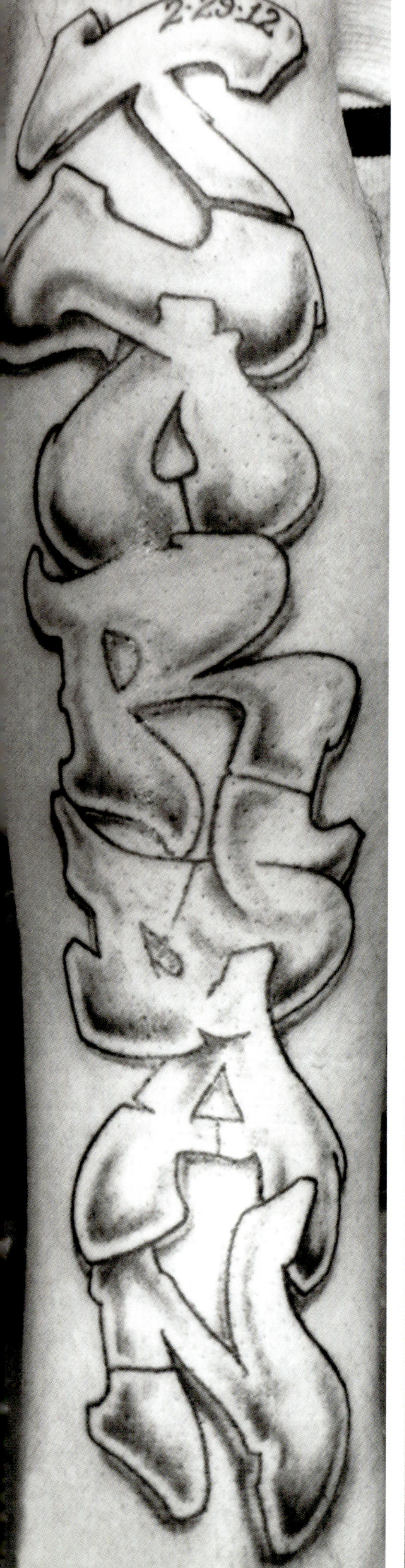
2-29-12

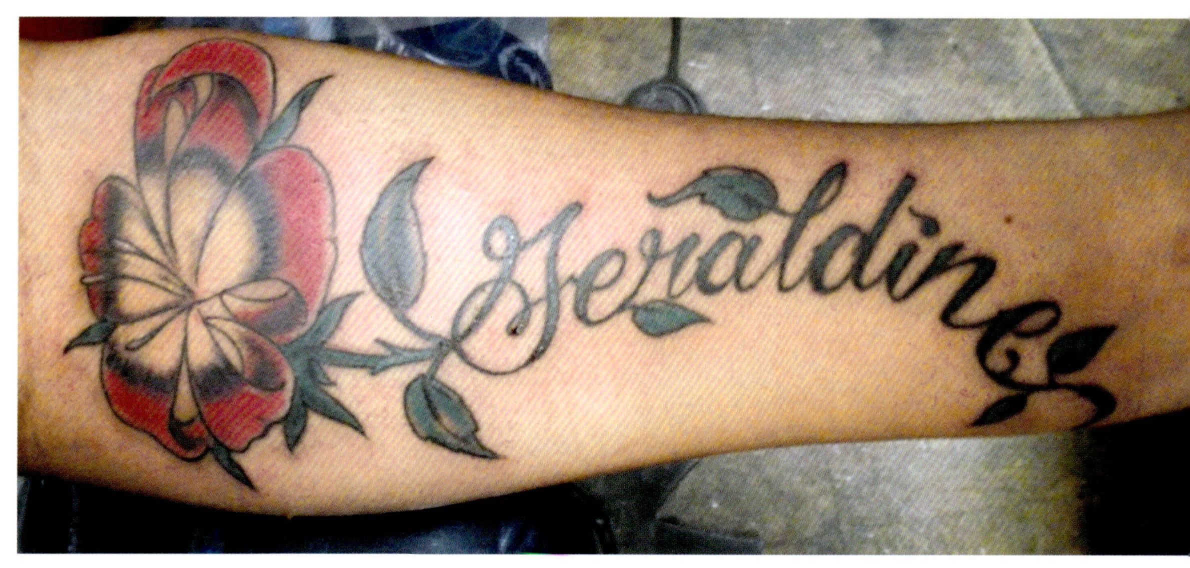
Geraldine

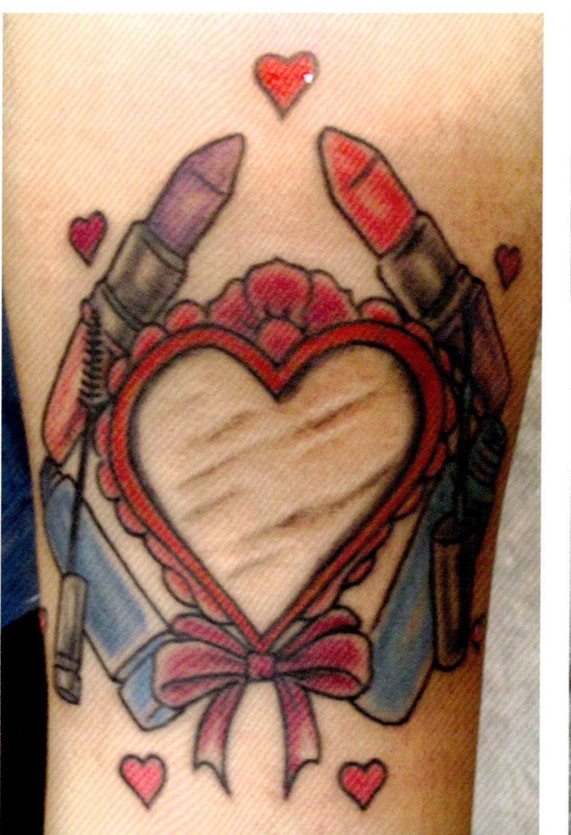

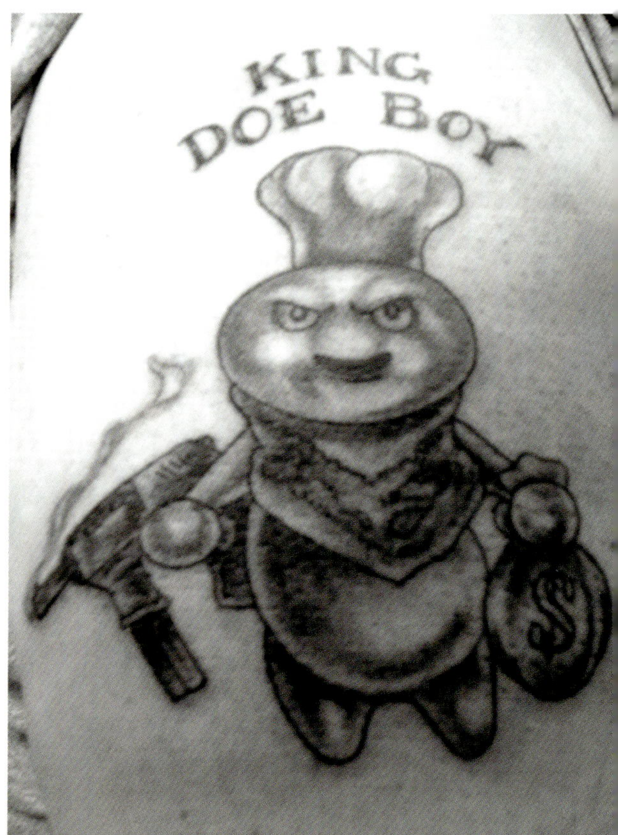
KING
DOE BOY

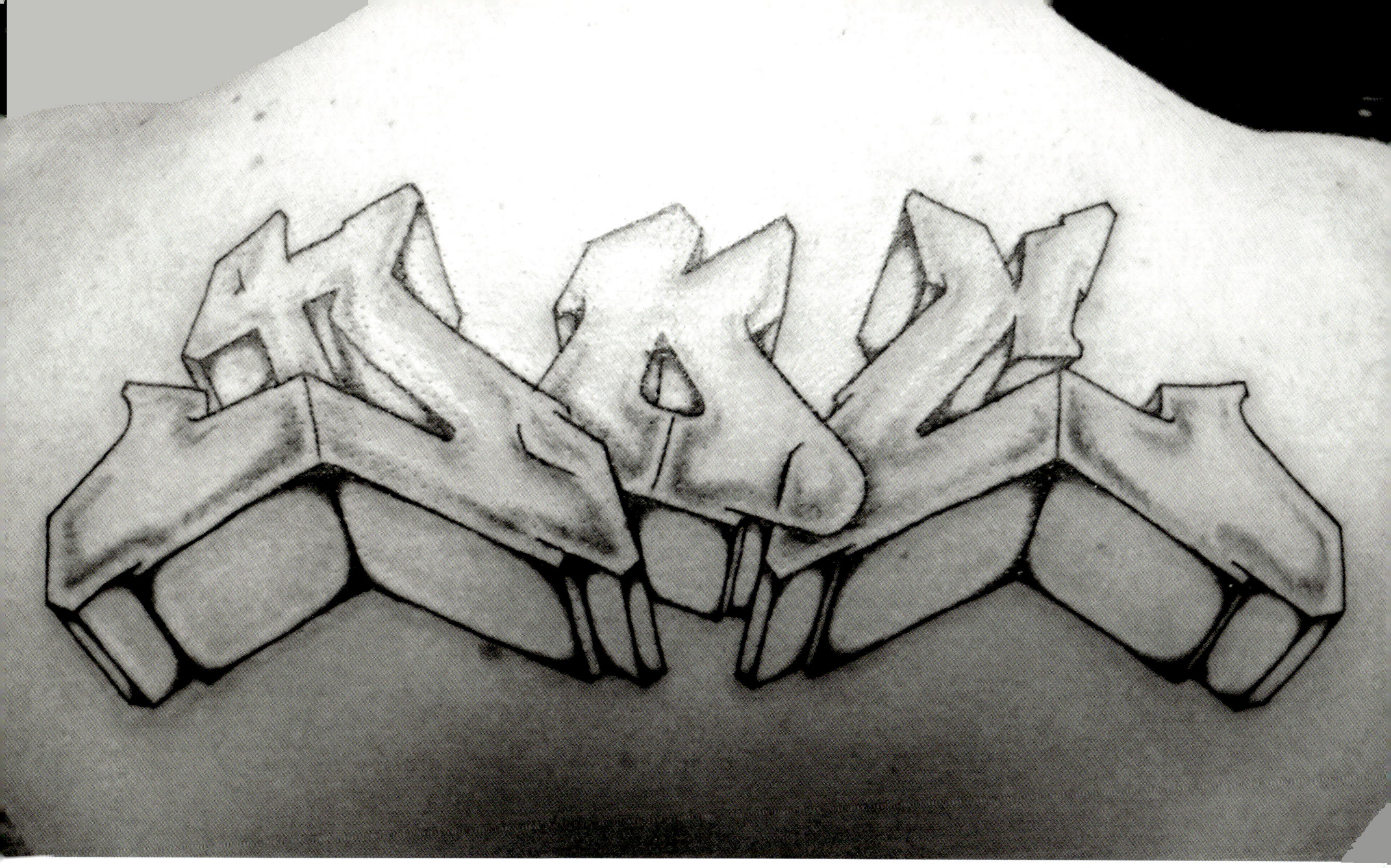

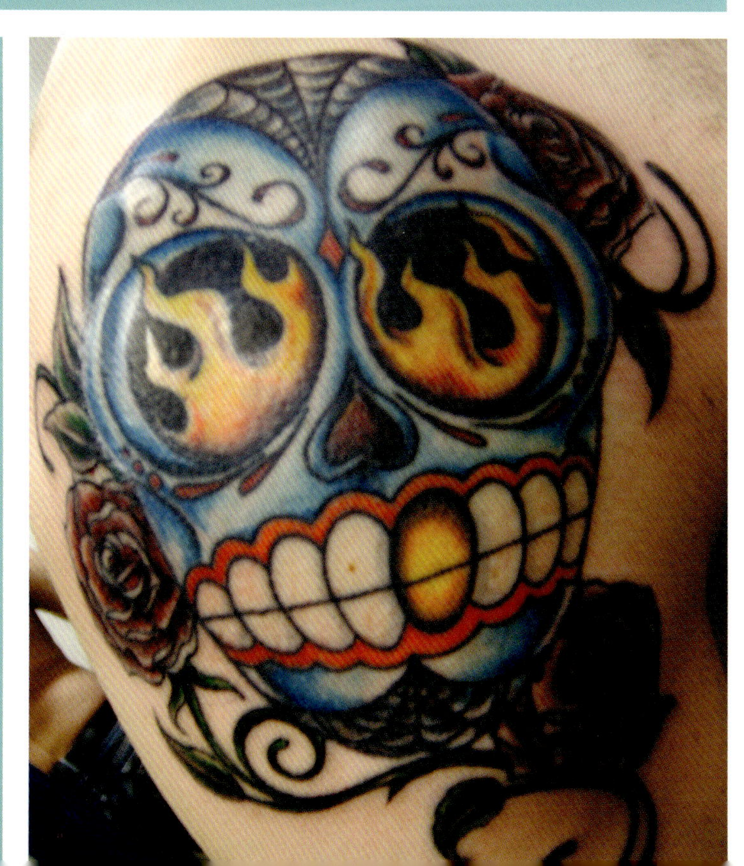

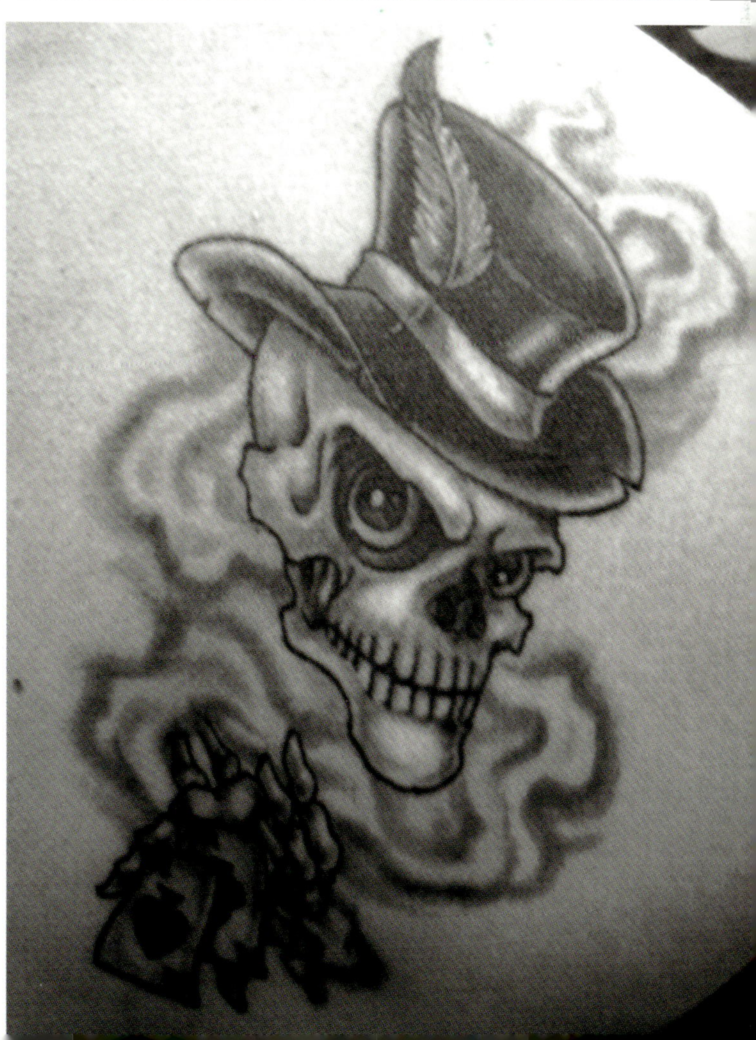

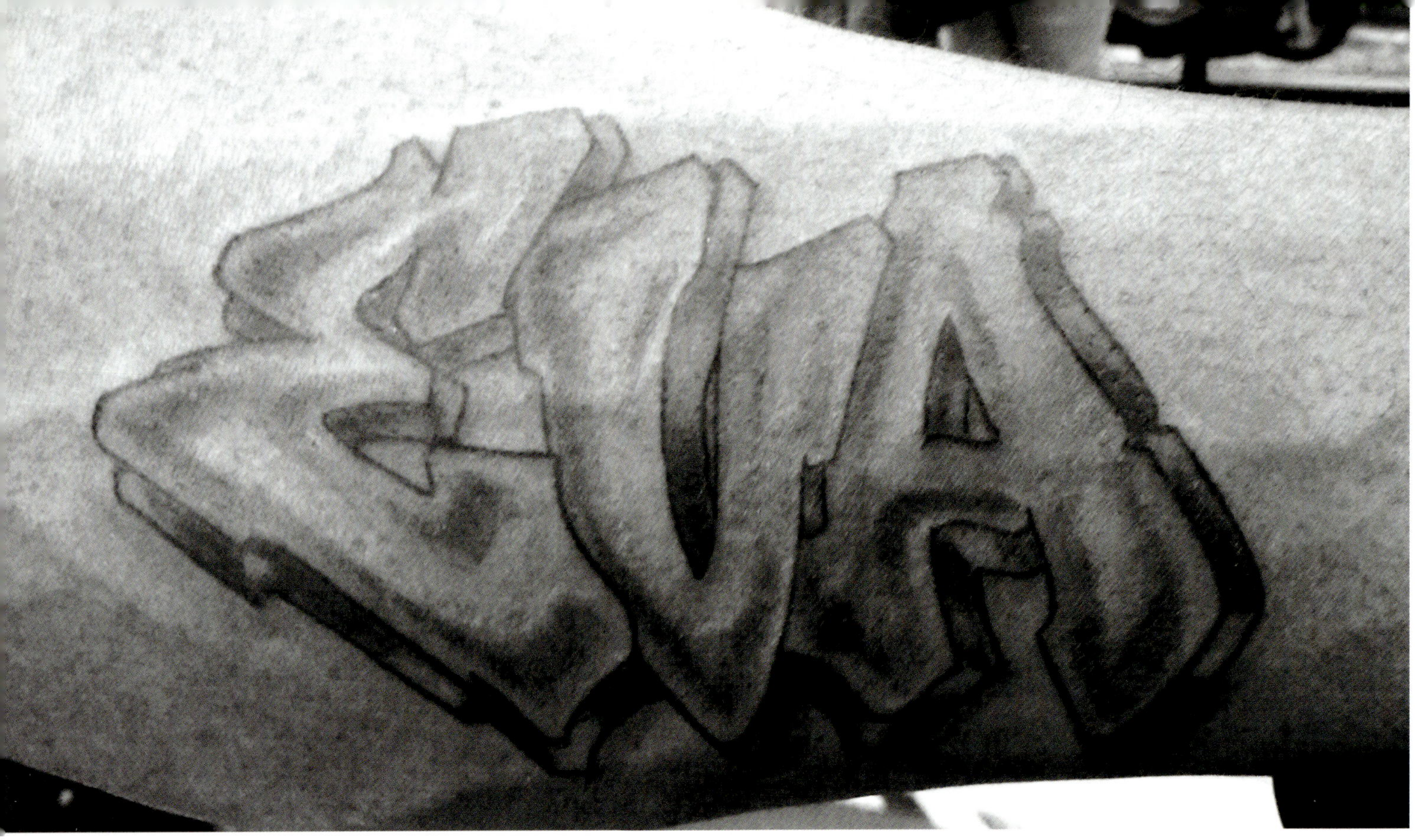

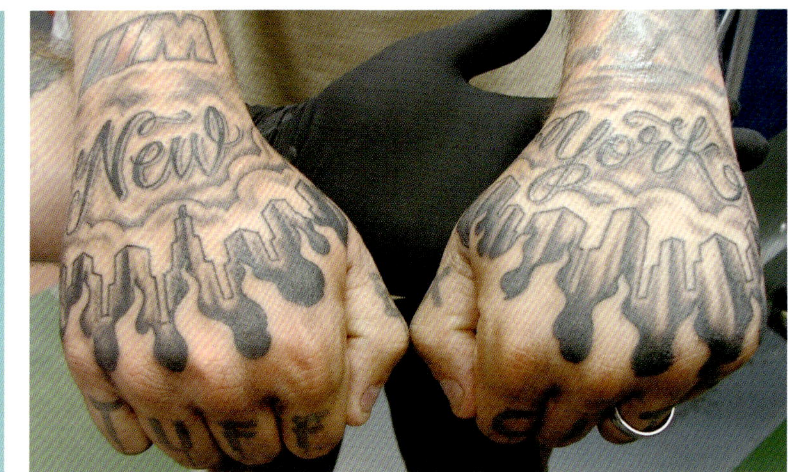

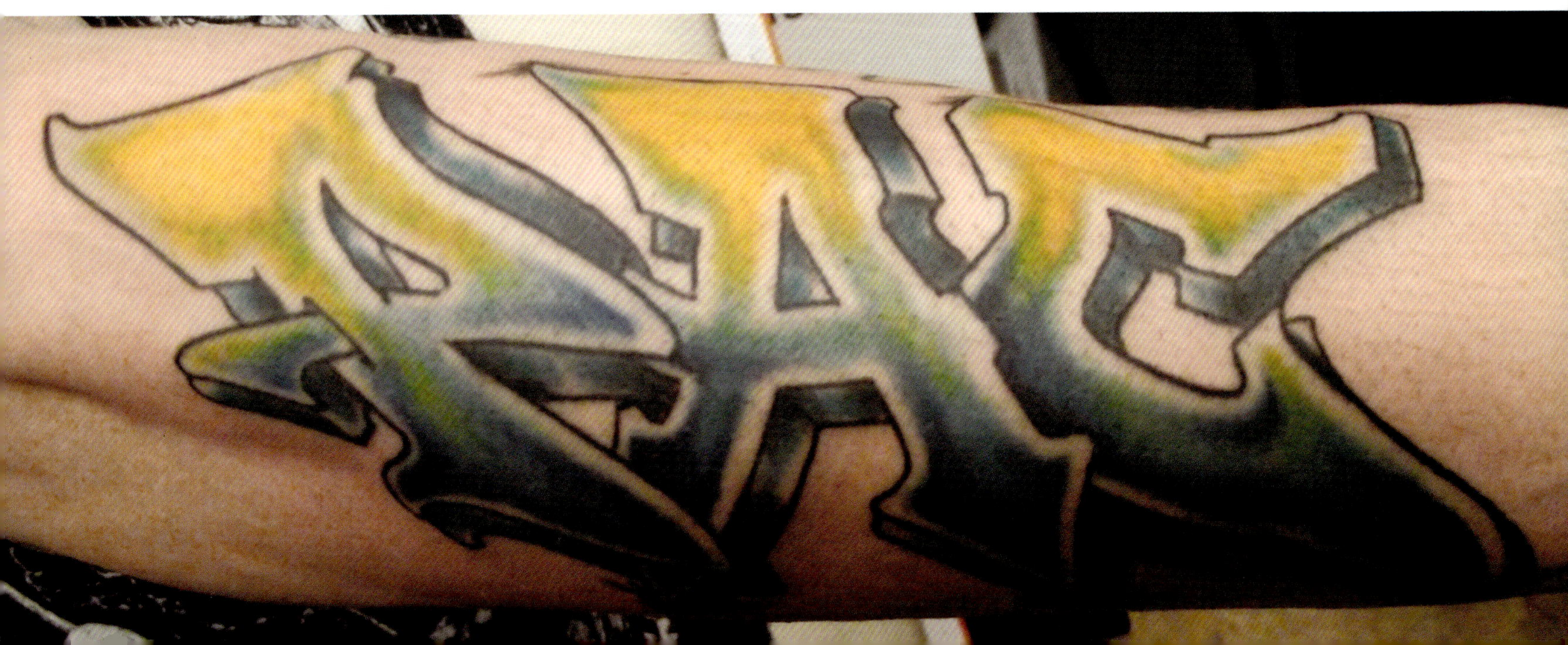

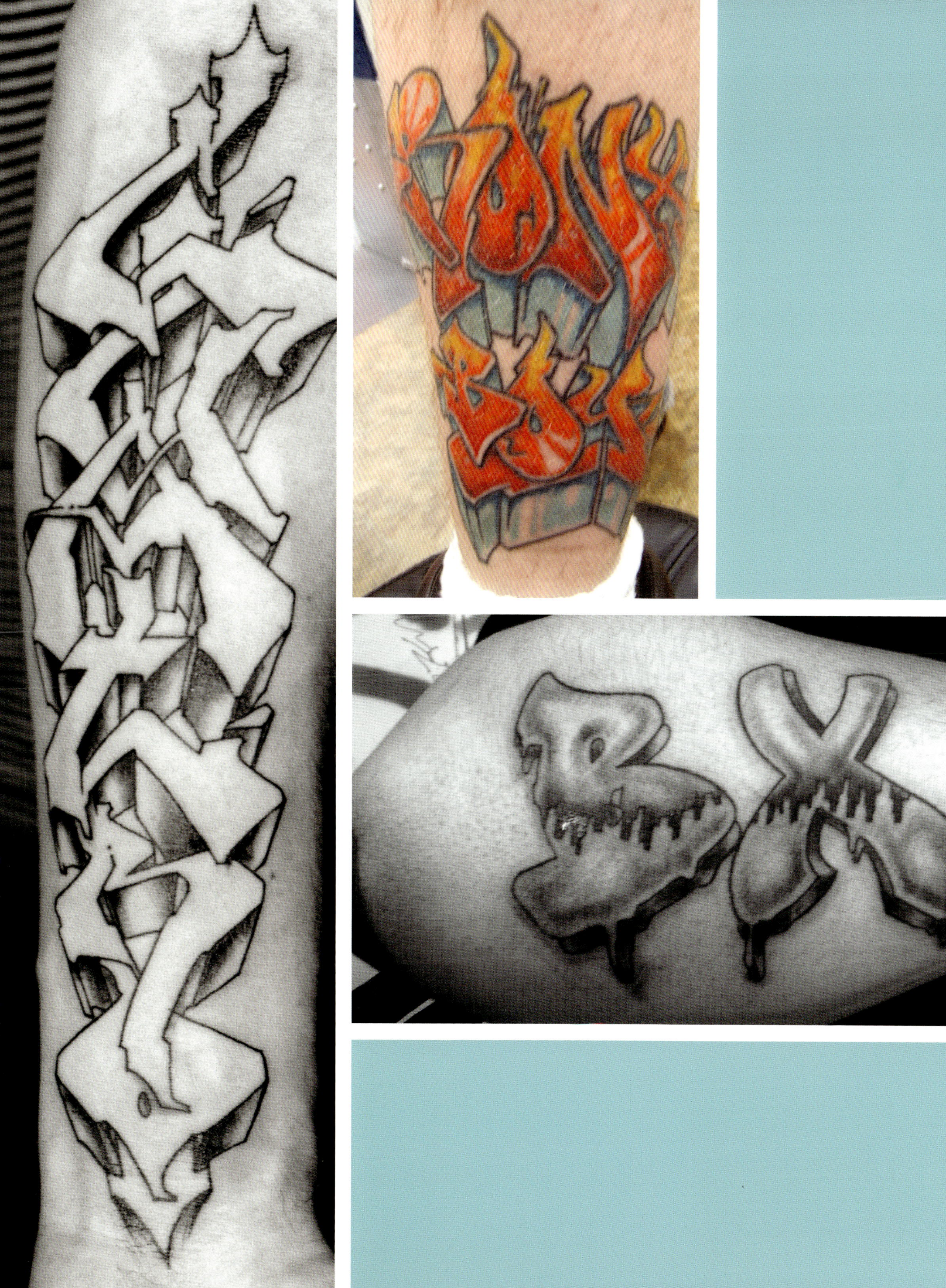

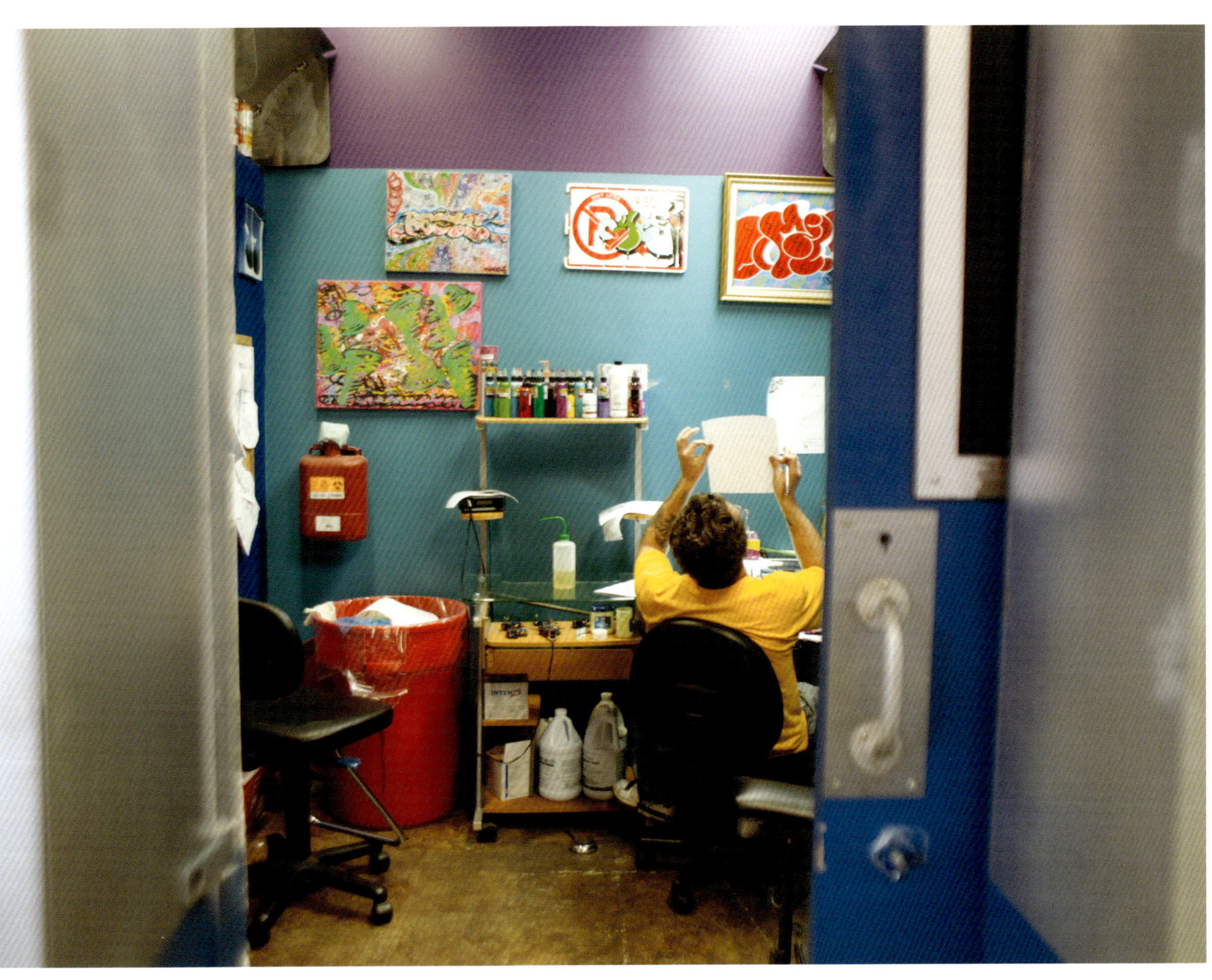

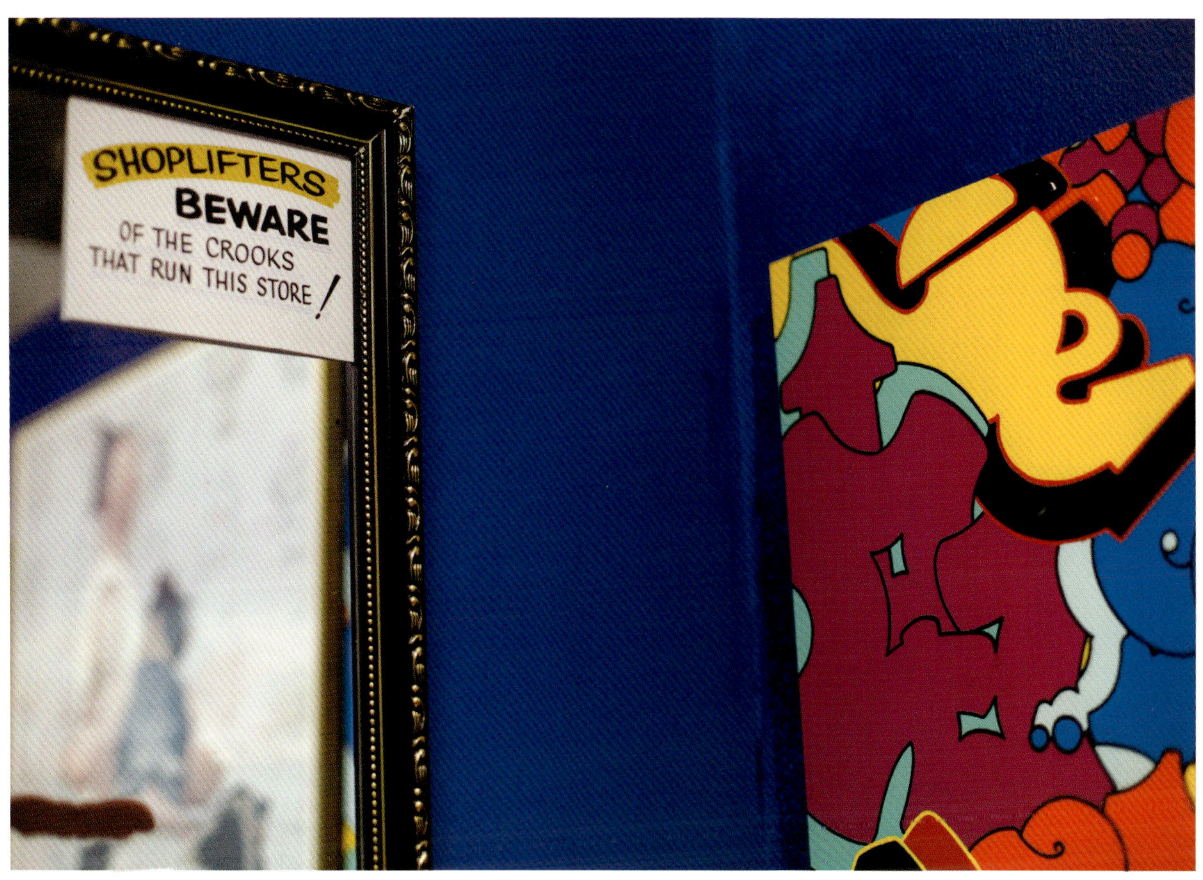

SHOPLIFTERS
BEWARE
OF THE CROOKS
THAT RUN THIS STORE !

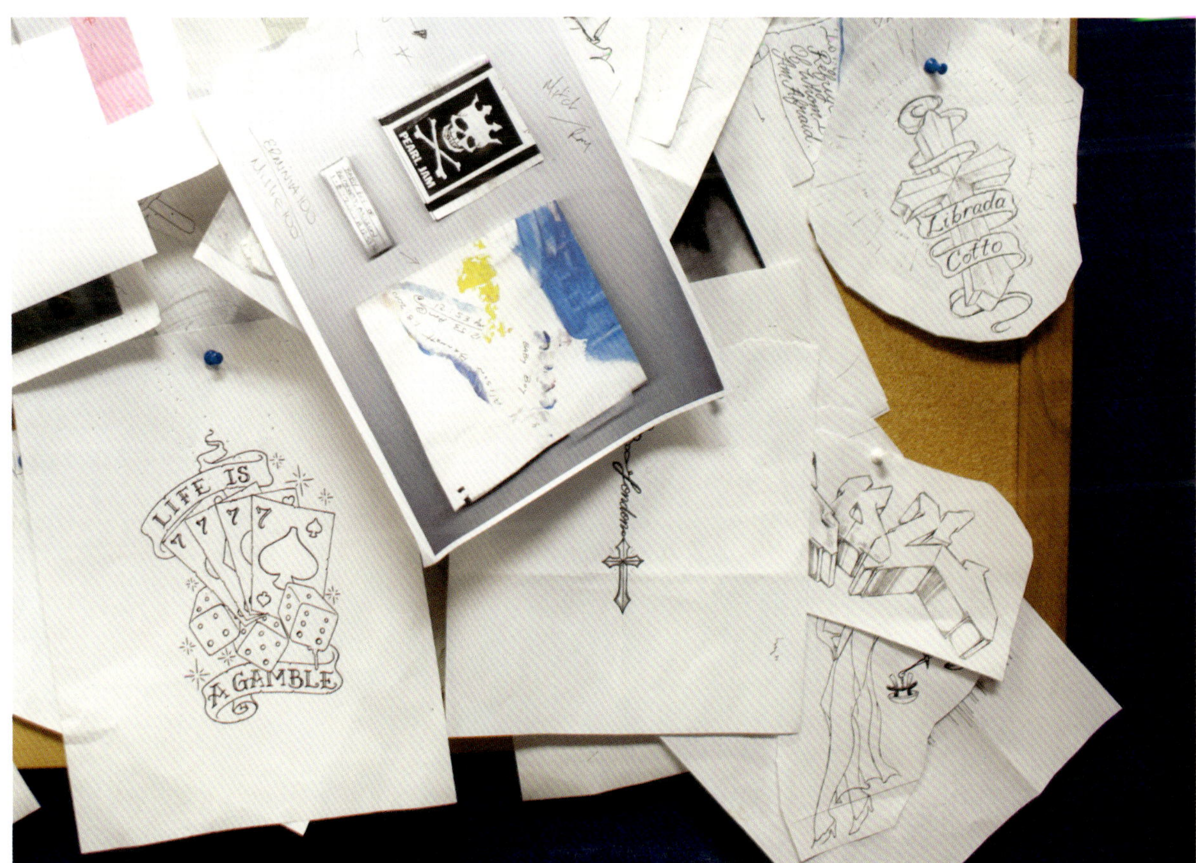

PEARL JAM
LIFE IS
7 7 7
A GAMBLE
Librada
Cotto

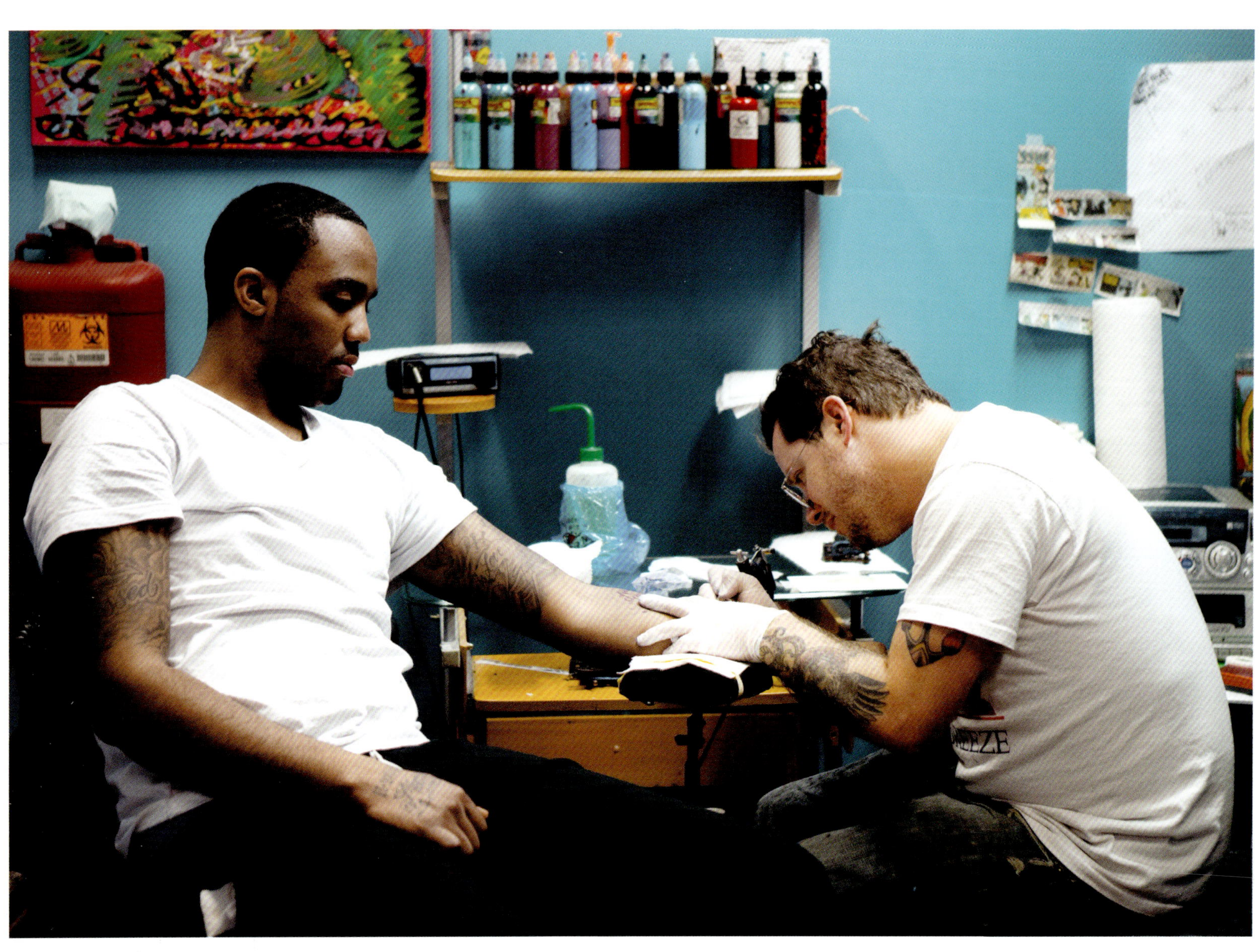

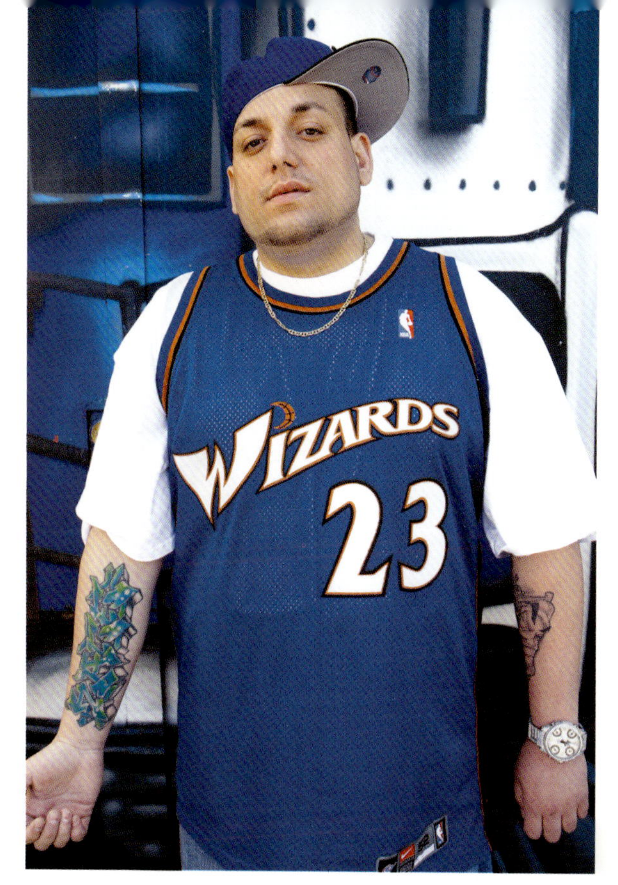

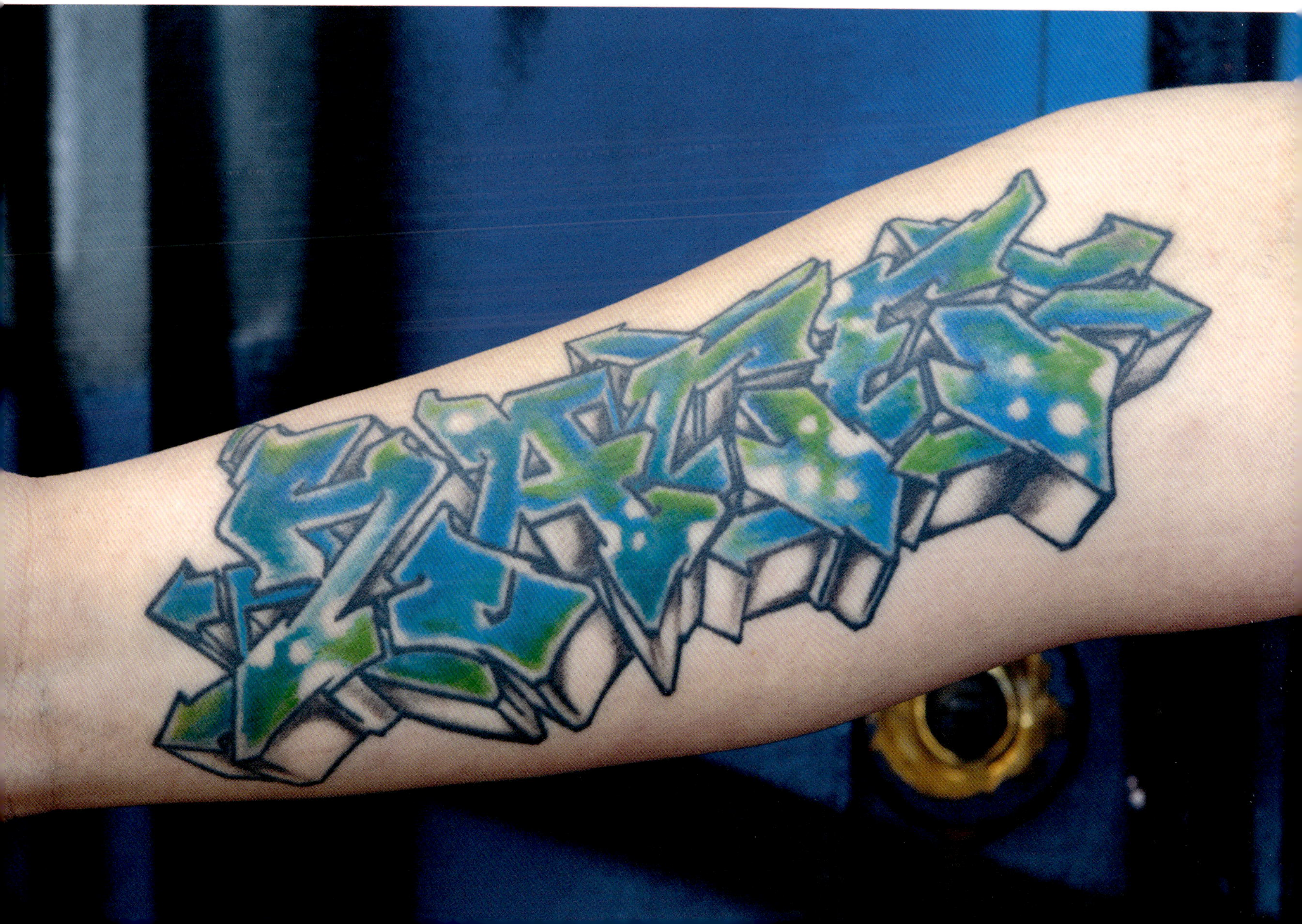

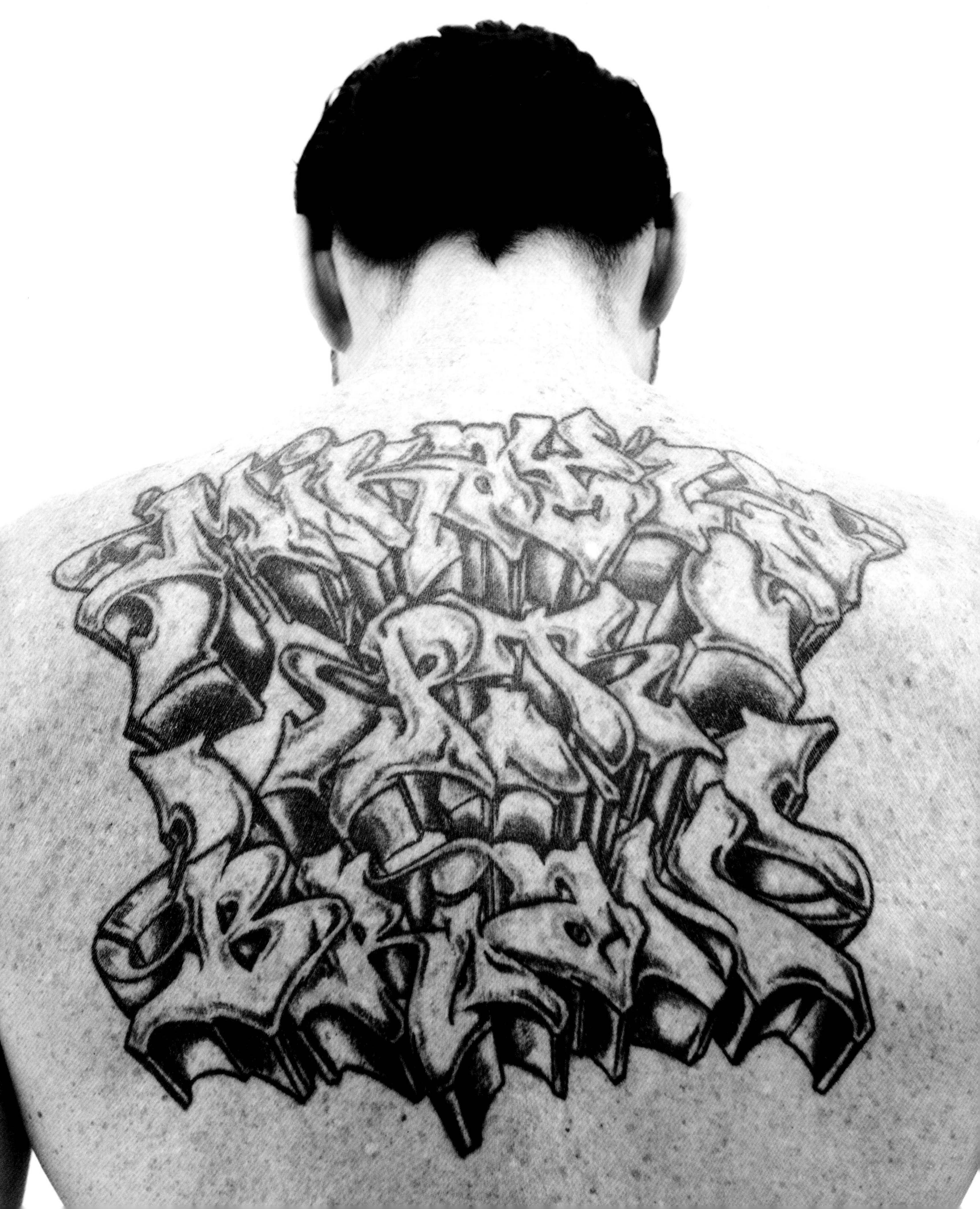

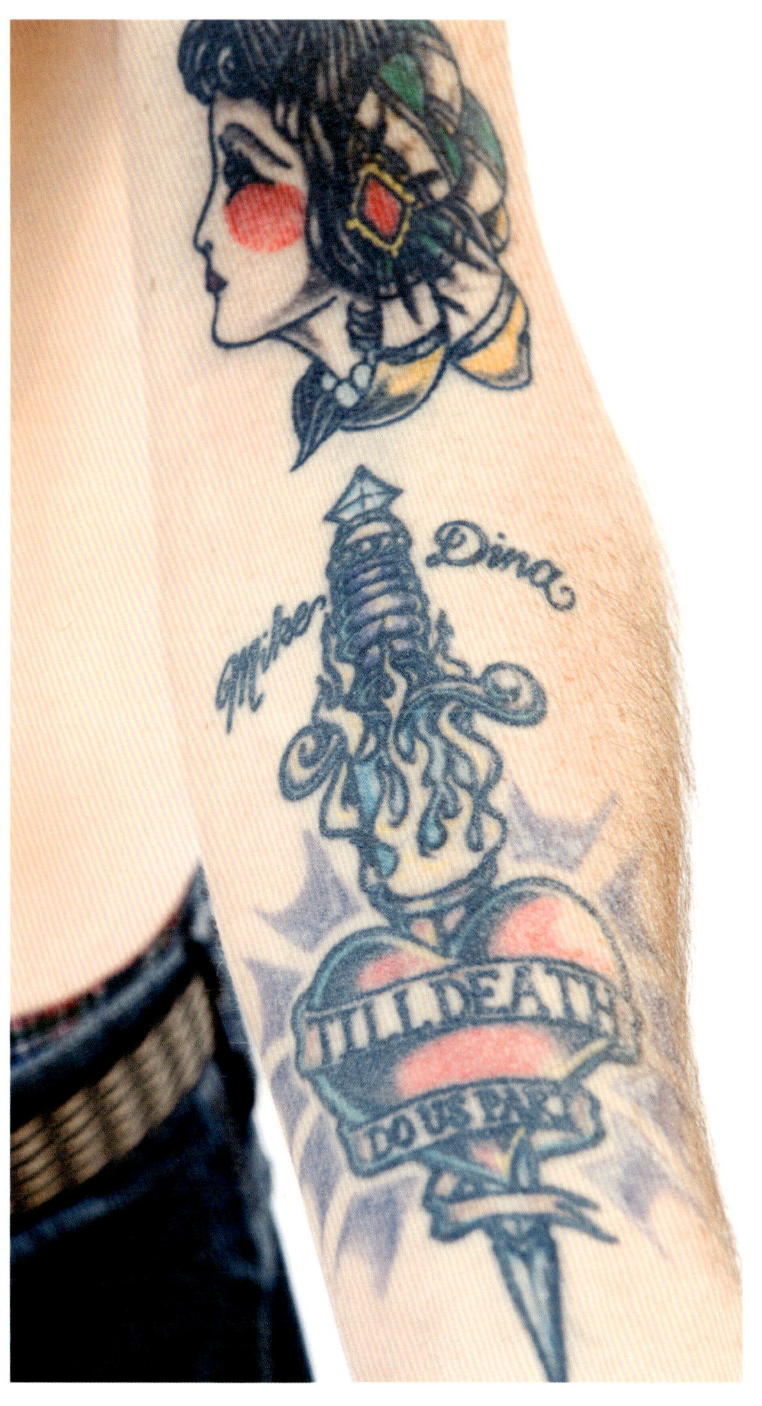
Mike
Dina
TILL DEATH
DO US PART

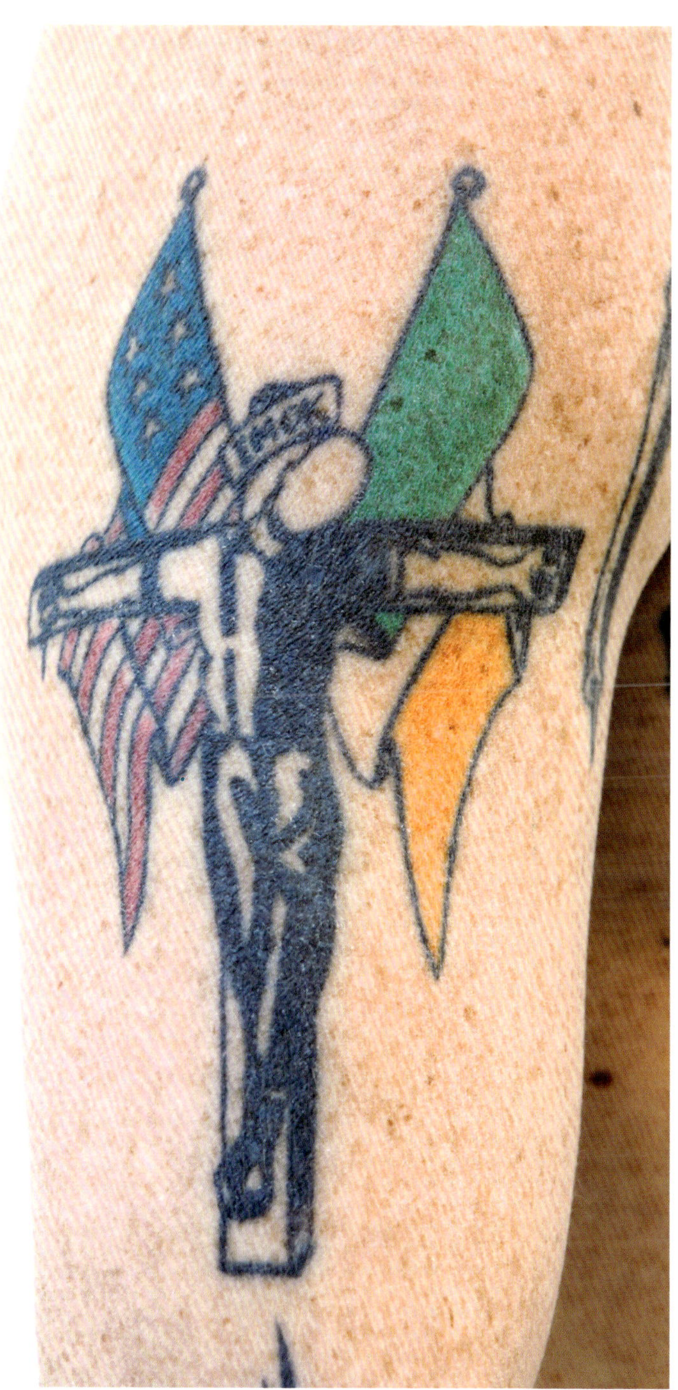

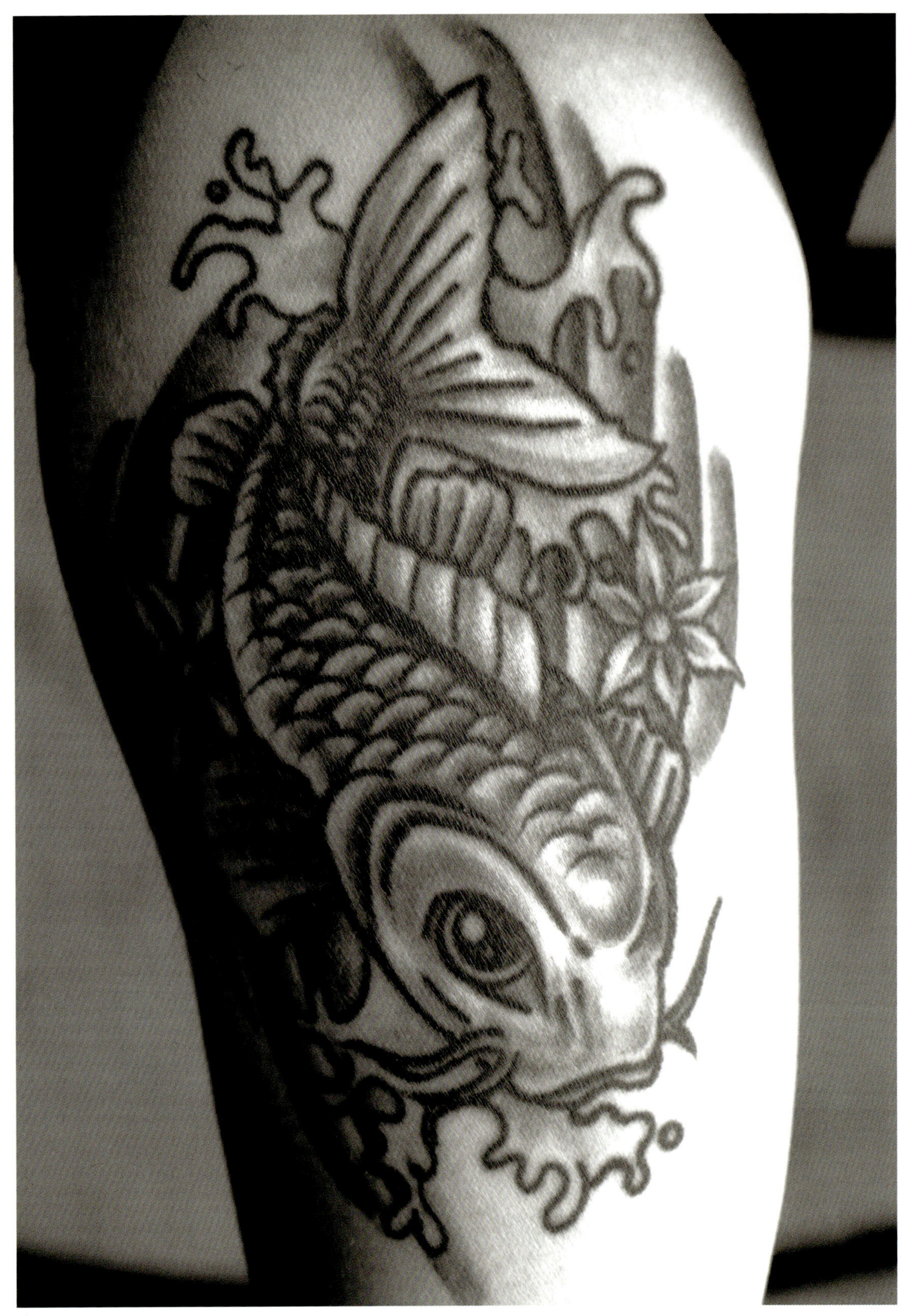

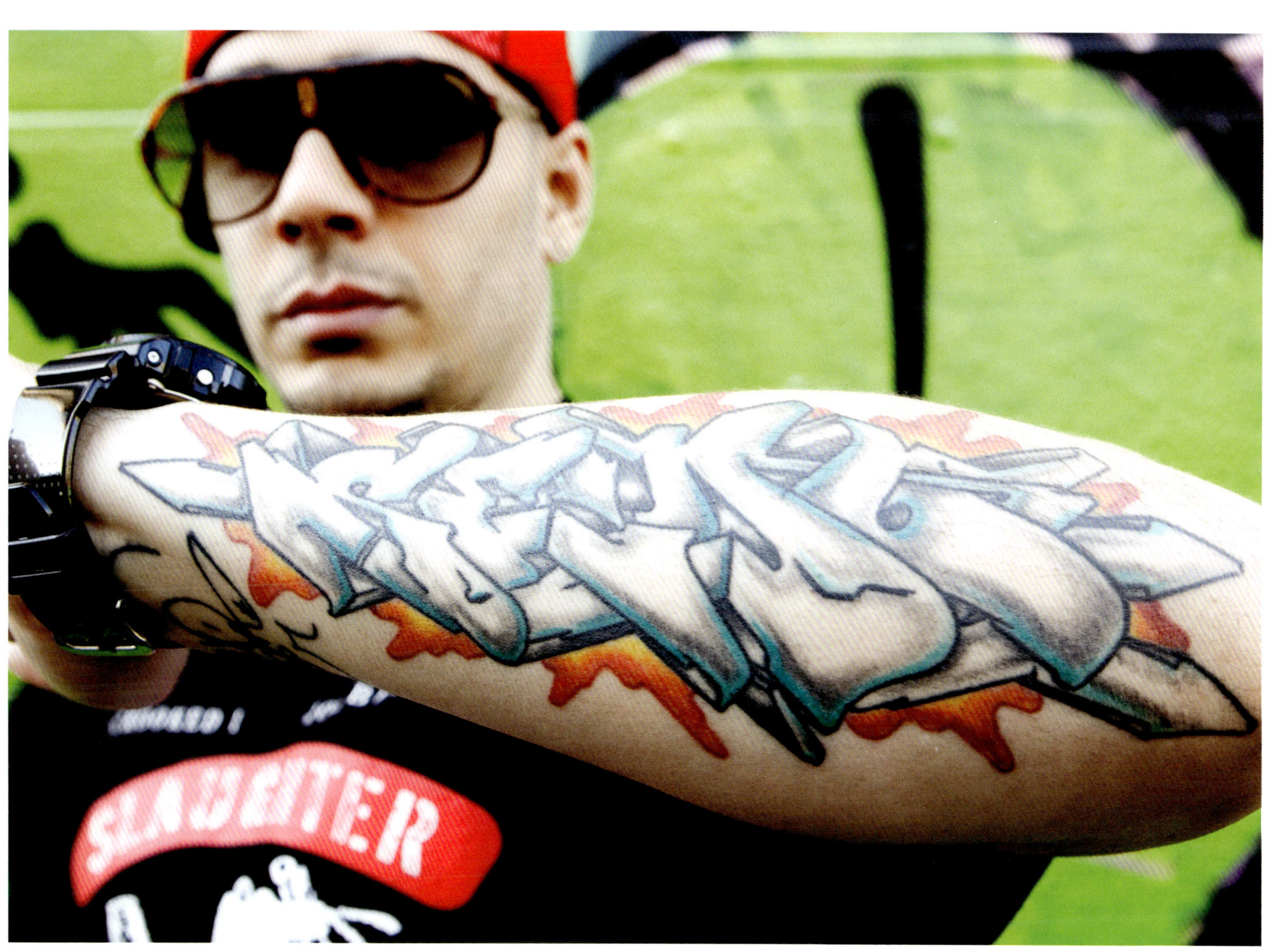

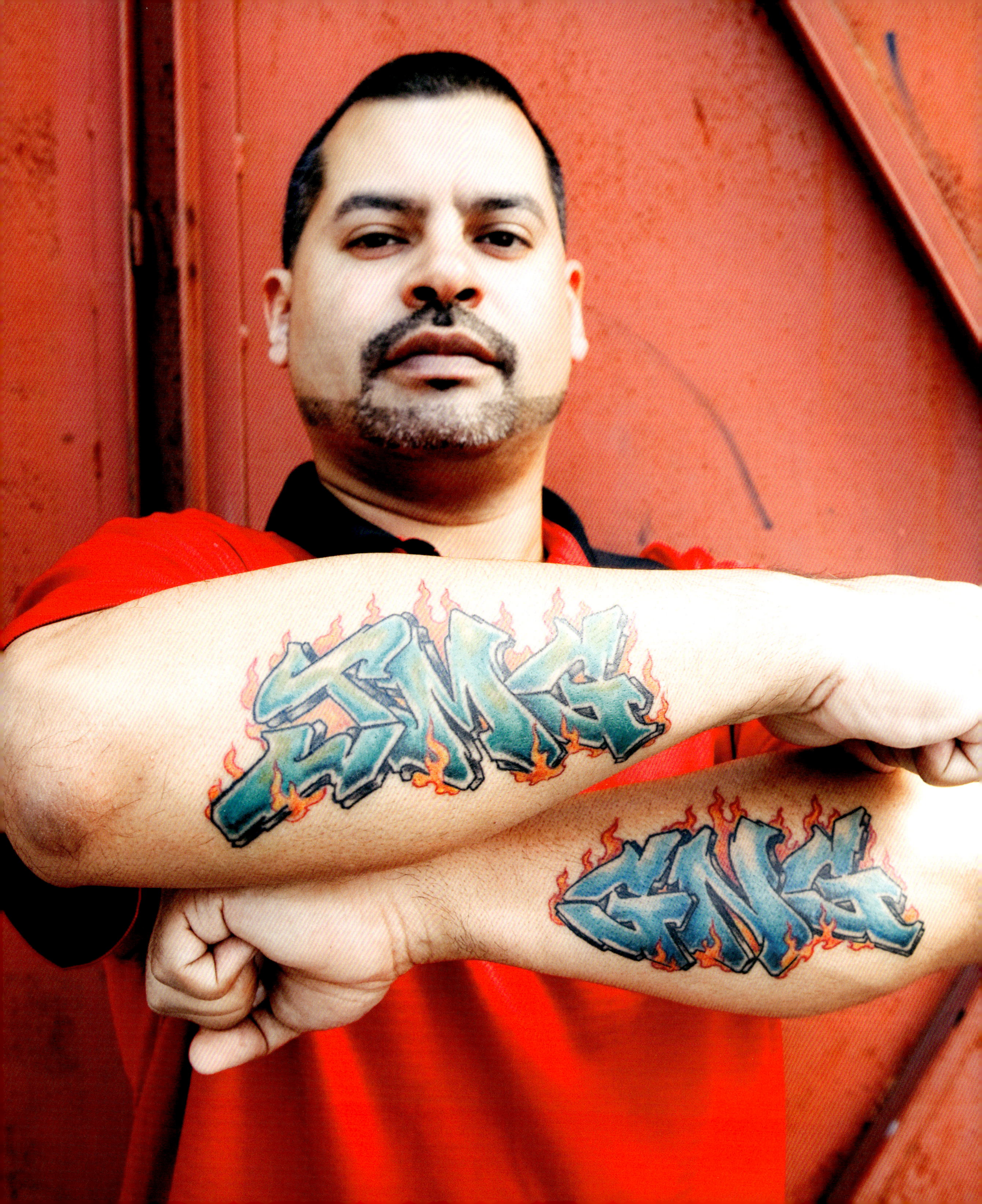

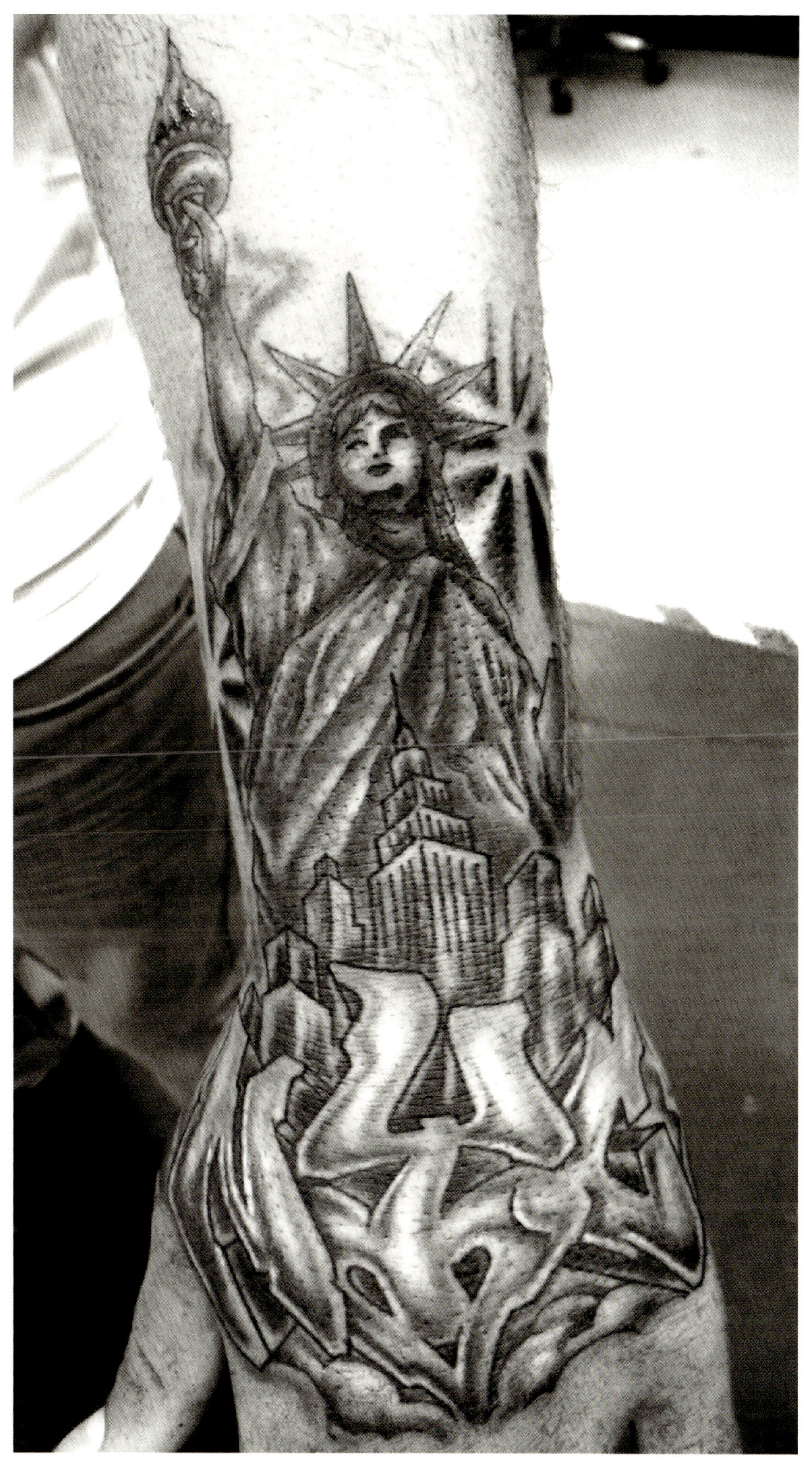

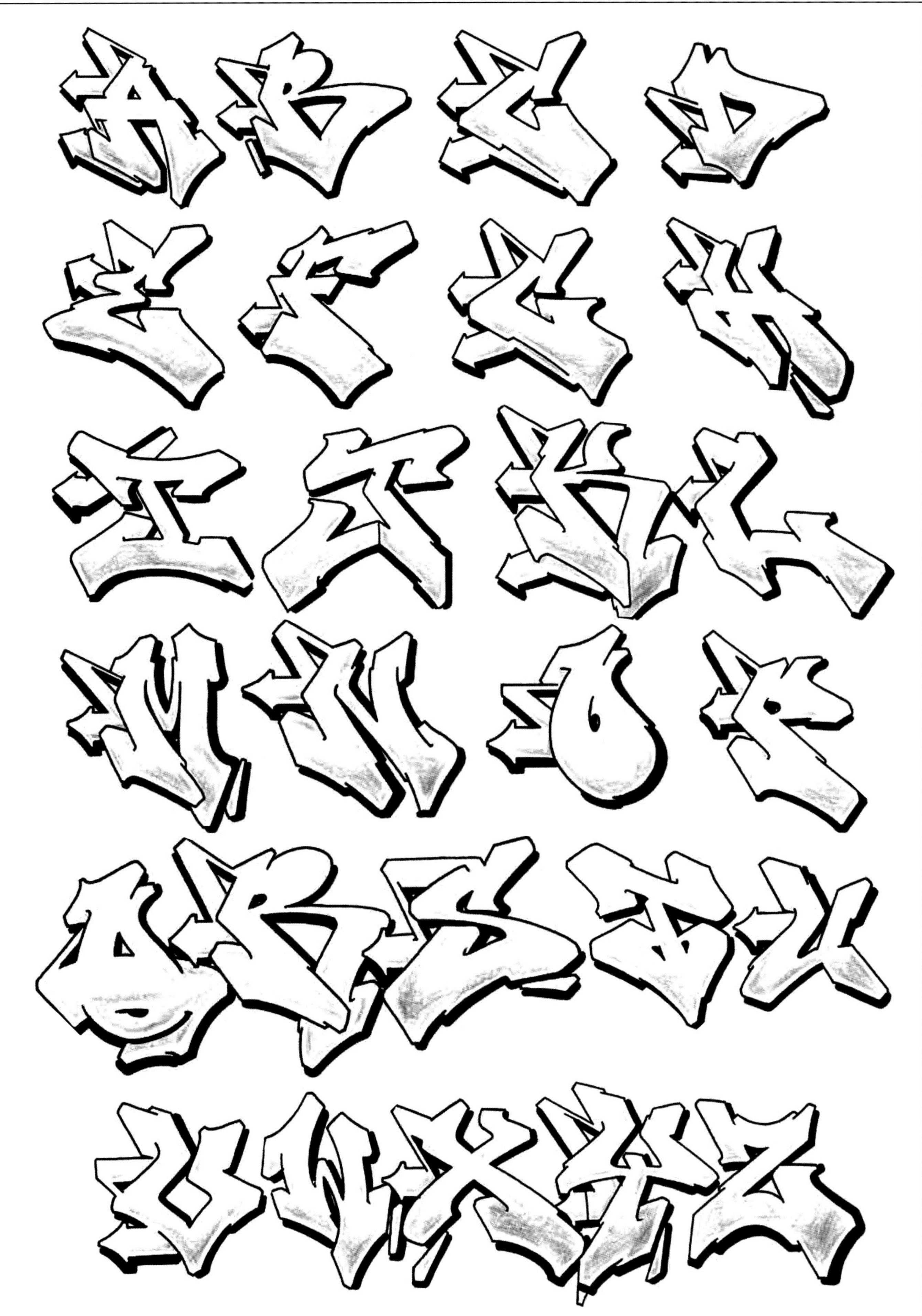

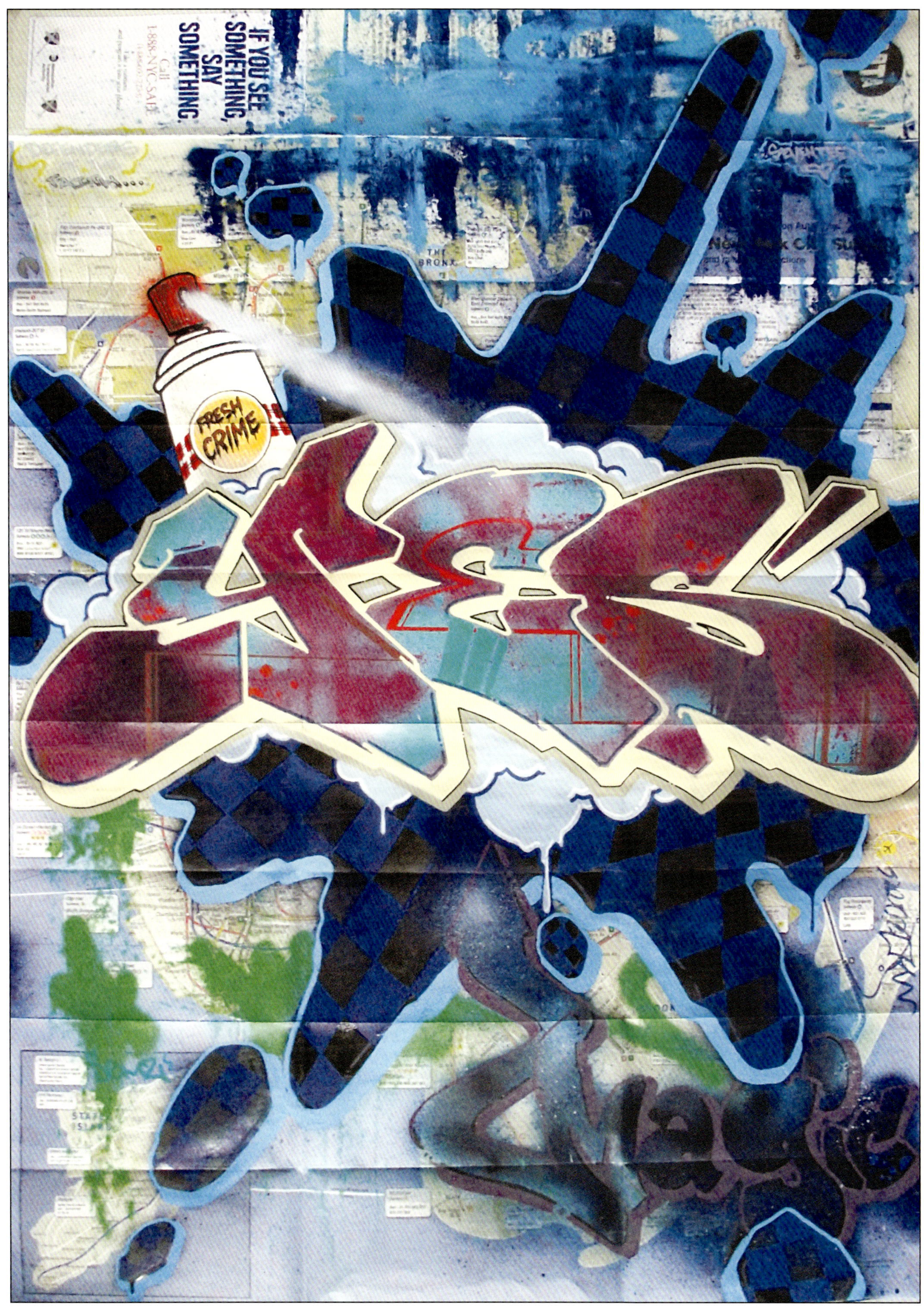

IF YOU SEE
SOMETHING,
SAY
SOMETHING.
Call
1-888-NYC-SAFE
FRESH
CRIME

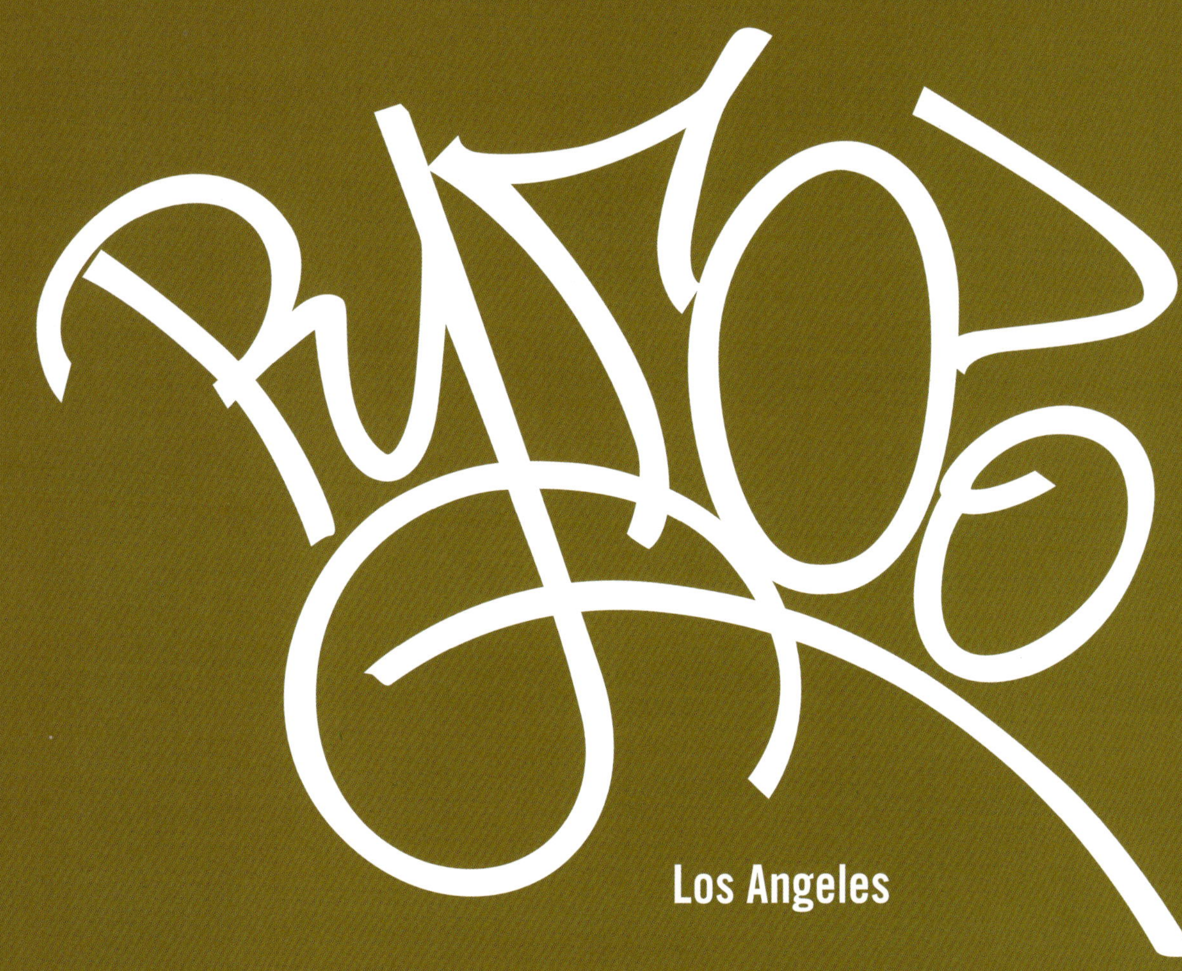

Los Angeles

"A lot of people say they want a 'tattoo machine tattoo' or design, and I'll take that and I'll make it this warped, wicked thing. I'll envision it on a train or a bus or a wall before I draw it, and give it that motion that you see in graffiti and that life that graffiti has."

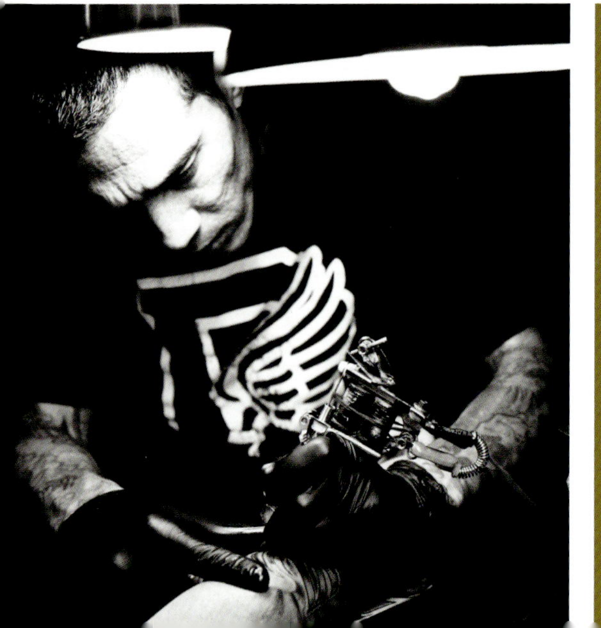

PYRO

Pyro got his name off the side of a disposable lighter when he was a kid. The year was 1983. Gang graffiti and mainstream advertisements were greeted by an equal amount of eyeballs during that stretch of Los Angeles history. Pyro soaked it all in. He took a deep breath and dove headfirst into Henry Chalfant and Martha Cooper's seminal tome, *Subway Art*. After years of writing and also working in the music biz, Pyro found himself hanging out in tattoo parlors. Pyro has created his own unique vocabulary by blending traditional graffiti and prison-reared *cholo* gang style.

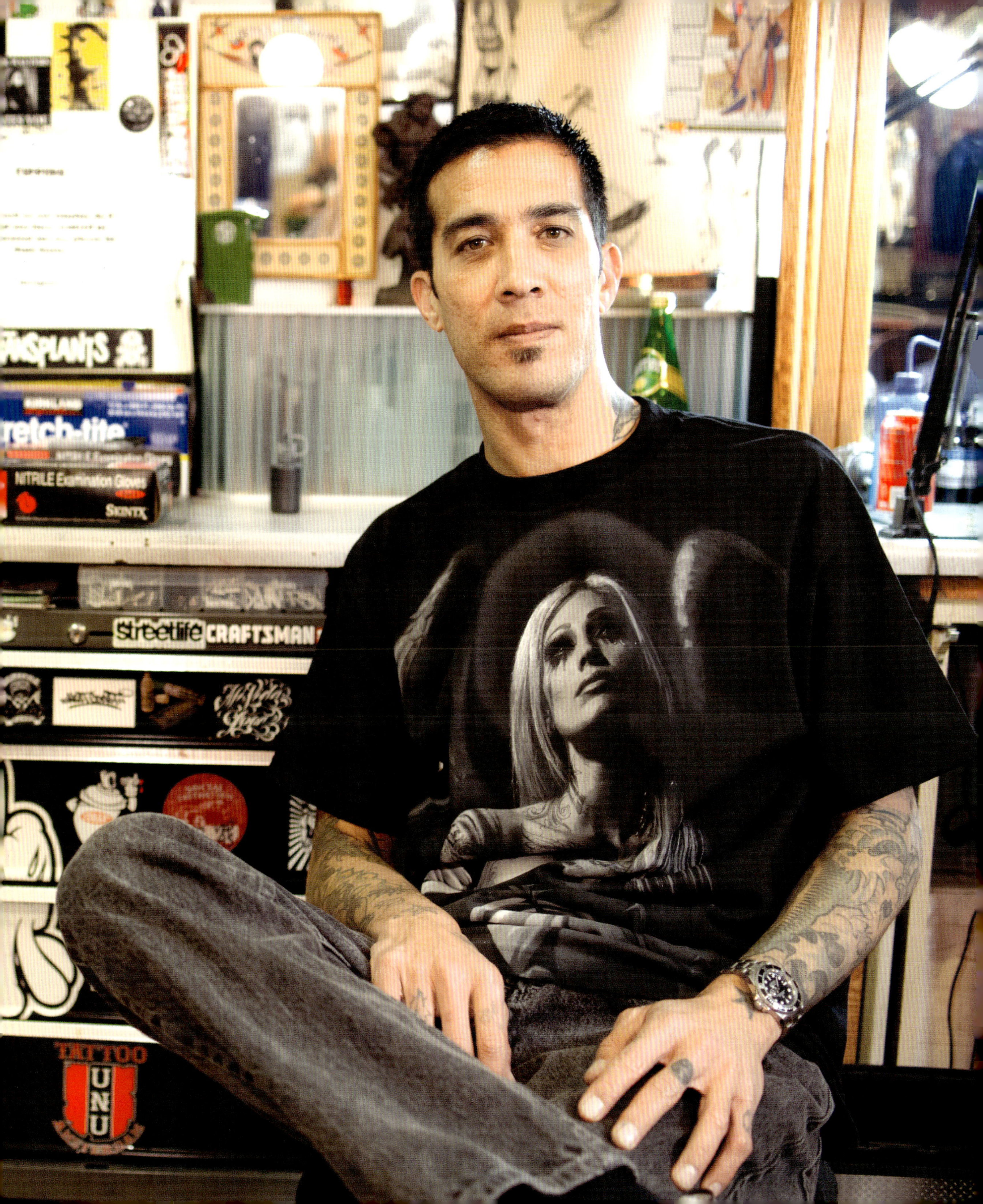

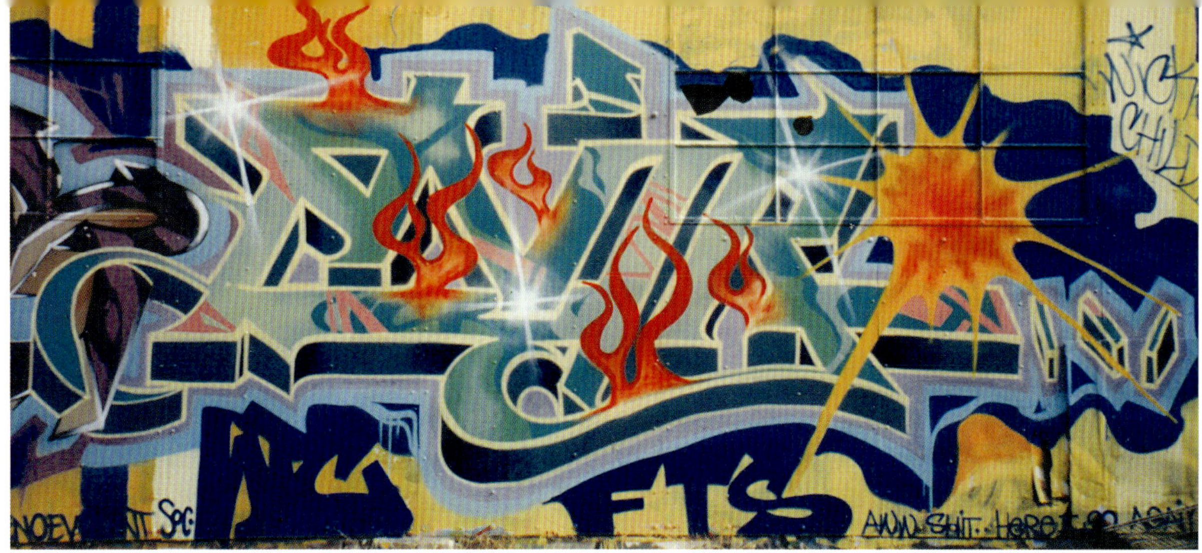

FROM LEFT: Pyro piece, Fairfax Avenue, Los Angeles, 1997; Pyro piece, Belmont, Long Beach, CA, 1986; Pyro, San Francisco, 1988

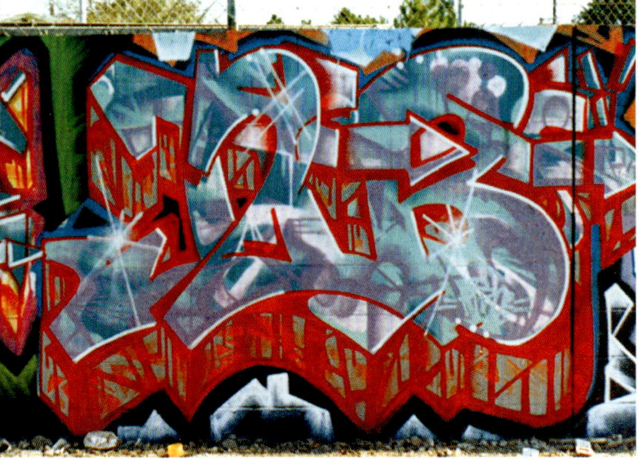

Pyro, *2B,* Los Angeles, 1986

My name is Pyro, West Coast Artists crew. I started writing in 1982, Los Angeles. I was influenced by the book *Subway Art*, as most of us were out here. I got a copy of that and was just amazed by it. I had started writing before that—just little names and nicknames and neighborhood shit.

I was really influenced by gang graffiti, block letters and the stylized tags—that stuff that was happening here in LA at the time. After I got *Subway Art*, I started trying to stylize myself a little bit more. I wouldn't say "wild style" but a little more flair to the letters and using colors and everything like that.

In '83 I started writing *Pyro* because I was hanging out at my sister's little store in Atwater at that time. I looked in my pocket and I had a little disposable lighter, and the shit was Pyro brand lighters. I was like, *ding*. There it is. And I was pretty much solo at that time. I wasn't with a crew. I was just hanging out, roaming around by myself, writing on shit. Around that time—late '84, early '85—West Coast Artists was formed. I didn't know them, but they were in the same neighborhood as me. I was really influenced by Rival, PJay, and Miner. They were actually influenced by Revlon from New York. That's where I got a lot of my influences. There were no trains here, so we hit the buses. Mad bus bombing, going to the bus yards, doing pieces on buses and the whole nine yards. I've been writing pretty much ever since.

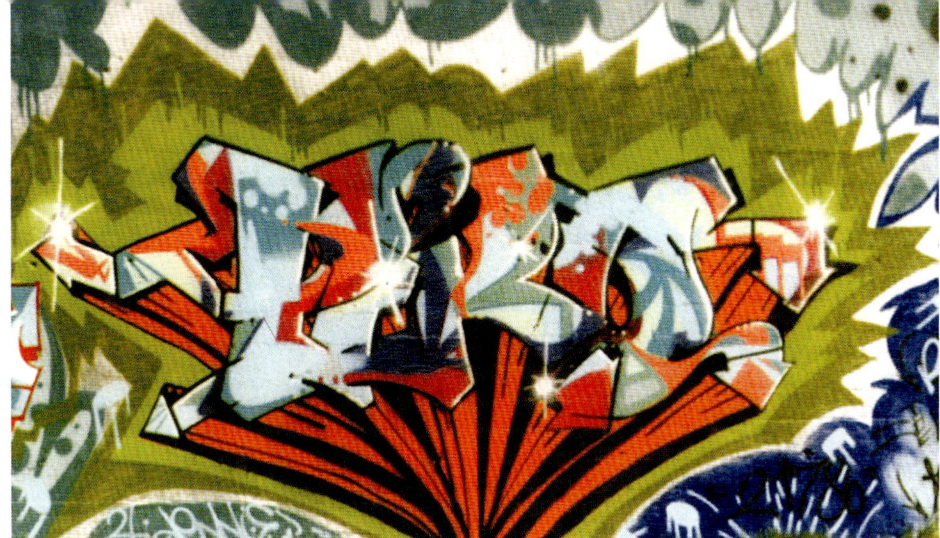

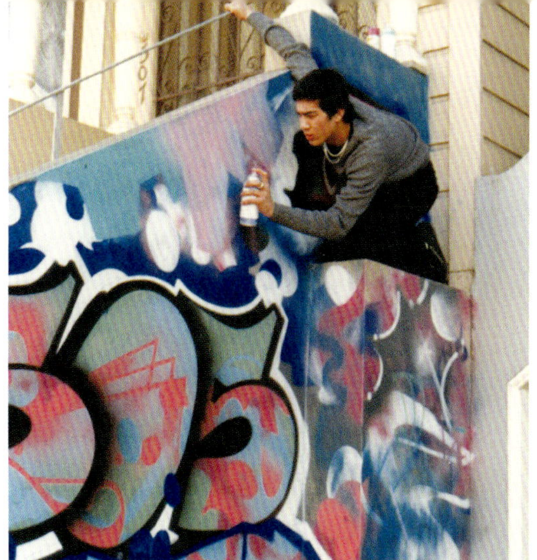

I took a break for a while. I've worked in music for a long time. In '96—actually prior to '96, like '93 to '95—I was hanging out a lot at Tattoo Mania up on the Sunset Strip. Back then it was Mark Mahoney, Tom Tilden, Gill Montie, Clay Decker, Tony DeCou, and a couple other people. I started hanging out with Clay, and basically Clay apprenticed me. He wasn't working full-time at the shop at that time. He was working out of his house, but I was pretty much his gofer for the most part, running around, taking care of errands for him and stuff like that. He taught me how to make machines, how to make needles, how to mix inks, and basically how to tattoo.

I started working at Tattoo Mania in '96. I only worked there for about a year and a half, and then I started working in music. I got an offer to tour and manage bands, so I was only tattooing part-time here and there. I worked in shops across the nation while I was on tour, but nothing full-time. I did that for about eight years, just tattooing part-time, doing tattoos out of my house for a while or working in shops for a week temporarily.

Then about six years ago, I quit doing music and I got back in tattooing full-time. I was in Vegas for about six years, had a shop in Pahrump [Nevada] called Body Magic. I was working up there and recently moved back to Los Angeles. I started tattooing at a couple of shops here and there and wound up here at Vintage Tattoo. I've been here ever since.

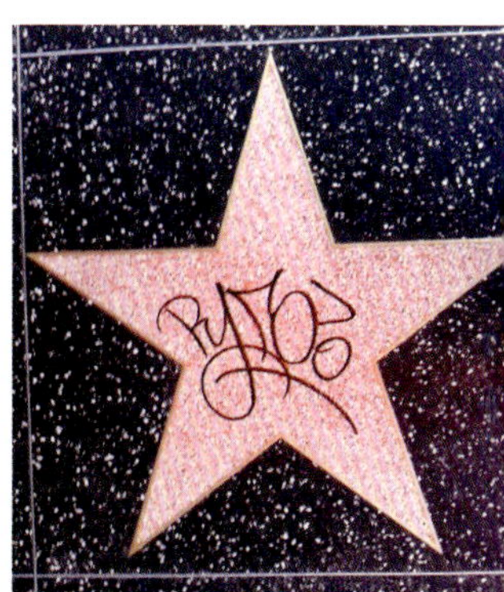

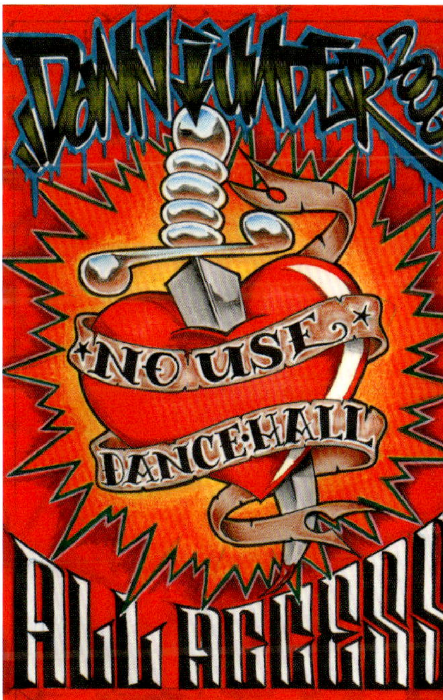

TOP: Pyro tag on Hollywood star
BOTTOM: Pyro tour pass art

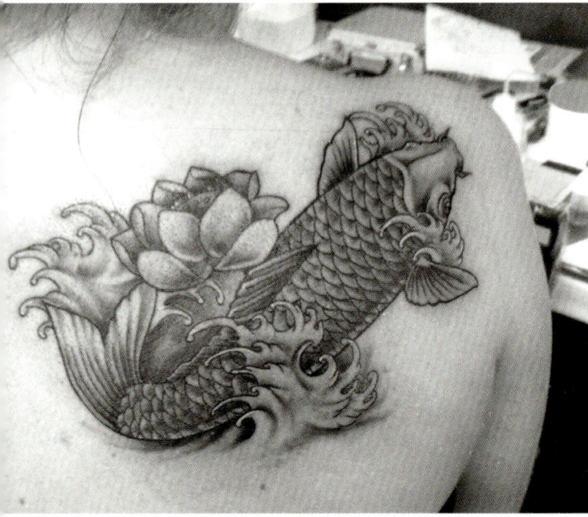

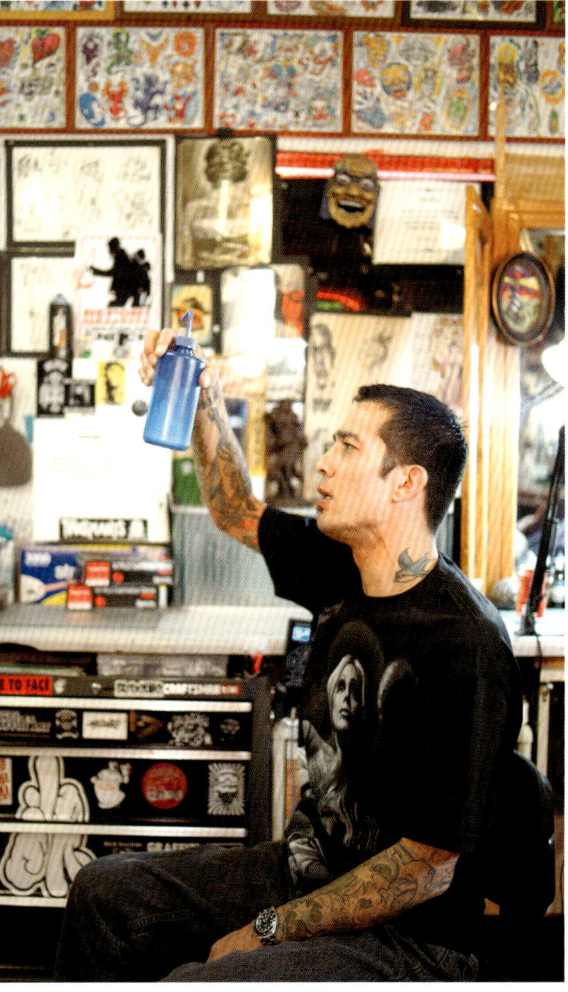

My graffiti background is definitely one of my two big influences. The other is the black and gray prison *cholo* style, which is so prominent here in California. Having been around Mark Mahoney early in my tattooing career, I was really influenced by him and his black and gray work. But that's not completely who I was, considering I come from a graffiti background. It's almost completely the opposite, completely crazy, wild-style colors and flourishes, your own adaptations of things. I like doing both.

Graffiti influences my color schemes and influences my perspective on things. A lot of people say they want a "tattoo machine tattoo" or design, and I'll take that and I'll make it this warped, wicked thing. I'll envision it on a train or a bus or a wall before I draw it, and give it that motion that you see in graffiti and that life that graffiti has. What I love to do is writing. I love coming up with my own designs, my own letters, incorporating wild style and tagging into gang graffiti and Old English and mixing the two.

Being able to draw something and putting it on someone's body forever, that's like the ultimate honor. I'm not into the whole political thing of the who's who and this person's that and yadda, yadda, yadda. I couldn't give a shit. It doesn't mean anything to me. To me, it's all about the person. If they're cool, they're down to earth, and they're real, then I'm cool with them. And if they've got a big head or an ego and walk around like they're a prima donna, fuck them. I don't give a fuck who they are.

The politics was definitely part of why I took a step back from tattooing for a while and just did music and graffiti. And now the whole graffiti scene has gotten so much more political with this new resurgence of it. There's so much money and mainstream companies involved. I try and stay clear of that. I do my own thing, and if people like it, people like it. If people don't, people don't. The main thing is, I do it for me. I do graffiti artwork and tattooing. It's my own personal pleasure. I love to do it, and that's what drives me.

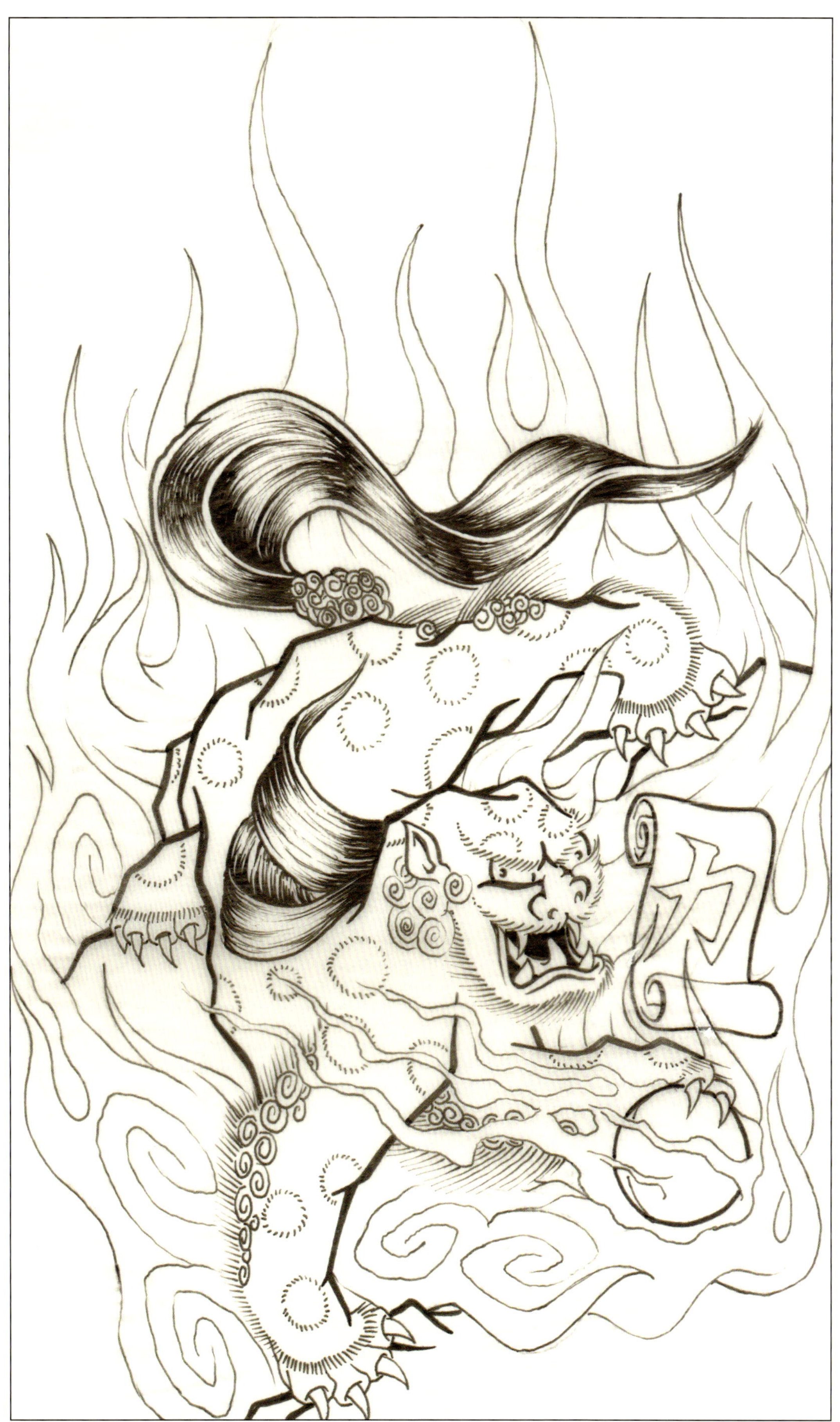

Pyro tattoo sketch

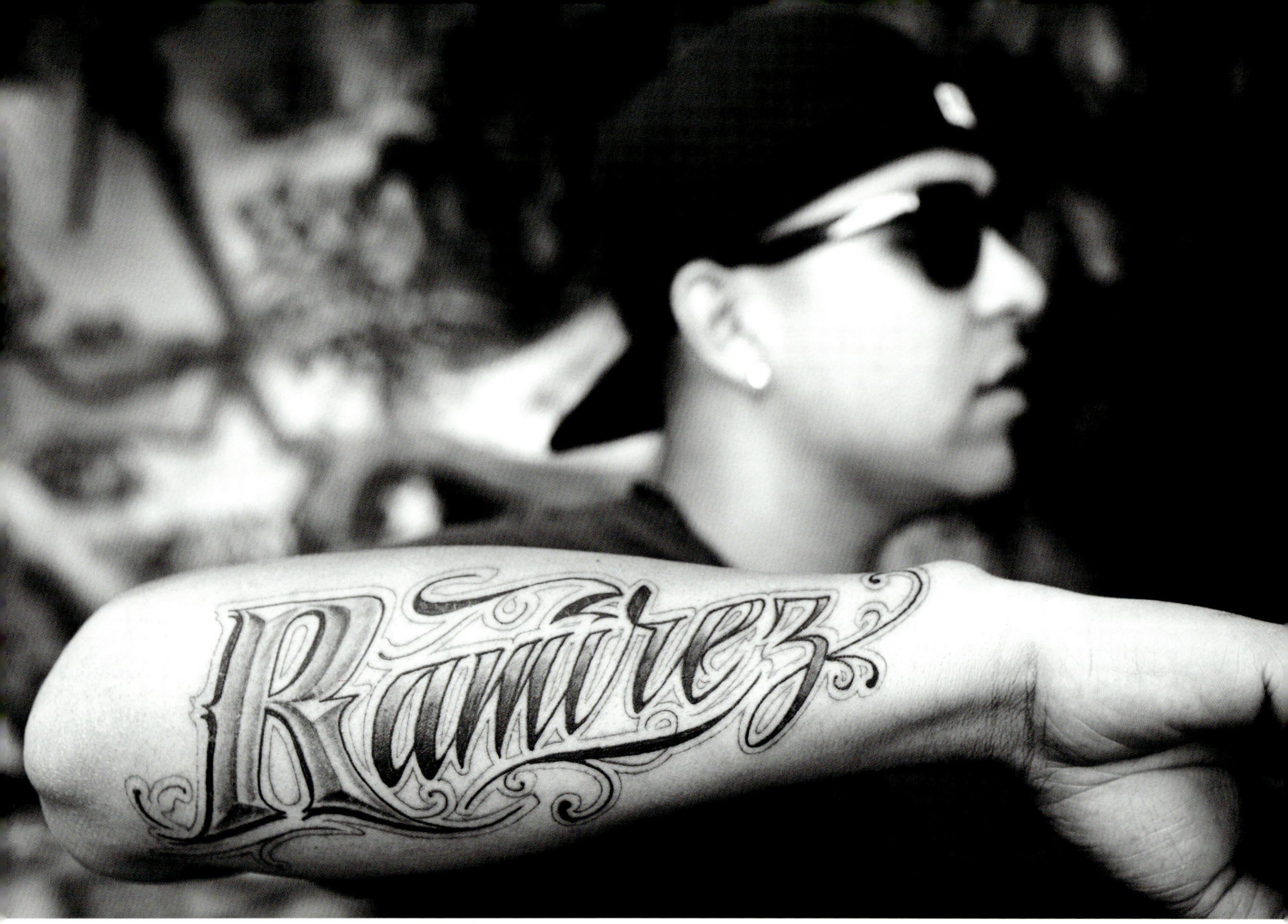

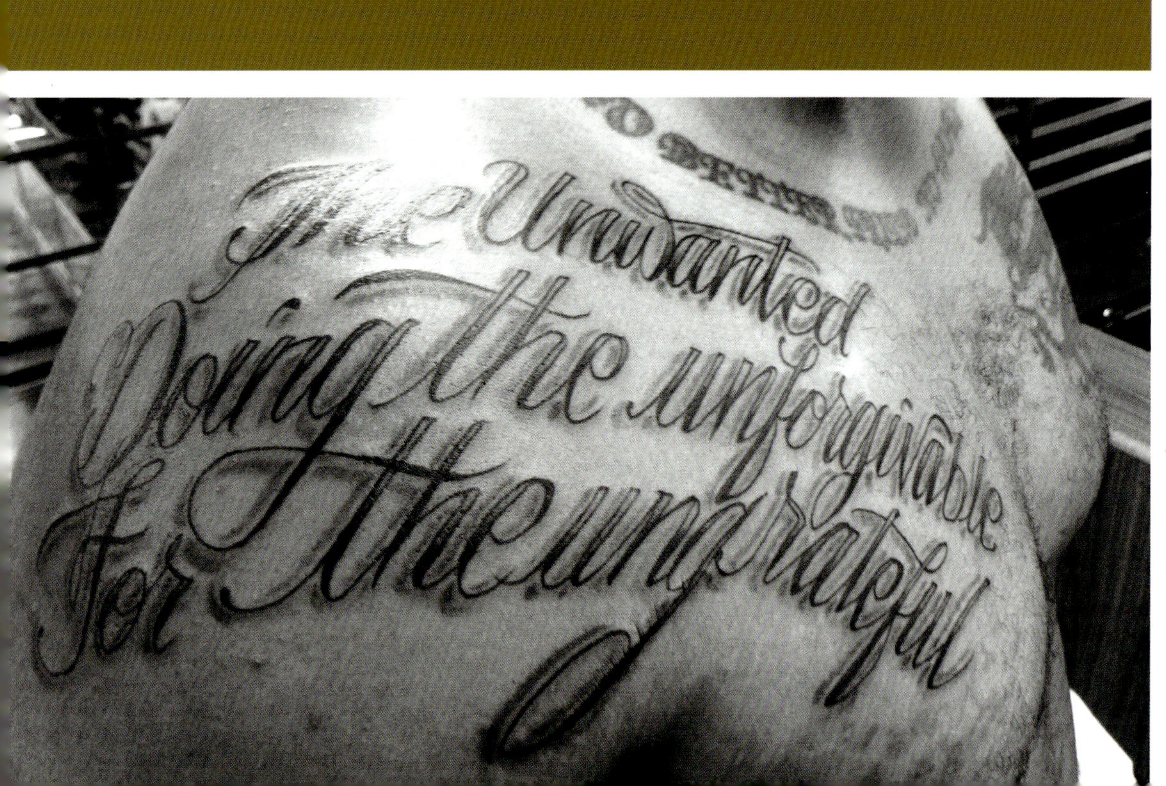
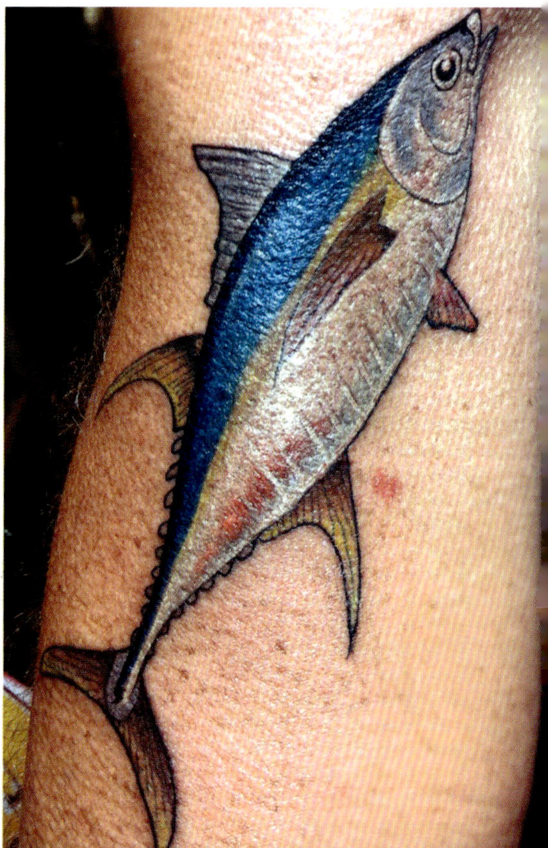

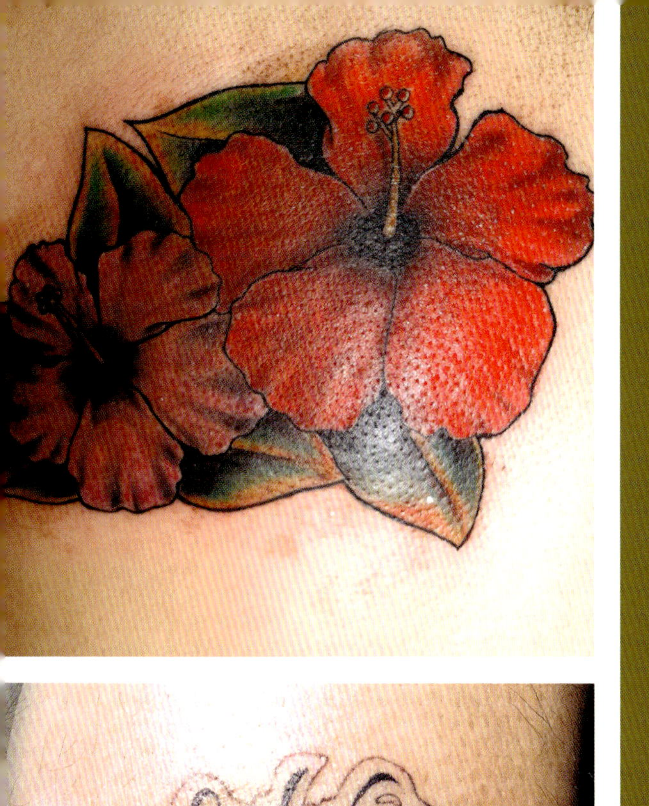
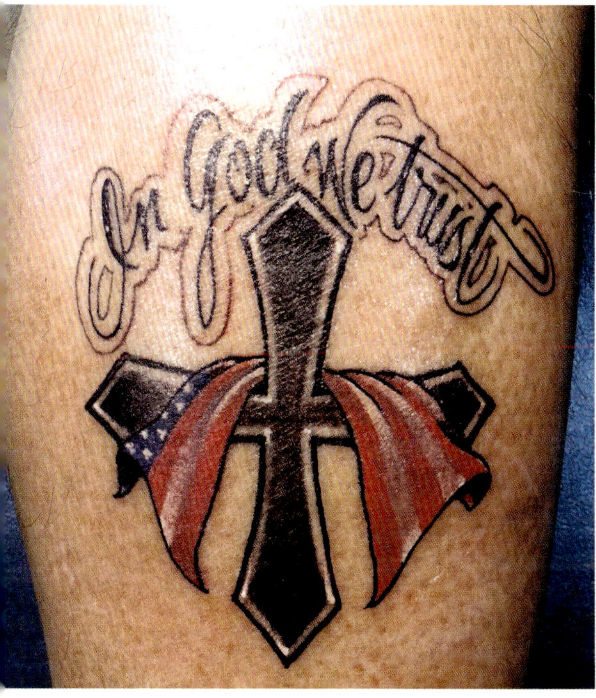
In God we trust
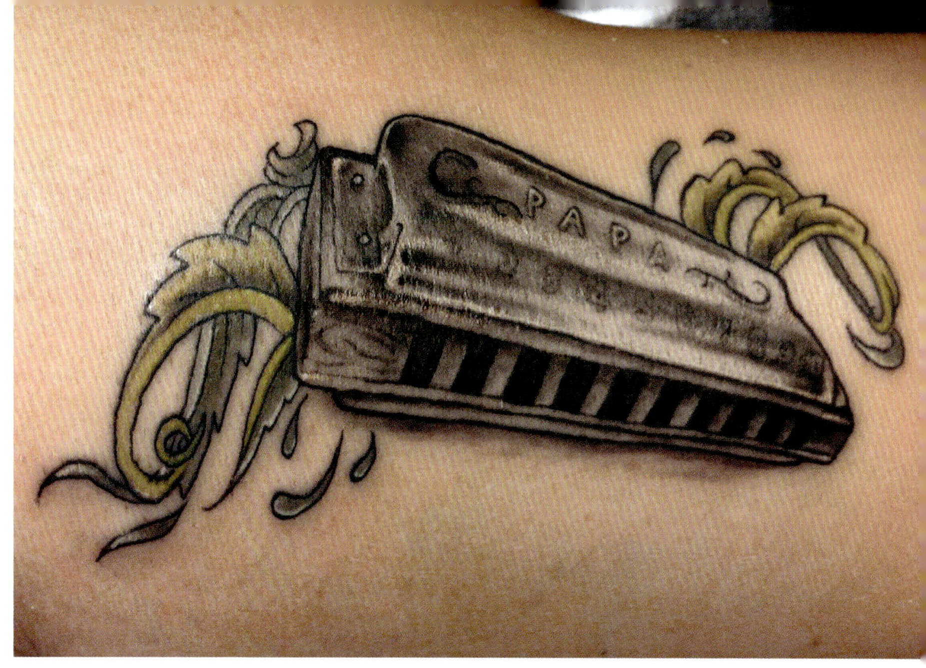
PAPA
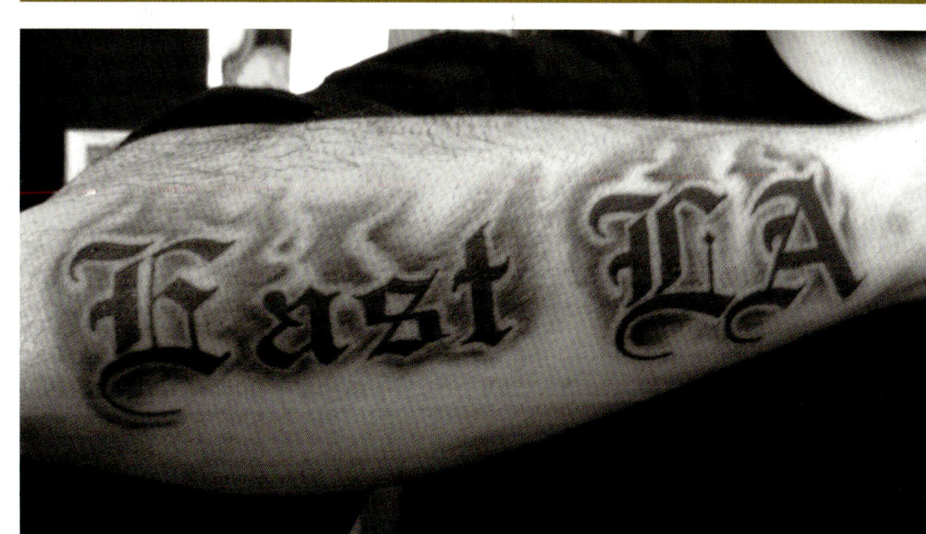
East LA
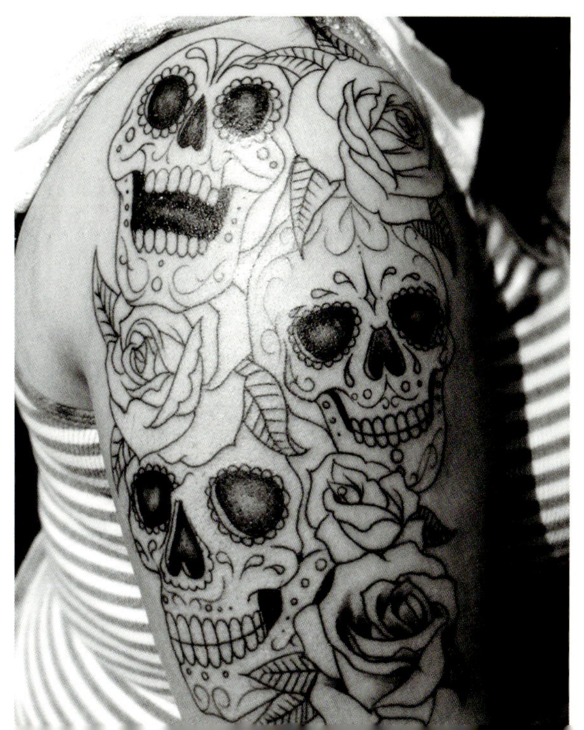

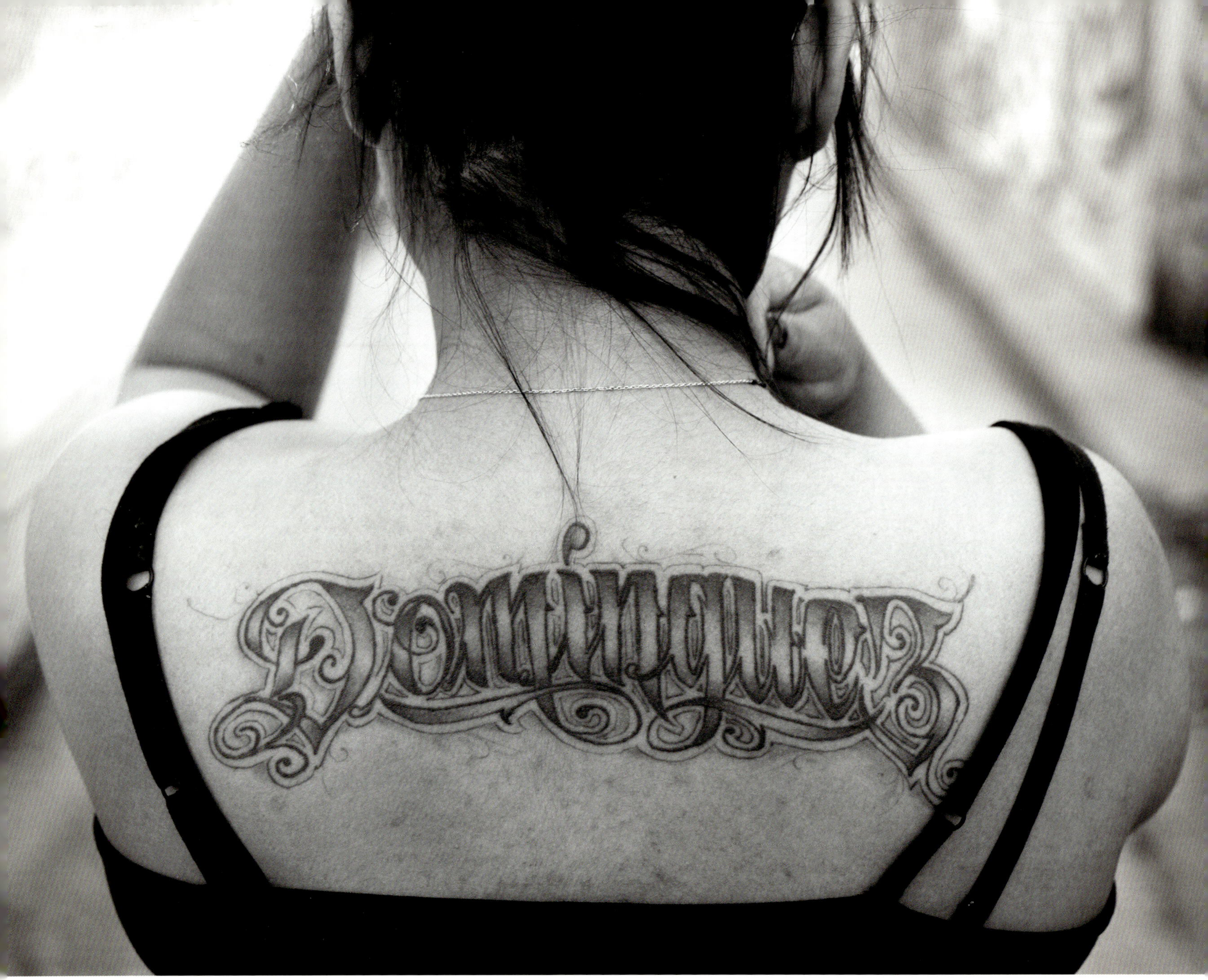

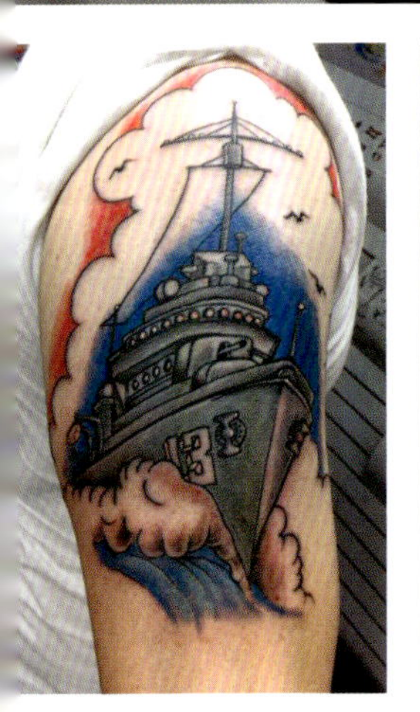

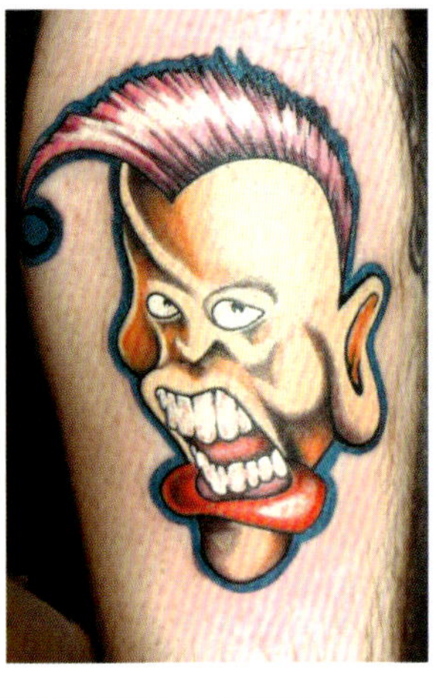

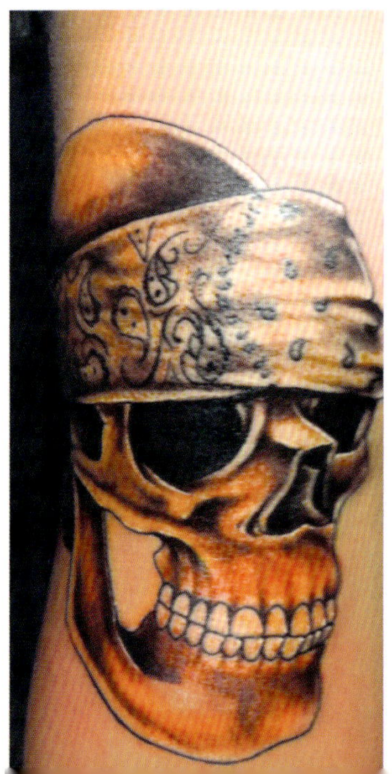

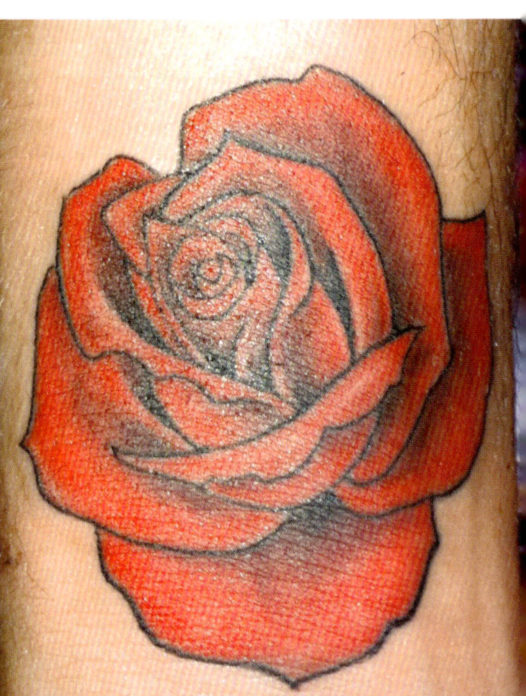

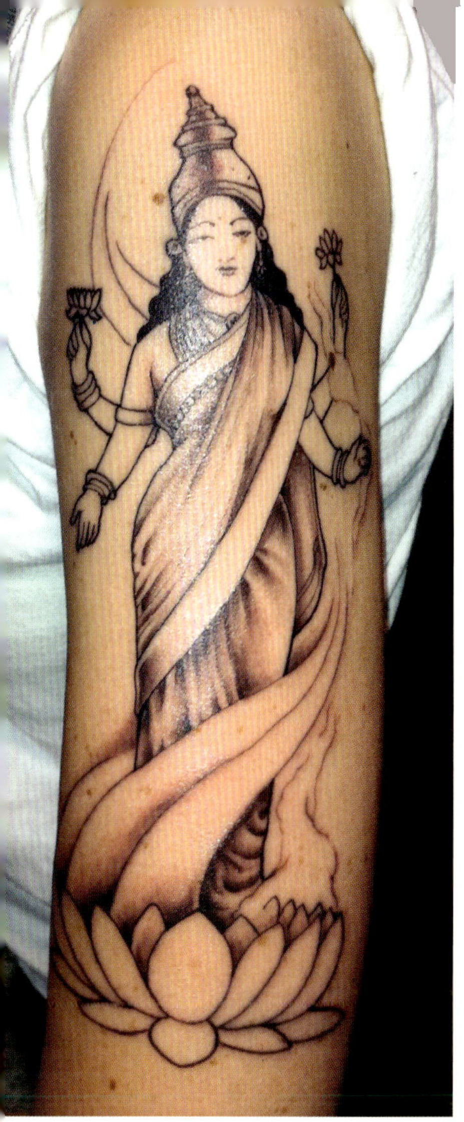

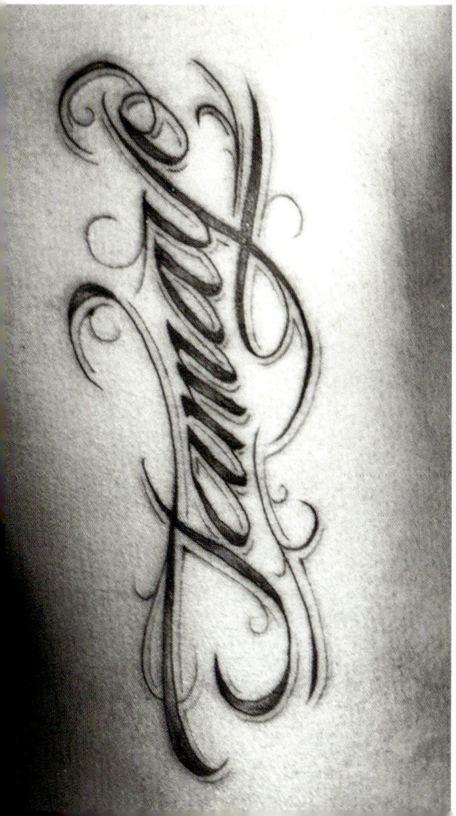

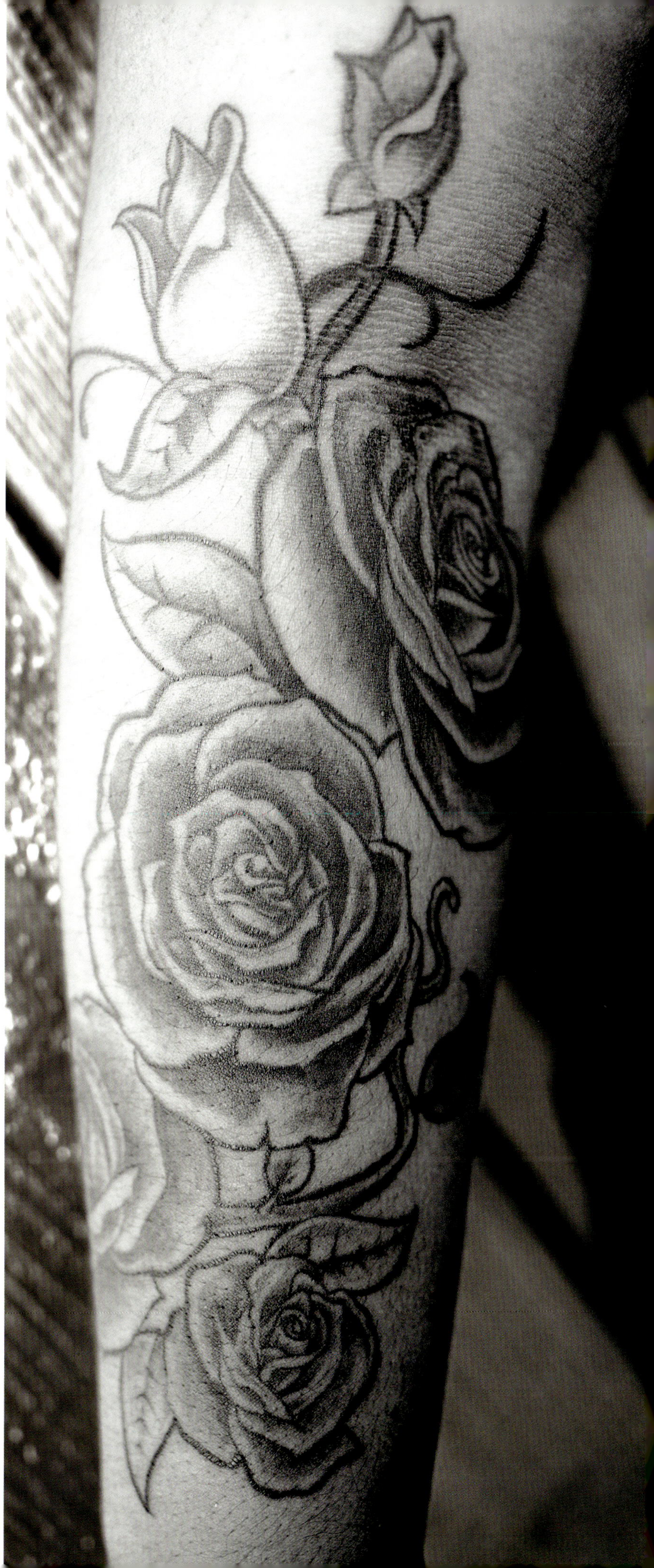

Kamal

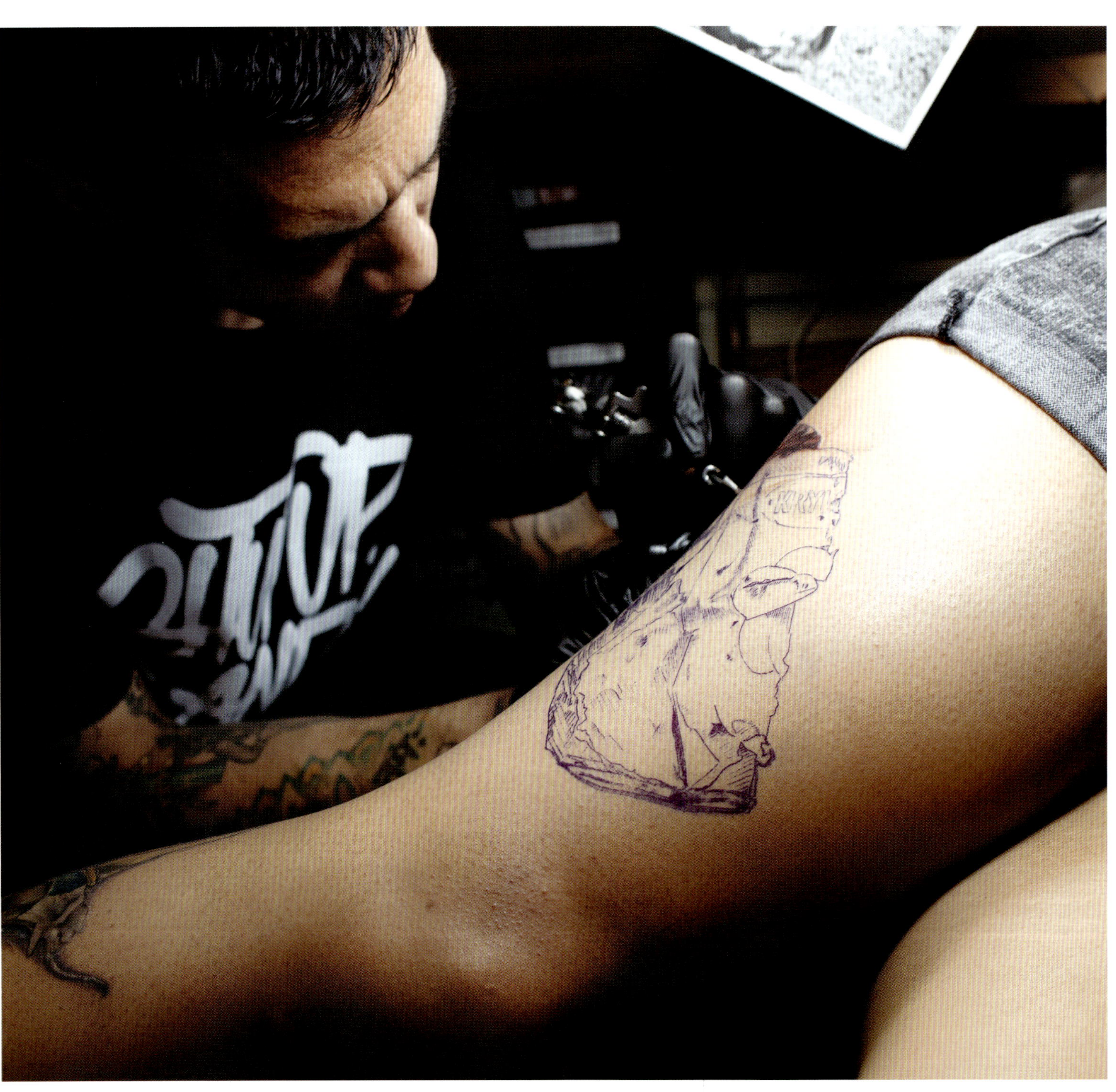

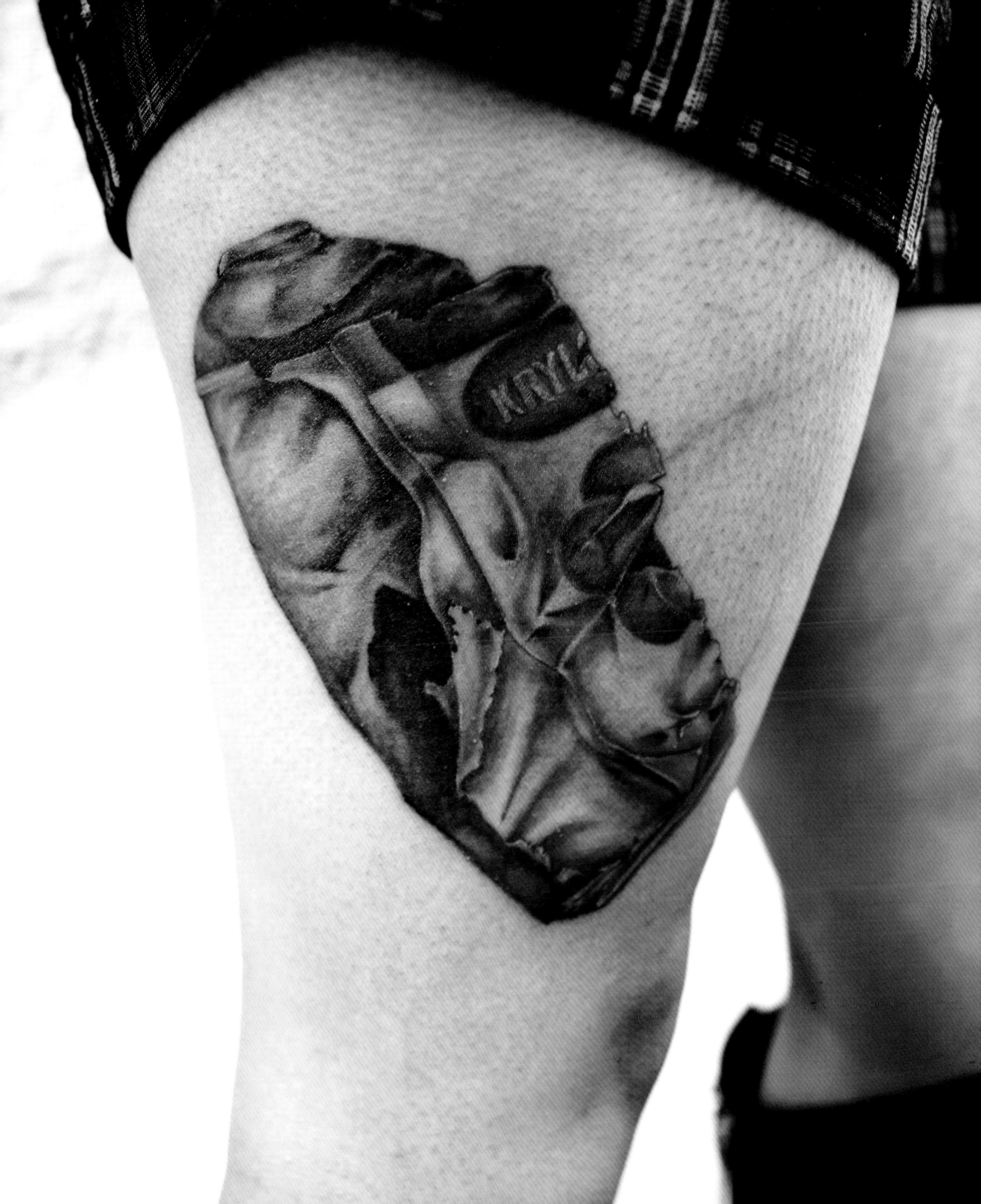

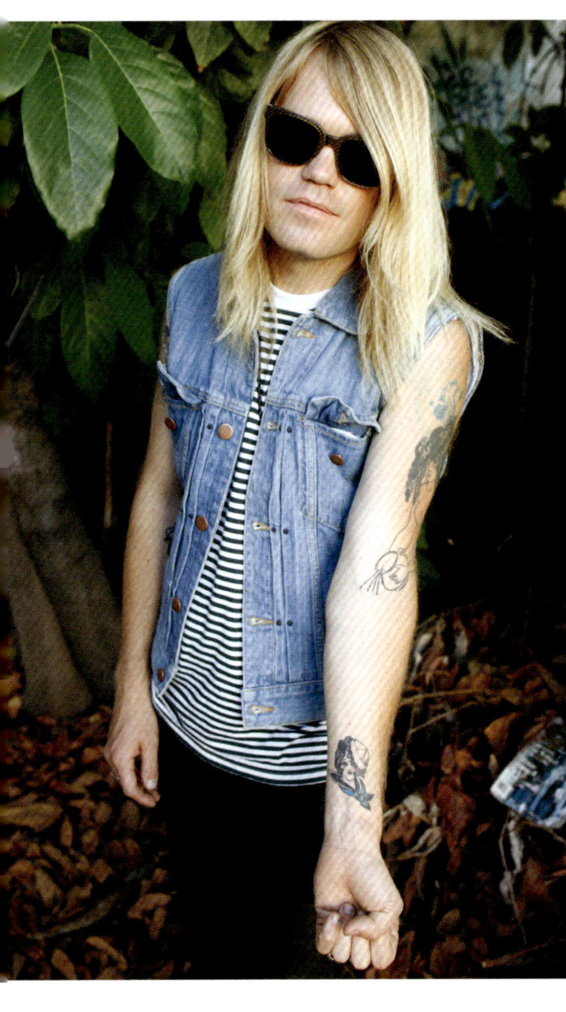

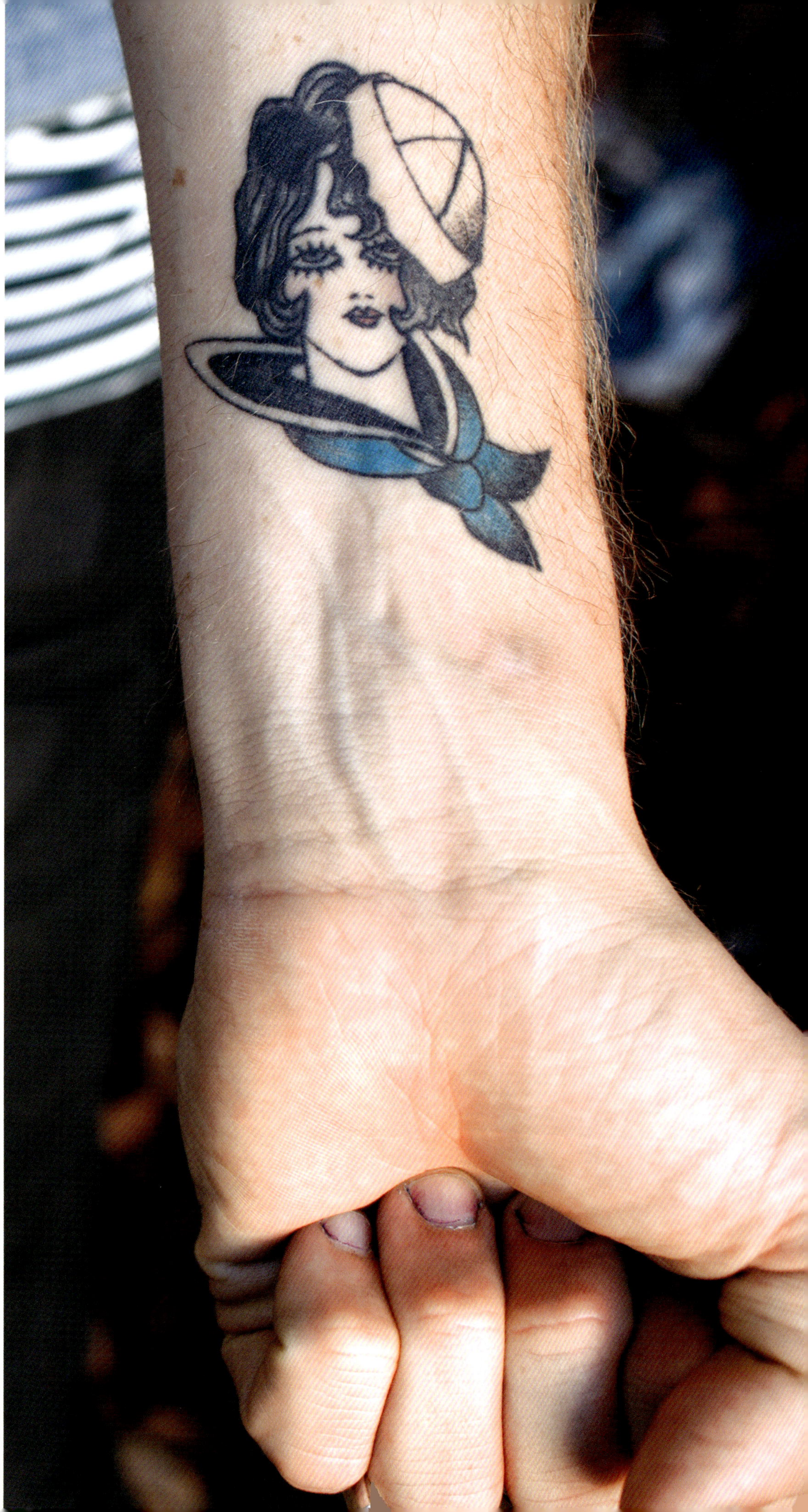

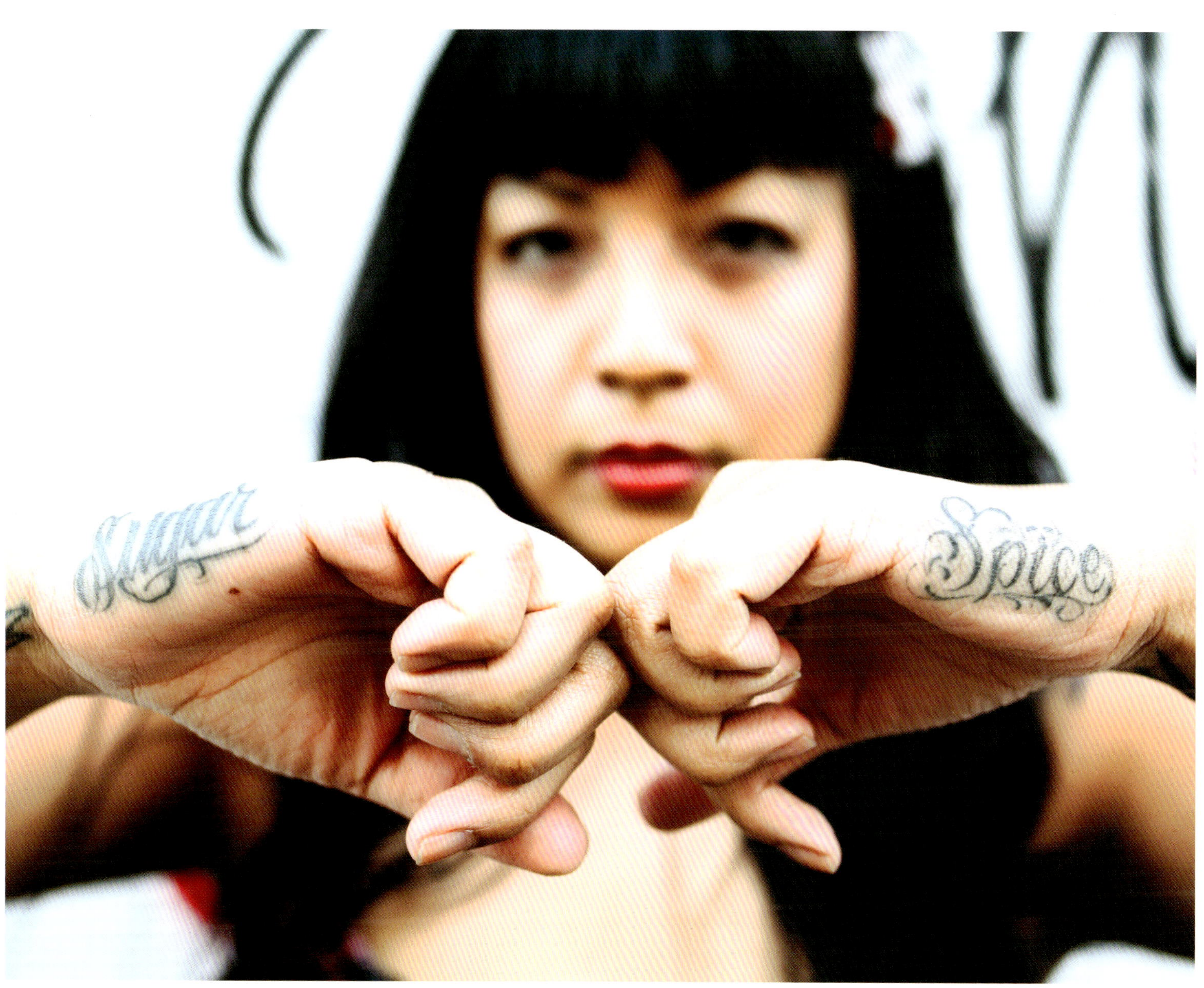

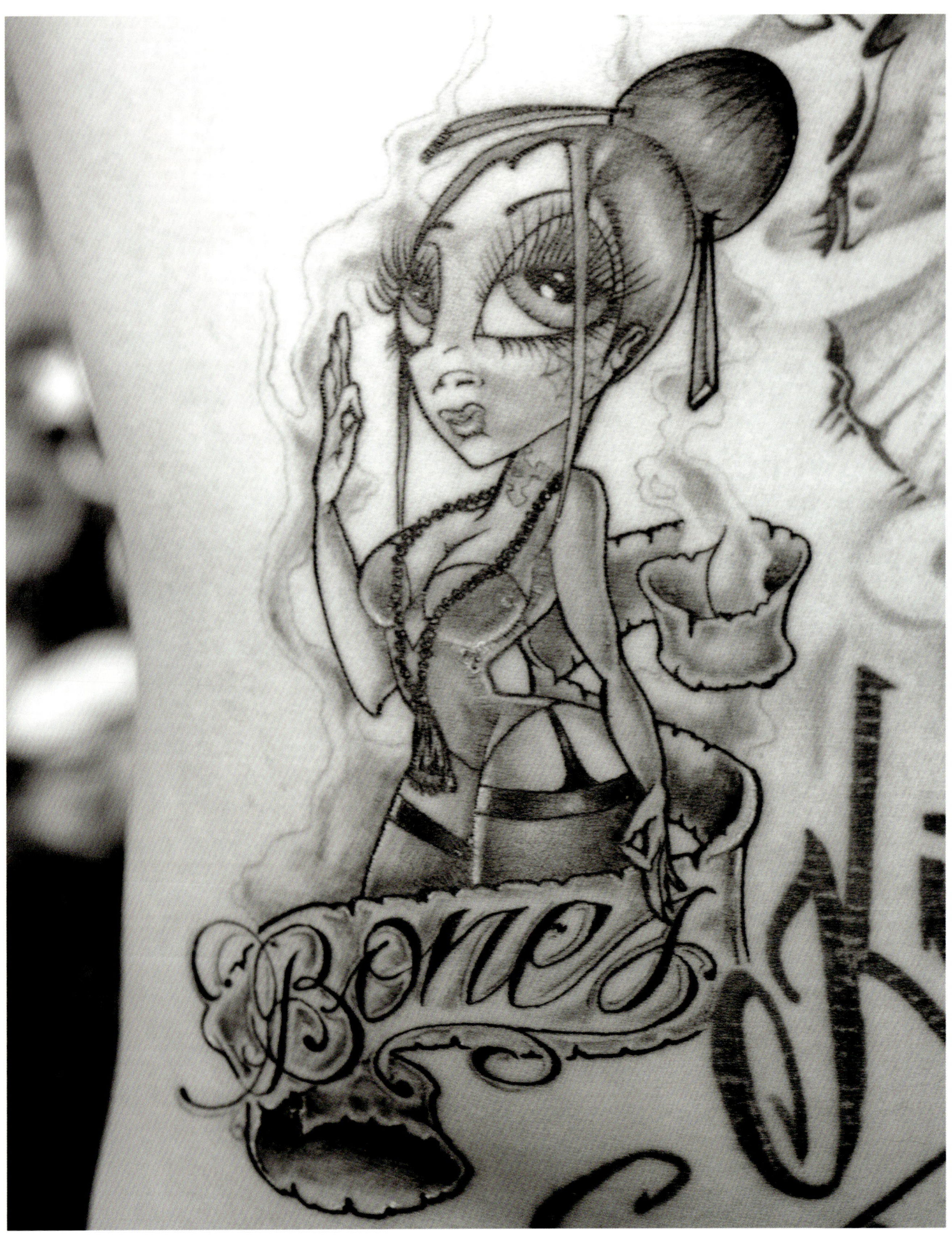

Bones

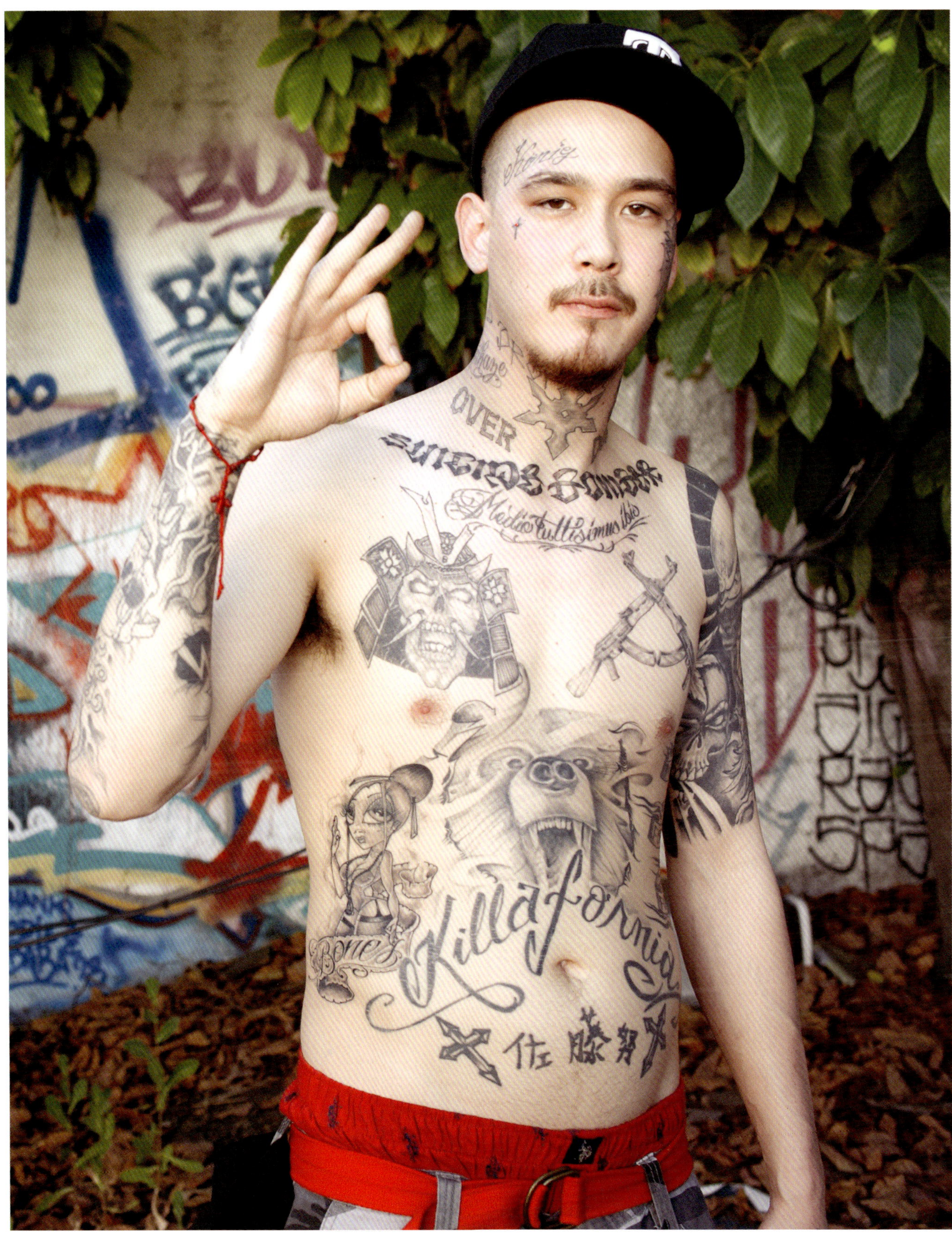

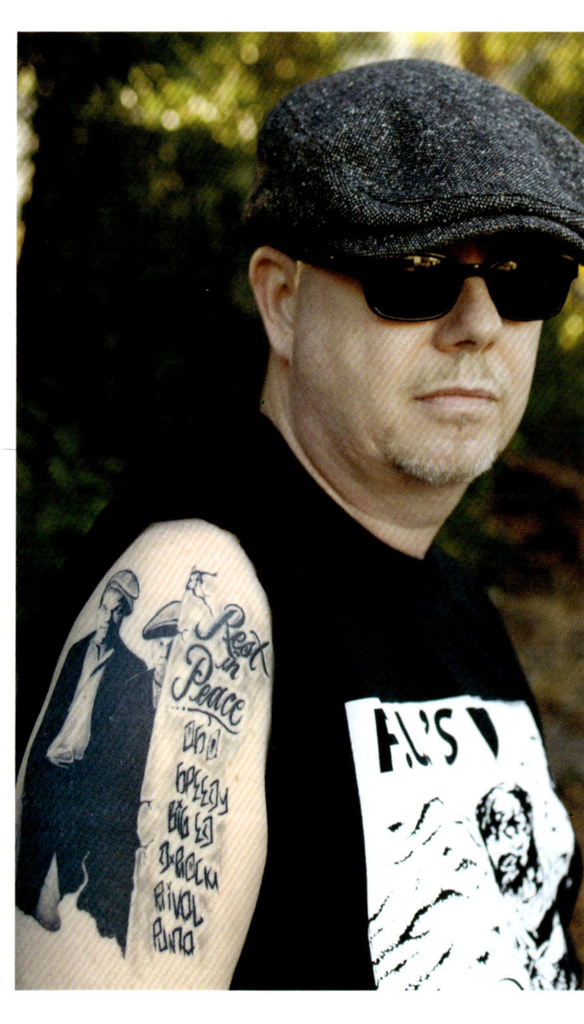

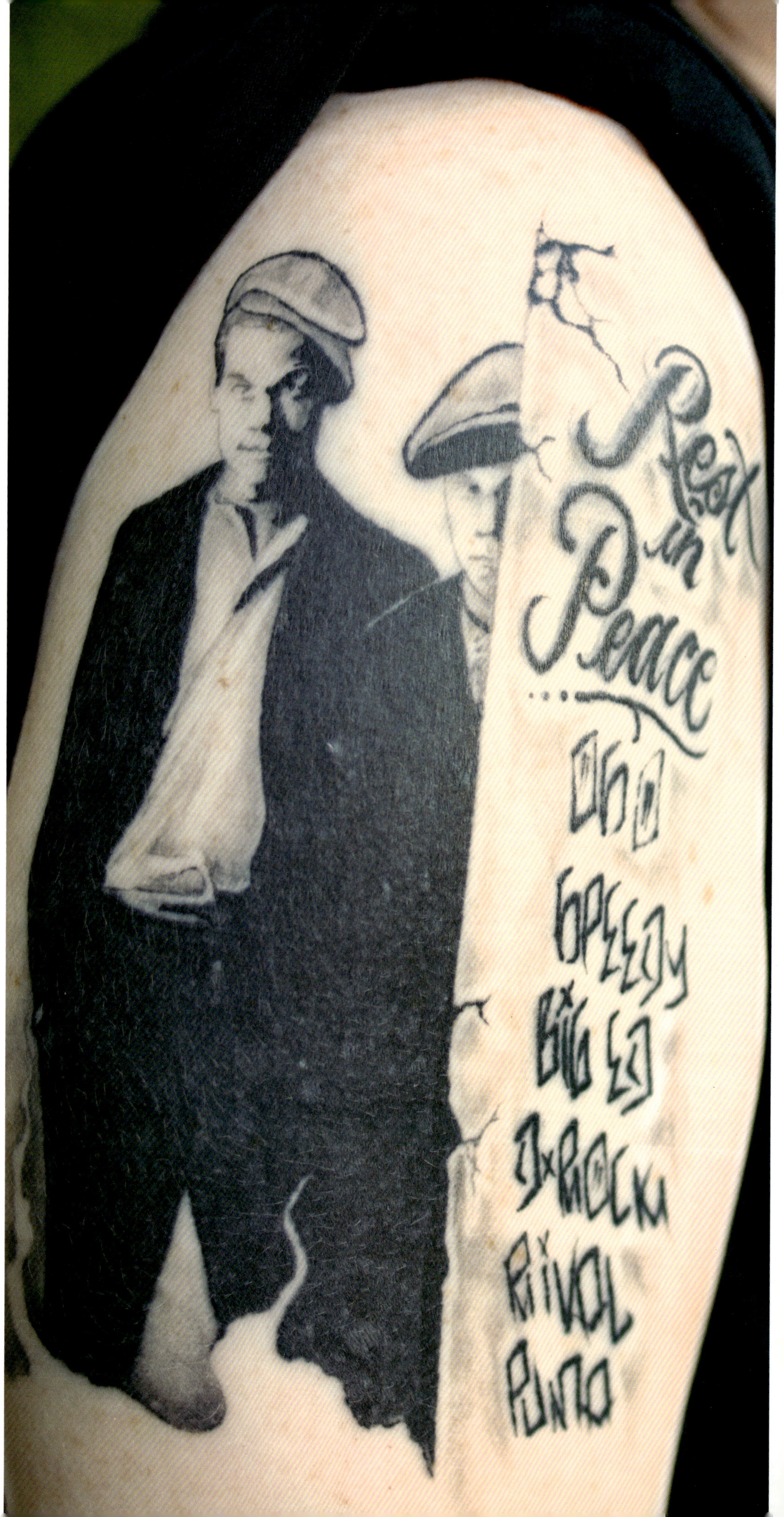

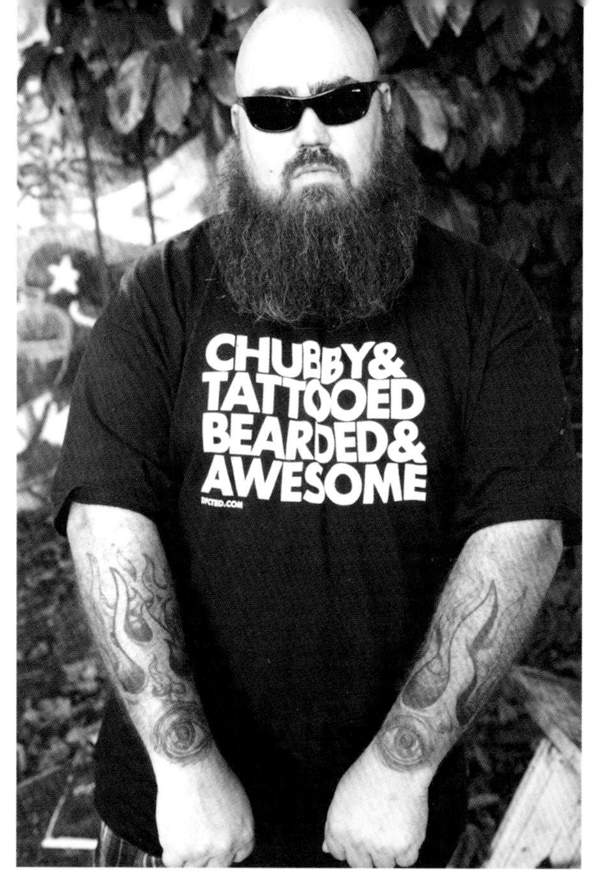

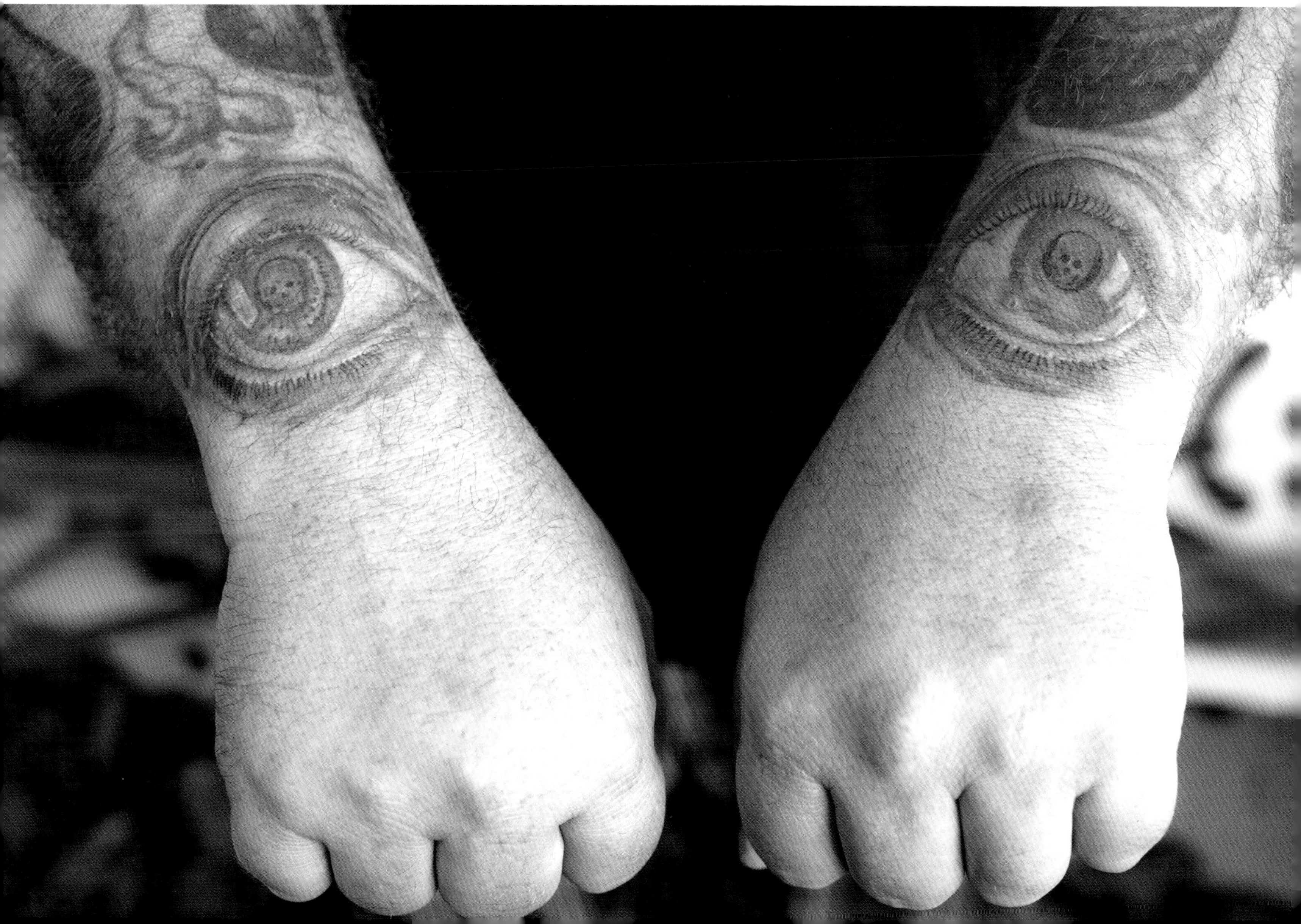

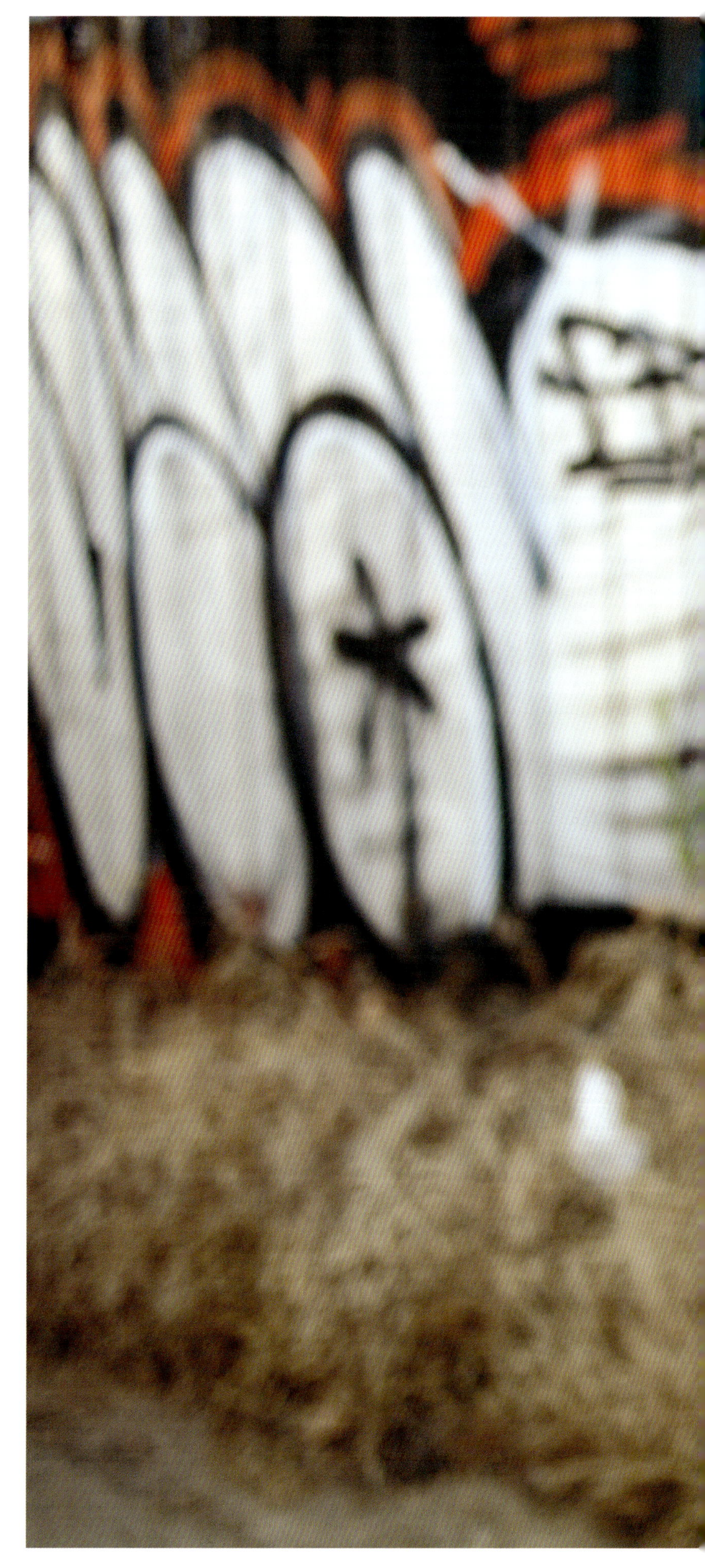

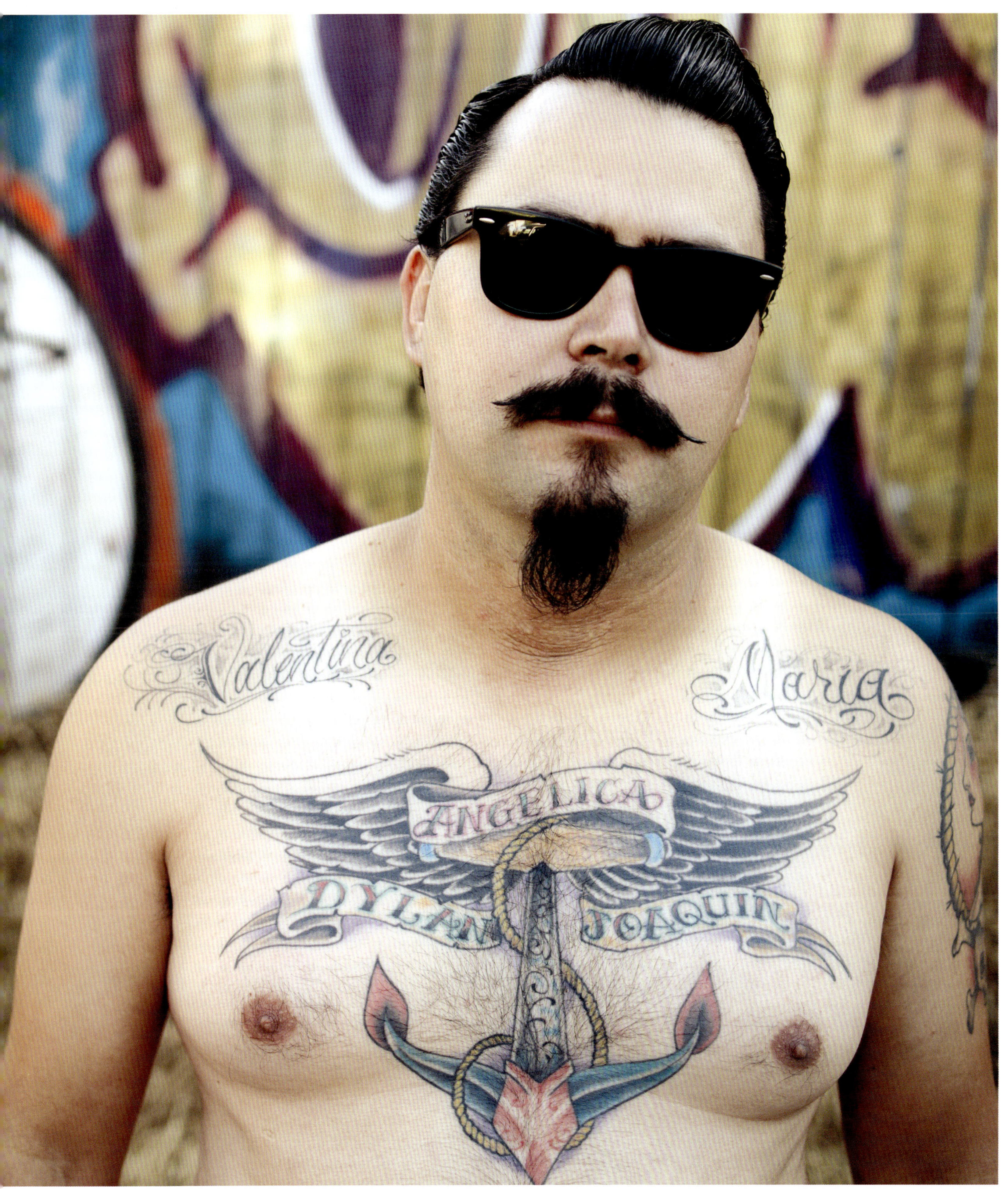
Valentina
Maria
ANGELICA
DYLAN JOAQUIN

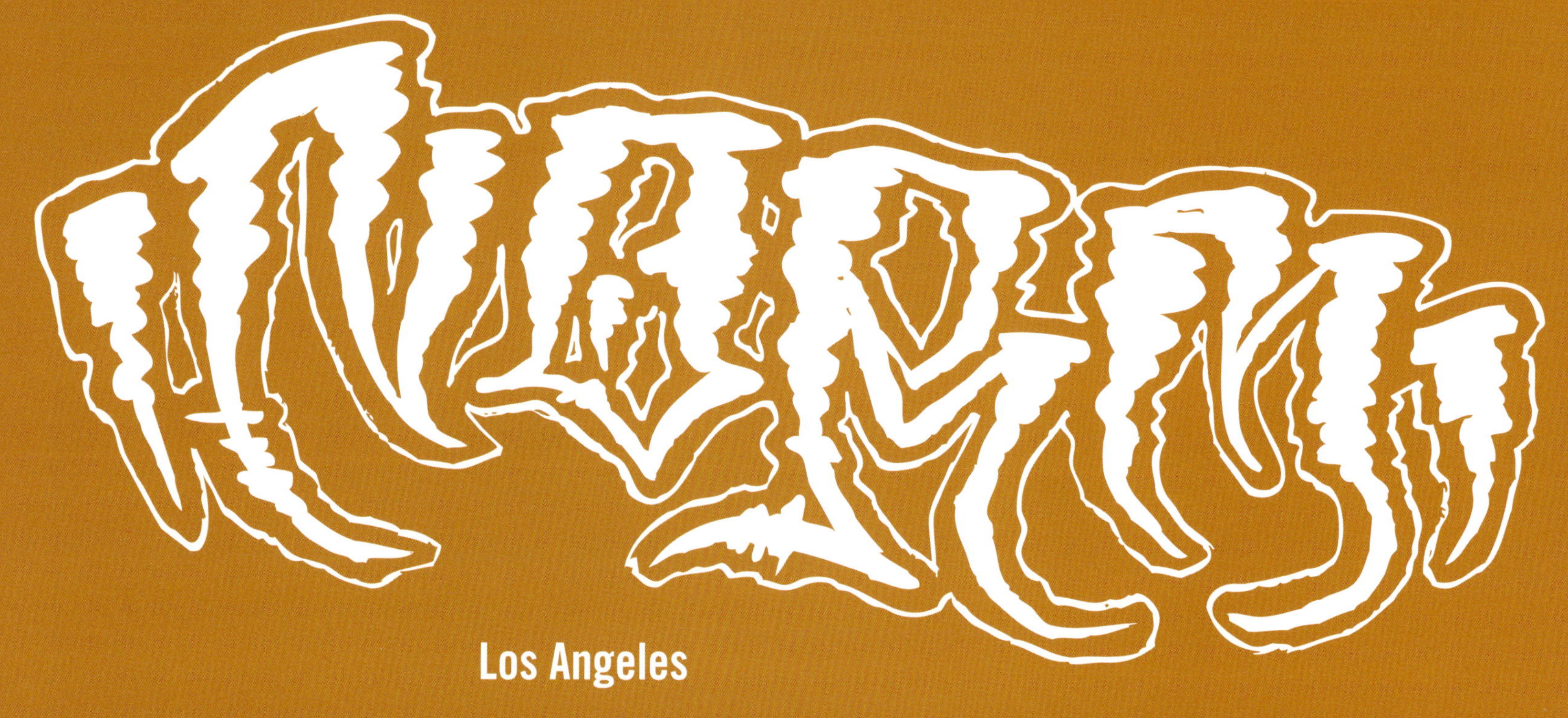

Los Angeles

> *"The name of the shop, Will Rise, is from my crew,*
> *Angels Will Rise. Without my crew, I would be nothing.*
> *They saved my life. Graffiti saved my life.*
> *Crime does pay, I guess, at the end of the day."*

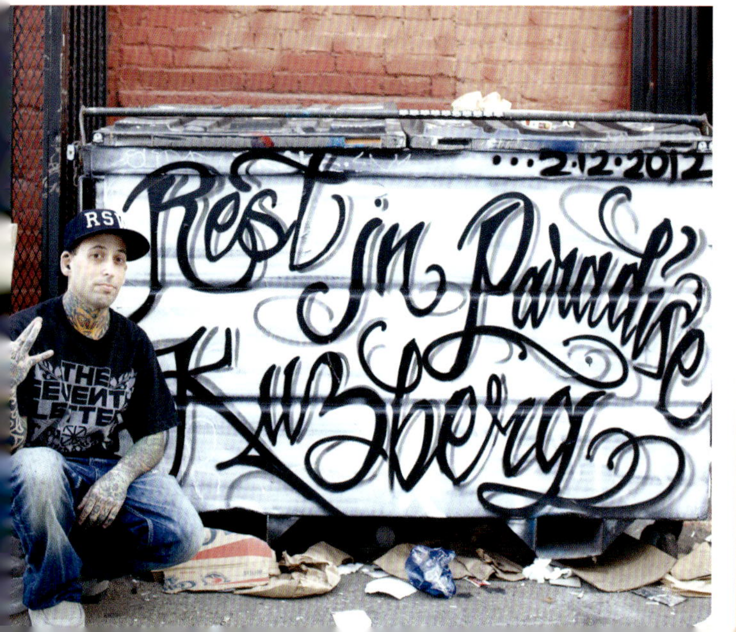

NORM

Norm is a student first. He lives life to the fullest, pushes the boundaries, reels it all in just in time to make a statement, and doesn't speak until he knows that he has a good command of his craft. He is the perfect portrait of a graffiti writer–turned–artist, the payoff on the promise that if you stay true to what it means to be a writer and you stay focused on letters, you will become a champion. Norm lives in Los Angeles and represents his AWR/MSK family to the fullest. On top of his impeccable lettering and tattoo work, he's a scientist when it comes to crafting his own tattoo machines.

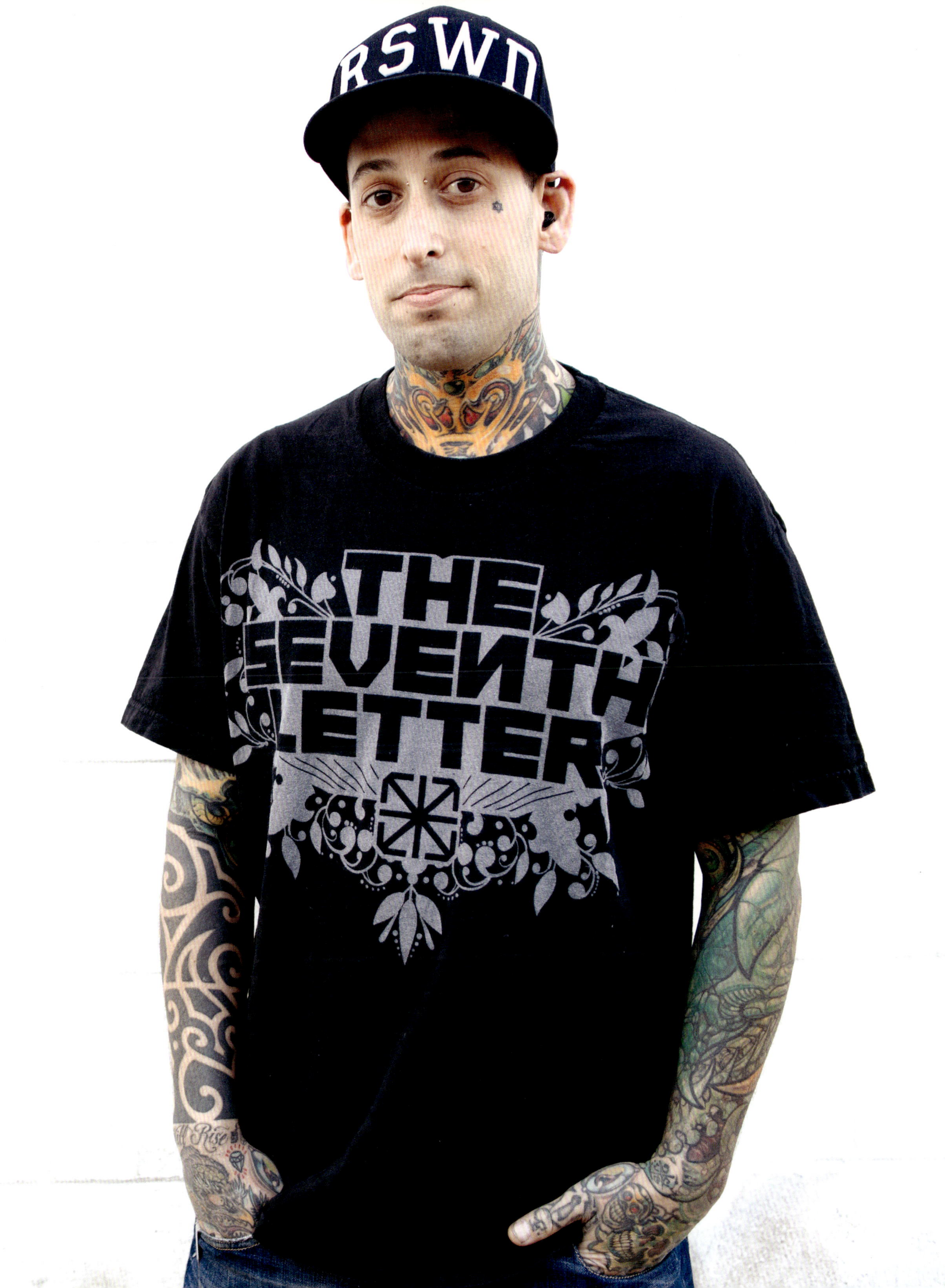
RSWD
THE
SEVENTH
LETTER

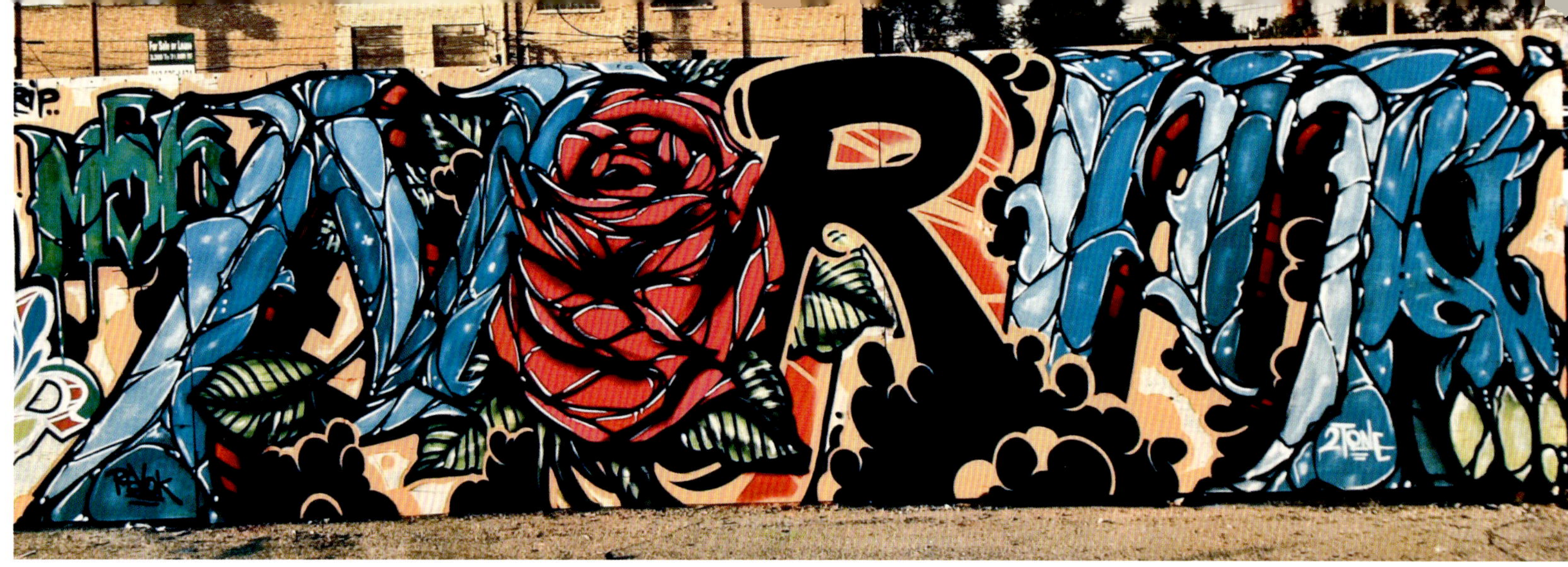

Norm piece, Chicago, 2012

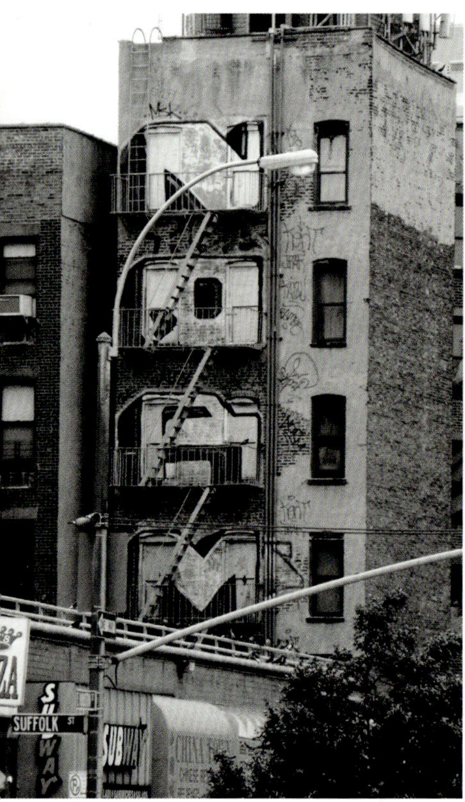

Norm piece, New York City, 2005

I started writing graffiti in San Francisco in 1998. I actually saw what Fate and Saber and Revok were doing in San Francisco at that time. I don't think I realized then how crazy graffiti could be, you know, climbing gnarly shit and getting in trouble and all of that—I really fell in love with that, I think. The crazy ledges and just all the tactical insane shit that goes on, like what MSK [Mad Society Kings] was doing in San Francisco.

Saber tried to convince me so many times not to do it. He basically begged me not to write graffiti. He'd say, "We're going to be friends, we're all going to hang out, but you don't need to do what we do." And I just kept doing it, I mean the ugliest graffiti you would ever see in your life. But I put it in places where they were like, whoa, wow, this dude actually wants to try to be a part of this. Then they finally stopped telling me not to do it and encouraged me, and from there, it just went crazy.

Fate was my mentor. Fate was the guy who brought me into all of this. Saber and Revok, same thing. Then I met Eclipse, and everybody just started coming to San Francisco. Like monthly, it'd be a different person, and they'd need a place to stay so they stayed with us. There was always somebody from the crew staying at the house, so I learned from them and painted with them. I was a toy so I had to paint around the corner from them. One day Revok did some letters for me and I filled them in around the corner while they painted a nice production or whatever. As time went by, I ended up painting with them. These are people that I look up to on a graffiti level, but they're also my friends, so everything just kind of came full circle. At that time I was a really bad junkie. I was battling this crazy shit and still painting all this graffiti but still being a complete idiot at the same time and getting arrested all the time. Finally I had just had enough. I went to a piercing shop and I had a job, so everything was good. I was working, but I was a mess.

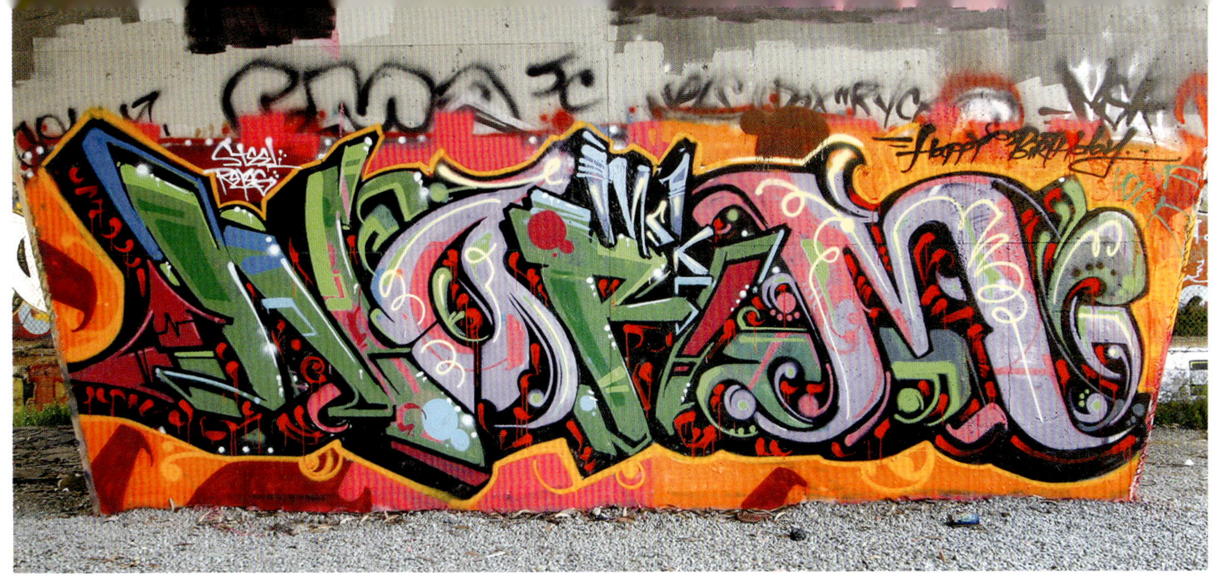

Norm piece, Los Angeles, 2011

Everybody came together and said, "This is it, you have to clean your act up. You could be doing a lot with your life and you have started to move in that direction, but you're a fuck-up, so get your shit together." It took a little a while and there were some bumps in the road. But I've been clean for years now. I was lucky enough to be able to learn how to tattoo.

I was taught by a bunch of people—everybody at the AWR shop when I was there. Everybody just helped, and then when I went out on the road, they sent me to different places. I would go to New York and stay with Civ and work with him. Then I would stay with Bert Krak and work with him, and I learned all these different aspects of tattooing that I didn't know.

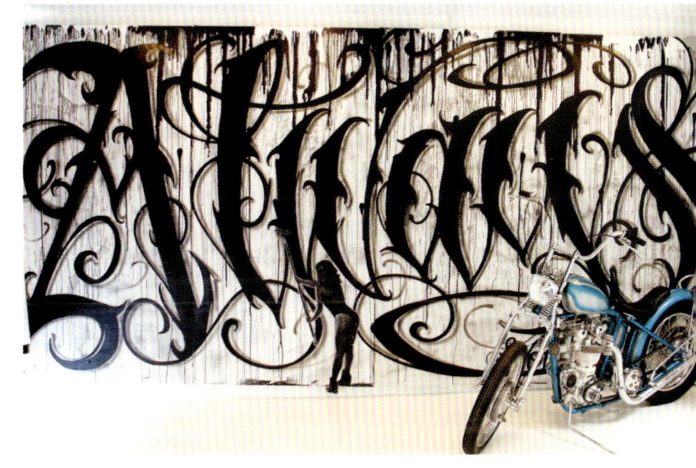

Norm, *Always*, Tokyo, 2010

Writing graffiti is so much different than tattooing because you can actually go back over graffiti and get rid of it. You can paint black over white, white over black, whatever. Tattooing is so permanent and it's one shot. In that one shot, that's the only chance you get. It's a lot different. I had to learn how to draw. I just tried to adapt and use the things that I'm good at. Graffiti, when you get down to it, is all basically the same. You don't like this part of your letter, you play it off with something else. With a tattoo, if you don't like this part of the skull, maybe you play it off with a rose or something.

Lettering is definitely my favorite thing to do. I try to draw it all on. My influences from my lettering, of course, would be Jack Rudy—he's a major influence. Mike Brown, of course, rest in peace, is amazing. Cartoon is also somebody I look up to as far as lettering goes.

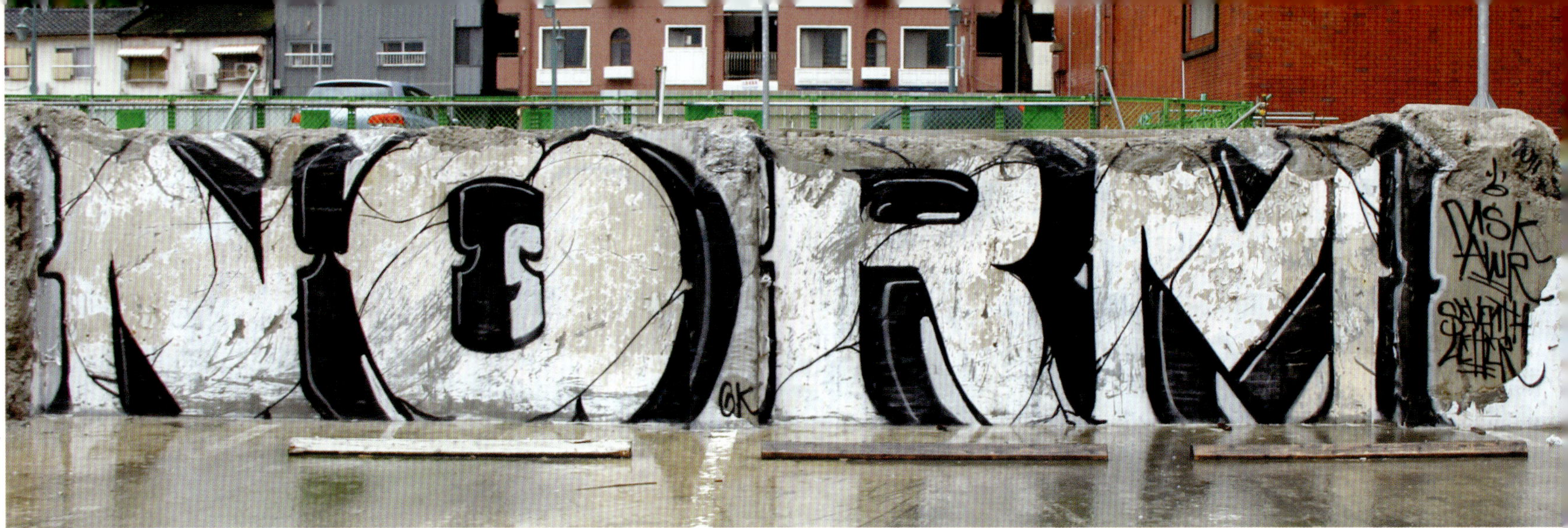

Norm piece, Tokyo, 2011

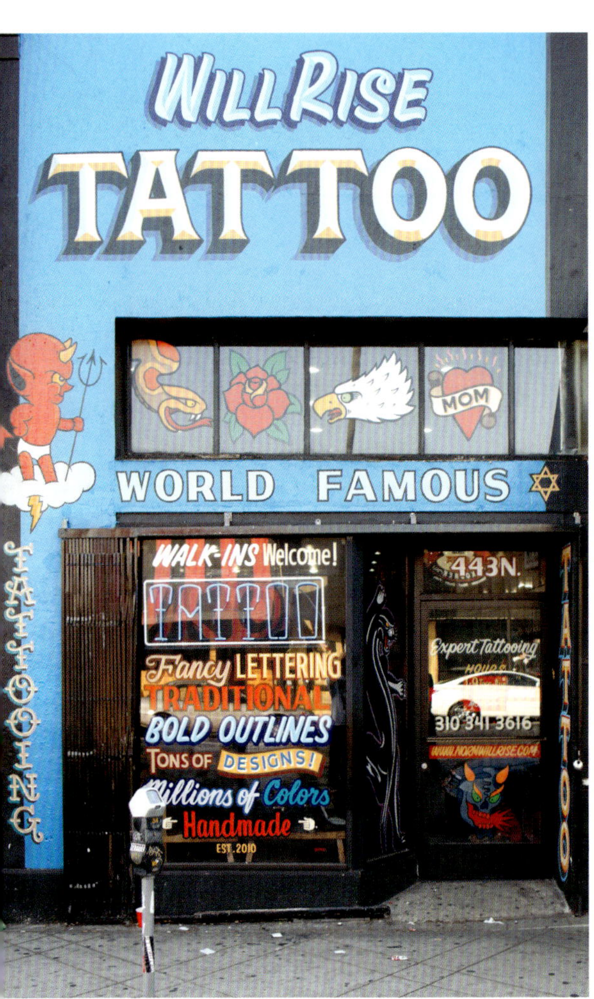

Will Rise Tattoo, Los Angeles, 2012

Tattoo politics are way different than graffiti. I think I liked the graffiti ones better if you have to compare the two. I'm a different kind of person. I came from graffiti, so this whole world is different to me. The tattoo community is new to me. I'm new to them, and what I bring to the table, I think I bring it in a different way. But I'm still doing the classic tattoo stuff and I'm just trying to put my spin on it. As far as the lettering goes, it all came from graffiti. That's where it's going to keep moving for me, and hopefully I can keep coming up with new shit so I don't get squashed.

Opening a tattoo shop was definitely not what I wanted to do because of how much work it is, dealing with all these artists and everything like that, but I guess it's kind of a home for people who don't want to work someplace else or whatever, and I'm picking up stragglers. Some dude needs help and that's just me, I want to help everybody out and I want everyone to come up. The name of the shop, Will Rise, is from my crew, Angels Will Rise. Without my crew, I would be nothing. They saved my life. Graffiti saved my life. Crime does pay, I guess, at the end of the day.

I get weird requests. Sometimes people want to buy a machine just to have it. I'm like, "Oh, that's cool and all, but I can't just sell you a tattoo machine because they're intended for the art." So I'll leave a wire out or something [so it won't work]. I had some kid in here the other day. He was like, "Well, I'm tattooing at my house." I'm like, "You put me in a bad position, homes. Just go get a job at a shop, dude. That's what you have to do. Pay your dues."

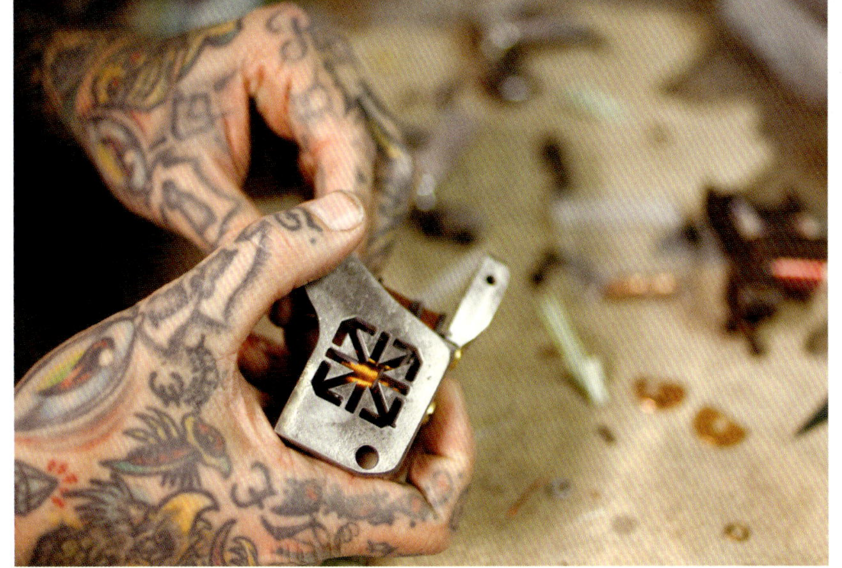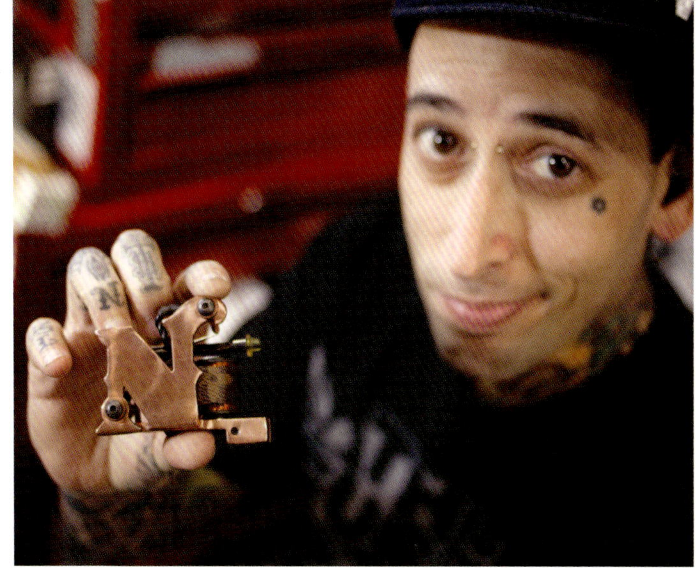

Two custom tattoo machines designed by Norm

If you want to start tattooing the right way, at the house is not the way to do it. You need to go and do a proper apprenticeship. I did an apprenticeship for three years. It could've gone on for longer. It's not something that you can just stay at your house and learn. And it's not hygienic. In the beginning, there are basic things that a tattooer needs to learn. And there's no "practice," either. Your practice is permanent. People need to take it seriously, as serious as it is. I work nine days a week. I take this job as seriously as I possibly can. It's the most important thing in my life.

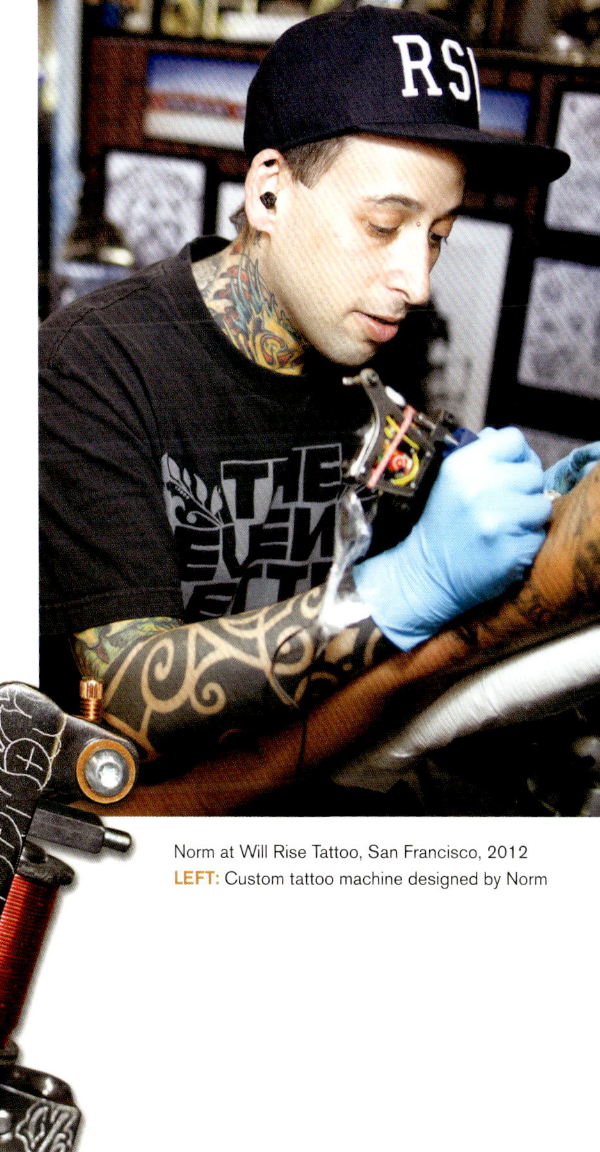

Norm at Will Rise Tattoo, San Francisco, 2012
LEFT: Custom tattoo machine designed by Norm

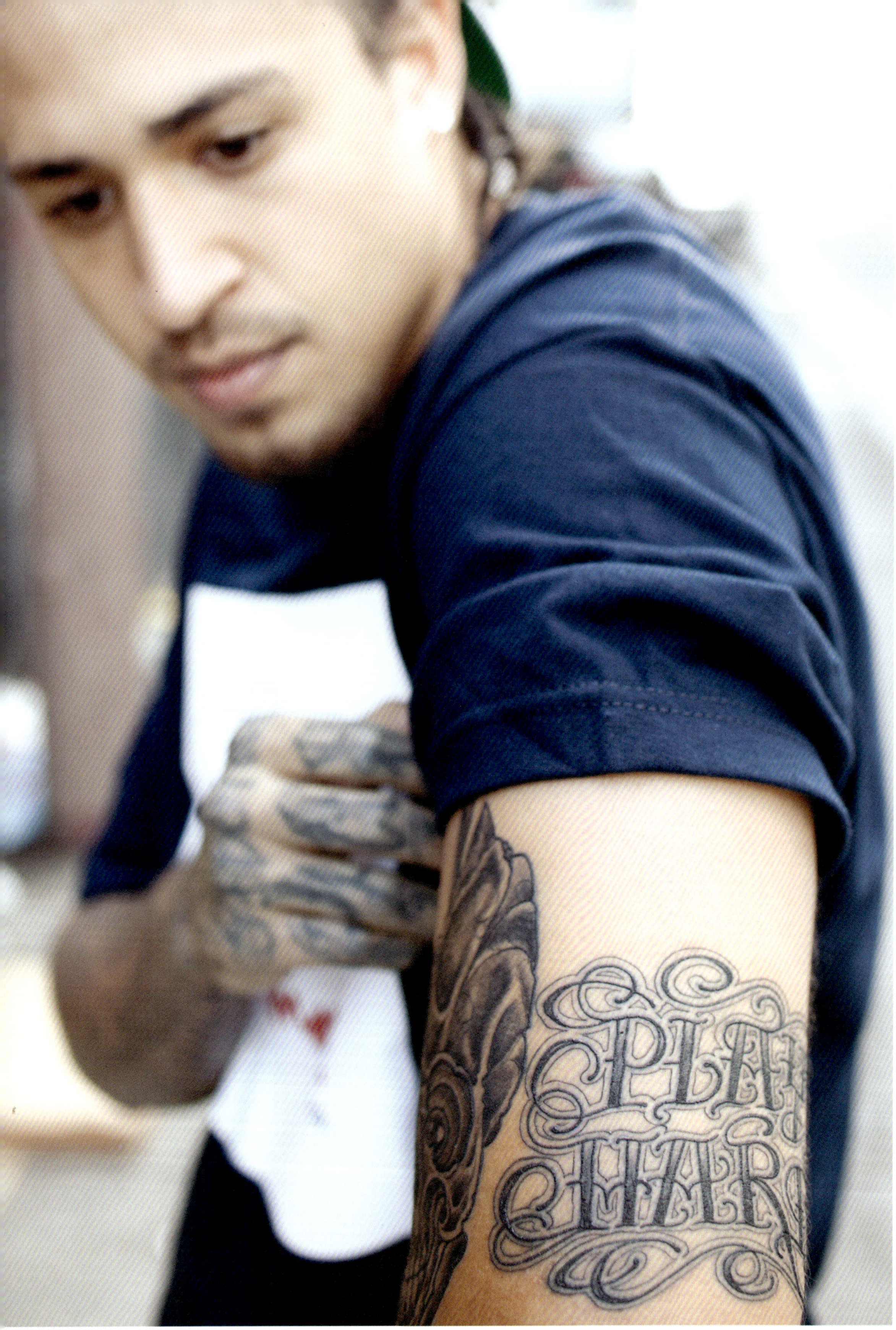

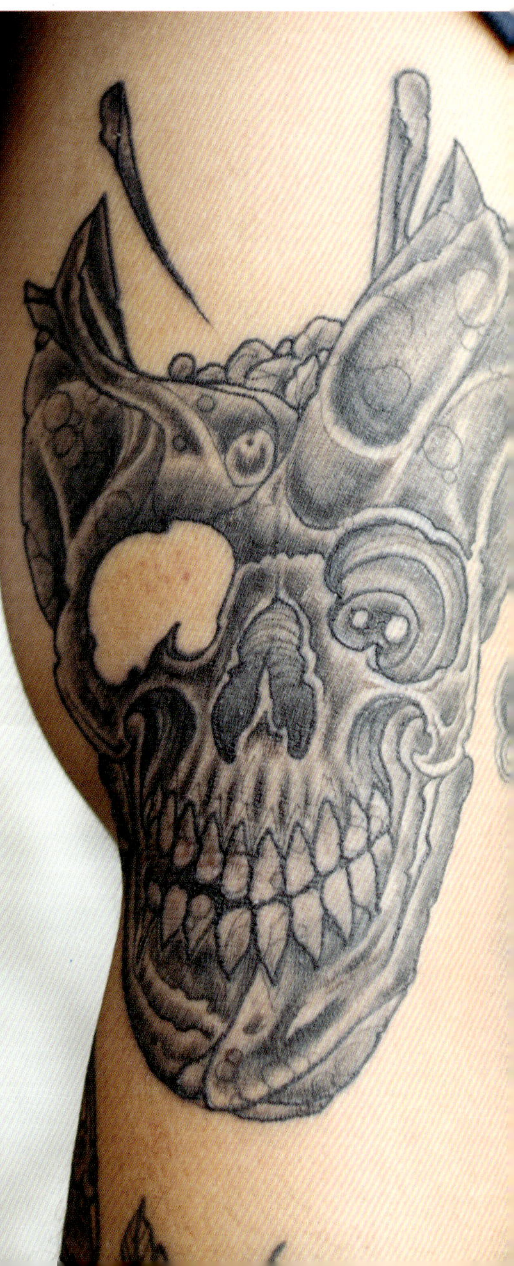

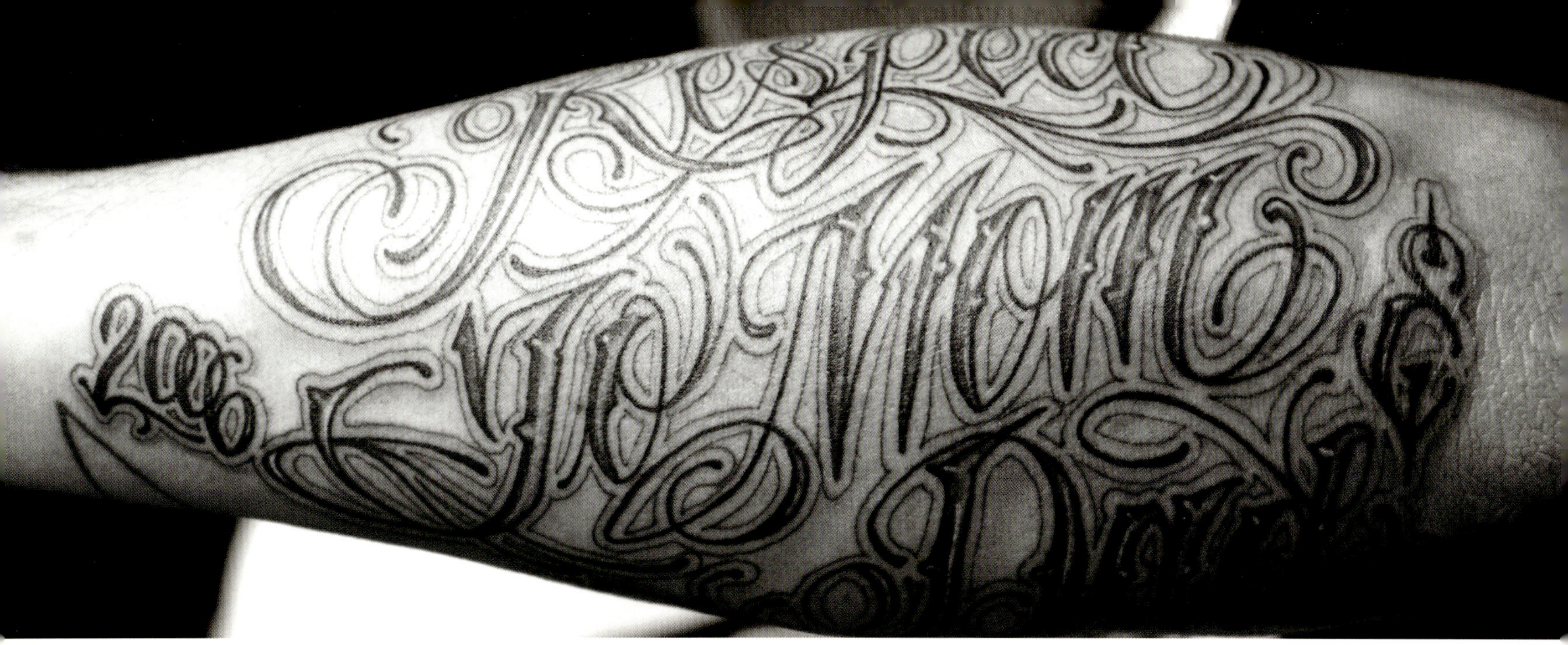

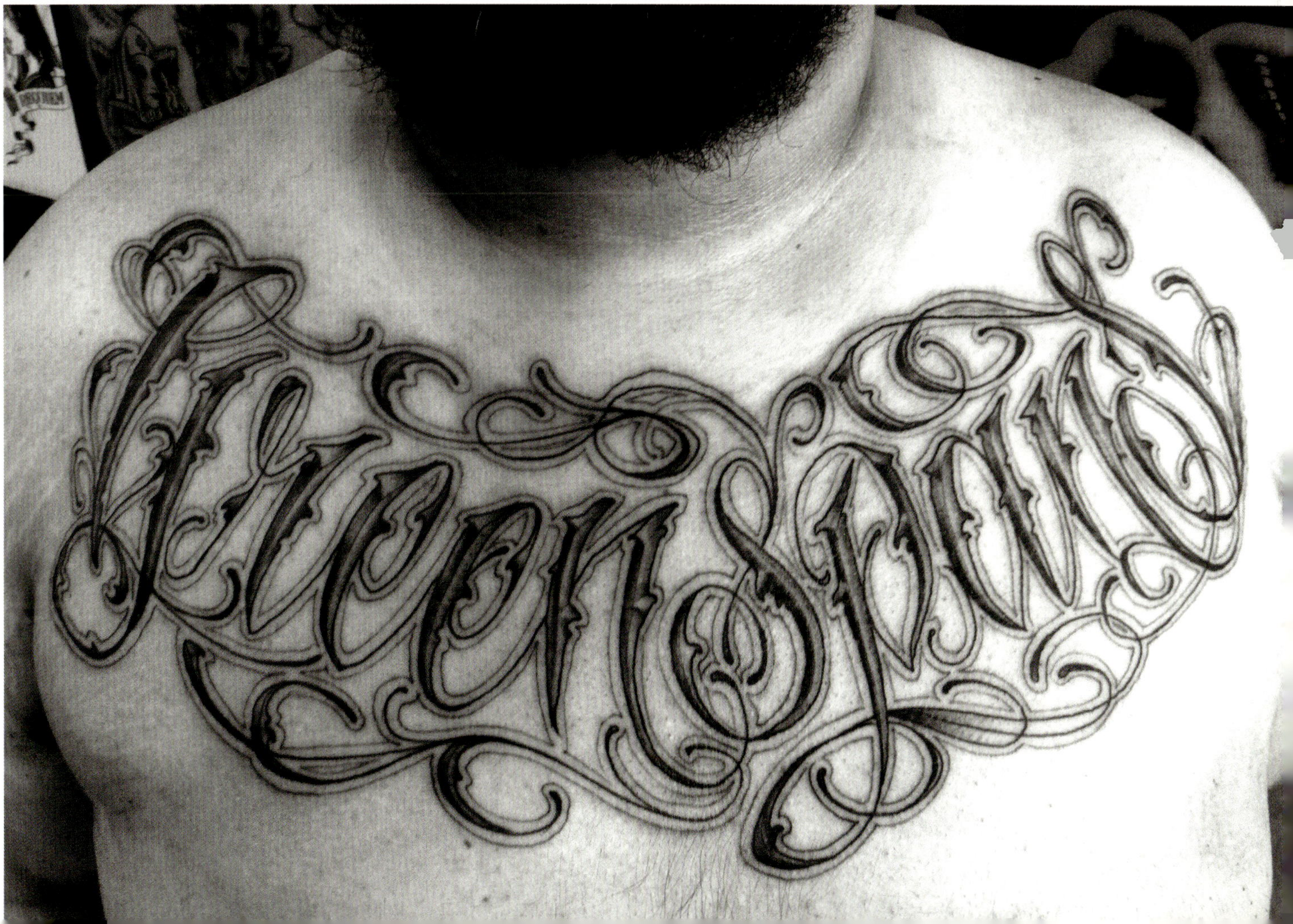

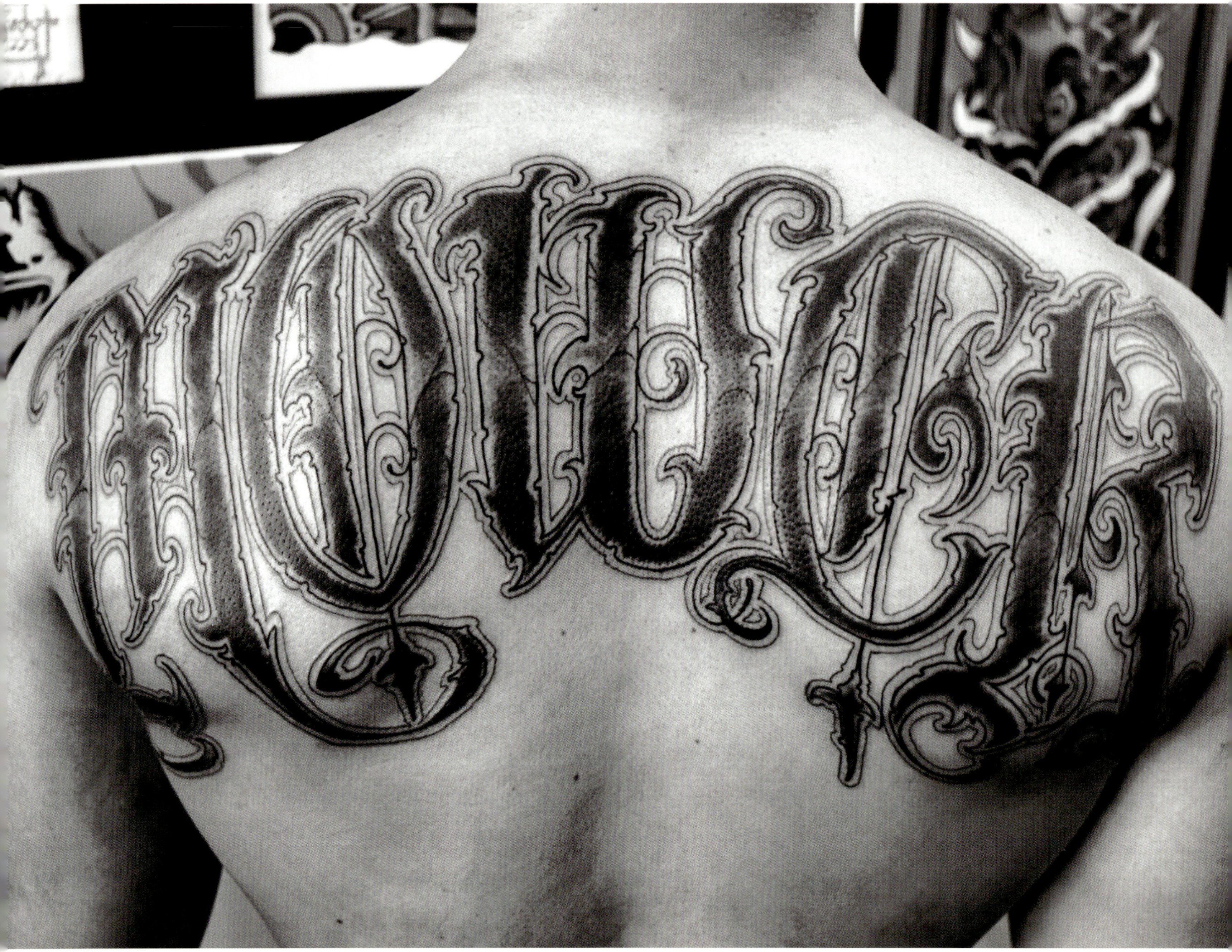

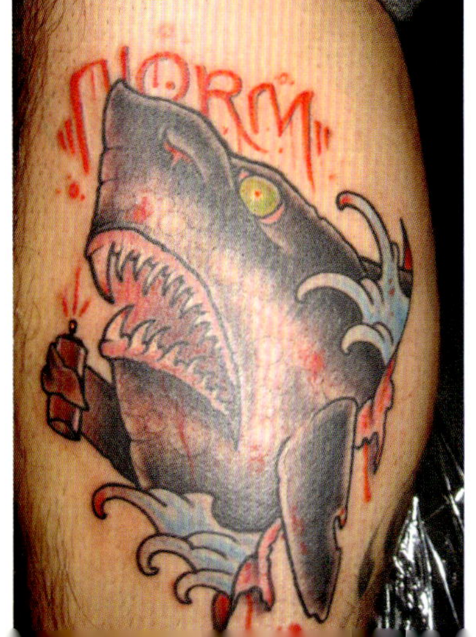
NORM

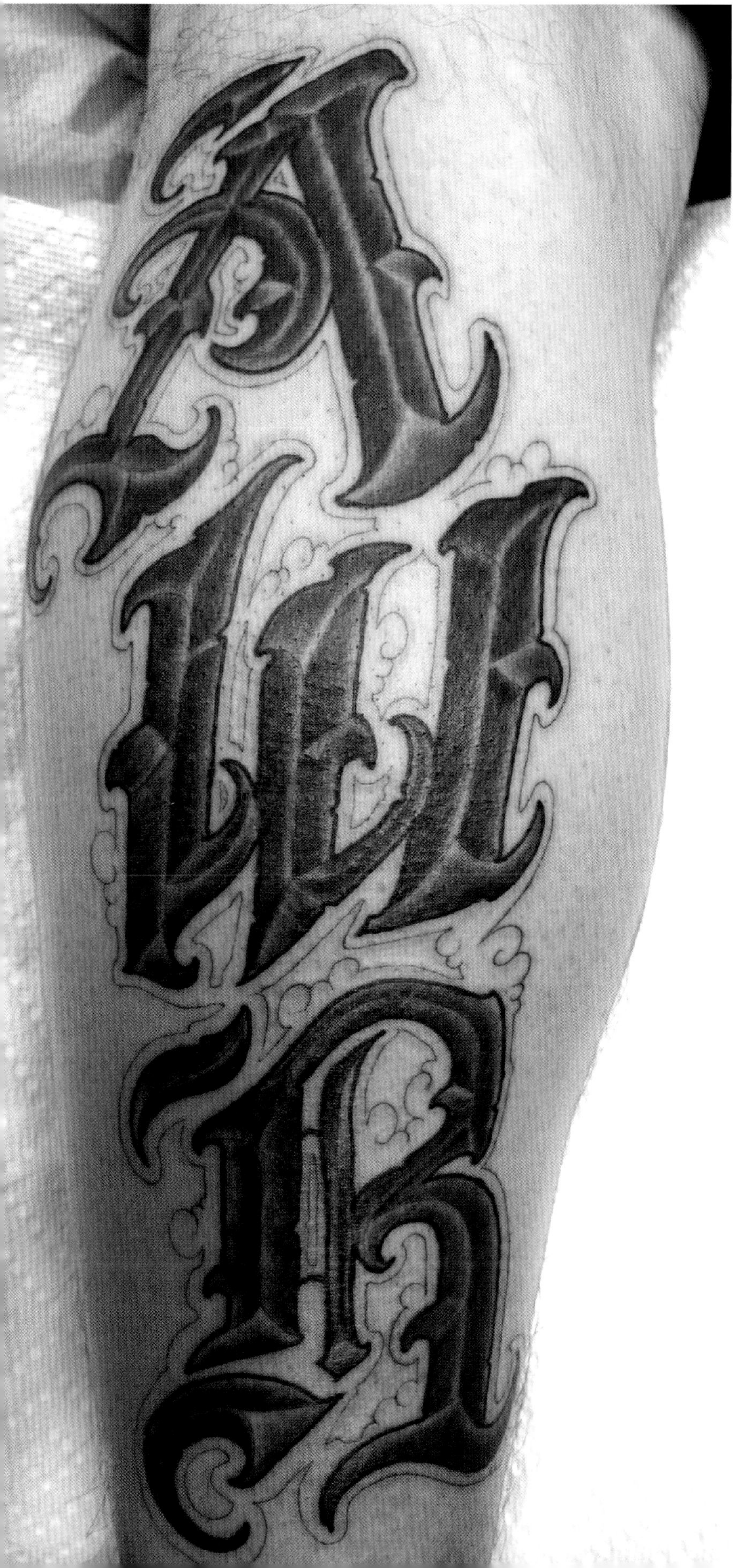

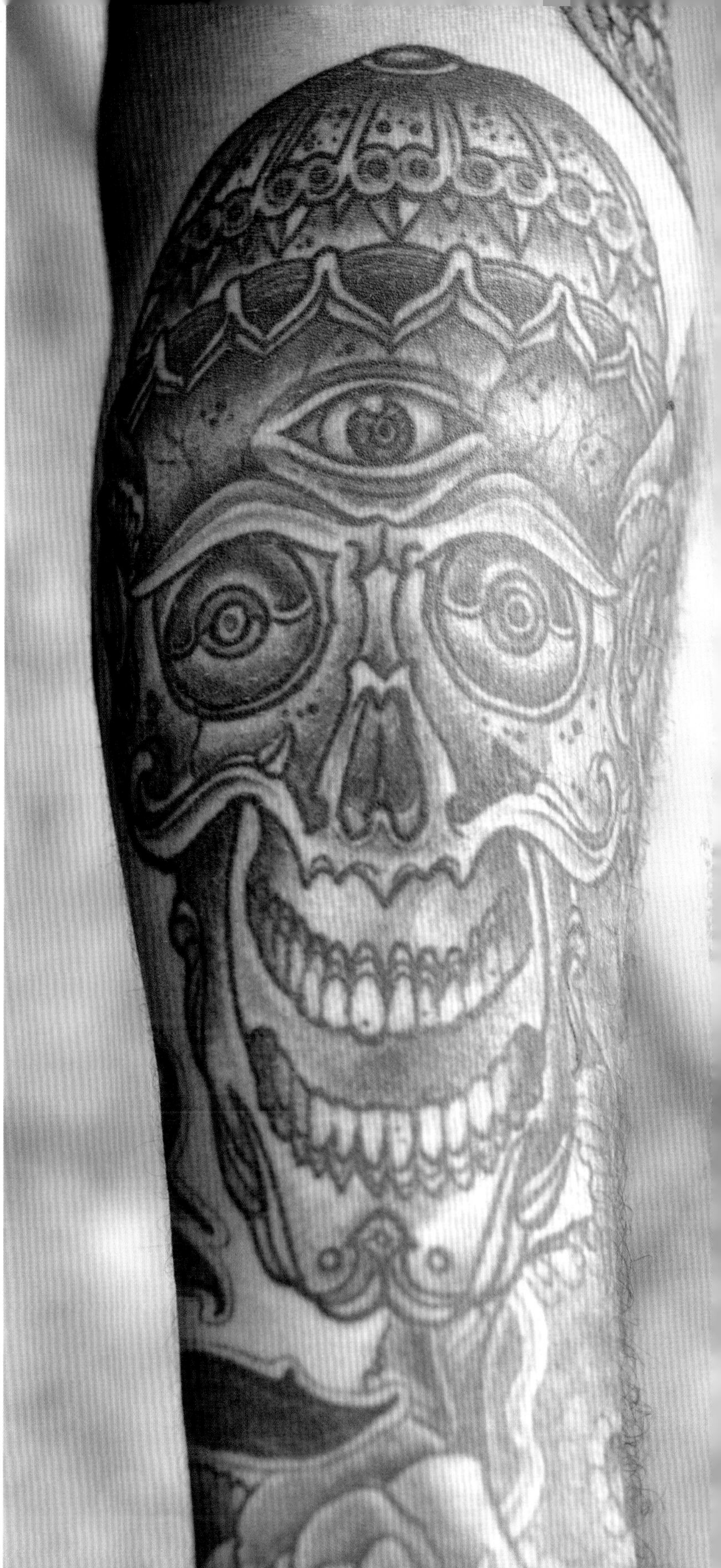

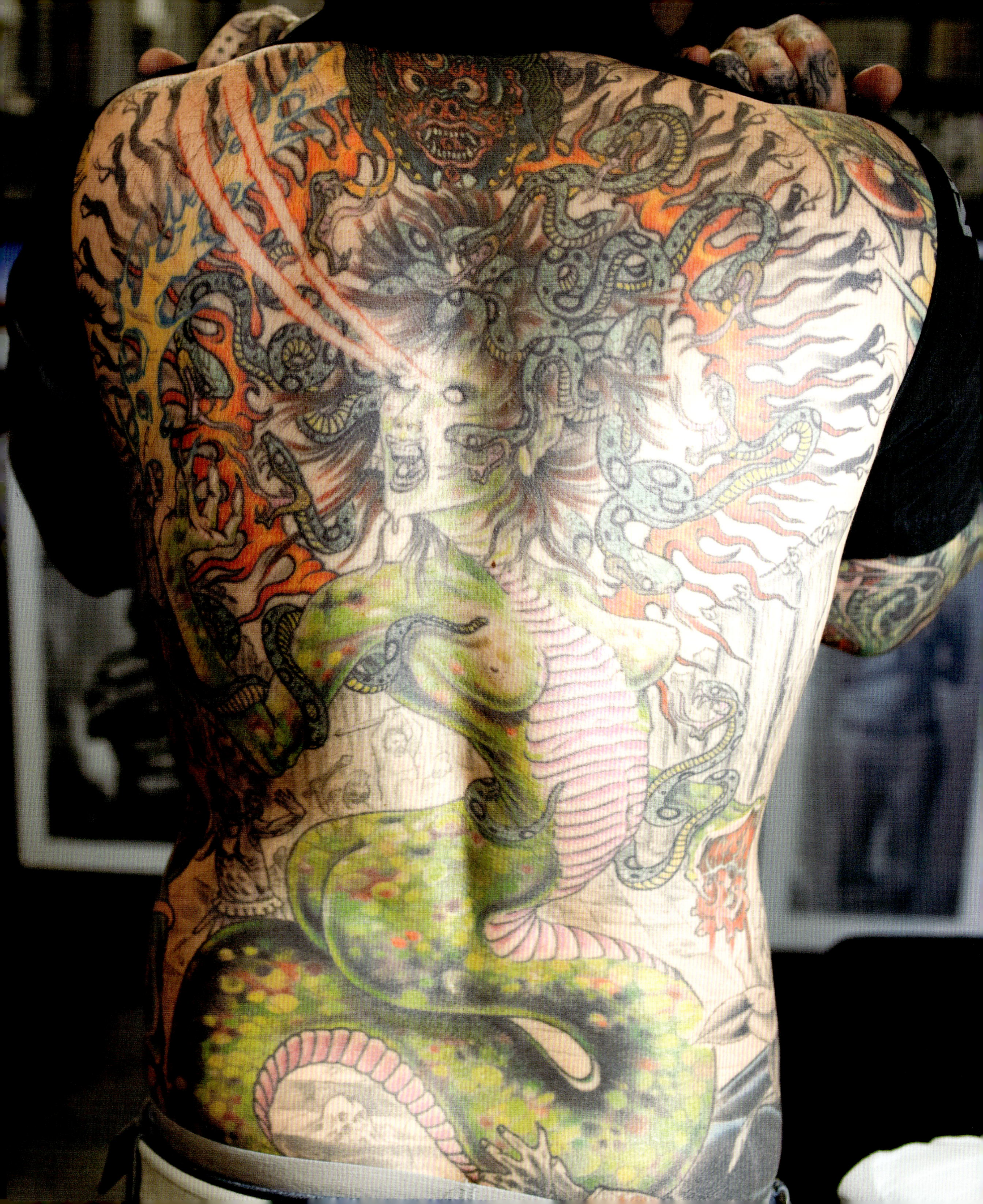

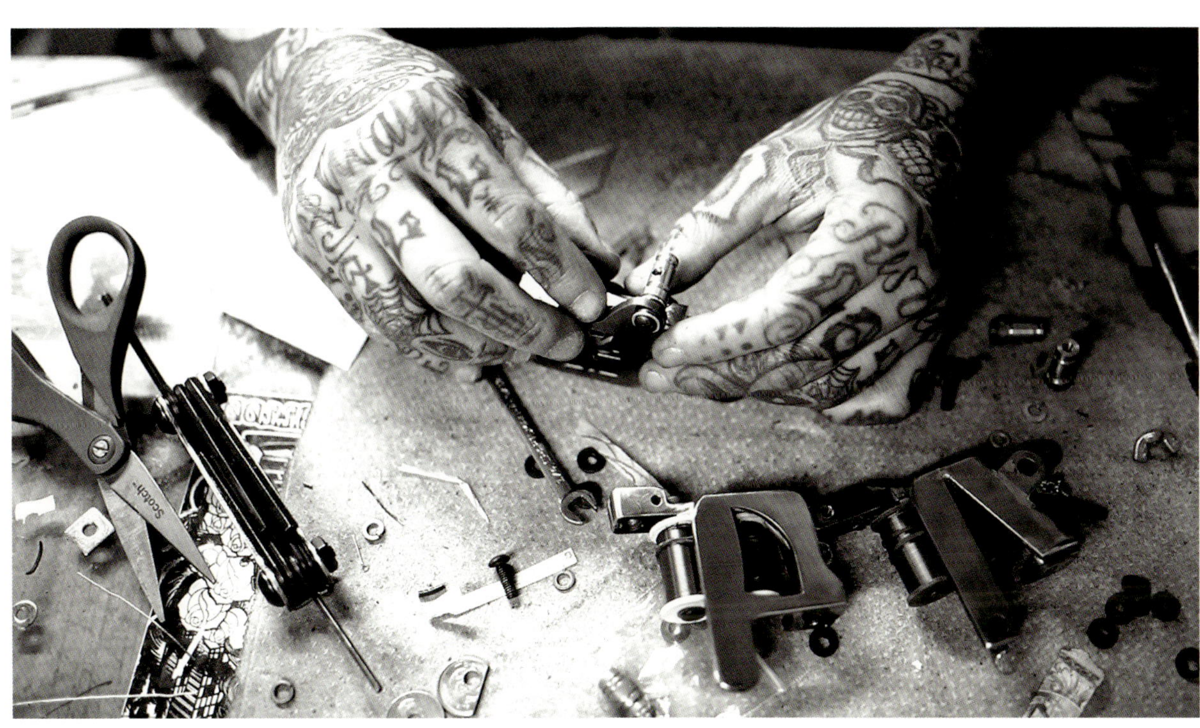

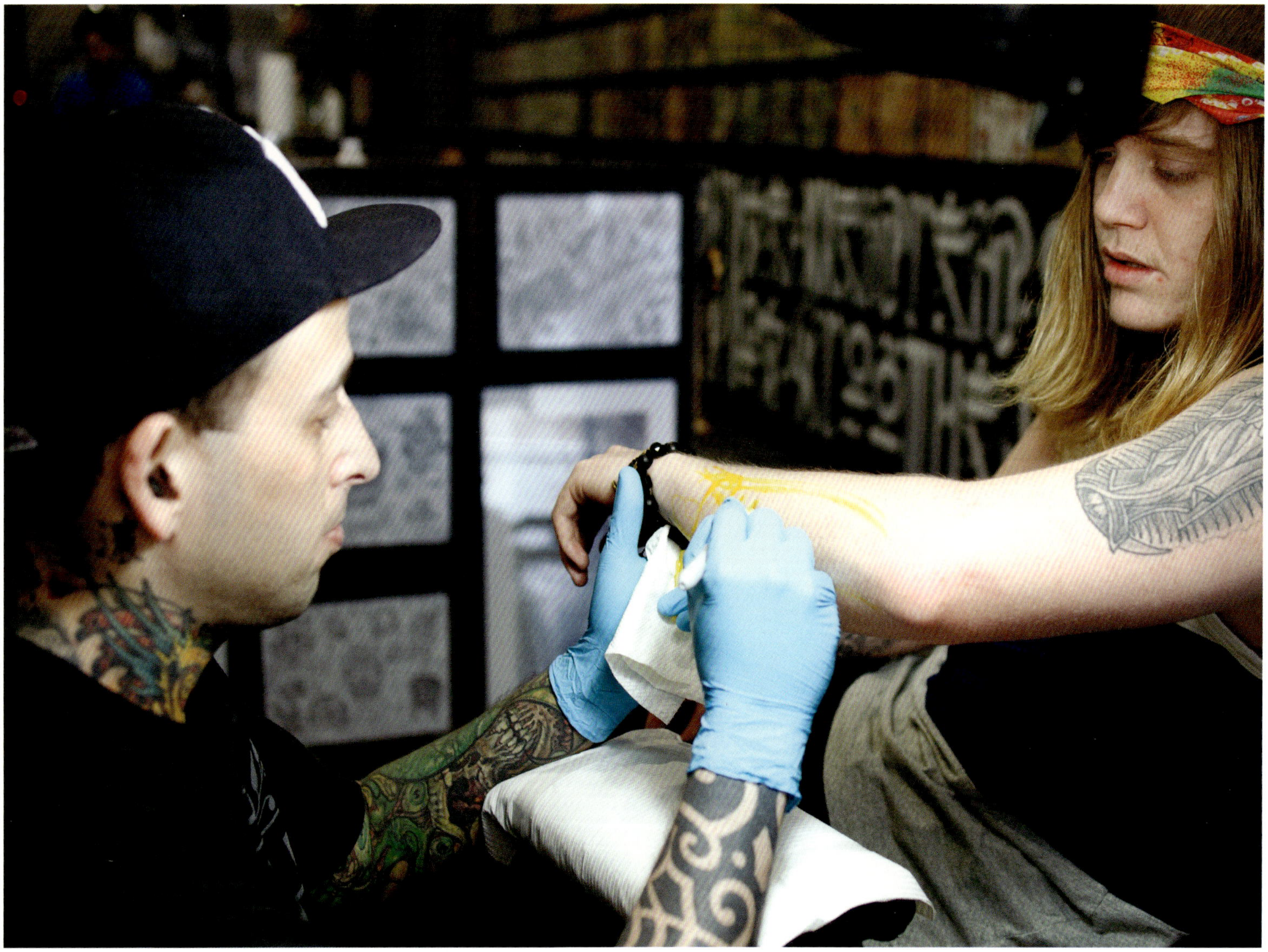

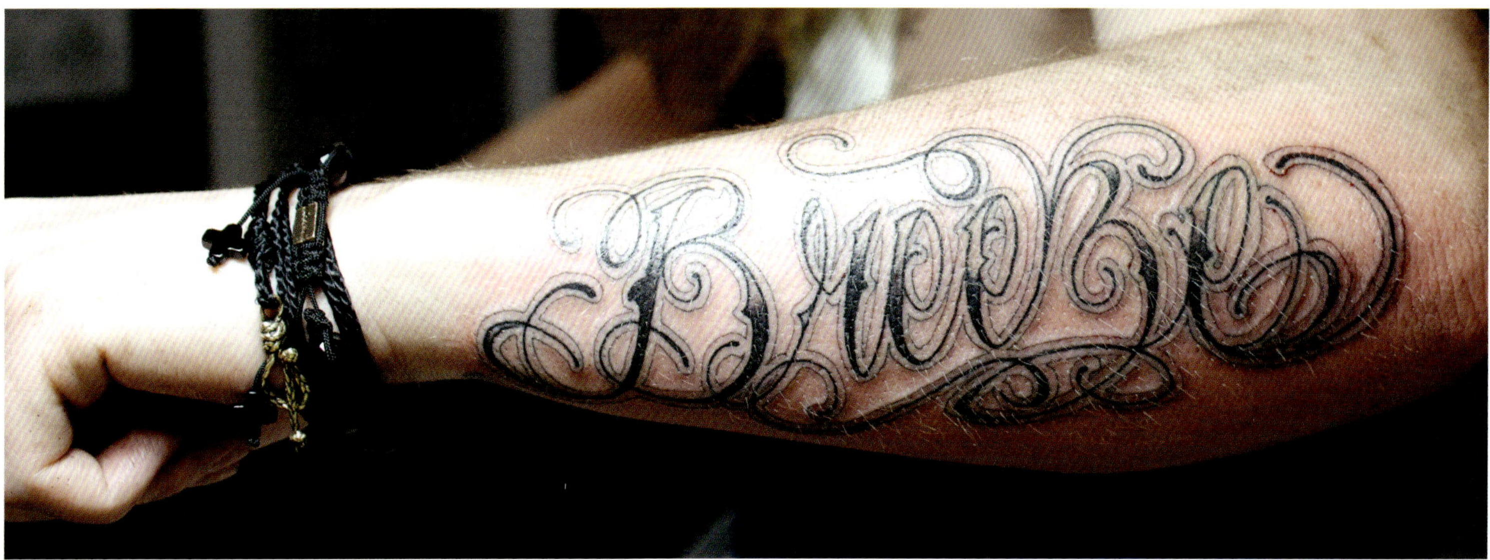

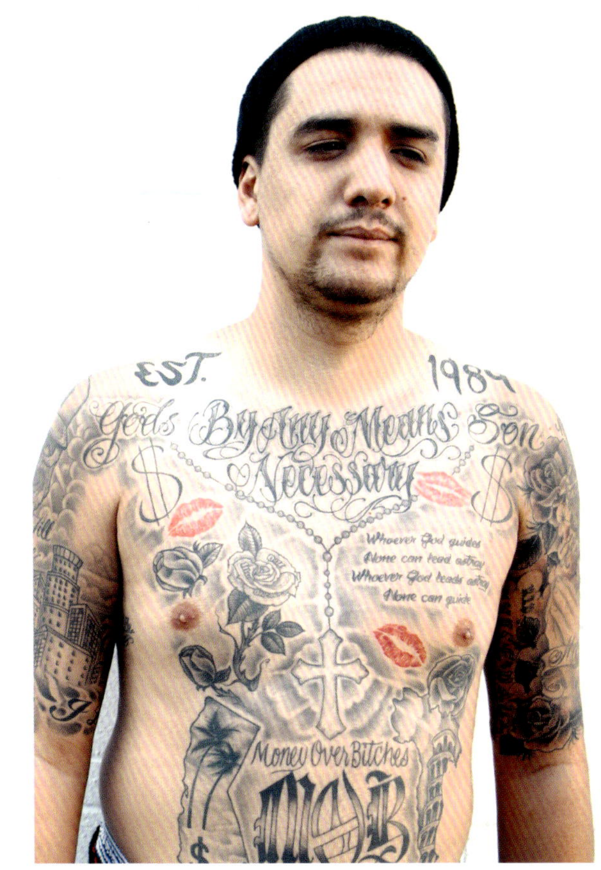

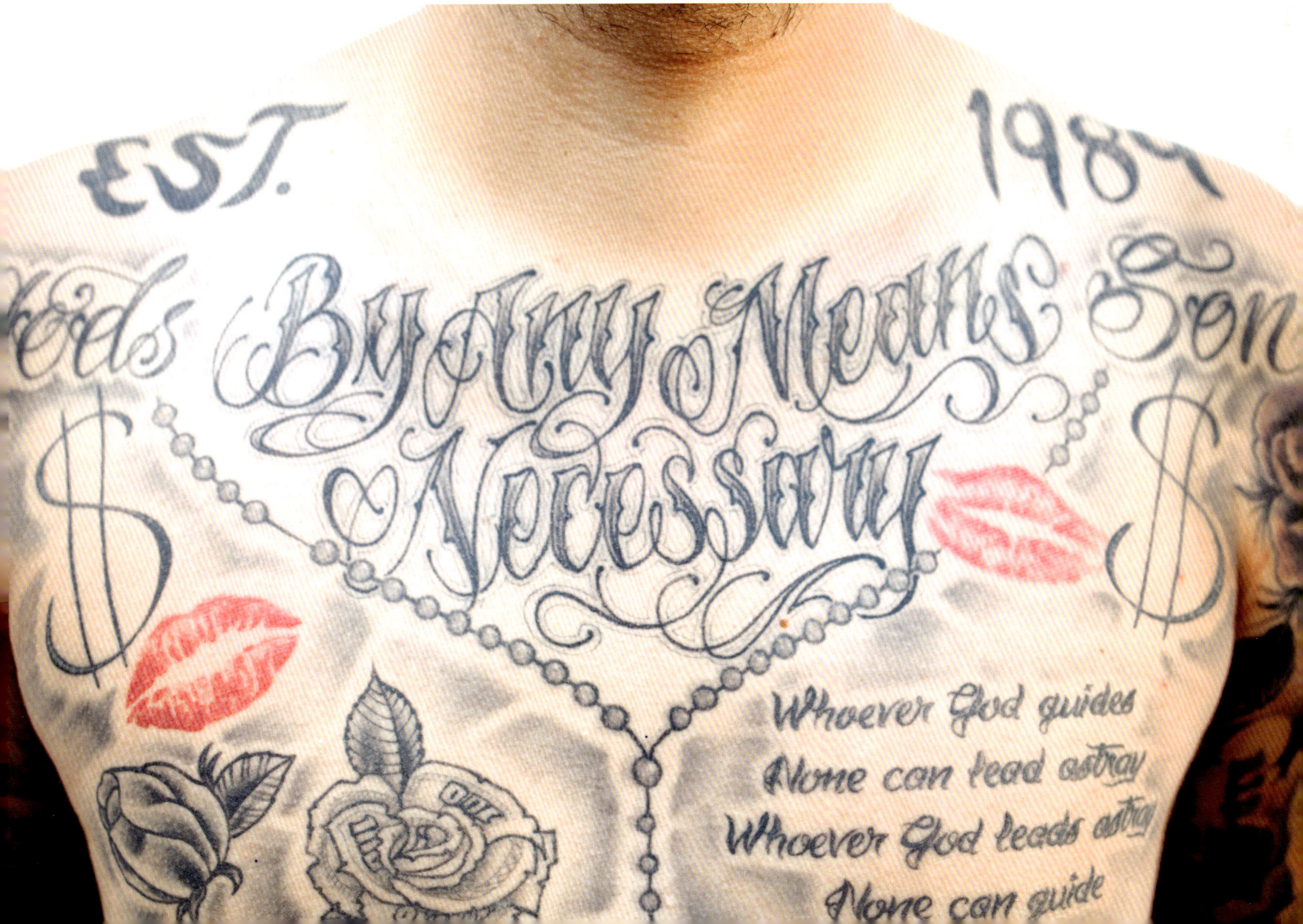

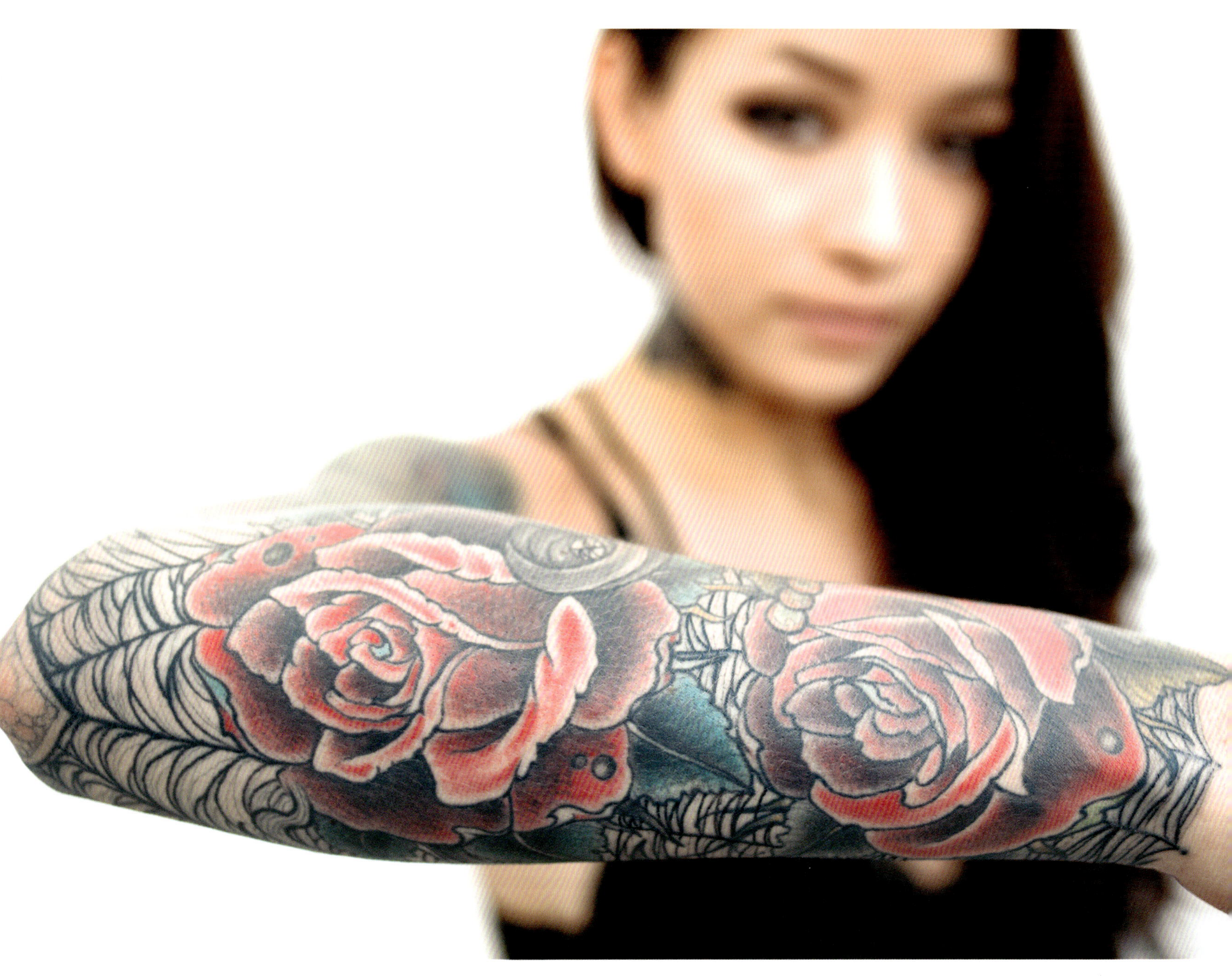

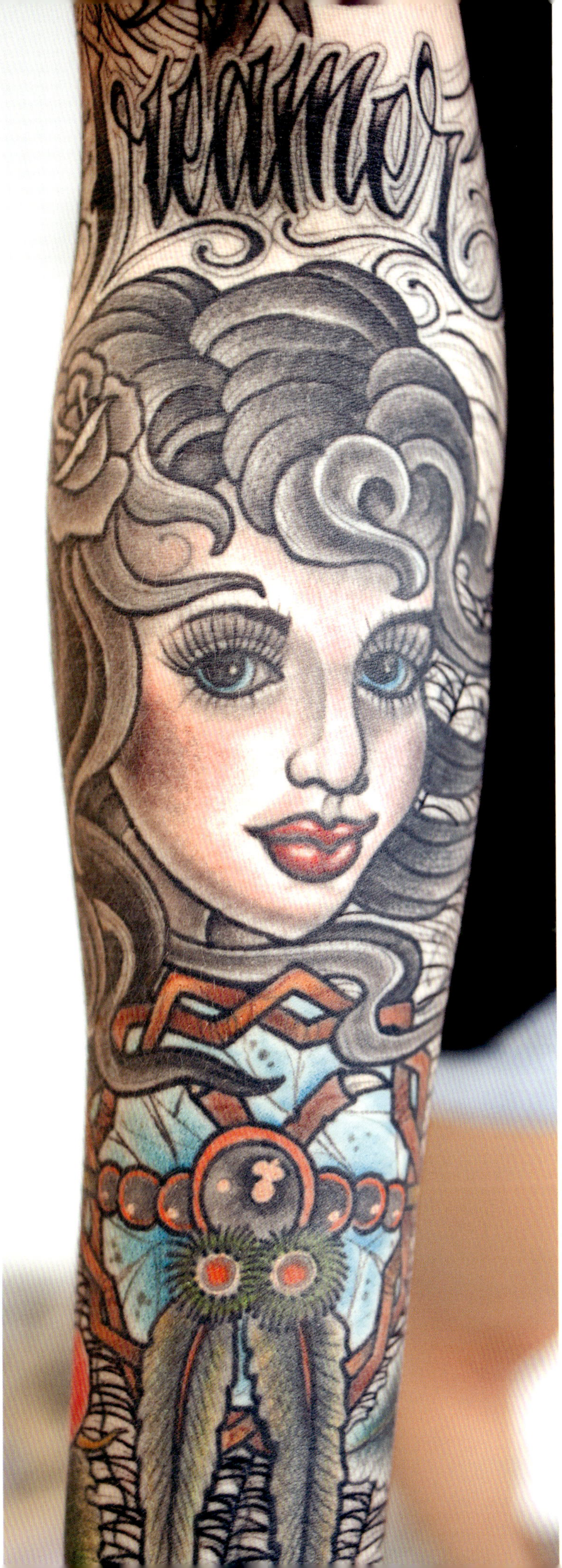

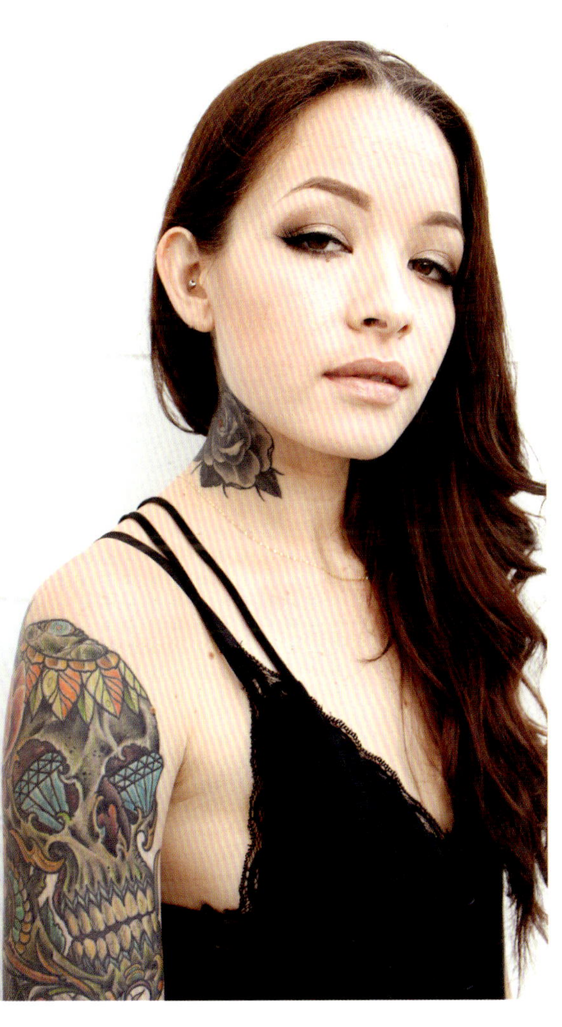

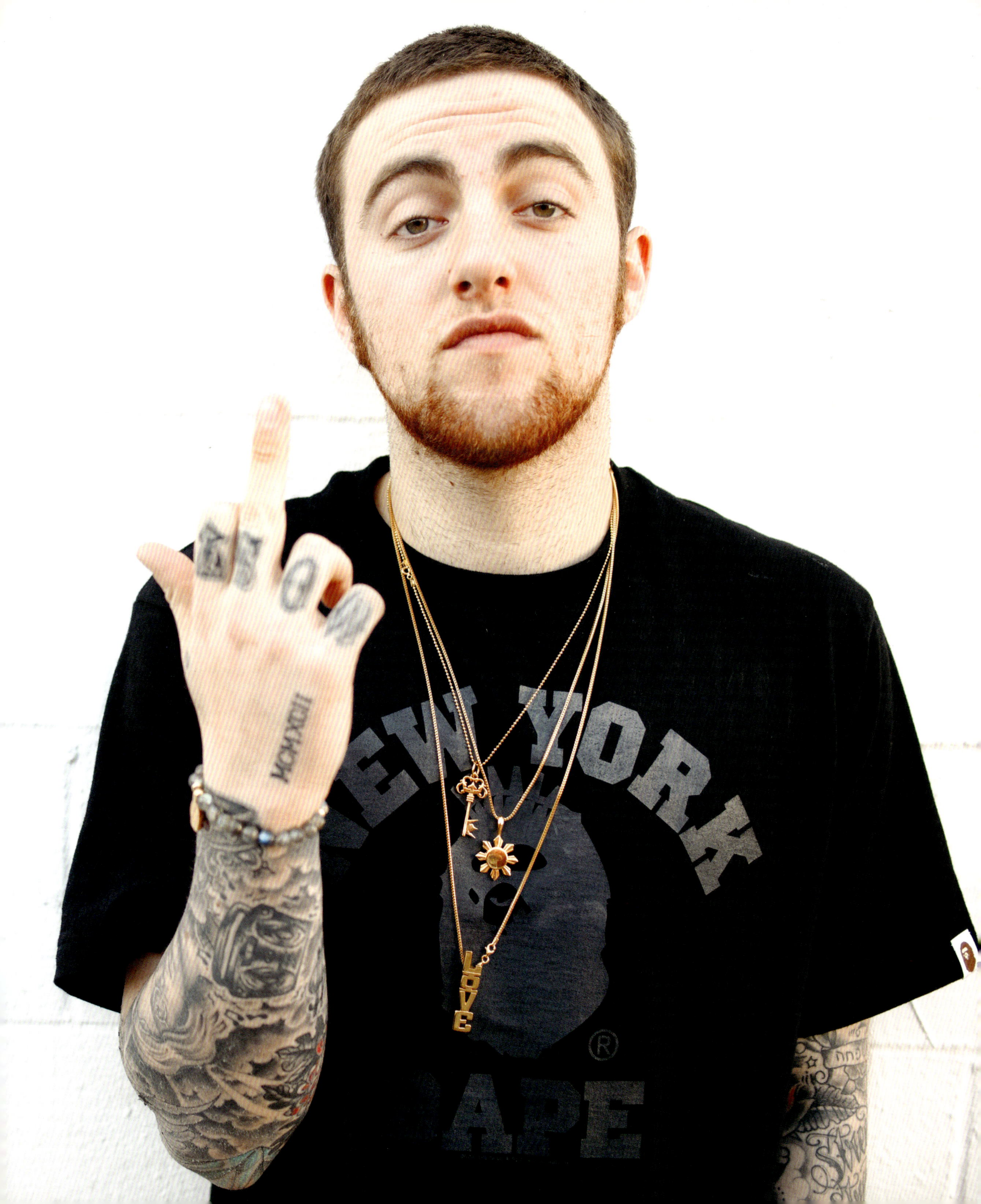

NEW YORK
APE
LOVE

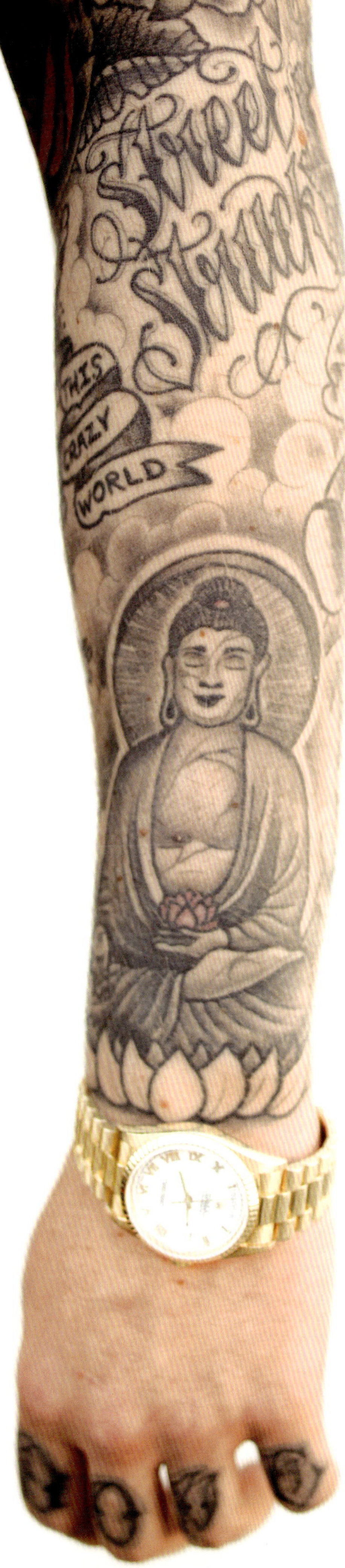

Street
Struck
THIS
CRAZY
WORLD

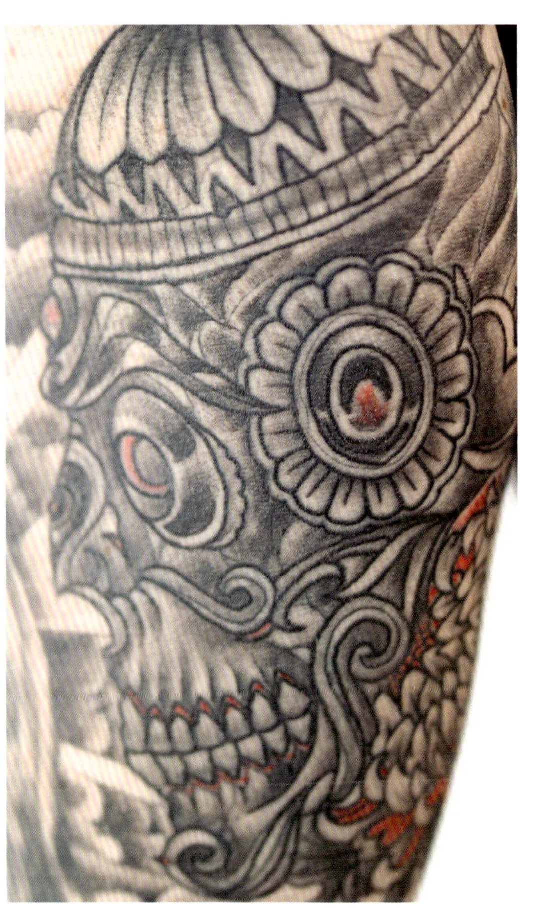

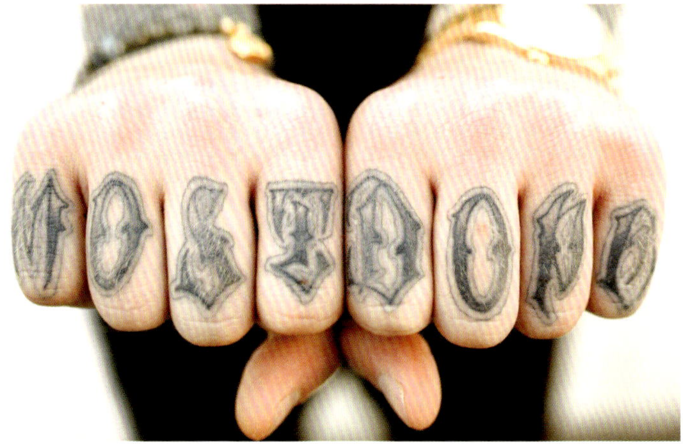

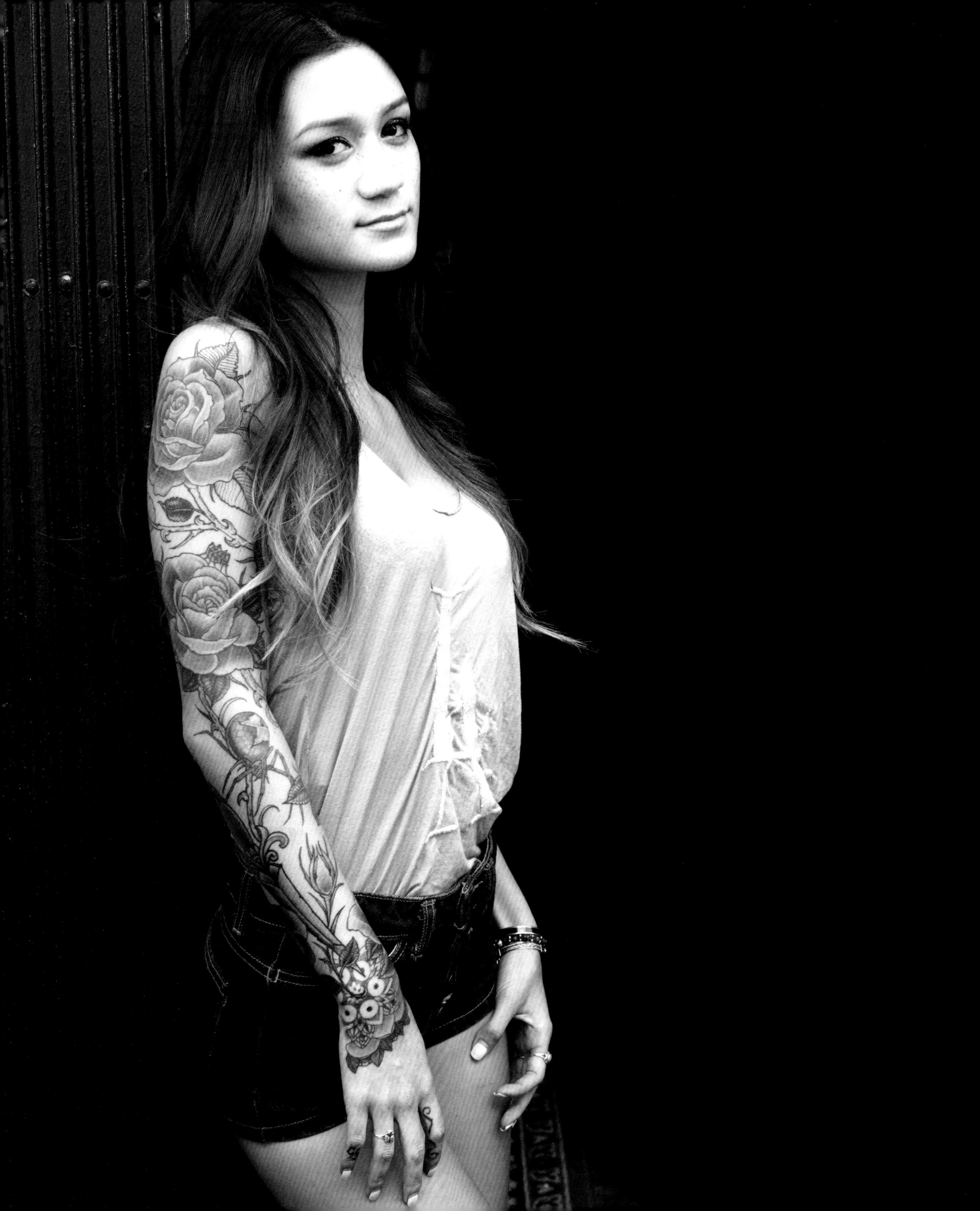

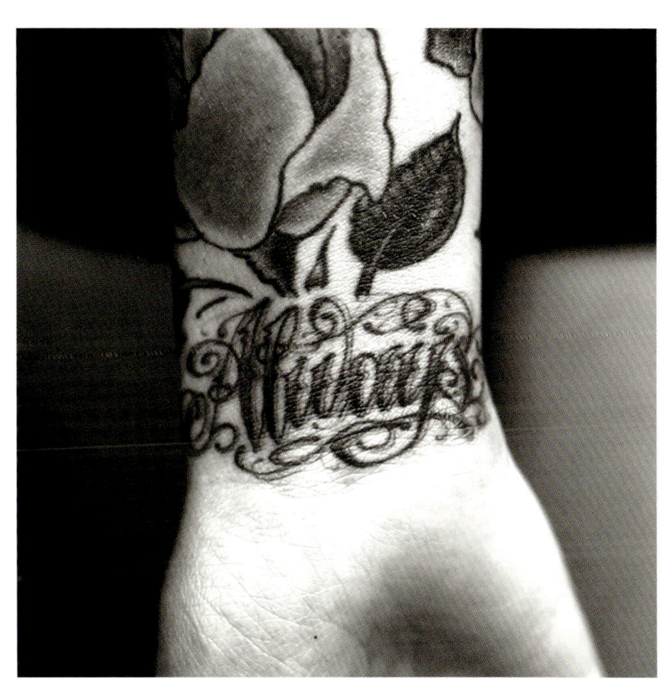

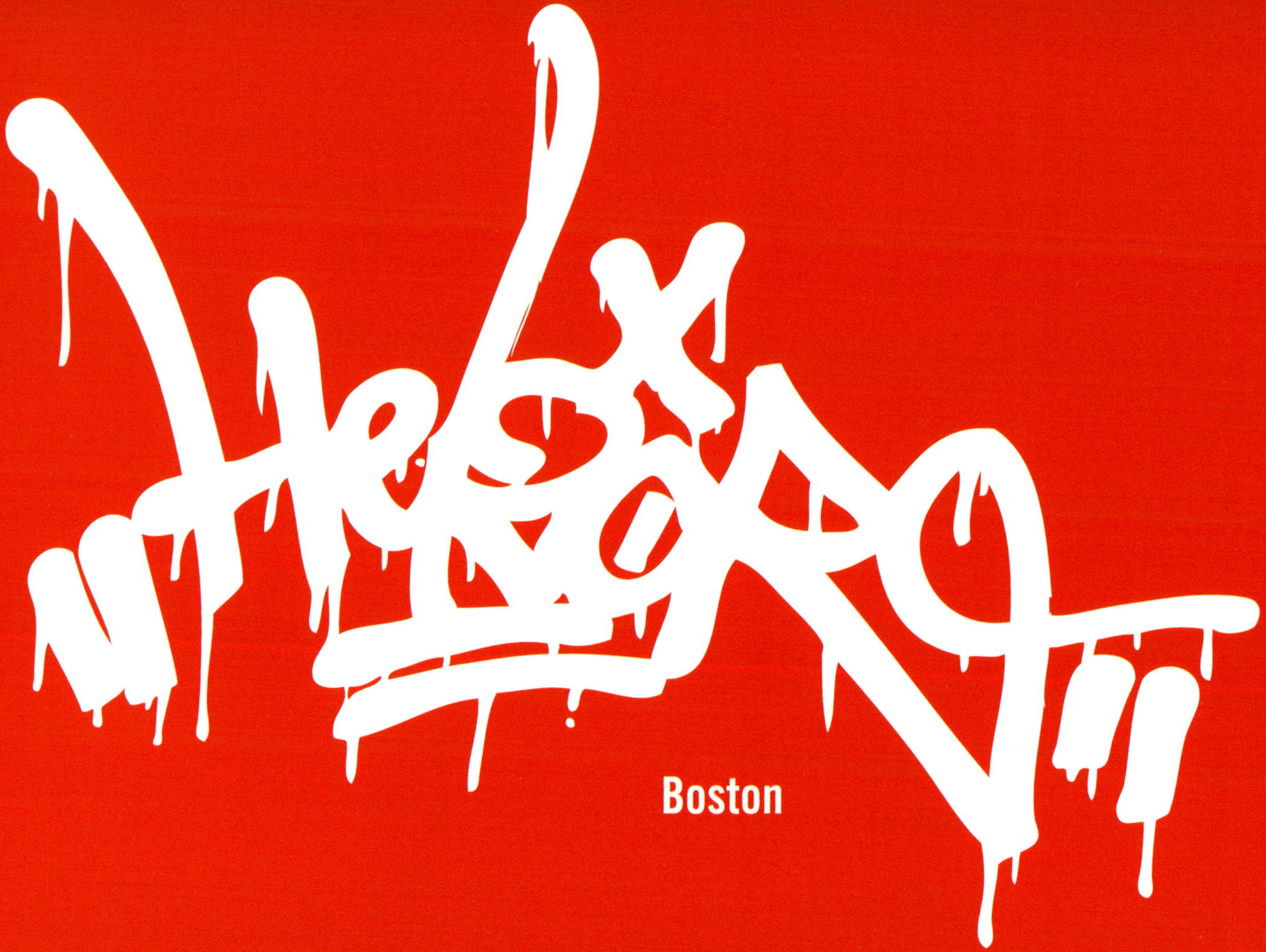

HELX ZORO

Boston

> "I put a hundred percent in every tattoo I do, and it's very flattering to have people come from across the country to get a piece from me.... I'm proud to accommodate these people with beautiful pieces of artwork that will live forever...at least until their time is up."

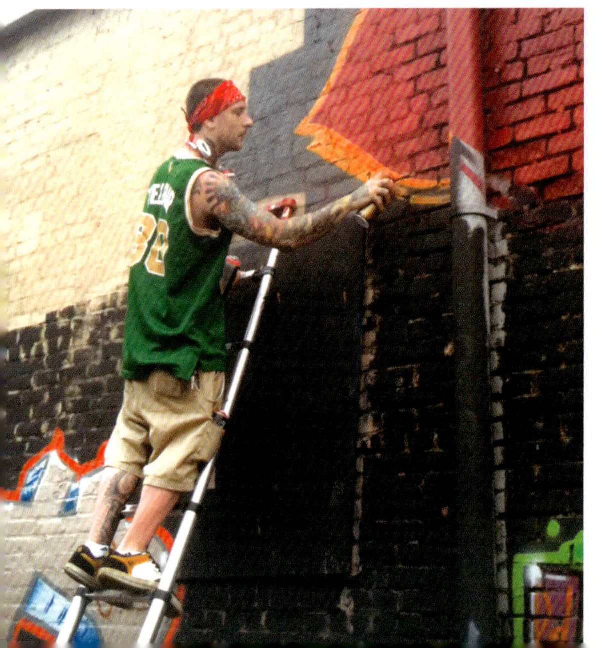

HELZ

Art has always been a refuge for Helz. In grade school, he loved to draw the wild and woolly Eddie, Iron Maiden's official mascot, as seen on the band's elaborate album covers. Helz's renderings of Eddie were impressive, and the respect he received because of his talents pleased him. Soon the respect he earned on the streets of Boston by way of his graffiti career would push him to the fringes of society, where the tattooed need to get more tattoos.

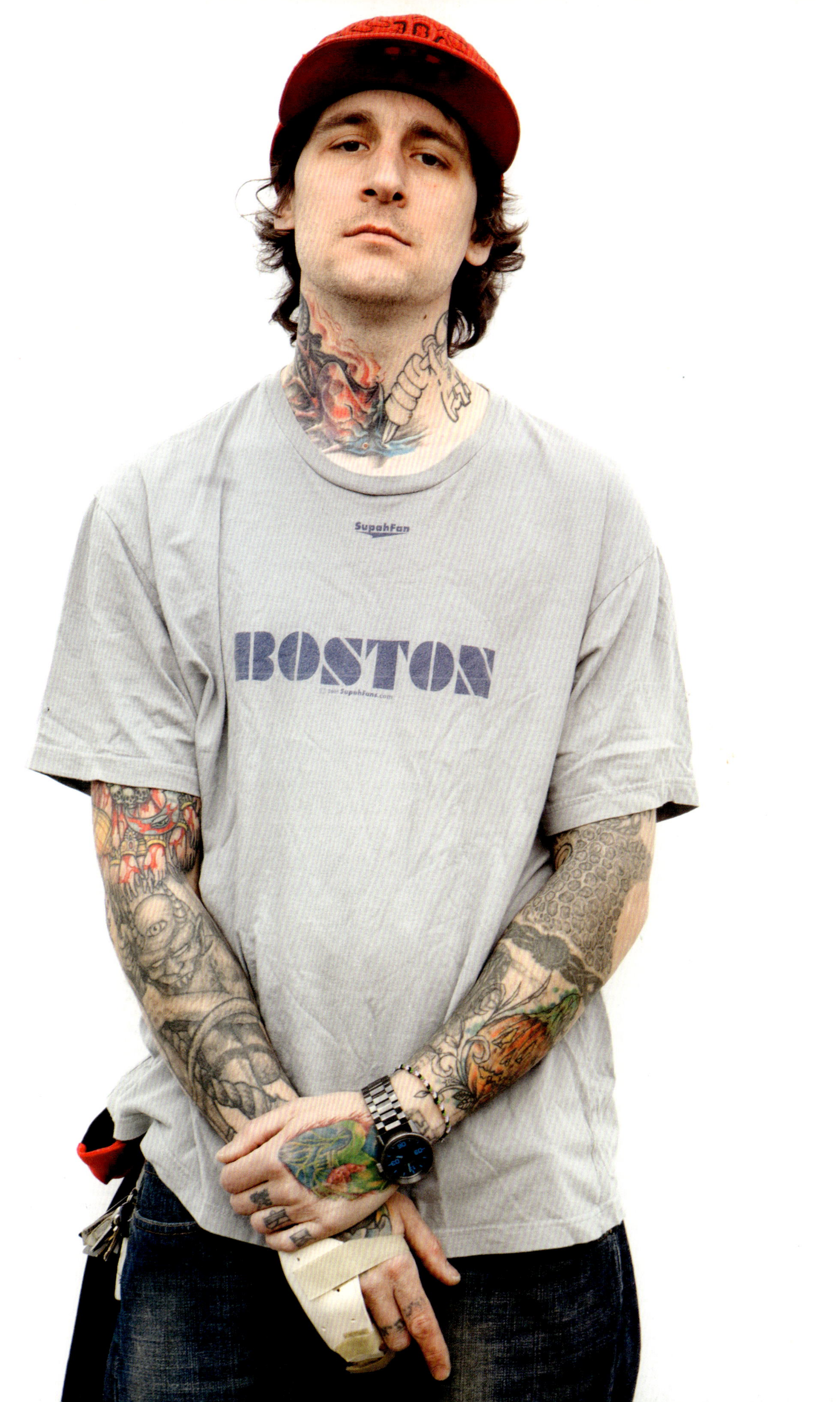
SupahFan
BOSTON
© 2001 SupahFans.com

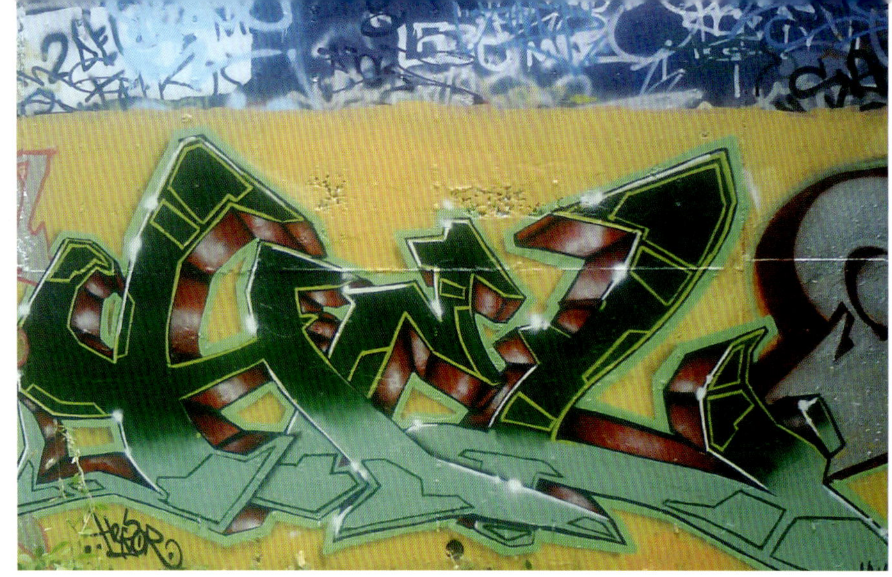
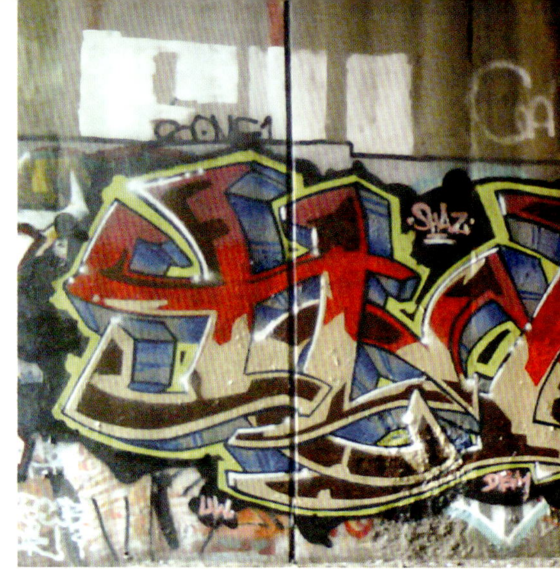

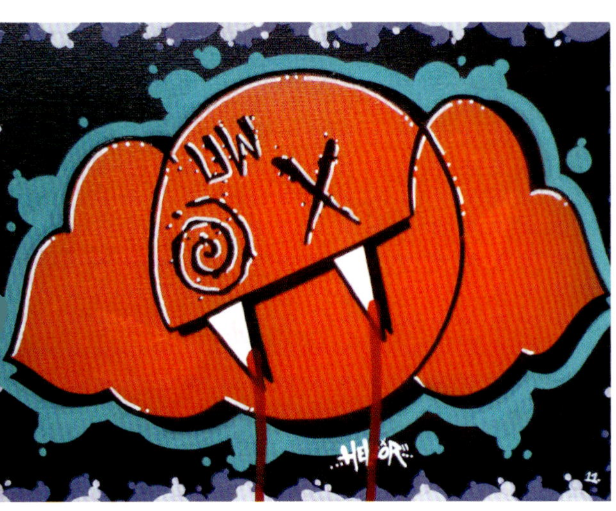

Helz painting, 2011

I write *Helz*. I'm originally from Dorchester, Massachusetts. It's south of Boston. I grew up in a little neighborhood with a bunch of friends that always got harassed by cops. I got serious about writing in '91. That's when I really started to kind of get out, sneaking out of my parents' house and going off bombing and stuff like that.

I was going to school in Quincy, which is straight next to Dorchester, and taking the train, a Red Line train from Ashmont into Quincy. Along the line by the JFK/UMass station there were all of these walls down by the tracks and they were filled with burners. All kinds of cats would go down there and just do burners. This was right before I started writing and it just blew my mind. In high school I ran into a buddy who wrote *Code*, and he kind of took me under his wing and showed me about graffiti. He was like my partner in crime for years.

I had been drawing since I was a little kid. Before I started doing graffiti, I would draw pictures of Eddie from Iron Maiden album covers. Me and a buddy in junior high school would always see who could draw the best Eddie. I've always been into drawing and stuff, and that eventually led me into a life of art.

When I first started getting up and stuff, I was just getting up for myself so I could go around and see everything that I'd bombed. I could be pleased with what I did, or sometimes I saw stuff I might learn to correct and grow from. I mean, for me, it was just kind of an escape from my life, all the bullshit that I had going on. [Graffiti] turned into more of a positive thing than what was going on in my personal life. It wasn't really for fame or venting. It was just something that really intrigued me. That's how I got started, and it grew from there.

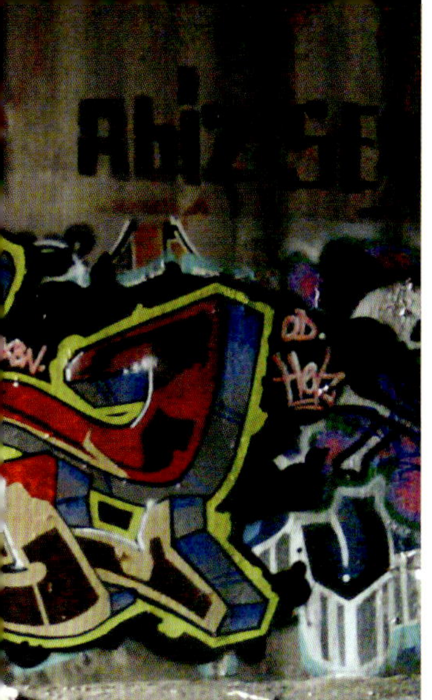

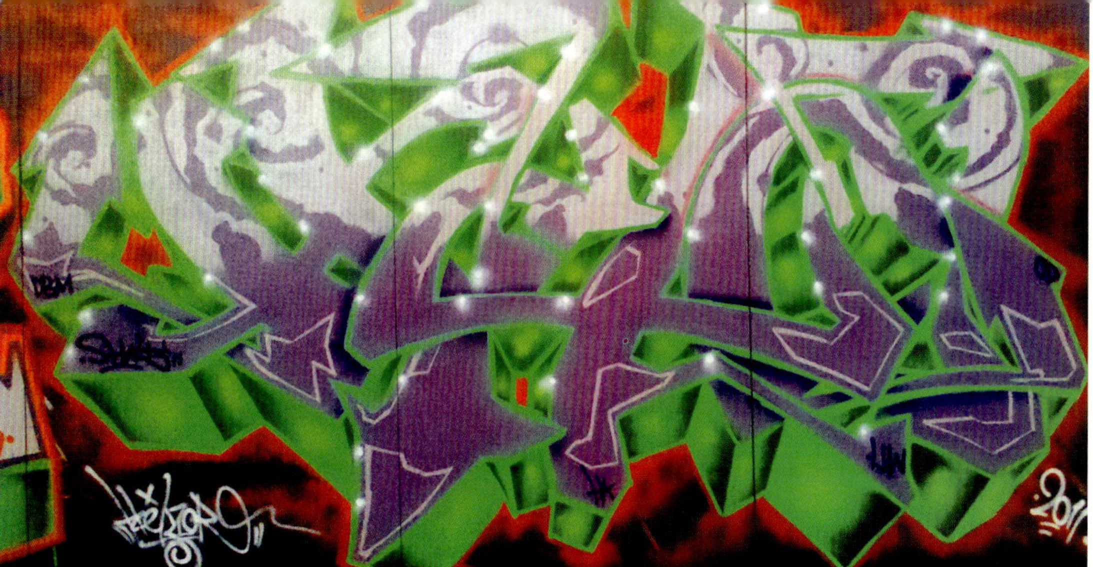

I lived with my mom for years. My dad was a big coke dealer in Boston, and he fucked up and got arrested and went to prison. I moved around from house to house with my mom, and she was a heavy vodka drinker. She'd wake up with screwdrivers every morning, so she didn't really stay on top of me about schoolwork or anything else. I guess she kind of had that as a getaway of her own.

I started my own crew. It was BSA—Boston Street Artists. I remember having a conversation with Code one time. We were down at this place called the Grove, it was like a trolley overpass. It was a bridge, and in the underpass we would do pieces. We're talking, and Code asked if there were any crews I wanted to be down with. I said I'd like to be down with OD [Over Dose] like Alone and Resent and to study with the OD crew. They have their own style. And then from that point I got introduced to YSB [Young Street Burners] crew in Dorchester, and they turned out to be my main homies, or my crew. Through them I met Lost and Alone and Curse and Alert and all these guys that I looked up to.

I was pretty much influenced around Boston, seeing what people were doing, how people would lay colors down, how people were doing letter construction and stuff like that. Of course I wouldn't bite their shit, but I would see how they were doing it and how I would make it my own to make my pieces pop. Eventually I went from doing negative-style pieces to more bold-letter-type things.

In New York there's bombers and there's pieces artists. There's cats that go bombing, and they don't do murals. Then there are cats that do murals that don't bomb and can't write tags. In Boston it's totally different. The graffiti culture where I grew up, you had to know both,

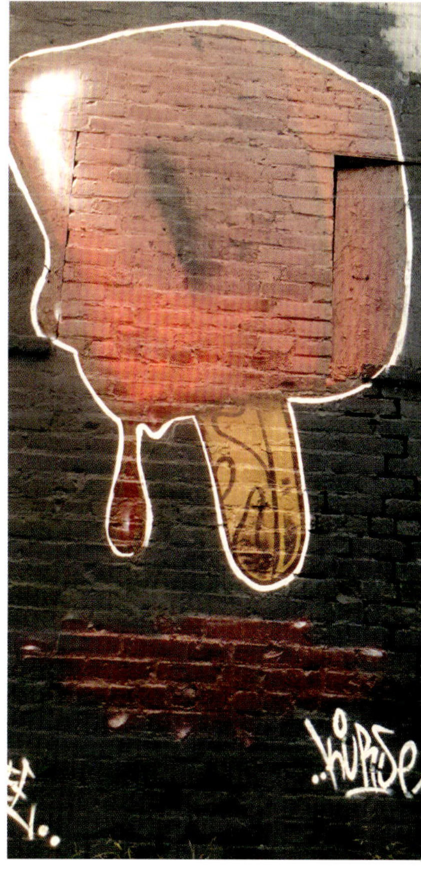

Helz piece on OD reunion wall, Boston, 2011

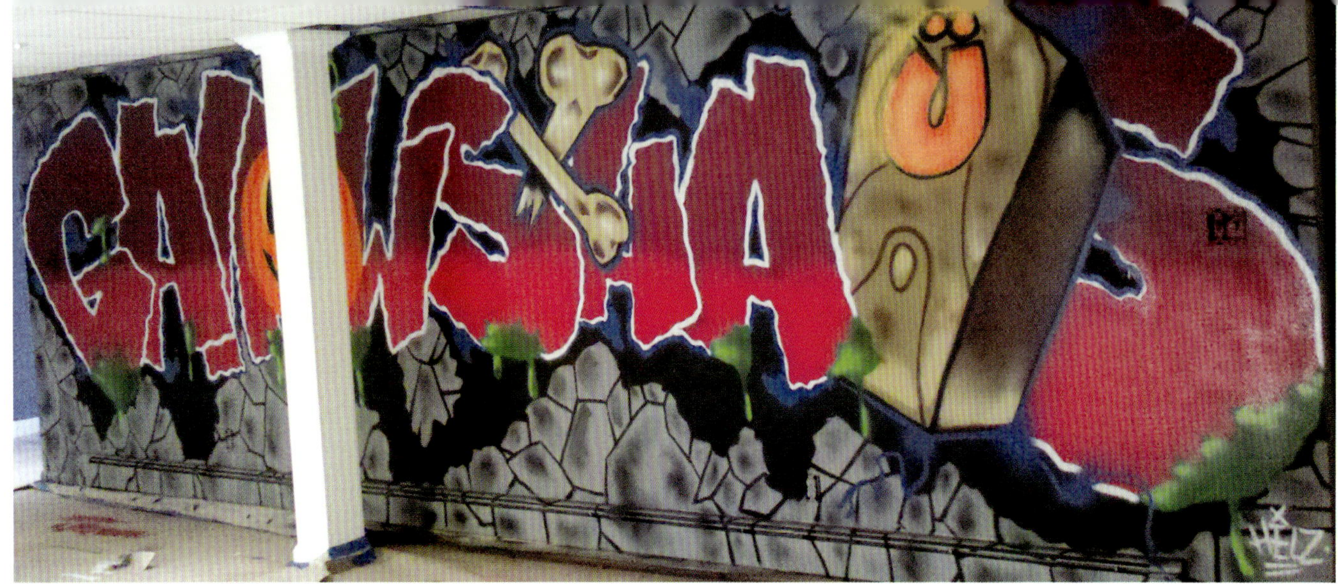

Helz, *Gallows Haüs*, Salem, MA, 2012

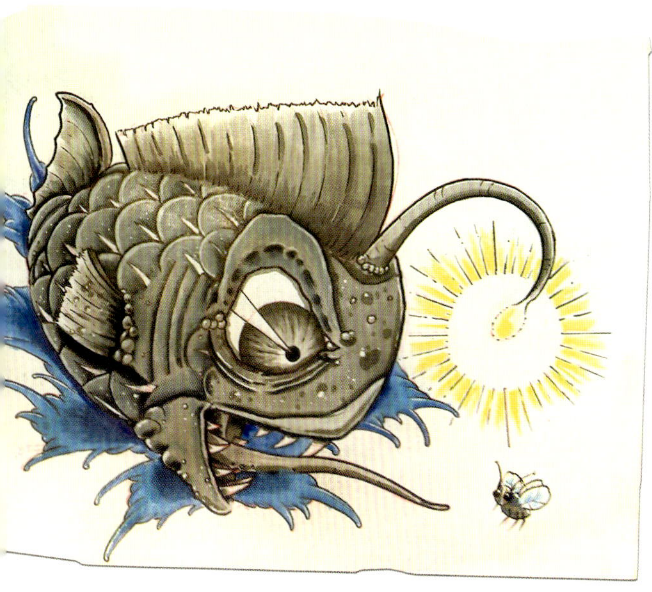

Helz, *Evil Angler Fish* drawing, 2012

and everybody did both. If you were a good writer, you have to build hand styles and you can do a burner in your sleep. That was the discipline that was in Boston. You got to get your hand styles down and from there you got to get your pieces down, and then you start getting noticed.

We were over at Alone's house, and Vase and Wizart came by. I can't remember who brought the acid that we all ended up taking, but we were hanging out and chilling and drawing and shit. Wizart showed us a tattoo that he did. He did like a big, fat Pilot marker that he tattooed on his calf. He's like, "Check this out. I just did this tattoo here and I'm thinking about starting to do tattoos." After that night of crazy debauchery and whatnot, me and Alone talked about it. We're like, hey, do you want to split the cost of a tattoo kit? At the time we bought a small ring and rod kit, which was like $500. I was tattooing almost ten years with that machine.

Eventually more and more people wanted my work because I was getting better and better. That was a very easy transition because in Boston, when we drew in our black books, we would draw with ball-point pens. So to make pieces with defined lines or thicker lines, we'd have to go over them and over them and make sure everything was tight. I feel that helped me a lot with tattooing, with my outlining, making sure that everything's tight from my days of black-book drawing.

For a while I was just tattooing out of my house and out of other people's houses, and I had a bunch of graffiti charges on me because out here in Boston, they don't have to catch you red-handed for you to get locked up. They had the vandals law, and [Lieutenant] Nancy O'Loughlin ran the vandal squad out here. She was taught by a New York vandal squad cop back in the early eighties. She could've been a writer, but she arrested writers. She knew every fucking writer, where they lived, what their names were, what their hand styles were, everything. What she would do is she would see people who looked like writers walking around with backpacks on, and she'd pull over, stop us, and go through our bags, go through our black books, see what we write. Then she would put our shit back in our bags and let us go on our way. From there, whenever we got up and she saw, she kept a little book, and she knew who to go after.

There were a couple of times I got caught red-handed. One time I was doing this rooftop, and the way to get to the rooftop was a fire escape, and the fire escape went up to this door. There was a big fence to block people from getting on the rooftop, so you had to ninja yourself over the fence. I was with Keen and I went first. I'm all quiet, and all of a sudden I hear a big thud. He like jumped off the top of the fence and landed on the parking roof. Meanwhile, the place is open 24 hours, and they called the cops because they think someone's trying to rob the place. Lots of cops showed up, guns out, they headed over the fence. I'm running to the end of the roof, throwing my cans off, and they're yelling, "Get the fuck on the ground!" with guns to our heads. Eventually, when we're getting interrogated, we said, "We're graffiti writers," and they're like, "Shit, if we knew you were going to write your name, we would have let you go. We thought you were robbing the place. Oh well, it's too late now. It's already called in. We're bringing you in." It turned out that one of the cops was Keen's friend in high school's brother. We totally could've gotten off. It was a fucking trip.

I put a hundred percent in every tattoo I do, and it's very flattering to have people come from across the country to get a piece from me. This woman came down from Iceland just to get a tattoo from me once. It's very flattering, and I'm proud to accommodate these people with beautiful pieces of artwork that will live forever…at least until their time is up.

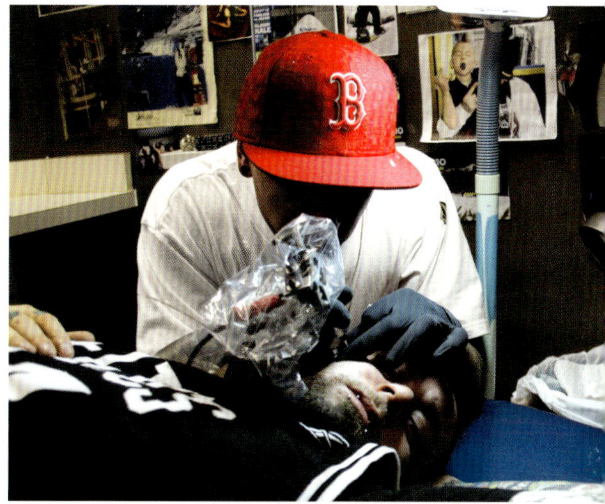

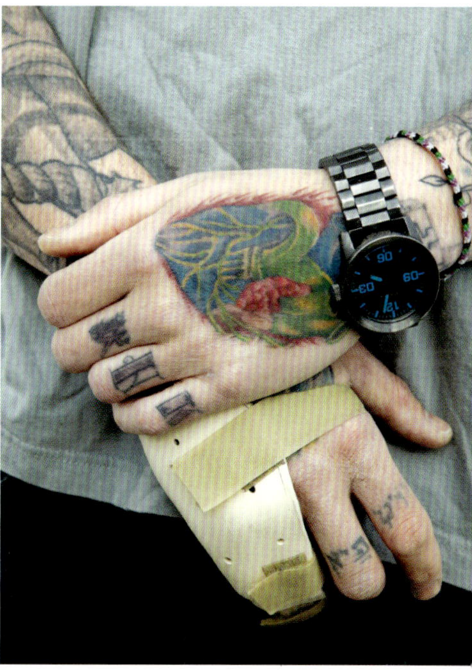

TOP: Helz tattooing Lord Dunce's face, 2007
BOTTOM: Helz with broken pinky finger from a skateboarding accident, 2012

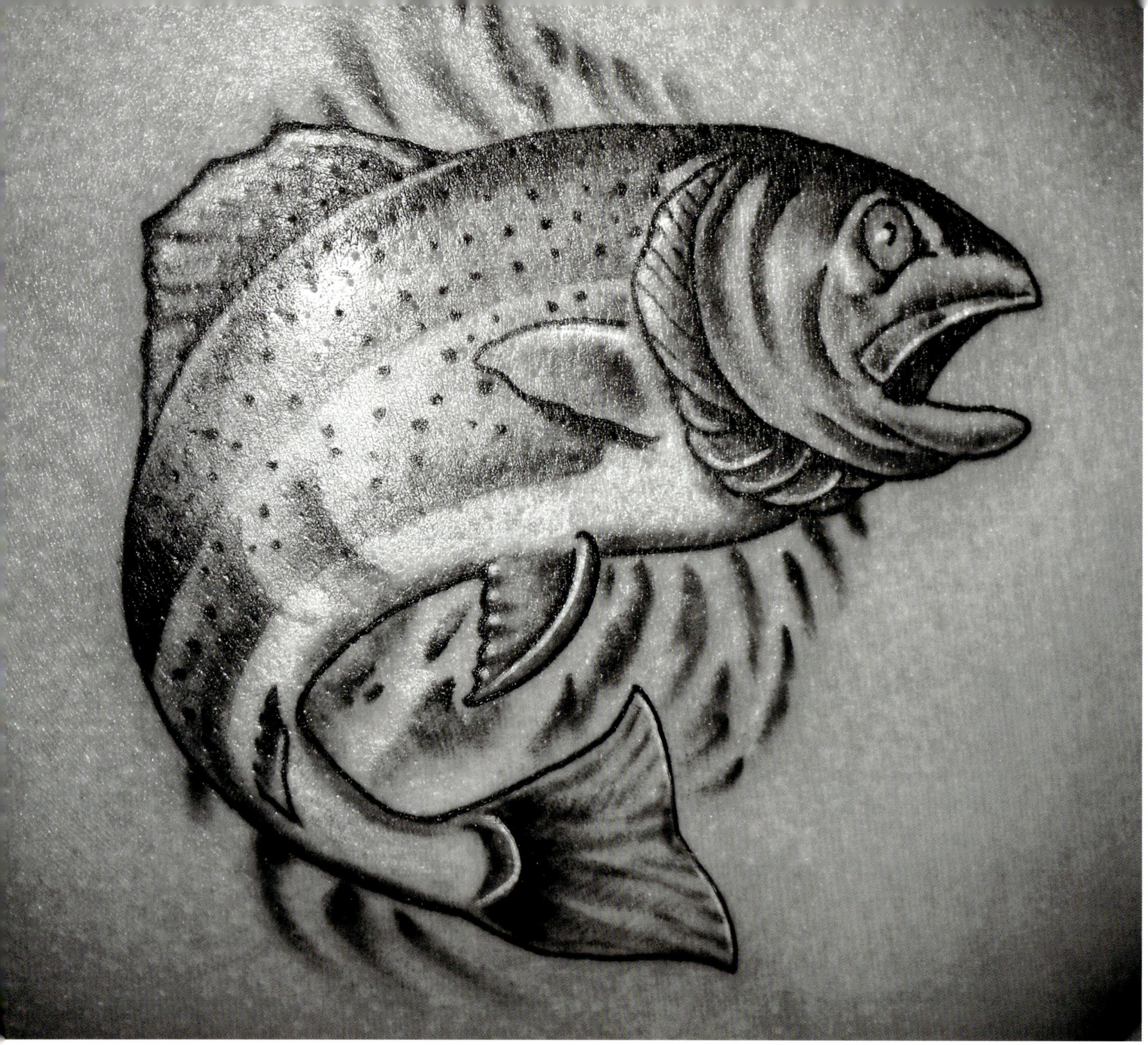

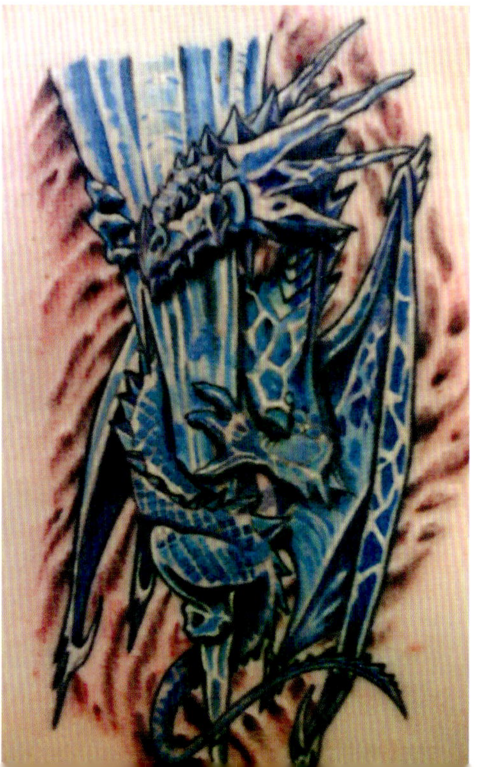
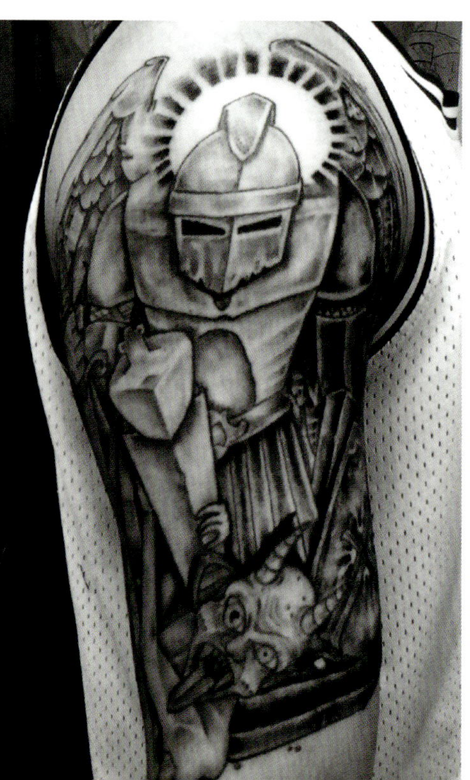

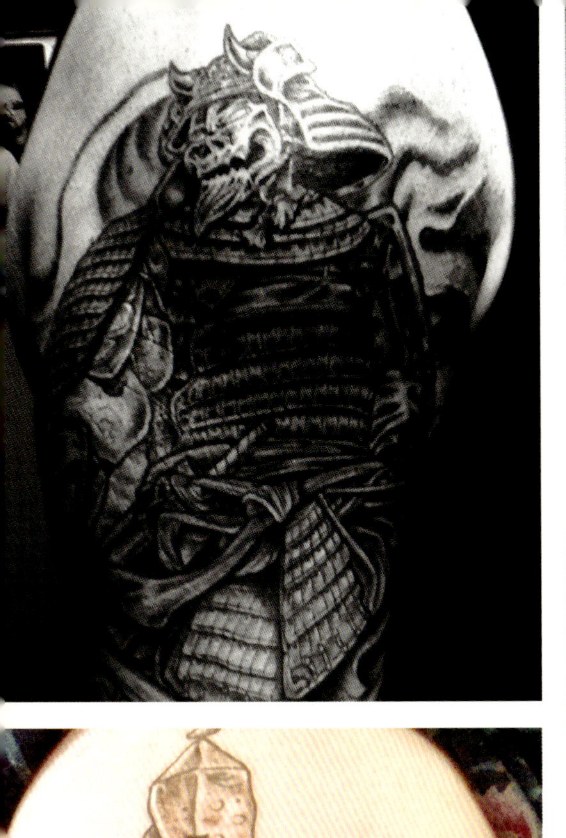
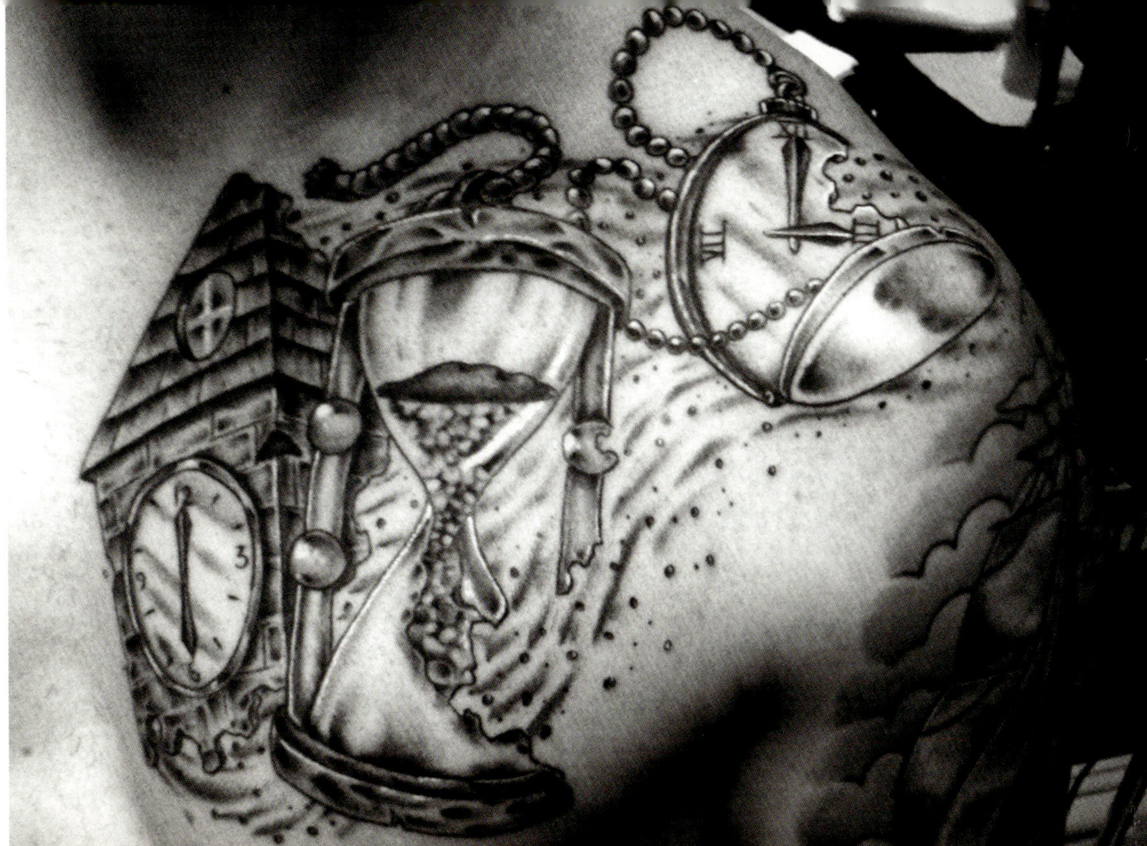
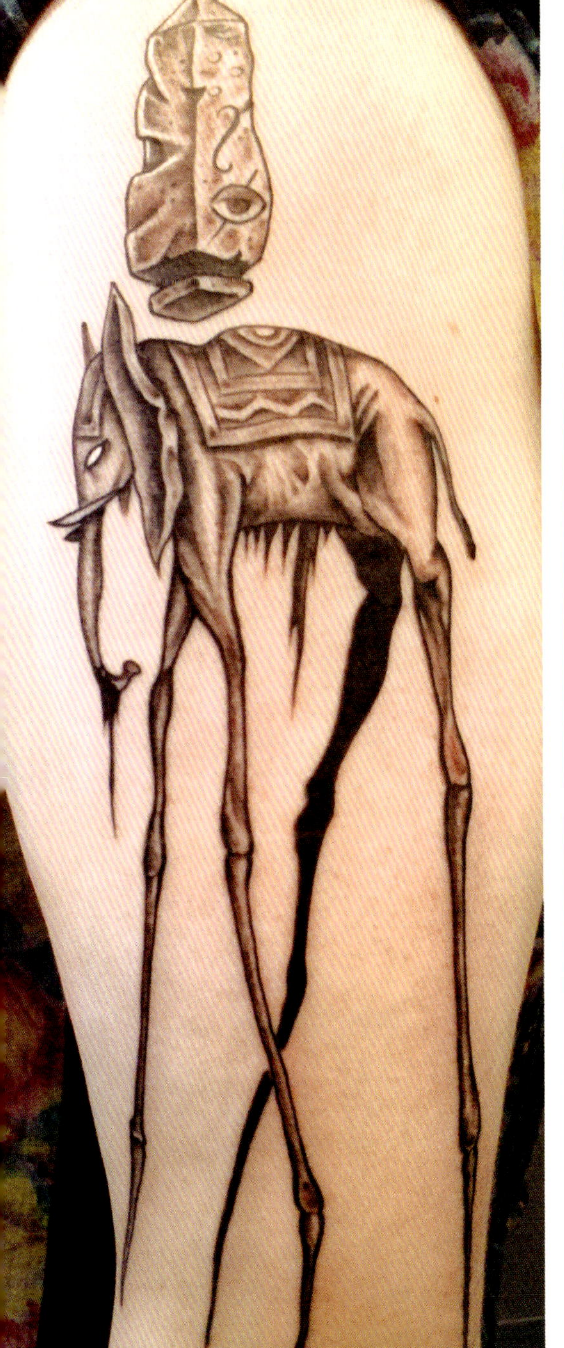
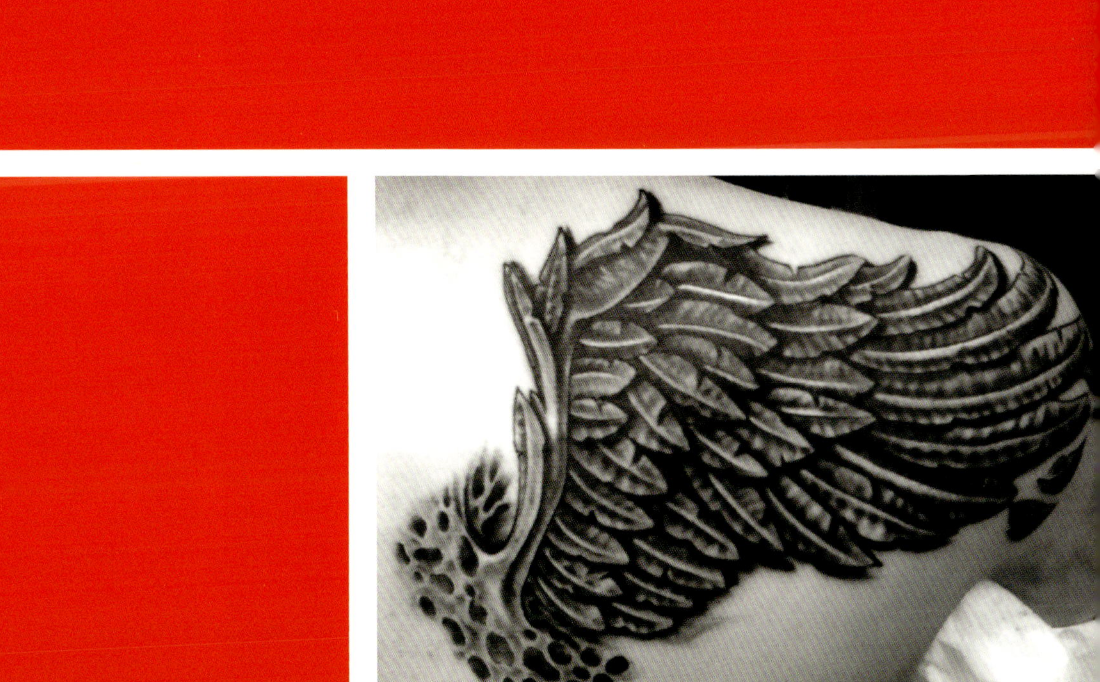

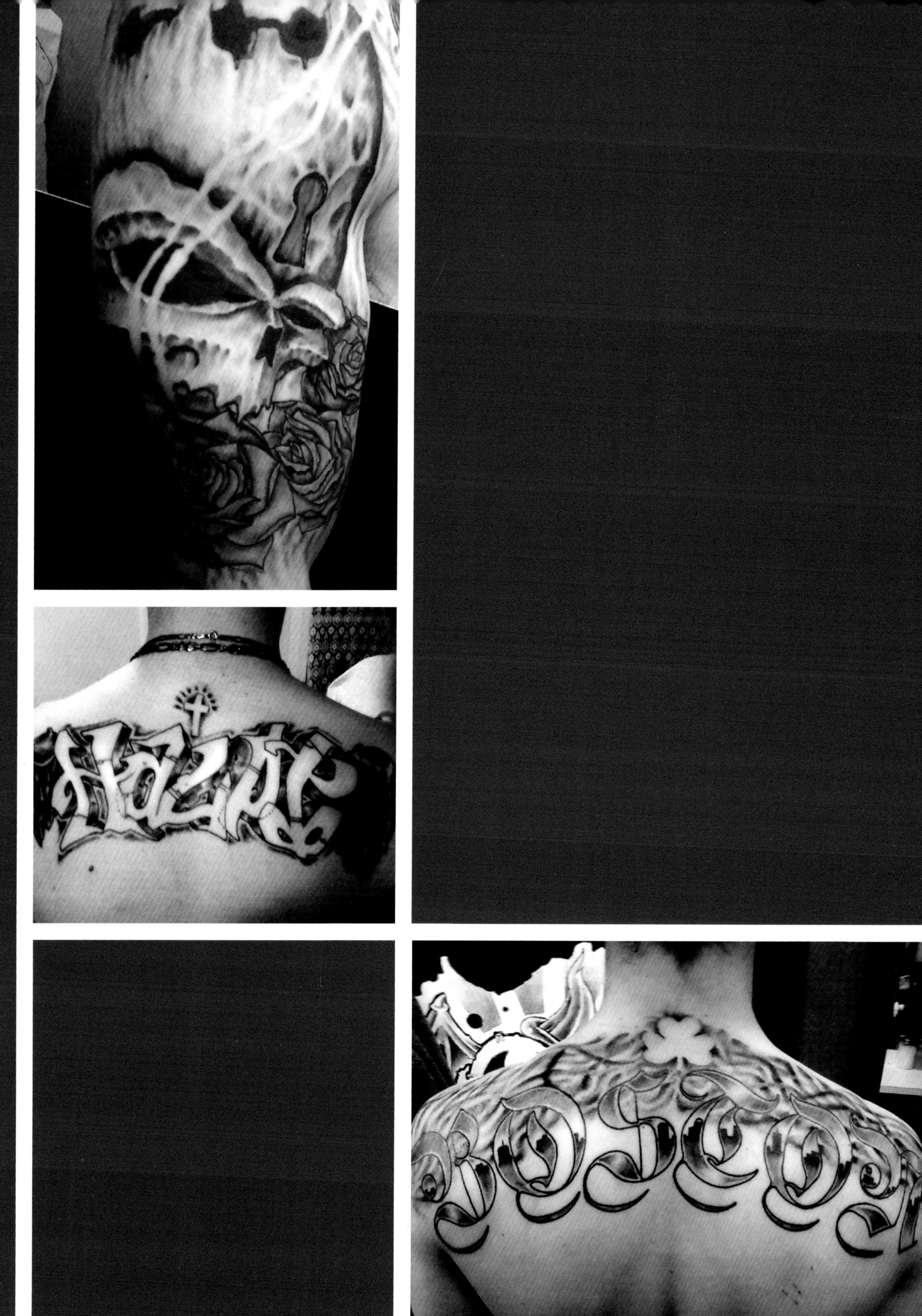

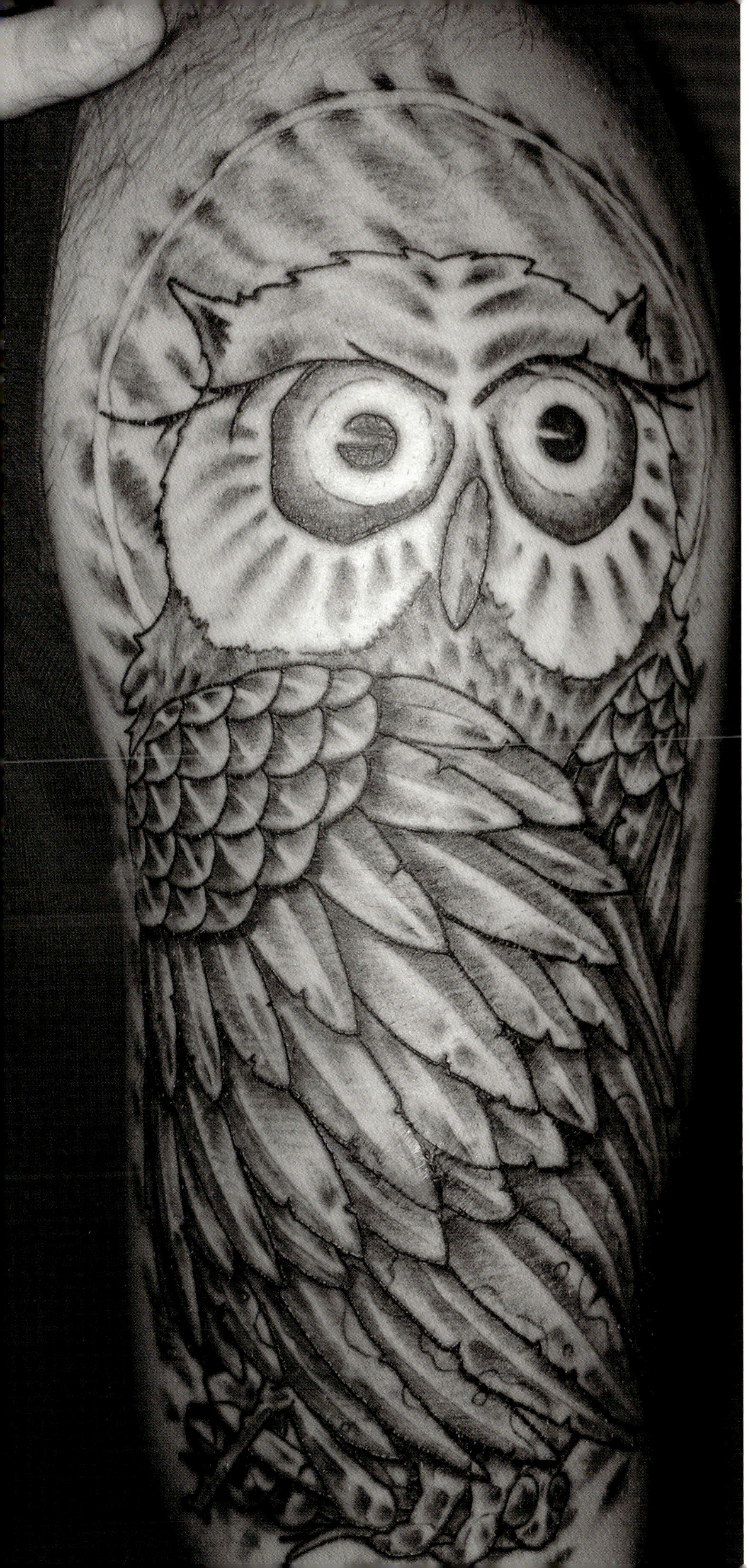

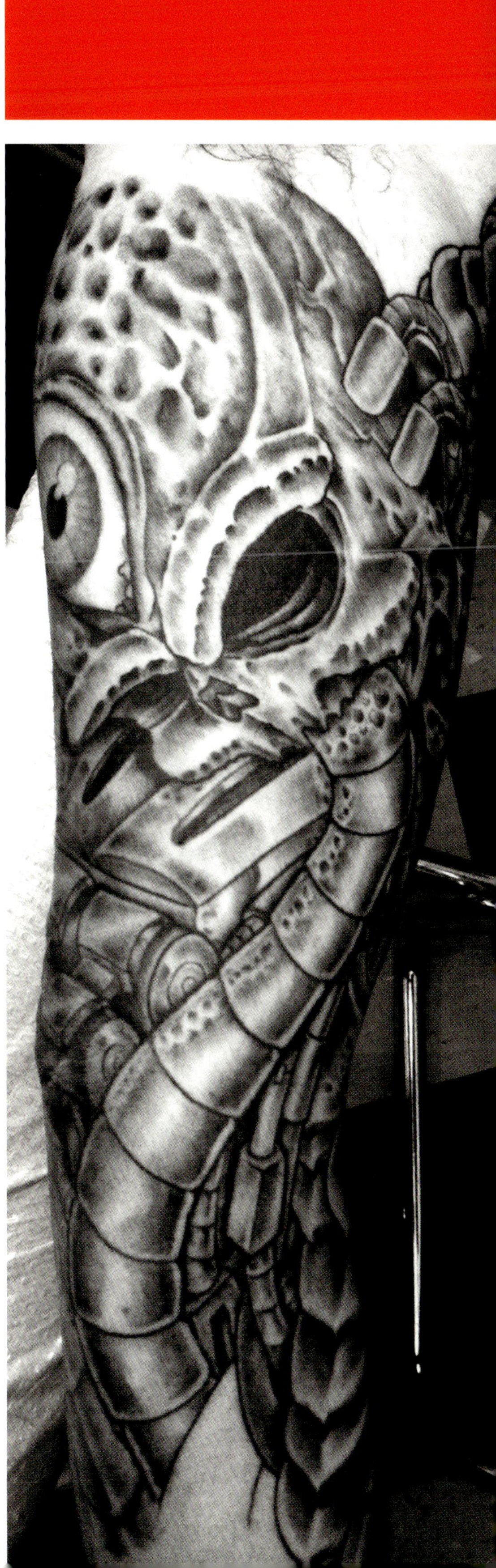

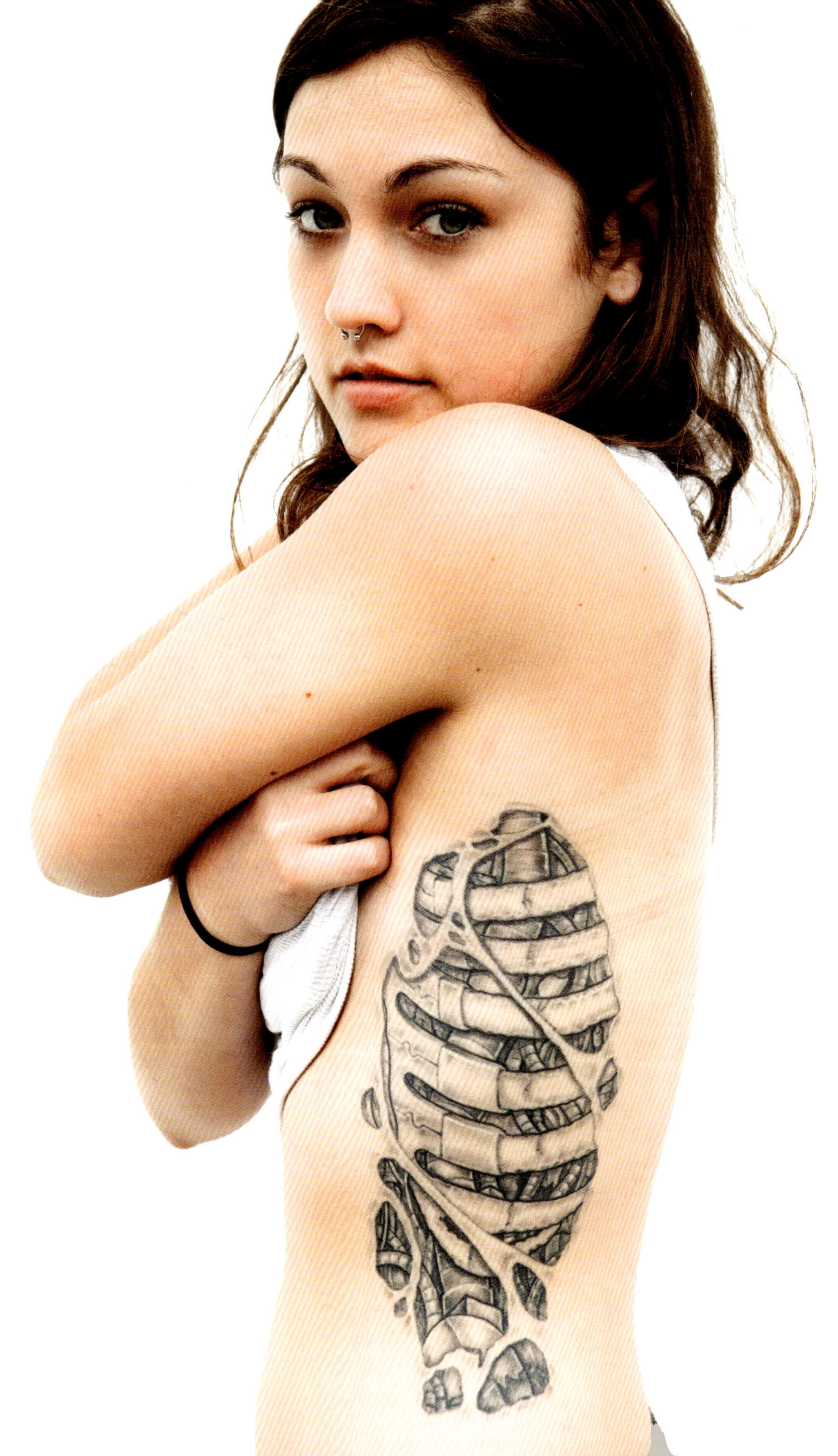

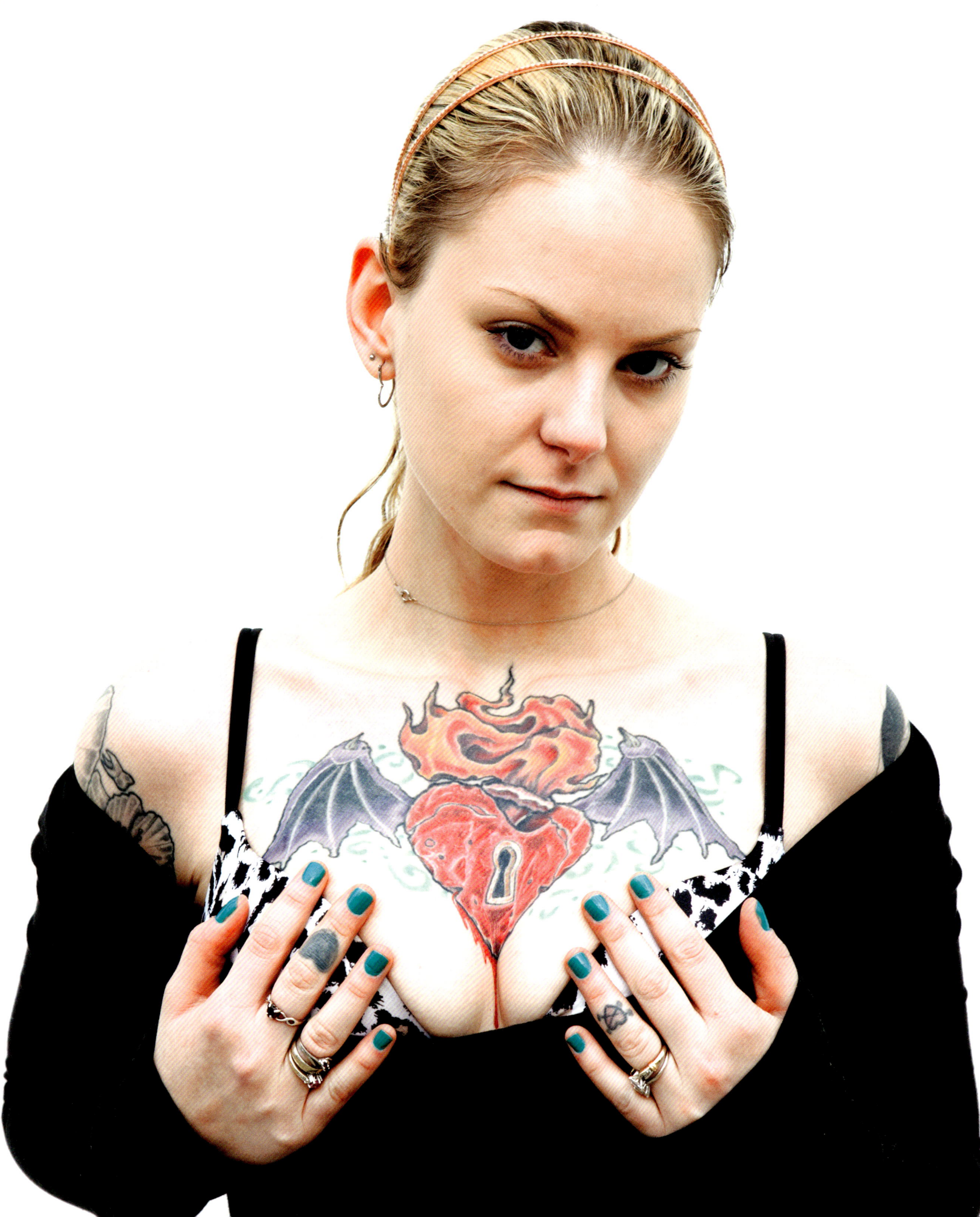

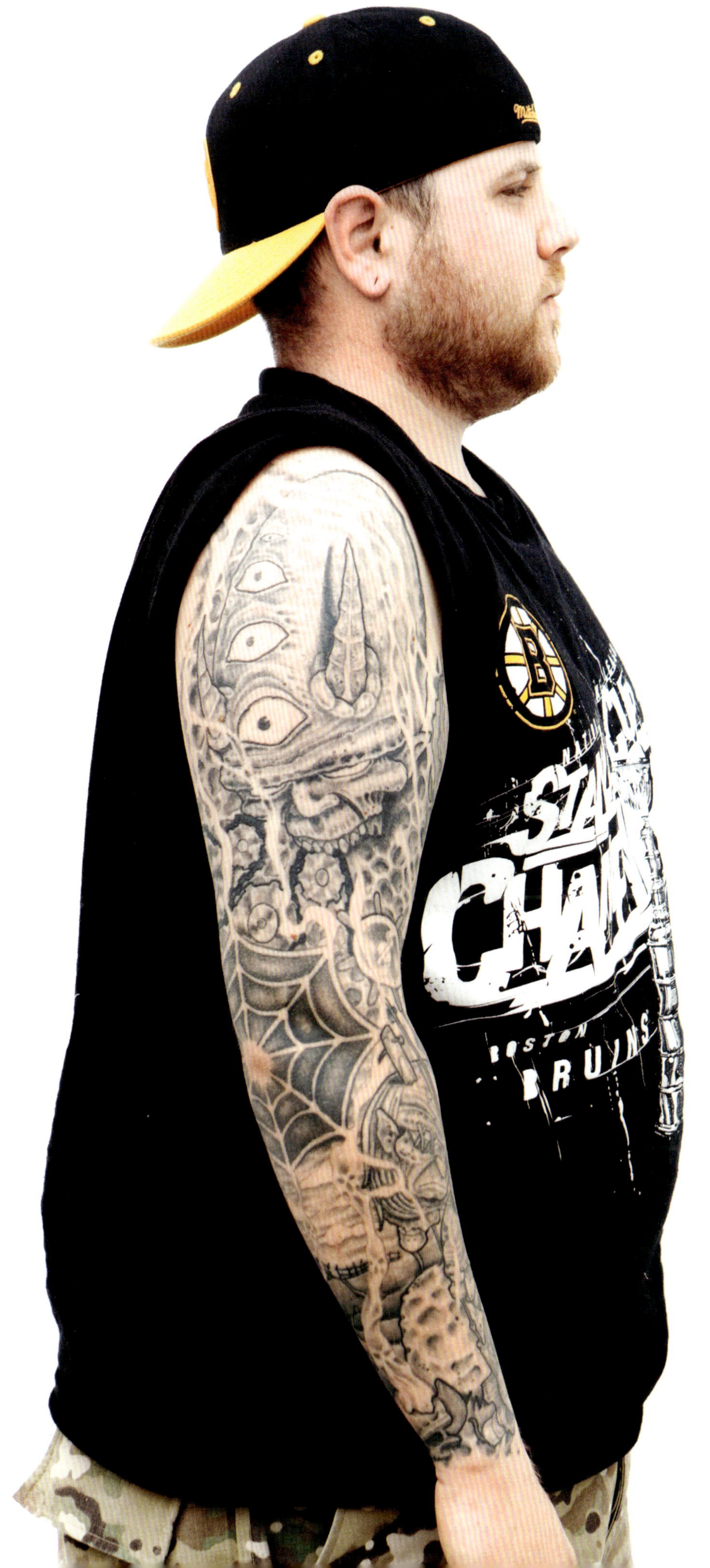

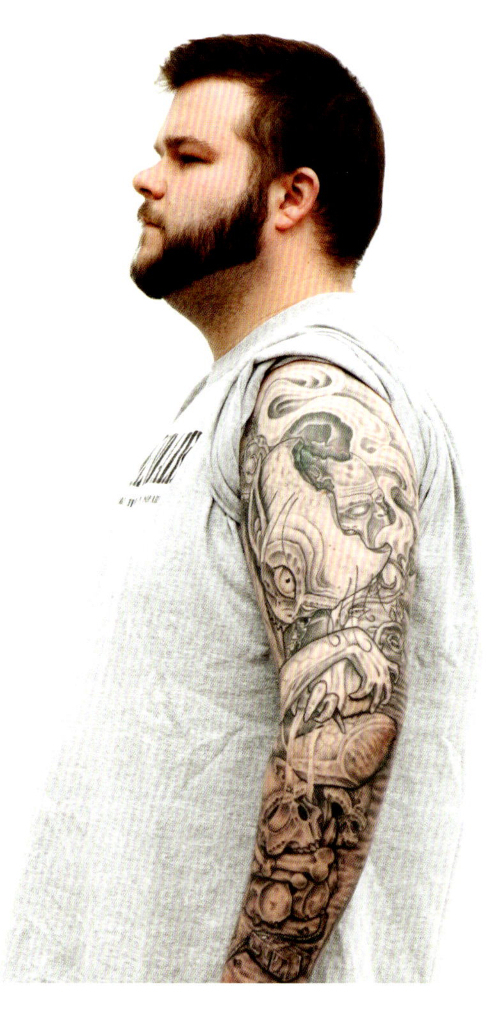

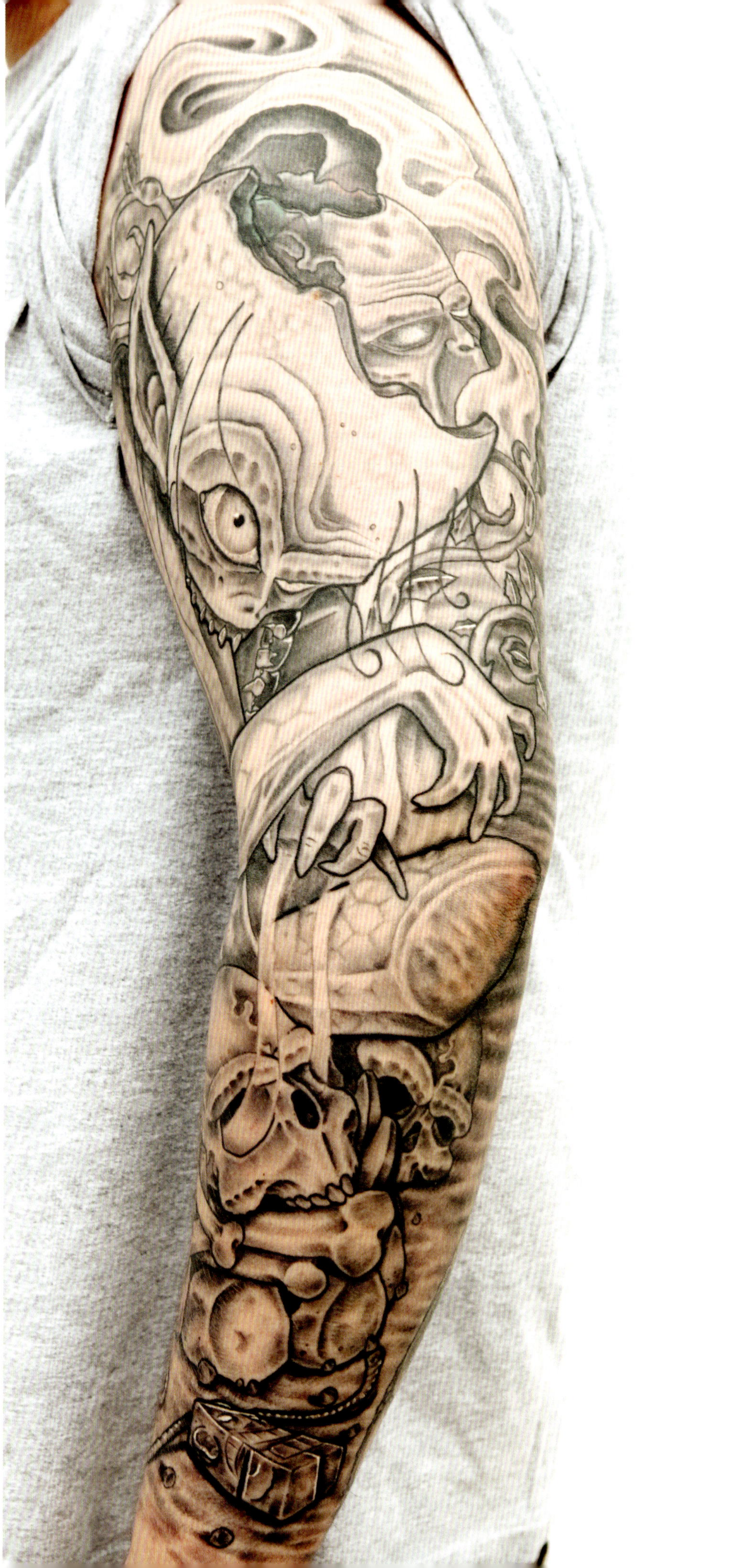

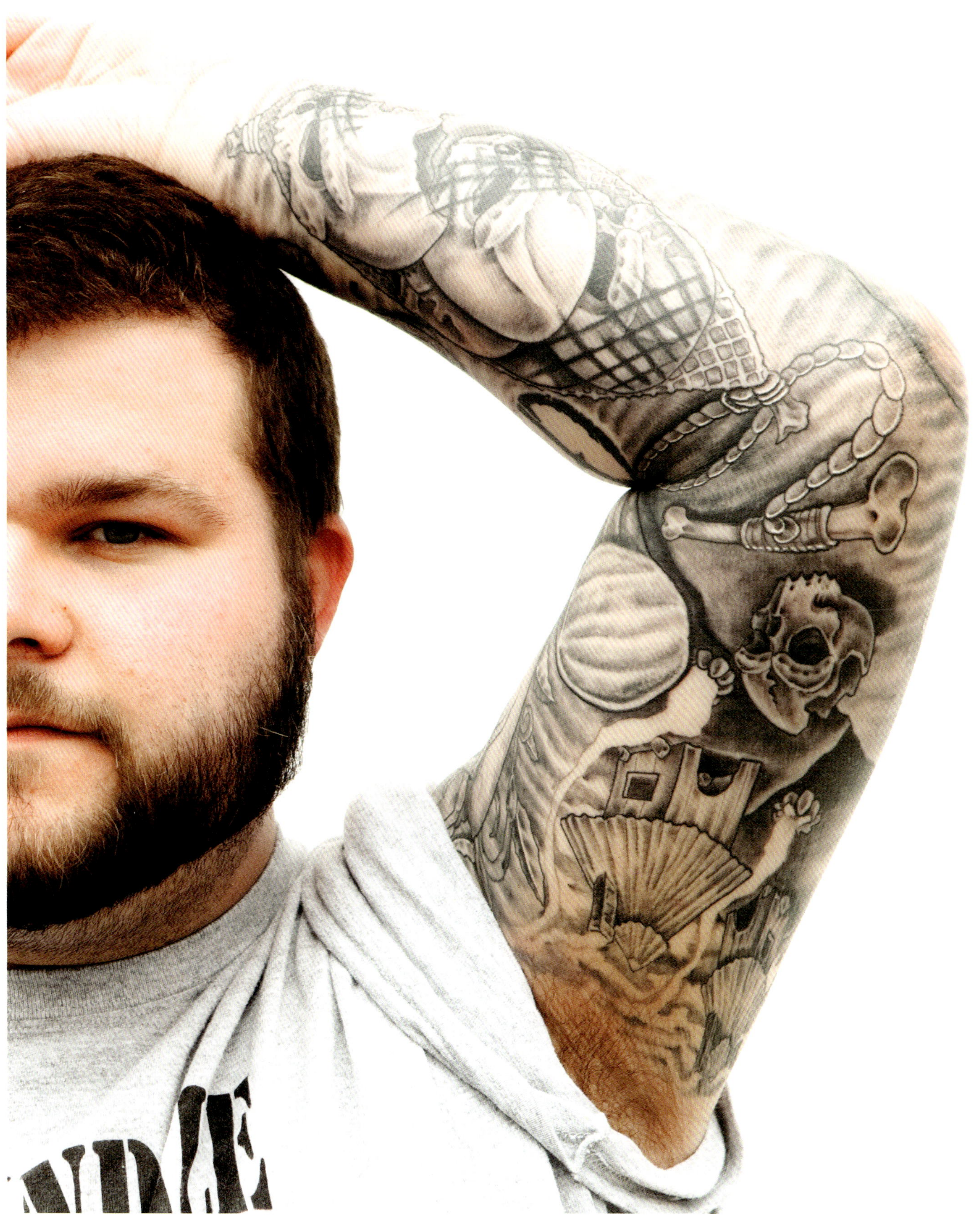

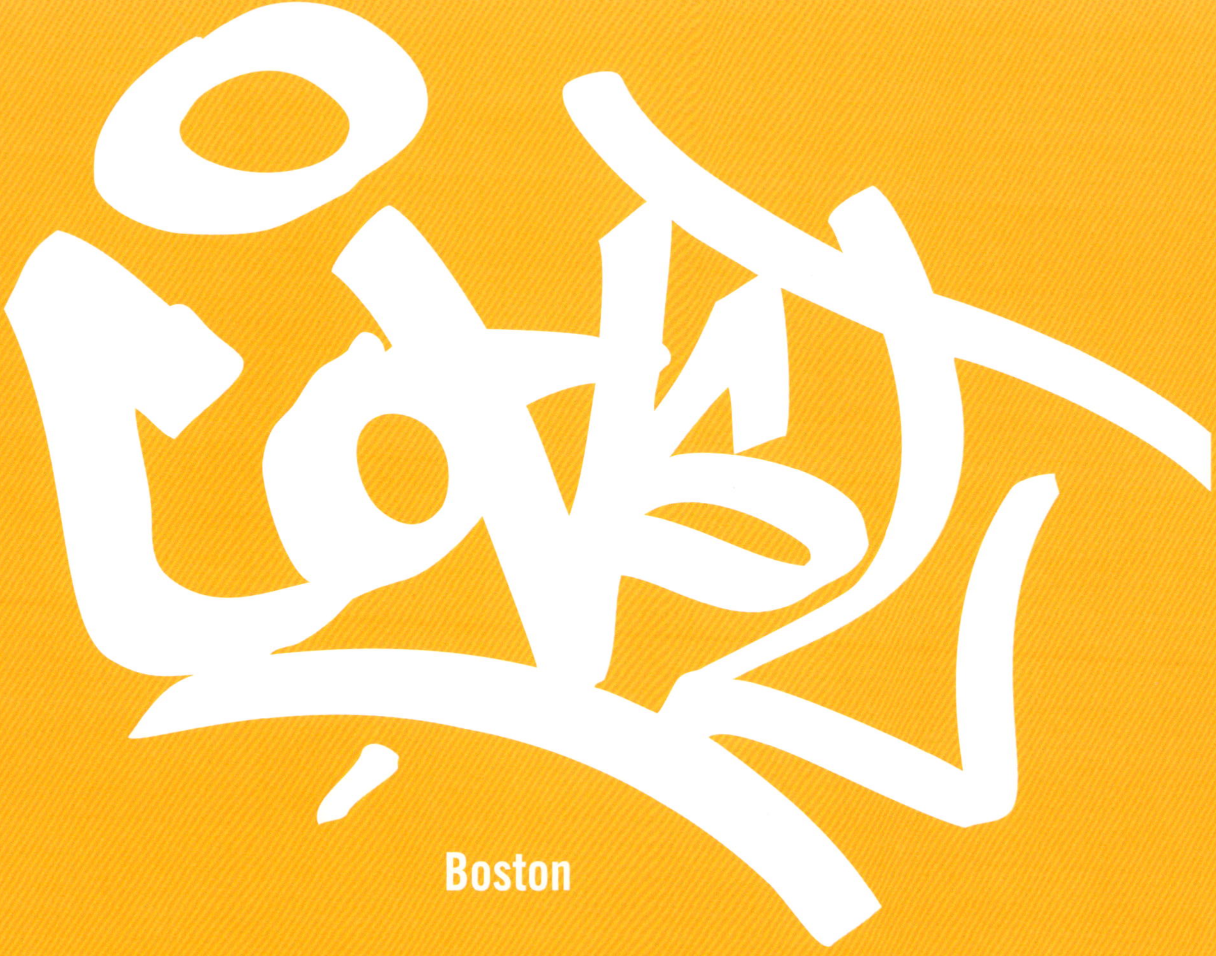

"There's definitely a similarity between getting where you want to be with graffiti and getting where you want to be with tattooing. When you start doing graffiti, you have no can control, things are dripping, you're not feeding things right, you can't get the right cuts… there are definitely some similarities in terms of obstacles, like what paint do I use for this kind of wall, or what needle do I use for this area of skin?"

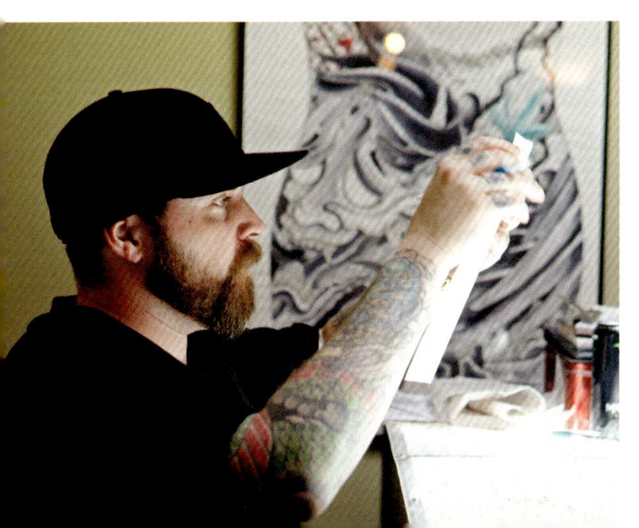

COAST

Coast was schooled in the ways of punk and hip-hop early in life. It was these two mind-sets that would inform his output inside the world of tattoo. Inspired by the greats of Boston graffiti, Coast stepped up and stepped out pretty hardcore, leaving a trail of his handiwork all over the Bean. A string of arrests and summonses would force him to flee to New York City, where he would develop his voice as a tattooist.

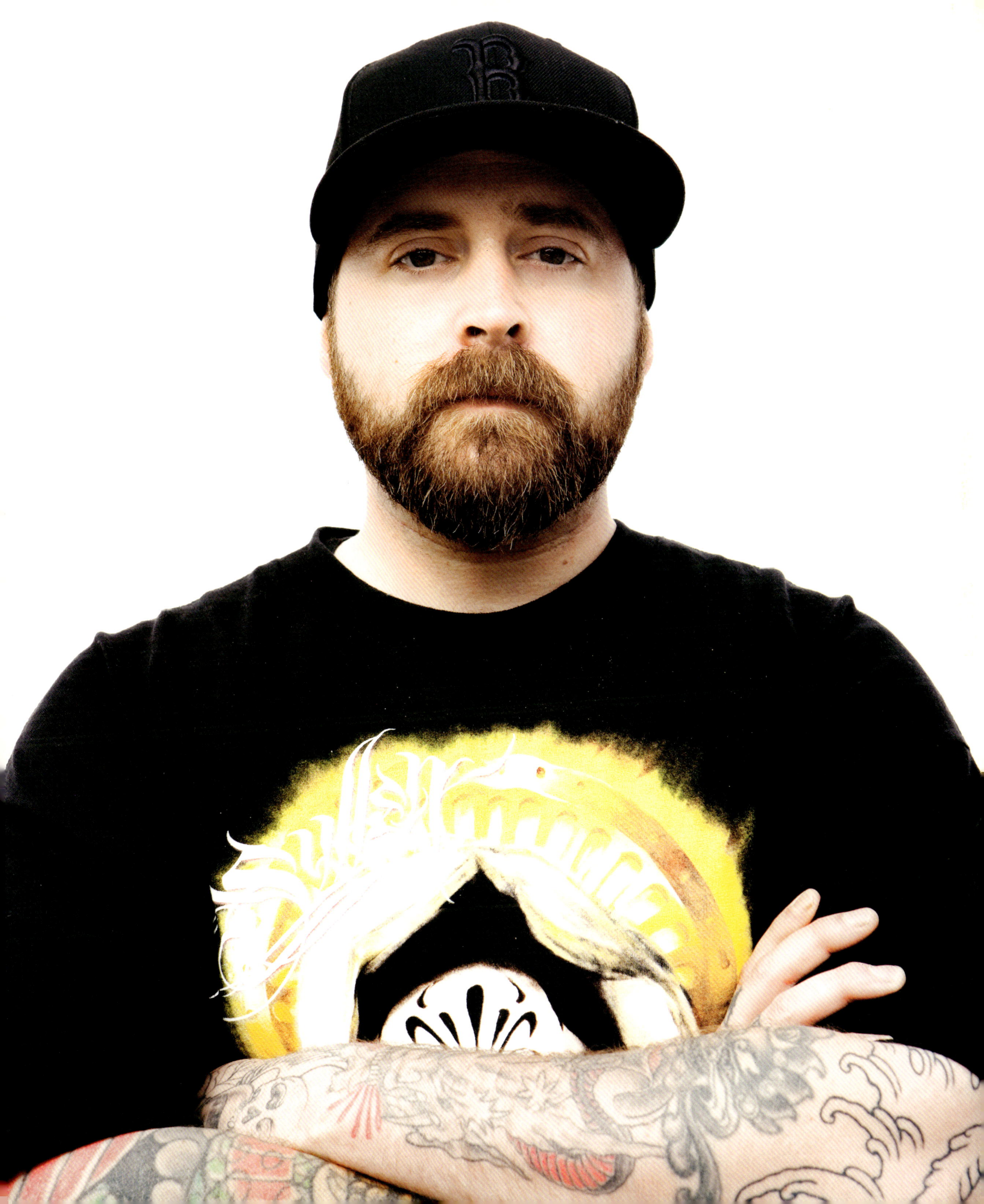

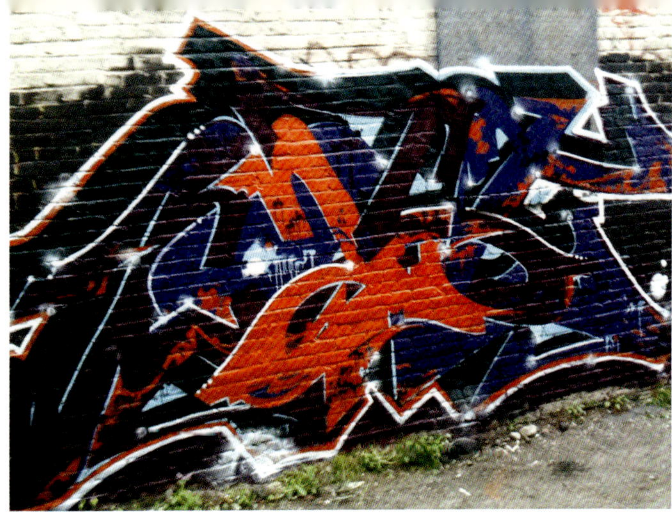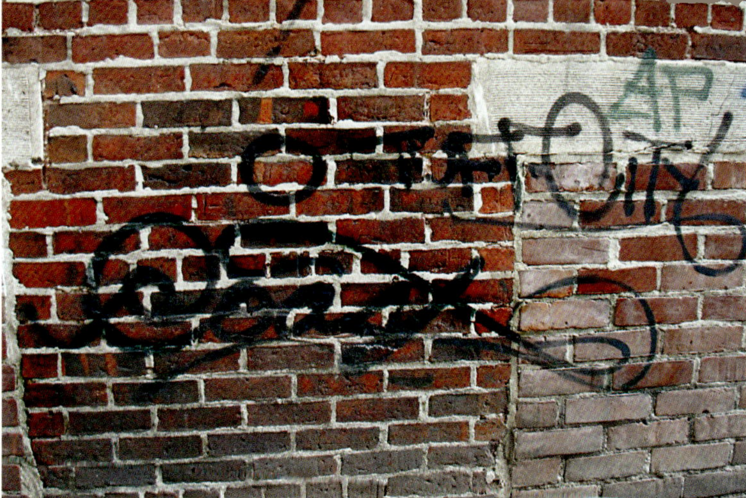

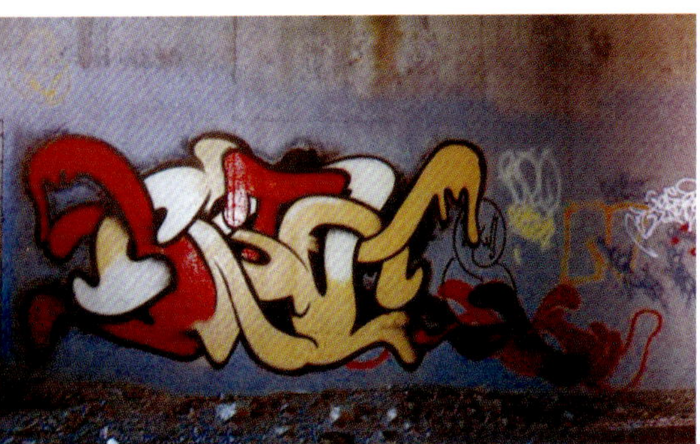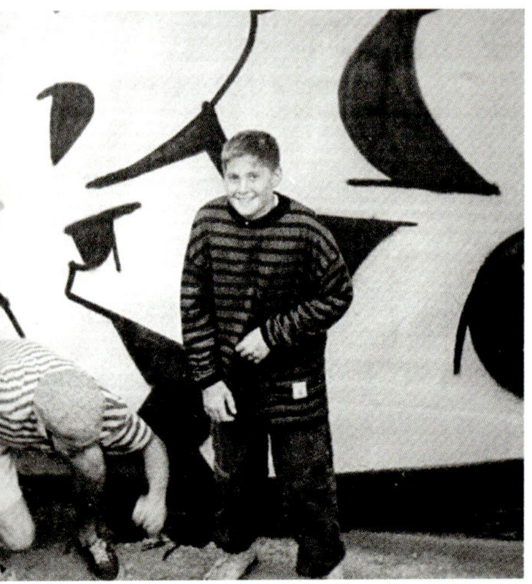

I'm from Boston originally. Actually I'm still in Boston; I have a shop here in Cambridge. I grew up on the line out here called the Mattapan-Ashmont line. Back in the eighties that was *the* line. It was just being killed. It was like, Click and Hang and Zone and all these legends of Boston. I started doing graffiti in probably '87 or '88—just tagging around, catching tags here and there. I was really influenced by some good artists. I mean, Click had the Mattapan-Ashmont line down and his stuff was beautiful. So I just started walking the tracks, checking it out, and one thing led to another.

The Boston graffiti scene in comparison to the New York graffiti scene is a midget, you know. Brooklyn alone is bigger than Boston, and then you got the Bronx, Queens, Manhattan. We did have artists on the same scale, for sure. But in terms of trains, getting killed and pieces everywhere, it wasn't that extreme, but it was still good.

The style in Boston definitely has its own feel, like every city. In Boston we had what we called bar letters—you know, lots of angled and sharp cuts. That's what really took off here. There were a lot of blockbusters back then too—huge blockbusters—and that was our style. And then as the nineties came in, it got a little different. Alert started doing stuff that just blew people's minds. I don't know where he came up with it or how he got it, but he started doing something completely new and it definitely changed the scene. He did things with letters that I've never seen before. In most cities a lot of the graffiti artists were influenced by

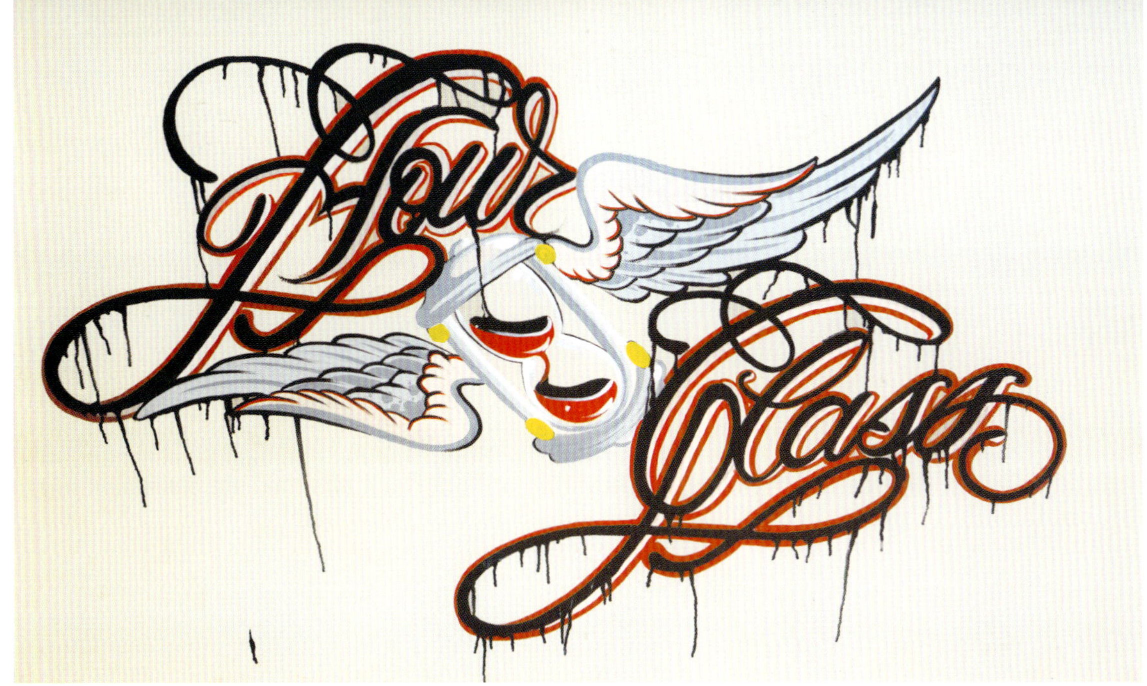

Coast, *Hour Glass*, Boston, 2010

Subway Art and things like that. A lot of the letters and the connections mimicked that time period. Alert kind of futurized the style a bit and people started following suit. It was a good time for a change.

As far as graf, I had a lot of early influences. In Boston I always saw Click pieces. In my neighborhood there were big Click pieces. Hang was his partner back then—they were always side by side. Zone started doing stuff, Wombat and Sly were doing stuff. There were a lot of people back then who were doing nice work. They definitely influenced me to keep going.

By '97 my house had been raided three times. I had cases and cases and cases concurrent. Five years' probation, ninety days here, a week or two there—too much trouble. For me, it wasn't good. They found out who I was. I was in New York for a while because I had to leave Boston…basically because of graffiti. My father said, "Pack your bags. Go. They're going to put you away. They want you in jail. Get out of here." So I left.

I ended up in New York. I had a backpack and a couple hundred bucks in my pocket. And I do work on cars, so I got a job working on cars and went to a bar here and there. I met a [tattoo] shop owner who took me under his wing—Chris Torres. He was like, "Yeah, come with me, man." And that's how I started. It was in Alphabet City. I mean, I had people showing me things before that, but like I said, it was Boston, it

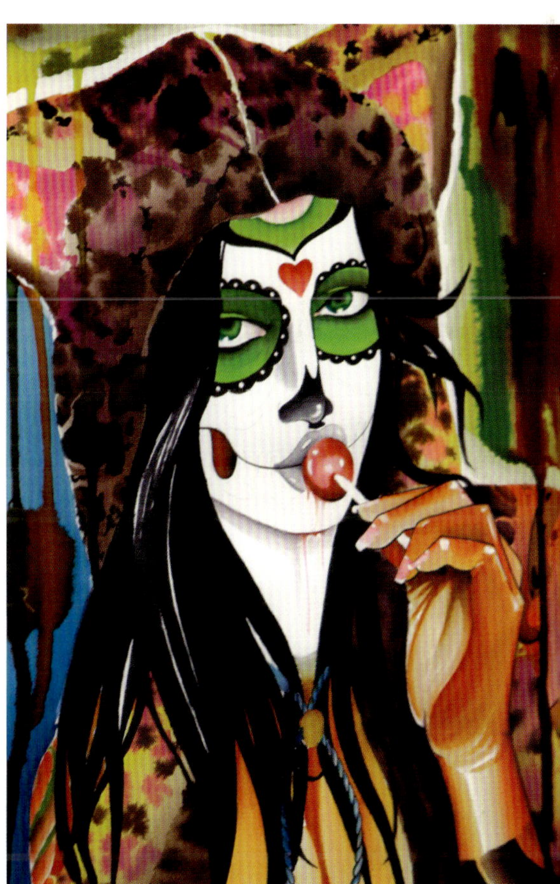

Coast watercolor, 2010

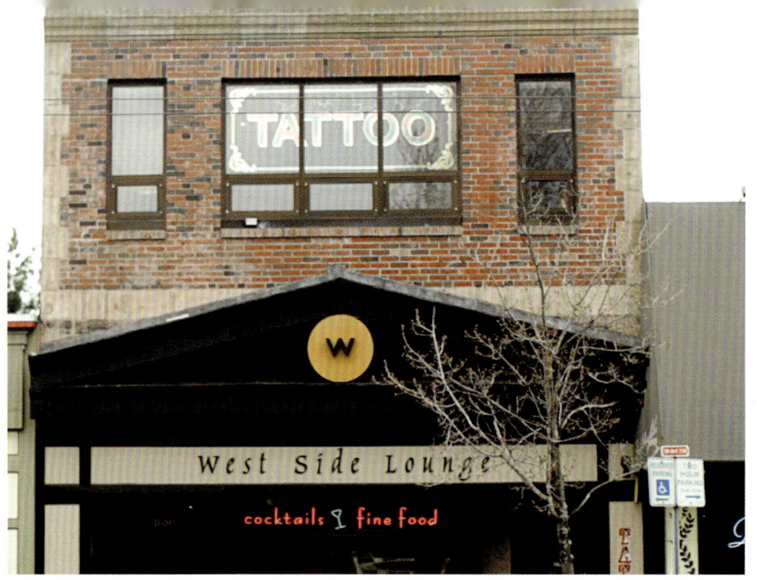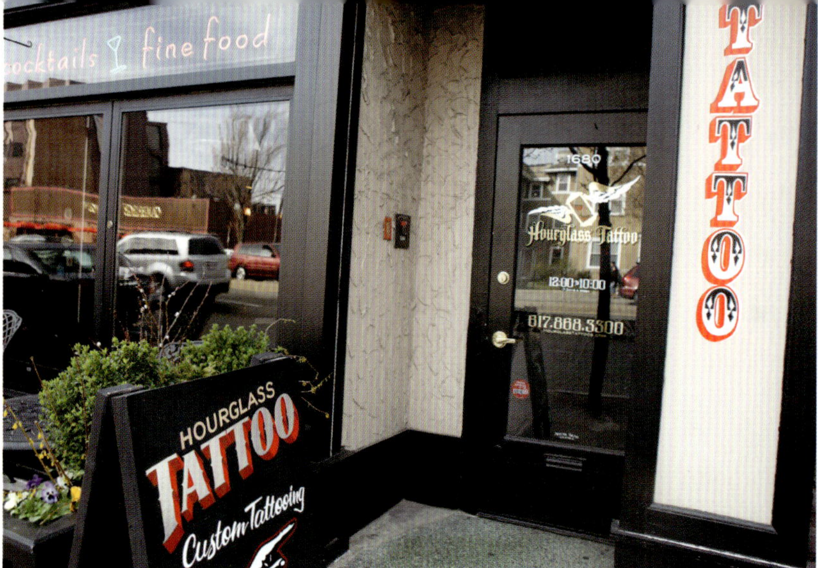

FROM LEFT: Exteriors of Hourglass Tattoo and Art Gallery, Boston, 2012

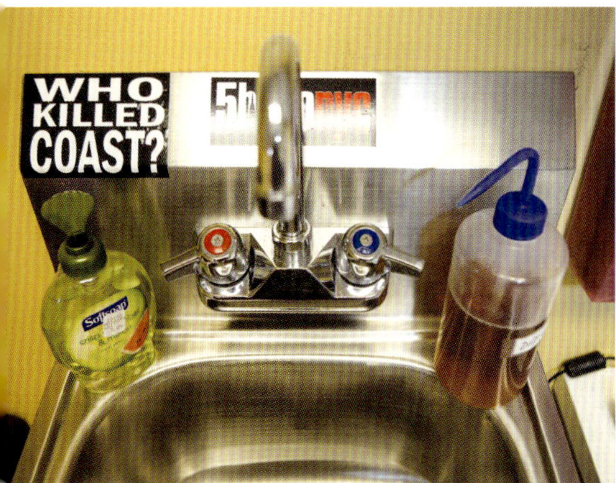

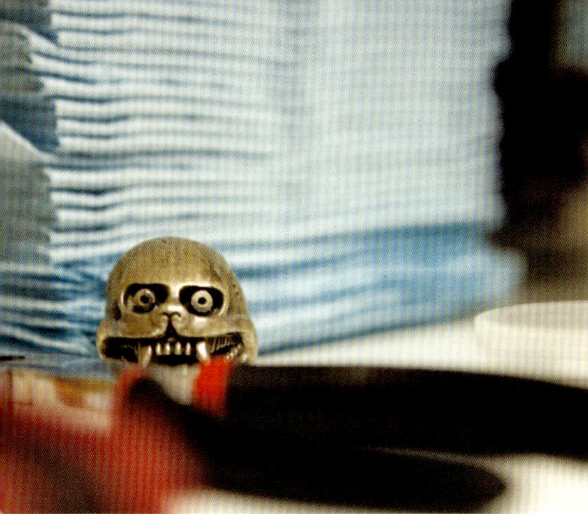

Interiors of Hourglass Tattoo, Boston, 2012

was illegal, it was underground, and it was just people trying to help me get started. But in New York, Alphabet City was the first legal shop, and I was sitting and watching what people were doing and being taught what to do.

I was always around tattoos. I was a little punk-rock derelict, you know, so I would go to hardcore shows when I was like ten. Everyone there was tattooed and they all looked out for me, you know? I started seeing everybody's artwork. "I like that, man. That looks good." Before you know it, so many people I knew were tattooing. In Boston it was illegal back then, so it was just house-party style, you know, setting up shops in apartments. I was always around it. A lot of people tried to influence me to get into it even back when I was fourteen or fifteen. But I wanted to do it the right way if I was going to do it. I didn't know later on I'd end up where I am. I started getting tattooed when I was like fifteen years old, and a few years later I was apprenticing, so one thing led to another. I came back to Boston around 2002 or 2003. Tattooing became legal here in 2001, I think. I decided that I had a lot of friends here growing up, and my clientele would be good here. I opened up my shop two years ago, in 2010. Business is good. I got great people working with me and the atmosphere is just laughs, jokes, and having a good time.

There's definitely a similarity between getting where you want to be with graffiti and getting where you want to be with tattooing. When

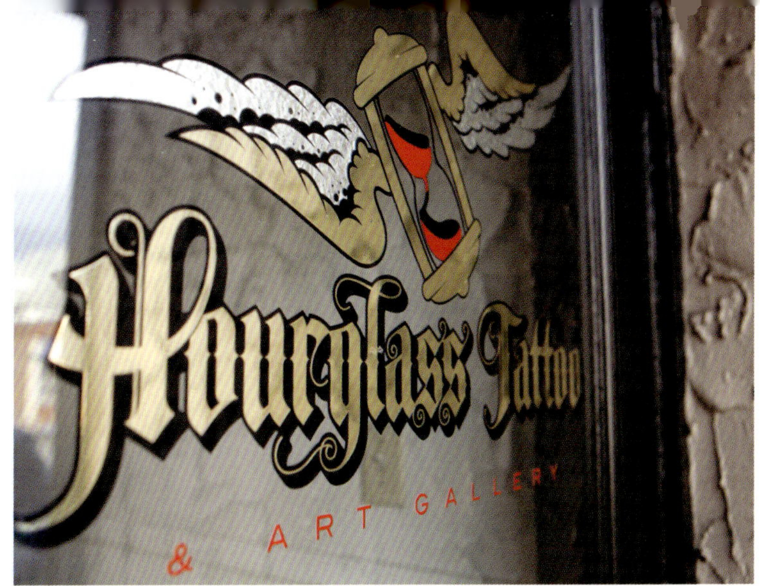 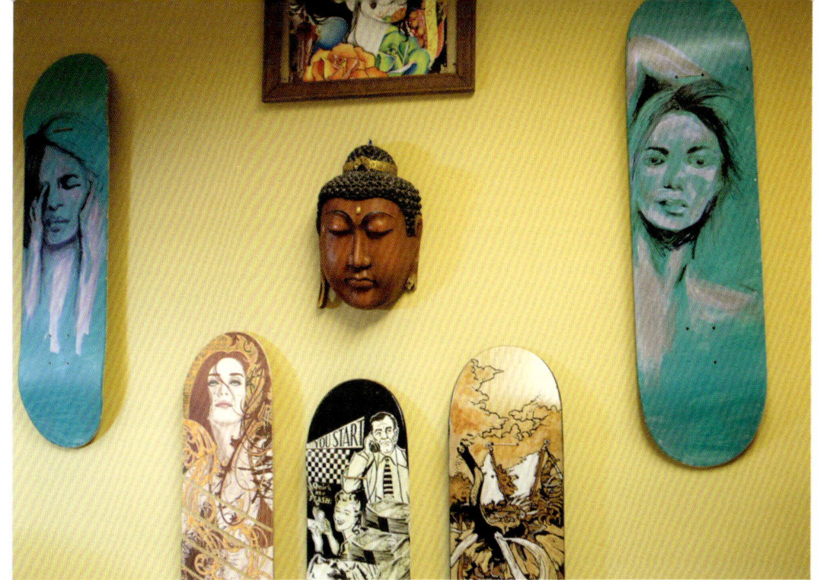

Custom skateboard decks designed by Coast, Hourglass Tattoo, Boston

you start doing graffiti, you have no can control, things are dripping, you're not feeding things right, you can't get the right cuts. It's very similar with tattooing because you don't know what needles to use on certain things, just like in graffiti when you don't know what caps to use on certain things. So there are definitely some similarities in terms of obstacles, like what paint do I use for this kind of wall, or what needle do I use for this area of skin?

When you're getting ready to do a piece, you might draw it out first and get some colors together, and then you go and do it. With tattooing, it's the same aspect. You've got to draw it out first, plan it out, see where it's going. The only difference with graffiti is that you're out there doing it for you. With tattooing, it's "Do you like it, the size, colors, and everything work for you?" Those are really the only differences to me. You definitely have more creative freedom with graffiti than you do with tattooing. But it all depends on the client.

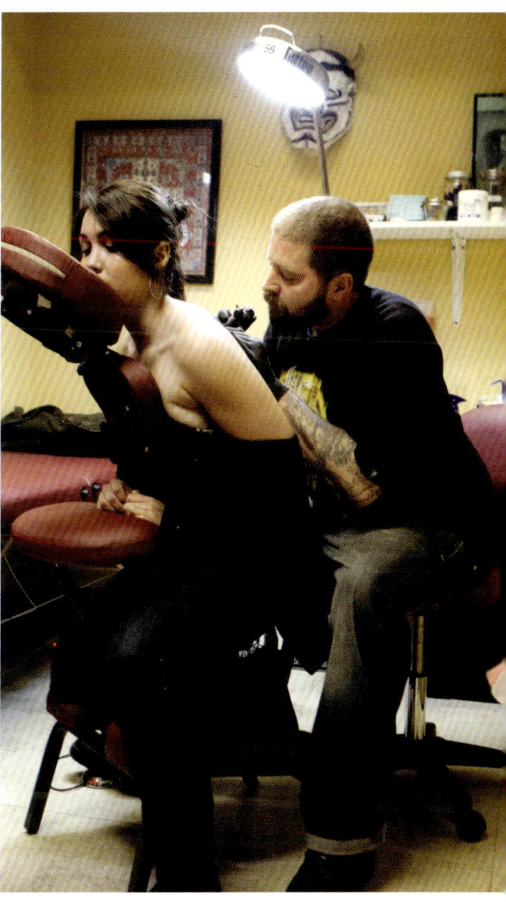

Coast at Hourglass Tattoo, Boston, 2012

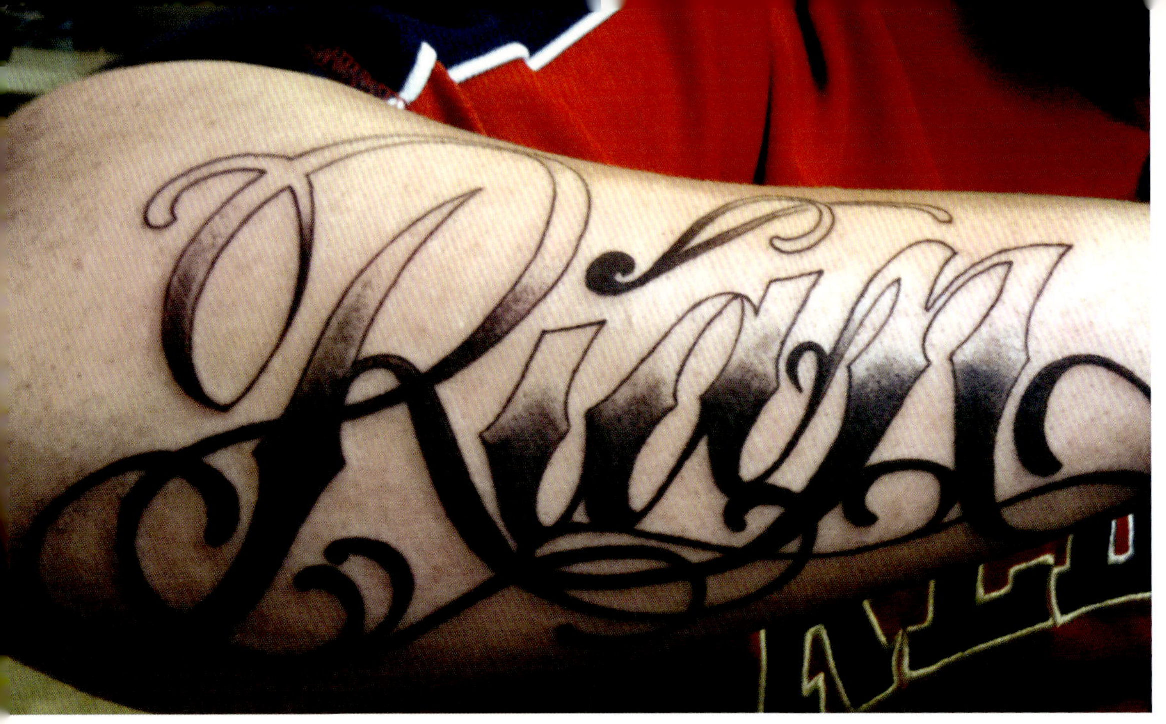

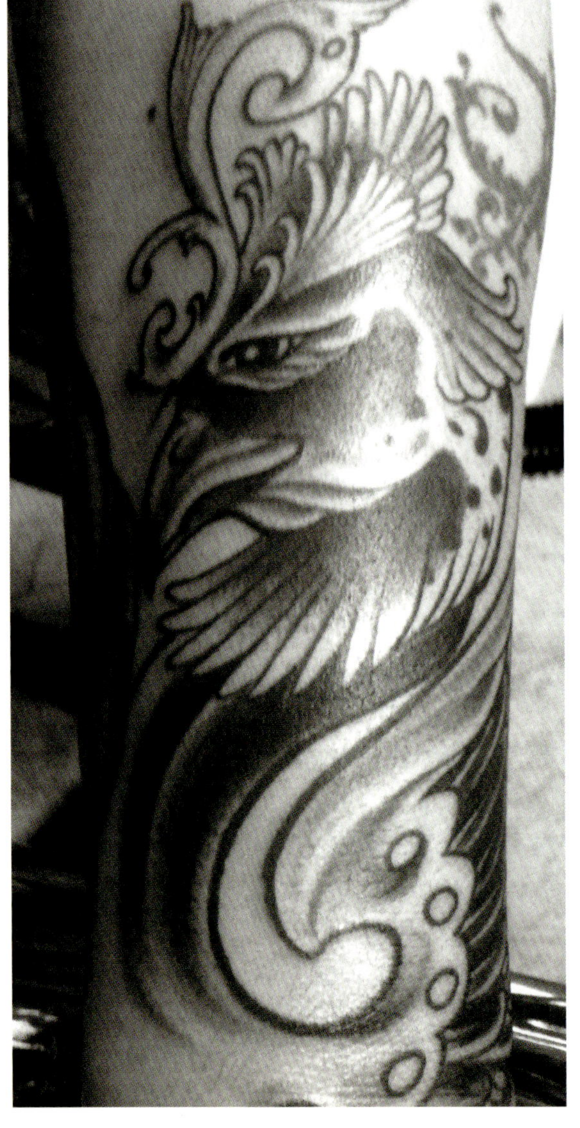

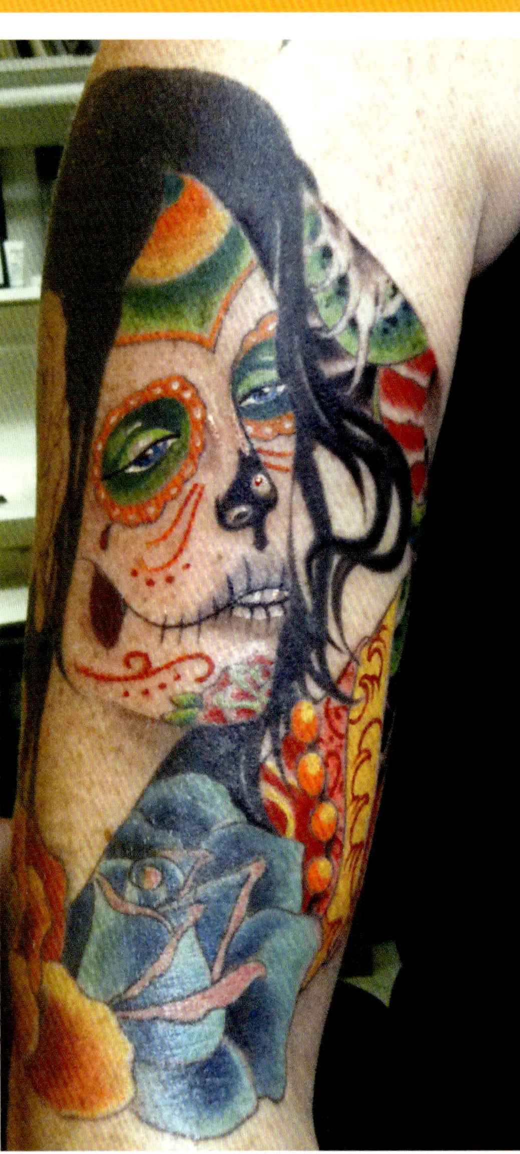

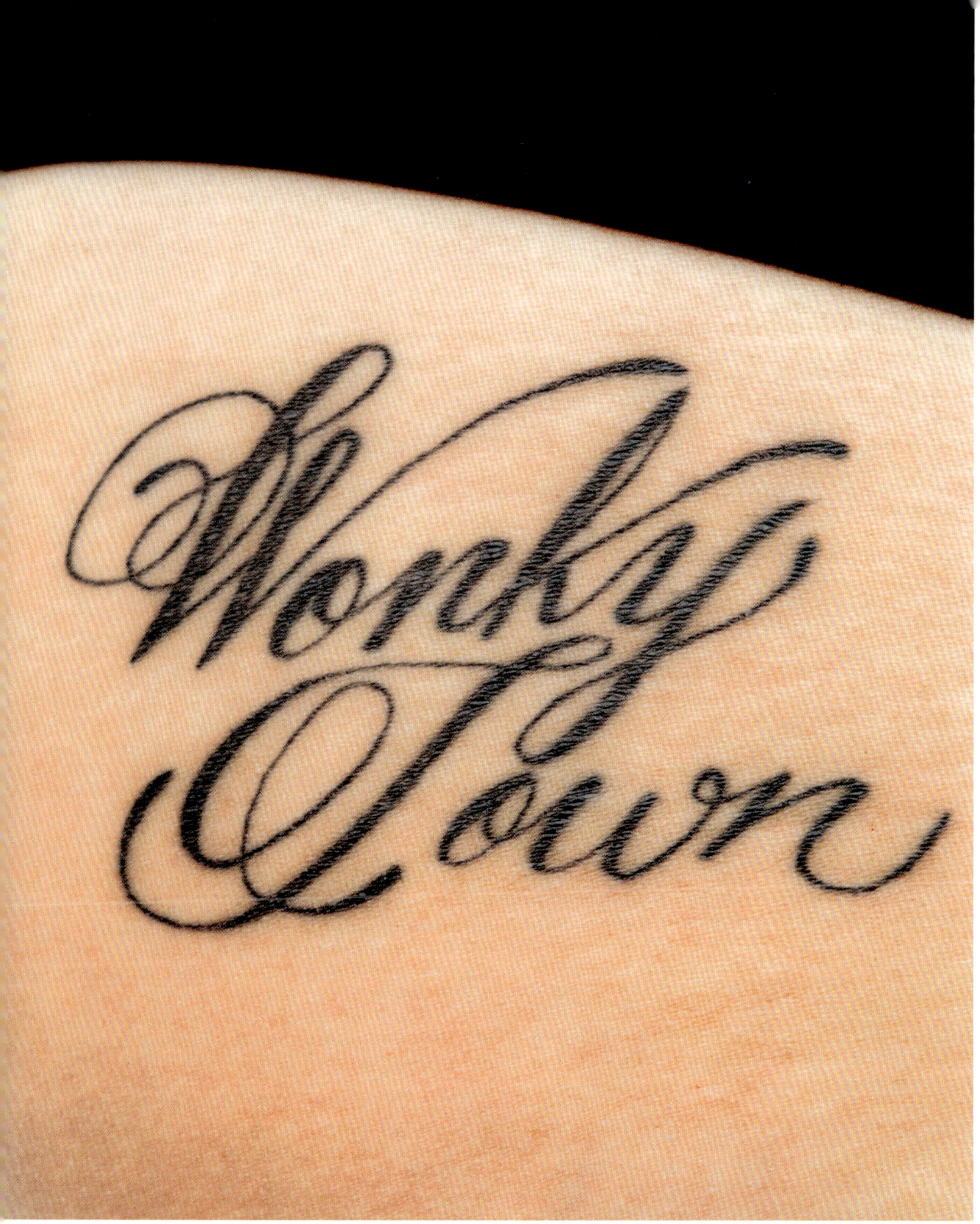

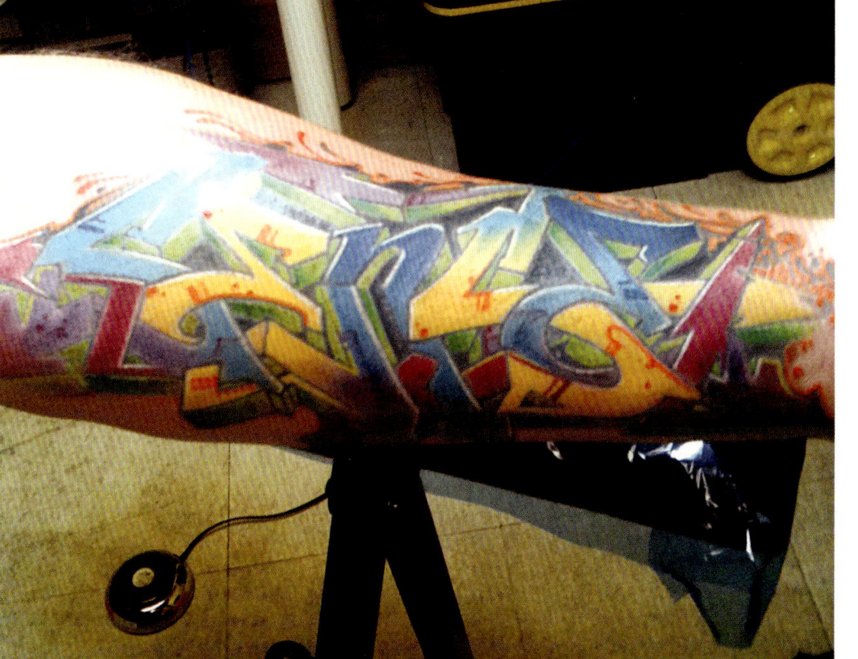

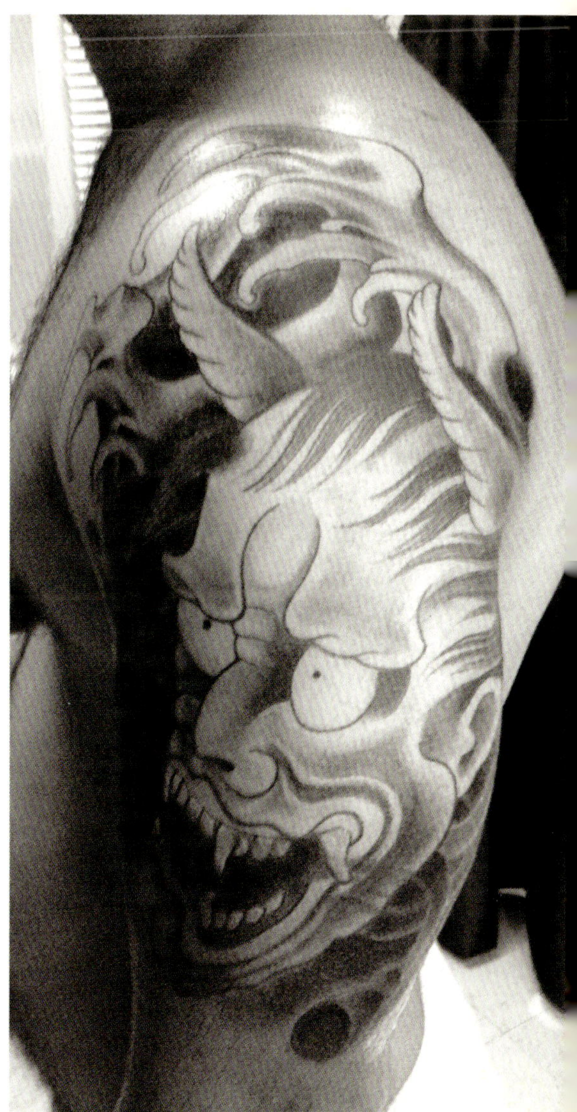

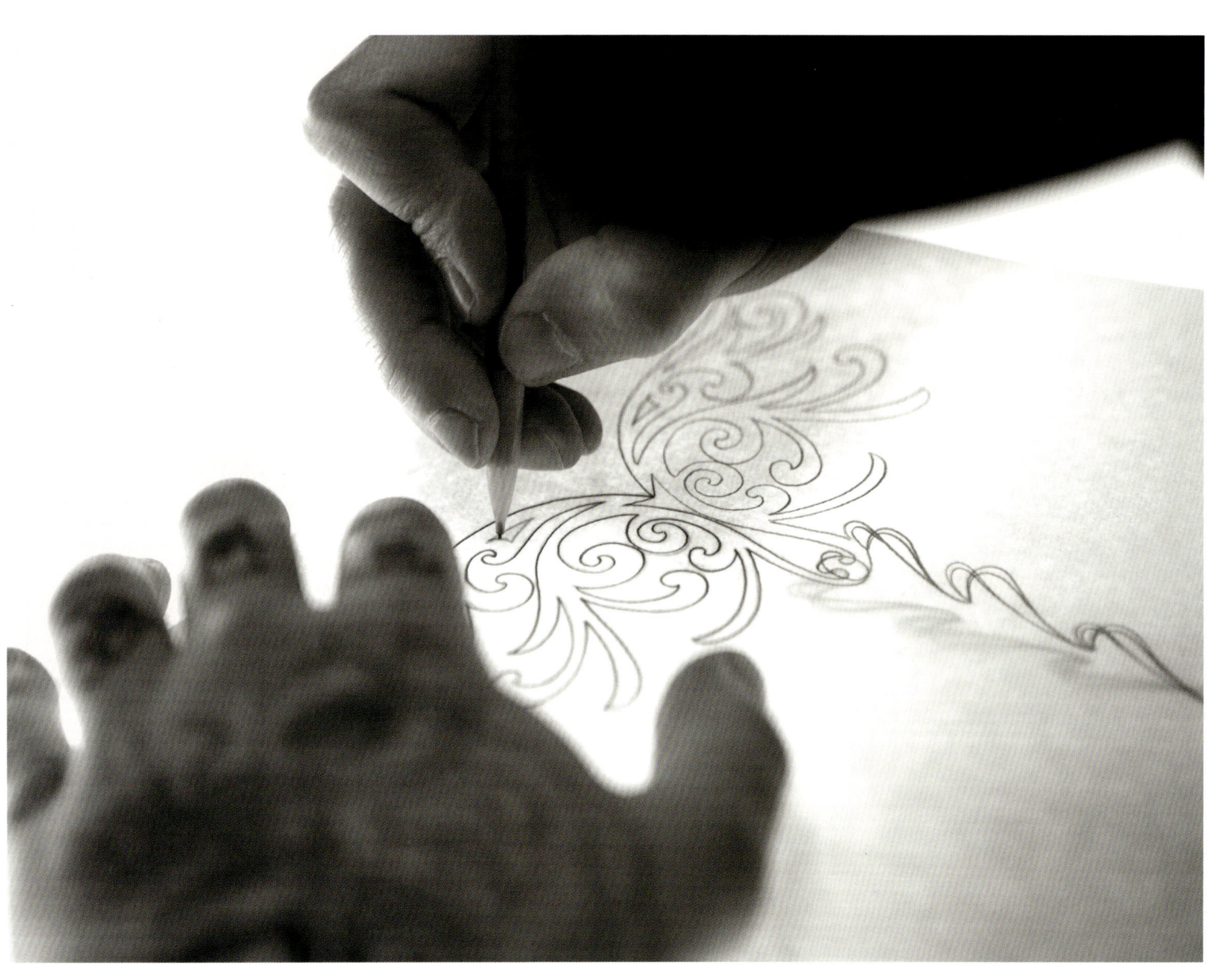

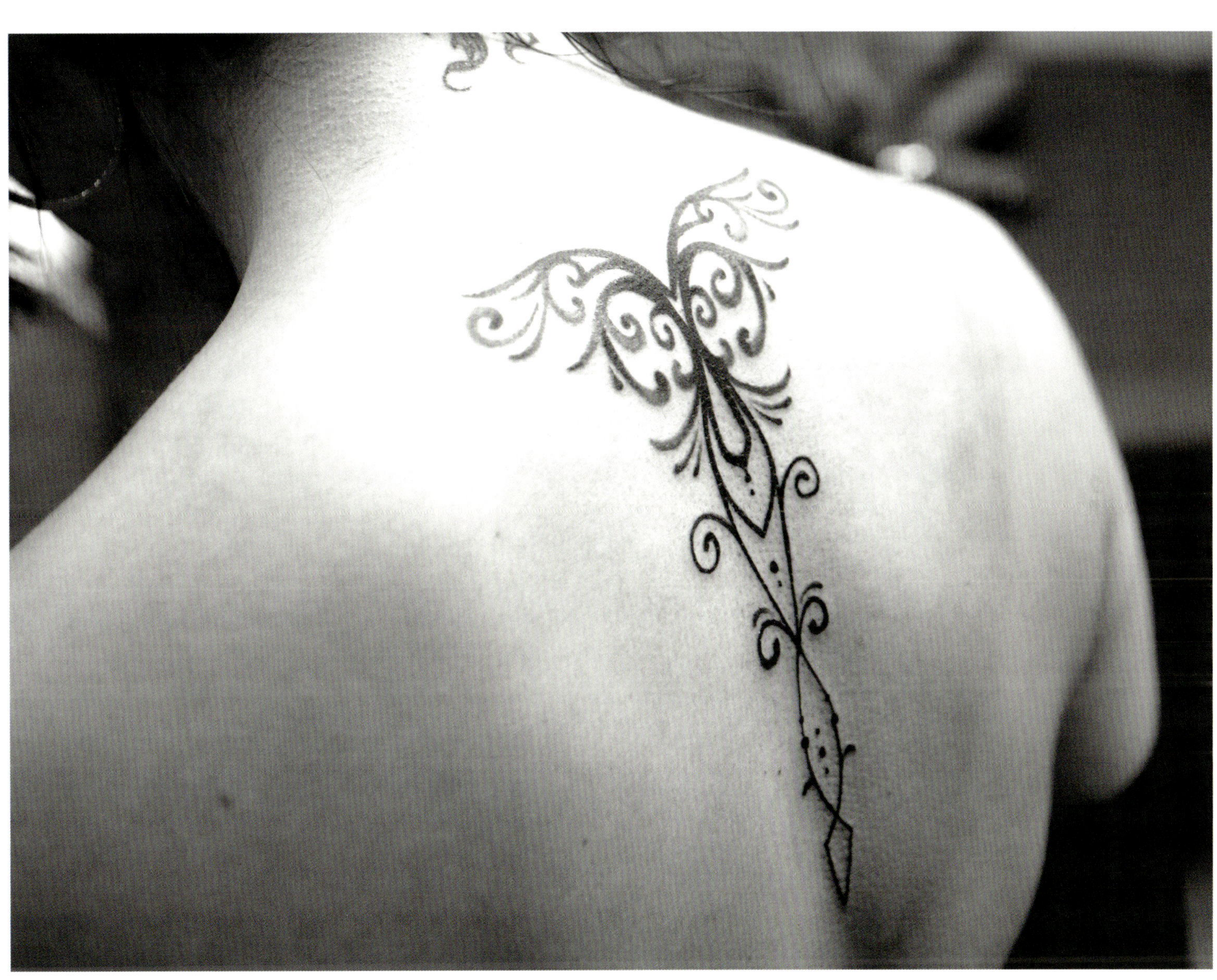

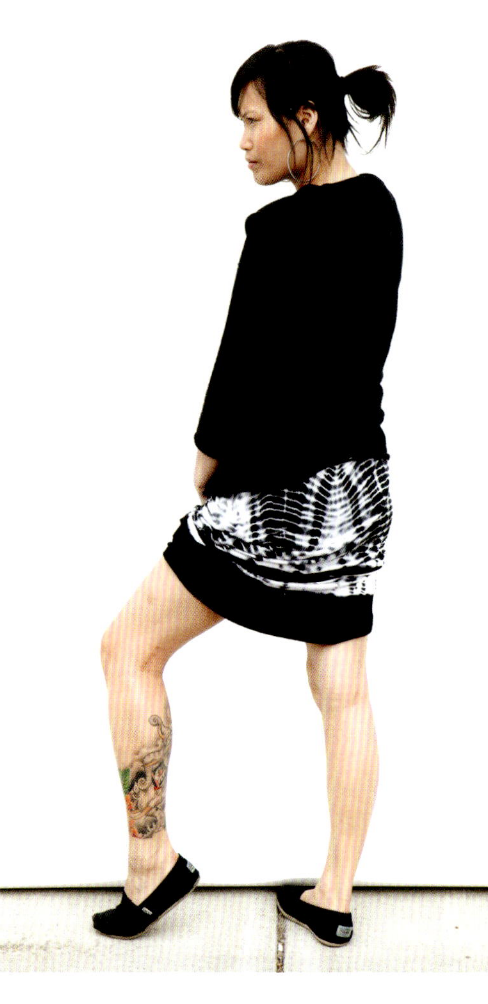

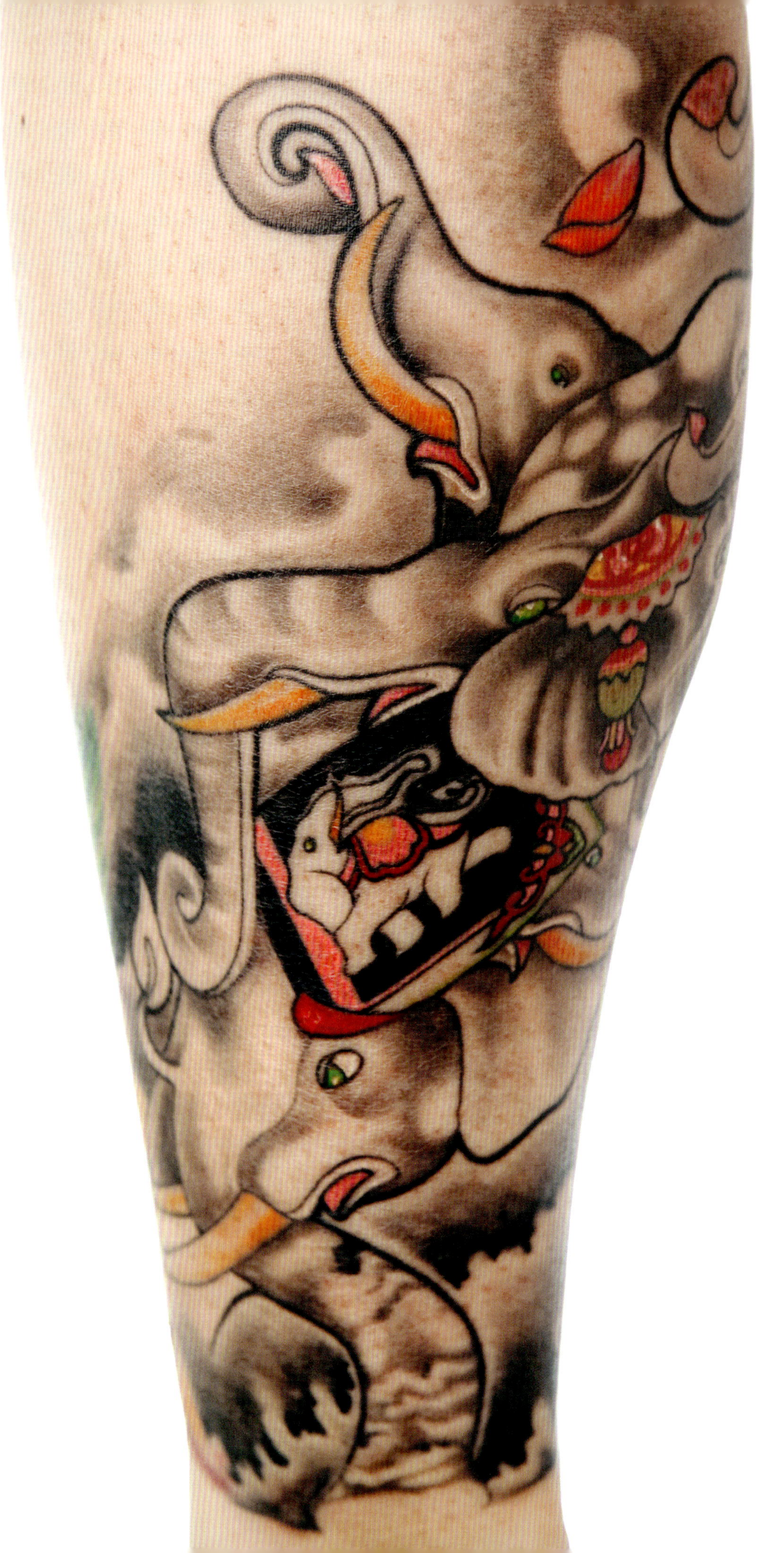

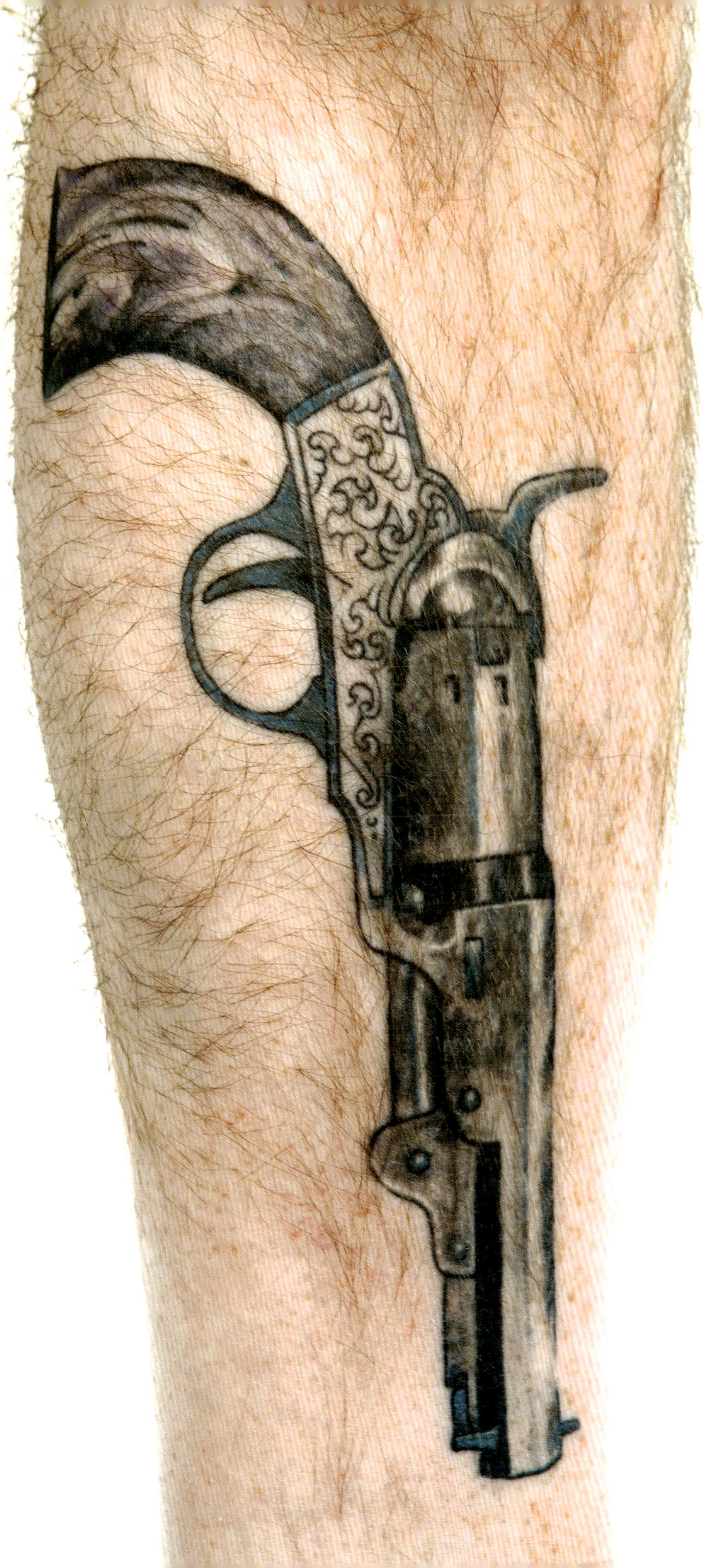

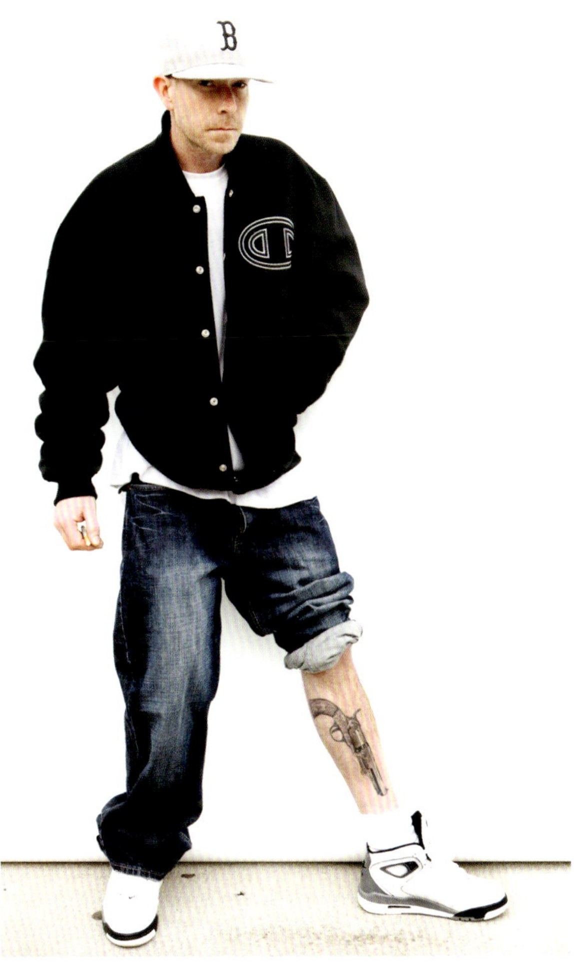

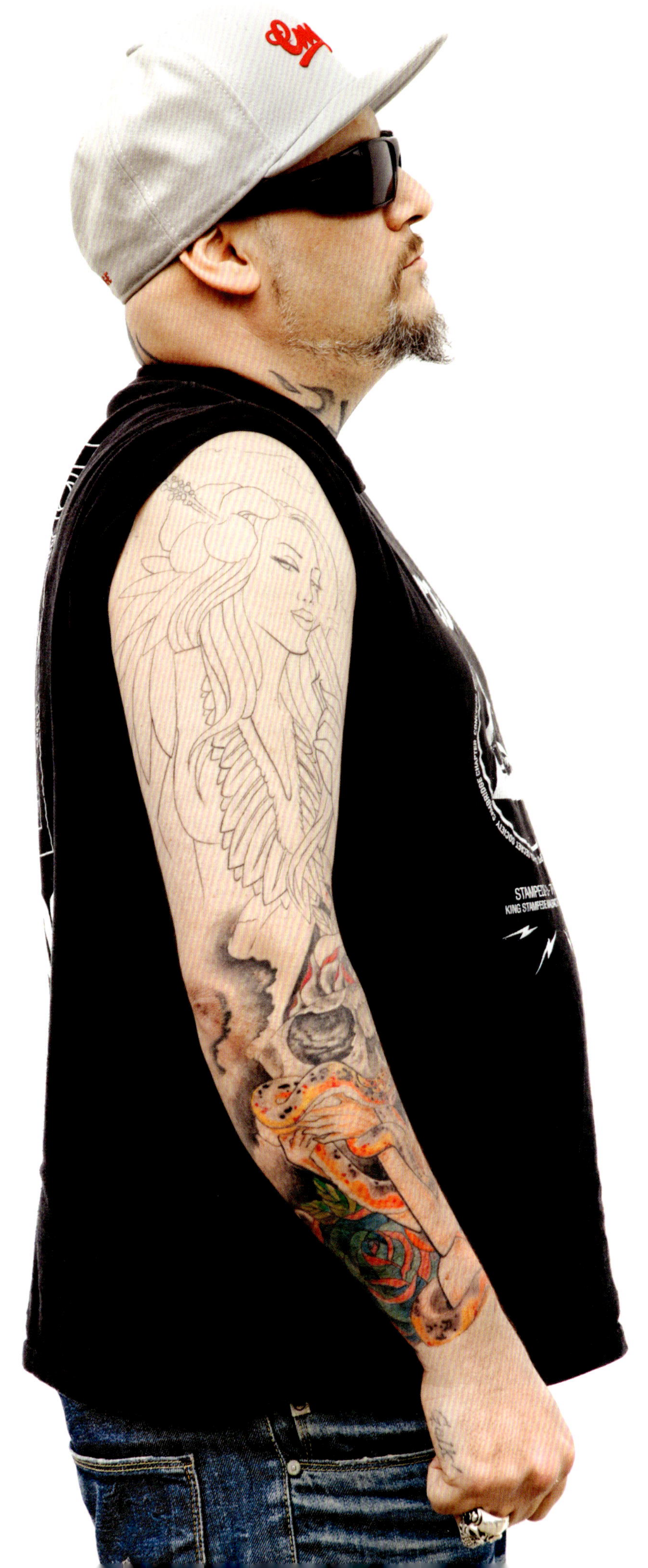

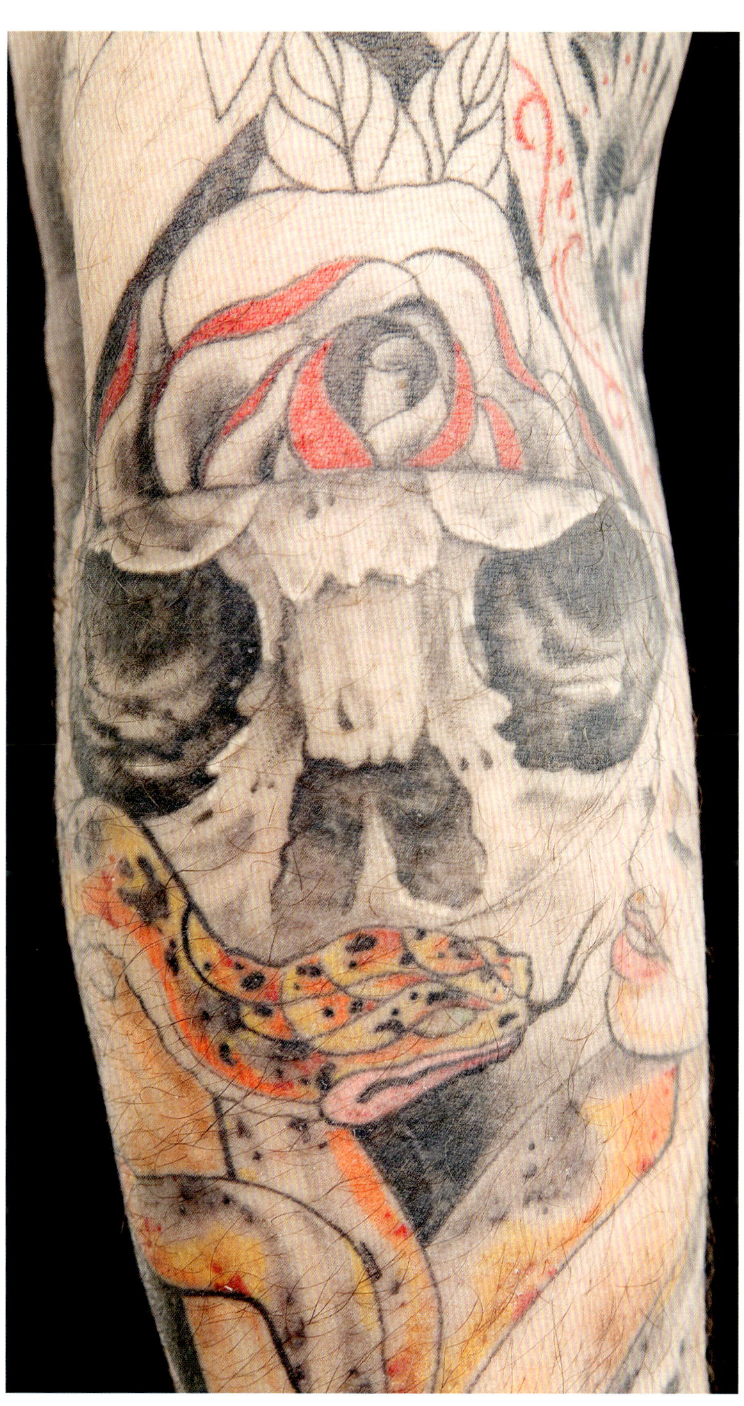
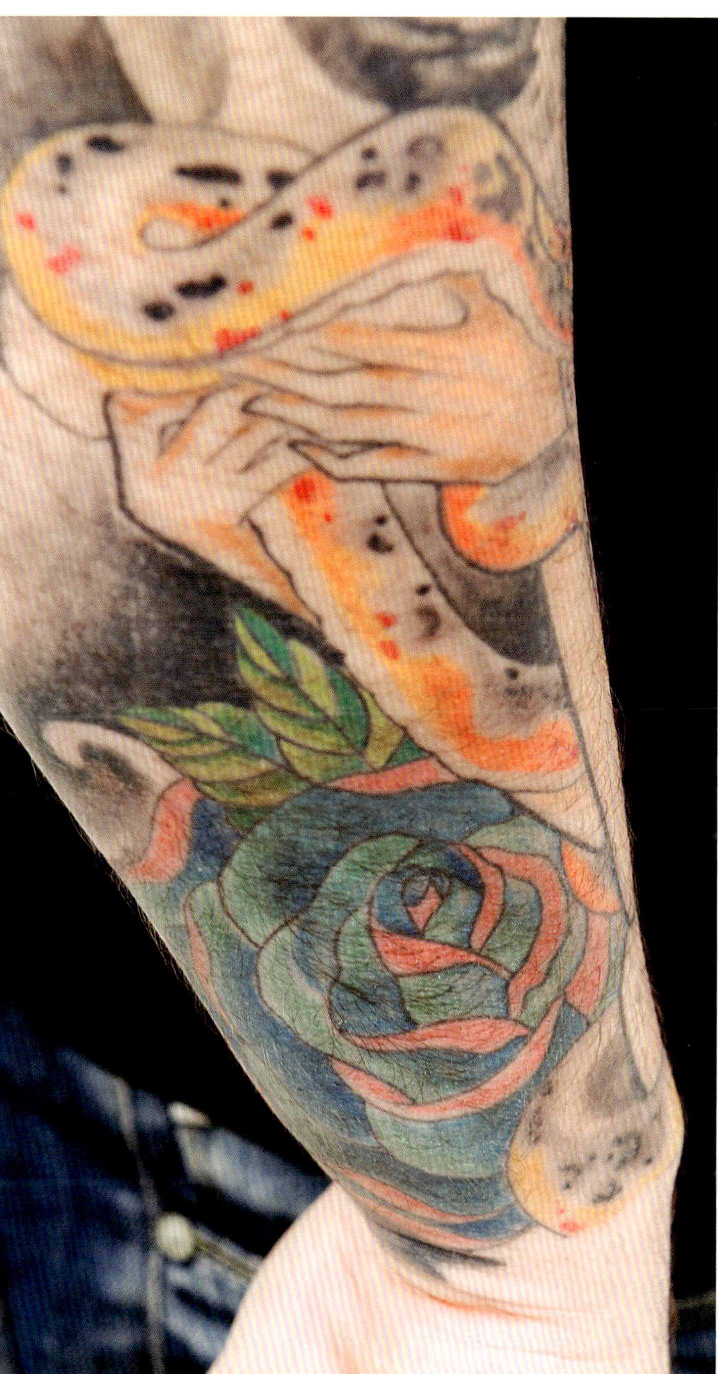

ACKNOWLEDGMENTS

The making of this book was a three-year process of hard work by a very dedicated and accomplished team of designers, photographers, and artists. We would like to thank our families and our friends, who are always such a great source of inspiration and support.

KAVES AND BILLY WOULD SINCERELY LIKE TO THANK:

Donna McLeer, Sacha Jenkins and SHR Airlines, Mark Mahoney, Joel Brick, Craig Wetherby, Kelly Gravel, Estevan Oriol, Angela Boatwright, Henry Chalfant, and James Prigoff.

We'd like to thank our friends at Prestel Publishing, especially Karen Levine, Ryan Newbanks, Stephen Hulbert, and Samantha Waller. Thanks to Nerissa Dominguez Vales of the Production Department and to Dianne Woo. We would also like to thank Chris Lyon and Mr. Monacelli for their support.

KAVES:

Donna, Blaise, Quinn, Dylan, Ruby, the McLeer family, the Cintorrino family, Peter Arbeeny, Bryce Romer, Howie Abrams, Steve Mona, Freddy Negrete, Isaiah Negrete, Cody Mac, Danny O'Connor, Danny Singer, Jon Rauch, Kevin and Fran Lyman, Alicia Galehdari, the Tadross family, and the Brooklyn Made Tattoo family.

BILLY:

Bill and Donna Burke, The Bean, Lauren DelVecchio Zaleski, Matt Johnson, James McLaughlin, Debbie Millman, J'aime Cohen, and Brian Joyce.

A very special thanks to Mario Barth and Intenze Products.

MICHAEL "KAVES" MCLEER is a world-renowned graffiti artist and musician turned tattooist. Having left his mark, literally, on the New York City transit system from the age of ten, Kaves eventually turned his attention to legal art in the form of tattooing and fine art as well as acting. He has created original pieces for companies such as Nike, Adidas, and Jaguar and for the Beastie Boys and Metallica, not to mention the 2011 Beaujolais Nouveau wine label for Georges Duboeuf. He owns and operates Brooklyn Made Tattoo in his hometown of Bay Ridge, Brooklyn, from which he exports all of his unique work.

BILLY BURKE is a producer/director whose six-episode series *Marked* (a collaboration with the tattooist Mario Barth) premiered on the History Channel in 2009. Barth and Burke's 2008 film *Under the Skin* won numerous awards, including Best Documentary Director from the Los Angeles Film Festival and Best Documentary from the New York Independent Film Festival.

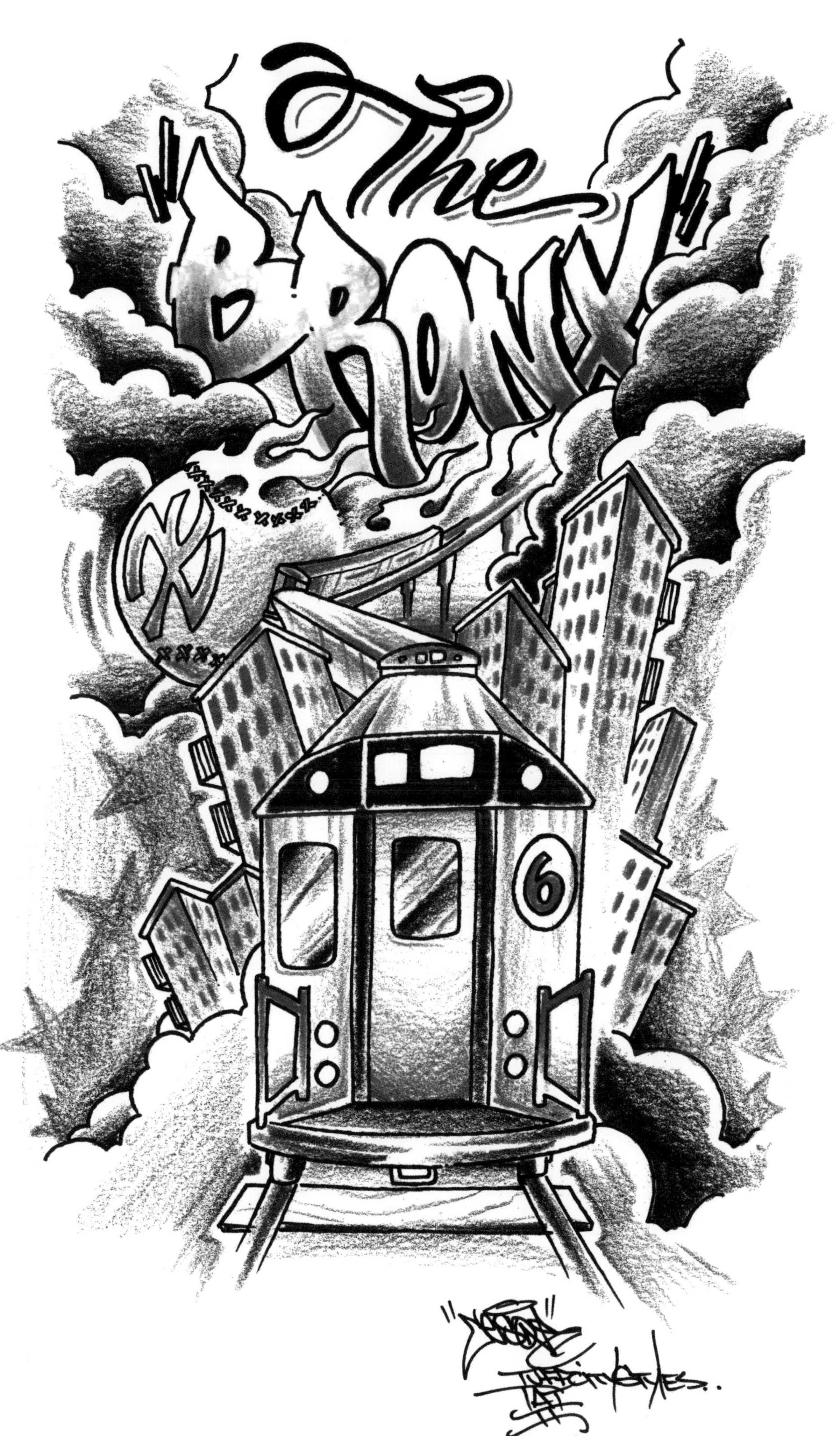
The
BRONX
6

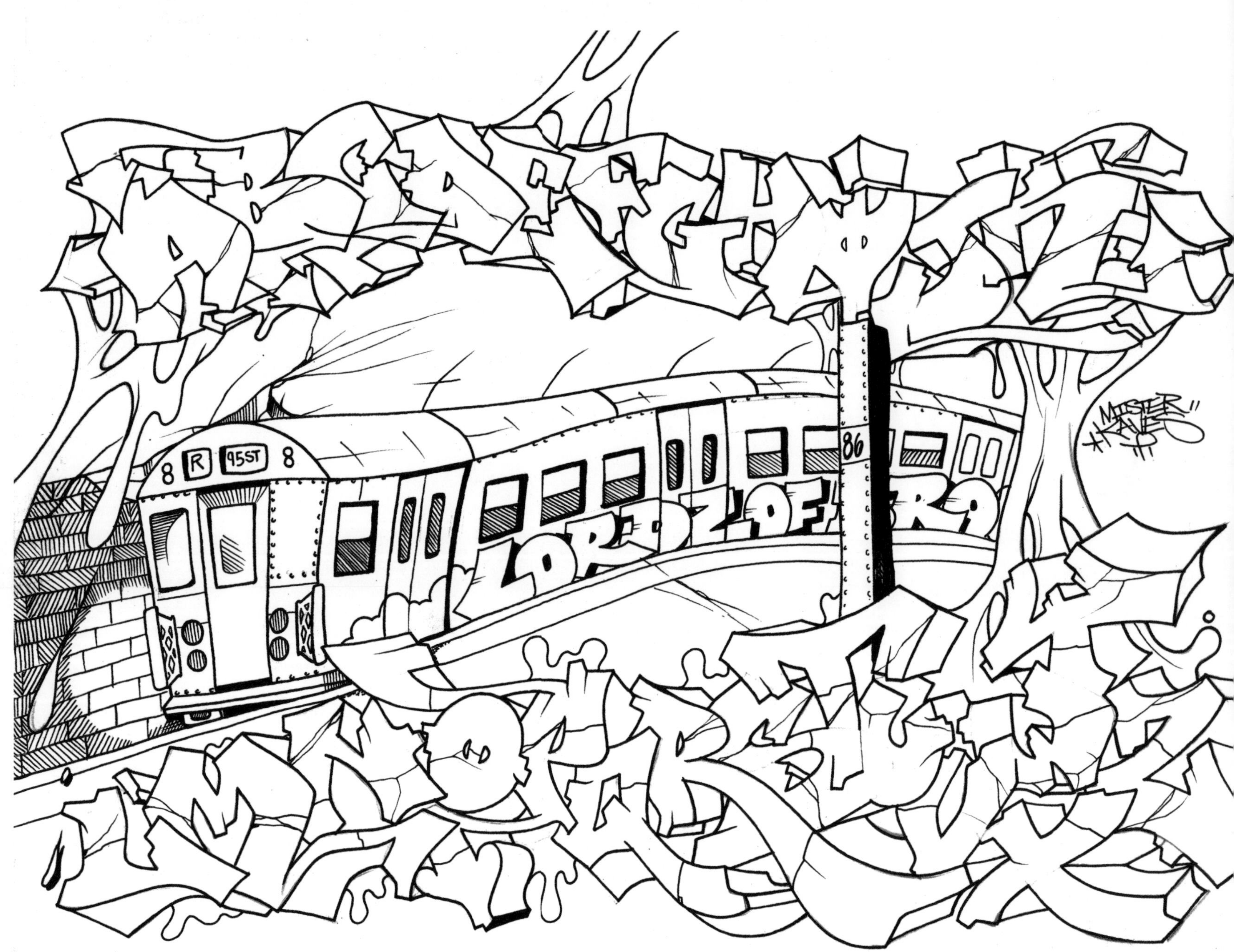

8 R 95ST 8
86
LORDZOFFR9
MISTER
RAVE